Virtues of the Imām Aḥmad ibn Ḥanbal

Volume Two

Letter from the General Editor

The Library of Arabic Literature series offers Arabic editions and English translations of key works of classical and pre-modern Arabic literature, as well as anthologies and thematic readers. Books in the series are edited and translated by distinguished scholars of Arabic and Islamic studies, and are published in parallel-text format with Arabic and English on facing pages. The Library of Arabic Literature includes texts from the pre-Islamic era to the cusp of the modern period, and encompasses a wide range of genres, including poetry, poetics, fiction, religion, philosophy, law, science, history, and historiography.

Supported by a grant from the New York University Abu Dhabi Institute, and established in partnership with NYU Press, the Library of Arabic Literature produces authoritative Arabic editions and modern, lucid English translations, with the goal of introducing the Arabic literary heritage to scholars and students, as well as to a general audience of readers.

Philip F. Kennedy
General Editor, Library of Arabic Literature

مناقب
أبي عبد الله أحمد بن محمّد بن حنبل

المجلّد الثاني

من تأليف

أبي الفرج عبد الرحمن بن عليّ بن محمّد بن الجوزيّ

LIBRARY OF
المكتبة
ARABIC
العربية
LITERATURE

Virtues of the Imām Aḥmad ibn Ḥanbal

Volume Two

Ibn al-Jawzī

Edited and translated by
Michael Cooperson

Volume editor
Tahera Qutbuddin

NEW YORK UNIVERSITY PRESS
New York and London

NEW YORK UNIVERSITY PRESS
New York and London

Library of Congress Cataloging-in-Publication Data

Ibn al-Jawzi, Abu al-Faraj ʻAbd al-Rahman ibn ʻAli, approximately 1116-1201.
[Manaqib al-Imam Ahmad ibn Hanbal. English]
Virtues of the Imam Ahmad ibn Hanbal / Ibn al-Jawzi ; edited and translated by Michael Cooperson.
volumes cm
Includes bibliographical references and index.
ISBN 978-0-8147-3894-8 (cl : alk. paper) -- ISBN 978-0-8147-7195-2 (e-book) -- ISBN 978-0-8147-3787-3 (e-book) 1. Ibn Hanbal, Ahmad ibn Muhammad, 780-855. 2. Islamic law--Biography. I. Cooperson, Michael, editor, translator. II. Title.
KBP310.I2653I26513 2013
297.1'4092--dc23
[B]
2013007686

New York University Press books are printed on acid-free paper, and their binding materials are chosen for strength and durability.

Series design by Titus Nemeth.

Typeset in Tasmeem, using DecoType Naskh and Emiri.

Typesetting and digitization by Stuart Brown.

Manufactured in the United States of America
c10 9 8 7 6 5 4 3 2 1

Table of Contents

مناقب
أبي عبد الله أَحمد بن محمّد بن حنبل

المجلّد الثاني

Virtues of the Imām Aḥmad ibn Ḥanbal

Volume Two

الباب الحادي والخمسون في ذكر حبه للفقر والفقراء

١،٥١ أخبرنا محمّد بن أبي منصور قال: أخبرنا عبد القادر بن محمّد قال: أنبأنا إبراهيم بن عُمر قال: أنبأنا عبد العزيز بن جعفر قال: أخبرنا أحمد بن محمد الخلّال قال:

أخبرني محمّد بن الحسين أن أبا بكر المرُّوذي حدثهم قال: كان أبو عبد الله يحب الفقراء لم أرَ الفقير في مجلسٍ أحدٍ أعزّ منه في مجلسه.

قال الخلّال:

٢،٥١ وأخبرنا أبو بكر المرُّوذي قال: قال لي أبو عبد الله – وذكر رجلاً فقيراً مريضاً – فقال لي: اذهب إليه وقُل[١]: أيّ شيء تشتهي حتى نعمل لك؟ ودفع إليَّ طِيباً وقال لي: طَيّبه.

٣،٥١ أخبرنا محمّد بن أبي منصور قال: أخبرنا المبارك بن عبد الجبار قال: أخبرنا أبو بكر محمّد بن عليّ الخياط قال: أنبأنا ابن أبي الفوارس قال: أخبرنا أحمد بن جعفر بن سَلْم قال: حدثنا أحمد بن محمد بن عبد الخالق قال:

أخبرنا أبو بكر المرُّوذي قال: قال أبو عبد الله أحمد بن حنبل: ما أعدِلُ بالفَقر شيئاً، ما أعدل بالفقر شيئاً، ما أعدل بالفقر شيئاً،[٢] أنا أفرح إذا لم يكن عندي شيء.

وذكرتُ له رجلاً صَبوراً على الفقر في أطمار فكان يسألني عنه ويقول: اذهب حتى تأتيني[٣] بخبره، سبحان الله، الصبر على الفقر، الصبر على الفقر، ما أَعدِل بالصبر على الفقر شيئاً، تَدري الصبر على الفقر أيّ شيء هو؟ وقال: كم بين من يُعطَى من الدنيا ليفتتن إلى آخر تزوي عنه.

وذكرتُ لأبي عبد الله الفُضيل وعُريَه وفَتحاً الموصلي وعريه[٤] وصبره فتغَرغرت عينه وقال: رحِمهم الله، كان يُقال: عند ذكر الصالحين تنزل الرحمة.

---

١ تركي: قل له. ٢ جاءت العبارة مرتين في د ومرة واحدة فقط في ش. ٣ هـ : يأتيني

٤ هـ : عَرَيه (مشكّلة) وفي ش:عريه.

Chapter 51: His Love of Poverty and His Affection for the Poor

We cite Muḥammad ibn Abī Manṣūr, who cites ʿAbd al-Qādir ibn Muḥammad, who was informed by Ibrāhīm ibn ʿUmar, who was informed by ʿAbd al-ʿAzīz ibn Jaʿfar, who cites Aḥmad ibn Muḥammad al-Khallāl, who cites Muḥammad ibn al-Ḥusayn, who heard Abū Bakr al-Marrūdhī report: 51.1

[Al-Marrūdhī:] Aḥmad loved the poor. I never saw poor men treated as well as they were when sitting in his company.

Al-Khallāl cites Abū Bakr al-Marrūdhī, who reports: 51.2

[Al-Marrūdhī:] Aḥmad once mentioned someone who was poor and ill, and told me, "Go and ask him what he wants us to do for him."

Then he handed me some scent and said, "Put this on him."

We cite Muḥammad ibn Abī Manṣūr, who cites al-Mubārak ibn ʿAbd al-Jabbār, who cites Abū Bakr Muḥammad ibn ʿAlī l-Khayyāṭ, who was informed by Ibn Abī l-Fawāris, who cites Aḥmad ibn Jaʿfar ibn Salm, who heard Aḥmad ibn Muḥammad ibn ʿAbd al-Khāliq report that he heard Abū Bakr al-Marrūdhī report: 51.3

[Al-Marrūdhī:] Aḥmad ibn Ḥanbal once said, "Nothing does as much good as poverty—nothing! When there's no money here I rejoice."

I once mentioned someone who bore poverty steadfastly despite living in rags. After that he would ask me about him, saying, "Go and see how he's doing! God be praised: there's nothing like bearing poverty—nothing like it at all. Do you understand what it means?"

Once he said, "Some people have the things of this world given to them in order to test them. It's much better when the world leaves you alone!"

I once mentioned how al-Fuḍayl and Fatḥ al-Mawṣilī had lived in destitution but bore up without complaint. "God have mercy on them," he said, as his eyes filled with tears. "They used to say that when the righteous are recalled, God's grace descends."

One day he said, "When there's no money here, I'm glad."

وقال لي أبو عبد الله يوماً: إني لأفرح إذا لم يكن عندي شيء. فجاءه ابنه الصغير بعَقب هذا الكلام فطلب منه فقال: ليس عند أبيك قطعة ولا عندي شيء.

الباب الثاني والخمسون في ذكر تواضعه

١،٥٢ أخبرنا أبو منصور عبد الرحمن بن محمّد قال: أخبرنا أحمد بن عليّ بن ثابت قال: أخبرني محمّد بن أحمد بن يعقوب قال: حدثنا محمّد بن عبد الله بن حَمْدُويَه قال: قرأت بخطّ أبي عمرو المُسْتَمْلي سمعت عبد الله بن بِشر الطّالَقاني يقول:

سمعتُ محمّد بن طارق البغدادي يقول: كنتُ جالساً إلى جنب أحمد بن حنبل فقلتُ: يا أبا عبد الله أستمدّ من مِحْبَرتك؟ فنظر إليّ وقال: لم يبلغ ورعي وورعك هذا. وتبسّم.

٢،٥٢ أخبرنا إسماعيل بن أحمد ومحمّد بن عبد الباقي قالا: أخبرنا حَمْد بن أحمد قال: حدثنا أحمد بن عبد الله قال: حدثنا سليمان بن أحمد قال: حدثنا عبد الله بن أحمد بن حنبل قال: سمعتُ عبّاس بن محمّد الدُوري يقول:

سمعتُ يحيى بن مَعِين يقول: ما رأيتُ مثل أحمد بن حنبل، صَحِبناه[1] خمسين سنة ما افتخر علينا بشيء مما كان فيه من الصلاح والخير.

٣،٥٢ أخبرنا محمّد بن أبي منصور قال: أخبرنا عبد القادر بن محمّد بن يوسف قال: أخبرنا إبراهيم بن عمر البرمكي قال: أخبرنا عليّ بن مَرْدَك قال: حدثنا أبو محمّد بن أبي حاتم قال:

حدثنا صالح قال: كان أبي ربما أخذ القَدوم وخرج إلى دار السكّان يعمل الشيء بيده وربما خرج إلى البقّال فيشتري الجُرْزة الحطب[2] والشيء فيحمله بيده.

---

١ د: صحبته. ٢ ش: من الحطب.

No sooner had he said it than his little son came to ask him for something. "Your father doesn't have a single coin," he replied, "or anything else."

Chapter 52: His Humility

We cite Abū Manṣūr ʿAbd al-Raḥmān ibn Muḥammad, who cites Aḥmad ibn ʿAlī ibn Thābit, who cites Muḥammad ibn Aḥmad ibn Yaʿqūb, who heard Muḥammad ibn ʿAbd Allāh ibn Ḥamduwayh report that he read a report in the handwriting of Abū ʿAmr al-Mustamlī (the amanuensis), who heard ʿAbd Allāh ibn Bishr al-Ṭālqānī say that he heard Muḥammad ibn Ṭāriq al-Baghdādī say: **52.1**

[Muḥammad ibn Ṭāriq:] I was sitting next to Aḥmad ibn Ḥanbal and I asked him if I could use his inkpot.

He looked at me. "Neither one of us is as scrupulous as all that," he said with a smile.

We cite Ismāʿīl ibn Aḥmad and Muḥammad ibn ʿAbd al-Bāqī, who cite Ḥamd ibn Aḥmad, who heard Aḥmad ibn ʿAbd Allāh report that he heard Sulaymān ibn Aḥmad report that he heard Aḥmad ibn Ḥanbal's son ʿAbd Allāh report that he heard ʿAbbās ibn Muḥammad al-Dūrī say that he heard Yaḥyā ibn Maʿīn say: **52.2**

[Yaḥyā ibn Maʿīn:] I never met anyone like Aḥmad ibn Ḥanbal. We sat with him for fifty years, and never once did he hold his piety and goodness over us.

We cite Muḥammad ibn Abī Manṣūr, who cites ʿAbd al-Qādir ibn Muḥammad ibn Yūsuf, who cites Ibrāhīm ibn ʿUmar al-Barmakī, who cites ʿAlī ibn Mardak, who heard Abū Muḥammad ibn Abī Ḥātim report that he heard Ṣāliḥ report: **52.3**

[Ṣāliḥ:] I often saw my father pick up an adze and go over to the tenants' rooms to take care of jobs with his own two hands. He would go to the grocers and buy a bundle of kindling or whatever, and carry it back himself.

قال أبو محمد: ٤،٥٢

وأخبرنا عبد الله بن أحمد فيما كتب إليّ قال: رأيت أبي إذا جاءه الشيخ والحَدَث من قريش أو غيرهم من الأشراف لا يخرج من باب المسجد حتى يخرجهم فيكونون هم يتقدّمونهم ثم يخرج بعدهم بي.[1]

أخبرنا محمد بن أبي منصور قال: أخبرنا أبو الحسين بن عبد الجبار قال: أخبرنا محمد بن عبد الواحد بن جعفر ٥،٥٢ الحريري قال: أخبرنا أبو عمر بن حَيُّوَيْه قال: حدثنا عبد الله بن محمد بن إسحاق المَرْوَزي قال: حدثنا العبّاس ابن محمد الدُّوري قال:

حدثنا عارِم بن الفضل قال: كان أحمد بن حنبل ها هنا عندنا بالبصرة فجاء ني بمِعْضَدة له - أو قال: صرّة فيها دراهم - فكان كلَّ قليلٍ يجيء فيأخذ منها فقلت له: يا أبا عبد الله بلغني أنك رجل من العرب فمن أيّ العرب أنت؟ فقال لي: يا أبا النُّعمان نحن قوم مساكين.

فكان كلّما جاء أعدتُ عليه فيقول لي هذا الكلام ولا يُخبرني حتى خرج من البصرة.

قال الخلال: ٦،٥٢

وأخبرني إسماعيل بن إسحاق الثقفي قال: قلتُ لأبي عبد الله أول ما رأيتُه يا أبا عبد الله ائذن لي أقبّل رأسك؟ فقال: لم أبلغ أنا ذلك.

قال الخلال: ٧،٥٢

وأخبرني أبو بكر المَرُّوذي قال: قلت لأبي عبد الله: الرجل يُقال له في وجهه أحيَيْتَ السنّة؟

قال: هذا فساد لقلب الرجل.

[1] الخبر في هـ فقط.

Abū Muḥammad said that among the things Ibn Ḥanbal's son ʿAbd Allāh wrote to him was the following: 52.4

[ʿAbd Allāh:] I remember that whenever any tribesman of Quraysh, young or old, or anyone of the Prophet's family came to see him, he'd refuse to walk through the doorway of the mosque until after they had gone through ahead of him.

We cite Muḥammad ibn Abī Manṣūr, who cites Abū l-Ḥusayn ibn ʿAbd al-Jabbār, who cites Muḥammad ibn ʿAbd al-Wāḥid ibn Jaʿfar al-Ḥarīrī, who cites Abū ʿUmar ibn Ḥayyuwayh, who heard ʿAbd Allāh ibn Muḥammad ibn Isḥāq al-Marwazī report that he heard al-ʿAbbās ibn Muḥammad al-Dūrī report that he heard ʿĀrim ibn al-Faḍl report: 52.5

[ʿĀrim ibn al-Faḍl:] Aḥmad ibn Ḥanbal was here with us in Basra. He had come to me with a knapsack—or maybe a knotted bundle—with some dirhams in it, and every so often he would come and take a little out. One day I said, "Aḥmad, I hear you're an Arab. What tribe are you from?"

"A poor one," he would say.

Every time he came over, I would ask him the same question and he would give me the same answer. It wasn't until he left Basra that I found out the truth.[1]

Al-Khallāl cites Ismāʿīl ibn Isḥāq al-Thaqafī, who reports: 52.6

[Al-Thaqafī:] The first time I saw Aḥmad, I asked if I could kiss his head. He said, "I've done nothing to deserve your respect."

Al-Khallāl cites Abū Bakr al-Marrūdhī, who reports: 52.7

[Al-Marrūdhī:] I asked Aḥmad whether you can tell a man to his face that he's revived the *sunnah*.

"You'll just give him a swelled head," he replied.

قال الخلال: ٨،٥٢

وأخبرني محمّد بن موسى بن أبي موسى[١] قال: رأيتُ أبا عبد الله وقد قال له خراساني: الحمد لله الذي رأيتُك. فقال له: اقعد! أيّ شيء ذا؟ من أنا؟

قال الخلال: ٩،٥٢

وأخبرني أحمد بن الحسين بن حَسّان قال: دخلنا على أبي عبد الله فقال له شيخ من أهل خراسان: يا أبا عبد الله، الله الله! فإنّ الناس يحتاجون إليك قد ذهب الناس فإن كان الحديث لا يمكن فمسائل فإنّ الناس مضطرّون إليك. فقال أبو عبد الله: إليّ أنا؟ واغتمّ من قوله وتنفّس صُعَداء فرأيت في وجهه أثر الغمّ.

وقيل لأبي عبد الله: جزاك الله عن الإسلام خيرًا فقال: لا بل جزى الله الإسلام عني خيرًا. ثمّ قال: ومن أنا؟ وما أنا؟

ودُفع إلى أبي عبد الله كتاب من رجل يسأله أن يدعو الله له فقال: فإذا دعونا لهذا نحن من يدعو لنا؟

قال الخلال: ١٠،٥٢

وأخبرني محمّد بن أحمد بن واصل قال: سمعتُ أبا عبد الله غير مرة يقول: من أنا حتّى تجيئون إليّ؟ من أنا حتى تجيئوا إليّ؟ اذهبوا اطلبوا الحديث!

قال الخلال: ١١،٥٢

وأخبرنا عليّ بن عبد الصمد الطَّيالسي قال: مسحتُ يدي على أحمد بن حنبل ثمّ مسحتُ يدي على بدني وهو ينظر فغضب غضبًا شديدًا وجعل ينفُض يده ويقول: عن من[٢] أخذتم هذا؟ وأنكره إنكارًا شديدًا.

١٢،٥٢ أخبرنا محمّد بن أبي منصور قال: أخبرنا المبارك بن عبد الجبار قال: أخبرنا عليّ بن عمر القَزْويني قال: أخبرنا محمّد

١ د: هرون. ٢ تركي: عَمَّن

Al-Khallāl cites Muḥammad ibn Mūsā ibn Abī Mūsā, who reports: 52.8

[Ibn Abī Mūsā:] A man from Khurasan once said to Aḥmad, "I thank God that I've met you!"

"Come off it," he replied. "What's all this? I'm nobody."

Al-Khallāl cites Aḥmad ibn al-Ḥusayn ibn Ḥassān, who reports: 52.9

[Al-Ḥusayn ibn Ḥassān:] We went in to see Aḥmad ibn Ḥanbal, and an elderly man from Khurasan said, "For God's sake, think of us! We need you. There's no one left who knows anything. If you can't teach Hadith, then answer legal questions. People need your help!"

"Mine?" he replied. He sighed and his face fell. To me he looked miserable.

Once someone said to him, "May God reward you for all you've done for Islam!"

"No," he replied, "may He reward Islam for what it's done for me!" Then he added, "Who am I? No one!"

He was once handed a note from a man asking him to pray for him. "If I do that," he said, "who will pray for me?"

Al-Khallāl cites Muḥammad ibn Aḥmad ibn Wāṣil, who reports: 52.10

[Muḥammad ibn Aḥmad:] More than once I heard Aḥmad say, "Who am I that you should come to me? Who am I that you should come to me? Go seek Hadith!"

Al-Khallāl cites ʿAlī ibn ʿAbd al-Ṣamad al-Ṭayālisī, who reports: 52.11

[Al-Ṭayālisī:] I once laid my hand on Aḥmad ibn Ḥanbal and then ran it down my body for a blessing. He saw me do it and grew furious. Flapping his hands as if to shake something off them, he said, "Who taught you to do that?"

It was clear that he didn't approve at all.

We cite Muḥammad ibn Abī Manṣūr, who cites al-Mubārak ibn ʿAbd al-Jabbār, who cites ʿAlī ibn ʿUmar al-Qazwīnī, who cites Muḥammad ibn al-ʿAbbās ibn Ḥayyuwayh, who heard Jaʿfar ibn Muḥammad al-Ṣandalī report that he was informed by Khaṭṭāb ibn Bishr: 52.12

ابن العباس بن حَيُّويه قال: حدثنا جعفر بن محمد الصَّنْدلي قال:

أخبرني خَطّاب بن بِشر قال: قال أبو عثمان الشافعي لأبي عبد الله أحمد بن حنبل: لا يزال الناس بخير ما منّ الله عليهم ببقائك، وكلام من هذا النحو كثير. فقال: لا تَقُل هذا يا أبا عثمان، لا تقل هذا يا أبا عثمان، ومن أنا في الناس؟

قال خَطّاب: وسألتُه عن شيء من الورع فرأيتُه قد أظهر الاغتمام وتبيّن عليه في وجهه إزراءً على نفسه واغتماماً بأمره حتى شقّ عليّ فقلت لرجل كان معي حين خرجنا: ما أراه ينتفع بنفسه أيّاماً، جدّدنا عليه غمّاً.

١٣،٥٢ أخبرنا محمد بن ناصر قال: أخبرنا عبد القادر بن محمد والمبارك بن عبد الجبار قالا: أخبرنا أبو بكر محمد بن عليّ الخيّاط قال: أخبرنا محمد بن أحمد بن أبي الفوارس قال: أخبرنا أحمد بن جعفر بن سَلْم قال: حدثنا أحمد بن محمد ابن عبد الخالق قال:

حدثنا أبو بكر أحمد بن محمد المَرُّوذي قال: سمعتُ أبا عبد الله أحمد بن محمد بن حنبل وذكر أخلاق الوَرِعين فقال: أسأل الله أن لا يَمقُتنا، أين نحن من هؤلاء؟

وقلت لأبي عبد الله: ما أكثر الداعين لك! فتغرغرت عينه وقال: أخاف أن يكون هذا استدراجاً، أسأل الله أن يجعلنا خيراً مما يظنّون ويغفر لنا مالا يعلمون.

قلت لأبي عبد الله: إنّ بعض المحدّثين قال لي: أبو عبد الله لم يَزْهد في الدراهم وَحدها، قد زَهِد في الناس. فقال أبو عبد الله: ومن أنا حتى أزهد في الناس؟ الناس يريدون يزهدون فيّ.

١٤،٥٢ أخبرنا المبارك بن أحمد الأنصاري قال: أخبرنا عبد الله بن أحمد السَّمَرْقَنْدي قال: أخبرنا أحمد بن عليّ بن ثابت قال: أخبرنا عليّ بن أحمد بن عمر المُقْرئ قال: أخبرنا إسماعيل بن عليّ الخُطَبي قال:

حدثنا عبد الله بن أحمد بن حنبل قال: رأيتُ أبي إذا جاءه الشيخ والحَدَث من قُريش أو غيرهم من الأشراف لا يخرج من باب المسجد حتّى يُخرجهم فيكونون[1] هم يتقدّمونه ثمّ يخرج بعدهم.

١ ش: فيكون؛ تركي: يكونوا.

[Khaṭṭāb ibn Bishr:] Abū ʿUthmān al-Shāfiʿī once began lavishing praise on Aḥmad ibn Ḥanbal, saying things like, "Everyone will be all right as long as God keeps you here with us."

"Don't say those things, Abū ʿUthmān," said Aḥmad. "I'm no one at all."

Another time I asked him a question about being scrupulous. I saw his face fall and assume such a mournful expression of self-reproach that I felt sorry for him. I said to someone who was with me, "Some days he seems so despondent, and all I did was make him feel worse."

We cite Muḥammad ibn Naṣir, who cites ʿAbd al-Qādir ibn Muḥammad, who along with al-Mubārak ibn ʿAbd al-Jabbār cites Abū Bakr Muḥammad ibn ʿAlī l-Khayyāṭ, who cites Muḥammad ibn Aḥmad ibn Abī l-Fawāris, who cites Aḥmad ibn Jaʿfar ibn Salm, who heard Aḥmad ibn Muḥammad ibn ʿAbd al-Khāliq report that he heard Abū Bakr Aḥmad ibn Muḥammad al-Marrūdhī report: **52.13**

[Al-Marrūdhī:] Once, after mentioning men famous for being scrupulous, Aḥmad ibn Ḥanbal said, "I hope God doesn't despise me. How can I compare with men like that?"

Once I said to him, "So many people are praying for you!"

"I'm afraid it may be a ruse to make me feel complacent," he said. "I pray to God to make me better than they think I am and forgive the sins they don't know I've committed."

Another time I told him that a Hadith-man had said, "Aḥmad has given up more than money: he's given up other people, too."

"Who am I to renounce anyone?" he said. "They should be renouncing me!"

We cite al-Mubārak ibn Aḥmad al-Anṣārī, who cites ʿAbd Allāh ibn Aḥmad al-Samarqandī, who cites Aḥmad ibn ʿAlī ibn Thābit, who cites ʿAlī ibn Aḥmad ibn ʿUmar al-Muqriʾ, who cites Ismāʿīl ibn ʿAlī l-Khuṭabī, who heard Aḥmad ibn Ḥanbal's son ʿAbd Allāh report: **52.14**

[ʿAbd Allāh:] I remember that whenever any tribesman of Quraysh, young or old, or anyone of the Prophet's family came to see him, he'd refuse to walk through the doorway of the mosque until after they had gone through ahead of him.

وقد روى أحمد بن عليّ الأبّار قال: ١٥،٥٢

سمعتُ أبا عبد الله[١] أحمد بن حنبل وسأله رجل: حَلفتُ بيمين ما أدري أيّ شيء هي، فقال: ليت لي[١] أنك إذا دَريتَ أنت[٢] دريتُ أنا.

الباب الثالث والخمسون في إجابته الدعوة وخروجه لرؤية المنكَر

أخبرنا محمّد بن ناصر قال: أخبرنا المبارك بن عبد الجبار قال: أخبرنا إبراهيم بن عمر البرمكي قال: أخبرنا أبو عبد ١،٥٣
الله بن بَطّة قال: حدثنا محمّد بن أيوب قال:

حدثنا إبراهيم الحَرْبي قال: كان أحمد بن حنبل يأتي العُرس والإملاك والخِتان يجيب ويأكل.

أخبرنا ابن ناصر قال: أنبأنا أبو عليّ الحسن بن أحمد قال: أخبرنا أبو الفتح بن أبي الفوارس قال: أخبرنا عثمان ٢،٥٣
ابن أحمد قال:

حدثنا أبو شُعيب صالح بن عِمْران الدّعّاء قال: دعا رجل أحمد بن حنبل فقال له: ترى أن تُعفيني بعد الإجابة؟ فقال: لا.

فذهب الرجل فأقعد مع أحمد من لم يشتهِ أحمد أن يقعد معه فقال أحمد عند ذلك: رحم الله ابن سيرين فإنّه قال: لا تُكرم أخاك بما يشُقّ عليه ولكن أخي هذا أكرمني بما يشق عليّ.

أخبرنا إسماعيل بن أحمد ومحمّد[٣] بن أبي القاسم قالا: أخبرنا حَمْد بن أحمد قال: حدثنا أحمد بن عبد الله الحافظ ٣،٥٣
قال: حدثنا محمّد بن جعفر قال: حدثنا محمّد بن إسماعيل قال:

---

١ في ش فقط. ٢ في د فقط. ٣ سقطت من تركي.

Aḥmad ibn ʿAlī l-Abbār reported: 52.15

[Al-Abbār:] I once heard a man tell Aḥmad ibn Ḥanbal, "I've sworn an oath but I don't know what kind of oath it is."

"If you ever figure it out," replied Aḥmad, "maybe I will too."

Chapter 53: His Accepting Invitations and His Withdrawal upon Seeing Things He Disapproved Of

We cite Muḥammad ibn Nāṣir, who cites al-Mubārak ibn ʿAbd al-Jabbār, who cites Ibrāhīm 53.1
ibn ʿUmar al-Barmakī, who cites Abū ʿAbd Allāh ibn Baṭṭah, who heard Muḥammad ibn Ayyūb report that he heard Ibrāhīm al-Ḥarbī report:

[Al-Ḥarbī:] Aḥmad ibn Ḥanbal would accept invitations to marriages, weddings, and circumcisions, and eat what was served.

We cite Ibn Nāṣir, who was informed by Abū ʿAlī l-Ḥasan ibn Aḥmad, who cites Abū 53.2
l-Fatḥ ibn Abī l-Fawāris, who cites ʿUthmān ibn Aḥmad, who heard Abū Shuʿayb Ṣāliḥ ibn ʿImrān al-Daʿʿāʾ report:

[Al-Daʿʿāʾ:] A man once invited Aḥmad ibn Ḥanbal to an event and Aḥmad accepted. Later, he tried to back out of it, but the man wouldn't take no for an answer. At the event the man went and seated Aḥmad next to someone he did not want to sit with. "Ibn Sīrīn, God bless him, had it right," said Aḥmad. "He said, 'Never try to honor your brother by doing something that will cause him hardship.' That's what this brother of mine has done to me."

We cite Ismāʿīl ibn Aḥmad and Muḥammad ibn Abī l-Qāsim, who cite Ḥamd ibn Aḥmad, 53.3
who heard Aḥmad ibn ʿAbd Allāh al-Ḥāfiẓ report that he heard Muḥammad ibn Jaʿfar report that he heard Muḥammad ibn Ismāʿīl report that he heard Aḥmad's son Ṣāliḥ report:

حدثنا صالح بن أحمد قال: كان رجل يختلف إلى عفّان يقال له أحمد بن الحكم العطّار فختن بعض ولده فدعا يحيى وأبا خَيْثَمَة وجماعة من أصحاب الحديث وطلب إلى أبي يحضر فمضوا ومضى أبي بعدهم وأنا معه فلمّا دخل أُجلس في بيت ومعه جماعة من أصحاب الحديث فقال له رجل: يا أبا عبد الله ها هنا آنية من فضّة.

فالتفت فإذا كرسي فقام فخرج وتبعه من كان في البيت وأُخبر الرجل فخرج فلحق أبي وحلف أنه ما علم بذلك ولا أمر به وجعل يطلب إليه فأبى وجاء عَفّان فقال له الرجل: يا أبا عثمان اطلب إلى أبي عبد الله يرجع فكلّمه عفّان فأبى أن يرجع ونزل بالرجل أمر عظيم.

٤،٥٣ أخبرنا محمد بن ناصر قال: أخبرنا أبو الحسين بن عبد الجبار قال: أخبرنا محمد بن عبد الواحد الحريري قال: أخبرنا أبو عُمر بن حَيّويه أن أبا مُزاحم الخاقاني أخبرهم قال: حدثني أبو بكر بن مكرم الصَّفّار قال:

حدثني عليّ بن أبي صالح السَّوّاق قال: كنا في وَلِيمةِ باب المقيّر قال: فجاء أحمد بن حنبل. فلما دخل نظر إلى كرسي في الدار عليه فضّة فخرج فلحقه صاحب المنزل فنفض يده في وجهه وقال: زِيُّ المجوس زيّ المجوس وخرج.

الباب الرابع والخمسون في ذكر إيثاره العُزلة والوَحدة

١،٥٤ أخبرنا إسماعيل بن أحمد ومحمّد بن أبي القاسم قالا: أخبرنا حَمْد بن أحمد قال: حدثنا أبو نُعَيم الحافظ قال: حدثنا أبي قال: حدثنا أحمد بن محمّد بن عمر قال:

[Ṣāliḥ:] There was man called Aḥmad ibn al-Ḥakam al-ʿAṭṭār who used to frequent the circle of ʿAffān. When it came time for him to circumcise one of his sons, he invited Yaḥyā, Abū Khaythamah, and a number of other Hadith-men, including my father. The others went ahead and my father and I came along after them. When we arrived, we were given a seat in a room with several other Hadith-men. At some point one of them said, "Aḥmad, there's something made of silver here." My father turned and saw a chair.[2] So he got up and left, and everyone who was in the room with him followed him out.

Hearing of this, the host, al-ʿAṭṭār, rushed out and caught up with him, swearing that he hadn't brought the item in and didn't know it was there, and asking my father to come back. My father refused. When ʿAffān came along, al-ʿAṭṭār asked him to speak with my father and persuade him to return. ʿAffān spoke with him but it did no good, and al-ʿAṭṭār was devastated.

We cite Muḥammad ibn Nāṣir, who cites Abū l-Ḥusayn ibn ʿAbd al-Jabbār, who cites Muḥammad ibn ʿAbd al-Wāḥid al-Ḥarīrī, who cites Abū ʿUmar ibn Ḥayyuwayh, who cites Abū Muzāḥim al-Khāqānī, who reports that he heard Abū Bakr ibn Makram al-Ṣaffār report that he heard ʿAlī ibn Abī Ṣāliḥ al-Sawwāq report: 53.4

[Al-Sawwāq:] We were at the banquet at the Pitch-Worker's Gate[3] when Aḥmad ibn Ḥanbal arrived. As soon as he set foot in the house, he saw a chair with silver ornamentation, and went out again. The host came out after him, but Aḥmad waved him away and left, saying, "Magian finery! Magian finery!"

Chapter 54: His Preference for Solitude

We cite Ismāʿīl ibn Aḥmad and Muḥammad ibn Abī l-Qāsim, who cite Ḥamd ibn Aḥmad, who heard Abū Nuʿaym al-Ḥāfiẓ report that he heard his father report that he heard Aḥmad ibn Muḥammad ibn ʿUmar report that he heard Aḥmad ibn Ḥanbal's son ʿAbd Allāh report: 54.1

حدثنا عبد الله بن أحمد بن حنبل قال: كان أبي أَصْبَرَ الناس على الوحدة وبِشْر رحمه الله فيما كان فيه لم يكن يصبر على الوحدة فكان يخرج إلى ذا ساعةً وإلى ذا ساعة.

قال أبو نعيم: وحدثنا سليمان بن أحمد قال: ٢،٥٤

قال عبد الله: لم يرَ أحدٌ أبي إلا في مسجد أو حضور جنازة أو عيادة مريض وكان يكره المشي في الأسواق.

أخبرنا ابن ناصر قال أنبأنا الحسن بن أحمد الفقيه قال: أخبرنا أبو القاسم الأَزْهَري قال: أخبرنا القَطيعي قال: ٣،٥٤

حدثنا عبد الله بن أحمد[1] قال: كان أبي أصبر الناس على الوحدة لم يرَه أحد إلا في مسجد أو حضور جنازة أو عيادة مريض وكان يكره المشي في الأسواق.

أخبرنا محمّد بن عبد الباقي قال: أنبأنا محمّد بن أبي نصر قال: أخبرنا أبو عليّ إسماعيل بن أحمد بن الحسين قال: ٤،٥٤
أخبرنا أبي قال: أخبرنا أبو عبد الله محمّد بن عبد الواحد[2] الحافظ قال سمعتُ أبا الطيِّب محمّد بن أحمد الذُهْلي قال: سمعتُ أبا العباس محمّد بن إسحاق يقول:

سمعتُ فتح بن نوح يقول: سمعتُ أحمد بن حنبل يقول: أشتهي ما لا يكون، أشتهي مكانًا لا يكون فيه أحد من الناس.

أخبرنا محمّد بن أبي منصور قال: أخبرنا عبد القادر بن محمّد قال: أنبأنا إبراهيم بن عمر البرمكي قال: أنبأنا عبد العزيز ٥،٥٤
ابن جعفر قال: أخبرنا أحمد بن محمّد الخلاّل قال:

أخبرنا أبو بكر المَرُّوذي قال: قال لي أبو عبد الله: ما أُبالي أن لا يراني أحد ولا أراه وإن كنتُ لأشتهي أن أرى عبد الوهّاب.

قال الخلاّل: وأخبرني عبد الملك بن عبد الحميد المَيْموني قال: ٦،٥٤

---

١ د: أخبرنا أبو القاسم أخبرنا القَطيعي أخبرنا عبد الله بن أحمد الأزهري ٢ د، ش: عبد الله.

['Abd Allāh:] My father could bear solitude better than anyone. Bishr,[4] great as he was, couldn't stand to be alone: he would go out visiting an hour here, an hour there.

Abū Nu'aym heard Sulaymān ibn Aḥmad report that he heard Aḥmad ibn Ḥanbal's son 'Abd Allāh say: 54.2

['Abd Allāh:] The only places anyone saw my father were in the mosque, at a funeral, or at the home of someone taken ill. He hated walking through the markets.

We cite Ibn Nāṣir, who was informed by al-Ḥasan ibn Aḥmad al-Faqīh, who cites Abū l-Qāsim al-Azharī, who cites al-Qaṭī'ī, who heard Aḥmad's son 'Abd Allāh report: 54.3

['Abd Allāh:] My father could bear solitude better than anyone. The only places anyone saw him were in the mosque, at a funeral, or at the home of someone taken ill. He hated walking through the markets.

We cite Muḥammad ibn 'Abd al-Bāqī, who was informed by Muḥammad ibn Abī Naṣr, who cites Abū 'Alī Ismā'īl ibn Aḥmad ibn al-Ḥusayn, who cites his father, who cites Abū 'Abd Allāh Muḥammad ibn 'Abd al-Wāḥid al-Ḥāfiẓ, who heard Abū l-Ṭayyib Muḥammad ibn Aḥmad al-Dhuhlī report that he heard Abū l-'Abbās Muḥammad ibn Isḥāq say that he heard Fatḥ ibn Nūḥ say: 54.4

[Fatḥ ibn Nūḥ:] I heard Aḥmad ibn Ḥanbal say, "I wish for something I'll never have: a place with no one in it at all."

We cite Muḥammad ibn Abī Manṣūr, who cites 'Abd al-Qādir ibn Muḥammad, who was informed by Ibrāhīm ibn 'Umar al-Barmakī, who was informed by 'Abd al-'Azīz ibn Ja'far, who cites Aḥmad ibn Muḥammad al-Khallāl, who cites Abū Bakr al-Marrūdhī, who reports: 54.5

[Al-Marrūdhī:] Aḥmad said to me, "I don't care if I never saw anyone and no one saw me—though I would miss 'Abd al-Wahhāb."[5]

Al-Khallāl cites 'Abd al-Malik ibn 'Abd al-Ḥamīd al-Maymūnī, who reports: 54.6

قال ابن[1] حنبل: رأيت الخلوة أروح لقلبي.

قال الخلاّل: ٧،٥٤

وأخبرني عبد الرحمن بن داوود الفارسي أن الفضل بن عبد الصمد الأصبهاني حدّثهم قال: حضرتُ باب أبي عبد الله فاستأذنت عليه فجاء ابنه عبد الله فدخل فقال له رجل: تُعلِم أبا عبد الله أن فلاناً مات وجنازته تُحمل بعد العصر.

فأخبره عبد الله ثم خرج فقال للرجل: أخبرتُه وترحّم عليه ودعا له، إنه يكره أن يعلم الناس بخروجه فيكثروا عليه.

قال الخلال: ٨،٥٤

وأخبرنا أبو عبد الله أحمد بن محمّد المُسَيّبي قال: قلت لأبي عبد الله: إني أحبّ أن آتيك فأُسلّم عليك ولكني أخاف أن تكره الرِّجل.

فقال: إنّا لنكره ذلك.

قال الخلال: ٩،٥٤

وأخبرنا أبو بكر المرُّوذي قال: ذكرتُ لأبي عبد الله عبد الوهّاب على أن يلتقيا فقال: أليس قد كره بعضهم اللقاء؟

وقال: يتزيّن لي وأتزين له، كفى بالعزلة عِلماً والفقيه الذي يخاف الله.

وسمعتُ أبا عبد الله يقول: أريد النزول بمكة أُلقي نفسي في شِعب من تلكَ الشِّعاب حتى لا أُعرَف.

---

١ د: قال احمد بن.

[Al-Maymūnī:] Ibn Ḥanbal said, "I've found that being alone is easier for me."

Al-Khallāl cites ʿAbd al-Raḥmān ibn Dāwūd al-Fārisī, who heard al-Faḍl ibn ʿAbd al-Ṣamad al-Iṣfahānī report: 54.7

[Al-Iṣfahānī:] I was once at Aḥmad's door waiting to be given permission to go in. At one point his son ʿAbd Allāh appeared. A man who was there said to him, "Tell your father that So-and-So died and we're carrying him to the cemetery this afternoon."

ʿAbd Allāh went in, came out again, and said to the man, "I told him. He asked for God's mercy on the deceased and prayed for him. But he doesn't like to go out when people know he's coming because he'll draw a crowd."

Al-Khallāl cites Abū ʿAbd Allāh Aḥmad ibn Muḥammad al-Musayyabī, who reports: 54.8

[Al-Musayyabī:] I once said to Aḥmad, "I'd like to visit you and pay my respects, but I'm afraid you wouldn't want me to."[6]

"I don't like that sort of thing," he said.

Al-Khallāl cites Abū Bakr al-Marrūdhī, who reports: 54.9

[Al-Marrūdhī:] I once suggested to Aḥmad that he meet up with ʿAbd al-Wahhāb.

"Didn't some of the pious avoid meetings?" he said. Then he added, "He would make an effort to be pleasant with me and I with him. No, solitude is a better teacher. The one with true understanding fears God."[7]

I once heard Aḥmad say, "I want to go down to Mecca and throw myself into one of those ravines where no one will ever find me."

الباب الخامس والخمسون في ذكر إيثاره خمول الذكر واجتهاده في ستر الحال

١،٥٥ أخبرنا محمّد بن أبي منصور قال: أخبرنا عبد القادر بن محمّد قال: أخبرنا إبراهيم بن عمر البَرمكي قال: أخبرنا عليّ بن مَرْدَك قال: حدثنا عبد الرحمن بن أبي حاتم قال: حدثنا أبي قال: حدثنا أحمد بن أبي الحَواري قال:

حدثني عُبيد القارئ قال: دخل عمّ أحمد بن حنبل على أحمد بن حنبل ويده تحت خدّه فقال له: يا ابن أخي أيّ شيء هذا الغمّ؟ أي شيء هذا الحزن؟

فرفع أحمد رأسه فقال: يا عم طوبى لمن أخمل الله عزّ وجلّ ذِكْرَه.

٢،٥٥ قال ابن أبي حاتم:

وسمعت أبي يقول: كان أحمد بن حنبل إذا رأيتَه تعلم أنه لا يُظهر النُسك، رأيتُ عليه نعلاً لا يشبه نعل القُرّاء له رأس كبير معقَّف وشِراكه مُسبَل كأنه اشتُري له من السوق ورأيت عليه إزارًا وجُبّة بُرد[١] مُخطّطة أسمارجون.[٢]

قال عبد الرحمن: أراد بهذا والله أعلم ترك التزيّي بزِيّ القرّاء وإزالته عن نفسه ما يشتهر به.

٣،٥٥ أخبرنا محمّد بن أبي منصور قال: أخبرنا عبد القادر بن محمّد قال: أنبأنا إبراهيم بن عمر قال: أنبأنا عبد العزيز بن جعفر قال: حدثنا أبو بكر الخلّال قال:

قال أبو بكر المرُّوذي: قال لي أبو عبد الله: قُل لعبد الوهاب أَخمِلْ ذِكرك فإني أنا قد بُليت بالشهرة.

وسمعته يقول: والله لو وجدتُ السبيل إلى الخروج لم أُقم في هذه المدينة ولخرجتُ منها حتى لا أُذكر عند هؤلاء ولا يذكروني.

---

١ د: وبرد. ٢ تركي: أسمان جون.

Chapter 55: His Wish to Live in Obscurity and His Efforts to Remain Unnoticed

We cite Muḥammad ibn Abī Manṣūr, who cites ʿAbd al-Qādir ibn Muḥammad, who cites Ibrāhīm ibn ʿUmar al-Barmakī, who cites ʿAlī ibn Mardak, who heard ʿAbd al-Raḥmān ibn Abī Ḥātim report that he heard his father report that he heard Aḥmad ibn Abī l-Ḥawārī report that he heard ʿUbayd al-Qāriʾ report: 55.1

[ʿUbayd al-Qāriʾ:] Aḥmad ibn Ḥanbal's uncle once went to see him and found him with his chin cupped in his hand. "Nephew," he asked, "what's troubling you? Why so glum?"

"Uncle," Aḥmad replied, "happiness is when God makes sure that no one's ever heard of you."

Ibn Abī Ḥātim reports that he heard his father say: 55.2

[Abū Ḥātim:] My father said, "All you had to do was look at Aḥmad ibn Ḥanbal to see that he wasn't trying to show off how ascetic he was. I saw him wearing sandals that didn't look like the sandals that the Qur'an-readers[8] wear. The toe-end was big and curled back and the strap hung loose. They looked like something bought for him from the market. I also saw him wearing a breechclout and a striped gown of a sky-blue color."[9]

By dressing this way Aḥmad was trying to avoid—or so I think, though God alone knows the truth—looking like a Qur'an-reader, in the hope of losing his reputation for piety.

We cite Muḥammad ibn Abī Manṣūr, who cites ʿAbd al-Qādir ibn Muḥammad, who was informed by Ibrāhīm ibn ʿUmar, who was informed by ʿAbd al-ʿAzīz ibn Jaʿfar, who heard Abū Bakr al-Khallāl report that Abū Bakr al-Marrūdhī said: 55.3

[Al-Marrūdhī:] Aḥmad once said to me, "Tell ʿAbd al-Wahhāb to hide his light under a bushel. Fame has brought me nothing but suffering."

[Al-Khallāl:] I heard him say, "I swear that if I knew a way to leave this city, I'd leave it. Then no one would mention me to them, and they'd forget about me."[10]

قال الخلّال: وأخبرنا محمّد بن العباس بن إبراهيم قال: حدثنا الحسن بن عبد الوهّاب قال: ٤،٥٥

حدثني إسحاق بن إبراهيم بن يونس قال: رأيتُ أحمد بن حنبل وقد صلّى الغداة فدخل منزله وقال: لا تتبعوني مرة أخرى.

قال الخلّال: ٥،٥٥

وأخبرني محمّد بن الحسن بن هارون قال: رأيتُ أبا عبد الله إذا مشى في الطريق يكره أن يتبعه أحد.

أخبرنا ابن ناصر قال: أنبأنا الحسن بن أحمد قال: أخبرنا أبو الحسن عليّ بن أحمد المُقرئ قال: أخبرنا الخُطَبي قال: ٦،٥٥

أخبرنا عبد الله بن أحمد قال: كان أبي إذا خرج في يوم الجمعة لا يدع أحداً يتبعه وربما وقف حتى ينصرف الذي يتبعه.

أخبرنا محمّد بن أبي منصور قال: أخبرنا محمّد بن عبد الملك بن عبد القاهر قال: أنبأنا عُبيد[1] الله بن أحمد بن عثمان ٧،٥٥ قال: حدثنا عبيد الله بن عثمان قال: حدثنا عليّ بن محمّد المصري قال:

أخبرني أبو يعقوب إسحاق ابن إبراهيم قال: رأيتُ أحمد بن حنبل يمشي وحده متواضعاً.

الباب السادس والخمسون في ذكر خوفه من الله عزّ وجلّ

أخبرنا إسماعيل بن أحمد السمرقندي ومحمّد بن عبد الباقي قالا: أخبرنا حمد بن أحمد قال: أخبرنا أبو نعيم أحمد ١،٥٦ ابن عبد الله قال: حدثنا محمّد بن جعفر قال: حدثنا محمّد بن إسماعيل بن أحمد قال:

---

١ د: عبد.

Al-Khallāl cites Muḥammad ibn al-ʿAbbās ibn Ibrāhīm, who heard al-Ḥasan ibn ʿAbd al-Wahhāb report that he heard Isḥāq ibn Ibrāhīm ibn Yūnus report: 55.4

[Isḥāq:] I once saw Aḥmad ibn Ḥanbal going back inside his house after praying the dawn prayer. He was telling people, "Stop following me around!"

Al-Khallāl cites Muḥammad ibn al-Ḥasan ibn Hārūn, who reports: 55.5

[Ibn Hārūn:] I remember that Aḥmad didn't like it when people followed him down the street.

We cite Ibn Nāṣir, who was informed by al-Ḥasan ibn Aḥmad, who cites Abū l-Ḥasan ʿAlī ibn Aḥmad al-Muqriʾ, who cites al-Khuṭabī, who cites Aḥmad's son ʿAbd Allāh, who reports: 55.6

[ʿAbd Allāh:] When my father went out on Fridays he wouldn't let anyone follow him. He would often stop and wait until they gave up and went away.

We cite Muḥammad ibn Abī Manṣūr, who cites Muḥammad ibn ʿAbd al-Malik ibn ʿAbd al-Qāhir, who was informed by ʿUbayd Allāh ibn Aḥmad ibn ʿUthmān, who heard ʿUbayd Allāh ibn ʿUthmān report that he heard ʿAlī ibn Muḥammad al-Miṣrī, who cites Abū Yaʿqūb Isḥāq ibn Ibrāhīm, who reports: 55.7

[Isḥāq:] I saw Aḥmad ibn Ḥanbal walking all by himself as if he were a man of no importance.

Chapter 56: His Fear of God

We cite Ismāʿīl ibn Aḥmad al-Samarqandī and Muḥammad ibn ʿAbd al-Bāqī, who cite Ḥamd ibn Aḥmad, who cites Abū Nuʿaym Aḥmad ibn ʿAbd Allāh, who heard Muḥammad ibn Jaʿfar report that he heard Muḥammad ibn Ismāʿīl ibn Aḥmad report that he heard Aḥmad ibn Ḥanbal's son Ṣāliḥ report: 56.1

حدثنا صالح بن أحمد بن حنبل قال: كان أبي إذا دعا له رجل يقول: الأعمال بخواتيمها. وكنتُ أسمعه كثيرًا يقول: اللّٰهُمَّ سَلِّمْ سَلِّمْ.[1]

وحدثني قال: حدثنا[2] يونس بن محمّد قال: حدثنا حمّاد بن زيد قال: زعم يحيى بن سعيد أنّ سعيد بن المسيَّب كان يقول: اللّٰهمّ سلِّمْ سلِّمْ.[3]

وحدثني أيضاً قال: حدثنا زيد بن الحُباب قال: حدثني عَيّاش بن عُقْبة قال: بلغني أن عمر بن عبد العزيز كان يُكثِر أن يقول: اللّٰهمّ سَلِّمْ سَلِّمْ.

٢،٥٦ أخبرنا إسماعيل ومحمّد قالا: أخبرنا حمد بن أحمد قال: حدثنا أبو نُعَيم قال: حدثنا أبي قال: حدثنا أحمد بن محمّد ابن عمر قال:

حدثنا عبد الله بن أحمد بن حنبل قال: سمعتُ أبي يقول: وَدِدتُ أني نجوتُ من هذا الأمر كَفافًا لا عليّ ولا لي.

٣،٥٦ أخبرنا محمّد بن أبي منصور قال: أخبرنا عبد القادر بن محمّد قال: أنبأنا إبراهيم بن عمر قال: أنبأنا عبد العزيز بن جعفر قال: أخبرنا أحمد بن محمّد الخلّال قال:

حدثنا محمّد بن الحسين أن أبا بكر المَرُّوذي حدثهم قال: أدخلتُ إبراهيم الحُصَري على أبي عبد الله، وكان رجلاً صالحًا، فقال: إن أُمّي رأت لك كذا وكذا وذكرت الجنّة فقال: يا أخي إنَّ سَهْل بن سَلامة كان الناس يُخبرونه بمثل هذا وخرج سهل إلى سفك الدماء، وقال: الرؤيا تَسُرّ[4] المؤمن ولا تَغرّه.

٤،٥٦ قال المَرُّوذي:

وسمعتُ محمّد بن حازم يقول: كنتُ عند أبي عبد الله فأتاهُ رجل شيخ فقال: يا أبا عبد الله مررتُ بقوم فذكروك فقالوا: أحمد ابن حنبل من خير الناس. فما اكترث لذلك.

---

١ ش: اللهم سلم اللهم سلم. ٢ ليس في د. ٣ ش: اللهُمَّ سَلِّم. ٤ ش: بُشرى.

[Ṣāliḥ:] Whenever someone said a prayer for my father, he would say, "Call no man blessed until his work is done."

I often heard him say, "God save us! God save us!"

I heard him report that he heard Yūnus ibn Muḥammad report that he heard Ḥammād ibn Zayd report that Yaḥyā ibn Saʿīd claimed that Saʿīd ibn al-Musayyab used to say, "God save us! God save us!" I also heard him report that he heard Zayd ibn al-Ḥubāb report that he heard ʿAyyāsh ibn ʿUqbah report that ʿUmar ibn ʿAbd al-ʿAzīz often used to say, "God save us! God save us!"

We cite Ismāʿīl and Muḥammad, who cite Ḥamd ibn Aḥmad, who heard Abū Nuʿaym report that he heard his father report that he heard Aḥmad ibn Muḥammad ibn ʿUmar report that he heard Aḥmad ibn Ḥanbal's son ʿAbd Allāh report that he heard his father say: 56.2

[ʿAbd Allāh:] All I want is to come out of this even, without winning or losing.[11]

We cite Muḥammad ibn Abī Manṣūr, who cites ʿAbd al-Qādir ibn Muḥammad, who was informed by Ibrāhīm ibn ʿUmar, who was informed by ʿAbd al-ʿAzīz ibn Jaʿfar, who cites Aḥmad ibn Muḥammad al-Khallāl, who heard Muḥammad ibn al-Ḥusayn report that he heard Abū Bakr al-Marrūdhī report: 56.3

[Al-Marrūdhī:] I brought Ibrāhīm al-Ḥuṣarī, who was a righteous man, to meet Aḥmad. Ibrāhīm told him that his mother had dreamed of him and said something about the Garden. "Brother," said Aḥmad, "People used to say the same kind of thing about Sahl ibn Salāmah, but he went on to shed blood."[12] He added, "A believer should find joy in dreams but never trust them."

Al-Marrūdhī reports that he heard Muḥammad ibn Ḥāzim say: 56.4

[Muḥammad ibn Ḥāzim:] Once when I was at Aḥmad's an elderly man came to see him. "Aḥmad," he said, "I overheard some people talking about you and saying you were among the best." Aḥmad ignored him.

قال المرّوذي: ٥،٥٦

وسمعتُ أبا عبد الله يقول: الخوف يمنعني من أكل الطعام والشراب فما أشتهيته.

قال المرّوذي: واراد أبو عبد الله أن يبول في مرضه الذي مات فيه فدعا بطَسْت فجئتُ[١] به فبال دماً عَبيطاً فأريتُه عبد الرحمن المتطِبب فقال: هذا رجل قد فتّت الغمّ - أو قال: الحزن - جوفه.

وبلغنا عن أبي بكر المرّوذي قال: ٦،٥٦

دخلتُ على أحمد يوماً فقلت: كيف أصبحت؟ فقال كيف أصبح مَن ربّه يُطالبه بأداء الفرض ونبيّه يطالبه بأداء السنّة والملكان يطالبانه بتصحيح العمل ونفسه تطالبه بهواها وإبليس يطالبه بالفحشاء وملَك الموت يطالبه بقبض روحه وعياله يطالبونه بالنفقة؟

الباب السابع والخمسون في ذكر غلبة الفكر والهمّ على قلبه

أخبرنا محمّد بن أبي منصور أخبرنا عبد القادر بن محمّد قال: أنبأنا إبراهيم بن عمر قال: أنبأنا عبد العزيز بن جعفر ١،٥٧
قال: حدثنا أحمد بن محمّد الخلّال قال:

أخبرنا أبو بكر المرّوذي قال: دخلتُ موضعاً وأبو عبد الله مُتوكِّئ على يدي[٢] فاستقبلتنا امرأة بيدها طُنبور مكشوف فتناولتُه منها فكسرتُه وجعلتُ أدوسه وأبو عبد الله واقف مُنكِّس الرأس إلى الأرض فلم يَقُل شيئاً وانتشَر أمر الطنبور فقال أبو عبد الله: ما علمتُ بهذا ولا علمت أنك كسرت طنبوراً بحضرتي إلى الساعة.

---

[١] ش: جيئ. [٢] ش: عليّ.

Al-Marrūdhī reports that he heard Abū ʿAbd Allāh say: 56.5

[Al-Marrūdhī:] I once heard Aḥmad say, "I'm too fearful of God to eat or drink, and now I don't want to eat at all."

During his final illness, Aḥmad needed to urinate, and called for a basin. I brought one, and saw that his urine was bright red. When I showed ʿAbd al-Raḥmān the physician, he said, "That's a man with innards torn apart by worry"—or "by sorrow."

We have heard it said that Abū Bakr al-Marrūdhī said: 56.6

[Al-Marrūdhī:] One morning I went in to see Aḥmad and asked him how he was.

"How can a man be," he answered, "with his Lord imposing obligations, his Prophet demanding that he follow the *sunnah*, his two angels waiting for good deeds, his soul clamoring for what it wants, the Devil goading him to lust, the Angel of Death seeking his life, and his family asking for money?"

Chapter 57: His Preoccupation and Absentmindedness

We cite Muḥammad ibn Abī Manṣūr, who cites ʿAbd al-Qādir ibn Muḥammad, who was 57.1 informed by Ibrāhīm ibn ʿUmar, who was informed by ʿAbd al-ʿAzīz ibn Jaʿfar, who heard Aḥmad ibn Muḥammad al-Khallāl report that he heard Abū Bakr al-Marrūdhī report:

[Al-Marrūdhī:] I once went out with Aḥmad leaning on my arm. We were approached by a woman carrying a long-necked lute[13] out in the open. I took it from her, broke it, and started stamping on it. The whole time, Aḥmad stood there staring at the ground and saying nothing. Soon everyone knew about the incident—everyone except for Aḥmad, who said, "I have no recollection of you ever breaking a lute in my presence."

الباب الثامن والخمسون في ذكر تعبّده

١،٥٨ أخبرنا المحمّدان: ابن عبد الملك وابن ناصر قالا: أخبرنا أحمد بن الحسن المعدّل قال: أنبأنا ابن شاذان قال: أخبرنا ابن عَمّ قال:

سمعتُ صالح بن أحمد يقول: كان أبي لا يدع أحدًا يستقي له الماء لوضوئه إلا هو وكان إذا خرجت الدّلو ملأى قال: الحمد لله.

قلتُ: يا أبة أيّ شيء الفائدة في هذا؟ فقال: يا بُني أما سمعتَ الله عزّ وجلّ يقول: ﴿قُلْ أَرَأَيْتُمْ إِنْ أَصْبَحَ مَاؤُكُمْ غَوْرًا فَمَن يَأْتِيكُم بِمَاءٍ مَّعِينٍ﴾.

٢،٥٨ أخبرنا إسماعيل بن أحمد ومحمّد بن عبد الباقي قالا: أخبرنا حَمَد بن أحمد قال[١]: حدثنا أبو نعيم أحمد بن عبد الله قال: حدثنا سليمان بن أحمد قال:

حدثنا عبد الله بن أحمد بن حنبل قال: كان أبي يصلّي في كلّ يوم وليلة ثلاث مائة ركعة فلمّا مرض من تلك الأسواط أضعفته فكان يصلّي في كل يوم وليلة مائة وخمسين ركعة وقد كان قرُب من[٢] الثمانين وكان يقرأ في كل يوم سُبعًا يختم في كل سبعة أيام، وكانت له خَتمة في كلّ سبع ليال سوى صلاة النهار وكان ساعةَ يصلي عشاء الآخرة ينام نومة خفيفة ثم يقوم إلى الصباح يصلّي ويدعو.

٣،٥٨ أخبرنا محمّد بن ناصر قال: أنبأنا أبو عليّ الحسن بن أحمد قال: حدثنا أبو القاسم الأزهَري قال: حدثنا عليّ بن عمر الدّارَقُطني قال: حدثنا أبو بكر النَّيسابوري قال: حدثنا عبد الملك الميموني قال:

قال لي القاضي محمّد بن محمّد بن إدريس الشافعي: قال لي أحمد بن حنبل: أبوك أحد الستّة الذين أدعو لهم سَحَرًا.

٤،٥٨ أخبرنا محمّد بن أبي القاسم قال: أخبرنا حمد بن أحمد قال: حدثنا أبو نُعَيم الحافظ قال: حدثنا عثمان بن محمّد قال: حدثنا أبو الحسين محمّد بن عبد الله الرازي قال:

---

١ د: أخبرنا حمد قال. ٢ د: من زمن.

Chapter 58: His Devotions

We cite the two Muḥammads, Ibn ʿAbd al-Malik and Ibn Nāṣir, who cite Aḥmad ibn al-Ḥasan al-Muʿaddal, who was informed by Ibn Shādhān, who cites Ibn ʿAlam, who heard Aḥmad's son Ṣāliḥ say: 58.1

[Ṣāliḥ:] My father would never let anyone else draw the water for his ablutions. Whenever the bucket came up full, he would say, "Praise God!"

I asked him what the reason was.

"Son," he replied, "haven't you heard what God says? «Say, 'Have you considered if your water were to sink into the ground, who could then bring you flowing water?'»"[14]

We cite Ismāʿīl ibn Aḥmad and Muḥammad ibn ʿAbd al-Bāqī, who cite Ḥamd ibn Aḥmad, who heard Abū Nuʿaym Aḥmad ibn ʿAbd Allāh report that he heard Sulaymān ibn Aḥmad report that he heard Aḥmad ibn Ḥanbal's son ʿAbd Allāh report: 58.2

[ʿAbd Allāh:] My father used to pray three hundred cycles every twenty-four hours. After he was flogged he could no longer manage so many, so he started doing only 150. At that time he was nearly eighty. Every day he'd read a seventh of the Qur'an, finishing it all in a week, and so every seven nights he'd have completed a full reading of the Qur'an in addition to the ritual prayers he'd performed during the daytime. When he'd finish the evening prayer he'd take a nap then pray until morning.

We cite Muḥammad ibn Nāṣir, who was informed by Abū ʿAlī l-Ḥasan ibn Aḥmad, who heard Abū l-Qāsim al-Azharī report that he heard ʿAlī ibn ʿUmar al-Dāraquṭnī report that he heard Abū Bakr al-Naysābūrī report that he heard ʿAbd al-Malik al-Maymūnī report that the judge Muḥammad ibn Muḥammad ibn Idrīs al-Shāfiʿī said to him: 58.3

[Ibn al-Shāfiʿī:] Aḥmad ibn Ḥanbal once told me, "Your father is one of the six people I pray for just before dawn."[15]

We cite Muḥammad ibn Abī l-Qāsim, who cites Ḥamd ibn Aḥmad, who heard Abū Nuʿaym al-Ḥāfiẓ report that he heard ʿUthmān ibn Muḥammad report that he heard Abū l-Ḥusayn Muḥammad ibn ʿAbd Allāh al-Rāzī report that he heard Yūsuf ibn al-Ḥusayn report: 58.4

حدثني يوسف بن الحسين قال: سَألني أحمد بن حنبل عن شيوخ الرّي وقال: أيّ شيء خبر أبي زُرْعة حفظه الله؟

فقلت: خير.

فقال: خمسة أدعو لهم في دُبُر كل صلاة أبوايَ والشافعيّ وأبو زُرْعة وآخر ذهب عنّي اسمه.

أخبرنا ابن ناصر قال: أنبأنا الحسن بن أحمد الفقيه قال: أخبرنا أبو محمّد الحسن بن محمّد قال: حدثنا يوسف بن ٥،٥٨
عمر قال: حدثنا أحمد بن جعفر قال: حدثنا أبو محمّد بن يونس بن عبد السميع قال:

سمعتُ هِلال بن العَلاء يقول: خرج الشافعي ويحيى بن مَعِين وأحمد بن حنبل إلى مكّة فلما أن صاروا بمكة نزلوا في موضع فأمّا الشافعي فإنه استلقى ويَحيى بن مَعِين أيضاً استلقى وأحمد بن حنبل قائم[١] يصلّي.

فلمّا أصبحوا قال الشافعي: لقد عملتُ للمسلمين مِائتي[٢] مَسألة.

وقيل ليحيى بن مَعِين: أي شيء عملتَ؟

قال: نفيتُ عن النبي صلى الله عليه وسلم مِائتي كذّاب.

وقيل لأحمد بن حنبل: فأنت؟

قال: صلّيتُ ركعات ختمتُ فيها القرآن.

أخبرنا ابن ناصر قال: أخبرنا عبد الملك بن محمّد البُرُوغَانيّ قال: أخبرنا عليّ بن عمر القَزْوِيني قال: حدثنا يوسف ٦،٥٨
ابن عمر القَوّاس قال: حدثنا أبو عبد الله محمّد بن القاسم ابن بنت كَعْب قال:

حدثنا جعفر بن أبي هاشم قال: سمعت أحمد بن حنبل يقول: ختمتُ القرآن في يوم فعددتُ موضع الصبر فإذا هو نيف وتسعون.

أخبرنا محمّد بن أبي منصور قال: أخبرنا عبد القادر بن محمّد بن يوسف قال: أخبرنا إبراهيم بن عمر البرمكي قال: ٧،٥٨
حدثنا عليّ بن عبد العزيز بن مَرْدَك قال: حدثنا عبد الرحمن بن أبي حاتم قال:

---

١ د: قام. ٢ ش: مايه.

[Yūsuf ibn al-Ḥusayn:] Aḥmad ibn Ḥanbal once asked me about the elders of Rey. "How is Abū Zurʿah, may God protect him?"

"He's well," I said.

He said: "There are five people I pray for at the end of every prayer." He told me who they were: his parents, al-Shāfiʿī, Abū Zurʿah, and one more whose name I've forgotten.

We cite Ibn Nāṣir, who was informed by al-Ḥasan ibn Aḥmad al-Faqīh, who cites Abū Muḥammad al-Ḥasan ibn Muḥammad, who heard Yūsuf ibn ʿUmar report that he heard Aḥmad ibn Jaʿfar report that he heard Abū Muḥammad ibn Yūnis ibn ʿAbd al-Samīʿ report that he heard Hilāl ibn al-ʿAlāʾ say: 58.5

[Hilāl ibn al-ʿAlāʾ:] Al-Shāfiʿī, Yaḥyā ibn Maʿīn, and Aḥmad ibn Ḥanbal went to Mecca. As soon as they reached the place where they were staying, al-Shāfiʿī lay down to rest and so did Yaḥyā ibn Maʿīn. Aḥmad, on the other hand, stayed up to pray.

The next morning al-Shāfiʿī said, "I've worked out a hundred legal problems for us Muslims."

"What did you do?" they asked Yaḥyā.

"I've refuted a hundred lies told of the Prophet."

"What about you?" they asked Aḥmad ibn Ḥanbal.

"I prayed two cycles and recited the entire Qurʾan."[16]

We cite Ibn Nāṣir, who cites ʿAbd al-Malik ibn Muḥammad al-Buzūghāʾī, who cites ʿAlī ibn ʿUmar al-Qazwīnī, who heard Yūsuf ibn ʿUmar al-Qawwās (the bowyer) report that he heard Abū ʿAbd Allāh Muḥammad ibn al-Qāsim, whose maternal grandfather was Kaʿb, report that he heard Jaʿfar ibn Abī Hāshim report: 58.6

[Ibn Abī Hāshim:] I heard Aḥmad ibn Ḥanbal say, "I've read through the whole Qurʾan in a day and counted how many times the word 'fortitude' comes up. It's over ninety."[17]

We cite Muḥammad ibn Abī Manṣūr, who cites ʿAbd al-Qādir ibn Muḥammad ibn Yūsuf, who cites Ibrāhīm ibn ʿUmar al-Barmakī, who heard ʿAlī ibn ʿAbd al-ʿAzīz ibn Mardak report that he heard ʿAbd al-Raḥmān ibn Abī Ḥātim report that he heard Ṣāliḥ report: 58.7

حدثنا صالح قال: كانت لأبي قَلَنْسُوَة قد خاطها بيده فيها قُطن فإذا قام من الليل لبسها، وكنت أسمع أبي كثيرًا يلتو سورة الكهف.

أخبرنا ابن ناصر قال: أخبرنا أبو سعد محمد بن أحمد الأصبهاني قال: وجدتُ بخط أبي بكر محمد بن عبيد[1] الله حدثنا محمد بن[2] القاسم بن حَسْنُويه قال: قُرِئَ على أبي الحسن عليّ بن عمر بن عبد العزيز وأنا حاضر أسمع: حدثكم أبو محمد عبد الرحمن بن محمد بن عمر البزّاز قال: حدثنا أحمد بن كثير قال: ٨،٥٨

حدثنا أبو بكر محمّد بن أبي عبد الله قال: حدثنا إبراهيم بن هانئ - وكان أبو عبد الله حيث تَوارى من السلطان توارى عنده - فحكى أنه لم يرَ أحدًا أقوى على الزهد والعبادة وجهد النفس من أبي عبد الله أحمد بن حنبل.

قال: كان يصوم النهار ويُعجل الإفطار ثم يصلّي بعد العشاء الآخرة ركعات ثمّ ينام نومة خفيفة ثم يقوم فيتطهّر ولا يزال يصلّي حتى يطلع الفجر ثم يوتِر بركعة. فكان هذا دأبه طول مقامه عندي ما رأيته فتَرَ ليلة واحدة وكنت لا أقوى معه على العبادة وما رأيتُه مفطرًا إلا يومًا واحدًا أفطر واحتجم.

أخبرنا محمد بن أبي منصور قال: أخبرنا عبد القادر بن محمد قال: أنبأنا أبو إسحاق البرمكي قال: أنبأنا عبد العزيز ابن جعفر قال: حدثنا أحمد بن محمد الخلّال قال: حدثنا محمد بن عليّ قال: حدثنا العباس بن أبي طالب قال: ٩،٥٨

سمعتُ إبراهيم بن شماس قال: كنتُ أعرف أحمد بن حنبل وهو غلام وهو يُحيي اللّيل.

قال الخلّال: ١٠،٥٨

وأخبرنا عبد الله بن أحمد قال: رأيتُ أبي لما كبر وأسنّ اجتهد في قراءة القرآن وكثرة الصلاة بين الظهر والعصر فإذا دخلتُ عليه انفتل من الصلاة وربما تكلّم

١ د: ابي بكر بن عبيد الله؛ ش: ابي بكر محمّد بن عبد الله. ٢ ش: بن ابي.

[Ṣāliḥ:] My father had a cap he had sewed himself, lined with cotton. When he stayed up at night to pray he would wear it. I often used to hear him reciting the Chapter of the Cave.[18]

We cite Ibn Nāṣir, who cites Abū Sa'd Muḥammad ibn Aḥmad al-Iṣfahānī, who found a report in the handwriting of Abū Bakr Muḥammad ibn 'Ubayd Allāh that he heard Muḥammad ibn al-Qāsim ibn Ḥasnuwayh report that he was present when a report was read aloud to Abū l-Ḥasan 'Alī ibn 'Umar ibn 'Abd al-'Azīz to the effect that he had heard Abū Muḥammad 'Abd al-Raḥmān ibn Muḥammad ibn 'Umar al-Bazzāz report that he heard Aḥmad ibn Kathīr report that he heard Abū Bakr Muḥammad ibn Abī 'Abd Allāh report: 58.8

[Abū Bakr Muḥammad ibn Abī 'Abd Allāh:] When Aḥmad was on the run from the authorities, he hid in the house of Ibrāhīm ibn Hāni'. I heard Ibrāhīm report that he never saw anyone deny himself so much, pray as earnestly, or push himself as hard as Aḥmad ibn Ḥanbal.

"He would fast all day," he recalled, "and then have a quick meal. After evening prayer he would do more cycles then take a nap. Then he would perform his ablutions and pray straight through until dawn. At dawn he'd pray a single *witr* cycle. That was his routine the whole time he stayed with me. He never let up for a single night. I couldn't keep up with him. I never saw him break his fast, except one day when he had himself cupped and then ate something."

We cite Muḥammad ibn Abī Manṣūr, who cites 'Abd al-Qādir ibn Muḥammad, who was informed by Abū Isḥāq al-Barmakī, who was informed by 'Abd al-'Azīz ibn Ja'far, who heard Aḥmad ibn Muḥammad al-Khallāl report that he heard Muḥammad ibn 'Alī report that he heard al-'Abbās ibn Abī Ṭālib report that he heard Ibrāhīm ibn Shammās report: 58.9

[Ibrāhīm ibn Shammās:] I knew Aḥmad ibn Ḥanbal when he was a boy. Even then he'd stay up at night praying.

Al-Khallāl cites Aḥmad ibn Ḥanbal's son 'Abd Allāh, who reports: 58.10

['Abd Allāh:] After my father grew old, he pushed himself to read the Qur'an more and more often and to pray more frequently between the noon and late afternoon prayers. Whenever I went into his room he would stop praying. Sometimes he would talk to me and sometimes he would sit quietly.

وربما سكت فإذا رأيت ذلك خرجت فيعود لصلاته ورأيتُه وهو مختفٍ أكثَر ذلك يقرأ القرآن.

قال الخلال:

١١،٥٨ وأخبرني أبو النَّضْر إسماعيل بن عبد الله العِجلي قال: أتيتُ أبا عبد الله آخر ما رأيتُه فخرج فقعد في دِهليز فقلتُ: يا أبا عبد الله كنتُ أراك تقف عن أشياء في الفقه، بانَ لك فيها قولٌ؟

فقال: يا أبا النّضر هذا زمان مبادرة، هذا زمان عمل.

وأخذ في نحوٍ من هذا[1] الكلام إلى أن قُمنا.

١٢،٥٨ أخبرنا عبد الوهّاب بن المبارك قال: أخبرنا عاصم بن الحسن قال: حدثنا أبو عمر بن مهدي قال: أخبرنا عثمان ابن أحمد الدقاق قال:

حدثنا جعفر بن أحمد المؤدّب قال: رأيتُ بشر بن الحارث يصلّي بعد الجمعة أربعًا لا يفصل بينهنّ بسلام، ورأيتُ أحمد بن حنبل يصلّي بعد الجمعة ستّ ركعات ويفصل بين[2] كل ركعتَين.

١٣،٥٨ أخبرنا عبد الرحمن بن محمّد القزّاز قال: أخبرنا أحمد بن عليّ بن ثابت قال: أخبرنا أبو الحسن محمّد بن عبد الواحد قال: حدثنا عمر بن محمّد بن عليّ الناقد قال: حدثنا الحسن بن إبراهيم بن تَوْبة الخلال قال:

سمعتُ أبا بكر بن عَنبَر الخُراساني قال: تبعتُ أحمد بن حنبل يوم الجمعة إلى مسجد الجامع فقام عند قُبّة الشعراء يركع وكان يتطوع ركعتين ركعتين فمرّ بين يديه سائل فمنعه منعاً شديداً فأراد السائل أن يمرّ بين يديه فقُمنا إلى السائل فنحّيناه.

١٤،٥٨ أخبرنا ابن ناصر قال: أخبرنا المبارك بن عبد الجبار قال: أخبرنا إبراهيم ابن عمر البرمكي قال: أخبرنا ابن بَطّة قال: حدثنا عمر بن محمّد بن رجاء قال:

---

١ ش، د: في نحو هذا من. ٢ ش، د: في.

If he was quiet, I'd leave him and he'd go back to his prayers. When he was in hiding, I remember seeing him spend most of the time reading the Qur'an.

Al-Khallāl cites Abū l-Naḍr Ismāʿīl ibn ʿAbd Allāh al-ʿIjlī, who reports: 58.11

[Al-ʿIjlī:] The last time I saw Aḥmad, he came out and sat with me in an anteroom.

I said, "I remember there were some law questions you were thinking about. Have you reached any answers?"

"This is the time to make haste," he said, "to *live* by the law." He continued in that vein until we rose to go.

We cite ʿAbd al-Wahhāb ibn al-Mubārak, who cites ʿĀṣim ibn al-Ḥasan, who heard Abū ʿUmar ibn Mahdī, who cites ʿUthmān ibn Aḥmad al-Daqqāq, who heard Jaʿfar ibn Aḥmad al-Mu'addib report: 58.12

[Al-Mu'addib:] I saw Bishr ibn al-Ḥārith pray four cycles after the Friday prayer without breaking them up by doing the salutation after the first two. But I saw Aḥmad ibn Ḥanbal pray six cycles after the Friday prayer and do the salutation after every two.[19]

We cite ʿAbd al-Raḥmān ibn Muḥammad al-Qazzāz, who cites Aḥmad ibn ʿAlī ibn Thābit, who cites Abū l-Ḥasan Muḥammad ibn ʿAbd al-Wāḥid, who heard ʿUmar ibn Muḥammad ibn ʿAlī l-Nāqid report that he heard al-Ḥasan ibn Ibrāhīm ibn Tawbah al-Khallāl report that he heard Abū Bakr ibn ʿAnbar al-Khurāsānī report: 58.13

[Abū Bakr ibn ʿAnbar:] One Friday I followed Ibn Ḥanbal to the mosque of al-Manṣūr. He stood by the Poets' Cupola and started praying supererogatory prayers two cycles at a time. A beggar came and stood in front of him, and Aḥmad gestured at him angrily to go away. Then the beggar tried to pass in front of him, and we rushed over and pulled him aside.[20]

We cite Ibn Nāṣir, who cites al-Mubārak ibn ʿAbd al-Jabbār, who cites Ibrāhīm ibn ʿUmar al-Barmakī, who cites Ibn Baṭṭah, who heard ʿUmar ibn Muḥammad ibn Rajā' report that he heard Aḥmad ibn Ḥanbal's son ʿAbd Allāh say: 58.14

سمعتُ عبد الله بن أحمد بن حنبل يقول: لمّا قدم أبو زُرْعة نزل عند أبي فكان كثير المذاكرة له فسمعتُ أبي يوماً يقول: ما صلّيتُ اليومَ غير الفَرض، استأثرتْ بمذاكرة أبي زُرعة على نوافلي.

وقال إسحاق بن إبراهيم بن هانئ: ١٥،٥٨

خرجتُ مع أبي عبد الله إلى[١] الجامع فسمعته يقرأ سورة الكهف.

الباب التاسع والخمسون في ذكر عدد حِجّاته

أخبرنا إسماعيل بن أحمد ومحمّد بن أبي القاسم قالا: أخبرنا حَمْد بن أحمد قال: حدثنا أبو نُعَيم أحمد بن عبد الله قال: حدثنا سليمان بن أحمد قال: ١،٥٩

حدثنا عبد الله بن أحمد بن حنبل قال: حَجّ أبي خمس حِجّات، ثلاث حِجَج ماشياً واثنتين راكباً وأنفق في بعض حجاته عشرين دِرْهماً.

أخبرنا محمّد بن أبي منصور قال: أخبرنا عبد القادر بن محمّد بن يوسف قال: أخبرنا أبو إسحاق بن عمر البرمكي؛ ٢،٥٩
وأخبرنا عبد الله بن عليّ المُقرئ قال: أخبرنا عبد الملك بن أحمد السُّيُوري قال: حدثنا عبد العزيز بن عليّ بن الفضل قالا: حدثنا عليّ بن عبد العزيز بن مَرْدَك قال: حدثنا عبد الرحمن بن أبي حاتم قال:

حدثنا صالح بن أحمد بن حنبل قال: سمعتُ أبي يقول: حججتُ خمس حجج منها ثلاث راجلاً أنفقتُ في إحدى هذه الحجج ثلاثين درهماً.

أخبرنا ابن ناصر قال: أخبرنا المبارك بن عبد الجبار قال: أخبرنا أبو بكر محمّد بن عليّ الخياط قال: أخبرنا محمّد بن أبي الفَوارس قال: أخبرنا أحمد بن جعفر بن سَلْم قال: أخبرنا أحمد بن محمّد بن عبد الخالق قال: ٣،٥٩

---

١ ليس في هـ.

['Abd Allāh:] When Abū Zur'ah came to Baghdad, he stayed with my father. He kept him so busy comparing reports and their transmissions[21] that my father said at one point, "Today all I've prayed is the ritual prayers. I've let all this comparing with Abū Zur'ah take the place of the rest."[22]

Isḥāq ibn Ibrāhīm ibn Hāni' reports: 58.15

[Ibn Hāni':] I went with Aḥmad to the Friday mosque and overheard him reading the Chapter of the Cave.[23]

Chapter 59: His Performances of the Pilgrimage

We cite Ismā'īl ibn Aḥmad and Muḥammad ibn Abī l-Qāsim, who cite Ḥamd ibn Aḥmad, 59.1
who heard Abū Nu'aym Aḥmad ibn 'Abd Allāh report that he heard Sulaymān ibn Aḥmad report that he heard Aḥmad ibn Ḥanbal's son 'Abd Allāh report:

['Abd Allāh:] My father made five pilgrimages: three on foot and two riding. On some of them he spent only twenty dirhams.

We cite Muḥammad ibn Abī Manṣūr, who cites 'Abd al-Qādir ibn Muḥammad ibn Yūsuf, 59.2
who cites Abū Isḥāq ibn 'Umar al-Barmakī; and we cite 'Abd Allāh ibn 'Alī l-Muqri', who cites 'Abd al-Malik ibn Aḥmad al-Suyūrī, who heard 'Abd al-'Azīz ibn 'Alī ibn al-Faḍl, who along with al-Barmakī heard 'Alī ibn 'Abd al-'Azīz ibn Mardak report that he heard 'Abd al-Raḥmān ibn Abī Ḥātim report that he heard Aḥmad ibn Ḥanbal's son Ṣāliḥ say:

[Ṣāliḥ:] I heard my father say, "I made five pilgrimages, three of them on foot. On one of them I spent only thirty dirhams."

We cite Ibn Nāṣir, who cites al-Mubārak ibn 'Abd al-Jabbār, who cites Abū Bakr 59.3
Muḥammad ibn 'Alī l-Khayyāṭ, who cites Muḥammad ibn Abī l-Fawāris, who cites Aḥmad ibn Ja'far ibn Salm, who cites Aḥmad ibn Muḥammad ibn 'Abd al-Khāliq, who heard Abū Bakr al-Marrūdhī report:

حدثنا أبو بكر المرُّوذي قال: قال لي أبو عبد الله: قد كفى بعضَ الناس من مَكة إلى ها هنا أربعة عشر درهماً.

قلتُ: من يا أبا عبد الله؟

قال: أنا.

٤،٥٩ أنبأنا يحيى بن الحسن قال: أنبأنا القاضي أبو يَعْلى محمد بن الحسين قال: نقلتُ من خطّ أبي إسحاق بن شَاقلا أخبرني أبو حَفص عمر بن عليّ بن جعفر الرزّاز جارنا قال: سمعتُ أبا جعفر محمد بن المولى يقول:

سمعتُ عبد الله بن أحمد بن حنبل يقول: كان في دِهْليزنا دُكّان وكان إذا جاءنا إنسان يريد أبي يخلو[1] معه أجلسه على الدكان وإذا لم يُرِد أن يخلو معه أخذ بعضادتي الباب وكلّمه.

فلمّا كان ذات يوم جاءنا إنسان فقال لي: قُل له: أبو إبراهيم السائح[2] فجلسا[3] على الدكان فقال لي أبي: سَلِّم عليه فإنه من كبار المسلمين، أو من خِيار المسلمين.

فسلّمت عليه فقال له أبي: حدثني يا أبا إبراهيم.

فقال: خرجتُ إلى الموضع الفلاني بقُرب الدَّير الفلاني فأصابتني علّة منعتني من الحركة فقلت في نفسي: لو كنتُ بقرب الدير لعلّ من فيه من الرهبان يداويني فإذا أنا بسبع عظيم يقصد نحوي حتى جاءني فاحتملني على ظهره حَملاً رفيقاً حتى ألقاني عند الدير فنظر الرهبان إلى حالي مع السبع فأسلموا كلُّهم وهم أربع مائة راهب.

ثم قال أبو إبراهيم لأبي: حدّثني يا أبا عبد الله.

فقال له: إني كنتُ قبل الحجّ بخمس ليال، أو أربع ليال، فبينا أنا نائم إذ رأيتُ النبي صلى الله عليه وسلم فقال لي: يا أحمد حُجّ.

فانتبهتُ، وكان من شأني إذا أردتُ سفراً جعلت في مِزْوَد لي فتيتاً ففعلتُ ذلك فلما أصبحتُ قصدت نحو الكوفة فلما تَقضّى بعض النهار إذا أنا بالكوفة فدخلتُ مسجد الجامع فإذا أنا بشاب حسن الوجه طيّب الريح فقلت: سلام عليكم.

---

[1] ش: أن يخلو. [2] تركي: فخرج إليه أبي. [3] ش: جلسنا.

[Al-Marrūdhī:] Aḥmad once said to me, "Some people can make it from Mecca back to Baghdad on only fourteen dirhams."

"Like who?" I asked.

"Me."

We were informed by Yaḥyā ibn al-Ḥasan, who was informed by Judge Abū Yaʿlā Muḥammad ibn al-Ḥusayn, who transcribed from the handwriting of Abū Isḥāq ibn Shāqlā, who cites his neighbor Abū Ḥafṣ ʿUmar ibn ʿAlī ibn Jaʿfar al-Razzāz, who reports that he heard Abū Jaʿfar Muḥammad ibn al-Mawlā say that he heard Aḥmad ibn Ḥanbal's son ʿAbd Allāh say: **59.4**

[ʿAbd Allāh:] In the anteroom of our house was a bench. When my father had a visitor he wanted to sit with privately, he would offer him a seat on the bench. With other callers, he would stand in the doorway with his hands on the doorposts and talk from there. One day a man came to the house and said, "Tell your father it's Abū Ibrāhīm the Wanderer."

The two of them sat down on the bench.

"Say hello to a great Muslim," my father told me (or "one of the best of the Muslims"). So I said hello. Then my father said, "Talk to us, Abū Ibrāhīm."

"I was passing through Such-and-Such a place," he said, "near the monastery there, when I got too sick to walk. I remember thinking that if I were closer to the monastery one of the monks might treat me. Suddenly a great lion appeared, walked up to me, and carried me along gently on its back until we reached the monastery, where it let me down. When the monks saw me arrive on the back of a lion, all four hundred of them embraced Islam.

"Now *you* talk to me, Abū ʿAbd Allāh!"

"Four or five nights before the pilgrimage," said my father, "I dreamed of the Prophet, God bless and keep him. He said, 'Aḥmad, make the pilgrimage.' Then I woke up. Whenever I prepare to travel, I put some crumbled bread in a bag. So I did that. The next morning, I started for Kufa, and got there later the same day. In the Friday mosque, I met a handsome young man with a pleasant scent. I greeted him and then said 'God is great' to begin my prayer. When I finished I asked him whether anyone was still leaving for the pilgrimage. He told me to wait until one of his brethren came along. When

ثم كبّرت أصلّي فلمّا فرغت من صلاتي قلت له: رحمك الله هل بقي أحد يخرج إلى الحجّ؟

فقال: انتظر حتى يجيء أخ من إخواننا. فإذا أنا برجل في مثل حالي.

فلم نزل نسير فقال له الذي معي: رحمك الله إن رأيتَ أن ترفق بنا؟

فقال له الشابّ: إن كان معنا أحمد بن حنبل فسوف يُرفق بنا.

قال أبو عبد الله: فوقع في نفسي أنه الخَضِر فقلت للذي معي: هل لك في الطعام؟

فقال لي: كُل مما تعرف وأكُل مما أعرف. وإذا أصبنا من الطعام غاب الشابّ من بين أيدينا ثم يرجع بعد فراغنا فلمّا كان بعد ثلاث إذا نحن بمكّة.

الباب الستون في ذكر دعائه ومناجاته

١،٦٠ أخبرنا المحمّدان ابن ناصر وابن عبد الباقي قالا: أخبرنا حَمْد بن أحمد قال: أخبرنا أبو نُعَيم الحافظ قال: حدثنا أبو عليّ عيسى بن محمد الجُرَيجي قال:

حدثنا عبد الله بن أحمد بن حنبل قال: كنتُ أسمع أبي كثيرًا يقول في دُبر صلاته: اللّهمّ كما صُنتَ وجهي عن السجود لغيرك فَصُنْ وجهي عن المسألة لغيرك. فقلتُ له: أسمعك تُكثر من هذا الدعاء فعندك فيه أثر؟ قال: فقال لي: نعم كنتُ أسمع وَكيع بن الجرّاح كثيرًا يقول هذا في سجوده فسألته كما سألتني فقال: كنتُ أسمع سفيان الثوري يقول هذا كثيرًا في سجوده فسألته فقال لي: كنتُ أسمع منصور بن المُعتَمِر يقوله.

٢،٦٠ أخبرنا عبد الرحمن بن محمد القزاز قال: أخبرنا أحمد بن عليّ بن ثابت قال: أخبرني الأزهري قال: حدثنا أحمد ابن إبراهيم بن شاذان قال:

he came, he turned out to be a man in the same situation as I was. As we walked along, he asked the young man if we would be carried.[24]

"'If Aḥmad ibn Ḥanbal is with us,' said the young man, 'then we will.'

"At that moment I realized that he was al-Khaḍir. Then I asked the man with me if he wanted something to eat.

"'Go ahead and eat your sort of food,' he said, 'and I'll eat mine.'

"Whenever we ate, the young man would disappear then return when we were done. Three days later we were in Mecca."[25]

Chapter 60: His Extemporaneous Prayers and Supplications

We cite the two Muḥammads, Ibn Nāṣir and Ibn ʿAbd al-Bāqī, who cite Ḥamd ibn Aḥmad, who cites Abū Nuʿaym al-Ḥāfiẓ, who heard Abū ʿAlī ʿĪsā ibn Muḥammad al-Jurayjī report that he heard Aḥmad ibn Ḥanbal's son ʿAbd Allāh report: 60.1

[ʿAbd Allāh:] At the end of his ritual prayers, my father often used to say, "God, you have safeguarded me from prostrating myself before any but You. Safeguard me likewise from seeking anything from any but You."

Finally I said, "I hear you saying that a lot. Are you following a precedent?"

"Yes," he answered. "Wakīʿ ibn al-Jarrāḥ used to say it often, so I asked him about it, just as you asked me now. He said that he heard Sufyān al-Thawrī say it and that Sufyān, when he asked him about it, said that he heard it from Manṣūr ibn al-Muʿtamir."

We cite ʿAbd al-Raḥmān ibn Muḥammad al-Qazzāz, who cites Aḥmad ibn ʿAlī ibn Thābit, who cites al-Azharī, who heard Aḥmad ibn Ibrāhīm ibn Shādhān report that he heard Abū ʿĪsā ʿAbd al-Raḥmān ibn Zādhān al-Razzāz report: 60.2

حدثنا أبو عيسى عبد الرحمن بن زاذان الرزّاز قال: صلّينا وأبو عبد الله أحمد ابن حنبل حاضر فسمعته يقول: اللّٰهمَّ من كان على هوى أو على رأي وهو يظنّ أنه على الحقّ وليس هو على الحق فردَّه إلى الحقّ حتّى لا يَضلَّ من هذه الأُمة أحدٌ.

اللّٰهمَّ لا تشغل قلوبنا بما تكفّلت لنا به ولا تجعلنا في رزقك خَوَلًا لغيرك.

ولا تمنعنا خيرَ ما عندك بشرِّ ما عندنا.

ولا ترانا حيث نهيتنا ولا تفقدنا من حيث أمرتّنا.

أَعِزَّنا ولا تُذِلَّنا أعزّنا بالطاعة ولا تذلّنا بالمعاصي.

وجاء إليه رجل فقال له شيئاً لم أفهمه فقال له: اصبر فإنّ النصر مع الصبر. ثم قال: سمعتُ عفّان بن مسلم يقول: أخبرنا همّام عن ثابت عن أَنَس عن النبي صلى الله عليه وسلم أنه قال: النَّصرُ مَعَ الصَّبْرِ والفَرَجُ معَ الكَرْبِ و ﴿إِنَّ معَ العُسْرِ يُسرًا إنَّ مَعَ العُسْرِ يُسرًا﴾.

أخبرنا عبد الوهاب بن المبارَك قال: أخبرنا أبو الحُسين بن عبد الجبّار قال: أخبرنا إبراهيم بن عمر البرمكي قال: ٣،٦٠
أخبرنا أبو بكر محمّد بن إسماعيل الوَرّاق قال: حدثنا أبو محمّد عبد الله بن إسحاق البَغَوي قال:

حدثنا أبو جعفر محمّد بن يَعقوب الصفّار قال: كُنّا عند أبي عبد الله أحمد بن حنبل فقلتُ: ادعُ الله لنا. فقال: اللّٰهمَّ إنّك تعلم أنّا نعلم أنّك لنا على أكثر ممّا نُحبّ فاجعلنا لك على ما تحبّ.

قال: ثم سكت ساعة فقيل: يا أبا عبد الله زِدْنا.

فقال: اللّٰهمَّ إنّا نسألك بالقدرة التي قلتَ للسماوات والأرض: ﴿أئتِيَا طَوْعًا أَوْ كَرْهًا قَالَتَا أَتَيْنَا طَائِعِينَ﴾، اللّٰهمَّ وفِّقْنا لمرضاتك، اللّٰهمَّ إنا نعوذ بك من الفقر إلاّ إليك ونعوذ بك من الذلّ إلا لك، اللّٰهمَّ لا تُكثِر علينا فنطغَى ولا تُقَلِل علينا فننسى، وهَبْ لنا من رحمتك وَسَعة من رزقك ما يكون بَلاغًا لنا وغنًى من فضلك.

[Al-Razzāz:] Once when we were praying with Aḥmad ibn Ḥanbal, I heard him say, "God, if anyone has followed a caprice or an independent judgment, believing that he is right when he is mistaken, return him to the truth so that no member of this community goes astray.

"God, let us not trouble ourselves over the sustenance that You have undertaken to provide, nor make us dependent on others for that sustenance that comes from You.

"Let us achieve the best of those things that You have promised without being deterred by the worst.

"May You never see us doing what You have forbidden, nor find us shirking from what You have commanded.

"Ennoble us and do not abase us: ennoble us through obedience to You, and do not abase us through disobedience of You."

One time a man came to him and asked him something I couldn't make out. Aḥmad answered, "Hold out as long as you can; in strength is victory." Then he added, "The Prophet, God bless and keep him, said, 'In strength is victory, and after suffering comes relief. «Surely with every hardship there is ease; surely with every hardship there is ease.»'"[26]

We cite ʿAbd al-Wahhāb ibn al-Mubārak, who cites Abū l-Ḥusayn ibn ʿAbd al-Jabbār, who cites Ibrāhīm ibn ʿUmar al-Barmakī, who cites Abū Bakr Muḥammad ibn Ismāʿīl al-Warrāq, who heard Abū Muḥammad ʿAbd Allāh ibn Isḥāq al-Baghawī report that he heard Abū Jaʿfar Muḥammad ibn Yaʿqūb al-Ṣaffār report: 60.3

[Al-Ṣaffār:] We were at Aḥmad ibn Ḥanbal's, and I asked him to pray for us. He said, "You know that we know that You desire for us most of what we seek for ourselves; make us rather seek for ourselves only what You desire for us."

He fell silent. Then someone said, "Give us more."

"God," he said, "we ask You, by that power You spoke of when You said to the heavens and the earth, «Come willingly or unwillingly, and they both said, 'We come willingly,'»[27] to guide us to what pleases You. We seek Your protection against all need except the need for You, and all subjection except to You. Give us not so much that we wax arrogant, nor so little that we become heedless. Grant us, in Your mercy, a sustenance that will suffice us, and a bounty that leaves us dependent on none but You."

٤،٦٠ أنبأنا عليّ بن عبيد الله قال: أنبأنا علي بن أحمد البُندار عن أبي عبد الله بن بَطّة قال: حدثنا أبو صالح محمد بن أحمد بن ثابت قال: حدثني أبو نصر عِصْمة بن أبي عِصْمة قال:

سَمعتُ سِندي الخَواتيمي يقول: دخلتُ على أحمد بعد أن ضُرِب وقد أُخرج من دار الخليفة[١] فرأيتُه مكبوبًا على وجهه في منزله وهو يدعو فسمعته يقول: يا شاكرًا ما يصنع[٢] اصنَعْ بي ما تشكرني عليه.

وبلغني عن المَرُّوذي أنه قال: اجتمع جماعة إلى أحمد فقالوا له: ادعُ فقال: اللّٰهمَّ لا تطالبنا بوفاء الشكر فيما أنعمتَ به علينا.[٣]

وبلغني عن محمّد بن يعقوب الصفّار قال: كان أحمد يدعو في دُبُر كل صلاة: اللّٰهمَّ إني أسألك موجبات رحمتك وعزائم مغفرتك والغنيمة من كلّ بِرّ والسلامة من كل إثم والفوز بالجنّة والنّجاة من النار ولا تدع لنا ذنبًا إلا غفرتَه ولا همًا إلا فرّجته ولا حاجة إلا قضيتها.

٥،٦٠ أخبرنا محمّد بن أبي منصور قال: أنبأنا أبو عليّ الحسن بن أحمد قال: أخبرنا هلال بن محمّد الحفّار قال: حدثني أبو عمرو عثمان بن أحمد السمّاك قال: حدثني أبو أحمد القَزويني قال:

سمعتُ القاسم بن الحسين الورّاق يقول: أراد رجل الخروج إلى طَرَسوس فقال لأحمد: زوّدني دعوة فإني أريد الخروج.

فقال له: قُل: يا دليل الحيارى دُلّني على طريق الصادقين واجعلني من عبادك الصالحين.

قال: فخرج الرجل فأصابته شدة وانقطع عن أصحابه فدعا بهذا الدعاء فلحق أصحابه فجاء إلى أحمد فأخبره بذلك فقال له أحمد: اكْتُمها[٤] علي.

٦،٦٠ أخبرنا عبد الرحمن بن محمّد قال: أخبرنا أحمد بن عليّ بن ثابت قال: أخبرنا أبو بكر أحمد بن عليّ بن محمّد الأصبهاني قال: حدثنا أبو بكر محمّد بن إبراهيم بن يعقوب البُخاري قال: حدثنا أبو النَّضر محمّد بن إسحاق الرَّشادي قال:

---

١ ش: الخلافة. ٢ د: نصنع، تركي: يُصنع. ٣ الخبر ناقص في ش. ٤ ش: اكتم.

We were informed by ʿAlī ibn ʿUbayd Allāh, who was informed by ʿAlī ibn Aḥmad al-Bundār, citing Abū ʿAbd Allāh ibn Baṭṭah, who heard Abū Ṣāliḥ Muḥammad ibn Aḥmad ibn Thābit report that he heard Abū Naṣr ʿIṣmah ibn Abī ʿIṣmah report that he heard Sindī l-Khawātīmī say: 60.4

[Al-Khawātīmī:] After Aḥmad Ibn Ḥanbal had been flogged and then sent out of the caliph's palace, I went to visit him. I found him lying face down in the house, praying. I overheard him say, "O You who reward us for what You do,[28] do to me whatever makes me deserving of Your reward."

I heard that al-Marrūdhī said that a group had gathered at Aḥmad's and asked him to pray. "God," he said, "do not demand from us a gratitude equal to Your blessings."

I heard Muḥammad ibn Yaʿqūb al-Ṣaffār say, "At the the end of every prayer, Aḥmad would say, 'God, I ask You to treat us as mercifully as Your mercy demands, and to forgive as as You have resolved to do. I ask You to let us reap the reward of our good deeds and to safeguard us from iniquity. I ask You to let us enter the Garden in triumph and to escape the Fire. If we sin, pardon us; if we worry, dispel our care. Let us want for nothing, but provide.'"

We cite Muḥammad ibn Abī Manṣūr, who was informed by Abū ʿAlī l-Ḥasan ibn Aḥmad, who cites Hilāl ibn Muḥammad al-Ḥaffār, who heard Abū ʿAmr ʿUthmān ibn Aḥmad al-Sammāk report that he heard Abū Aḥmad al-Qazwīnī report that he heard al-Qāsim ibn al-Ḥusayn al-Warrāq say: 60.5

[Al-Warrāq:] When we were in Tarsus we met someone who was leaving the city and asked Aḥmad to supply him with a prayer. He told him to say, "O guide to the errant! Lead me to the path where the truthful walk, and make of me a righteous servant."

The man left. On the road, he ran into some trouble and was separated from his companions. He uttered the prayer Aḥmad had taught him and shortly afterward caught up with the party. Later he came to Aḥmad and told him what had happened.

"Keep it a secret," said Aḥmad.

We cite ʿAbd al-Raḥmān ibn Muḥammad, who cites Aḥmad ibn ʿAlī ibn Thābit, who cites Abū Bakr Aḥmad ibn ʿAlī ibn Muḥammad al-Iṣfahānī, who heard Abū Bakr Muḥammad ibn Ibrāhīm ibn Yaʿqūb al-Bukhārī report that he heard Abū Naḍr Muḥammad ibn Isḥāq al-Rashādī report that he heard Saʿd ibn Masʿadah say: 60.6

سمعتُ سعد[1] بن مَسْعَدة يقول: سمعتُ طَلْحة بن عُبيد الله البغدادي وكان يسكن مصر يقول: وافق ركوبي ركوب أحمد بن حنبل في السفينة فكان يُطيل السكوت فإذا تكلم قال: اللّهمَّ أمِتْنا على الإسلام والسنّة.

الباب الحادي والستون في ذكر كراماته وإجابة سؤاله

١،٦١ أخبرنا إسماعيل بن أحمد ومحمّد بن أبي القاسم قالا: أخبرنا حَمْد بن أحمد قال: أخبرنا أحمد بن عبد الله قال: حدثنا أبي قال: حدثنا أحمد بن محمّد بن عمر قال:

حدثنا عبد الله بن أحمد بن حنبل قال: رأيتُ أبي حرّج على النمل أن يخرج من داره ثم رأيتُ النمل قد خرجن بعد ذلك نملاً سوداً فلم أرَهم بعد ذلك.

٢،٦١ أخبرنا محمّد بن أبي منصور قال: أخبرنا عبد القادر بن محمّد قال: أنبأنا إبراهيم بن عمر قال: أنبأنا عبد العزيز بن جعفر قال: حدثنا أحمد بن محمّد الخلّال قال:

حدثنا محمّد بن عليّ السِّمسار قال: رأيتُ أبا عبد الله بالليل قد جاء إلى منزل صالح وابن صالح تسيل الدماء من منخريه وقد جُمع له الطب[2] وهم يُعالجونه بالفتل وغيرها والدم يغلبهم.

فقال له أبو عبد الله: أيّ شيء حالك يا بُنيّ؟

فقال: يا جدّي هو ذا أموت، ادعُ الله لي.

فقال له: ليس عليك بأس. ثم جعل يحرك يده كأنه يدعو له فانقطع الدم وقد كانوا يئسوا منه لأنه كان يَرْعُف دائماً.

١ د: سعيد. ٢ هـ ود: هكذا، ش: الطبيب.

[Saʿd ibn Masʿadah:] I heard Ṭalḥah ibn ʿUbayd Allāh al-Baghdādī, who lived in Egypt, report that he and Aḥmad happened to travel by ship together. Aḥmad did not speak except to say, "God, let me die a Muslim and a follower of the *sunnah*."

Chapter 61: His Manifestations of Grace and the Effectiveness of His Prayers

We cite Ismāʿīl ibn Aḥmad and Muḥammad ibn Abī l-Qāsim, who cite Ḥamd ibn Aḥmad, who cites Aḥmad ibn ʿAbd Allāh, who heard his father report that he heard Aḥmad ibn Muḥammad ibn ʿUmar report that he heard Aḥmad ibn Ḥanbal's son ʿAbd Allāh report: **61.1**

[ʿAbd Allāh:] Once I saw my father threaten some ants and ask them to leave his house. They left in a great dark mass and never returned.

We cite Muḥammad ibn Abī Manṣūr, who cites ʿAbd al-Qādir ibn Abī Muḥammad, who was informed by Ibrāhīm ibn ʿUmar, who was informed by ʿAbd al-ʿAzīz ibn Jaʿfar, who heard Aḥmad ibn Muḥammad al-Khallāl report that he heard Muḥammad ibn ʿAlī l-Simsār report: **61.2**

[Muḥammad ibn ʿAlī l-Simsār:] One night Aḥmad went over to Ṣaliḥ's house because Ṣaliḥ's son was bleeding from the nose. The doctors[29] had come and were treating him with a twisted cord and so on,[30] but the blood was coming too fast.

"What's wrong, son?" said Aḥmad.

"Grandpa, I'm going to die!" said the boy. "Call to God for me."

"You'll be all right," said Aḥmad. He moved a hand as if praying for him and the blood stopped. This was after everyone had given the boy up for dead, since he had been bleeding continuously.

قال الخلال: ٣،٦١

وحدثنا أبو طالب عليّ بن أحمد قال: دخلتُ يوماً على أبي عبد الله وهو يُملي عليّ وأنا أكتب فاندقّ قلمي فأخذ قلماً فأعطانيه فجئتُ بالقلم إلى أبي عليّ الجعفري فقلت: هذا قلم أبي عبد الله أعطانيه فقال لغلامه: خُذ القلم فضعه في النخلة عسى تحمل. فوضعه في النخلة فحملت النخلة.

أخبرنا إسماعيل بن أحمد ومحمّد بن أبي القاسم قالا: أخبرنا حمد بن أحمد قال: أخبرنا أحمد بن عبد الله الحافظ ٤،٦١
قال: حدثنا سليمان بن أحمد قال: حدثنا الهَيْثَم بن خَلَف الدُوري قال:

حدثنا العباس بن محمّد الدوري[1] قال: حدثني عليّ بن أبي حَرارة – جار لنا – قال: كانت أُمّي مُقعدةً نحو عشرين سنة فقالت لي يوماً: اذهب إلى أحمد بن حنبل فَسَلْه أن يدعو الله لي، فسرت إليه فدققتُ عليه الباب وهو في دهليزه فلم يفتح لي وقال: من هذا؟

فقلت: أنا رجل من أهل ذاك الجانب سألتني أمّي وهي زَمِنة مُقْعَدة أن أسألك أن تدعو الله لها.

فسمعتُ كلامه كلامَ رجلٍ مُغْضَب فقال: نحن أحوج إلى أن تدعو الله لنا.

فوليتُ منصرفاً فخرجت عجوز من داره فقالت: أنت الذي كلّمت أبا عبد الله؟

قلتُ: نعم.

قالت: قد تركتُه يدعو الله لها.

قال: فجئتُ من فوري إلى[2] البيت فدققتُ الباب فخرجتْ على رجليها تمشي حتى فتحت الباب فقالت: قد وهب الله لي العافية.

أخبرنا محمّد بن أبي منصور قال: أخبرنا عبد القادر بن محمّد قال: أنبأنا إبراهيم بن عمر قال: أنبأنا عبد العزيز بن ٥،٦١
جعفر قال: حدثنا أبو بكر أحمد بن محمد الخلّال قال: حدثنا محمّد بن هارون بن مَكْرَم الصفّار قال:

---

١ حدثنا العباس بن محمّد الدوري: ليس في ش. ٢ ليس في د.

Al-Khallāl reports he also heard Abū Ṭālib ʿAlī ibn Aḥmad report: 61.3

[Abū Ṭālib:] Once I was taking dictation from Aḥmad and my pen snapped. He gave me one of his own. Later I showed it to Abū ʿAlī l-Jaʿfarī, telling him that it was a pen that Aḥmad had given me. "Take it," he told his serving boy, "and lay it on the palm tree: let's see if that will fertilize it."

The boy did as he was asked and the tree grew fruit.

We cite Ismāʿīl ibn Aḥmad and Muḥammad ibn Abī l-Qāsim, who cite Ḥamd ibn Aḥmad, who cites Aḥmad ibn ʿAbd Allāh al-Ḥāfiẓ, who heard Sulaymān ibn Aḥmad report that he heard al-Haytham ibn Khalaf al-Dūrī report that he heard al-ʿAbbās ibn Muḥammad al-Dūrī report: 61.4

[Al-ʿAbbās ibn Muḥammad:] One of my neighbors, a man named ʿAlī ibn Abī Ḥarārah, told me this story.

"My mother had been unable to walk for almost twenty years. One day she said, 'Go ask Aḥmad ibn Ḥanbal to pray to God for me.'

"I went to his house and knocked on the door. He was in the anteroom but he didn't open up.

"'Who is it?' he called out.

"I told him I lived in the neighborhood and my mother was an invalid who couldn't walk and wanted him to pray for her. Through the door came an angry reply: 'She's the one who should be praying for me!'

"I turned away. As I was leaving an old woman came out of the house and said, 'Are you the one who was talking to Abū ʿAbd Allāh?'

"'Yes.'

"'I just heard him praying for her.'

"I rushed home. When I knocked on the door, my mother came out walking on her own two feet to open it, saying, 'God cured me!'"

We cite Muḥammad ibn Abī Manṣūr, who cites ʿAbd al-Qādir ibn Muḥammad, who was informed by Ibrāhīm ibn ʿUmar, who was informed by ʿAbd al-ʿAzīz ibn Jaʿfar, who heard Abū Bakr Aḥmad ibn Muḥammad al-Khallāl report that he heard Muḥammad ibn Hārūn ibn Makram al-Ṣaffār report that he heard Ibrāhīm ibn Hāniʾ report: 61.5

حدثني إبراهيم بن هانئ قال: حدثني فلان النسّاج ساكن لأبي عبد الله قال: كنتُ أشتكي فكنت أئنّ بالليل فخرج أبو عبد الله في جوف الليل فقال: من هذا عندكم يشتكي؟

فقيل له فلان، فدعا لي[1] وقال: اللّهمَّ اشفِه. ودخل فكأنّه كان نارًا صُبّ عليه ماء.

٦،٦١ أخبرنا محمّد بن أبي منصور قال: أنبأنا الحسن بن أحمد الفقيه قال: أخبرنا أبو القاسم عبد العزيز بن محمّد قال: حدثنا أبو بكر[2] بن شاذان قال: حدثنا أبو عيسى أحمد بن يعقوب قال:

حدثتني فاطمة بنت أحمد بن حنبل قالت: وقع الحريق في بيت أخي صالح وكان قد تزوّج إلى[3] قوم مياسير فحملوا إليه جهازًا شبيهاً بأربعة آلاف دينار فأكلته النار فجعل صالح يقول: ما غمّني ما ذهب منّي إلا ثوب لأبي كان يصلّي فيه أتبرّك به وأُصلّي فيه.

قالت: فطفئ الحريق ودخلوا فوجدوا الثوب على سرير قد أكلت النار ما حواليه والثوب سليم.

٧،٦١ قلت: وهكذا بلغني عن قاضي القضاة عليّ بن الحسين الزّينبي أنه حكى أن الحريق وقع في دارهم فاحترق ما فيها إلا كتاب كان فيه شيء بخطّ أحمد.

قلتُ: ولما وقع الغرق ببغداد في سنة أربع وخمسين وخمس مائة وغرقت كتبي سلِم لي مجلّد فيه ورقتان بخطّ الإمام أحمد.

٨،٦١ أنبأنا يحيى بن الحسن قال: أنبأنا محمّد بن الحسين قال: أخبرنا أبو الحسن عليّ بن محمّد الحِنّائيّ قال: أخبرنا أبو محمّد عبد الله بن محمّد قال: أخبرنا أبو بكر محمّد بن عيسى قال: حدثنا العباس قال:

وحدثني اللّكّاف قال: حدثني عبد الله بن موسى وكان من أهل السنّة قال: خرجتُ أنا وأبي في ليلة مظلمة نزور أحمد فاشتدّت الظلمة فقال أبي: يا بُني تعالَ حتى نتوسّل إلى الله تعالى بهذا العبد الصالح حتى يُضيء لنا الطريق فإني مُنذ ثلاثين سنة ما توسّلت به إلا قُضِيت حاجتي.

---

١ د: له. ٢ أبو بكر: ليس في هـ. ٣ من هنا إلى لفظة (يا هذا اتّقِ الله) في ٥،٦٨ ناقص في الصورة الضوئية لـ هـ .

[Ibrāhīm ibn Hāniʾ]: So-and-So the weaver, who rented from Abū ʿAbd Allāh, told me: "Once when I was sick I kept moaning all night. In the middle of the night Aḥmad came out and said, 'Who's that in pain over there?'

"They told him, and he prayed for me. 'God, cure him!' he said, and went back inside. The pain suddenly stopped, as if someone had poured water on a fire."

We cite Muḥammad ibn Abī Manṣūr, who was informed by al-Ḥasan ibn Aḥmad al-Faqīh, who cites Abū l-Qāsim ʿAbd al-ʿAzīz ibn Muḥammad, who heard Abū Bakr ibn Shādhān report that he heard Abū ʿĪsā Aḥmad ibn Yaʿqūb report that he heard Aḥmad ibn Ḥanbal's daughter Fāṭimah report: 61.6

[Fāṭimah:] My brother Ṣāliḥ had a fire in his house. He'd married into a wealthy family who sent over a dowry that looked like it was worth four thousand dirhams, but all of it went up in smoke. Ṣāliḥ said, "All I care about is losing the robe that my father used to wear when he prayed. I liked to put it on for a blessing and pray in it."

When the fire was put out, they went back in. On the bed they found the robe. Everything around it had burned up but the robe was unharmed.

[The author:] I heard a similar story from the chief judge, ʿAlī ibn al-Ḥusayn al-Zaynabī. He had a fire and everything in the house burned up except a book that had some of Aḥmad's writing in it. 61.7

As for myself, when Baghdad was flooded in 554 [1159–60] and my books were ruined, one thing that was spared was a volume containing two sheets in Aḥmad's handwriting.

We were informed by Yaḥyā ibn al-Ḥasan, who was informed by Muḥammad ibn al-Ḥusayn, who cites Abū l-Ḥasan ʿAlī ibn Muḥammad al-Ḥinnāʾī, who cites Abū Muḥammad ʿAbd Allāh ibn Muḥammad, who cites Abū Bakr Muḥammad ibn ʿĪsā, who heard al-ʿAbbās report that he heard al-Lakkāf (the pack-saddler) report: 61.8

[Al-Lakkāf:] ʿAbd Allāh ibn Mūsā, who was a good Sunni, told me: "One dark night, my father and I went out to visit Aḥmad, but it got too dark to see. My father said, 'Let's call on God, invoking His righteous servant Aḥmad, and ask Him to light our way. For thirty years, everything I've asked for in his

فدعا أبي وأمّنت أنا على دعائه فأضاءت السماء كأنها ليلة مُقمرة حتى وصلنا إليه.

أخبرنا محمّد بن ناصر قال: أنبأنا يحيى بن عبد الوهاب بن مَنْدَه قال: أخبرنا محمّد بن الخطّاب قال: أخبرنا محمّد بن علي بن عمرو الحمّامي قال: أخبرنا أحمد بن بُندار بن إسحاق الرازي قال: ٩،٦١

سمعتُ عليّ بن سعيد الرازي قال: صرنا مع أحمد بن حنبل إلى باب المتوكّل فلمّا أدخلوه من باب الخاصّة قال لنا أحمد: انصرفوا عافاكم الله فما مرض منا أحدٌ منذ ذلك اليوم.[١]

الباب الثاني والستون في ذكر عدد زوجاته

أخبرنا محمّد بن أبي منصور قال: أخبرنا عبد القادر بن محمّد قال: أنبأنا إبراهيم بن عمر قال: أنبأنا عبد العزيز بن جعفر قال: حدثنا أبو بكر أحمد بن محمّد بن هارون قال: ١،٦٢

سمعتُ أبا بكر المَرُّوذي يقول: سمعتُ أحمد بن حنبل يقول: ما تزوّجتُ إلا بعد الأربعين.

قلتُ: وأول زوجاته عبّاسة[٢] بنت الفَضْل أمّ صالح.

أخبرنا محمّد بن ناصر قال: أخبرنا عبد القادر قال: أنبأنا أبو إسحاق البرمكي قال: أنبأنا عبد العزيز بن جعفر قال: حدثنا أبو بكر الخلّال قال: ٢،٦٢

أملى علينا زُهَيْر بن صالح بن أحمد بن حنبل قال: تزوّج جَدّي رحمه الله أمَّ أبي عبّاسة[٣] بنت الفضل من العرب من الرَّبَض ولم يولد له منها غير أبي ثم تُوفيت.

---

١ الخبر في ش فقط. ٢ د: عائشة. ٣ د: عائشة.

name has been granted.' My father prayed and I said 'Amen.' The sky lit up as if it were a moonlit night and stayed that way until we arrived."

We cite Muḥammad ibn Nāṣir, who was informed by Yaḥyā ibn 'Abd al-Wahhāb ibn Mandah, who cites Muḥammad ibn al-Khaṭṭāb, who cites Muḥammad ibn 'Alī ibn 'Amr al-Ḥammāmī, who cites Aḥmad ibn Bundār ibn Isḥāq al-Rāzī, who heard 'Alī ibn Sa'īd al-Rāzī report: **61.9**

[Al-Rāzī:] A group of us accompanied Aḥmad ibn Ḥanbal as far as al-Mutawakkil's gate. He was admitted at the Intimates' Gate, but before going in, he said, "All of you can go back now. May God keep you in health!"

Since that day, not one of us has fallen ill.

Chapter 62: The Number of Wives He Had

We cite Muḥammad ibn Abī Manṣūr, who cites 'Abd al-Qādir ibn Muḥammad, who was informed by Ibrāhīm ibn 'Umar, who was informed by 'Abd al-'Azīz ibn Ja'far, who heard Abū Bakr Aḥmad ibn Muḥammad ibn Hārūn report that he heard Abū Bakr al-Marrūdhī say: **62.1**

[Al-Marrūdhī:] I heard Aḥmad say, "I didn't marry until I was forty."

[The author:] His first wife was 'Abbāsah bint al-Faḍl, who was Ṣāliḥ's mother.

We cite Muḥammad ibn Nāṣir, who cites 'Abd al-Qādir, who was informed by Abū Isḥāq al-Barmakī, who was informed by 'Abd al-'Azīz ibn Ja'far, who heard Abū Bakr al-Khallāl report: **62.2**

[Al-Khallāl:] Aḥmad ibn Ḥanbal's grandson Zuhayr dictated the following to us. "My grandfather, God have mercy on him, married my father's mother, 'Abbāsah bint al-Faḍl, an Arab from just outside Medina. She had only one child—my father—and then she died."

أخبرنا أبو منصور القزاز قال: أخبرنا أبو بكر أحمد بن عليّ بن ثابت قال: حدثني الأزهري قال: حدثنا عُبيد الله ٣،٦٢
ابن محمد بن حمدان قال: حدثنا ابن مخلد قال: حدثنا المرُّوذي قال:

سمعتُ أبا عبد الله أحمد بن حنبل يقول: أقامت معي أم صالح ثلاثين سنة فما اختلفتُ أنا وهي في كلمة.

الزوجة الثانية رَيحانة أمّ عبد الله

أخبرنا ابن ناصر قال: أخبرنا عبد القادر بن محمد قال: أنبأنا البرمكي قال: أنبأنا عبد العزيز بن جعفر قال: حدثنا ٤،٦٢
أحمد بن محمد الخلّال قال:

حدثنا زُهَير قال: لما ماتت عبّاسة[1] أمّ صالح تزوّج جدّي بعدها امرأة من العرب يُقال لها رَيحانة فولدت له عمّي عبد الله لم يولد له منها غيره.

قال الخلال: وحدثني محمد بن العباس قال: ٥،٦٢

حدثني محمّد بن بَحر قال: حدثني عمّي قال: لما اجتمعنا لتزويج أبي عبد الله بأُخت محمّد بن ريحان قال له أبوها: يا أبا عبد الله إنها – ووضع أُصبعه على عينه يعني أنها بفرد عين – فقال له أبو عبد الله: قد علمتُ.

قال الخلال: وحدثنا أحمد بن محمّد بن خالد البَراثي قال: ٦،٦٢

أخبرني أحمد ابن عَنبَر[2] قال: لما ماتت أُمّ صالح قال أحمد لامرأة عندهم: اذهبي إلى فلانة ابنة عمّي فاخطُبيها لي من نفسها.

قالت: فأتيتُها فأجابته.

فلمّا رجعت إليه قال: كانت أُختها تسمع كلامك؟ — قال: وكانت بعين واحدة. — فقالت له: نعم.

قال: فاذهبي فاخطُبي تلك التي بعين واحدة.

---

١ د: عائشة. ٢ تركي: عنبر.

We cite Abū Manṣūr al-Qazzāz, who cites Abū Bakr Aḥmad ibn ʿAlī ibn Thābit, who heard al-Azharī report that he heard ʿUbayd Allāh ibn Muḥammad ibn Ḥamdān report that he heard Ibn Makhlad report that he heard al-Marrūdhī report: **62.3**

[Al-Marrūdhī:] I heard Aḥmad say, "Ṣāliḥ's mother and I lived together for thirty years and never had an argument."[31]

His Second Wife, Rayḥānah, ʿAbd Allāh's Mother[32]

We cite Ibn Nāṣir, who cites ʿAbd al-Qādir ibn Muḥammad, who was informed by al-Barmakī, who was informed by ʿAbd al-ʿAzīz ibn Jaʿfar, who heard Aḥmad ibn Muḥammad al-Khallāl report that he heard Zuhayr report: **62.4**

[Zuhayr:] After Ṣāliḥ's mother, ʿAbbāsah, died, my father married an Arab woman named Rayḥānah. She bore him only one child: my uncle ʿAbd Allāh.

Al-Khallāl heard Muḥammad ibn al-ʿAbbās report that he heard Muḥammad ibn Baḥr report: **62.5**

[Muḥammad ibn Baḥr:] I heard my uncle report: "When we all gathered to marry Aḥmad and Muḥammad ibn Rayḥān's sister, her father said to him, 'Abū ʿAbd Allāh, she's—' and laid a finger on his eye, meaning 'She's one-eyed.'

"Aḥmad said, 'I knew that.'"

Al-Khallāl heard Aḥmad ibn Muḥammad ibn Khālid al-Barāthī, who cites Aḥmad ibn ʿAnbar, who reports: **62.6**

[Aḥmad ibn ʿAnbar:] When Ṣāliḥ's mother died, Aḥmad said to one of the women of the house, "Go to my cousin So-and-So and ask her if she'll agree to marry me."

The cousin reported: "So I went and asked, and she agreed. But when I came back, he asked, 'Was her sister listening?'

"I told him that the sister"—who was one-eyed—"had been listening. He said, 'Go back and ask for the one with one eye.' So I did, and she accepted."

فأتتها فأجابته وهي أُمّ عبد الله ابنه.[1]

فأقام معها سبعاً ثم قالت له: كيف رأيتَ يا ابن عمّي؟ أنكرتَ شيئاً؟

قال: لا إلا أنّ نعلك هذه تصرّ.

٧،٦٢ قال الخلال: وأحفظ أنّ خطاب بن بشر قال: قالت امرأة أحمد لأحمد بعد ما دخلت إليه بأيّام: هل تنكر شيء؟

قال: لا إلا أنّ هذه النّعل التي تلبسينها ولم تكن على عهد رسول الله صلّى الله عليه وسلّم.

قال: فباعتها واشترت مقطوعاً فكانت تلبسه.

قال الخلال: وهي هذه المرأة، يعني أمّ عبد الله.

قال الخلّال: وسمعتُ أبا بكر المرُّوذي يقول: سمعتُ أبا عبد الله - وذكر أهله فترحّم عليها - وقال: مكثنا عشرين سنة ما اختلفنا في كلمة.

قال الخلال: وهي هذه المرأة يعني أمّ عبد الله.

٨،٦٢ قلت: قد ذكرنا عنه أنّه قال: أقامت معي أمّ صالح ثلاثين سنة، وفي هذه الرواية: مكثنا عشرين سنة، وكلتا الروايتين عن المرُّوذي، وإحدى الرِّوايتين غلط بلا شك لأنّ أحمد لم يتزوّج إلا بعد الأربعين ولم يتزوج بعد أم صالح حتى ماتت فلو أقام معها ثلاثين ومع الأُخرى عشرين تمّ له تسعون سنة وكلّ ما عاش سَبعاً وسبعين ثمّ كان يكون قد تزوّج أم عبد الله بعد السبعين ومعلوم أنه لم يمت إلا وعبد الله يروي عنه ويسافر معه، وكان يقول: ابني عبد الله محظوظ من حفظ الحديث، وقد طلب الحديث وسمع من العلماء في حياة أبيه الكثير، والذي أراه أنّ الإشارة بقوله مكثنا عشرين سنة إلى أم صالح والله أعلم.

وهاتان زوجتان وما عرفنا أنه تزوج ثالثة.

---

١ د: ابن عمه.

This was ʿAbd Allāh's mother. After seven years of marriage, she asked him, "Cousin, how do things seem to you? Is there anything you don't like?"

"Nothing," he answered, "except that those sandals of yours squeak."

Al-Khallāl also said: "I remember Khaṭṭāb ibn Bishr saying that one of Aḥmad's wives said to him a few days after she came into the household: 'Is there anything I'm doing wrong?' **62.7**

"'No,' he answered, 'except that those sandals you're wearing didn't exist at the time of the Prophet, God bless and keep him.'"

So she sold them and bought a *maqṭūʿ*,[33] which she would wear.

Al-Khallāl added that the woman he was talking about is this one: that is, ʿAbd Allāh's mother.

He also heard al-Marrūdhī say that he heard Aḥmad mention a wife and ask God to have mercy on her. Then he said, "We lived together for twenty years and never had an argument."

That's this woman: ʿAbd Allāh's mother.

[The author:] I've already quoted Aḥmad as saying that Ṣāliḥ's mother lived with him for thirty years, and this last report says that he and a wife lived together for twenty. Although both reports are attributed to al-Marrūdhī, one of them must be wrong. Aḥmad did not marry at all until he was forty and did not marry again until after Ṣāliḥ's mother had died. If he spent thirty years with her and another twenty with the second wife, he would have to have lived for ninety years. Yet he only lived to be seventy-seven. Moreover, he would need to have married ʿAbd Allāh's mother when he was over seventy, but we know that by the time he died, ʿAbd Allāh was already transmitting his reports and traveling with him. Aḥmad used to say that ʿAbd Allāh—who had already begun seeking Hadith and had heard many teachers while his father was still alive—had a good head for memorizing Hadith. Therefore, I think that the person Aḥmad lived with for twenty years was Ṣāliḥ's mother—though God knows best. **62.8**

These, in any case, are the two wives he is known to have had. We have not heard of a third.

الباب الثالث والستّون في ذكر سراريه

كان رضي الله عنه قد اشترى جارية اسمها حُسْن. ١،٦٣

أخبرنا محمّد بن أبي منصور قال: أخبرنا عبد القادر بن محمّد قال: أنبأنا البرمكي قال: أنبأنا عبد العزيز قال: أنبأنا عبد العزيز قال: أنبأنا أبو بكر الخلّال قال: حدثني محمّد بن العبّاس حدثنا محمّد بن عليّ حدثني أبو بكر[1] بن يحيى قال: ٢،٦٣

قال لي أبو يوسف بن بُختان: لمّا أمرَنا أبو عبد الله أن نشتري له الجارية مضيت أنا وفُوران فتبعني أبو عبد الله فقال لي: يا أبا يوسف يكون لها لحم.

قال الخلال: ٣،٦٣

وحدّثنا زُهَير بن صالح قال: لما توفّيت أمّ عبد الله اشترى حُسْنَ فوَلدت منه أمّ عليّ واسمها زينب، ثمّ ولدت الحسن والحسين توأماً وماتا بالقُرب من ولادتهما ثم ولدت الحسن ومحمّدا فعاشا حتى صارا من السنّ إلى نحو الأربعين سنة ثم ولدت بعدهما سعيداً.

قال الخلّال: وحدثنا محمّد بن عليّ بن بحر قال: ٤،٦٣

سمعت حُسْنَ أمّ وَلَد أبي عبد الله تقول: قلتُ لمولاي: يا مولاي أصرف فرد[2] خلخالي؟ قال: وتَطيب نفسكِ؟ قلت: نَعم.

قال: الحمدُ لله الذي وَفقك لهذا.

قالت: فأعطيته أبا الحسن بن صالح فباعه بثمانية دنانير ونصف وفرّقها وقتَ حملي.

فلما ولدتُ حَسناً أعطى مولايَ كَرّامة درهماً، وهي امرأة كبيرة كانت تخدمهم، وقال لها[3]: اذهبي إلى ابن شُجاع، جار لنا قصّاب، يشتري لك بهذا رأساً فاشترى

---

١ د: ابو عبد الله. ٢ هـ: فردة. ٣ ليس في د، ش.

Chapter 63: His Concubines

Aḥmad, God have mercy on him, bought a concubine named Ḥusn. 63.1

We cite Muḥammad ibn Abī Manṣūr, who cites ʿAbd al-Qādir ibn Muḥammad, who was informed by al-Barmakī, who was informed by ʿAbd al-ʿAzīz, who was informed by Abū Bakr al-Khallāl, who heard Muḥammad ibn al-ʿAbbās report that he heard Muḥammad ibn ʿAlī report that he heard Abū Bakr ibn Yaḥyā report that Abū Yūsuf ibn Bukhtān said: 63.2

[Abū Yūsuf ibn Bukhtān:] When Aḥmad asked us to buy the girl for him, Fūrān and I went. As we were leaving, Aḥmad came after me and said, "Make sure she's got some meat on her."

Al-Khallāl also heard Ṣāliḥ's son Zuhayr report: 63.3

[Zuhayr:] When ʿAbd Allāh's mother died, Aḥmad bought Ḥusn. She bore him Umm ʿAlī, whose name was Zaynab. Later she bore al-Ḥasan and al-Ḥusayn, who were twins, but they died soon after they were born. Then she bore Muḥammad and al-Ḥasan, who lived till about forty. After them she bore Saʿīd.

Al-Khallāl also heard Muḥammad ibn ʿAlī ibn Baḥr report that he heard Ḥusn, who bore one of Abū ʿAbd Allāh's sons, say: 63.4

[Ḥusn:] I asked my master whether I should sell one of my anklets. He asked if I really meant it, and I said I did.

"Praise God," he said, "who led you to make this choice."

So I gave the anklet to Ṣāliḥ's son Abū l-Ḥasan, who sold it for eight-and-a-half dinars. When I got pregnant, my master distributed the money. When I had Ḥasan, he gave a dirham to Karrāmah—an old woman who served us—and told her to go to Ibn Shujāʿ—a neighbor of ours who was a butcher—and tell him to take it and buy a head.[34] He bought the head, she brought it home, and we ate it.

"Ḥusn," he said to me, "all I have left is this dirham, and this is the only day you'll get anything from me."[35]

لنا رأساً وجاءت به فأكلنا فقال لي: يا حُسن ما أملك غير هذا الدرهم وما لك عندي غير هذا اليوم.

قالت: وكان إذا لم يكن عند مولاي شيء فرِح يومَه ذلك.

قالت: ودخل مولاي يوماً فقال لي: أريد أحتجم اليوم وليس معي شيء. فجئتُ إلى جرّة لي فيها قريب من نصف مَنّاً[1] غزل فأخرجته فبعثت به إلى بعض الحاكة فباعه بأربعة دراهم فاشتريتُ لحماً بنصف درهم وأعطى الحجّام درهماً واشتريتُ طيباً بدرهم.

ولما خرج مولاي إلى سُرّ مَن رأى كنت قد غزلت غزلاً ليّناً وعملت ثوباً حسناً فلمّا قدم أخرجتُ إليه ذلك الثوب الحسن وكنت قد أُعطيتُ كِراه خمسة عشر درهماً من الغلّة فلمّا نظر إليه قال: ما أريده.

قلت: يا مولاي عندي غير هذا من قطن غيره.

فدفعت الثوب إلى فُوران فباعه باثنين وأربعين درهماً واشتريتُ منه قطناً فغزلته ثوباً كبيراً فلما أعلمته قال: لا تقطعيه، دعيه. فكان كفنه، كُفِّنَ فيه، وأخرجت الغليظ فقطعه.[2]

قالت: وخبزتُ يوماً لمولاي وهو في مرضه الذي تُوفّي فيه فقال: أين خبزتيه؟

قلت: في بيت عبد الله.

قال: ارفعيه. ولم يأكل منه.

٥،٦٣ قلتُ: ما عرفنا أن أحمد رضي الله عنه تزوّج سوى المرأتين اللتين ذكرناهما: أمّ صالح وأُم عبد الله ولا تسرّى إلا بهذه الجارية التي ذكرنا أخبارها واسمها حُسْن إلا أن أبا الحُسين أحمد بن جعفر بن المنادي ذكر في كتاب فضائل أحمد أنّ أحمد استأذن أهله أن يتسرى طلباً للاتّباع فأذنت له فاشترى جارية بثمن يسير وسمّاها ريحانة استناناً برسول الله صلى الله عليه وسلم فعلى هذا يكون قد اشترى جاريتين وتكون إحداهما في حياة زوجته، والله أعلم.

---

١ هكذا في جميع النسخ، وفي تركي: منّ. ٢ ش: قطعته.

Whenever there was no money in the house my master was happy all day.

One day he came in and said he needed a cupping but had no money. So I went to my jar, took out half a *mann*[36] of weaving I kept there, and sent it out to one of the weavers, who sold it for four dirhams. I spent half a dirham on meat, and he spent a dirham on the cupping. I also bought some perfume for another dirham.

When my master went out to Samarra, I wove a length of soft cloth and used it to make a beautiful robe. When he came back I brought out the robe—this was after I'd been paid fifteen dirhams for it out of the rental income[37]—but when he saw it he said, "I don't want it."

"Master," I said, "I have other things I made from different cotton."

So I gave the robe to Fūrān, who sold it for forty-two dirhams. With that I bought some cotton and wove it into a large gown. When I told Aḥmad, he said, "Don't cut—leave it be!" He ended up using it as his shroud and they wrapped him up in it. I took out the coarse material and he cut it.[38]

Once when he was sick at the end I baked something for him.

"Where did you bake this?" he asked.

"At ʿAbd Allāh's," I said.

"Take it away," he said, and refused to eat it.

[The author:] As far as we know, Aḥmad married only two women—Ṣāliḥ's 63.5
mother and ʿAbd Allāh's—and had only the one concubine whose reports we have cited. Her name is Ḥusn. Yet, in his *Virtues of Aḥmad*,[39] Abū l-Ḥusayn Aḥmad ibn Jaʿfar ibn al-Munādī reports that Aḥmad asked his wife for permission to buy a concubine in order to emulate the practice of the Prophet. She gave her permission and he bought an inexpensive girl he named Rayḥānah, following the *sunnah* of the Prophet. If this is right, he must have bought two slaves, one during his wife's lifetime. But God alone knows best![40]

الباب الرابع والستون في ذكر عدد[1] أولاده

١،٦٤ قد ذكرنا أن صالحاً من أُمّ وعبد الله من أمّ وأن حُسْناً[2] الجارية ولدت له الحَسَن والحُسَين ثم ولدت ثالثاً يسمّى بالحسن أيضاً ثم ولدت محمّدا وولدت سعيداً وزَيْنب، وتُكنى أمّ علي.

٢،٦٤ أخبرنا ابن أبي منصور قال: أخبرنا عبد القادر بن محمّد قال: أنبأنا أبو إسحاق البرمكي قال: أنبأنا عبد العزيز بن جعفر قال: حدثنا أحمد بن محمّد الخلال قال:

أخبرني أبو غالب عليّ بن أحمد قال: قال لي صالح: جعل أبي يعتذر إليّ من حَسَن[3] وسعيد ويقول: كلّ ما أخذ الله تعالى ميثاقه فلا بدّ أن يخرج إلى الدنيا.

٣،٦٤ قال الخلال: وأخبرني الخَضِر بن أحمد بن المثنى الكِندي قال:

حدثنا عبد الله بن أحمد قال: وُلد لأبي مولود فأعطاني عبد الأعلى رُقعة يُهنّيه فرمى بالرقعة أبي وقال: ليس هذا كتاب عالِمٍ ولا مُحدِّث، هذا كتابُ كاتب!

٤،٦٤ أنبأنا محمّد بن أبي منصور قال: أخبرنا المبارك بن عبد الجبار قال: أخبرنا عبيد الله بن عمر بن شاهين قال: حدثني أبي قال: حدثنا أحمد بن محمّد بن الفضل قال:

سمعتُ أبا محمّد فُوران يقول: كنتُ أصحبُ أحمد بن حنبل ويأنس إليّ ومنّي يستقرض فإذا جاء مولود بالليل وأنا لا أعلم يجيء في السحر فيقعد على باب داري لا يدق الباب وأنا ليس أعلم به حتى أخرج إلى الصلاة فيقوم إليَّ فيصحبني فأقول له: في أيّ شيء جئت يا أبا عبد الله الساعة؟

فيقول: قد جاءنا مولود.

---

١ ليس في هـ. ٢ هكذا في جميع النسخ. ٣ مشكّلة في هـ ، وفي ش، د : حُسن، مشكّلة أيضا.

Chapter 64: The Number of His Children

We have already mentioned that Ṣāliḥ was born to one mother and ʿAbd Allāh to another, and that Ḥusn the slave bore him al-Ḥasan and al-Ḥusayn, then a third child also named al-Ḥasan, then Muḥammad, Saʿīd, and Zaynab, who was called Umm ʿAlī. 64.1

We cite Ibn Abī Manṣūr, who cites ʿAbd al-Qādir ibn Muḥammad, who was informed by Abū Isḥāq al-Barmakī, who was informed by ʿAbd al-ʿAzīz ibn Jaʿfar, who heard Aḥmad ibn Muḥammad al-Khallāl, who cites Abū Ghālib ʿAlī ibn Aḥmad, who reported that Ṣāliḥ said to him: 64.2

[Ṣāliḥ:] My father once started apologizing to me for Ḥasan and Saʿīd, saying, "Every soul that acknowledged God as his Lord has to be born sooner or later."[41]

Al-Khallāl cites al-Khaḍir ibn Aḥmad ibn al-Muthannā l-Kindī, who heard Aḥmad's son ʿAbd Allāh report: 64.3

[ʿAbd Allāh:] When one of the babies was born, ʿAbd al-Aʿlā gave me a note of congratulations to deliver to my father. But my father flung it away, saying, "No man of learning would write a note like that, or any Hadith-man either. It's what you'd expect from a scribe!"

We were informed by Muḥammad ibn Abī Manṣūr, who cites al-Mubārak ibn ʿAbd al-Jabbār, who cites ʿUbayd Allāh ibn ʿUmar ibn Shāhīn, who heard his father report that he heard Aḥmad ibn Muḥammad ibn al-Faḍl report that he heard Abū Muḥammad Fūrān say: 64.4

[Fūrān:] I was a close associate of Aḥmad ibn Ḥanbal. He felt comfortable with me and he would even borrow money from me.

Whenever he had a baby born at night when I wasn't there to hear about it, he would come in the very early morning and sit by my door. But he wouldn't knock, so I never knew he was there until I came out to pray. Then he would get up and join me. I'd ask him what he was doing there so early and he'd say, "We had a baby."

فيمضي هو وأُصلي أنا الغداة وأخرج إلى القَنْطَرة أو باب التبْن فآخذ ما يصلح للنساء وأبعث به إليه.

الباب الخامس والستون في ذكر أخبار أولاده وعَقِبه

ذكر صالح بن أحمد بن حنبل وأولاده وعَقِبه[1]

١،٦٥ كان صالح يُكنى أبا الفضل وهو أكبر أولاد أحمد وُلد سنة ثلاث ومائتين وكان أحمد يحبّه ويُكرمه وابتُلي بالعيال على حداثة سنّه فقلّت روايته عن أبيه على أنه قد روى عنه كثيرًا[2] وروى عن أبي الوليد الطَّيالِسي وإبراهيم بن الفضل الذارع وعلي بن المَديني، وروى عنه ابنه زُهير والبَغَوي ومحمّد ابن مَخْلد في آخرين. وولي قضاء أصفهان فخرج إليها فمات بها.

٢،٦٥ وأخبرنا عبد الرحمن بن محمّد القزاز قال: أخبرنا أحمد بن عليّ بن ثابت قال: حُدِّثت عن عبد العزيز بن جعفر قال: حدثنا أبو بكر الخلّال قال: كان صالح بن أحمد بن حنبل سَخيًا جدًا، أخبرني الحسن بن عليّ الفقيه بالمصيِّصَة قال: كان صالح قد افتصد فدعا إخوانَه وأنفق في ذلك اليوم نحوًا من عشرين دينارًا في طيب وغيره.

وأحسب أنه قال: كان في الدعوة ابن أبي مريم.

وإذا أبو عبد الله قد دقّ الباب فقال له ابن أبي مريم: أسبِلْ علينا السِّتر لا نفتضح ولا يشمّ أبو عبد الله رائحة الطيب!

---

١ ليس في هـ. ٢ ليس في ش.

Then he'd leave and I'd pray the morning prayer. Afterward I'd go to the bridge[42] or the Straw Gate[43] to buy what the women needed and have it delivered to his house.

Chapter 65: The Lives of His Children and Descendants

Ṣāliḥ ibn Aḥmad ibn Ḥanbal, His Children, and His Descendants

Ṣāliḥ, who was called Abū l-Faḍl, was the oldest of Aḥmad's children. He was born in 203 [818–19]. His father loved him and treated him generously. Burdened with children when he was still young, Ṣāliḥ was unable to transmit as many of his father's reports as he might have, though he still transmitted quite a few, along with reports he learned from Abū l-Walīd al-Ṭayālisī, Ibrāhīm ibn al-Faḍl al-Dhāriʿ (the taker of measures)[44], and ʿAlī ibn al-Madīnī. Transmitting in turn from him were his son Zuhayr, al-Baghawī, and Muḥammad ibn Makhlad, among others. He moved to Isfahan after being appointed judge there, and there he died. 65.1

We cite ʿAbd al-Raḥmān ibn Muḥammad al-Qazzāz, who cites Aḥmad ibn ʿAlī ibn Thābit, who reported that he heard a report credited to ʿAbd al-ʿAzīz ibn Jaʿfar, who heard Abū Bakr al-Khallāl report: 65.2

[Al-Khallāl:] Ṣāliḥ was always eager to spend money. Al-Ḥasan ibn ʿAlī l-Faqīh told me in Miṣṣīṣah that Ṣāliḥ once had his blood let and afterward invited his friends to celebrate his recovery. He must have spent twenty dinars on scent and that sort of thing.

I think it was also al-Ḥasan who told me the following.

At one point Aḥmad knocked on the door. One of the guests, Ibn Abī Maryam, said to Ṣāliḥ, "Let down that curtain so we don't get in trouble with your father! And don't let him smell the scent!"

فدخل أبو عبد الله فقعد في الدار وسأله عن حاله وقال له: خُذ هذين الدرهمين وأنفقهما اليوم. وقام فخرج.

فقال ابن أبي مريم لصالح: فعل الله بك وفعل! لِمَ أردتَ أن تأخذ الدراهم هذه؟[1]

٣،٦٥ أخبرنا عبد الرحمن بن محمّد القزاز قال: أخبرنا أحمد بن عليّ بن ثابت قال: حدثني محمّد بن الحُسين بن محمّد قال: ذكر أبو بكر الخلال قال: أخبرني محمّد بن العباس قال:

حدثني محمّد بن عليّ قال: لما صار صالح إلى أصفهان وكنت معه بدأ بالمسجد[2] الجامع فدخله وصلى ركعتين واجتمع الناس والشيوخ وجلس وقُرئ عهده الذي كتب له الخليفة فجعل يبكي بُكاءً[3] شديداً حتى غلبه فبكى الشيوخ الذين قربوا منه.

فلمّا فُرغ من قراءة العهد جعل المشايخ يدعون له يقولون: ما ببلدنا أحد إلّا ويحبّ أبا عبد الله ويميل إليك.

فقال لهم: تدرون ما أبكاني؟ ذكرتُ أبي أن يراني في مثل هذا[4] الحال، وكان عليه السَّواد، وكان أبي يبعث خلفي إذا جاءه رجل زاهد أو متقشّف لأنظر عليه، يحبّ أن أكون مثله أو يَراني مثله، ولكنّ الله يعلم ما دخلتُ في هذا الأمر إلا لدَيْن قد غلبني وكثرة عيال أحمد.[5]

وكان صالح غير مرة إذا انصرف من مجلس الحكم ينزع سواده ويقول لي: تراني أموت وأنا على هذا؟

توفّي صالح في رمضان سنة خمس وستين ومائتين بأصفهان.

٤،٦٥ فأما زهير بن صالح فإنه حدث عن أبيه[6] وروى عنه ابن أخيه محمّد بن أحمد ابن صالح وأحمد بن سلمان[7] النجّاد. وقال الدارقطني: زهير ثقة.

قال أحمد بن كامل القاضي: توفّي زهير بن صالح في ربيع الأول سنة ثلاث وثلاث مائة.

---

١ تركي: منه. ٢ ش، د: المسجد. ٣ ما بعدها يستأنف في الورقة رقم ١٢٢ من هـ على غير ترتيب. ٤ د: هذه.
٥ تركي: أحمد الله. ٦ د: حدث عن ابيه وروى عن ابيه. ٧ د: سليمان.

Aḥmad came in, sat down, and asked Ṣāliḥ how he was feeling. Then he said, "Here, take these two dirhams and spend them on yourself today." With that, he got up and left.

"You so-and-so!" said Ibn Abī Maryam to Ṣāliḥ. "How could you think of taking those dirhams?"

We cite ʿAbd al-Raḥmān ibn Muḥammad al-Qazzāz, who cites Aḥmad ibn ʿAlī ibn Thābit, who heard Muḥammad ibn al-Ḥusayn ibn Muḥammad report that Abū Bakr al-Khallāl mentioned that Muḥammad ibn al-ʿAbbās heard Muḥammad ibn ʿAlī report: 65.3

[Muḥammad ibn ʿAlī:] I was with Ṣāliḥ when he arrived in Isfahan. The first place he went was the Friday mosque, where he prayed two cycles. Then, when the notables and elders had gathered, he sat down to hear the letter of appointment that the caliph had given him. As the letter was being read he began to weep uncontrollably. Soon the elders sitting near him were weeping as well. When the reading was finished, they prayed aloud for him. "Everyone in our town treasures the memory of Abū ʿAbd Allāh," they told him, "and wishes you the best."

"Do you know," he asked them, "why I'm crying? I imagined my father seeing me like this"—dressed, that is, in the black robes of his office. "Whenever a shabby ascetic would come to visit him, my father would send for me so I could meet him. He wanted me to be like that—or look like that. As God is my witness, I had no choice but to take this position: I have a debt to pay and all my father's children to feed."[45]

More than once, as he left the judicial session and removed his black robe, Ṣāliḥ said to me, "Just think: I might die in these clothes!"

Ṣāliḥ died in Ramaḍān 265 [April–May 879] in Isfahan.

His son Zuhayr transmitted reports from him, and Zuhayr's reports, in turn, were transmitted by his nephew Muḥammad ibn Aḥmad ibn Ṣāliḥ and by Aḥmad ibn Sulaymān al-Najjād. Al-Dāraquṭnī describes Zuhayr as reliable. According to Judge Aḥmad ibn Kāmil, he died in Rabīʿ I 303 [September–October 915]. 65.4

محمّد بن أحمد بن صالح بن أحمد بن حنبل

يُكنى أبا جعفر روى عن أبيه وعن عمّه زهير وإبراهيم بن خالد الهِسِنْجَانِي في ٥،٦٥
جماعة وروى عنه الدَّارَقُطني وتوفّي سنة ثلاثين وثلاث مائة.

ذكر عبد الله بن أحمد بن حنبل

كان يُكنى أبا عبد الرحمن وكان أروى الناس عن أبيه وسمع معظم تصانيفه وحديثه ٦،٦٥
وسمع من عبد الأعلى بن حمّاد وكامل بن طلحة ويحيى بن مَعِين وأبي بكر وعثمان ابنَيْ أبي شَيْبة وشَيبان بن فَرّوخ في خلق كثير.

وكان له حظٌ وافر من الحفظ وكان أحمد يقول: ابني عبد الله محظوظ من علم الحديث، أو: من حفظ الحديث.

ولمّا مرض قيل له: أين تحب أن تُدفن؟ فقال: صحّ عندي أن بالقَطيعة نبيّاً مدفونًا ولأن أكون في جوار نبي أحبّ إليّ من أن أكون في جوار أبي.

وتوفّي يوم الأحد لتسع بقين من جمادى الآخرة سنة تسعين ومائتين ودُفن في آخر النهار في مقابر باب التِّبن وصلّى عليه زُهير ابن أخيه وكان له جمع عظيم.

ذكر سَعيد بن أحمد بن حنبل

قال حنبل بن إسحاق: وُلد سعيد قبل موت أحمد بنحو من خمسين يوماً. وقال غيره: ٧،٦٥
ولي سعيد قضاء الكوفة وتوفي سنة ثلاث وثلاث مائة.

قلتُ: وهذا لا يصحّ فإنّ أبا منصور القزاز أخبرنا قال: أخبرنا أحمد بن عليّ بن ثابت قال: سعيد بن أحمد بن حنبل حكى عن أبي مُجالد أحمد بن الحسين الضرير، روى عنه القاضي أبو عمران موسى بن القاسم الأشْيَب ومات سعيد قبل وفاة أخيه عبد الله بدهر طويل.

Muḥammad ibn Aḥmad ibn Ṣāliḥ ibn Aḥmad ibn Ḥanbal

Called Abū Jaʿfar, he transmitted reports he learned from his father, his uncle Zuhayr, and Ibrāhīm ibn Khālid al-Hisinjānī, among others. Transmitting in turn from him was al-Dāraquṭnī. He died in 330 [941–42]. 65.5

ʿAbd Allāh ibn Aḥmad ibn Ḥanbal

Called Abū ʿAbd al-Raḥmān, he transmitted more of his father's reports than anyone else, having heard most of his compilations and his Hadith. He also heard reports from ʿAbd al-Aʿlā ibn Ḥammād, Kāmil ibn Ṭalḥah, Yaḥyā ibn Maʿīn, Abū Shaybah's sons Abū Bakr and ʿUthman, Shaybān ibn Farrūkh, and many others. 65.6

He had a very retentive memory. His father used to say, "My son ʿAbd Allāh has a gift for learning"—or "memorizing"—"Hadith."

In his last illness, he was asked where he wanted to be buried. He replied, "I'm certain that there's a prophet buried somewhere in the Qaṭīʿah, and I'd rather be near a prophet than near my father."

He died on Sunday, the twenty-first of Jumādā II 290 [May 22, 903], and in the late afternoon was buried in the Straw Gate cemetery. His nephew Zuhayr prayed over him with a great crowd in attendance.

Saʿīd ibn Aḥmad ibn Ḥanbal

According to Ḥanbal ibn Isḥāq, Saʿīd was born about fifty days before Aḥmad died. According to others, Saʿīd was appointed judge in Kufa and died in 303 [915–16]. 65.7

[The author:] This is incorrect. I cite Abū Manṣūr al-Qazzāz, who reports hearing Aḥmad ibn ʿAlī ibn Thabit say that Saʿīd ibn Aḥmad ibn Ḥanbal repeated reports he had heard from Abū Mujālid Aḥmad ibn al-Ḥusayn al-Ḍarīr, and Judge Abū ʿImrān Mūsā ibn al-Qāsim al-Ashyab transmitted reports from *him*. Saʿīd died quite a long time before his brother ʿAbd Allāh.

قلت: وقد ذكرنا في باب ثناء العلماء على الإمام أحمد أنّ إبراهيم الحربي جاء إلى عبد الله يُعزّيه بأخيه سعيد.

٨،٦٥ قلت: فأما الحسن ومحمّد فلا نعرف من أخبارهما شيئًا وأما زينب فقد ذكرنا لها حديثًا في باب ورعه وأنها قالت لإسحاق بن إبراهيم: خُذ هذه الدجاجة فِبعها فإن أبي يحتاج أن يحتجم وما عنده شيء. وقد قال إسحاق: رأيتُ أبا عبد الله يضرب ابنته على اللّحن وينتهرها.

٩،٦٥ وأخبرنا محمّد بن أبي منصور قال: أخبرنا عبد القادر بن محمّد قال: أخبرنا أبو بكر محمّد بن عليّ الخيّاط قال: أخبرنا أبو الفتح بن أبي الفَوارس قال: أخبرنا أبو بكر أحمد بن جعفر بن محمّد بن سَلْم[1] الخُتَّلي[2] قال:

حدثنا أبو بكر المرُّوذي قال: دخلتُ على أبي عبد الله فرأيت امرأة تمشط صبيّة له فقلتُ للماشِطة: بعد وصلتِ رأسَها بقرامِل؟

فقالت: لم تَترُكني الصبية، قالت: إنّ أبي نهاني.

وقالت: يغضب.

وقد رُوي لنا أنّه كانت له بنت اسمها فاطمة والظاهر أنّها غير زينب. إلا أنّا قد ذكرنا عن زهير عدد أولاده ولم يذكرها فيهم فيحتمل أن تكون هي زينب لأنّ المرأة قد تُسمى باسمين ويحتمل أن تكون غيرها.

١٠،٦٥ وقد ذكرنا لفاطمة حديثًا في باب كراماته وقد أنبأنا أبو بكر بن عبد الباقي قال: أنبأنا أبو إسحاق البرمكي قال: وجدتُ في كتاب أبي: حدثنا أبو بكر بن شاذان قال: حدثنا أبو عيسى أحمد بن يعقوب قال:

حدثتني فاطمة بنت أحمد بن حنبل قالت: وقع الحريق في بيت أخي صالح فدخلوا فإذا ثوب كان لأبي قد أكلت النار ما حوله وهو سليم.

---

١ د: مسلم. ٢ ليس في ش.

I have also mentioned, in the chapter on those learned men who praised Aḥmad, that Ibrāhīm al-Ḥarbī visited ʿAbd Allāh to express his condolences on the death of his brother Saʿīd.

Regarding al-Ḥasan and Muḥammad we have no information at all. As for Zaynab, we have reported, in the chapter on Aḥmad's scrupulosity, the story where she tells Isḥāq ibn Ibrāhīm, "Take this chicken and sell it! My father needs a cupping but he has no money." Said Isḥāq, "I saw Aḥmad beat his daughter and scold her for speaking bad Arabic."[46] 65.8

We cite Muḥammad ibn Abī Manṣūr, who cites ʿAbd al-Qādir ibn Muḥammad, who cites Abū Bakr Muḥammad ibn ʿAlī l-Khayyāṭ, who cites Abū l-Fatḥ ibn Abī l-Fawāris, who cites Abū Bakr Aḥmad ibn Jaʿfar ibn Muḥammad ibn Salm al-Khuttalī, who heard Abū Bakr al-Marrūdhī report: 65.9

[Al-Marrūdhī:] I went in to see Aḥmad and found a woman there combing the hair of one of his daughters.

"Have you put ties[47] in her hair yet?" I asked the woman.

"She won't let me," came the reply. "She said, 'My daddy said I can't.'"

"He'd get mad," said the girl.

It is reported that Aḥmad had a daughter named Fāṭimah, who is apparently someone other than Zaynab. On the other hand, Zuhayr's report, cited earlier, on the number of Aḥmad's children does not mention her. Fāṭimah may be the same person as Zaynab, since women sometimes have two names, or she may be someone else. In the chapter on Aḥmad's manifestations of grace, we cited Fāṭimah in this report:

We cite Abū Bakr ibn ʿAbd al-Bāqī, who was informed by Abū Isḥāq al-Barmakī, who found in a document of his father's that he had heard Abū Bakr ibn Shādhān report that he heard Abū ʿĪsā Aḥmad ibn Yaʿqūb report that he heard Aḥmad ibn Ḥanbal's daughter Fāṭimah report:[48] 65.10

[Fāṭimah:] My brother Ṣāliḥ had a fire in his house. Afterward they went in and found that a robe that had belonged to my father was untouched even though everything around it had burned.

الباب السادس والستون في ذكر ابتداء المِحْنة وسببها

١،٦٦ لم يزَلِ الناس على قانون السلف وقولهم إنّ القُرآن كلامُ الله غير مخلوق حتى نبغت المعتزلة فقالت بخَلْق القرآن وكانت تستُر ذلك، وكان القانون محفوظًا في زمن الرشيد.

٢،٦٦ فأخبرنا عبد الرحمن بن محمّد القزاز قال: أخبرنا أحمد بن عليّ بن ثابت قال: أخبرنا محمّد بن أحمد بن أبي طاهر الدقّاق قال: أخبرنا أبو بكر أحمد بن سليمان النجّاد قال: حدثنا عبد الله بن أحمد بن حنبل قال: حدثنا أحمد ابن إبراهيم الدّوْرَقي قال:

حدثني محمّد بن نوح قال: سمعتُ هارون أمير المؤمنين يقول: بلغني أنّ بشرًا المَرِيسي زعَمَ أنّ القُرآن مخلوق، ولِلهِ عليّ إن أظفرني به لأقتلنّه قِتْلَةً ما قتلتُها أحدًا قطّ.

٣،٦٦ أخبرنا عبد الملك بن أبي القاسم قال: أخبرنا عبد الله بن محمّد الأنصاري قال: حدثنا يحيى بن عمّار بن يحيى قال: حدثنا محمّد بن إبراهيم ابن جَنَاح الأصمّ قال: حدثنا أحمد بن محمّد بن سهل قال: حدثنا إبراهيم ابن إسحاق الأنصاري قال: حدثنا أحمد بن إبراهيم الدورقي قال:

سمعتُ محمّد بن نوح يحدّث عن المسعودي قاضي بغداد قال: سمعتُ هارون الرشيد يقول: بلغني أن بِشْر بن غِياث يقول: القُرآن مخلوق ولِلهِ عليّ لئن أظفرني به لأقتلنّه قِتْلة ما قَتلتُها أحدًا.

قال أحمد: فكان بشرٌ متواريًا أيّام هارون نحوًا من عشرين سنة حتى مات هارون فظهر ودعا إلى الضلالة وكان من المحنة ما كان.

٤،٦٦ قلت: فلما تُوفّي الرشيد كان الأمر كذلك في زمن الأمين فلمّا ولي المأمون خالَطه قوم من المعتزلة فحسّنوا له القول بخلق القرآن وكان يتردّد في حمل الناس على

Chapter 66: How and Why the Inquisition Began

Before the rise of the Secessionists, there was general agreement on the ancestral principle that the Qur'an is the speech of God and not created.[49] Even when the Secessionists adopted the belief that the Qur'an is created, they kept it a secret. Thus the principle remained inviolate down through the reign of al-Rashīd.[50] 66.1

We cite ʿAbd al-Raḥmān ibn Muḥammad al-Qazzāz, who cites Aḥmad ibn ʿAlī ibn Thābit, who cites Muḥammad ibn Aḥmad ibn Abī Ṭāhir al-Daqqāq, who cites Abū Bakr Aḥmad ibn Sulaymān al-Najjād, who heard Aḥmad ibn Ḥanbal's son ʿAbd Allāh report that he heard Aḥmad ibn Ibrāhīm al-Dawraqī report that he heard Muḥammad ibn Nūḥ report: 66.2

[Muḥammad ibn Nūḥ:][51] I heard Hārūn al-Rashīd, the Commander of the Faithful, say, "I hear that Bishr al-Marīsī claims the Qur'an is created. If God puts him in my hands, I swear I'll kill him more painfully than I've ever killed anyone."

We cite ʿAbd al-Malik ibn Abī l-Qāsim, who cites ʿAbd Allāh ibn Muḥammad al-Anṣārī, who heard Yaḥyā ibn ʿAmmār ibn Yaḥyā report that he heard Muḥammad ibn Ibrāhīm ibn Janāḥ al-Aṣamm report that he heard Aḥmad ibn Muḥammad ibn Sahl report that he heard Ibrāhīm ibn Isḥāq al-Anṣārī report that he heard Aḥmad ibn Ibrāhīm al-Dawraqī report: 66.3

[Al-Dawraqī:] I heard Muḥammad ibn Nūḥ report, citing al-Masʿūdī, judge in Baghdad: "I hear that Bishr al-Marīsī claims the Qur'an is created. If God puts him in my hands, I swear I'll kill him more painfully than I've ever killed anyone."

Bishr thus remained in hiding for twenty years. When Hārūn died, he reappeared and began advocating his misguided belief. That's how the Inquisition started.

[The author:] Even after al-Rashīd died and al-Amīn became caliph, the official position remained the same. But when al-Maʾmūn came to power, a number of Secessionists insinuated themselves into his company and 66.4

ذلك ويُراقب بقايا الأشياخ ثم قوي عزمه على ذلك فحمل الناس عليه.

أخبرنا عبد الرحمن بن محمد القزاز قال: أخبرنا أحمد بن عليّ بن ثابت قال: أخبرنا القاضي أبو بكر أحمد بن الحسن ٥،٦٦
الحِيري وأبو سعيد محمد بن موسى الصَّيْرَفي قالا: حدثنا أبو العباس محمد بن يَعقوب الأصمّ قال: حدثنا يحيى بن أبي طالب قال: أخبرني الحسن بن شاذان الواسطي قال: حدثني ابن عَرْعَرة قال:

حَدثني ابن أكثم قال: قال لنا المأمون: لولا مكان يزيد بن هارون لأظهرتُ أنّ القُرآن مَخلوق. فقال بعضُ جُلسائه: يا أمير المؤمنين ومن يزيد حتّى يكون يُتّقى؟

قال: فقال: ويحك! إني أخاف إن أظهرتُه فيردّ عليّ فيختلف الناس وتكون فتنة وأنا أكره الفِتنة.

قال: فقال الرجل: فأنا أخبر ذلك منه. فقال له: نعم.

فخرج إلى واسط فجاء إلى يزيد فدخل عليه المسجد وجلس إليه فقال له: يا أبا خالد إن أمير المؤمنين يُقرئك السلام ويقول لك: إني أريد أن أظهر أن القرآن مخلوق.

قال: فقال: كذبتَ على أمير المؤمنين، أمير المؤمنين لا يحمل الناس على ما لا يعرفونه فإن كنتَ صادقًا فاقعُد إلى المجلس فإذا اجتمع الناس فَقُل.

قال: فلما أن كان الغد اجتمع الناس فقام فقال: يا أبا خالد - رضي الله عنك - إنّ أمير المؤمنين يُقرئك السلام ويقول لك: إني أردت أن أُظهر أن القرآن مخلوق فما عندك في ذلك؟ قال: كذبتَ على أمير المؤمنين، أمير المؤمنين لا يحمل الناس على ما لا يعرفونه وما لم يقُل به أحد.

قال: فقدم فقال: يا أمير المؤمنين كنتَ أعلم، كان من القصّة كيتَ وكيت. فقال له: ويحك تلعّب بك!

persuaded him to adopt the view that the Qur'an is created. Fearful of those elders who were still alive, al-Ma'mūn hesitated to call for assent to the new creed. Eventually, though, he resolved to impose it on the community.[52]

We cite ʿAbd al-Raḥmān ibn Muḥammad al-Qazzāz, who cites Aḥmad ibn ʿAlī ibn Thābit, who cites the judge Abū Bakr Aḥmad ibn al-Ḥasan al-Ḥīrī, who along with Abū Saʿīd Muḥammad ibn Musā l-Ṣayrafī heard Abū l-ʿAbbās Muḥammad ibn Yaʿqūb al-Aṣamm report that he heard Yaḥyā ibn Abī Ṭālib, who cites al-Ḥasan ibn Shādhān al-Wāsiṭī, who heard Ibn ʿArʿarah report that he heard Ibn Aktham report: **66.5**

[Ibn Aktham[53]:] Al-Ma'mūn once remarked that if not for Yazīd ibn Hārūn, he would proclaim that the Qur'an is created. One of those present asked whether Yazīd was really someone to worry about.

"Fool!" said the caliph. "What if I make a statement and he condemns it? People will have to choose sides. And if there's one thing I hate, it's conflict."

"Let me go and see for myself," said the man.

"You go ahead," said al-Ma'mūn.

So the man traveled to Wāsiṭ, where he found Yazīd in his mosque and sat down with him.

"Yazīd," said the man, "the caliph sends his regards and wants you to know that he intends to declare that the Qur'an is created."

"You're lying," said Yazīd. "The caliph would never force people to take a position they don't understand or accept. If you want to see for yourself, come back when the study circle gathers. When everyone's here, you can tell them what you told me."

The next day the man waited for the people to gather and then said, "God be pleased with you, Yazīd! The caliph sends his regards and wants you to know that he intends to declare that the Qur'an is created. What do you have to say about that?"

"You're lying," said Yazīd. "The caliph would never force people to take a position they don't understand or accept, and that no one has ever believed in before."

So the man came back and said to the caliph, "You were right! Here's what happened," and told the story.

"Now do you see?" said al-Ma'mūn. "He played you perfectly."

الباب السابع والستون في ذكر قصّته مع المأمون

١،٦٧ قال العلماء بالسِّير: كتب المأمون وهو بالرَّقّة إلى إسحاق بن إبراهيم وهو صاحب الشرطة ببغداد بامتحان الناس فامتحنهم.

٢،٦٧ أخبرنا المحمّدان: ابن ناصر وابن عبد الباقي قالا: أخبرنا حَمْد بن أحمد قال: أخبرنا أبو نُعيم أحمد بن عبد الله قال: حدثنا محمّد بن جعفر وعلي بن أحمد قالا: حدثنا محمّد بن إسماعيل بن أحمد، وأخبرنا هِبة الله بن الحسين بن الحاسب قال: أخبرنا الحسن بن أحمد بن[1] البنّا قال: أخبرنا أبو الفتح بن أبي الفوارس قال: أخبرنا أحمد بن جعفر ابن سَلْم قال: حدثنا عمر بن محمّد بن عيسى الجَوْهَري قالا:

حدثنا صالح بن أحمد بن حنبل قال: سمعتُ أبي يقول: لما أُدخلنا على إسحاق ابن إبراهيم للمحنة قُرِئ علينا كتابُ الذي صار إلى طَرَسوس - يعني المأمون - فكان فيما قُرِئ علينا ﴿ليسَ كمِثْلِه شَيْء﴾ و﴿هُوَ خَالِقُ كُلِّ شَيْءٍ﴾ فقلت: ﴿وهو السميعُ البَصير﴾.

قال صالح: ثم امتحن القوم فوجّه بمن امتنع إلى الحبس فأجاب القوم جميعاً غير أربعة: أبي ومحمّد بن نوح وعُبيد الله بن عمر القَواريري والحسن بن حمّاد سَجّادة. ثم أجاب عُبيد الله بن عمر والحسن بن حماد وبقي أبي ومحمّد بن نوح في الحبس فمكثا[2] أيّاماً في الحبس ثمّ ورد الكتاب من طرسوس بحملهما فحُملا مُقيَّدَين زميلَين.

٣،٦٧ أخبرنا المحمّدان ابن ناصر وابن عبد الباقي قالا: أخبرنا حمد بن أحمد قال: أخبرنا أبو نعيم الحافظ قال: حدثنا سليمان بن أحمد، وأخبرنا ابن ناصر قال: أنبأنا أبو عليّ الحسن بن أحمد قال: أخبرنا عليّ بن أحمد بن عمر الحمّامي قال: أخبرنا ابن الصوّاف قالا: حدثنا عبد الله بن أحمد بن حنبل قال:

---

١ ليس في هـ. ٢ د: فمكث.

Chapter 67: His Experience with al-Maʾmūn[54]

According to his biographers, al-Maʾmūn sent a letter from al-Raqqah[55] to the chief of the Baghdad police, Isḥāq ibn Ibrāhīm, telling him to put the community to the test, which he did. 67.1

We cite the two Muḥammads, Ibn Nāṣir and Ibn ʿAbd al-Bāqī, who cite Ḥamd ibn Aḥmad, who cites Abū Nuʿaym Aḥmad ibn ʿAbd Allāh, who heard Muḥammad ibn Jaʿfar and ʿAlī ibn Aḥmad report that they heard Muḥammad ibn Ismāʿīl ibn Aḥmad; and we cite Hibat Allāh ibn al-Ḥusayn ibn al-Ḥāsib, who cites al-Ḥasan ibn Aḥmad ibn al-Bannā, who cites Abū l-Fatḥ ibn Abī l-Fawāris, who cites Aḥmad ibn Jaʿfar ibn Salm, who heard ʿUmar ibn Muḥammad ibn ʿĪsā l-Jawharī, who along with Muḥammad ibn Ismāʿīl ibn Aḥmad heard Aḥmad ibn Ḥanbal's son Ṣāliḥ report: 67.2

[Ṣāliḥ:] I heard my father say, "When they took us in to be questioned by Isḥāq ibn Ibrāhīm, the first thing they did was to read aloud the letter written by the one in Tarsus"—that is, al-Maʾmūn.[56] "They recited some verses to us, including «Nothing is like Him»[57] and «He is the creator of everything.»[58] When I heard 'Nothing is like Him,' I recited «He is the One who hears and sees.»[59]

"Then those present were put to the test. Those who withheld their assent were taken away and locked up. Of them all, only four resisted. Their names are Muḥammad ibn Nuḥ; ʿUbayd Allāh ibn ʿUmar al-Qawārīrī; al-Ḥasan ibn Ḥammād, called Sajjādah; and my father. Later ʿUbayd Allāh ibn ʿUmar and al-Ḥasan ibn Ḥammād gave in too, leaving only Muḥammad ibn Nūḥ and my father in confinement. There they stayed until, several days later, a letter arrived from Tarsus ordering the two of them to be transported there. They were duly sent, shackled one to the other."

We cite the two Muḥammads, Ibn Nāṣir and Ibn ʿAbd al-Bāqī, who cite Ḥamd ibn Aḥmad, who cites Abū Nuʿaym al-Ḥāfiẓ, who heard Sulaymān ibn Aḥmad report; and we cite Ibn Nāṣir, who was informed by Abū ʿAlī l-Ḥasan ibn Aḥmad, who cites ʿAlī ibn Aḥmad ibn ʿUmar al-Ḥammāmī, who cites Ibn al-Ṣawwāf, who along with Sulaymān ibn Aḥmad heard Aḥmad ibn Ḥanbal's son ʿAbd Allāh report that he heard Abū Maʿmar al-Qaṭīʿī report: 67.3

حدثني أبو مَعْمَر القَطِيعي قال: لما حضرنا في دار السلطان أيّامَ المحنة وكان أبو عبد الله أحمد بن حنبل قد أُحضِر وكان رجلاً ليّناً فلمّا رأى الناس يُجيبون انتفخت أوداجه واحمرّت عيناه وذهب ذلك اللِّين الذي كان فيه، فقلتُ: إنه قد غضب لله.

قال أبو مَعْمَر: فلمّا رأيت ما به قلت: يا أبا عبد الله أبشر، حدثنا محمّد بن فُضيل ابن غَزْوان عن الوليد بن عبد الله بن جُمَيع عن أبي سَلَمَة بن عبد الرحمن بن عَوْف قال: كان من أصحاب النبي صلى الله عليه وسلم من إذا أُريدَ على شيء من دينه رأيتَ حَماليق عينيه في رأسه تدور كأنّه مجنون.

٤،٦٧ أخبرنا عبد الملك بن أبي القاسم قال: أخبرنا عبد الله بن محمّد الأنصاري قال: أخبرنا أبو يعقوب قال: أخبرنا الحسين بن محمّد بن سعيد الخَفّاف قال:

سمعتُ ابن أبي أُسامة يقول: حُكي[١] لنا أنّ أحمد بن حنبل قيل له أيّام المحنة: يا أبا عبد الله ألا تَرى الحقّ كيف ظهر عليه الباطل؟ فقال: كلاّ إن ظهور الباطل على الحق أن تنتقل القلوب من الهدى إلى الضلالة وقلوبنا بعدُ لازمة للحق.

٥،٦٧ أخبرنا هبة الله بن الحسين بن الحاسب قال: أخبرنا الحسن بن أحمد بن البنّا قال: أخبرنا أبو الفتح بن أبي الفوارس قال: حدثنا أبو بكر أحمد بن جعفر بن سَلْم قال: حدثنا عمر بن محمّد بن عيسى الجوهري. وأخبرنا ابن ناصر قال: أخبرنا عبد القادر بن محمّد قال: أخبرنا أبو إسحاق البرمكي قال: أخبرنا عليّ بن مَرْدَك قال: حدثنا ابن أبي حاتم قالا:

حدثنا صالح بن أحمد قال: حُمِل أبي ومحمّد بن نوح مقيّدين فصِرنا معهما إلى الأنبار فسأل أبو بكر الأحولُ أبي فقال: يا أبا عبد الله إن عُرِضتَ على السيف تُجيب؟

قال: لا. ثم سُيِّرا.

قال: فسمعت أبي يقول: لمّا صرنا إلى الرّحبة ورحلنا منها وذلك في جَوف الليل عَرَض لنا رجل فقال: أيّكم أحمد بن حنبل؟ فقيل له: هذا. فقال للجَمّال: على رِسْلِك

---

١ د: يحكي.

[Abū Maʿmar al-Qaṭīʿī:] I was there when Aḥmad ibn Ḥanbal was brought to the palace during the Inquisition. He had always been a meek man, but when he saw the members of the community giving their assent, his veins swelled, his eyes went red, and all the meekness was gone. Seeing him, I remember thinking to myself, “He’s standing up for God.”

“Abū ʿAbd Allāh,” I told him, “this is good news! Haven’t we heard Muḥammad ibn Fuḍayl ibn Ghazwān report, citing al-Walīd ibn ʿAbd Allāh ibn Jumayʿ, citing Abū Salamah ibn ʿAbd al-Raḥmān ibn ʿAwf, who said, ‘Among the Prophet’s Companions were some who, if challenged on any matter of religion, would glower and roll their eyes like madmen’?”

We cite ʿAbd al-Malik ibn Abī l-Qāsim, who cites ʿAbd Allāh ibn Muḥammad al-Anṣārī, who cites Abū Yaʿqūb, who cites al-Ḥusayn ibn Muḥammad ibn Saʿīd al-Khaffāf, who heard Ibn Abī Usāmah say: 67.4

[Ibn Abī Usāmah:] I remember hearing that during the Inquisition, someone said to Aḥmad ibn Ḥanbal, “See? Right loses and wrong wins!”

“Never!” he retorted. “Wrong wins only if people’s hearts wander off and lose their way, but ours haven’t done that yet.”

We cite Hibat Allāh ibn al-Ḥusayn ibn al-Ḥāsib, who cites al-Ḥasan ibn Aḥmad ibn al-Bannā, who cites Abū l-Fatḥ ibn Abī l-Fawāris, who heard Abū Bakr Aḥmad ibn Jaʿfar ibn Salm report that he heard ʿUmar ibn Muḥammad ibn ʿĪsā l-Jawharī report; and we cite Ibn Nāṣir, who cites ʿAbd al-Qādir ibn Muḥammad, who cites Abū Isḥāq al-Barmakī, who cites ʿAlī ibn Mardak, who heard Ibn Abī Ḥātim, who along with al-Jawharī heard Aḥmad’s son Ṣāliḥ report: 67.5

[Ṣāliḥ:] My father and Muḥammad ibn Nūḥ were carried off in chains and we went with them as far as al-Anbār. There Abū Bakr al-Aḥwal asked my father, “Abū ʿAbd Allāh, if they threaten you with a sword, will you give in?”

“No,” he answered. Then he and Muḥammad ibn Nūḥ were taken away.

Later my father told me:

“When we got to al-Raḥbah[60] it was the middle of the night. As we were leaving, a man came up to us and said, ‘Which of you is Aḥmad ibn Ḥanbal?’

“Someone pointed me out. ‘Slow down,’ said the man to the camel-driver. Then to me: ‘Listen, you! What does it matter if they kill you right here and

ثم قال: يا هذا ما عليك أن تُقتل ها هنا وتدخل الجنة ها هنا. ثم قال: أستودعك الله. ومضى.

قال أبي: فسألتُ عنه فقيل لي: هذا رجل من العرب من ربيعة يعمل الشِّعر في البادية يُقال له جابر بن عامر، يُذكَر بخير.

أخبرنا ابن ناصر قال: أخبرنا أبو الحسين بن عبد الجبّار قال: أخبرنا محمّد بن عبد الواحد بن جعفر قال: أخبرنا أبو عمر بن حيّويه قال: حدثنا عبد الله بن محمّد بن إسحاق المرْوَزي قال: ٦٧،٦

حدثنا عبد الله[1] بن سعيد المروزي عن صالح بن أحمد في حديث المحنة قال: لما رحلنا إلى طرسوس للمحنة قال أبي: لما نزلنا الرَّحْبة ورحلنا منها في جوف الليل عرض لي رجل فقال: أيّكم أحمد بن حنبل؟

فقيل له: هذا.

فسلّم عليّ ثم قال: يا هذا ما عليك أن تُقتل ها هنا وتَدخل الجنة. ثم سلّم وانصرف.

فقلت: من هذا؟

فقيل لي: رجل من العرب من رَبيعة يقول الشِّعر بالبادية يُقال له جابر بن عامر.

قال المرْوَزي: وحدثنا المَعْمَري عن أحمد بن أبي الحَواري قال: حدثنا إبراهيم بن عبد الله قال: ٦٧،٧

قال أحمد بن حنبل: ما سمعتُ كلمة منذ وقعتُ في الأمر الذي وقعتُ فيه أقوى من كلمة أعرابي كلّمني بها في رَحْبة طَوْق قال لي: يا أحمد إن يقتلك الحقّ متَّ شهيداً وإن عشتَ عشتَ حميداً.

قال: فقوّى قلبي.

أخبرنا محمّد بن أبي منصور قال: أخبرنا عبد القادر بن محمّد قال: أخبرنا إبراهيم بن عمر قال: أخبرنا عليّ بن عبد العزيز قال: ٦٧،٨

---

[1] هـ: عبيد الله.

now? You'll enter the Garden, here and now.' Then he said, 'I leave you in the care of God,' and left.

"I asked who he was and they told me: 'He's an Arab of Rabī'ah named Jābir ibn 'Āmir who composes poetry in the wilderness. People speak highly of him.'"

We cite Ibn Nāṣir, who cites Abū l-Ḥusayn ibn 'Abd al-Jabbār, who cites Muḥammad ibn 'Abd al-Wāḥid ibn Ja'far, who cites Abū 'Umar ibn Ḥayyuwayh, who heard 'Abd Allāh ibn Muḥammad ibn Isḥāq al-Marwazī report that he heard 'Abd Allāh Sa'īd al-Marwazī report, citing Aḥmad's son Ṣāliḥ, talking about the Inquisition: 67.6

[Ṣāliḥ:] "On our way to Tarsus to be questioned"—said my father—"we stopped at al-Raḥbah. In the middle of the night, as we were leaving, a man came up to me and asked, 'Which of you is Aḥmad ibn Ḥanbal?'

"When someone pointed me out, the man greeted me and said, 'Listen, you! What does it matter if they kill you right here and now? You'll enter the Garden!'

"He said good-bye and left. I asked who he was, and they told me he was an Arab of Rabī'ah named Jābir ibn 'Āmir who composed poetry in the wilderness."

Al-Marwazī reports that he heard al-Ma'marī, citing Aḥmad ibn Abī l-Ḥawārī, who heard Ibrāhīm ibn 'Abd Allāh report: 67.7

[Ibrāhīm ibn 'Abd Allāh:] Aḥmad ibn Ḥanbal said, "The most powerful thing anyone said to me during my ordeal was what a desert Arab said to me at Raḥbat Ṭawq: 'Aḥmad, if you die for the truth you die a martyr, and if you live you live a hero.'"

With that he strengthened my resolve.

We cite Muḥammad ibn Abī Manṣūr, who cites 'Abd al-Qādir ibn Muḥammad, who cites Ibrāhīm ibn 'Umar, who cites 'Alī ibn 'Abd al-'Azīz, who cites 'Abd al-Raḥmān ibn Abī Ḥātim, who heard his father report that he heard Aḥmad ibn Abī l-Ḥawārī, citing one of his companions, report that Aḥmad ibn Ḥanbal said: 67.8

أخبرنا عبد الرحمن بن أبي حاتم قال: حدثنا أبي قال: حدثنا أحمد بن أبي الحَواري عن بعض أصحابه. قال: قال أحمد بن حنبل: ما سمعتُ كلمة كانت أوقع في قلبي من كلمة سمعتها من أعرابي في رَحبة طوق قال لي: يا أحمد إن قتلك الحقّ متّ شهيداً وإن عشتَ عشتَ حميداً.

قال ابن أبي حاتم: قال أبي: فكان كما قال، لقد رفع الله عزّ وجلّ شأن أحمد بن حنبل بعد ما امتُحن وعظُم عند الناس وارتفع أمره جدّاً.

٩،٦٧ قلتُ: وقد بلغنا عن الشافعي رضي الله عنه أنّه رأى رسول الله صلّى الله عليه وسلّم في المنام يُخبره بما سيلقى أحمد من الامتحان في خلق القرآن ويأمره أن يُعلم أحمد بذلك وسيأتي هذا مُسنداً في باب المنامات التي رئيت لأحمد بن حنبل.[1]

١٠،٦٧ أخبرنا محمّد بن ناصر قال: أنبأنا أحمد بن أبي سعد[2] النَّيْسابوري قال: سمعتُ عبد الله بن يوسف يقول: سمعتُ أبا العباس الأصمّ يقول: سمعتُ العباس بن محمّد الدُّوري يقول:

سمعتُ أبا جعفر الأنباري يقول: لما حُمِل أحمد بن حنبل إلى المأمون أُخبرتُ فعبرت الفرات فإذا هو جالس في الخان فسلّمت عليه فقال: يا أبا جعفر تعنّيتَ. فقلتُ: ليس في[3] هذا عناء. وقلتُ له: يا هذا أنت اليوم رأس والناس يقتدون بك فوالله لئن أجبتَ إلى خلق القرآن ليُجيبَنّ بإجابتك خلق[4] من خلق الله وإن أنت لم تُجب ليَمتنعنّ خلق من الناس كثير، ومع هذا فإنّ الرجل إن لم يقتلك فإنك تموت ولابد من الموت فاتّقِ الله ولا تُجبهم إلى شيء. فجعل أحمد يبكي ويقول: ما شاء الله، ما شاء الله!

ثم قال لي أحمد: يا أبا جعفر أعِدْ عليّ ما قلت. فأعدتُ عليه فجعل يقول: ما شاء الله، ما شاء الله!

١١،٦٧ أخبرنا المحمّدان: ابن أبي منصور وابن أبي القاسم قالا: أخبرنا أبو الفضل حمد بن أحمد قال: أخبرنا أحمد بن عبد الله قال: حدثنا محمّد ابن جعفر وعلي بن أحمد قالا: حدثنا محمّد بن إسماعيل بن أحمد، وأخبرنا هِبة الله

---

١ الخبر في ش فقط. ٢ د: سعيد. ٣ د: ليس هذا عناء، ش: ما هذا عناء. ٤ ش: خلق كثير.

[Aḥmad:] "Nothing has ever made more of an impression on me than the words of a desert Arab from Raḥbat Ṭawq: 'Aḥmad, if you die for the truth you die a martyr, and if you live you live a hero.'"

Ibn Abī Ḥātim quoted his father as saying, "In the end he was right. By the time the Inquisition was over, God had made Aḥmad ibn Ḥanbal a name to be reckoned with."

[The author:] We have also heard that al-Shāfiʿī, may God be pleased with him, had a dream where the Prophet asked him to warn Aḥmad that he would be tried regarding the creation of the Qur'an. This report will be given along with its chain of transmitters in the chapter on dreams. 67.9

We cite Muḥammad ibn Nāṣir, who was informed by Aḥmad ibn Abī Saʿd al-Naysābūrī, who heard ʿAbd Allāh ibn Yūsuf say that he heard Abū l-ʿAbbās al-Aṣamm say that he heard al-ʿAbbās ibn Muḥammad al-Dūrī say that he heard Abū Jaʿfar al-Anbārī say: 67.10

[Al-Anbārī:] When I found out that Aḥmad ibn Ḥanbal was being taken to see al-Ma'mūn, I crossed the Euphrates and found Aḥmad sitting in a caravanserai. When I greeted him he said, "Abū Jaʿfar, you shouldn't have troubled yourself!"

"It was no trouble," I told him. Then I said, "Listen here! As of today, you have people prepared to follow your example. If you say the Qur'an is created, many of them will say the same. If you resist, many of them will too. Think about it: even if that man doesn't kill you, you're going to die sooner or later anyway. So fear God and don't give in!"

"God's will be done!" said Aḥmad, weeping. "God's will be done!" Then he said, "Abū Jaʿfar, repeat what you said for me."

So I repeated it, and again he said "God's will be done! God's will be done!"

We cite the two Muḥammads, Ibn Abī Manṣūr and Ibn Abī l-Qāsim, who cite Abū l-Faḍl Ḥamd ibn Aḥmad, who cites Aḥmad ibn ʿAbd Allāh, who heard Muḥammad ibn Jaʿfar and ʿAlī ibn Aḥmad report that they heard Muḥammad ibn Ismāʿīl ibn Aḥmad; and we cite Hibat Allāh ibn al-Ḥusayn ibn al-Ḥāsib, who cites al-Ḥasan ibn Aḥmad ibn al-Bannā, who cites Abū l-Fatḥ ibn Abī l-Fawāris, who heard Aḥmad ibn Jaʿfar ibn Salm report that 67.11

ابن الحسين بن الحاسب قال: أخبرنا الحسن بن أحمد بن البنّا قال: أخبرنا أبو الفتح بن أبي الفوارس قال: حدثنا أحمد بن جعفر بن سَلْمٍ قال: حدثنا عمر بن عيسى الجَوهري، قالا:

حدثنا صالح بن أحمد قال: قال أبي: لما صِرنا إلى أَذَنَة ورحلنا منها وذلك في جوف الليل وفُتح لنا بابها فإذا رجل قد دخل وقال: البُشرى! قد مات الرجل. قال أبي: وكنْتُ أدعو الله أن لا أراه.

١٢،٦٧ أخبرنا عبد الملك الكَرُوخي قال: أخبرنا عبد الله بن محمد الأنصاري قال: أخبرنا أبو يعقوب قال: حدثنا أبو عليّ ابن أبي بكر المروَزي قال: حدثنا أبو عبد الله محمد بن الحسن بن عليّ البُخاري قال:

سمعت محمّد بن إبراهيم البُوشَنْجي يقول: سمعتُ أحمد بن حنبل يقول: دعوتُ ربّي ثلاث دعوات فتبيّنتُ الإجابة في ثنتين، دعوته أن لا يجمع بيني وبين المأمون ودعوته أن لا أرى المتوكّل، فلم أرَ المأمون، مات بالبَذَنْدون وهو نهر الروم وأحمد محبوس بالرَّقّة حتى بويع المعتصم بالروم ورجع فرُدّ أحمد إلى بغداد في سنة ثمان عشرة ومائتين والمعتصم امتحنه فأمّا المتوكّل فإنه لما أحضر أحمدَ دار الخلافة ليحدّث ولده قَعد له المتوكل في خَوخة حتى نَظر إلى أحمد ولم يَره أحمد.

١٣،٦٧ أخبرنا محمّد بن أبي منصور قال: أخبرنا عبد القادر بن محمّد قال: أخبرنا إبراهيم بن عمر قال: أخبرنا عليّ بن عبد العزيز قال: حدثنا عبد الرحمن بن أبي حاتم قال:

حدثنا صالح بن أحمد قال: لمّا صار أبي ومحمّد بن نوح إلى طَرسوس رُدّا في أقيادهما فلما صارا إلى الرقّة حُملا في سفينة فلما وصلا إلى عانات توفّي محمّد بن نوح فأُطلق عنه قيدُه وصلّى عليه أبي.

١٤،٦٧ أخبرنا عبد الرحمن بن محمد القزاز قال: أخبرنا أحمد بن عليّ بن ثابت قال: أخبرنا محمّد بن أحمد بن رزق قال: حدثنا عثمان بن أحمد الدقّاق قال:

he heard 'Umar ibn 'Īsā l-Jawharī, who along with Muḥammad ibn Ismā'īl ibn Aḥmad heard Aḥmad's son Ṣāliḥ report:

[Ṣāliḥ:] My father told me: "We were just leaving Adana when the city gate opened behind us and someone called out: 'Good news! That man is dead!'[61]

"I had been praying I would never meet him."

We cite 'Abd al-Malik al-Karūkhī, who cites 'Abd Allāh ibn Muḥammad al-Anṣārī, who cites Abū Ya'qūb, who heard Abū 'Alī ibn Abī Bakr al-Marwazī report that he heard Abū 'Abd Allāh Muḥammad ibn al-Ḥasan ibn 'Alī l-Bukhārī report that he heard Muḥammad ibn Ibrāhīm al-Būshanjī say: 67.12

[Al-Būshanjī:] I heard Aḥmad ibn Ḥanbal say, "Three times I've asked God for something and twice seen my request granted. I asked Him to keep me away from al-Ma'mūn, and I told Him I didn't want to see al-Mutawakkil. Well, I never saw al-Ma'mūn."[62]

Al-Ma'mūn died at the Badhandūn—a river in Byzantine territory—while Aḥmad was locked up in al-Raqqah. Al-Mu'taṣim received the oath of allegiance in Anatolia and returned to Iraq. Aḥmad was brought back to Baghdad in 218 [833], and it was al-Mu'taṣim who tried him. As for al-Mutawakkil, when he brought Aḥmad to the palace to instruct his children in Hadith, he observed him from a secret compartment, meaning that he saw Aḥmad but Aḥmad never saw him.

We cite Muḥammad ibn Abī Manṣūr, who cites 'Abd al-Qādir ibn Muḥammad, who cites Ibrāhīm ibn 'Umar, who cites 'Alī ibn 'Abd al-'Azīz, who heard 'Abd al-Raḥmān ibn Abī Ḥātim report that he heard Aḥmad's son Ṣāliḥ report: 67.13

[Ṣāliḥ:] My father and Muḥammad ibn Nūḥ were sent back from Tarsus still in irons. When they reached al-Raqqah, they were put onto a boat. At 'Ānāt,[63] Muḥammad ibn Nūḥ died and his chains were removed. My father prayed over his body.

We cite 'Abd al-Raḥmān ibn Muḥammad al-Qazzāz, who cites Aḥmad ibn 'Alī ibn Thābit, who cites Muḥammad ibn Aḥmad ibn Rizq, who heard 'Uthmān ibn Aḥmad al-Daqqāq report that he heard Ḥanbal ibn Isḥāq report that he heard Abū 'Abd Allāh Aḥmad ibn Ḥanbal say: 67.14

حدثنا حنبل بن إسحاق قال: سمعتُ أبا عبد الله أحمد بن حنبل يقول: ما رأيتُ أحداً على حداثة سنّه وقلّة عِلمه أقوم بأمر الله من محمّد بن نوح وإني لأرجو أن يكون الله قد ختم له بخير، قال لي ذات يوم وأنا معه خِلْوَين: يا أبا عبد الله، اللهَ اللهَ، إنّك لست مثلي أنت رجل يُقتَدَى بك وقد مدّ الخلق أعناقهم إليك لِما يكون منك فاتقِ الله واثْبت لأمر الله، أو نحو هذا من الكلام. فعجبتُ من تقويته لي وموعظته إيّاي، فانظر بما خُتم له: مَرض وصار إلى بعض الطريق فمات فصلّيتُ عليه ودَفنته - أظنّه قال: بعانَة.

قال أحمد بن عليّ بن ثابت: وكانت وفاته سنة ثمان عشرة ومائتين.

الباب الثامن والستون في ذكر ما جرى له بعد موت المأمون

قد ذكرنا أنه لمّا جاء الخبر بموت المأمون رُدّ أحمد بن حنبل ومحمّد بن نوح في أقيادهما فمات محمّد بن نوح في الطريق ورُدّ أحمد إلى بغداد مقيّداً. ١،٦٨

أخبرنا عبد الملك بن أبي القاسم قال: أخبرنا عبد الله بن محمّد الأنصاري قال: أخبرنا أبو يعقوب قال: أخبرني جدّي قال: أخبرنا محمّد بن أبي جعفر المُنذري وأبو أحمد بن أبي أُسامة قالا: ٢،٦٨

سمعنا محمّد بن إبراهيم البُوشَنْجي يقول: أُخذ أحمد أيّام المأمون ليُحمل إلى المأمون ببلاد الروم فبلغ أحمد الرقّة ومات المأمون بالبَذَندون قبل أن يلقاه أحمد وذلك في سنة ثمان عشرة ومائتين.

فأخبرني أبو العباس الرقّي وكان من حفّاظ أهل الحديث أنهم دخلوا على أحمد

[Ḥanbal:] I heard Aḥmad ibn Ḥanbal say: "I never saw anyone so young or so unlearned stand up for God more bravely than Muḥammad ibn Nūḥ. I hope God saved him when he died!

"One day, when the two of us were alone, he said to me, 'Aḥmad, fear God! Fear God! We're nothing alike, you and I. You're a man people follow and everyone is watching and waiting to see what you'll do. Fear God, and stand firm!'—or words to that effect. Imagine him trying to keep me strong and warn me to do the right thing! And look what happened to him: he fell sick and ended up dying by the side of a road somewhere. I prayed over him and buried him."

He may have added: "That was in 'Ānāh."

Aḥmad ibn 'Alī ibn Thābit reported that Muḥammad ibn Nūḥ died in 218 [833].

Chapter 68: What Happened after the Death of al-Ma'mūn

As soon as al-Ma'mūn's death was announced, Aḥmad ibn Ḥanbal and Muḥammad ibn Nūḥ were sent back to Iraq in irons, as we have seen. Muḥammad ibn Nūḥ died on the way and Aḥmad, still in chains, completed the journey. 68.1

We cite 'Abd al-Malik ibn Abī l-Qāsim, who cites 'Abd Allāh ibn Muḥammad al-Anṣārī, who cites Abū Ya'qūb, who cites his grandfather, who cites Muḥammad ibn Abī Ja'far al-Mundhirī, who along with Abū Aḥmad ibn Abī Usāmah heard Muḥammad ibn Ibrāhīm al-Būshanjī say: 68.2

[Al-Būshanjī:] During the reign of al-Ma'mūn, Aḥmad was taken away to the Byzantine frontier. He had traveled as far as al-Raqqah when al-Ma'mūn died at al-Badhandūn, so the two never met.[64] That was in 218 [833].

Abū l-'Abbās al-Raqqī, a Hadith scholar, told me that he and some others went to visit Aḥmad during his imprisonment in al-Raqqah. There they

بالرقّة وهو محبوس فجعلوا يذاكرونه[1] ما يُروَى في التقيّة من الأحاديث فقال أحمد: وكيف تصنعون بحديث خَبّاب: إنَّ مَنْ كانَ قَبْلَكُم كانَ يُنْشَر أحدُهم بالمِنشارِ ثمّ لا يَصِدّه ذلِكَ عن دِينِه؟

قال: فيئسنا منه.

فقال أحمد: لستُ أُبالي بالحبس، ما هو ومنزلي إلّا واحد، ولا قتلًا بالسيف، إنما[2] أخاف فتنة بالسوط وأخاف أن لا أصبر. فسمعه بعض أهل الحبس وهو يقول ذلك فقال: لا عليك يا أبا عبد الله فما هو إلّا سَوْطان ثم لا تدري أين يقع الباقي. فكأنه سُرّي عنه.

ورُدّ من الرقّة وحُبس.

٣،٦٨ أخبرنا هِبة الله بن الحسين بن الحاسب قال: أخبرنا الحسن بن أحمد بن البنّا قال: أخبرنا أبو الفتح بن أبي الفَوارِس قال: حدثنا أحمد بن جعفر بن سَلْم قال: حدثنا عمر بن محمّد بن عيسى الجَوْهَري قال:

حدثنا صالح بن أحمد قال: لما جاء نَعِيُّ المأمون رُدّ أبي ومحمّد بن نوح في أقيادهما إلى الرقّة وأُخرجا في سفينة مع قوم محبسين[3] فلمّا صارا بعانات توفّي محمّد بن نوح ودُفن بها.

ثم صار أبي إلى بغداد وهو مُقيّد فمكث بالياسِريّة أيّامًا.

ثم صار إلى الحبس في دار اكتُرِيت له عند دار عُمارة.

ثم نُقل بعد ذلك إلى حبس العامّة في درب المَوْصِلي، وفي رواية في درب يُعرف بالمَوْصِليّة.

٤،٦٨ أخبرنا محمّد بن أبي منصور قال: أخبرنا أبو الفضل الحداد قال: حدثنا أبو نُعَيم الحافظ قال: حدثنا محمّد بن جعفر قال: حدثنا محمّد بن إسماعيل ابن أحمد قال:

حدثنا صالح بن أحمد قال: قال أبي: كنتُ أُصلّي بأهل السجن[4] وأنا مقيّد.

---

[1] هـ: يذكرونه. [2] د: وانما. [3] هكذا في هـ، د، وناقص في ش. [4] ش: الحبس.

confronted him with the reports that allow a Muslim to conceal his beliefs when his life is in danger.

"But what do you do," responded Aḥmad, "with Khabbāb's report that says: 'Before your time there were believers who could be sawed in half without renouncing their faith'?"

When they heard that they gave up hope.

"I don't care if they keep me locked up," he went on. "My house is already a prison. I don't care if they kill me by the sword, either. The only thing I'm afraid of is being flogged. What if I can't take it?"

One of the prisoners had overheard him. "Don't worry, Aḥmad," he said. "After two lashes you don't feel the rest."

Aḥmad looked relieved.

After that he was brought back from al-Raqqah and jailed in Baghdad.

We cite Hibat Allāh ibn al-Ḥusayn ibn al-Ḥāsib, who cites al-Ḥasan ibn Aḥmad ibn al-Bannā, who cites Abū l-Fatḥ ibn Abī l-Fawāris, who heard Aḥmad ibn Jaʿfar ibn Salm report that he heard ʿUmar ibn Muḥammad ibn ʿĪsā l-Jawharī report that he heard Aḥmad's son Ṣāliḥ report: **68.3**

[Ṣāliḥ:] When the news came that al-Ma'mūn had died, Muḥammad ibn Nūḥ and my father, still in chains, were sent back to al-Raqqah. From there they continued their journey on a prison ship. When they reached ʿĀnāt, Muḥammad ibn Nūḥ died and they buried him there. Finally my father, still in chains, reached Baghdad.

First he stayed for a few days in Yāsiriyah.[65] Then they held him in a house rented for that purpose near the Palace of ʿUmārah.[66] After that he was transferred to the Commoners' Prison[67] in Mawṣilī Street—or, according to another report, a street called al-Mawṣiliyyah.[68]

We cite Muḥammad ibn Abī Manṣūr, who cites Abū l-Faḍl al-Ḥaddād, who heard Abū Nuʿaym al-Ḥāfiẓ report that he heard Muḥammad ibn Jaʿfar report that he heard Muḥammad ibn Ismāʿīl ibn Aḥmad report that he heard Aḥmad's son Ṣāliḥ report: **68.4**

[Ṣāliḥ:] My father said, "I used to lead the prisoners in prayer with the chains still on me."[69]

٥،٦٨ أخبرنا عبد الرحمن بن محمد القزاز قال: أخبرنا أحمد بن عليّ بن ثابت قال: أخبرني الحسن بن عليّ التَّميمي قال: حدثنا عمر بن أحمد الواعِظ قال: حدثنا أحمد بن محمّد بن مَسْعَدة الأَصْبَهاني قال: حدثنا أبو يحيى مكّي ابن عبد الله بن يوسف الثَّقفي قال:

حدثنا أبو بكر الأَعْيَن قال: قلتُ لآدم العَسْقَلاني: إني أُريد أن أخرج إلى بغداد أَفَلَكَ[1] حاجة؟

قال: نعم، إذا أتيتَ بغداد فَأْتِ[2] أحمد بن حنبل فَأَقْرِئه منّي السلام وقل له: يا هذا اتّقِ الله وتقرّب إليه بما أنت فيه ولا يستفزنّك أحد فإنّك إن شاء الله مُشرف على الجنّة، وقل له: حدّثنا الليثُ بن سعد عن محمّد بن عَجْلان عن أبي الزّناد عن الأعرج عن أبي هُريرة قال: قال رسول الله صلّى الله عليه وسلّم : مَنْ أرادَكُم عَلى مَعْصِيَةِ اللهِ فَلا تُطيعوه.

فأتيتُ أحمد بن حنبل في السجن فدخلت عليه فسلّمت عليه وأَقْرَأْته السلام وقلت له هذا الكلام والحديث فأطرق أحمد إطراقةً ثم رفع رأسه فقال: رحمه الله حيّاً وميتاً، فلقد أحسن النصيحة.

٦،٦٨ أخبرنا عبد الملك بن أبي القاسم قال: أخبرنا عبد الله بن محمّد الأنصاري قال: أخبرنا إسحاق بن إبراهيم السَّرَخْسي قال: أخبرنا محمّد بن عُبيد الله اللأَّل:[3] حدثنا محمّد بن إبراهيم الصرّام قال: حدثنا إبراهيم بن إسحاق الغَسِيلي[4] قال:

حدّثنا أبو بكر محمّد بن طَريف الأعين قال: أتيتُ آدم بن أبي إياس فقلت له: إنّ عبد الله بن صالح يُقرِئك السلام.

قال: لا تُقْرِئْني منه السلام ولا تُقْرِئه منّي السلام.

فقلت: ولِمَ؟

قال: لأنه قال: القرآن مخلوق.

فقلت له: إنه قد اعتذر اليومَ وأخبر الناس برجوعه عن ذلك.

قال: إنْ كان كذلك فأقرئه منّي السلام.

---

١ د: فلك. ٢ ش: فاتيت. ٣ د: الدلال. ٤ د: العُسيلي.

We cite ʿAbd al-Raḥmān ibn Muḥammad al-Qazzāz, who cites Aḥmad ibn ʿAlī ibn Thābit, who cites al-Ḥasan ibn ʿAlī l-Tamīmī, who heard ʿUmar ibn Aḥmad al-Wāʿiẓ report that he heard Aḥmad ibn Muḥammad ibn Masʿadah al-Iṣfahānī report that he heard Abū Yaḥyā Makkī ibn ʿAbd Allāh ibn Yūsuf al-Thaqafī report that he heard Abū Bakr al-Aʿyan report: 68.5

[Abū Bakr al-Aʿyan:] I told Ādam al-ʿAsqalānī I was traveling to Baghdad and asked him if he wanted anything.

"Yes," he said. "When you get there, go to Aḥmad ibn Ḥanbal, greet him for me, and tell him this. 'You there! Fear God, and seek closeness to Him, by staying the course. Let no one dismay you: you stand—God willing—at the very gate of the Garden.' And tell him: 'We heard al-Layth ibn Saʿd report, citing Muḥammad ibn ʿAjlān, citing Abū l-Zinād, citing al-Aʿraj, citing Abū Hurayrah, that the Prophet, God bless and keep him, said: "If any ask you to disobey God, heed him not."'"

So I went to see Aḥmad ibn Ḥanbal in jail. When I found him, I greeted him, conveyed al-ʿAsqalānī's greeting, and repeated his words, along with the Hadith. Aḥmad lowered his gaze for a time, then raised his head and said, "God have mercy on him in life and death alike! His is good counsel indeed."

We cite ʿAbd al-Malik ibn Abī l-Qāsim, who cites ʿAbd Allāh ibn Muḥammad al-Anṣārī, who cites Isḥāq ibn Ibrāhīm al-Sarakhsī, who cites Muḥammad ibn ʿUbayd Allāh al-La''āl (the pearl merchant), who heard Muḥammad ibn Ibrāhīm al-Ṣarrām report that he heard Ibrāhīm ibn Isḥāq al-Ghasīlī report that he heard Abū Bakr Muḥammad ibn Ṭarīf al-Aʿyan report: 68.6

[Al-Aʿyān:] I went to Ādam ibn Abī Iyās [al-ʿAsqalānī] and told him that ʿAbd Allāh ibn Ṣāliḥ had sent him his regards.

"Convey no greetings to me from him," he said, "or to him from me!"

"Why not?" I asked.

"Because he said that the Qur'an is created."

"He's just explained that he didn't mean it," I said, "and he's announced to everyone that he takes back what he said."

"In that case, convey my greetings."

As I was leaving, I told al-ʿAsqalānī I was going to Baghdad and asked him if he wanted anything.

فلما فرغتُ قلت له: إني أُريد الخُروج إلى بغداد فهل لك من حاجة؟

قال: نعم، ائتِ أحمدَ بن حنبل فاقرأ عليه مني السلام وقل له: يا هذا اتقِ الله وتقرّب إلى الله بما أنت عليه ولا يستفزنّك أحد عن دينك فإنّك إن شاء الله مشرف على الجنّة.

وقل له: حدّثنا الليث بن سعد عن ابن عَجلان عن أبي الزناد عن الأعرج عن أبي هريرة قال: قال رسول الله صلى الله عليه وسلم: مَن أرادكم على مَعصية الله فلا تُطيعوه.

فأتيتُه وهو في السجن فأقرأته السلام وأَخبرته بالكلام والحديث فأطرق مليّاً ثم قال: يرحمه الله حيّاً وميتاً، قد أحسن النصيحة.

الباب التاسع والستون في ذكر قصّته مع المعتصِم

لمّا مات المأمون رُدّ أحمد إلى بغداد فسُجن إلى أن امتحنه المعتصم وكان أحمد بن أبي ١،٦٩
دُؤاد على قضاء القضاة فحمله على امتحان الناس بخلق القرآن.

قال أبو بكر المرُّوذي: ٢،٦٩

لما سُجن أحمد بن حنبل جاء السجّان فقال له: يا أبا عبد الله، الحديث الذي رُوي في الظَّلَمة وأعوانهم صحيح؟

قال: نعم.

قال السجّان: فأنا من أعوان الظّلمة؟

قال أحمد: فأعوان الظّلمة من يأخذ شَعرك ويغسل ثوبك ويصلح طعامك ويبيع ويشتري منك فأمّا أنت فمِن أنفُسهم.[1]

[1] الخبر في ش فقط.

"Yes," he said. "Go to Ibn Ḥanbal and give him my regards. Tell him this: 'You there! Fear God, and seek closeness to Him, by staying the course. Let no one dismay you: you stand—God willing—at the very gate of the Garden.' And tell him: 'We heard al-Layth ibn Saʿd report, citing Muḥammad ibn ʿAjlān, citing Abū l-Zannād, citing al-Aʿraj, citing Abū Hurayrah, that the Prophet, God bless and keep him, said: "If any ask you to disobey God, heed him not."'"

So I went to see Aḥmad ibn Ḥanbal in jail. When I found him, I conveyed al-ʿAsqalānī's greeting and his advice, along with the Hadith. Aḥmad lowered his gaze for a moment, then said, "God have mercy on him in life and death alike! His is good counsel indeed."

Chapter 69: His Experience with al-Muʿtaṣim

When al-Ma'mūn died, Aḥmad was brought back to Baghdad and impris- 69.1
oned there. Then he was tried by al-Muʿtaṣim. The chief judge at the time
was Aḥmad ibn Abī Du'ād, who had persuaded the caliph to test people's 69.2
belief that the Qur'an is created.[70]

Al-Marrūdhī said:

When Aḥmad ibn Ḥanbal was put in prison, the jailer came and asked him whether the Hadith about tyrants and those who serve them was authentic.[71] Aḥmad told him it was.

"Am I one of those who serve them?" asked the jailer.

"Those who serve are the ones who cut your hair, wash your clothes, prepare your food, and do business with you. What *you* are is one of the tyrants."

٣،٦٩ أخبرنا محمّد بن أبي منصور قال: أخبرنا عبد القادر بن محمّد قال: أخبرنا إبراهيم بن عمر قال: أخبرنا عليّ بن عبد العزيز قال: أخبرنا عبد الرحمن[١] بن أبي حاتم قال: حدثنا صالح بن أحمد قال:

قال أبي: لمّا كان في شهر رمضان سنة تسع عشرة حُوّلتُ إلى دار إسحاق بن إبراهيم يُوجّه إليّ في كل يوم بِرَجُلَيْن؛ أحدهما يقال له أحمد بن رَباح والآخر أبو شُعيب الحجّام فلا يزالان يناظراني حتى إذا أرادا الانصراف دُعي بقيد فزيد في قيودي. فصار في رجله أربعة أقياد.

قال أبي: فلمّا كان في اليوم الثالث دخل عليّ أحد الرجلين فناظرني فقلت له: ما تقول في علم الله؟

قال: علم الله مخلوق.

فقلتُ له: كفرتَ.

فقال الرسول الذي كان يحضر من قِبل إسحاق بن إبراهيم: إنّ هذا رسول أمير المؤمنين!

فقلتُ له: إنّ هذا قد كفر.

٤،٦٩ فلمّا كان في الليلة الرابعة وَجّه - يعني المعتصم - بِبُغا الذي كان يُقال له الكبير إلى إسحاق فأمره بحملي إليه فأُدخلت إلى إسحاق فقال: يا أحمد إنّها والله نفسك، إنه لا يقتُلك بالسيف، إنه قد آلى إن لم تُجبْه أن يضربك ضَرباً بعد ضرب وأن يُلقيك في موضع لا ترى فيه الشمس، أليس قد قال الله عز وجل: ﴿إِنَّا جَعَلْنَاهُ قُرْآنًا عَرَبِيًّا﴾ أفيكون مجعولاً إلّا مخلوقاً؟

فقلت له: قد قال الله عزّ وجلّ: ﴿فَجَعَلَهُمْ كَعَصْفٍ مَأْكُولٍ﴾ أَخَلَقهم؟

قال: فسكت ثم قال: اذهبوا به.

٥،٦٩ قال أبي: فلما صرنا إلى الموضع المعروف بباب البستان أُخرجت وجيء بدابّة فحُملتُ عليها وعليّ الأقياد، ما معي أحد يُمسكني فكدت غير مرة أن أَخِرّ على وجهي لِثقل القيود، فجيء بي - يعني إلى دار المعتصم - فأُدخلت حجرة وأُدخلت[٢] إلى بيت وأُقفل

[١] هـ: عبد الرحيم. [٢] حجرة وأُدخلت: ليس في هـ.

We cite Muḥammad ibn Abī Manṣūr, who cites ʿAbd al-Qādir ibn Muḥammad, who cites Ibrāhīm ibn ʿUmar, who cites ʿAlī ibn ʿAbd al-ʿAzīz, who cites ʿAbd al-Raḥmān ibn Abī Ḥātim, who heard Aḥmad's son Ṣāliḥ report that his father said: 69.3

[Aḥmad:] In Ramadan of '19 [September or October 834] I was moved to Isḥāq ibn Ibrāhīm's house. Every day they sent over two men—Aḥmad ibn Rabāḥ, one was called, and the other was Abū Shuʿayb al-Ḥajjām—to debate with me. When they were ready to leave they would call for a fetter and add it to the fetters that I already had on me. I ended up with four fetters on my legs.[72]

On the third day one of the two came and started debating with me. At one point I asked, "What do you say about God's knowledge?"[73]

"God's knowledge is created," he replied.

"You're an unbeliever!"

Present also was a man sent by Isḥāq ibn Ibrāhīm. When he heard me, he said, "You're talking to the emissary of the Commander of the Faithful!"

"Whoever he is," I replied, "he's still an unbeliever."

On the fourth night, he—that is, al-Muʿtaṣim—sent Bughā, called the Elder, to fetch me from Isḥāq's. On the way out, I was taken to see Isḥāq, who said, "By God, Aḥmad, it's your life we're talking about here. He won't behead you and be done with it: he's sworn that if you don't do as he asks he'll flog you senseless and then throw you where you'll never see the sun. Now look here: doesn't God say «We have made it an Arabic Qur'an?»[74] How could He make it without creating it?" 69.4

I answered with a different verse: «He made them like stubble cropped by cattle.»[75] Then I asked him whether "made them" meant "created them." He didn't know how to answer me so he said nothing. Finally he said, "Take him away!"

When we got to the place called the Orchard Gate, they took me out.[76] Then they brought a riding animal and put me on it, fetters and all. There was no one with me to hold me up, and more than once I nearly fell over with the weight of the fetters. They took me inside—inside al-Muʿtaṣim's palace, that is—put me in a room, and locked the door. I wanted to clean myself off for prayer, but it was the middle of the night and there was no lamp in the room. 69.5

الباب عليّ وذلك في جوف الليل وليس في البيت سراج فأردتُ أن أتمسّح للصلاة فمَددت يدي فإذا أنا بإناء فيه ماء وطَسْت موضوع فتوضّأت للصلاة وصلّيت.

٦،٦٩ فلمّا كان من الغد أَخرجتُ تِكّتي من سَراويلي وشددتُ بها الأقياد أحملها وعطفتُ سراويلي فجاء رسول المعتصم فقال: أجب. فأخذ بيدي فأدخلني عليه والتكّة بيدي أحمل بها الأقياد، وإذا هو جالس وابن أبي دؤاد حاضر وقد جمع خلقاً كثيراً من أصحابه.

٧،٦٩ أخبرنا إسماعيل بن أحمد ومحمّد بن أبي القاسم قالا: أخبرنا حَمْد بن أحمد قال: حدثنا أحمد بن عبد الله الحافظ قال: حدثنا الحسين بن محمّد قال: حدثنا عبد الرحمن بن الفيض قال:

سمعت إبراهيم بن محمّد بن الحسن يقول: أُدخل أحمد بن حنبل على الخليفة وعنده ابن أبي دُؤاد وأبو عبد الرحمن الشافعي فأُجلس بين يدي الخليفة وكانوا هوّلوا عليه وقد كانوا ضربوا عُنق رجلين، فنظر أحمد إلى أبي عبد الرحمن الشافعي فقال: أيّ شيء تحفظ عن الشافعي في المسح؟ فقال ابن أبي دُؤاد: انظروا رجلاً هو ذا يُقدم به لضرب العنق يناظر في الفقه!

٨،٦٩ أخبرنا عبد الملك بن أبي القاسم قال: أخبرنا عبد الله بن محمّد الأنصاري قال: أخبرنا أبو يعقوب قال: أخبرنا جدّي قال: أخبرنا محمّد بن أبي جعفر المنذري وأبو أحمد بن أبي أُسامة قالا:

سَمعنا محمّد بن إبراهيم البُوشَنْجي قال: قَدم المعتصم من بلادِ الروم بَغداد في شهر رمضان سنة ثمان عشرة فامتحن فيها أحمد وضُرب بين يديه.[1]

٩،٦٩ أخبرنا ابن ناصر قال: أخبرنا عبد القادر بن محمّد[2] قال: أخبرنا البرمكي[3] قال: أخبرنا ابن مَردَك قال: حدثنا ابن أبي حاتم قال:

---

١ ليس في ش. ٢ بن محمد: ليس في د. ٣ ما بعدها في هـ يستأنف في الورقة رقم ١٢٩ على غير ترتيب.

But when I stuck out my hand I found a pitcher of water and a basin nearby. So I did my ablutions and prayed.

The next morning, I pulled the drawstring out of my trousers and used it to tie the fetters together so I could lift them, leaving my trousers hanging down on one side. Then al-Muʿtaṣim's messenger came, took me by the arm, and told me to come along. So I appeared before al-Muʿtaṣim holding up my fetters with the cord. He was sitting there with Ibn Abī Duʾād and a crowd of his associates. **69.6**

We cite Ismāʿīl ibn Aḥmad and Muḥammad ibn Abī l-Qāsim, who cite Ḥamd ibn Aḥmad, who heard Aḥmad ibn ʿAbd Allāh al-Ḥāfiẓ report that he heard al-Ḥusayn ibn Muḥammad report that he heard ʿAbd al-Raḥmān ibn al-Fayḍ report that he heard Ibrāhīm ibn Muḥammad ibn al-Ḥasan say: **69.7**

[Ibrāhīm ibn Muḥammad:] Aḥmad ibn Ḥanbal was brought before the caliph. Aḥmad ibn Abī Duʾād and Abū ʿAbd al-Raḥmān, the disciple of al-Shāfiʿī, were there too. Aḥmad was given a seat in front of the caliph. They had said things to frighten him, and they had just finished beheading two men. Upon seeing Abū ʿAbd al-Raḥmān, Ibn Ḥanbal asked, "Do you know any reports from al-Shāfiʿī on passing hands over one's shoes?"[77]

"Look at that!" exclaimed Ibn Abī Duʾād. "We bring him here to behead him, and he wants to discuss jurisprudence!"

We cite ʿAbd al-Malik ibn Abī l-Qāsim, who cites ʿAbd Allāh ibn Muḥammad al-Anṣārī, who cites Abū Yaʿqūb, who cites his grandfather, who cites Muḥammad ibn Abī Jaʿfar al-Mundhirī, who along with Abū Aḥmad ibn Abī Usāmah heard Muḥammad ibn Ibrāhīm al-Būshanjī report: **69.8**

[Al-Būshanjī:] Al-Muʿtaṣim returned to Baghdad from the Byzantine front in Ramadan of '18. It was then that he tried Aḥmad and had him flogged in open court.[78]

We cite Ibn Nāṣir, who cites ʿAbd al-Qādir ibn Muḥammad, who cites al-Barmakī, who cites Ibn Mardak, who heard Ibn Abī Ḥātim report that he heard Aḥmad's son Ṣāliḥ report that his father said:[79] **69.9**

حدثنا صالح بن أحمد قال: قال أبي: لما دخلتُ عليه قال لي- يعني المعتصم: ادْنُه ادْنُه! فلم يَزل يُدنيني حتى قربت منه. ثم قال: اجلس. فجلست وقد أثقلتني الأقياد فمكثتُ قليلاً ثم قلتُ: تأذن[١] في الكلام؟

فقال: تكلّم.

فقلتُ: إلى ما دعا الله ورسوله؟

فسكت هُنيهةً ثم قال: إلى شَهادة أن لا إله إلاّ الله.

فقلتُ: فأنا أشهدُ أن لا إله إلاّ الله.

ثم قلتُ: إنّ جدّك ابن عباس يقول: لما قدِم وفد عبد القَيْس على النبيّ صلّى الله عليه وسلّم سألوه عن الإيمان فقال: أتدرون ما الإيمان؟ قالوا: الله ورسوله أعلم. قال: شَهادَةُ أَنْ لا إله إلاّ الله وأَنَّ محمّدا رَسولُ اللهِ وإِقامُ الصَّلاةِ وإِيتاءُ الزَّكاةِ وأَن تُعطُوا الخُمسَ مِنَ المَغْنَم.

فقال أبي: فقال، يعني المعتصم: لولا أنّي وجدتك في يد مَن كان قبلي ما عرضتُ لك. ثم قال: يا عبد الرحمن بن إسحاق أَلَمْ آمُرْكَ أن ترفع المحنة؟

قال أبي: فقلتُ: الله أكبر إنّ في هذا لَفَرجاً للمسلمين.

ثم قال لهم، يعني المعتصم: ناظروه، كلّموه. ثم قال: يا عبد الرحمن كلِّمه. ١٠،٦٩

فقال لي عبدُ الرحمن: ما تقول في القُرآن؟

قلت له: ما تقول في علم الله عزّ وجلّ؟

فسكت، فقال لي بعضهم: أليس قال الله عزّ وجلّ: ﴿اللهُ خَالِقُ كُلِّ شَيْءٍ﴾ والقرآن أليس هو شيء[٢]؟

قال أبي: فقلتُ: قال الله عزّ وجلّ: ﴿تُدَمِّرُ كُلَّ شَيْءٍ بِأَمْرِ رَبِّهَا﴾ فدمّرت إلا ما أراد الله عزّ وجل.

وقال بعضهم: قال الله عز وجل: ﴿ما يَأْتِيهِم مِّن ذِكْرٍ مِّن رَّبِّهِم مُّحْدَثٍ﴾ أفيكون محدثٌ[٣] إلا مخلوقاً؟

---

١ هـ: أتأذن. ٢ هكذا في جميع النسخ. ٣ ش: مخلوقاً.

[Aḥmad:] When I came before al-Muʿtaṣim, he kept telling me to come closer. When I got up close to him he told me to sit, and I did, weighed down by the fetters. After a time I asked if I might speak.[80]

"Go ahead," he said.

"What did the Prophet call on us to do?" I asked.

After a moment of silence, he replied: "To testify that there is no god but God."

"Well, I testify that there is no god but God." Then I went on: "Your grandfather Ibn ʿAbbās reports that when the delegation from the tribe of Qays came to see the Prophet, they asked him about faith. He answered, 'Do you know what faith is?'

"'God and His Emissary know best,' they said.

"'It means testifying that there is no god but God, and Muḥammad is His Emissary. It means holding the ritual prayer, paying the alms tax, and giving up one-fifth of your spoils.'"[81]

"If my predecessor hadn't left you for me to deal with," said al-Muʿtaṣim, "I wouldn't be doing this to you." Then, turning to ʿAbd al-Raḥmān ibn Isḥāq, he said, "Didn't I ask you to stop the Inquisition?"

"Thank God!" I thought to myself. "The Muslims' suffering is over!" 69.10

But then he said to them, "Debate with him. Talk to him!" and then again to ʿAbd al-Raḥmān: "Talk to him!"

"What do you say about the Qurʾan?" asked ʿAbd al-Raḥmān.

"What do you say about God's knowledge?" I asked. He fell silent.

One of the others broke in. "But didn't God say, «God is the creator of all things»?[82] And isn't the Qurʾan a thing?"

"God also mentioned a wind," I said, "that would «destroy everything at the behest of its Lord,»[83] but it destroyed only what He wanted it to."[84]

Then another one spoke up: "God says, «Whenever any new admonition comes to them from their Lord.»[85] How can something be new without having been created?"

I replied: "God also said, «*Ṣād*. By the Qurʾan, containing the admonition.»[86] This admonition is the Qurʾan. In the other verse there's no 'the.'"

One of them cited the Hadith of ʿImrān ibn Ḥuṣayn that God created the remembrance. "That's wrong," I said. "I have it on more than one source that he said, 'God wrote the remembrance.'"

قال أبي: فقلت له: قال الله عزّ وجلّ: ﴿صٓ وَالقُرآنِ ذِي الذِّكرِ﴾ والذِكر هو القرآن وتلك ليس فيها ألف ولا لام.

قال أبي: وذكر بعضهم حديث عِمران بن حُصَين: إن الله عز وجل خلق الذِكر.

فقلتُ: هذا خطأ، حدّثنا غير واحد: إنَّ الله عزَّ وجلَّ كَتَبَ الذِكرَ.

واحتجّوا عليّ بحديث ابن مسعود: ما خَلَقَ اللهُ عزَّ وجلَّ مِن جَنّةٍ ولا نارٍ ولا سَماءٍ ولا أَرضٍ أَعظَمَ من آيةِ الكُرسي. قال أبي: فقلتُ: إنّما تُوقعُ[1] الخلق على الجنة والنار والسماء والأرض ولم يقع على القرآن.[2]

قال: فقال بعضهم حديث خبّاب: يا هَنَتَاه تَقرّبْ إلى الله بما اسْتَطَعْتَ فإنّك لن تَتَقَرّبَ إليه بشيءٍ أَحَبَّ إلَيْهِ مِنْ كَلامِه.

قال أبي: هذا كذا هو.

فجعل ابن أبي دُؤاد ينظر إليه كالمغضب.

١١،٦٩ قال: وكان يتكلم هذا فأَردّ عليه ويتكلم هذا فأردّ عليه فإذا انقطع الرجل منهم اعترض ابن أبي دؤاد فيقول: يا أمير المؤمنين هو والله ضالّ مُضلّ مبتدِع.

قال أبي: فيقول: كلِّموه، ناظروه.

فيكلّمني هذا فأردّ عليه ويكلّمني هذا فأَردّ عليه، فإذا انقطعوا يقول لي، يعني المعتصم: ويحك يا أحمد! ما تقول؟ فأقول: يا أمير المؤمنين أعطوني شيئاً من كتاب الله عزّ وجلّ أَو سُنّة رسول الله صلّى الله عليه وسلّم حتى أقولَ به.

فيقول ابن أبي دؤاد: وأنت لا تقول إلا ما في كتاب الله أو سنّة رسول الله؟

فقلت له: تأوّلتَ تأويلاً فأنت أَعلم وما تأولتُ، ما يُحبَس عليه ويُقيّد عليه.

١٢،٦٩ أخبرنا عبد الملك بن أبي القاسم قال: أخبرنا عبد الله بن محمّد الأنصاري قال: أخبرنا أبو يعقوب قال: أخبرني جدّي قال: أخبرنا محمّد بن أبي جعفر المُنذِري وأبو أحمد بن أبي أُسامة قالا:

سمعنا محمّد بن إبراهيم البُوشَنْجي قال: حدثني بعض أصحابنا أنّ ابن أبي دُؤاد أقبل

---

[1] ش: يوقع، مهملة في د. [2] د: على حرف القرآن.

Next they tried arguing with me using the Hadith of Ibn Mas'ūd: "God has created nothing—not the Garden or the Fire or the heavens or the earth—greater than the Throne Verse."

I said: "The word 'created' applies to the Garden, the Fire, the heavens, and the earth, but not to the Qur'an."

One of them cited the Hadith of Khabbāb: "You there! Try as you may to come nearer to God, you will find nothing dearer to Him by which to approach Him than His word."[87]

"Yes," I said, "that's what it says."

Ibn Abī Du'ād glared at me.

And so it went. One of them would say something, and I would rebut him. 69.11
Then another would speak and I would rebut him too. Whenever one of his men was stymied, Ibn Abī Du'ād would interrupt: "Commander of the Faithful! By God, he's misguided, and misleading, and a heretical innovator!"

But al-Mu'taṣim kept saying, "Talk to him! Debate him!"

So again one of them would say something, and I would rebut him. Then another would speak and I would rebut him too. When none of them had anything left to say, he—meaning al-Mu'taṣim—said, "Come on, Aḥmad! Speak up!"

"Commander of the Faithful," I replied, "give me something I can agree to—something from the Book of God or the *sunnah* of His Emissary."

At that, Ibn Abī Du'ād exclaimed, "What! You only repeat what's in the Qur'an or the *sunnah* of His Emissary?"

"You have an interpretation," I said, "and that's your affair, but it's nothing to lock people up for, or put them in chains."

We cite 'Abd al-Malik ibn Abī l-Qāsim, who cites 'Abd Allāh ibn Muḥammad al-Anṣārī, 69.12
who cites Abū Ya'qūb, who cites his grandfather, who cites Muḥammad ibn Abī Ja'far al-Mundhirī, who along with Abū Aḥmad ibn Abī Usāmah heard Muḥammad ibn Ibrāhīm al-Būshanjī report:

[Al-Būshanjī:] One of my associates reported that Ibn Abī Du'ād confronted Aḥmad and tried to engage him in debate but Aḥmad ignored him.

على أحمد يكلّمه فلم يلتفت إليه أحمد حتى قال المعتصم لأحمد: ألا تُكلّمُ أبا عبد الله؟ فقال أحمد: لستُ أعرفه من أهل العِلم فأُكلّمه.

١٣،٦٩ أخبرنا ابن ناصر قال: أخبرنا ابن[١] يوسف قال: أخبرنا البرمكي قال: حدثنا ابن مردك قال: حدثنا ابن أبي حاتم قال:

حدثنا صالح بن أحمد قال: جعل ابن أبي دؤاد يقول: يا أمير المؤمنين والله لئن أجابك لَهو أحبُّ إليّ من مائة ألف دينار ومائة ألفِ دينار - فيعدّ من ذلك ما شاء الله - قال: فقال، يعني المعتصم: واللهِ لئن أجابني لأُطلقنّ عنه بيدي ولأركبنّ إليه بجُندي ولأطأنّ عَقِبَه. ثم قال: يا أحمد والله إنّي عليك لَشفيق وإنّي لأُشفق عليك كشفقتي على هارون ابني، ما تقول؟ فأقول: أعطوني شيئاً من كتاب الله عزّ وجلّ أو سنّة رسوله.

١٤،٦٩ فلما طال المجلس ضَجِر وقال: قوموا! وحبسني وعبد الرحمن بن إسحاق يكلّمني وقال: وِيحك، أَجِبْني!

وقال لي: ما أعرفك ألم تكن تأتينا؟

فقال له عبد الرحمن بن إسحاق: يا أمير المؤمنين أعرفه منذ ثلاثين سنة يرى طاعتك والجهاد والحجّ معكم.

قال: فيقول: واللهِ إنه لَعالم وإنّه لَفقيه، وما يسوؤني[٢] أن يكون مثلُه معي يردّ عني أهل المِلَل.

ثم قال لي: ما كنت تعرف صالحاً الرشيدي؟

قال: قلت: قد سمعت باسمه.

قال: كان مؤدِّبي وكان في ذلك الموضع جالساً - وأشار إلى ناحية من الدار - فسألتُه عن القرآن فخالفني فأمرت به فوُطئ وسُحب.

ثم قال لي: يا أحمد أجبني إلى شيء لك فيه أدنى فرَج حتى أُطلق عنك بيدي.

---

١ د: ابو. ٢ ش: يسُرني.

Eventually al-Muʿtaṣim asked Aḥmad why he wouldn't address Ibn Abī Du'ād.

"I speak only with men of learning," said Aḥmad.

We cite Ibn Nāṣir, who cites Ibn Yūsuf, who cites al-Barmakī, who heard Ibn Mardak report that he heard Ibn Abī Ḥātim report that he heard Aḥmad's son Ṣāliḥ report: 69.13

[Aḥmad:] "Commander of the Faithful," said Ibn Abī Du'ād, "seeing him capitulate to you would mean more to me than a hundred thousand dinars, and another hundred thousand dinars,"[88] and so on, throwing out one number after another.

"If he tells me what I want to hear," said al-Muʿtaṣim, "I swear I'll unchain him with my own hands. Then I'll lead my troops to him and march along behind him." Then he said, "Aḥmad, I want what's best for you, the same as if you were my son Hārūn. Come on, now: What can you tell me?"[89]

"Give me something from the Book of God," I said, "or the *sunnah* of His Emissary."

As the session dragged on, al-Muʿtaṣim grew bored and restless. "Go!" he said to the scholars. Then he ordered ʿAbd al-Raḥmān ibn Isḥāq and me to stay behind so he could talk to me. 69.14

"Come on!" he said. "Why don't you give up?" Then he said, "I don't recognize you. Have you never come here before?"

"I know him, Commander of the Faithful," said ʿAbd al-Raḥmān ibn Isḥāq. "For thirty years, he's been saying that Muslims owe obedience to you and should follow you in the holy war and join you on the pilgrimage."

"By God," said al-Muʿtaṣim, "he's a man of learning—a man of understanding! I wouldn't mind having someone like him with me to argue against people from other religions." Then, turning to me, "Did you know Ṣāliḥ al-Rashīdī?"

"I've heard of him," I said.

"He was my tutor, and he was sitting right there," he said, pointing to a corner of the room. "I asked him about the Qur'an and he contradicted me, so I had him trampled and dragged out. So Aḥmad: find something—anything—you can agree to, and I'll unchain you with my own hands."

"Give me something from the Book of God," I said, "or the *sunnah* of His Emissary."

قال: قلت: أعطوني شيئاً من كتاب الله عز وجل أو سنّة رسوله.

فطال المجلس فقام فدخل ورددت إلى الموضع الذي كنت فيه. ١٥،٦٩

فلمّا كان بعد المغرب وجّه إليّ برجلين من أصحاب ابن أبي دُؤاد يبيتان عندي ويناظراني ويقيمان معي حتى إذا كان وقت الإفطار جيء بالطعام ويجتهدان بي أن أفطر فلا أفعل.

قال أبي: ووجه إليّ، يعني المعتصم، ابن أبي دُؤاد في بعض الليل فقال: يقول لك أمير المؤمنين: ما تقول؟ فأردّ عليه نحواً ممّا كنت أردّ.

فقال ابن أبي دؤاد: والله لقد كتب اسمك في السبعة، يحيى بن مَعين وغيره، فمحوته -والسبعة يحيى بن مَعين وأبو خَيْثمة[1] وأحمد الدَّورقي والقَواريري وسَعدويه وسَجادة وأحمد بن حنبل وقيل خَلَف المخزومي - ولقد سائني أخذهم إياك، ثم يقول: إن أمير المؤمنين قد حلف أن يضربك ضرباً بعد ضرب وأن يُلقيك في موضع لا ترى فيه الشمس ويقول: إن أجابني جئتُ إليه حتى أُطلق عنه بيدي. ثم انصرف.

فلمّا أصبح، وذلك في اليوم الثاني، جاء رسوله فأخذ بيدي حتّى ذهب بي إليه ١٦،٦٩ فقال لهم: ناظروه، كلّموه.

فجعلوا يناظروني ويتكلم هذا من ها هنا فأردّ عليه ويتكلّم هذا من ها هنا فأردّ علي، فإذا جاؤوا بشيء من الكلام ممّا ليس في كتاب الله عزّ وجلّ ولا سنّة رسوله ولا فيه خبر قلت: ما أدري ما هذا.

قال: يقولون: يا أمير المؤمنين إذا توجّهتْ[2] له الحُجّة علينا ثبت وإذا كلّمناه بشيء يقول: لا أدري ما هذا فيقول: ناظروه!

فقال رجل: يا أحمد أراك تذكر الحديث وتَنْتَحِله. ١٧،٦٩

قلتُ: ما تقول في ﴿يُوصِيكُمُ اللَّهُ فِي أَوْلَادِكُمْ لِلذَّكَرِ مِثْلُ حَظِّ الْأُنْثَيَيْنِ﴾؟

فقال: خصّ الله عزّ وجلّ بها المؤمنين.

---

١ ش: يحيى ابو خيثمة. ٢ مشكلة في ش.

The session dragged on. Finally al-Muʿtaṣim rose and went back inside, and I was sent back to the place where they had been keeping me. 69.15

After sunset prayers, two of Ibn Abī Du'ād's associates were sent in to spend the night there and continue debating with me. They stayed until it was time to break the fast.[90] When the meal arrived they pressed me to eat but I wouldn't. Then, at some point during the night, al-Muʿtaṣim sent over Ibn Abī Du'ād.

"The Commander of the Faithful wants to know if you have anything to say."

I gave him my usual answer.

"You know," he said, "your name was one of the seven—Yaḥyā ibn Maʿīn and the rest—but I rubbed it out."[91]

The seven were Yāḥyā ibn Maʿīn, Abū Khaythamah, Aḥmad al-Dawraqī, al-Qawārīrī, Saʿduwayh, and—in some accounts—Khalaf al-Makhzūmī.[92]

Ibn Abī Du'ād continued: "I was sorry to see them arrest you." Then he said, "The Commander of the Faithful has sworn to give you a good long beating and then throw you somewhere where you'll never see the sun. But he also says that if you capitulate he'll come and unchain you himself."

Then he left.

The next morning—on my second day there—al-Muʿtaṣim's envoy came, took me by the arm, and brought me before him. Again al-Muʿtaṣim ordered them to debate me. "Talk to him!" he said. 69.16

So the debate began again. One of them would speak from over here and I would answer him, and another from over there and I'd answer him too. Whenever they mentioned anything not in the Book of God or the *sunnah* of His Emissary, or in a report about the early Muslims, I would say, "I don't know what you mean."

"Commander of the Faithful," they would protest, "when he has an argument against us he stands his ground, but whenever we make a point he says he doesn't know what we're talking about."

"Keep debating him!" said al-Muʿtaṣim.

"All I see you doing," said one of them, "is citing Hadith and claiming to know what it means." 69.17

"What do you say," I asked him, "about the verse «Concerning your children, God enjoins you that a male shall receive a share equivalent to that of two females»?"[93]

فقلتُ: ما تقولُ إن كان قاتلاً أو عَبدًا أو يَهوديًا؟

قال: فسكت. وإنّما احتججتُ عليهم بهذا لأنّهم كانوا يحتجّون بظاهر القرآن وحيث قال لي: أراك تنتحل الحديث.

فلم يزالوا كذلك إلى أن قرُب الزوال فلما ضجر قال لهم: قوموا! وخلا بي وبعبد الرحمن[1] بن إسحاق فلم يزل يكلّمني ثمّ قام فدخل ورُدِدْتُ إلى الموضع.

أخبرنا المحمّدان ابن ناصر وابن عبد الباقي قالا: أخبرنا حَمْد قال: حدثنا أبو نُعَيم الحافظ قال: حدثنا سليمان بن أحمد قال: حدثنا عبد الله بن أحمد بن حنبل قال: ١٨،٦٩

كتب إليّ الفتح بن شَخْرَف بخطّ يده قال: قال ابنُ حُطَيط، رجلٌ قد سمّاه من أهل الفضل من أهل خُراسان: حُبِس أحمد بن حنبل وبعض أصحابه في المحنة في دار قبل أن يُضرب.

قال أحمد بن حنبل: فلمّا كان الليل نام من كان معي من أصحابي وأنا متفكّر في أمري قال: فإذا أنا برجل طويل يتخطّى الناس حتى دنا منّي فقال: أنت أحمد بن حنبل؟

فسكتُّ فقالها ثانية فسكتّ فقالها ثالثة: أنت أبو عبد الله أحمد بن حنبل؟

قلتُ: نعم.

قال: أصبِر ولك الجنّة.

قال أحمد: فلمّا مَسّني حَرّ السَّوط ذكرتُ قول الرجل.

أخبرنا ابن ناصر قال: أخبرنا ابن يوسف قال: أخبرنا البرمكي قال: حدثنا ابن مردك قال: حدثنا ابن أبي حاتم قال: حدثنا صالح بن أحمد قال: ١٩،٦٩

قال أبي: فلمّا كانت الليلة الثالثة قلت: خليق أن يحدث غدًا من أمري شيء.

---

١ هـ، د: خلا لي ولعبد الرحمن.

"It applies only to believers," he said.

I asked him: "What about murderers, slaves, or Jews?"

He fell silent. I had resorted to that tactic for one reason: they had been arguing on the basis of the plain text of the Qur'an while accusing me of citing Hadith for no good reason.[94]

They kept at it until nearly noon. When al-Muʿtaṣim had had enough, he sent everyone away except for ʿAbd al-Raḥmān ibn Isḥāq, who continued to argue with me. Finally al-Muʿtaṣim rose and went back inside, and I was sent back to the place where they had been holding me.

We cite the two Muḥammads, Ibn Nāṣir and Ibn ʿAbd al-Bāqī, who cite Ḥamd, who heard Abū Nuʿaym al-Ḥāfiẓ report that he heard Sulaymān ibn Aḥmad report that he heard Aḥmad ibn Ḥanbal's son ʿAbd Allāh report: 69.18

[ʿAbd Allāh:] Al-Fatḥ ibn Shakhraf wrote to me in his own hand saying that he heard from Ibn Ḥuṭayṭ—a man of learning from Khurasan, whose name he gave in full—that before Aḥmad ibn Ḥanbal was flogged, he and some of his fellow victims of the Inquisition were kept in confinement in a house somewhere.

"Night fell," said Aḥmad, "and the others went to sleep, but I couldn't stop thinking about what would happen to me. Then I saw a tall man picking his way around the sleepers toward me.

"'Are you Aḥmad ibn Ḥanbal?' he asked.

"I said nothing and he asked again. When I didn't answer, he asked a third time: 'Are you Aḥmad ibn Ḥanbal?'

"'Yes.'

"'Only endure,' he said, 'and the Garden is yours.'

"Later, when I felt the burning of the whips, I remembered what he'd told me."

We cite Ibn Nāṣir, who cites Ibn Yūsuf, who cites al-Barmakī, who heard Ibn Mardak report that he heard Ibn Abī Ḥātim report that he heard Aḥmad's son Ṣāliḥ report: 69.19

[Aḥmad:] I remember thinking to myself on the third night that something was bound to happen the next day. I asked one of the men who were

فقلتُ لبعض من كان معي الموكّل بي: أرتَدْ لي[1] خيطاً. فجاءني بخيط فشددتُ به الأقياد ورددتُ التكّة إلى سراويلي مخافة أن يحدث من أمري شيء فأتعرّى.

٢٠،٦٩ فلمّا كان من الغد في اليوم الثالث وجّه إليّ فأُدخلتُ[2] فإذا الدار غاصَّة فجعلت أدخل من موضع إلى موضع وقوم معهم السيوف وقوم معهم السياط وغير ذلك ولم يكن في اليومين الماضيين كبير[3] أحد من هؤلاء. فلمّا انتهيتُ إليه قال: اقعُد. ثم قال: ناظروه، كلِّموه.

قال: فجعلوا يناظروني ويتكلم هذا فأردّ عليه. ويتكلم هذا فأردّ عليه وجعل صوتي يعلو أصواتهم فجعل بعض من على رأسه قائم يُومئ إليّ بيده.

فلما طال المجلس نحّاني ثم خلا بهم ثم نحّاهم وردّني عليه وقال: ويحك يا أحمد! أَجِبْني حتى أُطلق عنك بيدي.

فرددت عليه نحواً ممّا كنتُ أردّ فقال لي: عليك - ! وذكر اللعن. ثم قال: خُذوه واسحبوه وخلّعوه.

قال: فسُحبت ثم خُلّعت.

٢١،٦٩ قال: وقد كان صار إليّ شَعر من شعر النبي صلّى الله عليه وسلّم فصررتُه في كمّ قميصي فوجّه إليّ إسحاق بن إبراهيم: ما هذا المصرور في كمّ قميصك؟ فقلت: شعر من شعر النبي صلى الله عليه وسلم. قال: وسعى بعض القوم إلى القميص ليخرقه عليّ فقال لهم، يعني المعتصم: لا تخرقوه. فنُزِع القميص عنّي. قال: فظننتُ أنه إنما دُرِئ عن القميص الخرق بسبب الشعر الذي كان فيه.

٢٢،٦٩ قال أبي: وجلس على كُرسي، يعني المعتصم، ثم قال: العُقابَين والسياط فجيء بالعقابين فمُدّت يداي فقال بعض من حضر خلفي: خُذ نابَيِ[4] الخشبتين بيديك وشُدّ عَليهما. فلم أفهم ما قال، فتخلّعت يداي.

---

١ ش: اريد لي. ٢ د: فادخلت عليه. ٣ د: كثير. ٤ د: نابى، ش: يابي عبد الله، تركي: ناتئ.

assigned to me to find me a cord. He found one and I used it to pull up my chains. Then I put the drawstring back on my trousers to hold them up so I wouldn't be exposed if something happened to me.

On the morning of the third day,[95] al-Muʿtaṣim sent for me again. I entered the hall to find it packed with people. As I came slowly forward, I saw people with swords, people with whips, and so on—many more than on the first two days. When I reached him, he told me to sit down. "Debate him," he told the others. "Talk to him!" 69.20

They began to argue with me. One would talk and I would answer him, and then another would talk and I'd answer him too. Soon I was winning.[96] One of the men standing near al-Muʿtaṣim began pointing at me. After the session had gone on for a while, al-Muʿtaṣim had me led away to one side so he could confer with them alone. Then he sent them to the side and had me brought over.

"Come on, Aḥmad!" he said. "Tell me what I want to hear, and I'll unchain you with my own hands."

When I gave him my usual answer, he cursed me, then said, "Drag him away and strip him!"

I was dragged away and stripped.[97]

Some time before, I had acquired some of the Prophet's hair. Noticing that I had something knotted up in the sleeve of my shirt, Isḥāq ibn Ibrāhīm sent someone over to ask what it was. I told him it was some of the Prophet's hair. When they started tearing my shirt off, al-Muʿtaṣim told them to stop and they pulled it off me without ripping it. I think he held back because of the hair that was knotted up inside. 69.21

Sitting down on a chair, al-Muʿtaṣim called for the posts and the whips. They brought out the posts and made me stretch out my arms. From behind me someone said, "Hold on to the tusks and pull," but I didn't understand, so I ended up spraining both my wrists.[98] 69.22

٦٩، ٢٣ أخبرنا عبد الملك بن أبي القاسم قال: أخبرنا عبد الله بن محمّد الأنصاري قال: أخبرنا أبو يعقوب قال: أخبرنا جدّي قال: أخبرنا محمّد بن أبي جعفر المُنذِري وأبو أحمد بن أبي أُسامة قالا:

سمعنا محمّد بن إبراهيم البُوشَنْجي يقول: ذكروا أنّ المعتصم لان في أمر أحمد لمّا عُلّق في العقابين ورأى ثبوته وتصميمه وصلابته في أمره حتى أغراه ابن أبي دؤاد وقال له: إن تركته قيل إنّك تركت مذهب المأمون. وسَخِطتَ قولَه فهاجَه ذلك على ضربه.

٦٩، ٢٤ أخبرنا ابن ناصر قال: أخبرنا ابن يوسف قال: أخبرنا البرمكي قال: أخبرنا ابن مَرْدَك قال: حدثنا ابن أبي حاتم قال: حدثنا صالح قال:

قال أبي: لما جيء بالسياط نظر إليها المعتصم فقال: ائتوني بغيرها.

فأُتي بغيرها ثم قال للجلّادين: تقدّموا.

قال: فجعل يتقدّم إليّ الرجل منهم فيضربني سوطين فيقول له، يعني المعتصم: شُدّ، قطع الله يدك! ثم يَتَنحّى ثم يتقدم الآخر فيضربني سوطين وهو في كل ذلك يقول لهم: شدّوا، قطع الله أيديكم!

٦٩، ٢٥ فلما ضُربت تسعة عشر سوطاً قام إليّ، يعني المعتصم، فقال: يا أحمد علامَ تقتل نفسك؟ إنّي والله عليك شفيق.

قال: فجعل عُجَيْف ينخسني بقائم سيفه وقال: تريد أن تغلب هؤلاء كلّهم؟

وجعل بعضهم يقول: ويلك، الخليفة على رأسك قائم!

وقال بعضهم: يا أمير المؤمنين دمهُ في عنقي، اقتله!

وجعلوا يقولون له: يا أمير المؤمنين أنت صائم وأنت في الشمس قائم.

فقال لي: ويحك يا أحمد، ما تقول؟

فأقول: أعطوني شيئاً من كتاب الله عزّ وجلّ أو سنّة رسوله صلى الله عليه وسلم أقول به.

قال: ثم رجع فجلس ثم قال للجلاد: تقدم أَوْجِعْ قطع الله يدك!

We cite ʿAbd al-Malik ibn Abī l-Qāsim, who cites ʿAbd Allāh ibn Muḥammad al-Anṣārī, who cites Abū Yaʿqūb, who cites his grandfather, who cites Muḥammad ibn Abī Jaʿfar al-Mundhirī, who along with Abū Aḥmad ibn Abī Usāmah heard Muḥammad ibn Ibrāhīm al-Būshanjī say: 69.23

[Al-Būshanjī:] They say that when Aḥmad was suspended from the posts, al-Muʿtaṣim, seeing him undaunted, so admired his bravery that he was prepared to be lenient with him; but then Aḥmad ibn Abī Du'ād provoked him, saying, "If you let him go, people will say that you've renounced al-Ma'mūn's creed and are refusing to enforce it." It was this that pushed al-Muʿtaṣim to go ahead and flog him.

We cite Ibn Nāṣir, who cites Ibn Yūsuf, who cites al-Barmakī, who cites Ibn Mardak, who heard Ibn Abī Ḥātim report that he heard Ṣāliḥ report that his father said: 69.24

[Aḥmad:] When they brought the whips, al-Muʿtaṣim looked at them and said, "Bring different ones," which was done.[99] Then he said to the lictors,[100] "Proceed!"

One at a time, they came at me, and struck two lashes apiece, with al-Muʿtaṣim calling out, "Harder, damn you!" As each one stepped aside another would come up and hit me twice more, with him shouting all the while, "Harder, damn you all!"[101]

After I had been struck nineteen lashes, he—meaning al-Muʿtaṣim—rose 69.25
from his seat and walked up to me.

"Aḥmad," he said, "why are you killing yourself? I swear to God, I want what's best for you."

Then ʿUjayf began jabbing at me with the hilt of his sword. "Do you think you can win against this whole lot?"

"For shame!" someone called out. "The caliph is standing there waiting for you."

"Commander of the Faithful!" cried another. "Kill him, and let his blood be on my hands!"

Then more of them chimed in. "Commander of the Faithful, you've been fasting, and now you're standing in the sun!"[102]

"Come on, Aḥmad," he said. "Say something!"

"Give me something I can believe," I said, "from the Book of God or the *sunnah* of His Emissary."

He went back to his chair and sat down.

ثم قام الثانية فجعل يقول: ويحك يا أحمد، أجبني. ٢٦،٦٩

فجعلوا يقبلون عليّ ويقولون: ويلك يا أحمد، إمامك على رأسك قائم!

وجعل عبد الرحمن يقول: من صنع من أصحابك في هذا الأمر ما تصنع؟

قال: وجعل يقول، يعني المعتصم: ويحك! أجبني إلى شيء لك فيه أدنى فرج حتى أُطلق عنك بيدي.

قال: فقلت: يا أميرَ المؤمنين أعطوني شيئاً من كتاب الله عزّ وجلّ أو سنّة رسوله حتى أقول به.

قال: فرجع فجلس فقال للجلادين: تقدموا.

فجعل الجلاد يتقدّم ويضربني سوطين ويتنحّى وهو في خلال ذلك يقول: شدّ قطع الله يدك!

قال أبي: فذهب عقلي.

فأفقتُ بعد ذلك فإذا الأقياد قد أُطلقتْ عنّي فقال لي رجل ممن حضر: إنا كببناك على وجهك وطرحنا على ظهرك باريّة ودُسْناك.

قال أبي: فما شعرتُ بذلك.

وأتوني بسَويق فقالوا لي: اشرب وتقيأ.

فقلت: لست أفطر.

٢٧،٦٩ ثم جيء بي إلى دار إسحاق بن إبراهيم فحضرت صلاة الظهر فتقدم ابن سَماعة فصلّى فلمّا انفتل من الصلاة قال لي: صلّيتَ والدم يسيل في ثوبك؟

فقلت: قد صلّى عُمر وجرحه يثعب دماً.

٢٨،٦٩ قال أبو الفضل: ثم خُلّي عنه فصار إلى منزله فمكث في السجن منذ أُخذ وحُمل إلى أن ضُرب وخُلّي عنه ثمانية وعشرين شهراً.

قال صالح: ولقد أخبرني أحد الرجلين اللذين كانا مع أبي، يعني في الحبس،[1] وكان هذا الرجل قد سمع ونظر ثم جاءني[2] بعد ذلك فقال لي: يا ابن أخي، رحمة

---

١ د: السجن. ٢ في كل النسخ: حال، صححها التركي.

"Proceed," he said to the lictor. "Let him feel it, damn you!"

Soon he rose a second time, saying, "Come on, Aḥmad! Tell me what I want to hear." 69.26

The others joined in, saying, "Shame on you, Aḥmad: your imam is standing here waiting for you."

"Which of your associates," asked ʿAbd al-Raḥmān, "is doing what you're doing?"

"Tell me whatever you can manage," al-Muʿtaṣim said to me, "and I'll unchain you with my own hands."

"Give me something I can believe," I said, "from the Book of God or the *sunnah* of His Emissary."

Again he went back to his chair and sat down. "Proceed," he said to the lictors. Again they came up one by one and struck me two lashes apiece, with al-Muʿtaṣim calling out, "Harder, damn you!" As each stepped aside another would come up and hit me twice more, with him shouting all the while, "Harder, damn you all!"

That's when I passed out.[103]

Some time later I came to my senses to find that my chains had been removed.

"We threw you face down," said one of the men who had been there. "Then we rolled you over on the ground and trampled you."

I had no memory of that.

They brought me some barley water and told me to drink it and vomit.

"I can't break the fast," I told them.

They took me back to Isḥāq ibn Ibrahīm's place, where I attended the 69.27
noon prayer.[104] Ibn Samāʿah stepped forward to lead the prayer. When he finished he asked me, "How could you pray when you're bleeding inside your clothes?"

"ʿUmar prayed with blood spurting from his wounds," I answered.

Ṣāliḥ said: 69.28

My father was released and went home. From the time he was first arrested to the time he was flogged and let go was twenty-eight months.

One of the two men who were with my father—in jail, that is—heard and saw everything. Later he came to see me and said, "Cousin, may God have mercy on Abū ʿAbd Allāh! I never saw anyone like him. When they sent food in, I would remind him that he was fasting, and tell him he was allowed

الله على أبي عبد الله والله ما رأيت أحداً يشبهه ولقد جعلت أقول له في وقت ما يُوَجَّه إلينا بالطعام: يا أبا عبد الله أنت صائم وأنت في موضع تَقِيَّة. ولقد عطش فقال لصاحب الشراب: ناولني، فناوله قَدحاً فيه ماء وثلج فأخذه ونظر إليه هُنَيّة ثم ردّه عليه ولم يشرب فجعلتُ أعجب من صبره على الجوع والعطش وهو فيما هو فيه من الهول.

٢٩،٦٩ قال صالح: وقد كنتُ ألتمس وأحتال أن أوصل إليه طعاماً أو رغيفاً أو رغيفين في تلك الأيّام فلم أقدر على ذلك، وأخبرني رجل حضره أنه تفقّده في هذه الثلاثة الأيّام وهم يناظرونه ويكلّمونه فما لحن في كلمة، قال: وما ظننت أن أحداً يكون في مثل شجاعته وشدّة قلبه.

٣٠،٦٩ أخبرنا عبد الملك بن أبي القاسم قال: أخبرنا عبد الله بن محمّد الأنصاري قال: أخبرنا أبو يعقوب قال: أخبرنا جدّي قال: أخبرنا محمّد بن أبي جعفر المنذري وأبو أحمد بن أبي أُسامة قالا:

سمعنا محمّد بن إبراهيم البُوشَنْجي قال: قدم المعتصم من بلاد الروم بغداد في شهر رمضان سنة ثمان عشرة فامتحن فيها أحمد وضُرب بين يديه. فحدثني من أثق به من أصحابنا عن محمّد بن إبراهيم بن مُصعب، وهو يومئذ على الشُّرَط للمعتصم خليفة إسحاق بن إبراهيم، أنه قال: ما رأيتُ أحداً لم يُداخل السلطان ولا خالط الملوك أثبت قلباً من أحمد يومئذ، ما نحن في عينه إلّا كأمثال الذُّباب.

٣١،٦٩ أخبرنا ابن ناصر قال: أخبرنا المبارك بن عبد الجبار قال: أخبرنا أبو محمّد الحسن بن محمّد الخلّال قال: حدثنا أبو الفضل عُبيد الله بن عبد الرحمن الزُّهري قال: قرأت في كتابي:

قال المَرُّوذي في محنة أحمد بن حنبل وهو بين الهُنْبَازَيْن: يا أستاذ قال الله تعالى: ﴿وَلا تَقْتُلوا أَنْفُسَكُم﴾.

فقال أحمد: يا مَرّوذي اخرج انظر أي شيء ترى.

قال: فخرجت إلى رحبة دار الخليفة فرأيت خَلقاً من الناس لا يُحصي عددهم إلّا الله والصحف في أيديهم والأقلام والمحابر في أذرعتهم فقال لهم المَرُّوذي: أيّ

to save himself.[105] I also remember that he was thirsty. He asked the attendant for something to drink. The man gave him a cup of water with ice in it. He took it and looked at it for a moment, but then he gave it back without drinking it. I was amazed that he could go without food or water even in that terrifying place."

Ṣāliḥ said: 69.29

At the time, I was doing everything I could to smuggle some food or a loaf or two of flatbread in to him, but none of my pleading did any good.

A man who was there told me that he kept his eye on him for the entire three days, and not once during all the argument and debate did he mispronounce a single word. "I didn't think it was possible for anyone to be as tough as he was."

We cite ʿAbd al-Malik ibn Abī l-Qāsim, who cites ʿAbd Allāh ibn Muḥammad al-Anṣārī, 69.30
who cites Abū Yaʿqūb, who cites his grandfather, who cites Muḥammad ibn Abī Jaʿfar al-Mundhirī, who along with Abū Aḥmad ibn Abī Usāmah heard Muḥammad ibn Ibrāhīm al-Būshanjī report:

[Al-Būshanjī:] Al-Muʿtaṣim returned to Baghdad from the Byzantine front in Ramadan of '18. It was then that he tried Aḥmad and had him flogged before him.

A trustworthy associate of mine reported to me what he was told by Ibrāhīm ibn Muṣʿab, who at that time was standing in for Isḥāq ibn Ibrāhīm as al-Muʿtaṣim's chief of police: "I've never seen anyone brought face to face with kings and princes show as little fear as Aḥmad did that day. To him we were nothing but a cloud of flies."

We cite Ibn Nāṣir, who cites al-Mubārak ibn ʿAbd al-Jabbār, who cites Abū Muḥammad 69.31
al-Ḥasan ibn Muḥammad al-Khallāl, who heard Abū l-Faḍl ʿUbayd Allāh ibn ʿAbd al-Raḥmān al-Zuhrī report:

[Al-Zuhrī:] I read from my own notes what al-Marrūdhī said at the trial of Aḥmad ibn Ḥanbal, as Aḥmad was hanging between the posts.[106]

"Master," said al-Marrūdhī, "God says, «Do not kill yourselves.»"[107]

"Marrūdhī," said Aḥmad, "go and look outside and tell me what you see."

Al-Marrūdhī reported: "I went out and there, in the courtyard of the caliph's palace, was a vast crowd of people—God only knows how

شيء تعملون؟ فقالوا: ننتظر ما يقول أحمد فنكتبه. فقال المروذي: مكانكم! فدخل إلى أحمد بن حنبل وهو قائم بين الهُنْبَارزين فقال له: رأيتُ قوماً بأيديهم الصحف والأقلام ينتظرون ما تقول فيكتبونه.

فقال: يا مروذي أُضِلّ هؤلاء كلّهم؟ أقتل نفسي ولا أضلّ هؤلاء كلّهم.

٣٢،٦٩ قلت: هذا رجل هانت عليه نفسه في الله تعالى فبذلها كما هانت على بلال نفسه، وقد روينا عن سعيد بن المُسَيَّب أنه كانت نفسه عليه في الله تعالى أهون من نفس ذُباب. وإنما تهون أنفسهم عليهم لتلمّحهم العواقب فعيون البصائر ناظرة إلى المآل لا إلى الحال، وشدّة ابتلاء أحمد دليل على قوّة دينه لأنه قد صحّ عن النبي صلّى الله عليه وسلّم أنّه قال: يُبْتَلَى الرَّجلُ على حَسَبِ دِينِه فسبحان من أيّده وبَصّره وقوّاه ونصره.

٣٣،٦٩ أخبرنا محمّد بن ناصر قال: أنبأنا الحسن بن أحمد الفقيه قال: أخبرنا عُبيد الله بن أحمد قال: حدثنا أبو بكر محمّد ابن عبيد الله الكاتب قال: حدثنا أبو عليّ الحسن بن محمّد بن عثمان الفَسَوي قال: حدثني داوود بن عَرَفَة قال:

حدثنا مَيْمون بن الأصبَغ قال: كنتُ ببغداد فسمعتُ ضجّة فقلت: ما هذا؟

فقالوا: أحمد بن حنبل يُمتحَن. فأتيتُ منزلي فأخذت مالاً له خطر فذهبت به إلى من يُدخلني إلى المجلس فأدخلوني.

فإذا بالسيوف قد جُرِدت وبالرّماح قد رُكزت وبالتّراس قد نُصبت وبالسياط قد طُرحت فألبسوني قَباء أسود ومنطقة وسيفاً ووقفوني حيث أسمع الكلام.

فأتى أمير المؤمنين فجلس على كرسي وأُتي بأحمد بن حنبل فقال له: وقرابتي من رسول الله صلّى الله عليه وسلّم لأضربنّك بالسياط أو تقول كما أقول. ثم التفت إلى جلاد فقال: خُذه إليك! فأخذه.

فلما ضُرب سوطاً قال: بسم الله.

فلما ضُرب الثاني قال: لا حول ولا قُوة إلا بالله.

many—with their sheets of paper, their pens, and their pots of ink. I asked them what they were doing, and they said, 'We're waiting to hear what Aḥmad says so we can write it down.'"

He told them to stay where they were, then went back inside, where Aḥmad was still hanging between the posts. He told him that he had seen a crowd of people holding pen and paper and waiting to write down whatever he would say.

"Can I mislead all those people?" asked Aḥmad. "I'd rather kill myself."[108]

[The author:] Here then is a man who, like Bilāl, was willing to give up his life for the sake of his God.[109] Of Saʿīd ibn al-Musayyab, similarly, it is reported that his life meant as little to him as the life of a fly. Such indifference to self is possible only when one has glimpsed the life that lies beyond this one and trained one's gaze on the future rather than the present. Aḥmad's great suffering is evidence of his strong faith, for, as the Prophet is known to have said, "A man suffers in proportion to his faith." Praise the One who helped Aḥmad, granted him the gift of perception, strengthened his resolve, and came to his aid. 69.32

We cite Muḥammad ibn Nāṣir, who was informed by al-Ḥasan ibn Aḥmad al-Faqīh, who cites ʿUbayd Allāh ibn Aḥmad, who heard Abū Bakr Muḥammad ibn ʿUbayd Allāh al-Kātib report that he heard Abū ʿAlī l-Ḥasan ibn Muḥammad ibn ʿUthmān al-Fasawī report that he heard Dāwūd ibn ʿArafah report that he heard Maymūn ibn al-Aṣbagh report: 69.33

[Ibn al-Aṣbagh:] I was in Baghdad and heard a clamor. I asked what it was about and people told me that Aḥmad ibn Ḥanbal was being tried. So I went home, collected a substantial sum of money, and bribed my way into the session. Inside the palace, I saw soldiers with their swords drawn, their spears fixed, their shields planted, and their whips at the ready. I was fitted out with a black cloak, a sash, and a sword, and given a seat close enough that I could hear what was being said.

The caliph appeared and seated himself in a chair. Then Ibn Ḥanbal was brought in.

"I swear by my ancestor the Prophet," said the caliph, "that if you don't say as I say, I'll have you flogged!"

Turning to the lictor, he said, "Take him away!"

At the first blow, Aḥmad said, "In the name of God!"

فلما ضُرب الثالث قال: القُرآن كلام الله غير مخلوق.

فلما ضُرب الرابع قال: ﴿قُل لَن يُصِيبَنَا إِلَّا مَا كَتَبَ اللهُ لَنَا﴾. فضربه تسعةً وعشرين سوطاً.

وكانت تِكّة أحمد حاشية ثوب فانقطعت فنزل السراويل إلى عانته فقلتُ: الساعة ينهتك.

فرمى أحمدُ طرفه نحو السماء وحرّك شفتيه فما كان بأسرع من أن بقي السراويل لم ينزل.

قال ميمون: فدخلت إليه بعد سبعة أيّام فقلت: يا أبا عبد الله رأيتك يوم ضربوك قد انحلّ سراويلك فرفعتَ طرفك نحو السماء ورأيتك تحرّك شفتيك فأيّ شيء قلت؟

قال: قلت: اللّهمّ إني أسألك باسمك الذي ملأت به العرش إن كنت تعلم أنّي على الصواب فلا تهتك لي سِتْراً.

٣٤،٦٩ أخبرنا المحمّدان: ابن ناصر وابن عبد الباقي قالا: أخبرنا حَمْد قال: أخبرنا أبو نُعَيم الحافظ قال: أخبرنا عبد الله بن جعفر قال: حدثنا أبي قال: حدثنا أحمد بن أبي عُبيد الله قال:

قال أحمد بن الفرَج: حضرت أحمد لمّا ضُرب فتقدّم أبو الدَّنّ فضربه بضعة عشر سوطاً فأقبل الدم من أكتافه وكان عليه سراويل فانقطع خيطه فنزل السراويل فلحظته وقد حرّك شفتيه فعاد السراويل كما كان.

فسألتُه عن ذلك فقال: قلتُ: إلهي وسيّدي وقفتَني هذا الموقف فتهتكني على رؤوس الخلائق؟ فعاد السراويل كما كان.

٣٥،٦٩ أخبرنا المحمّدان: ابن ناصر وابن عبد الباقي قالا: أخبرنا حمد بن أحمد قال: حدثنا أبو نُعَيم الحافظ قال: حدثنا الحسين بن محمّد قال: حدثنا إبراهيم بن محمّد القاضي قال: حدثني أبو عبد الله الجوهري قال: حدثني يوسف ابن يعقوب بن الفَرَج قال:

سمعت عليّ بن محمد القُرَشي قال: لما قُدِّم أحمد بن حنبل ليضرب وجُرِّد وبقي في سراويله فبينا هو يُضرب انحلّ السراويل فجعل يحرّك شفتيه بشيء فرأيتُ يَدَيْن

At the second, he said, "There is no might or power except by God!"

At the third, he said, "The Qur'an is the speech of God, and uncreated!"

At the fourth he said, "«Say: we will suffer only what God has decreed for us!»"[110]

The lictor had struck him twenty-nine lashes when Aḥmad's trouser cord—which was made of nothing more than a strip of garment lining—broke. His trousers slipped down as far as his groin.

"He'll be left with nothing on," I thought to myself. But then he looked up to the heavens and moved his lips. Instantly the trousers stopped slipping and remained in place.

Seven days later, I went to see him. "Aḥmad," I asked, "I was there the day they beat you and your trousers came apart. I saw you look up and move your lips. What were you saying?"

He said, "I said, 'God, I call You by Your name, which has filled the Throne! If You know me to be in the right, do not expose my nakedness.'"

We cite the two Muḥammads, Ibn Nāṣir and Ibn ʿAbd al-Bāqī, who cite Ḥamd, who cites Abū Nuʿaym al-Ḥāfiẓ, who cites ʿAbd Allāh ibn Jaʿfar, who heard his father report that he heard Aḥmad ibn Abī ʿUbayd Allāh report that Aḥmad ibn al-Faraj said: **69.34**

[Aḥmad ibn al-Faraj:] I was there when Aḥmad was whipped. Abū l-Dann came up and struck him more than ten lashes. Blood started pouring from his shoulders. He was wearing a pair of trousers, and the cord broke. I noticed that as the trousers began to come down, he said something inaudible and they went back up.

Later I asked him about it, and he told me what he had said: "'My God and Lord, You've put me here, and now You're going to expose my nakedness to the world?' That's when my trousers came back up."[111]

We cite the two Muḥammads, Ibn Nāṣir and Ibn ʿAbd al-Bāqī, who cite Ḥamd ibn Aḥmad, who heard Abū Nuʿaym al-Ḥāfiẓ report that he heard al-Ḥusayn ibn Muḥammad report that he heard Ibrāhīm ibn Muḥammad al-Qāḍī report that he heard Abū ʿAbd Allāh al-Jawharī report that he heard Yūsuf ibn Yaʿqūb ibn al-Faraj report that he heard ʿAlī ibn Muḥammad al-Qurashī report: **69.35**

[Al-Qurashī:] When they brought Aḥmad ibn Ḥanbal forward to be flogged, they stripped him of everything but his trousers. As he was being

خرجتا من تحته وهو يُضرب فشدّتا السراويل.

فلما فرغوا من الضرب قلنا له: ما كنت تقول حيث انحلّ السراويل؟

قال: قلتُ: يا من لا يعلم العرش منه أين هو إلا هو إن كنتُ على الحقّ فلا تُبْدِ عورتي، فهذا الذي قلتُ.

أخبرنا ابن ناصر قال: أخبرنا أبو عليّ الحسن بن أحمد قال: حدثني القاضي أبو يَعْلَى محمّد بن الحسين قال: حدثنا أبو الحسن عليّ بن محمّد الحِنائيّ قال: حدثنا أبو محمد عبد الله بن محمّد بن إسماعيل الطَّرَسوسي قال: حدثنا أبو بكر محمّد بن عيسى قال: حدثنا أحمد بن طاهر قال: حدثنا العباس بن عبد الله قال: ٣٦،٦٩

سمعتُ جعفرًا الرازي يقول: كان إسحاق بن إبراهيم يقول: أنا والله رأيت يوم ضرب أحمد سراويله وقد ارتفع من بعد انخفاضه وانعقد من بعد انحلاله ولم يفطن بذلك لذهول عقل من حضره، وما رأيتُ يوماً كان أعظم على المعتصم من ذلك اليوم، والله لو لم يرفع عنه الضرب لم يبرح من مكانه إلا ميتاً.

أخبرنا عبد الملك بن أبي القاسم قال: أخبرنا عبد الله بن محمّد الأنصاري قال: أخبرنا محمّد بن المنتصر قال: أخبرنا أبو بكر بن أبي الفضل قال: حدثنا محمّد بن إبراهيم الصرّام قال: ٣٧،٦٩

حدثنا إبراهيم بن إسحاق الأنصاري قال: سمعت بعض الجلّادين يقول: لقد بطّل[١] أحمد بن حنبل الشُطّار، والله لقد ضربتُه ضربًا لو أُبرِكَ لي بعير فضربته ذلك الضرب لنقبتُ عن جوفه.

أخبرنا عبد الملك قال: أخبرنا عبد الله بن محمّد قال: أخبرني أبو يعقوب إجازة قال: حدثنا أبو عليّ منصور بن عبد الله قال: حدثنا بكر بن محمّد بن حمدان قال: حدثنا جعفر بن كِزال قال: سمعت محمّد بن إسماعيل بن أبي سَمينة قال: ٣٨،٦٩

سمعت شاباص التائب[٢] يقول: لقد ضربتُ أحمد بن حنبل ثمانين سَوطًا لو ضربتُه فيلاً لهدّتْه.[٣]

---

١ مشددة في هـ، د. ٢ ش: الثايب، د: النابت. ٣ هكذا في جميع النسخ.

flogged, the trousers came loose. His lips moved, and then I saw two hands appear from under him as he was being whipped and pull the trousers back up. When the flogging was over, we asked him what he had said when the trousers came loose. He told us, "I said, 'I call on You who alone knows where Your Throne is. If I'm in the right, do not expose my nakedness.' That's what I said."

We cite Ibn Nāṣir, who cites Abū ʿAlī l-Ḥasan ibn Aḥmad, who heard the judge Abū Yaʿlā Muḥammad ibn al-Ḥusayn report that he heard Abū l-Ḥasan ʿAlī ibn Muḥammad al-Ḥinnāʾī report that he heard Abū Muḥammad ʿAbd Allāh ibn Muḥammad ibn Ismāʿīl al-Ṭarasūsī report that he heard Abū Bakr Muḥammad ibn ʿĪsā report that he heard Aḥmad ibn Ṭāhir report that he heard al-ʿAbbās ibn ʿAbd Allāh report that he heard Jaʿfar al-Rāzī say: 69.36

[Al-Rāzī:] Isḥāq ibn Ibrāhīm used to say, "By God, I was there the day Aḥmad was flogged and his trousers came down and went up again, and reknotted themselves after coming loose. The people there with him were too preoccupied to notice. But I never saw a more terrible day for al-Muʿtaṣim. If he hadn't stopped the flogging, he would never have made it out alive."[112]

We cite ʿAbd al-Malik ibn Abī l-Qāsim, who cites ʿAbd Allāh ibn Muḥammad al-Anṣārī, who cites Muḥammad ibn al-Muntaṣir, who cites Abū Bakr ibn Abī l-Faḍl, who heard Muḥammad ibn Ibrāhīm al-Ṣarrām report that he heard Ibrāhīm ibn Isḥāq al-Anṣārī report: 69.37

[Al-Anṣārī:] I heard one of the lictors say, "Aḥmad ibn Ḥanbal turned out to be as tough as a bandit.[113] If a camel knelt down and I hit it as hard as I hit him, I would have split open its belly."

We cite ʿAbd al-Malik, who cites ʿAbd Allāh ibn Muḥammad, who with his permission cites Abū Yaʿqūb, who heard Abū ʿAlī Manṣūr ibn ʿAbd Allāh report that he heard Bakr ibn Muḥammad ibn Ḥamdān report that he heard Jaʿfar ibn Kuzāl report that he heard Muḥammad ibn Ismāʿīl ibn Abī Samīnah report that he heard Shābāṣ the Penitent say: 69.38

[Shābāṣ:] I struck Aḥmad ibn Ḥanbal eighty lashes. If I'd hit an elephant that hard I would've knocked it down.[114]

أنبأنا أبو عبد الله بن البَنّا عن القاضي أبي يعلى قال: أخبرني محمّد بن جعفر الراشدي قال: ٦٩، ٣٩

حدثني بعض أصحابنا قال: لمّا أخذتْ أبا عبد الله السياط قال: بك أستغيث يا جبّار السماء ويا جبّار الأرض!

أخبرنا عبد الملك بن أبي القاسم قال: أخبرنا عبد الله بن محمّد الأنصري قال: أخبرنا أبو يعقوب قال: سمعت إبراهيم ٦٩، ٤٠
ابن إسماعيل الخَلّالي قال: سمعت محمّد بن عبد الله بن شاذان يقول: سمعت أحمد بن الحسن بن عَبْدُويَه يقول:

سمعت عبد الله بن أحمد بن حنبل يقول: كنت كثيرًا أسمع والدي يقول: رحم الله أبا الهيثَم، غفرَ الله لأبي الهيثم، عفا الله عن أبي الهيثم! فقلت: يا أبة من أبو الهيثم؟

قال: لا تعرفه؟ قلت: لا.

قال: أبو الهيثم الحدّاد، اليوم الذي أخرجتُ فيه للسياط ومُدّت يداي للعقابَين إذا أنا بإنسان يجذب ثوبي من ورائي ويقول لي: تعرفني؟ قلت: لا.

قال: أنا أبو الهيثم العيّار اللصّ الطرّار، مكتوب في ديوان أمير المؤمنين أني ضُربت ثمانية عشر ألف سوط بالتفاريق وصبرتُ في ذلك على طاعة الشيطان لأجل الدنيا فاصبر أنت في طاعة الرحمن لأجل الدين.

قال: فضُربت ثمانية عشر سوطاً بدل ما ضُرب ثمانية عشر ألفاً، وخرج الخادم فقال: عفا عنه أمير المؤمنين.

وقد ذكر إبراهيم بن محمّد بن عَرَفة في تاريخه أنّ أحمد ضرب ستّة وثلاثين سوطاً.[1]

أخبرنا محمّد بن أبي منصور قال: أخبرنا المبارك بن عبد الجبّار قال: أخبرنا أبو محمّد الخلّال قال: أخبرنا عمر بن ٦٩، ٤١
شاهين قال: حدثنا شُعيب بن محمّد الذارع قال:

حدثنا يحيى بن نُعيم قال: لمّا أُخرج أحمد بن حنبل إلى المعتصم يوم ضُرب قال له العون الموكّل به: ادعُ على ظالمك. فقال: ليس بصابر من دعا على ظالمه.[2]

---

١ الجملة في ش فقط. ٢ د: ظالم.

We were informed by Abū ʿAbd Allāh ibn al-Bannā, citing the judge Abū Yaʿlā, who cites Muḥammad ibn Jaʿfar al-Rāshidī, who reports: **69.39**

[Al-Rāshidī:] One of my associates reported: "When the whips began to tear into Abū ʿAbd Allāh, he said, 'To You, Sovereign of the heavens and the earth, I cry for help!'"

We cite ʿAbd al-Malik ibn Abī l-Qāsim, who cites ʿAbd Allāh ibn Muḥammad al-Anṣārī, who cites Abū Yaʿqūb, who heard Ibrāhīm ibn Ismāʿīl al-Khallālī report that he heard Muḥammad ibn ʿAbd Allāh ibn Shādhān say that he heard Aḥmad ibn al-Ḥasan ibn ʿAbduwayh say that he heard Aḥmad ibn Ḥanbal's son ʿAbd Allāh say: **69.40**

[ʿAbd Allāh:] I often heard my father say, "God have mercy on Abū l-Haytham! God pardon Abū l-Haytham! God forgive Abū l-Haytham!"

"Dad," I finally asked, "who is Abū l-Haytham?"

"Don't you know?"

"No."

"It's Abū l-Haytham al-Ḥaddād. The day they took me and stretched my arms out for the flogging, I felt someone pulling at my clothes from behind.

"'Do you recognize me?' he asked.

"'No.'

"'I'm Abū l-Haytham, and I'm a bandit, a cutpurse, and a thief. At one time or another, I've been struck eighteen thousand lashes—all on record with the Commander of the Faithful—for the sake of Satan and the things of this world. So bear up and take your beating for God and Islam.'

"They struck me eighteen lashes instead of his eighteen thousand. Then the attendant came out and said, 'The Commander of the Faithful has pardoned him!'"

[The author:] In his *History*, Ibrāhīm ibn Muḥammad ibn ʿArafah reports that Aḥmad was struck thirty-six lashes.[115]

We cite Muḥammad ibn Abī Manṣūr, who cites al-Mubārak ibn ʿAbd al-Jabbār, who cites Abū Muḥammad al-Khallāl, who cites ʿUmar ibn Shāhīn, who heard Shuʿayb ibn Muḥammad al-Dhāriʿ report that he heard Yaḥyā ibn Nuʿaym report: **69.41**

[Yaḥyā ibn Nuʿaym:] As Aḥmad ibn Ḥanbal was being taken out to al-Muʿtaṣim to be flogged, the officer escorting him said, "Go ahead and curse whoever did this to you!"

"Cursing your oppressor," said Aḥmad, "shows a lack of fortitude."

٤٢،٦٩ أخبرنا أبو المعمَّر الأنصاري قال: أخبرنا محفوظ بن أحمد قال: أخبرنا أبو عليّ الحسن بن غالب قال: سمعت أبا الفضل التميمي يقول:

قال أبو القاسم البَغَوي: رأيت أحمد بن حنبل داخلاً إلى جامع المدينة وعليه كساء أخضر وبيده نعلاه حاسر الرأس، فرأيتُ شيخًا آدم طُوالاً أبيض اللحية.

وكان على دكّة المنارة قوم من أصحاب السلطان فنزلوا واستقبلوه وقبّلوا رأسه ويده وقالوا له: ادعُ على من ظلمك.

فقال: ليسَ بصابر من دعا على ظالم.

٤٣،٦٩ أخبرنا ابن ناصر قال: أخبرني أبو عليّ الحسن بن عبد الجبّار قال: أخبرنا أبو بكر محمد بن عليّ قال: أخبرنا محمد ابن أبي الفوارس قال: أخبرنا أحمد بن جعفر بن سَلْم قال: أخبرنا أحمد بن محمد بن عبد الخالق قال: حدثنا أبو بكر المرّوذي قال:

سمعت أبا عبد الله يقول: لما حُملت إلى الدار مكثت يومين لم أطعم، فلما ضُربت جاءوني بسويق فلم أشرب وأتممت صومي.

٤٤،٦٩ أخبرنا ابن ناصر قال: أنبأنا أبو عليّ الحسن بن أحمد قال: أخبرنا أبو القاسم الأزهري قال: أخبرنا أبو عمر محمد بن العباس قال: حدثني جعفر بن أبي عمران قال: حدثنا صدقة قال:

حدثني أبو عمرو[١] المخزومي[٢] قال: كنت بمكّة أطوف بالبيت مع سعيد بن منصور فإذا صوت من ورائي: ضُرب أحمد بن حنبل اليوم!

قال: فجاء الخبر أنه ضُرب في ذلك اليوم.

وفي رواية أُخرى: فقال لي سعيد بن منصور: أتسمع ما أسمع؟

قلت: نعم.

قال: فاعْرِفْ ذلك اليوم.

قال: فجاء الخبر أنه ضُرب في ذلك اليوم.

---

١ تركي: عمر. ٢ د: المحرمي.

We cite Abū l-Muʿammar al-Anṣārī, who cites Maḥfūẓ ibn Aḥmad, who cites Abū ʿAlī l-Ḥasan ibn Ghālib, who heard Abū l-Faḍl al-Tamīmī say that Abū l-Qāsim al-Baghawī said: 69.42

[Al-Baghawī:] I saw Aḥmad ibn Ḥanbal going into the mosque of al-Manṣūr wearing a green over-garment, his sandals in his hand, bare-headed. To me he looked to be a tall, dark-skinned, white-bearded old man. Sitting in the gallery of the minaret were members of the caliph's entourage. When they saw him, they came down to pay their respects. Kissing his head and hands, they said, "Curse the one who mistreated you."

"Cursing your oppressor," said Aḥmad, "shows a lack of fortitude."[116]

We cite Ibn Nāṣir, who cites Abū l-Ḥusayn ibn ʿAbd al-Jabbār, who cites Abū Bakr Muḥammad ibn ʿAlī, who cites Muḥammad ibn Abī l-Fawāris, who cites Aḥmad ibn Jaʿfar ibn Salm, who cites Aḥmad ibn Muḥammad ibn ʿAbd al-Khāliq, who heard Abū Bakr al-Marrūdhī report that he heard Abū ʿAbd Allāh say: 69.43

[Aḥmad:] When they took me to the palace I went without food for two days. After they flogged me they brought me some barley water, but I didn't have any so as not to break my fast.

We cite Ibn Nāṣir, who was informed by Abū ʿAlī l-Ḥasan ibn Aḥmad, who cites Abū l-Qāsim al-Azharī, who cites Abū ʿUmar Muḥammad ibn al-ʿAbbās, who heard Jaʿfar ibn Abī ʿImrān report that he heard Ṣadaqah report that he heard Abū ʿAmr al-Makhzūmī report: 69.44

[Al-Makhzūmī:] I was in Mecca walking around the Kaʿbah with Saʿīd ibn Manṣūr when I heard a voice behind me say: "Today is the flogging of Aḥmad ibn Ḥanbal."

Later I found out that he had been flogged that day.

In another telling:

Saʿīd ibn Manṣūr asked me, "Did you hear what I heard?"

I told him I had.

"Remember what day this is," he said.

Later we found out that he had been flogged that day.

أخبرنا أبو منصور القزاز قال: أخبرنا أبو بكر أحمد بن عليّ بن ثابت قال: أخبرنا الأزهري قال: أخبرنا عليّ بن محمد بن لؤلؤ قال: حدثنا هيثم[1] الدوري قال: ٦٩،٤٥

حدثنا محمّد بن سُويد الطحّان قال: كنا عند عاصم بن عليّ ومعنا أبو عُبيد القاسم ابن سلاّم وإبراهيم بن أبي الليث، وذكر جماعة، وأحمد بن حنبل يُضرب ذلك اليوم، فجعل عاصم يقول: ألا رجل يقوم معي فنأتي هذا الرجل فنكلّمه؟

قال: فما يُجيبه أحد، فقال إبراهيم بن أبي الليث: يا أبا الحسين أنا أقومُ معك.

فصاحَ: يا غلام خُفّي!

فقالَ له إبراهيم: يا أبا الحسين أبلغ إلى بناتي فأوصيهنّ وأُجدّد بهنّ عهداً.

قال: فظننّا أنه ذهب يتكفّن ويتحنّط.

ثم جاء فقال عاصم: يا غُلام خُفّي!

فقال: يا أبا الحسين إني ذهبت إلى بناتي فبكين.

قال: وجاء كتاب ابنتي عاصم من واسط: يا أبانا إنه بلغنا أنّ هذا الرجل أخذ أحمد بن حنبل فضربه بالسوط على أن يقول: القرآن مخلوق فاتّقِ الله ولا تُجبه إن سألك فوالله لأنْ يأتينا نعيّك أحبّ إلينا من أن يأتينا أنّك قلت.

أخبرنا محمّد بن أبي منصور قال: أخبرنا عبد القادر بن محمّد قال: أخبرنا محمّد بن عليّ الخيّاط قال: أخبرنا أحمد بن عبد الله بن الخضر قال: حدثنا أبو جعفر أحمد بن يعقوب الأصفهاني قال: حدثنا عمر بن الحسن الشيباني قال: ٦٩،٤٦

أخبرني أبو شُعيب الحرّاني قال: كنا مع أبي عُبيد القاسم بن سلاّم بباب المعتصم وأحمد بن حنبل يُضرب، قال: فجعل أبو عُبيد يقول: أيُضرب سيّدنا؟ لا صبرَ! أَيضرب سَيدنا؟ لا صبرَ!

قال أبو شُعيب: فقلت أنا:

ضَربوا ابْنَ حَنْبَلَ بالسّياطِ بظُلْمِهِمْ بَغيًا فَثُبِّتَ بالثّباتِ الأَنْوَرِ
قالَ المُوَفَّقُ حينَ مُدِّدَ بَيْنَهُمُ مَدَّ الأَديمِ على الصَّعيدِ القَرْقَرِ
إِنّي أَموتُ ولا أَبوءُ بفَجْرَةٍ تُصْلي بَوائِقُها مَحَلَّ المُفْتَري

[1] د: هشيم.

We cite Abū Manṣūr al-Qazzāz, who cites Abū Bakr Aḥmad ibn ʿAlī ibn Thābit, who cites al-Azharī, who cites ʿAlī ibn Muḥammad ibn Luʾluʾ, who heard Haytham al-Dūrī report that he heard Muḥammad ibn Suwayd al-Ṭaḥḥān report: 69.45

[Al-Ṭaḥḥān:] On the day Aḥmad ibn Ḥanbal was flogged, I was with Abū ʿUbayd al-Qāsim ibn Sallām, Ibrahīm ibn Abī l-Layth, and several others at the home of ʿĀṣim ibn ʿAlī.

"Will anyone come with me and talk to that man?" asked ʿĀṣim.[117] He repeated the question several times but no one answered, until finally Ibrāhīm said, "I'll come."

ʿĀṣim shouted to the servant boy to bring his boots. But then Ibrāhīm said, "Let me go and see my daughters first. I haven't seen them in a while and I have some things to tell them."

He left, and we suspected that he had gone to perfume himself and put on his shroud.

When he returned, ʿĀṣim again called for his boots.

"I went to see my daughters," said Ibrāhīm, "and they wept."

Then a letter came from ʿĀṣim's two daughters in Wāsiṭ. It read, "Father, we've heard that that man has taken Aḥmad ibn Ḥanbal and flogged him to make him say that the Qur'an is created. If he asks you to do the same thing, be fearful of God and refuse. By God, we'd rather hear that you'd died than that you gave in."

We cite Muḥammad ibn Abī Manṣūr, who cites ʿAbd al-Qādir ibn Muḥammad, who cites Muḥammad ibn ʿAlī l-Khayyāṭ, who cites Aḥmad ibn ʿAbd Allāh ibn al-Khaḍir, who heard Abū Jaʿfar Aḥmad ibn Yaʿqūb al-Iṣfahānī report that he heard ʿUmar ibn al-Ḥasan al-Shaybānī cite Abū Shuʿayb al-Ḥarrānī, who reports: 69.46

[Al-Ḥarrānī:] While Aḥmad was being flogged, Abū ʿUbayd al-Qāsim ibn Sallām and I were waiting at al-Muʿtaṣim's gate. Abū ʿUbayd started saying, "Are we going to let them do this to the best of us? It's unbearable!"

I said:

They had no right to flog him so
  But let them strike, for firm he stood,
And even as they stretched him flat
  As highland earth, he said, inspired:
"I may die, but you, not I, will burn
  With the liars in the pits of Hell!"

٤٧،٦٩ أخبرنا محمّد بن ناصر قال: أنبأنا أبو عليّ بن البَنّا قال: أخبرنا الحسن ابن أحمد قال: أخبرنا ابن السمّاك في الإجازة قال: حدثنا أبو جعفر محمّد بن أحمد قال:

سمعتُ أبا حاتم يقول: لمّا كان اليوم الذي ضُرب فيه أحمد قلتُ: أمرّ اليوم فأعرف خبر أحمد.

فبكّرت فإذا أنا بشيخ قائم وهو يقول: اللّهمّ ثبّته، اللّهمّ أعِنْه!

ثمّ لم يزل كالحيران ويقول: إن كان أجاب حتى أدخل فأقوم مقامه!

فخرج رجل فقال: لم يُجبْهم فقال: الحمد لله!

فقلتُ : من هذا؟

فقالوا: بشر بن الحارث.

٤٨،٦٩ قلت: وقد نُقل إلينا حكايات في قصّة ضربه لم يثبت عندنا صحّتها فتنكّبناها.[١]

سياق بيان فضله في صبره وما تمّ له

٤٩،٦٩ أخبرنا عبد الملك بن أبي القاسم الكَرُوخي قال: أخبرنا عبد الله بن محمّد الأنصاري قال: أخبرنا أحمد بن محمّد بن حَسان قال: أخبرنا أحمد بن محمّد بن شارَك قال: حدثنا محمّد بن عبد الرحمن السامي قال: حدثنا إسماعيل قال: حدثنا عمر بن شاكر قال: حدثنا أنس بن مالك قال:

قال رسول الله صلى الله عليه وسلم : يَأْتي عَلى النّاسِ زَمانٌ الصابرُ مِنهُم على دينِهِ لَهُ أَجرُ خَمْسينَ مِنْكُم.

قالوا: منّا؟

قال: منكم حتى أعادها ثلاث مرّات.

٥٠،٦٩ أخبرنا يحيى بن عليّ المُدير قال: أخبرنا أبو بكر الخيّاط قال: حدثنا أبو عليّ بن حَمكان قال: حدثنا أبو بكر النقّاش قال: حدثنا أبو نعيم الاستَراباذي قال: حدثنا الربيع بن سليمان قال:

---

١ تنكبناها ليس في ش.

We cite Muḥammad ibn Nāṣir, who was informed by Abū ʿAlī ibn al-Bannā, who cites al-Ḥasan ibn Aḥmad, who by permission cites Ibn al-Sammāk, who heard Abū Jaʿfar Muḥammad ibn Aḥmad report that he heard Abū Ḥātim say: 69.47

[Abū Ḥātim:] The day they flogged Aḥmad, I decided to go and see for myself what had happened to him. I arrived early and found an old man standing there saying, "God, give him strength! God, help him!" He continued, speaking as if caught in some terrible dilemma, "I need to know if he's given in and I have to go take his place."

Then someone came out, saying, "He didn't give in."

"Thank God!" said the old man.

I asked someone who the old man was.

"Bishr ibn al-Ḥārith," I was told.[118]

[The author:] We are aware of other accounts of the flogging, but we doubt their accuracy and have therefore omitted them.[119] 69.48

More on What He Achieved by Remaining Steadfast throughout His Ordeal

We cite ʿAbd al-Malik ibn Abī l-Qāsim al-Karūkhī, who cites ʿAbd Allāh ibn Muḥammad al-Anṣārī, who cites Aḥmad ibn Muḥammad ibn Ḥassān, who cites Aḥmad ibn Muḥammad ibn Shārak, who heard Muḥammad ibn ʿAbd al-Raḥmān al-Sāmī report that he heard Ismāʿīl report that he heard ʿUmar ibn Shākir report that he heard Anas ibn Mālik report: 69.49

The Prophet, God bless and keep him, said: "There will come a time when anyone who suffers bravely for his faith will be rewarded fifty times more than you."

"More than us?" asked his Companions.

"Yes," he said, repeating it three times.

We cite Yaḥyā ibn ʿAlī l-Mudīr, who cites Abū Bakr al-Khayyāṭ, who cites Abū ʿAlī ibn Ḥamakān, who heard Abū Bakr al-Naqqāsh report that he heard Abū Nuʿaym al-Astarābādhī report that he heard al-Rabīʿ ibn Sulaymān report that he heard al-Shāfiʿī say: 69.50

سمعت الشافعي يقول: أشدّ الأعمال ثلاثة: الجود من قلّة والورع في خلوة وكلمة الحقّ عند من يُرجى ويُخاف.

أخبرنا محمّد بن أبي منصور قال: أخبرنا عبد القادر بن محمّد قال: أخبرنا إبراهيم بن عمر قال: حدثنا عليّ بن عبد العزيز قال: حدثنا أبو محمّد بن أبي حاتم قال: ٦٩،٥١

سمعت أبا زُرْعة يقول: لم أزل أسمع الناس يذكرون أحمد بن حنبل بخير ويُقدّمونه على يحيى بن مَعِين وأبي خَيثمة غير أنه لم يكن مِن ذكره ما صار بعد أن امتحن فلمّا امتحن ارتفع ذكره في الآفاق.

قال ابن أبي حاتم: وحدثنا عبد الملك بن أبي عبد الرحمن قال: ٦٩،٥٢

سمعت أحمد بن يونس روى الحديث: في الجنّةِ قُصورٌ لا يَدْخُلها إلا نَبِيّ أو صِدّيق أو مُحكَّم في نَفْسِه. فقيل لأحمد بن يونس: من المحكّم في نفسه؟ قال: أحمد ابن حنبل المحكّم في نفسه.

قلت: هذا الحديثُ مرويّ عن كَعب الأحبار:

أخبرنا محمّد بن عبد الباقي ابن أحمد بن سَلمان قال: أخبرنا حَمد بن أحمد قال: أخبرنا أحمد بن عبد الله الأصبهاني قال: حدثنا عبد الله بن محمّد قال: حدثنا عبد الرحمن بن محمّد بن سَلْم قال: حدثنا هَنّاد بن السَّري قال:

حدثنا محمّد بن عُبيد عن سَلَمة بن نُبَيْط عن عبد الله بن أبي الجَعْد عن كعب الأحبار قال: إنّ لله عزّ وجلّ داراً دُرّة فوق دُرّة أو لُؤلؤة فوق لُؤلؤة، فيها سبعون ألف قصر في كلّ قصر سبعون ألف دار في كلّ دار سبعون أَلف بيت لا يسكنها إلّا نبيّ أو صِدّيقٌ أو شهيد أو إمام عادل أو مُحكَّمٌ في نَفسِه.

وقد رواه المحدّثون بكسر الكاف ونَصبها فمن فتح الكاف أراد به: الرجل يُخيّر بين الكُفر والقتل فيختار القتل، ذكره أبو عُبيد الهَرَوي، ومن كسر فالمرادُ به: المنصف من نَفسه، قاله وكيع.

[Al-Shāfiʿī:] "The hardest three things are these: being generous when you have little, being scrupulous when you're alone, and speaking truth to power."

We cite Muḥammad ibn Abī Manṣūr, who cites ʿAbd al-Qādir ibn Muḥammad, who cites Ibrāhīm ibn ʿUmar, who heard ʿAlī ibn ʿAbd al-ʿAzīz report that he heard Abū Muḥammad ibn Abī Ḥātim report that he heard Abū Zurʿah say: 69.51

[Abū Zurʿah:] I always used to hear people speaking highly of Ibn Ḥanbal and giving him precedence over Yaḥyā ibn Maʿīn and Abū Khaythamah, though never as much as after he was tried. After he was tried, his reputation knew no bounds.

Ibn Abī Ḥātim reports that he heard ʿAbd al-Malik ibn Abī ʿAbd al-Raḥmān report: 69.52

[Ibn Abī ʿAbd al-Raḥmān:] I heard Aḥmad ibn Yūnus recite the Hadith: "In the Garden are palaces open only to prophets, truth-tellers, or those given power over their own souls."

Someone asked, "Who are 'those given power over their own souls'?"

"Aḥmad ibn Ḥanbal, for example," he replied.

[The author:] This Hadith is traced back to Kaʿb al-Aḥbār, as follows:

We cite Muḥammad ibn ʿAbd al-Bāqī ibn Aḥmad ibn Sulaymān, who cites Ḥamd ibn Aḥmad, who cites Aḥmad ibn ʿAbd Allāh al-Iṣfahānī, who heard ʿAbd Allāh ibn Muḥammad report that he heard ʿAbd al-Raḥmān ibn Muḥammad ibn Salm report that he heard Hannād ibn al-Sarī report that he heard Muḥammad ibn ʿUbayd, citing Salamah ibn Nubayṭ, citing ʿAbd Allāh ibn Abī l-Jaʿd, citing Kaʿb al-Aḥbār, report:

[Kaʿb al-Aḥbār:] Belonging to God are dwellings of pearl upon pearl, or nacre upon nacre, in which are seventy thousand palaces. In each palace are seventy thousand courts, and in each court seventy thousand rooms, where none may live but prophets, truth-tellers, martyrs, just rulers, and those given power over their own souls.

[The author:] According to Hadith scholars, one of the words in this report may be pronounced two different ways. *Muḥakkam*, "given power," means—according to Abū ʿUbayd al-Harawī—someone who is asked to choose between death and unbelief and chooses death. If pronounced *muḥakkim*, it means, according to Wakīʿ, someone capable of judging himself.

٥٣،٦٩ أخبرنا محمّد بن أبي منصور قال: أخبرنا أبو الحسين بن عبد الجبّار قال: أخبرنا أبو محمد الخلّال قال: حدثنا عبيد الله بن عبد الرحمن الزُّهْري من ولد عبد الرحمن بن عَوف قال: سمعت أبي يقول:

سمعت عبد الله بن أحمد بن حنبل يقول: قال لي أبي: يا بُنيّ لقد أعطيتُ المجهود من نفسي، يعني في المحنة.

قال: وكتب أهل المطامير إلى أحمد بن حنبل: إن رجعت عن مقالتك ارتددنا عن الإسلام.

٥٤،٦٩ أخبرنا عبد الرحمن بن محمّد القزاز قال: أخبرنا أحمد بن عليّ بن ثابت قال: أخبرنا عليّ بن أحمد بن عمر المقرئ قال: أخبرنا أبو بكر محمّد بن عبد الله الشافعي قال:

حدثنا أبو غالب ابن بنت معاوية قال: ضُرب أحمد بن حنبل بالسِّياط في الله فقام مقام الصدّيقين في العَشر الأواخر من رمضان سنة عشرين ومائتين.

٥٥،٦٩ أخبرنا ابن ناصر قال: أخبرنا عبد الملك بن محمّد البُزُوغائي قال: أخبرنا عليّ بن عمر القَزويني قال: أخبرنا يوسف ابن عمر القوّاس قال: حدثنا محمّد بن القاسم ابن بنت كعب قال:

حدثنا جعفر بن أبي هاشم قال: مكث أحمد بن حنبل في السجن سنة سبع عشرة وثماني عشرة وتسع عشرة وأُخرج في رمضان.

سياق كيفية خروجه من دار المعتصم

٥٦،٦٩ أخبرنا محمّد بن ناصر قال: أخبرنا عبد القادر بن محمّد قال: أخبرنا إبراهيم بن عمر البرمكي قال: أخبرنا عليّ بن عبد العزيز بن مَرْدَك قال: أخبرنا عبد الرحمن بن أبي حاتم قال: حدثنا أبي قال: قال إبراهيم بن الحارث من ولد عُبادة بن الصّامت قال:

قال أبو محمّد الطُّفاوي لأحمد بن حنبل: يا أبا عبد الله أخبرني عمّا صَنعوا بك؟

قال: لما ضُربت بالسياط جاء ذاك الطويل اللّحية، يعني عُجيفاً، فضربني بقائم السيف فقلت: جاء الفرج تضرب عنقي وأستريح.

We cite Muḥammad ibn Abī Manṣūr, who cites Abū l-Ḥusayn ibn ʿAbd al-Jabbār, who cites Abū Muḥammad al-Khallāl, who heard ʿUbayd Allāh ibn ʿAbd al-Raḥmān al-Zuhrī, who was a descendant of ʿAbd al-Raḥmān ibn ʿAwf, report that he heard his father say that he heard Aḥmad ibn Ḥanbal's son ʿAbd Allāh say: 69.53

[ʿAbd Allāh:] My father once said to me, speaking of the Inquisition: "Son, I gave all I could."

He[120] also said that some Catacombers[121] wrote to Aḥmad ibn Ḥanbal saying, "If you change your mind about your creed, we'll change our minds about being Muslims."

We cite ʿAbd al-Raḥmān ibn Muḥammad al-Qazzāz, who cites Aḥmad ibn ʿAlī ibn Thābit, who cites ʿAlī ibn Aḥmad ibn ʿUmar al-Muqri', who cites Abū Bakr Muḥammad ibn ʿAbd Allāh al-Shāfiʿī, who heard Abū Ghālib, grandson of Muʿāwīyah, report: 69.54

[Abū Ghālib:] Aḥmad was flogged for the sake of God and stood where the truth-tellers stand during the last ten days of Ramadan 220 [mid- to late September 835].

We cite Ibn Nāṣir, who cites ʿAbd al-Malik ibn Muḥammad al-Buzūghā'ī, who cites ʿAlī ibn ʿUmar al-Qazwīnī, who cites Yūsuf ibn ʿUmar al-Qawwās, who heard Muḥammad ibn al-Qāsim, grandson of Kaʿb, report that he heard Jaʿfar ibn Abī Hāshim report: 69.55

[Jaʿfar ibn Abī Hāshim:] Ibn Ḥanbal was in jail through '17, '18, and '19, and was let out in Ramadan.

More on How He Left the Palace of al-Muʿtaṣim

We cite Muḥammad ibn Nāṣir, who cites ʿAbd al-Qādir ibn Muḥammad, who cites Ibrāhīm ibn ʿUmar al-Barmakī, who cites ʿAlī ibn ʿAbd al-ʿAzīz ibn Mardak, who cites ʿAbd al-Raḥmān ibn Abī Ḥātim, who heard his father report that Ibrāhīm ibn al-Ḥārith, who was a descendant of ʿUbādah ibn al-Ṣāmit, said: 69.56

[Ibn al-Ḥārith:] Abū Muḥammad al-Ṭufāwī asked Aḥmad ibn Ḥanbal to tell him what they had done to him.

"After they had flogged me," said Aḥmad, "that one with the long beard"—meaning ʿUjayf—"came up and jabbed me with the hilt of his sword. I remember thinking it was finally over. Let him cut my throat so I can rest!

فقال له ابن سَماعة: يا أمير المؤمنين اضرب عنقه ودمه في رقبتي.

فقال له ابن أبي دُؤاد: لا يا أمير المؤمنين، لا تفعل، فإنه إن قُتل أو مات في دارك قال الناس صبر حتى قُتل فاتّخذه الناس إماماً وثبتوا على ما هم عليه، لا ولكن أُطلقه الساعة فإن مات خارجاً من منزلك شكّ الناس في أمره وقال[1] بعضُهم لم يُجِبْه فيكون الناس في شكّ من أمره.

وقال ابن أبي حاتم: ٥٧،٦٩

وسمعت أبا زُرْعة يقول: دعا المعتصم بعمّ أحمد بن حنبل ثم قال للناس: تعرفونه؟

قالوا: نعم هو أحمد بن حنبل.

قال: فانظروا إليه أليس هو صحيح البدن؟

قالوا: نعم.

ولولا أنه فعل ذلك لكنت أخافُ أن يقع شرّ لا يُقام له، فلمّا قال: قد سلّمته إليكم صحيح البدن، هدأ الناس وسكنوا.

أخبرنا محمّد بن ناصر قال: أنبأنا الحسن بن أحمد الفقيه قال: حدثنا عبيد الله بن أحمد قال: حدثنا أبو بكر محمّد بن ٥٨،٦٩ عبيد الله الكاتب قال: حدثنا أبو عليّ الحسن بن محمّد بن عثمان قال: حدثني داوود بن عَرَفة قال:

حدثنا مَيمون بن الأَصْبغ قال: أُخرج أحمد بن حنبل بعد أن اجتمع الناس على الباب وضجّوا حتى خاف السلطان فخرج.

---

١ د: قال.

"Ibn Samāʿah said to the caliph, 'Commander of the Faithful! Behead him and let his blood be on my hands.'

"But then Ibn Abī Dū'ād said, 'Commander of the Faithful: better not to! If you kill him here or let him die inside the palace, they'll say he held out till the end. They'll make a hero of him and they'll think they've been proven right. No: let him go right away. If he dies outside they won't know what happened. Some will say he resisted[122] but no one will know for sure.'"[123]

Ibn Abī Ḥātim also reports that he heard Abū Zurʿah say: 69.57

[Abū Zurʿah:] Al-Muʿtaṣim summoned Aḥmad ibn Ḥanbal's uncle and asked the people, "Do you know who this is?"

"Yes," they said. "It's Aḥmad ibn Ḥanbal."

"Look at him. Do you see that he's unharmed?"

"Yes."

If he hadn't done that, I suspect that an unstoppable outburst of violence would have ensued.[124] When he said, "I give him to you unharmed," the people were mollified.

We cite Muḥammad ibn Nāṣir, who was informed by al-Ḥasan ibn Aḥmad al-Faqīh, who 69.58
heard ʿUbayd Allāh ibn Aḥmad report that he heard Abū Bakr Muḥammad ibn ʿUbayd Allāh al-Kātib report that he heard Abū ʿAlī l-Ḥasan ibn Muḥammad ibn ʿUthmān report that he heard Dāwūd ibn ʿArafah report that he heard Maymūn ibn al-Aṣbagh report:

[Ibn al-Aṣbagh:] Only after a crowd had gathered at the gate and begun to raise an outcry was Ibn Ḥanbal released. The authorities were frightened and let Aḥmad out.

الباب السبعون في ذكر تلقّي المشايخ إياه بعد انقضاء المحنة ودعائهم له

١،٧٠ أخبرنا إسماعيل بن أحمد السمرقندي ومحمّد بن عبد الباقي قالا: أخبرنا حَمْد بن أحمد قال: حدثنا أبو نُعَيْم الحافظ قال: حدثنا سليمان بن أحمد قال: حدثنا الحسين بن محمّد قال:

حدثنا مُهَنَّأ بن يحيى قال: رأيت يعقوب بن إبراهيم بن سعد الزُّهري[1] حين أُخرج أحمد من الحبس وهو يقبّل جبهة أحمد ووجهه ورأيت سليمان بن داوود الهاشمي يقبّل جبهة أحمد ورأسه.

٢،٧٠ أخبرنا عبد الملك بن أبي القاسم قال: أخبرنا عبد الله بن محمّد الأنصاري قال: حدثنا أبو يعقوب الحافظ قال: حدثنا أبو بكر بن أبي الفضل قال: حدثنا محمّد بن إبراهيم الصرّام قال: حدثنا إبراهيم بن إسحاق قال:

حدثني الحسن بن عبد العزيز الجَرَوي. قال: قلت للحارث ابن مسكين: إن هذا الرجل، أعني أحمد بن حنبل، قد ضُرب فاذهب بنا إليه. فذهبت أنا وهو فدخلنا عليه حِدْثانَ ضربه فقال لنا: ضُربتُ فسقطت وسمعت ذاك، يعني ابن أبي دُؤاد، يقول: يا أمير المؤمنين هو والله ضالّ مضلّ.

فقال له الحارث: أخبرني يوسف بن عمر بن يزيد عن مالك ابن أنس أن الزُّهري سُعِي به حتى ضُرب بالسياط فقيل لمالك بعد ذلك: إنّ الزُّهري قد أُقيم للناس وعُلّقت كتبه في عنقه فقال مالك: قد ضُرب سعيد ابن المُسيَّب بالسياط وحُلق رأسه ولحيته وضُرب أبو الزِّناد بالسياط وضرب محمّد بن المُنْكَدِر وأصحاب له في حمّام بالسياط. قال: وقال عُمر بن عبد العزيز: لا تغبطوا أحدًا لم يُصبه في هذا الأمر أذى قال: وما ذكر مالك نفسه.

قال: فأُعجب أحمد بقول الحارث.

٣،٧٠ قلت: وما زال الناس يُبتلون في الله تعالى ويصبرون وقد كانت الأنبياء تُقتل

---

[1] بن سعد الزهري: ليس في د.

Chapter 70: His Reception by the Elders after His Release, and Their Prayers for Him

We cite Ismāʿīl ibn Aḥmad al-Samarqandī and Muḥammad ibn ʿAbd al-Bāqī, who cite Ḥamd ibn Aḥmad, who heard Abū Nuʿaym al-Ḥāfiẓ report that he heard Sulaymān ibn Aḥmad report that he heard al-Ḥusayn ibn Muḥammad report that he heard Muhanna' ibn Yaḥyā report: 70.1

[Muhanna' ibn Yaḥyā:] I saw Yaʿqūb ibn Ibrāhīm ibn Saʿd al-Zuhrī kissing Aḥmad on the forehead and the face after he was released from jail. I also saw Sulaymān ibn Dāwūd al-Hāshimī kissing his head and forehead.

We cite ʿAbd al-Malik ibn Abī l-Qāsim, who cites ʿAbd Allāh ibn Muḥammad al-Anṣārī, who heard Abū Yaʿqūb al-Ḥāfiẓ report that he heard Abū Bakr ibn Abī l-Faḍl report that he heard Muḥammad ibn Ibrāhīm al-Ṣarrām report that he heard Ibrāhīm ibn Isḥāq report that he heard al-Ḥasn ibn ʿAbd al-ʿAzīz al-Jarawī report: 70.2

[Al-Jarawī:] I said to al-Ḥārith ibn Miskīn: "That man"—meaning Aḥmad ibn Ḥanbal—"is being flogged. Come on: let's go to him."

We arrived just as he was being flogged. Later he told us, "After they beat me I fell down and I heard that one"—meaning Ibn Abī Du'ād—"saying, 'Commander of the Faithful, he's gone astray, and will lead others astray.'"

Al-Ḥārith remarked: "Yūsuf ibn ʿUmar ibn Yazīd told me, citing Mālik ibn Anas, that al-Zuhrī was maliciously denounced to the authorities and then flogged. When he was told that al-Zuhrī had been subjected to a public inquisition with his books hanging around his neck, Mālik said, 'Saʿīd ibn al-Musayyab was flogged, and had his hair and beard shaved off. Abū l-Zinād and Muḥammad ibn al-Munkadir were also flogged. ʿUmar ibn ʿAbd al-ʿAzīz once said, "Do not envy anyone who hasn't suffered for Islam."' And Mālik didn't even mention himself."

Aḥmad was impressed with what al-Ḥārith told him.

[The author:] People have always suffered through ordeals for the sake of God. Many prophets were killed; and among the ancient nations, many good people were killed or immolated, with some of them being sawed in half without renouncing their faith. If not for my aversion to prolixity and 70.3

وأهل الخير في الأُمَم السالفة يُقتلون ويُحرقون ويُنشر أحدهم بالمنشار وهو ثابت على دينه ولولا كراهية التطويل لذكرتُ من ذلك بأسانيده ما يطول غير أني أُوثر الاختصار.

٤،٧٠ وقد سُمّ نبيّنا صلّى الله عليه وسلّم وسُمّ أبو بكر وقُتل عمر وعثمان وعليّ وسُمّ الحسن وقُتل الحسين وابن الزبير والضحّاك بن قيس والنعمان بن بشير وصُلب خُبيب بن عَديّ. وقتل الحجّاج عبدَ الرحمن بن أبي ليلى وعبدَ الله بن غالب الحُدّاني وسعيد بن جُبير وأبا البَختري الطائي وكُميل بن زياد وحُطيطًا الزيّات وماهان الحَنَفي صَلبه وصَلب قبله ابنَ الزبير وقتل الواثقُ أحمد بن نصر الخُزاعي وصَلبه.

٥،٧٠ فأمّا من ضُرب من كبار العلماء فعبدُ الرحمن بن أبي ليلى ضربه الحجّاج أربع مائة سوط ثم قتله.

سعيد بن المسيّب ضربه عبد الملك بن مروان مائة سوط لأنّه بعث ببيعة الوليد إلى المدينة فلم يبايع سعيدٌ فكتب أن يُضرب مائة سوط ويصبّ عليه جرّة ماء في يوم شاتٍ ويُلبس جبّة صوف ففُعل به ذلك.

خُبَيْب بن عبد الله بن الزبير ضربه عمر بن عبد العزيز بأمر الوليد مائة سوط وذلك أنّه حدّث عن النبي صلى الله عليه وسلم أنّه قال: إذا بلغ بَنو أبي العاص ثلاثينَ رَجُلًا اتّخذوا عبادَ الله خَوَلًا ومالَ الله دولًا.

فكان عمر إذا قيل له أَبْشِرْ قال: كيف بِخُبيب على الطريق؟

٦،٧٠ أبو الزِناد ضربه بنو أُمية. أبو عَمرو بن العَلاء ضربه بنو أُميّة خمس مائة سوط. رَبيعة الرأي ضَربه بنو أُميّة. عَطيّة العَوْفي ضَربه الحجّاج أربع مائة سوط. يزيد الضَّبّي ضربه الحجّاج أربع مائة سوط. ثابت البُناني ضربه ابن الجارود خليفة ابن زياد. عبد الله بن عَون ضربه بِلال بن أبي بُردة سبعين سوطًا. مالك بن أنس ضربه المنصور سبعين سوطًا في يَمين المكره وكان مالك يقول: لا تُلزِمه اليمين. أبو السوّار العَدوِي وعُقبة بن عبد الغافر ضُربا بالسياط.

ولأحمد بن حنبل في هؤلاء الأئمة أُسوة.

my preference for brevity, I would list the reports I have in mind, along with their chains of transmission.

The Prophet, God bless and keep him, was poisoned, as was Abū Bakr. 70.4
ʿUmar, ʿUthmān, and ʿAlī were assassinated. Al-Ḥasan was poisoned, and al-Ḥusayn, Ibn al-Zubayr, al-Ḍaḥḥāk ibn Qays, and al-Nuʿmān ibn Bashīr were assassinated. Khubayb ibn ʿAdī was crucified. Al-Ḥajjāj executed ʿAbd al-Raḥmān ibn Abī Laylā, ʿAbd Allāh ibn Ghālib al-Ḥuddānī, Saʿīd ibn Jubayr, Abū l-Bakhtarī l-Ṭāʾī, Kumayl ibn Ziyād, and Ḥuṭayṭ al-Zayyāt. He also crucified Māhān al-Ḥanafī, and before him Ibn al-Zubayr. And al-Wāthiq killed and crucified Aḥmad ibn Naṣr al-Khuzāʿī.

Among the great scholars who were flogged is ʿAbd al-Raḥmān ibn 70.5
Abī Laylā, who was struck four hundred lashes and then executed by Ibn al-Ḥajjāj.

Another is Saʿīd ibn al-Musayyab, who was struck one hundred lashes by ʿAbd al-Malik ibn Marwān for refusing to swear allegiance to al-Walīd in Medina. At ʿAbd al-Malik's orders, he was flogged, drenched with water on a cold day, and dressed in a woolen cloak.[125]

Another is Khubayb ibn ʿAbd Allāh ibn al-Zubayr, who was struck a hundred lashes by ʿUmar ibn ʿAbd al-ʿAzīz at the command of al-Walīd, all for reciting a Hadith where the Prophet—God bless and keep him—says, "When the descendants of Abū l-ʿĀṣ reach thirty in number, they will make God's servants their own, and take turns plundering His treasury."

Whenever ʿUmar was told, "Rejoice!" he would reply, "How can I rejoice with Khubayb blocking my way?"[126]

Others include Abū l-Zinād, who was flogged by the Umayyads; Abū ʿAmr 70.6
ibn al-ʿAlāʾ, struck five hundred lashes by the Umayyads; Rabiʿat al-Raʾy, flogged by the Umayyads; ʿAṭiyyah al-ʿAwfī, struck four hundred lashes by al-Ḥajjāj; Yazīd al-Ḍabbī, struck four hundred lashes by al-Ḥajjāj; Thābit al-Bunānī, flogged by Ibn al-Jārūd, the deputy of Ibn Ziyād; ʿAbd Allāh ibn ʿAwn, struck seventy lashes by Bilāl ibn Abī Burdah; Mālik ibn Anas, struck seventy lashes by al-Manṣūr for saying that a person who swears an oath under compulsion is not bound by it; and Abū l-Sawwār al-ʿAdawī and ʿUqbah ibn ʿAbd al-Ghāfir, who were both flogged.

Aḥmad ibn Ḥanbal thus had a formidable list of exemplars.[127]

سياق ذكر جعله للمعتصم في حِلّ من ضربه ومَن حضر

٧،٧٠ أخبرنا محمّد بن أبي منصور قال: أخبرنا عبد القادر بن محمّد قال: أخبرنا أبو إسحاق البرمكي قال: أخبرنا عليّ بن مردك قال: حدثنا ابن أبي حاتم قال:

قال صالح بن أحمد: سمعتُ أبي يقول: لقد جعلتُ الميّت في حِلّ من ضربه إيّاي. ثمّ قال: مررتُ بهذه الآية ﴿فَمَنْ عَفَا وَأَصْلَحَ فَأَجْرُهُ عَلَى اللهِ﴾ فنظرت في تفسيرها فإذا هو ما أخبرنا هاشم بن القاسم قال: أخبرنا المبارك بن فَضالة قال: أخبرني من سمع الحسن يقول: إذا كان يوم القيامة جَثَت الأُمم كلّها بين يَدي الله عزّ وجلّ ثم نُودي أن لا يقوم إلا من أجره على الله عزّ وجلّ.

قال: فلا يقوم إلا من عفا في الدنيا.

قال أبي: فجعلتُ الميّتَ في حل من ضربه إيّاي. وجعل يقول: وما على رجل أن لا يعذِّب الله بسببه أحداً؟

٨،٧٠ قال ابن أبي حاتم:

وحدثنا أحمد بن سنان قال: بلغني أن أحمد بن حنبل جعل المعتصم في حلّ في يوم فتح بابك[١] أو في يوم فتح عَمّوريّة فقال: هو في حل من ضربي.

٩،٧٠ أخبرنا محمّد بن أبي منصور قال: أخبرنا عبد القادر بن محمّد قال: أخبرنا إبراهيم بن عمر قال: أخبرنا عبيد الله بن عبد الرحمن قال: حدثنا أبو عبد الله الحسن بن عبد الله بن سِقّلاب قال:

حدثني عبد الله بن أحمد بن حنبل قال: قال لي أبي: وجّه إليّ الواثق أن أجعل المعتصم في حلّ من ضربه إيّاي فقلت: ما خرجتُ من داره حتى جعلته في حل، وذكرتُ قول النبيّ صلّى الله عليه وسلّم: لا يَقومُ يَوْمَ القِيامةِ إلّا مَنْ عَفا فعفوتُ عنه.

---

١ د وهامش هـ: بابل.

More on His Exempting al-Muʿtaṣim and the Others Present from Liability for Flogging Him

We cite Muḥammad ibn Abī Manṣūr, who cites ʿAbd al-Qādir ibn Muḥammad, who cites Abū Isḥāq al-Barmakī, who cites ʿAlī ibn Mardak, who heard Ibn Abī Ḥātim report that he heard Aḥmad's son Ṣāliḥ report: 70.7

[Ṣāliḥ:] I heard my father say, "I exempt that dead man[128] from liability for flogging me." Then he said, "I just came across the verse «Whoever pardons and amends will find his reward with God»[129] and looked into what it means. I cite Hāshim ibn Qāsim, who cites al-Mubārak ibn Faḍālah, who cites someone who heard al-Ḥasan say, 'On the Day of Resurrection, all the nations will come crawling before God, mighty and glorious. Then only those to whom God owes a reward will be called upon to rise.'

"He said: 'The only ones to rise will be those who forgave others.'

"So I decided to exempt the deceased from liability for flogging me."

Then he added, "I'd rather not have God torment anyone for my sake."

Ibn Abī Ḥātim reports that he heard Aḥmad ibn Sinān report: 70.8

[Aḥmad ibn Sinān:] I heard that Aḥmad ibn Ḥanbal forgave al-Muʿtaṣim the day he defeated Bābak, or the day he captured Amorium. He said, "I exempt him from any liability for flogging me."

We cite Muḥammad ibn Abī Manṣūr, who cites ʿAbd al-Qādir ibn Muḥammad, who cites Ibrāhīm ibn ʿUmar, who cites ʿUbayd Allāh ibn ʿAbd al-Raḥmān, who heard Abū ʿAbd Allāh al-Ḥasan ibn ʿAbd Allāh ibn Ṣiqlāb, who heard Aḥmad ibn Ḥanbal's son ʿAbd Allāh report that his father said: 70.9

[Aḥmad:] Al-Wāthiq sent me a message asking me to forgive al-Muʿtaṣim for flogging me. I responded, "I forgave him the moment I left the palace because of what the Prophet said: 'None will rise on Resurrection Day except those who forgive.'"

١٠،٧٠ أخبرنا ابن ناصر قال: أخبرنا المبارك بن عبد الجبار قال: أخبرنا أبو بكر محمد بن عليّ الخياط قال: أخبرنا محمد بن أبي الفوارس قال: أخبرنا أحمد بن جعفر بن سَلْم قال: أخبرنا أحمد بن محمد بن عبد الخالق حدثنا أبو بكر المَرُّوذي قال:

قال لي أبو عبد الله: قد سألني إسحاق بن إبراهيم أن أجعل أبا إسحاق في حلّ فقلت له: قد كنتُ جعلته في حلّ. ثمّ قال أبو عبد الله: تفكّرتُ في الحديث: إذا كانَ يومُ القِيامة نادَى مُنادٍ: لا يَقُمْ إلّا مَن عَفا. وذكرتُ قول الشَّعْبي: إن تعفُ عنه مرّة يكن لك من الأجر مرّتين.

١١،٧٠ أخبرنا عبد الملك بن أبي القاسم قال: أخبرنا عبد الله بن محمد الأنصاري قال: حدثنا محمد بن أحمد الجارودي قال: حدثنا الحسين بن عليّ بن جعفر قال: حدثني أبي قال:

حدثنا أبو عليّ الحسين بن عبد الله الخِرَقِي وقد رأى أحمد بن حنبل قال: بتّ مع أحمد بن حنبل ليلة فلم أره ينام إلّا يبكي إلى أن أصبح فقلت: أبا عبد الله كثر بكاؤك الليلة فما السبب؟ فقال لي: ذكرتُ ضرب المعتصم إياي ومرّ بي في الدَّرس: ﴿وَجَزَاءُ سَيِّئَةٍ سَيِّئَةٌ مِثْلُهَا فَمَنْ عَفَا وَأَصْلَحَ فَأَجْرُهُ عَلَى اللَّهِ﴾ فسجدتُ وأحللته من ضربي في السجود.

١٢،٧٠ أنبأنا محمد بن ناصر قال: أخبرنا المبارك بن عبد الجبّار قال: أخبرنا عُبيد الله بن عمر بن شاهين قال: حدثني أبي قال: سمعت عثمان بن عَبْدُوَيه يقول:

سمعتُ إبراهيم الحربي يقول: أحلّ أحمد بن حنبل من حضر ضربه وكلّ من شايع فيه والمعتصم وقال: لولا أنّ ابن أبي دؤاد داعية لأحللته.

١٣،٧٠ قال عمر بن شاهين: وحدثنا أحمد بن خالد المكَتِّب قال:

سمعت أبا العباس بن واصل المقرئ يقول: قال لي فُوران: وجّه إليّ أبو عبد الله أحمد بن حنبل في الليل فدعاني فقال لي: كيف أخبرتني عن فضل الأَنْماطي؟ قال: قلت: يا أبا عبد الله قال لي فضل: لا أجعل في حلّ من أمر بضربي

We cite Ibn Nāṣir, who cites al-Mubārak ibn ʿAbd al-Jabbār, who cites Abū Bakr Muḥammad ibn ʿAlī l-Khayyāṭ, who cites Muḥammad ibn Abī l-Fawāris, who cites Aḥmad ibn Jaʿfar ibn Salm, who cites Aḥmad ibn Muḥammad ibn ʿAbd al-Khāliq, who heard Abū Bakr al-Marrūdhī report that Abū ʿAbd Allāh told him: 70.10

[Aḥmad:] Isḥāq ibn Ibrāhīm asked if I would exempt Abū Isḥāq [al-Muʿtaṣim] from liability. I told him that I already had. I had been thinking about the Hadith that says: "On the Day of Resurrection a cry will sound: 'Let none rise but those who have forgiven!'" I also remembered what al-Shaʿbī said, "Forgive once and be rewarded twice."

We cite ʿAbd al-Malik ibn Abī l-Qāsim, who cites ʿAbd Allāh ibn Muḥammad al-Anṣārī, who heard Muḥammad ibn Aḥmad al-Jārūdī report that he heard al-Ḥusayn ibn ʿAlī ibn Jaʿfar report that he heard his father report that he heard Abū ʿAlī l-Ḥusayn ibn ʿAbd Allāh al-Khiraqī, upon seeing Aḥmad ibn Ḥanbal, report: 70.11

[Al-Khiraqī:] I once spent the night at Aḥmad ibn Ḥanbal's. Every time he lay down, he would weep, straight through until morning. I asked him why he had been weeping so much. He said, "I was thinking about how al-Muʿtaṣim had me flogged. Then during the lesson we came across the verse «Let harm be requited by an equal harm. But whoever pardons and amends will find his reward with God.»[130] So I prostrated myself and decided to forgive him."

We were informed by Muḥammad ibn Nāṣir, who cites al-Mubārak ibn ʿAbd al-Jabbār, who cites ʿUbayd Allāh ibn ʿUmar ibn Shāhīn, who heard his father report that he heard ʿUthmān ibn ʿAbduwayh say that he heard Ibrāhīm al-Ḥarbī say: 70.12

[Al-Ḥarbī:] Aḥmad ibn Ḥanbal forgave everyone, including al-Muʿtaṣim, who attended his flogging or helped carry it out under instructions from others. He said, "If Ibn Abī Duʾād weren't summoning others to unbelief, I would forgive him, too."

ʿUmar ibn Shāhīn reports that he heard Aḥmad ibn Khālid al-Muktib report that he heard Abū l-ʿAbbās ibn Wāṣil al-Muqriʾ say that Fūrān told him: 70.13

[Fūrān:] One night Aḥmad ibn Ḥanbal sent for me. When I arrived he asked, "You once reported something Faḍl al-Anmāṭī said. What was it?"

I told him, "Faḍl said to me: 'I will never forgive the one who ordered me flogged so I would say the Qurʾan is created, or the ones who carried out the

حتى أقول القرآن مخلوق ولا من تولّى الضرب ولا من سرّه ممّن حضر وغاب من الجَهْمِيَّة.

فقال لي أحمد بن حنبل: لكني جعلتُ المعتصم في حلّ ومن تولّى ضربي ومن غاب ومن حضر وقلت لا يُعذَّب فيّ أحد، وذكرتُ حديثين يُرويان عن النبيّ صلّى الله عليه وسلّم:

إنّ اللهَ عَزَّ وجلَّ يُنْشِئُ قصوراً فيَرْفَعُ الناسُ رُءوسَهم فيَقولونَ: لِمَنْ هذِهِ القُصورُ؟ ما أحسنها! فيُقالُ: لِمَنْ أَعْطَى ثَمَنَها. قيل: وما ثَمَنُها؟ قال: مَن عَفا عن أَخيه المُسْلِم.

ويَأْمُرُ اللهُ عَزّ وجلّ بِعَقْدِ لِواءٍ فيُنادي مُنادٍ: لِيَقُمْ تَحْتَ هذا اللِّواءِ إلى الجَنّةِ مَنْ لَهُ عِنْدَ اللهِ عَهْدٌ. فيُقال: بَيِّنْ بَيِّنْ مَنْ هُوَ؟ قال: مَنْ عَفا عن أخيه المُسْلِم.

١٤،٧٠ أخبرنا محمّد بن أبي منصور قال: أخبرنا محمّد بن عبد الملك بن عبد القاهر قال: أنبأنا عُبيد الله بن أحمد بن عثمان الصَّيْرَفي قال: أخبرنا أبو الحسن محمّد بن أحمد أنّ أبا عَمرو[1] بن السمّاك أخبرهم قال: أخبرنا محمّد بن سُفْيان بن هارون قال: حدثنا أبو جعفر محمّد بن صالح قال:

سمعتُ عمّي عبد الله بن أحمد يقول: قرأت على أبي رَوْح عن أَشْعَث عن الحسن: إن لله عزّ وجلّ باباً في الجنّة لا يدخله إلّا من عفا عن مَظْلَمَة.

فقال لي: يا بُنيّ ما خرجت من دار أبي إسحاق حتى أحللته ومن معه إلّا رجلين: ابن أبي دؤاد وعبد الرحمن بن إسحاق فإنهما طلبا دمي وأنا أهونُ على الله عزّ وجلّ من أن يعذِّب فيَّ أحداً، أُشهدك أنّهما في حِلّ.

---

١ د: عمر.

flogging, or any of the followers of Jahm—present or absent—who rejoiced in it.'"

Aḥmad said: "But I've forgiven al-Muʿtaṣim, the ones who flogged me, and anyone who was there, or who wasn't. I thought it was better not to have anyone tormented in the Fire on my account. I also remembered two Hadiths reported of the Prophet, God bless and keep him: 'God, mighty and glorious, will raise palaces, and people will lift their eyes to them and say, "Whose are these? How beautiful they are!"

"'The answer will come: "They belong to those who have paid for them."

"'"What price did they pay?"

"'"Forgiving a fellow Muslim."'

"The other report is: 'God, mighty and glorious, will order a banner to be raised and a crier to cry, "Let all who have a claim on God follow this banner into the Garden."

"'The people will ask, "Tell us who has a claim!"

"'The answer will come, "Whoever forgave his fellow Muslim."'"

We cite Muḥammad ibn Abī Manṣūr, who cites Muḥammad ibn ʿAbd al-Malik ibn ʿAbd al-Qāhir, who was informed by ʿUbayd Allāh ibn Aḥmad ibn ʿUthmān al-Ṣayrafī, who cites Abū l-Ḥasan Muḥammad ibn Aḥmad, who cites Abū ʿAmr ibn al-Sammāk, who cites Muḥammad ibn Sufyān ibn Hārūn, who heard Abū Jaʿfar Muḥammad ibn Ṣāliḥ report that he heard his uncle ʿAbd Allāh, Aḥmad's son, say: 70.14

[ʿAbd Allāh:] I once read to my father a report narrated by Rawḥ citing Ashʿath citing al-Ḥasan: "The Garden has a door that God has placed there only for those who have forgiven an injustice done them."

"Son," my father said, "the moment I left al-Muʿtaṣim's palace, I forgave him and everyone with him, with two exceptions: Ibn Abī Duʾād and ʿAbd al-Raḥmān ibn Isḥāq, who were calling for my blood. But I'm too insignificant in the eyes of God for Him to torment anyone on my account, so I declare them forgiven as well."

سياق ذكر بقاء أثر[1] الضرب عليه

أخبرنا محمد بن أبي منصور قال: أخبرنا عبد القادر بن محمد قال: أخبرنا إبراهيم بن عمر البرمكي قال: أخبرنا علي ابن عبد العزيز قال: أخبرنا عبد الرحمن بن أبي حاتم قال: ١٥،٧٠

حدثنا صالح بن أحمد بن حنبل قال: نظر إلي أبي رجل ممّن يُبصر الضرب والعلاج فقال: قد رأيت مَن ضُرب ألف سوط، ما رأيتُ ضربًا مثل هذا، لقد جَرّ[2] عليه من خلفه ومن قُدّامه.

ثم أخذ ميلاً فأدخله في بعض تلك الجراحات فنظر إليه فقال: لم يَثْقب[3]. وجعل يأتيه ويعالجه.

وقد كان أصاب وجهَه غير ضربة ومكث مُتكئًا على وجهه ما شاء الله.

ثم قال: إنّ هاهنا شيئًا أُريد أن أقطعه فجاء بحديدة فجعل يعلّق اللحم بها ويقطعه بسكّين معه وهو صابر لذلك يحمد الله عزّ وجلّ في ذلك فبرأ منه. ولم يزل يتوجّع من مواضع منه وكان أثر الضرب بيّنًا في ظهره إلى أن توفّي رحمه الله.

فسمعتُ أبي يقول: والله لقد أعطيتُ المجهود من نفسي ولَوددتُ أن أنجو من هذا الأمر الذي أخاف كِفافًا لا عليّ ولا لي.

قال ابن أبي حاتم: ١٦،٧٠

وسمعت أبي يقول: أتيتُ أحمد بن حنبل بعدما ضُرب بثلاث سنين أو نحوها فقلت له: ذهب عنك أثر الضرب؟

فأخرج يده اليسرى على كوعه اليمنى وقال: هذا! كأنّه يقول: خُلع، وأنّه يجد منها ألم ذلك.

وبلغني عن أبي الحسين بن المنادي قال: ١٧،٧٠

حدثني جدّي قال: لقيتُ أبا عبد الله بعد ما انكشف ذلك البلاء فرأيت بين

---

١ ليس في د. ٢ مشكلة في هـ، وفي تركي: جُرّ. ٣ معجمة في هـ، وفي تركي: تُثْقَب.

More on the Effects of the Flogging

We cite Muḥammad ibn Abī Manṣūr, who cites ʿAbd al-Qādir ibn Muḥammad, who cites Ibrāhīm ibn ʿUmar al-Barmakī, who cites ʿAlī ibn ʿAbd al-ʿAzīz, who cites ʿAbd al-Raḥmān ibn Abī Ḥātim, who heard Aḥmad ibn Ḥanbal's son Ṣāliḥ report: 70.15

[Ṣāliḥ:] A man who treated flogging victims came to look after my father.[131] "I've seen people who'd been struck a thousand lashes," he told us, "but nothing as bad as this. They struck him from the front as well as behind."

Then he took an instrument and probed some of the wounds. "They didn't puncture anything," he said.

He began to come regularly to treat my father. Some of the blows had struck him in the face, and he had been left lying face down for some time. At one point the man said, "There's something I want to remove." He took out a piece of metal and used it to fold back the flesh while cutting some of it away with a knife. My father bore it all, praising God the whole time, and eventually recovered. He continued to feel pain in certain places, and the scars were visible on his back until the day he died.

I heard him say, "By God, I have given all I could. I was afraid, and all I wished for was to come out of it even, not winning or losing."

Ibn Abī Ḥātim reports that he heard his father say: 70.16

[Abū Ḥātim:] I went to see Aḥmad ibn Ḥanbal three or so years after he was flogged.

"Do you still feel any pain?" I asked him.

He put his right hand on his left elbow and said, "Here," as if to say that it had been dislocated and still hurt.

We have heard it said that Abū l-Ḥusayn ibn Munādī heard his grandfather report: 70.17

[Ibn Munādī's grandfather:] After the ordeal was over, I saw Aḥmad sitting with a censer in front of him. He would take a rag he had wrapped around his hand and warm it over the fire then hold it to his side, where they

يديه مِجمَرة فيها جمر يضع خرقة ملفوفة في يده فيُسخنها بالنار ثم يجعلها على جنبه من الضرب الذي كان ضُرب فالتفت إليّ فقال: يا أبا جعفر ما كان في القوم أرأف[١] بي من المعتصم.

الباب الحادي والسبعون في ذكر[٢] تحديثه بعد موت المعتصم

١،٧١ أخبرنا الكَرُوخي قال: أخبرنا عبد الله بن محمّد الأنصاري قال: أخبرنا أبو يعقوب قال: أخبرنا جدّي قال: أخبرنا محمّد بن أبي جعفر المنذري قال:

سمعتُ محمّد بن إبراهيم البُوشَنْجي يقول: في سنة سبع وعشرين حدّث أحمد بن حنبل ببغداد ظاهرًا جَهرةً وذلك حين مات المعتصم، بلغنا انبساطه في الحديث ونحن بالكوفة فرجعتُ إليه فأدركته في رجب من هذه السنة وهو يحدّث ثم قطع الحديث لثلاث بقين من شعبان من غير منع من السلطان ولكن كتب الحسن بن عليّ بن الجَعد وهو يومئذ قاضي بغداد[٣] إلى ابن أبي دُؤاد إن أحمد قد انبسط في الحديث، فبلغ ذلك أحمد فأمسك عن الحديث من غير أن يُمنع ولم يكن حدّث أيّام المعتصم فيما بلغنا وكانت ولايته ثمان سنين وثمانية أشهر ثم لم يُحدث إلى أن توفّي.[٤]

---

١ ش: ارفق. ٢ ليس في هـ. ٣ د: قاضٍ ببغداد. ٤ د: مات.

had hit him. "Abū Jaʿfar," he said, turning to me, "no one showed more compassion for me that day than al-Muʿtaṣim."

Chapter 71: His Teaching of Hadith after the Death of al-Muʿtaṣim

We cite al-Karūkhī, who cites ʿAbd Allāh ibn Muḥammad al-Anṣārī, who cites Abū Yaʿqūb, who cites his grandfather, who cites Muḥammad ibn Abī Jaʿfar al-Mundhirī, who heard Muḥammad ibn Ibrāhīm al-Būshanjī say: **71.1**

[Al-Būshanjī:] In '27 [842], Aḥmad ibn Ḥanbal taught Hadith openly in Baghdad. That was right after al-Muʿtaṣim died. We were in Kufa when we heard the news. I headed back to Baghdad and caught up with him in Rajab of that year, while he was still teaching. Then, with three days left in Shaʿbān, he stopped of his own accord. The authorities hadn't told him to stop, but al-Ḥasan ibn ʿAlī ibn al-Jaʿd, who was then judge in Baghdad, had written to Ibn Abī Du'ād to tell him that Aḥmad was openly teaching Hadith. When Aḥmad learned of this, he stopped without having to be asked. As far as we know, he had not taught during al-Muʿtaṣim's reign, which lasted for eight years and eight days. After that he did not teach again at all until he died.

الباب الثاني والسبعون في ذكر قصته مع الواثق

١،٧٢ ولي الواثق أبو جعفر هارون بن المعتصم في ربيع الأوّل سنة سبع وعشرين ومائتين وحسّن له ابن أبي دُؤاد امتحان الناس بخلق القرآن ففعل ذلك ولم يعرض لأحمد إمّا لِمَا علم من صبره أو لِما خاف من تأثير عُقوبته لكنّه أرسل إلى أحمد بن حنبل: لا تُساكنّي بأرض. فاختفى أحمد بقيّة حياة الواثق فما زال يتنقّل في الأماكن ثم عاد إلى منزله بعد أشهر فاختفى فيه إلى أن مات الواثق.

٢،٧٢ أخبرنا أبو منصور القزاز قال:

أخبرنا أحمد بن عليّ بن ثابت قال: أقام أحمد بن حنبل مدة اختِفائه عند إسحاق ابن إبراهيم بن هانئ النَّيسابوري.

قلت: وقد رُوي: عند إبراهيم بن هانئ وبيت الوالد والولد واحد.

٣،٧٢ أخبرنا موهوب بن أحمد قال: أخبرنا عليّ بن أحمد بن البُسْري قال: حدثنا محمّد بن عبد الرحمن المُخَلِّص قال:

حدثنا البَغَوي قال: سمعت أبا عبد الله أحمد بن حنبل في سنة ثمان وعشرين في أولها وقد حدّث حديث معاوية عن النبيّ صلّى الله عليه وسلّم أنّه قال: لَمْ يَبْقَ مِنَ الدُّنيا إلّا بَلاءٌ وفِتْنَةٌ فَأَعِدّوا لِلبَلاءِ صَبراً.

فجعل يقول: اللّهمّ رضينا! اللّهمّ رضينا!

٤،٧٢ أخبرنا إسماعيل بن أحمد ومحمّد بن عبد الباقي قالا: أخبرنا حمد بن أحمد قال: حدثنا أحمد بن عبد الله قال: أخبرني جعفر بن محمّد الخُلْدي في كتابه قال: حدثني أبو حامد قَرابة أسد المعلّم قال:

قال إبراهيم ابن هانئ: اختفى عندي أحمد بن حنبل ثلاثة أيّام ثمّ قال: اطلبْ لي موضعاً حتّى أتحول إليه.

Chapter 72: His Experience with al-Wāthiq

In Rabīʿ I 227 [January 842], Abū Jaʿfar Hārūn al-Wāthiq, son of al-Muʿtaṣim, succeeded to the caliphate. Although Ibn Abī Duʾād persuaded him to continue putting people to the test over the createdness of the Qurʾan, he avoided another confrontation with Aḥmad, either because he was aware of his ability to withstand coercion or because he was afraid of what would happen if Aḥmad were punished. He did, however, write to him saying, "Take care that we never find each other in the same place." Aḥmad accordingly went into hiding for the remainder of al-Wāthiq's reign. After several months spent moving from one place to another, Aḥmad disappeared into his house, where he remained until al-Wāthiq died. 72.1

We cite Abū Manṣūr al-Qazzāz, who cites Aḥmad ibn ʿAlī ibn Thābit, who reports: 72.2

[Aḥmad ibn ʿAlī:] When he was a fugitive, Aḥmad ibn Ḥanbal stayed with Isḥāq ibn Ibrāhīm ibn Hāniʾ al-Naysābūrī.

[The author:] Isḥaq's father, Ibrāhīm ibn Hāniʾ, is sometimes named instead, but the house is one and the same.

We cite Mawhūb ibn Aḥmad, who cites ʿAlī ibn Aḥmad ibn al-Busrī, who heard 72.3
Muḥammad ibn ʿAbd al-Raḥmān al-Mukhalliṣ report that he heard al-Baghawī report:

[Al-Baghawī:] At the beginning of '28 [late in 842], I heard Aḥmad ibn Ḥanbal recite the Hadith reported by Muʿawiyah where the Prophet, God bless and keep him, says, "Nothing remains in this present world but adversity and tribulation, so prepare yourselves to be steadfast."

Afterward he said, "God, I accept Your charge," over and over.

We cite Ismāʿīl ibn Aḥmad and Muḥammad ibn ʿAbd al-Bāqī, who cite Ḥamd ibn Aḥmad, 72.4
who heard Aḥmad ibn ʿAbd Allāh cite a document written by Jaʿfar ibn Muḥammad al-Khuldī, who reports that he heard Abū Ḥāmid, a relative of Asad al-Muʿallim, report that he heard Ibrāhīm ibn Hāniʾ say:

[Ibrāhīm ibn Hāniʾ:] Aḥmad ibn Ḥanbal hid at my place for three days. Then he said, "Find me somewhere else to go."

قلت: لا آمَنُ عليك يا أبا عبد الله. فقال: افعلْ، فإذا فعلتَ أفدتُك. فطلبت له موضعاً فلمّا خرج قال لي: اختفى رسول الله صلّى الله عليه وسلّم في الغار ثلاثة أيّام ثم تحوّل وليس ينبغي أن يُتبع رسول الله في الرخاء ويُترك في الشدّة.

٥،٧٢ أخبرنا عبد الوهاب الحافظ وعلي بن أبي عمر قالا: أخبرنا رزق الله بن عبد الوهاب التميمي قال: حدثنا أحمد ابن محمّد بن يوسف قال: حدثنا جعفر بن محمّد بن نُصير قال: حدثنا أبو حامد أحمد بن مَخْلَد بن ماهان الحَذّاء قال: حدثنا فتح بن شَخْرَف قال:

قال لي إبراهيم بن هانئ النَّيْسابوري: اختفى عندي أحمد بن حنبل ثلاث ليال. ثم قال: اطلب لي مَوضعاً حتى أدور إليه. فقلت: لا آمنُ عليك يا أبا عبد الله. فقال لي: النبيّ صلّى الله عليه وسلّم اختفى في الغار ثلاثة أيّام ثمّ دار وليس ينبغي أن تُتبع سنّة رسول الله في الرخاء وتُترك في الشدة.

قال فتح: حدّثتُ به صالحاً وعبد الله فقالا: لم نسمع هذه الحكاية إلّا منك وحدثت بها إسحاق بن إبراهيم بن هانئ فقال: ما حدّثني أبي بها.

٦،٧٢ أخبرنا عبد الملك الكَرُوخي قال: أخبرنا عبد الله بن محمّد الأنصاري قال: أخبرنا إسحاق بن إبراهيم السَّرَخْسي قال: أخبرنا أحمد بن أبي عمران قال: أخبرنا أبو عليّ الحسين بن جعفر الخطيب قال: سمعت هارون بن عبد الرحمن يقول: سمعت تميم بن بُهْلول الرازي يقول:

سمعت أبا زُرْعة يقول: قلت لأحمد بن حنبل: كيف تخلصتَ من سيف المعتصم وسوط الواثق؟ فقال: لو وُضع الصدق على جُرح[1] لبرأ.

فصل

٧،٧٢ وقد رُوي أنّ الواثق ترك امتحان الناس بسبب مناظرة جرت بين يديه رأى بها أنّ الأولى ترك الامتحان.

---

[1] د: جراح.

I told him it wasn't safe, but he insisted, and promised to tell me something useful if I did as he asked. So I found a place for him to go. As he was leaving, he said, "The Emissary of God hid in a cave for three days and then moved elsewhere, and it's wrong to follow his example in good times but not in bad."[132]

We cite ʿAbd al-Wahhāb al-Ḥāfiẓ and ʿAlī ibn Abī ʿUmar, who cite Rizq Allāh ibn ʿAbd al-Wahhāb al-Tamīmī, who heard Aḥmad ibn Muḥammad ibn Yūsuf report that he heard Jaʿfar ibn Muḥammad ibn Nuṣayr report that he heard Abū Ḥāmid Aḥmad ibn Makhlad ibn Māhān al-Ḥadhdhāʾ report that he heard Fatḥ ibn Shakhraf report that Ibrāhīm ibn Hāniʾ al-Naysābūrī told him: 72.5

[Ibrāhīm ibn Hāniʾ:] Aḥmad ibn Ḥanbal hid at my place for three nights. Then he said, "Find me somewhere else to go."

I told him it wasn't safe. He replied, "The Prophet, God bless and keep him, hid in a cave for three days and then moved elsewhere, and it's wrong to follow his example in good times but not in bad."

Fatḥ added: I recited this report for Ṣāliḥ and ʿAbd Allāh, who said it was the first they had heard of it. I also recited it for Ibrāhīm's son Isḥāq, who said that his father had never said any such thing to him.

We cite ʿAbd al-Malik al-Karūkhī, who cites ʿAbd Allāh ibn Muḥammad al-Anṣārī, who cites Isḥāq ibn Ibrāhīm al-Sarakhsī, who cites Aḥmad ibn Abī ʿUmrān, who cites Abū ʿAlī l-Ḥusayn ibn Jaʿfar al-Khaṭīb, who heard Hārūn ibn ʿAbd al-Raḥmān say that he heard Tamīm ibn Buhlūl al-Rāzī say that he heard Abū Zurʿah say: 72.6

[Abū Zurʿah:] I asked Aḥmad ibn Ḥanbal how he had escaped al-Muʿtaṣim's sword and al-Wāthiq's lash. He said, "Apply truthfulness to any wound, and it heals."[133]

Addendum

It is reported that al-Wāthiq put an end to the Inquisition after watching a debate that persuaded him of the better course.[134] 72.7

٨،٧٢ فأخبرنا أبو منصور عبد الرحمن بن محمد القزاز قال: أخبرنا أحمد بن عليّ ابن ثابت قال: أخبرنا محمد بن الفرَج بن عليّ البزّاز قال: حدثنا عبد الله ابن إبراهيم بن ماسي قال: حدثنا جعفر بن شُعَيب الشاشي قال: حدثني محمد ابن يوسف الشاشي قال: حدثني إبراهيم بن مَنّة قال: سمعت طاهر بن خَلَف يقول:

سمعت محمّد بن الواثق الذي كان يُقال له المهتدي بالله يقول: كان أبي إذا أراد أن يقتل رجلاً أحضرنا ذلك المجلس. فأُتي بشيخ مخضوب مُقيَّد فقال أبي: ائذنوا لأبي عبد الله وأصحابه، يعني ابن أبي دُؤاد.

قال: فأُدخل الشيخ فقال: السلام عليك يا أمير المؤمنين.

فقال: لا سلّمَ[1] الله عليك!

فقال: يا أمير المؤمنين بئس ما أدّبك مؤدِّبك، قال الله تعالى: ﴿وَإِذَا حُيِّيتُم بِتَحِيَّةٍ فَحَيُّوا بِأَحْسَنَ مِنْهَا أَوْ رُدُّوهَا﴾، والله ما حيّيتني بها ولا بأحسن منها.

فقال ابن أبي دؤاد: يا أمير المؤمنين الرجل مُتكلّم.

فقال له: كلِّمه!

٩،٧٢ فقال: يا شيخ ما تقول في القُرآن؟

قال الشيخ: لم تُنصِفني، ولِّني[2] السؤال.

فقال له: سَل!

فقال له الشيخ: ما تقول في القرآن؟

قال: مخلوق.

فقال: هذا شيء علّمه النبيّ صلّى الله عليه وسلّم وأبو بكر وعمر وعثمان وعلي والخلفاء الراشدون أم شيء لم يعلموه؟

فقال: شيء لم يعلموه.

فقال: سبحان الله! شيء لم يعلمه النبي صلى الله عليه وسلم ولا أبو بكر ولا عمر ولا عثمان ولا عليّ ولا الخلفاء الراشدون عَلِمْتَه أنت!

قال: فخجل فقال: أَقِلْني.

---

١ ش: لا سلام ٢ د: ولى.

We cite Abū Manṣūr ʿAbd al-Raḥmān ibn Muḥammad al-Qazzāz, who cites Aḥmad ibn ʿAlī ibn Thābit, who cites Muḥammad ibn al-Faraj ibn ʿAlī l-Bazzāz, who heard ʿAbd Allāh ibn Ibrāhīm ibn Māsī report that he heard Jaʿfar ibn Shuʿayb al-Shāshī report that he heard Muḥammad ibn Yūsuf al-Shāshī report that he heard Ibrāhīm ibn Mannah report that he heard Ṭāhir ibn Khalaf say that he heard Muḥammad ibn al-Wāthiq, called al-Muhtadī, say: **72.8**

[Al-Muhtadī:] Whenever my father al-Wāthiq was going to execute anyone, we would attend the session. One day an elderly man with a dyed beard was brought in, weighed down with fetters. My father summoned Ibn Abī Du'ād and his associates, then had the man brought forward.

"Peace be upon you," said the elder.

"May God not grant you peace!" retorted my father.

"Commander of the Faithful," said the elder, "you've been poorly raised. God says «When you are greeted by anyone, respond with a better greeting or at least return it.»[135] But you neither returned my greeting nor offered a better one."

"It seems we have a debater on our hands," said Ibn Abī Du'ād.

"Debate him, then," said my father.

"Old man! What do you say regarding the Qur'an?" **72.9**

"That won't do. Let me ask first."

"Go ahead."

"What do you say regarding the Qur'an?"

"It's a created thing."

"Is that something that the Prophet, Abū Bakr, ʿUmar, ʿUthmān, ʿAlī, and the Righteous Caliphs were aware of, or not?"

"They weren't aware of it."

"God preserve us!" cried the elder. "The Prophet didn't know about it, and neither did Abū Bakr, or ʿUmar, or ʿUthmān, or ʿAlī, or the Righteous Caliphs, but you do!"

Ibn Abī Du'ād was stymied and abashed. "Give me a moment," he said.

قال: والمسألة بحالها؟

قال: نعم.

قال: ما تقول في القرآن؟

قال: مخلوق.

فقال: هذا شيء علمه النبي صلى الله عليه وسلم وأبو بكر وعمر وعثمان وعلي[1] والخلفاء الراشدون أم لم يعلموه؟

فقال: علموه ولم يدعوا الناس إليه.

فقال: أفلا وَسِعَك ما وسعهم؟

١٠،٧٢ قال: ثمّ قام أبي فدخل مجلس الخلوة واستلقى على قفاه ووضع إحدى رجليه على الأخرى وهو يقول: هذا شيء لم يعلمه النبيّ صلّى الله عليه وسلّم ولا أبو بكر ولا عمر ولا عثمان ولا عليّ ولا الخلفاء الراشدون علمته أنت، سبحان الله! شيء[2] علمه النبي صلى الله عليه وسلم وأبو بكر وعمر وعثمان وعلي والخلفاء الراشدون ولم يدعوا الناس إليه، أفلا وسعك ما وسعهم؟!

ثمّ دعا عَمّاراً الحاجب فأمر أن يرفع عنه القيود ويعطيه أربع مائة دينار ويأذن له في الرجوع، وسقط من عينه ابنُ أبي دؤاد ولم يمتحن بعد ذلك أحداً.

١١،٧٢ وقد رُويت لنا هذه القصة[3] على صفة أُخرى:

فأخبرنا أبو منصور عبد الرحمن بن محمّد القزاز وأبو السعود أحمد بن عليّ بن المُجَلّي قالا: أخبرنا أحمد بن عليّ بن ثابت قال: أخبرنا محمّد بن أحمد بن رزق قال: أخبرنا أحمد بن سِنْدي الحَدّاد قال: قُرِئ على أحمد بن الممتنع وأنا أسمع، قيل له:

أخبركم صالح بن عليّ بن يعقوب الهاشمي قال: حضرت المهتدي بالله أمير المؤمنين وقد جلس للنظر في أمور المتظلّمين في دار العامّة فنظرت إلى قصص الناس تُقرأ عليه من أوّلها إلى آخرها فيأمر بالتوقيع فيها ويُنشَأ الكتّابُ عليها وتُحرّر وتُختَم وتُدفَع إلى صاحبها بين يديه، فسرّني ذلك واستحسنت ما رأيت فجعلت

---

١ ليس في هـ. ٢ ليس في د. ٣ د: الحكاية.

"Same question again?"

"Yes."

"What do you say regarding the Qur'an?"

"It's a created thing."

"Is that something that the Prophet, Abū Bakr, ʿUmar, ʿUthmān, ʿAlī, and the Righteous Caliphs were aware of, or not?"

"They were aware of it," said Ibn Abī Du'ād, "but they didn't call on anyone to proclaim it."

"So why can't you do the same?" asked the elder.

My father rose, went into his private chamber, lay down, and crossed his legs, repeating to himself: "The Prophet didn't know about it, or Abū Bakr, or ʿUmar, or ʿUthmān, or ʿAlī, or the Righteous Caliphs, but you do! God preserve us! The Prophet, Abū Bakr, ʿUmar, ʿUthmān, ʿAlī, and the Righteous Caliphs did know about it, but they didn't call on anyone to proclaim it; why can't you do the same?" **72.10**

Then he summoned ʿAmmār the chamberlain and told him to remove the old man's fetters, give him four hundred dinars, and let him go. He lost all regard for Ibn Abī Du'ād and stopped the Inquisition then and there.

[The author:] I have heard a different telling of the story. **72.11**

We cite Abū Manṣūr ʿAbd al-Raḥmān ibn Muḥammad al-Qazzāz and Abū l-Saʿūd Aḥmad ibn ʿAlī ibn al-Mujallī, who cite Aḥmad ibn ʿAlī ibn Thābit, who cites Muḥammad ibn Aḥmad ibn Rizq, who cites Aḥmad ibn Sindī l-Ḥaddād, who reports that he heard read aloud back to Aḥmad ibn al-Mumtaniʿ his report that Ṣāliḥ ibn ʿAlī ibn Yaʿqūb al-Hāshimī said:

[Ṣāliḥ ibn ʿAlī:] I once saw the Caliph al-Muhtadī billāh presiding over the Grievance Court at Commoners' Gate. I watched the cases being read aloud to him from beginning to end, and saw him make a ruling on each one. I watched as the orders were issued, the wording settled, and the documents sealed and handed over to the petitioners under his supervision. It was a fine and impressive sight to see. At one point, al-Wāthiq caught me staring at him and I averted my eyes. The same thing happened twice more: when he

أنظر إليه، ففطن ونظر إليَّ فغضضتُ عنه حتى كان ذلك منّي ومنه مرارًا ثلاثًا إذا نظر غضضت وإذا شُغل نظرت. فقال لي: يا صالح!

قلت: لبَّيك يا أمير المؤمنين! وقمتُ قائمًا.

فقال: في نفسك منّا شيء تريد، أو قال: تحب، أن تقوله؟

قلت: نعم يا سيّدي.

فقال لي: عُد إلى موضعك.

فعدت حتى إذا قام قال للحاجب: لا يبرح صالح!

فانصرف الناس ثمّ أذن لي فدخلت فدعوت له.

فقال لي: اجلس!

فجلست، فقال: يا صالح تقول لي ما دار في نفسك أو أقول أنا ما دار في نفسي أنّه دار في نفسك؟

قلتُ: يا أمير المؤمنين، ما تعزم عليه وتأمر به.

فقال: أقول أنا إنّه دار في نفسي أنّك استحسنت ما رأيت منّا فقلتَ: أيّ خليفة خليفتنا إن لم يكن[1] يقول: القرآن مخلوق.

فورد على قلبي أمر عظيم ثم قلت: يا نفس هل تموتين قبل أجلك؟ وهل تموتين إلا مرّة؟ وهل يجوز الكذب في جدّ أو هزل؟ فقلت: يا أمير المؤمنين ما دار في نفسي إلّا ما قلت.

فأطرق مليًّا ثم قال: ويحك! إسمع منّي ما أقول فوالله لتسمعنّ الحق.

فَسُرّي عني فقلتُ: يا سيدي ومن أولى بقول الحق منك وأنت خليفة ربّ العالمين وابن عم سيّد المرسلين.

١٢،٧٢ فقال: ما زلت أقول إنّ القرآن مخلوق صدرًا من أيّام الواثق حتى أقدَم أحمد بن أبي دؤاد علينا شيخًا من أهل الشام من أهل أَذَنة فأُدخل الشيخ على الواثق مقيّدًا وهو جميل الوجه تامّ القامة حسن الشيبة فرأيتُ الواثق قد استحيا منه ورقّ له.

---

١ ليس في د.

looked at me I would look away, but then when he turned back to his work I would begin staring again. Finally he said, "Ṣāliḥ!"

I rose. "At your service, Commander of the Faithful!"

"You have something you want"—or "you would like"—"to tell me."[136]

"Yes, sire!"

"Resume your place."

So I went back and waited until he closed the session and said to the chamberlain, "Have Ṣāliḥ stay."

After everyone had left, I was admitted to his presence. I greeted him with a prayer for his well-being.

"Sit," he said.

I sat.

"Do you want to tell me what you were thinking, or do you want me to tell you what I think you were thinking?"

"Whichever you decide, Commander of the Faithful!"

"I'll tell you what I think, then. You approved of what you saw me doing and you thought, 'What a great caliph we have—if only he didn't believe that the Qur'an is created!'"

His words struck terror into my heart. But then I reminded myself that I wasn't going to die any earlier than God had already decreed, that I was only going to die once no matter what, and that lying is wrong, no matter how grave or how trivial the subject. So I said, "Commander of the Faithful, those were my thoughts exactly."

He bowed his head for a moment, then said, "Hmph! Well then, listen: I'll be honest with you."

With a great sense of relief, I said, "Who better, sire, to speak the truth than the deputy of the Lord of the Worlds and the nephew of the Chief of Prophets?"

Al-Muhtadī then told me the following story.

[Al-Muhtadī:] Beginning in the reign of al-Wāthiq, I always believed that **72.12**
the Qur'an was created. But then Aḥmad ibn Abī Du'ād brought in an elderly man—a Syrian, from Adana—weighed down with fetters, to face al-Wāthiq.

فما زال يُدنيه ويقرّبه حتى قرب منه فسلّم الشيخ فأحسن ودعا فأبلغ فقال له الواثق: اجلس!

فجلس فقال له: يا شيخ ناظِر ابن أبي دؤاد على ما يناظرك عليه.

ف فقال الشيخ: يا أمير المؤمنين ابن أبي دؤاد يصبأ[1] ويضعف عن المناظرة.

فغضب الواثق وعاد مكانَ الرقّة له غَضباً عليه وقال: أبو عبد الله بن أبي دؤاد يصبأ ويضعف عن مناظرتك أنت؟

فقال الشيخ: هوّن عليك يا أمير المؤمنين ما بك فَائذَنْ في مُناظرته.

فقال الواثق: ما دعوتُك إلّا للمناظرة.

فقال الشيخ: يا أمير المؤمنين إن رأيت أن تحفظ عليّ وعليه ما نقول.

قال: أفعل.

١٣،٧٢ قال الشيخ: يا أحمد، أخبرني عن مقالتك هذه، هي مقالة واجبة داخلة في عقد الدين فلا يكون الدين كاملاً حتى يقال فيه بما قلت؟

قال: نعم.

قال الشيخ: يا أحمد أخبرني عن رسول الله صلّى الله عليه وسلّم حين بعثه الله تعالى إلى عباده، هل ستر شيئاً مما أمره الله عزّ وجلّ به في أمر دينهم؟

قال: لا.

فقال الشيخ: فدعا رسول الله صلّى الله عليه وسلّم الأمّة إلى مقالتك هذه؟ فسكت ابن أبي دؤاد[2].

فقال الشيخ: تكلّم!

فسكت. فالتفت الشيخ إلى الواثق فقال: يا أمير المؤمنين، واحدة. فقال الواثق: واحدة.

فقال الشيخ: يا أحمد أخبرني عن الله تعالى حين أنزل القرآن على رسول الله فقال: ﴿الْيَوْمَ أَكْمَلْتُ لَكُمْ دِينَكُمْ وَأَتْمَمْتُ عَلَيْكُمْ نِعْمَتِي وَرَضِيتُ لَكُمُ الْإِسْلَامَ دِينًا﴾

---

١ تركي: يصبو. ٢ ما بعد (قال لا) إلى هاهنا ليس في ش.

He was a handsome fellow, well built, with a fine head of gray hair. I could see that al-Wāthiq had taken a liking to him and was uncomfortable with the thought of arguing with him. He beckoned him closer and closer. When he had come right up next to him, the elder greeted him most properly and intoned an eloquent prayer for his well-being. Al-Wāthiq invited him to sit down, then said, "Sir, I want you to debate whatever point Ibn Abī Du'ād raises with you."

The elder replied, "Commander of the Faithful, Ibn Abī Du'ād is an apostate[137] and too weak-witted to debate with me."

When al-Wāthiq heard this, his kindness toward the man disappeared, to be replaced by anger. "Ibn Abī Du'ād is an apostate and too weak-witted to debate with *you*?"

"Forget I mentioned it, Commander of the Faithful," he replied. "I'll debate with him."

"That's why I brought you here," said al-Wāthiq.

"Then would you mind keeping score, Commander of the Faithful?"

"Agreed."

"Tell me, Aḥmad," said the elder to Ibn Abī Du'ād,[138] "is this creed of yours an obligatory part of our religion, such that one's religion is incomplete unless one holds the same view as you do?" **72.13**

"Yes."

"Tell me, then: When God sent His Emissary to humankind, did the Emissary keep back anything that God had commanded him to tell us regarding our religion?"

"No."

"And did he summon the community to espouse this creed of yours?"

Ibn Abī Du'ād was left speechless.

"That's one for me, Commander of the Faithful," said the elder.

"All right then, one for you."

"Now then, Aḥmad," said the elder, "recall that when God revealed the Qur'an to His Emissary, he said: «Today I have perfected your religion for you and completed my blessing upon you; I am satisfied with Islam as a religion for you.»[139] Which of you is right: God, when He speaks of perfecting

هل كان الله تعالى الصادق في إكمال دينه أو أنت الصادق في نُقصانه حتى يقال فيه بمقالتك هذه؟

فسكت ابن أبي دؤاد.

فقال الشيخ: أَجِبْ يا أحمد!

فلم يجب، فقال الشيخ: يا أمير المؤمنين اثنتان.

فقال الواثق: اثنتان.

فقال الشيخ: يا أحمد أخبرني عن مقالتك هذه عَلِمَها رسول الله أم جهلها؟

قال ابن أبي دُؤاد: علمها.

قال: فدعا الناس إليها؟ فسكتَ.

فقال الشيخ: يا أمير المؤمنين ثلاث.

فقال الواثق: ثلاث.

فقال الشيخ: يا أحمد فاتّسع لرسول الله أنْ علمها وأمسك عنها كما زعمتَ ولم يطالب أمّته بها؟

قال: نعم.

قال الشيخ: واتّسع لأبي بكر الصدّيق وعمر ابن الخطّاب وعثمان بن عفّان وعلي ابن أبي طالب رضي الله عنهم؟

قال ابن أبي دُؤاد: نعم.

فأعرض الشيخ عنه وأقبل على الواثق فقال: يا أمير المؤمنين قد قدّمت القول إن ١٤،٧٢ أحمد يصبأ ويضعف عن المناظرة، يا أمير المؤمنين إن لم يتّسع لنا من الإمساك عن هذه المقالة بما زعم هذا أنّه اتسع لرسول الله ولأبي بكر وعمر وعثمان وعلي فلا وسَّع الله على من لم يتّسع له ما اتّسع لهم. فقال الواثق: نعم إن لم يتّسع لنا من الإمساك عن هذه المقالة ما اتّسع لرسول الله صلّى الله عليه وسلّم وأبي بكر وعمر وعثمان وعلي فلا وسّع الله علينا، اقطعوا قيد الشيخ!

فلمّا قطعوا القيد ضرب الشيخ بيده إلى القيد حتّى يأخذه فجاذبه الحدّاد عليه فقال

His religion; or you, when you say that something is missing and can only be completed by adding this doctrine of yours?"

Again Ibn Abī Du'ād was stymied.

"Say something," said the elder. But Ibn Abī Du'ād had nothing to say.

"That's two for me, then, Commander of the Faithful."

"Two it is."

"Now then, Aḥmad," said the elder, "tell me: Was the Emissary of God aware of this doctrine of yours, or not?"

"He was aware of it."

"And did he summon people to espouse it?"

Again, silence.

"That's three, Commander of the Faithful."

"Three it is," said al-Wāthiq.

"Now then, Aḥmad," said the elder, "you're claiming that the Emissary of God was content to know it but not press it upon the community?"

"Yes."

"And the same goes for Abū Bakr al-Ṣiddiq, 'Umar ibn al-Khaṭṭāb, 'Uthmān ibn 'Affān, and 'Alī ibn Abī Ṭālib, God be pleased with them all?"

"Right."

Thereupon the elder turned away and addressed al-Wāthiq. "As you may 72.14
recall, Commander of the Faithful, I said that Ibn Abī Du'ād is an apostate and too weak-minded to debate with me. If he's right, and we can't keep this doctrine back, even though the Emissary of God, 'Umar, 'Uthmān, and 'Alī all managed to, then I say: may God give no good to anyone who's too good to do what was good enough for them!"

"Why yes," said al-Wāthiq. "If we're too good to keep quiet about a doctrine that the Emissary of God, 'Umar, 'Uthmān, and 'Alī all kept quiet about, then may God be no good to us! Remove the man's fetters."

As the fetters were being removed, the elder reached for them but the blacksmith pulled them away.

الواثق: دَع الشيخَ يأخذه.

فأخذه فوضعه في كمّه فقال له الواثق: يا شيخ لم جاذبت الحدّاد عليه؟

قال: لأنّي نويتُ أن أتقدّم إلى من أُوصي إليه إذا أنا متّ أن يجعله بيني وبين كفني حتى أُخاصم به هذا الظالم عند الله يوم القيامة وأقول يا ربّ سَلْ عبدك هذا لِمَ قيّدني وروّع أهلي وولدي وإخواني بلا حقّ أوجب ذلك عليّ؟

وبكى الشيخ وبكى الواثق وبكينا.

ثم سأله الواثق أن يجعله في حِلّ وسعة ممّا ناله فقال له الشيخ: والله يا أمير المؤمنين لقد جعلتُك في حلّ وسعة من أوّل يوم إكراماً لرسول الله إذ كنتَ رجلاً من أهله.

فقال الواثق: لي إليك حاجة.

فقال الشيخ: إن كانت ممكنة فعلتُ.

فقال له الواثق: تقيم قِبَلَنا فننتفع بك وينتفع بك فتياننا.

فقال الشيخ: يا أمير المؤمنين إنّ ردّك إيّاي إلى الموضع الذي أخرجني عنه هذا الظالم أنفع لك من مقامي عليك، وأُخبرك بما في ذلك، أصير إلى أهلي وولدي فأكفّ دعاءهم عليك فقد خلّفتُهم على ذلك.

فقال له الواثق: فتقبّل منّا صِلة تستعين بها على دهرك.

فقال: يا أمير المؤمنين لا تحلّ لي، أنا عنها غنيّ وذو مِرّةٍ سَويّ.

فقال: سل حاجة.

فقال: أَوَتقضيها يا أمير المؤمنين؟

قال: نعم.

قال: تأذن أن يُخلى لي السبيل الساعة إلى الثّغر.

قال: قد أذنتُ لك. فسلّم وخرج.

قال المهتدي بالله: فرجعت عن هذه المقالة وأظنّ أنّ الواثق رجع عنها منذ ذلك الوقت.

"Let the man have them," said al-Wāthiq. The elder took them and put them into his sleeve.

"Why did you try to wrestle them away from the smith?" asked al-Wāthiq.

"Before I die," the elder said, "I intend to give them to my executor and tell him to put them inside my shroud so that when the Day of Resurrection comes, I can use them as proof before God against my abuser. 'Lord,' I'll say, 'ask this creature of yours why he chained me up and terrified my wife, my children, and my friends for no good reason at all?'"

He burst into tears, and so did al-Wāthiq, and so did we all. Then al-Wāthiq asked him to exempt him from any liability for what he had suffered at his hands.

"By God," said the elder, "I forgave you from the beginning, out of respect for the Emissary of God, since you're a descendant of his."

"Will you do something for me?"

"If I can."

"Stay here so that we and our children can learn from you."

"Commander of the Faithful," said the elder, "you're better off sending me back to where this abuser found me, and I'll tell you why: so I can stop my wife and children from cursing you, which is what they were doing when I left them."

"In that case," said al-Wāthiq, "let us give you something to make sure you're well taken care of."

"I can't accept it," he replied, "as I don't need it, and I'm able-bodied."

"Ask me for any other favor, then."

"And you'll grant it?"

"Yes."

"Let me go back to the frontier this minute."

"Granted."

The elder bid him farewell and went out. That's when I renounced the doctrine, and I think al-Wāthiq did too.

أخبرنا القزاز قال: أخبرنا أبو بكر الخطيب قال: أخبرنا أبو بكر عبد الله بن عليّ بن حَمُّوَيه قال: ١٥،٧٢

سمعتُ أبا بكر أحمد بن عبد الرحمن الشيرازي الحافظ أخبرنا بحديث الشيخ الأَذَني ومناظرته فقال: الشيخُ هو أبو عبد الرحمن عبد الله بن محمّد بن إسحاق الأَذْرَمِي.[1]

قلت: وقد روي أن الواثق رجع عن القول بخلق القرآن قبل موته.

أخبرنا أبو منصور القزاز قال: أخبرنا أبو بكر الخطيب قال: أَخبرني عبيد الله بن أبي الفتح قال: أخبرنا أحمد بن ١٦،٧٢
إبراهيم بن الحسن قال: حدثنا إبراهيم بن محمّد بن عَرَفَة قال:

حدثني حامد بن العباس عن رجل عن المهتدي بالله أنّ الواثق مات وقد تاب عن القول بخلق القرآن.

الباب الثالث والسبعون في ذكر قصّته مع المتوكِّل

١،٧٣ ولِي المتوكّل على الله بعد الواثق في يوم الأربعاء لستّ بقين من ذي الحجّة سنة اثنتين وثلاثين ومائتين وسِنّه ست وعشرون سنة يومئذ فأظهر الله عزّ وجلّ به السُنّة وكشف تلك الغمّة فشكره الناس على ما فعل.

أخبرنا أبو منصور عبد الرحمن بن محمّد قال: أخبرنا أحمد بن عليّ بن ثابت قال: أخبرنا محمّد بن عليّ بن إسحاق ٢،٧٣
الخازن قال: أخبرنا أحمد بن بشر بن سعيد الخِرَقي قال: حدثنا أبو روق الهِزّاني قال: سمعتُ محمّد بن خَلَف يقول:

كان إبراهيم بن محمّد التيّمي قاضي البصرة يقول:[2] الخلفاء ثلاثة، أبو بكر الصدّيق

---

١ ش: الأذني. ٢ الجملة ناقصة في د.

We cite al-Qazzāz, who cites Abū Bakr al-Khaṭīb, who cites Abū Bakr ʿAbd Allāh ibn ʿAlī ibn Ḥammuwayh as saying: 72.15

[Abū Bakr ʿAbd Allāh:] Abū Bakr Aḥmad ibn ʿAbd al-Raḥmān al-Shīrāzī l-Ḥāfiẓ reported the story of the elder from Adana and what happened at the debate. He added that the elder was Abū ʿAbd al-Raḥmān ʿAbd Allāh ibn Muḥammad ibn Isḥāq al-Adhramī.

[The author:] It is reported that before he died, al-Wāthiq disavowed the doctrine of the createdness of the Qurʾan.

We cite Abū Manṣūr al-Qazzāz, who cites Abū Bakr al-Khaṭīb, who cites ʿUbayd Allāh ibn Abī l-Fatḥ, who cites Aḥmad ibn Ibrāhīm ibn al-Ḥasan, who heard Ibrāhīm ibn Muḥammad ibn ʿArafah report that he heard Ḥāmid ibn al-ʿAbbās report, citing a man who had heard al-Muhtadī: 72.16

[Al-Muhtadī:] By the time he died, al-Wāthiq had renounced the doctrine of the createdness of the Qurʾan.[140]

Chapter 73: His Experience with al-Mutawakkil

On Wednesday, with six nights left in Dhu l-Hijjah 232 [August 11, 847], al-Mutawakkil ʿalā llāh, who was then twenty-six years of age, succeeded al-Wāthiq as caliph. Through him God brought about the triumph of the *sunnah* and put an end to the suffering caused by the Inquisition, much to the gratification of the people. 73.1

We cite Abū Manṣūr ʿAbd al-Raḥmān ibn Muḥammad, who cites Aḥmad ibn ʿAlī ibn Thābit, who cites Muḥammad ibn ʿAlī ibn Isḥāq al-Khāzin, who cites Aḥmad ibn Bishr ibn Saʿīd al-Khiraqī, who heard Abū Rawq al-Hizzānī report that he heard Muḥammad ibn Khalaf say that Muḥammad al-Taymī, judge in Basra, used to say: 73.2

[Al-Taymī:] There were three great caliphs: Abū Bakr, who fought the apostates until they surrendered; ʿUmar ibn ʿAbd al-ʿAzīz, who made good

قاتَل أهل الردّة حتى استجابوا له، وعمر بن عبد العزيز ردّ مظالم بني أميّة والمتوكّل محا البِدع وأظهر السُّنّة.

٣،٧٣ أخبرنا عبد الرحمن قال: أخبرنا أحمد بن عليّ قال: أخبرني الحسن بن شهاب العُكبَري في كتابه قال: حدثنا عبيد الله بن عبد الله بن أبي سُمرة[١] البُندار قال: حدثنا معاوية بن عثمان قال:

حدثنا عليّ بن حاتم حدثنا عليّ ابن الجهم قال: وجّه إِليّ أمير المؤمنين المتوكّل فأتيته فقال لي: يا عليّ رأيتُ النبيّ صلّى الله عليه وسلّم في المنام فقمت إليه فقال لي: تقوم إِليّ وأنت خليفة!

فقلت له: أبشر يا أمير المؤمنين أمّا قيامك إليه فقيامك بالسنّة وقد عدّك من الخلفاء.

فسُرّ بذلك.

٤،٧٣ أخبرنا عبد الرحمن قال: أخبرنا أحمد بن عليّ قال: حدثنا الأزهري قال: حدثنا عبيد الله بن محمد العُكبَري قال: حدثنا أبو الفضل محمّد بن أحمد بن سهل النَّيسابوري قال[٢]: حدثنا سعيد بن عثمان الخيّاط قال:

حدثني عليّ بن إسماعيل قال: رأيت جعفرًا المتوكّل بطرسوس في النوم وهو في النور جالس.

قلت: المتوكل؟

قال: المتوكل.

قلت: ما فعل الله بك؟

قال: غفر لي.

قلتُ: بماذا؟

قال: بقليل من السنّة أحييتُها.

قلت: أطفأ المتوكّل نيران البدعة وأوقد مصابيح السنّة.

---

١ مشكلة في ش. ٢ من (حدثنا عبيد الله) إلى هاهنا ناقص في ش.

the abuses of the Umayyads; and al-Mutawakkil, who abolished heretical innovations and publicly proclaimed the *sunnah.*

We cite ʿAbd al-Raḥmān, who cites Aḥmad ibn ʿAlī, who cites al-Ḥasan ibn Shihāb al-ʿUkbarī, who wrote that he heard ʿUbayd Allāh ibn ʿAbd Allāh ibn Abī Sumrah al-Bundār report that he heard Muʿāwiyah ibn ʿUthmān report that he heard ʿAlī ibn Ḥātim report that he heard ʿAlī ibn al-Jahm report: 73.3

[ʿAlī ibn al-Jahm:] The Caliph al-Mutawakkil sent for me and said, "ʿAlī, I dreamed I saw the Prophet. I rose to greet him, and he said, 'You're rising for me even though you're a caliph?'"

"It's a good dream, Commander of the Faithful," I said. "Your rising for him symbolizes your standing up for the *sunnah.* And he called you a caliph!"

Al-Mutawakkil was pleased.

We cite ʿAbd al-Raḥmān, who cites Aḥmad ibn ʿAlī, who heard al-Azharī report that he heard ʿUbayd Allāh ibn Muḥammad al-ʿUkbarī report that he heard Abū l-Faḍl Muḥammad ibn Aḥmad ibn Sahl al-Naysābūrī report that he heard Saʿīd ibn ʿUthmān al-Khayyāṭ report that he heard ʿAlī ibn Ismāʿīl report: 73.4

[ʿAlī ibn Ismāʿīl:] In Tarsus I dreamed that I saw al-Mutawakkil sitting in a place full of light.

"Al-Mutawakkil?" I asked.

"Yes," he said.

"What has God done with you?"

"He forgave me."

"Why?"

"Because of the little bit of *sunnah* I was able to restore."

[The author:] Al-Mutawakkil extinguished the fires of heretical innovation and lit the lamps of *sunnah.*

٥،٧٣ أخبرنا أبو منصور القزّاز قال: أخبرنا أبو بكر أحمد بن عليّ بن ثابت قال: أخبرني الأزهري قال: أخبرنا أحمد ابن إبراهيم قال:

حدثنا إبراهيم بن محمّد بن عَرَفة قال: في سنة أربع وثلاثين ومائتين أشخص المتوكّل الفُقهاء والمحدّثين وكان فيهم مُصْعَب الزُبيري وإسحاق بن أبي إسرائيل وإبراهيم بن عبد الله الهَرَوي وعبد الله وعثمان ابنا أبي شَيْبة فقُسّمت بينهم الجوائز وأُجريت عليهم الأرزاق وأمرهم المتوكّل أن يجلسوا للناس وأن يحدّثوا بالأحاديث التي فيها الردّ على المعتزِلة والجَهْمية وأن يحدّثوا بالأحاديث في الرّؤية فجلس عثمان بن أبي شيبة في مدينة المنصور ووُضع له منبر واجتمع عليه نحو من ثلاثين ألفاً من الناس وجلس أبو بكر بن أبي شيبة في مسجد الرُّصافة واجتمع عليه نحو من ثلاثين ألفاً.

٦،٧٣ أنبأنا أبو القاسم الحريري عن أبي إسحاق البرمكي قال: أخبرنا أبو الحسن بن الفُرات قال: أنشدنا القاضي أبو بكر بن كامل قال: أنشدني بكر الخليلي الزاهد قال: أنشدني أبو عبد الله غلام خليل قال:

أنشدني أبو جعفر الخَوّاص بعَبّادان بعد زوال المحنة:

ذَهَبتْ دَوْلَةُ أَصحابِ البِدَعْ وَوَهى حَبْلُهم ثُمّ[1] انقَطَعْ
وتَداعَى بانْصِرافٍ[2] جَمْعُهُمْ حِزبُ إبليسَ الّذي كانَ جَمَعْ
هَلْ لَهُمْ يا قَوْمُ في بِدعَتِهِمْ مِنْ فَقيهٍ أو إمامٍ يُتَّبَعْ
مِثْلَ سُفيانَ أخي الثَّوْرِ الّذي عَلَّمَ النّاسَ دَقيقاتِ الوَرَعْ
أو سُلَيْمانَ أخي التَّيْمِ الّذي تَرَكَ النَّوْمَ لِهَوْلِ المُطَّلَعْ
أو فَقيهِ الحَرَمَيْنِ مالِكٍ ذلِكَ البَحْرِ الغَزيرِ المُنْتَجَعْ
أو فَتَى الإسلامِ أعني أَحْمَدا ذاكَ لَوْ قارَعَهُ القُرّا قَرَعْ
لَمْ يَخَفْ سَوْطَهُمُ إذْ خَوَّفوا لا ولا سَيْفَهُمُ لَمّا لَمَعْ

١ ش: بانصرام. ٢ ش: حين.

We cite Abū Manṣūr al-Qazzāz, who cites Abū Bakr Aḥmad ibn ʿAlī ibn Thābit, who cites al-Azharī, who cites Aḥmad ibn Ibrāhīm, who heard Ibrāhīm ibn Muḥammad ibn ʿArafah report: 73.5

[Ibrāhīm ibn Muḥammad:] In 234 [848–49], al-Mutawakkil chose a number of jurists and Hadith-men, including Muṣʿab al-Zubayrī, Isḥāq ibn Abī Isrāʾīl, Ibrāhīm ibn ʿAbd Allāh al-Harawī, and ʿAbd Allāh and ʿUthmān, the sons of Ibn Abī Shaybah, to receive awards and regular stipends, and ordered them to hold public Hadith sessions to teach the reports that refute the Secessionists and the followers of Jahm, as well as the reports that describe seeing God. ʿUthmān ibn Abī Shaybah had a pulpit set up for him to lead a session inside the City of al-Manṣūr. Some thirty thousand people gathered to hear him. Abū Bakr ibn Abī Shaybah held his session in the mosque of al-Ruṣāfah, where another thirty thousand gathered to hear.[141]

We were informed by Abū l-Qāsim al-Ḥarīrī, citing Abū Isḥāq al-Barmakī, who cites Abū l-Ḥasan ibn al-Furāt, who heard Judge Abū Bakr ibn Kāmil recite a verse which he heard from the renunciant Bakr al-Khalīlī, who heard it from Abū ʿAbd Allāh Ghulām Khalīl: 73.6

[Ghulām Khalīl:] In ʿAbbādān, after the end of the Inquistion, Abū Jaʿfar al-Khawwāṣ recited for me:

The heretics' rope has frayed and snapped
  Their turn in power come and gone;
And gone with them is the Devil's horde
  That gathered round to cheer them on.
Tell me, friends: In all that lot
  Was there an exemplar? Even one?
One like Sufyān of Thawr, who taught us all
  What to accept and what to shun?
Or Sulaymān of Taym, who never slept,
  For fear of God's all-seeing gaze?
Or like Mālik, that sea, that pasture-ground
  Where the jurists come to graze?
Or Ibn Ḥanbal, Islam's brave young man,
  As stout a heart as God e'er made;
Who, though ringed about with whip and sword,
  Faced their clamor unafraid.[142]

فصــل

٧،٧٣ ثم بعث المتوكّل بعد مضيّ خمس سنين من ولايته يستزير[١] أحمد بن حنبل.[٢]

فأخبرنا محمّد بن أبي منصور قال: أخبرنا عبد القادر بن محمّد بن يوسف[٣] قال: أخبرنا إبراهيم بن عمر البرمكي قال: أخبرنا عليّ بن عبد العزيز قال: أخبرنا عبد الرحمن بن أبي حاتم قال:

حدثنا صالح بن أحمد بن حنبل قال: وجّه المتوكّل إلى إسحاق بن إبراهيم يأمره بحمل أبي إليه فوجّه إسحاق إلى أبي فقال له: إنّ أمير المؤمنين كتب إليّ يأمرني بإشخاصك إليه فتأهّبْ لذلك.

٨،٧٣ قال أبي: وقال لي: اجعلني في حِلّ من حضوري ضربك.

قلتُ: قد جعلت كلّ من حضر في حلّ.

قال أبي: وقال أسألك عن القرآن مسألةَ مسترشدٍ لا مسألة امتحان وليكن ذلك عندك مَستوراً، ما تقول في القرآن؟

فقلت: القرآن كلام الله غير مخلوق.

قال لي: من أين قلت غير مخلوق؟

فقلت: قال الله عز وجل: ﴿أَلا لَهُ الخَلْقُ والأَمْرُ﴾ ففرّق بين الخلق والأمر.

فقال إسحاق: الأمر مخلوق.

فقلت: يا سبحان الله أمخلوق يخلق مخلوقاً؟

فقال: وعمّن تحكي أنه ليس بمخلوق؟

فقلت: جعفر بن محمّد قال: ليس بخالق ولا مخلوق.

قال: فسكت.

فلمّا كان في الليلة الثانية وجّه إليّ فقال: ما تقول في الخُروج؟

فقلت: ذاك إليكم.

---

١ د: بتسيير. ٢ ش: بتسيُّر[هكذا] أحمد بن حنبل إليه. ٣ بن يوسف: ليس في د.

Addendum

Five months into his reign, al-Mutawakkil sent for Aḥmad ibn Ḥanbal. 73.7

We cite Muḥammad ibn Abī Manṣūr, who cites ʿAbd al-Qādir ibn Muḥammad ibn Yūsuf, who cites Ibrāhīm ibn ʿUmar al-Barmakī, who cites ʿAlī ibn ʿAbd al-ʿAzīz, who cites ʿAbd al-Raḥmān ibn Abī Ḥātim, who heard Aḥmad ibn Ḥanbal's son Ṣāliḥ report:

[Ṣāliḥ:] Al-Mutawakkil ordered Isḥāq ibn Ibrāhīm to send my father to him. So Isḥāq summoned my father and said: "The Commander of the Faithful requires your presence. Prepare yourself for a journey!"

My father said: 73.8

Isḥāq also asked me to forgive him for being present when I was flogged. I told him that I had already forgiven everyone who was there. Then he said he wanted to ask me about the Qur'an—not to test me, but because he genuinely wanted to know.

"Just between us, then: What do you say about the Qur'an?"

"It's the speech of God," I told him, "uncreated."

"Why uncreated?"

"God has said, «His is the creation, His the command,»[143] which shows that what He creates is not the same as what He commands."

"But His command is created," said Isḥāq.

"God help us!" I said. "Can one created thing create another?"

"But what authority tells you it isn't created?"

"Jaʿfar ibn Muḥammad says, 'It is neither a creator nor a created thing.'"

He fell silent.

The next night, he sent for me and asked, "How do you feel about going?"

"That's up to you."

وجاء إلى أبي جماعة من الأنصار والهاشميين عندما وجّه المتوكّل في حملة ٩،٧٣
فقالوا: تُكلّمه؟

فقال: قد نويت أن أكلّمه في أهله وفي الأنصار والمهاجرين وما فيه مصلحة للمسلمين.

وكان حمله إلى المتوكل في سنة سبع وثلاثين ومائتين.

فأُخرج حتى إذا صرنا في موضع يقال له بُصْرَى بات أبي في المسجد ونحن معه فلمّا كان في جوف الليل جاء النَّيْسابوري فقال: يقول لك ارجع!

فقلت له: يا أبتِ أرجو أن يكون خيرة.

فقال: لم أزل أدعو الله عزّ وجلّ.

سياق ما حدث بعد ذلك من تحريض الأعداء على أحمد أنه قد أخفى بعض العلويّين عنده

١٠،٧٣ لمّا أُخرج أحمد رضي الله عنه إلى المتوكّل رُدّ من بعض الطريق ثم توفّي إسحاق بن إبراهيم وولي مكانه ابنه عبد الله بن إسحاق فرفع الأعداء إلى المتوكّل أنّ عند أحمد علويّاً.

١١،٧٣ أخبرنا المحمّدان: ابن ناصر وابن عبد الباقي قالا: أخبرنا حمد بن أحمد قال: حدثنا أحمد بن عبد الله قال: حدثنا محمّد بن جعفر والحسين بن محمّد وعلي بن أحمد قالوا: حدثنا محمّد بن إسماعيل بن أحمد قال:

حدثنا صالح بن أحمد قال: لمّا ولي عبد الله بن إسحاق كتب المتوكّل إليه أنْ وجِّهْ إلى أحمد بن حنبل أنّ عندك طِلْبَة أمير المؤمنين. فوجّه بحاجبه مظفَّر وحضر معه صاحب البريد - وكان يُعرف بابن الكلبي - وكان قد كتب إليه أيضاً، فقال له مظفر: يقول لك الأمير: قد كتب إِليّ أمير المؤمنين أن عندك طِلْبَته. وقال له ابن الكلبي مثل ذلك وكان قد نام الناس.

[Ṣāliḥ continued:] 73.9

When al-Mutawakkil sent for my father, a number of Helpers and Hāshimī dignitaries came to see him and asked whether he would really speak to him.

"I had made up my mind to speak to him," said my father, "about his family, about the Helpers and Emigrants, and about the best interests of the Muslims."

It was in 237 [851–52] that my father was sent to al-Mutawakkil. He was taken out of Baghdad and made it as far as a place called Buṣrā, where we spent the night in a mosque. In the middle of the night, al-Naysābūrī arrived and said, "He says, 'Go back!'"

"I hope this is for the best," I said.

"I've been praying all this time," he said.

An Account of What Happened When Aḥmad's Enemies Denounced Him to the Authorities, Claiming That He Was Harboring a Partisan of ʿAlī

After Aḥmad was taken to see al-Mutawakkil and then sent back again, Isḥāq 73.10
ibn Ibrāhīm died and was succeeded by his son, ʿAbd Allāh ibn Isḥāq. Then Aḥmad's enemies denounced him to al-Mutawakkil, claiming that he was harboring a partisan of ʿAlī.[144]

We cite the two Muḥammads, Ibn Nāṣir and Ibn ʿAbd al-Bāqī, who cite Ḥamd ibn Aḥmad, 73.11
who heard Aḥmad ibn ʿAbd Allāh report that he heard Muḥammad ibn Jaʿfar, al-Ḥusayn ibn Muḥammad, and ʿAlī ibn Aḥmad report that they heard Muḥammad ibn Ismāʿīl ibn Aḥmad report that he heard Aḥmad's son Ṣāliḥ report:

[Ṣāliḥ:] The Caliph al-Mutawakkil sent a message to ʿAbd Allāh ibn Isḥāq, the new governor in Baghdad, telling him to warn Aḥmad ibn Ḥanbal against hiding anything from the caliph. The caliph then dispatched his chamberlain, Muẓaffar, as well as the chief of the courier service, a man named Ibn al-Kalbī, to whom he had sent the same message. Late at night, after most people had gone to bed, al-Muẓaffar and Ibn al-Kalbī confronted Aḥmad and passed on the message that ʿAbd Allāh ibn Isḥāq had conveyed to them: that is, that he should be wary of hiding anything from the caliph.

أخبرنا محمّد بن ناصر قال: أخبرنا عبد القادر بن محمّد قال: أخبرنا إبراهيم بن عمر قال: أخبرنا عليّ بن عبد العزيز ١٢،٧٣
قال: أخبرنا عبد الرحمن بن أبي حاتم قال:

حدثنا صالح بن أحمد بن حنبل قال: دقّوا الباب وأبي في إزار ففتح فلمّا قُرئ عليه الكتاب، وكأنّهم أَوْمَؤوا إلى أنّ عنده عَلويّاً، قال لهم: ما أعرف من هذا شيئاً وإني لأرى طاعته في العُسر واليُسر والمَنْشَط والمَكْرَه والأَثَرة وإنّي أتأسّف على تخلّفي عن الصلاة في جماعة وعن حضور الجمعة ودعوة المسلمين.

وقد كان إسحاق وجّه إليه قبل موته: الزم بيتك ولا تخرج إلى جمعة ولا جماعة وإلا نزل بك ما نزل بك في أيّام أبي إسحاق.

ثم قال له ابن الكلبي: قد أمرني أمير المؤمنين أن أُحلّفك أن ما عندك طلبته، فتحَلَّفْ!

قال: إن استحلفتموني حلفتُ.

فأحلفه بالله وبالطلاق أنّ ما عندك[1] طلبة أمير المؤمنين.

ثمّ قال له: أريد أن أفتّش منزلك، وكنت حاضراً، فقال: ومنزل ابنك.

فقام مُظفر وابن الكلبي وامرأتان معهما فدخلا ففتّشا البيت ثم فتّش[2] الامرأتان النساء ثم دخلوا منزلي ففتّشوه ودلّوا شمعة في البئر فنظروا ووجّهوا النِّسوة ففتّشوا الحرم ثم خرجوا.

فلمّا كان بعد يومين وردَ كتاب عليّ بن الجهم: إن أمير المؤمنين قد صحّ عنده براءتك ممّا قُرفت به وقد كان أهل البدع مدّوا أعينهم فالحمد لله الذي لم يُشمتهم بك، قد وجه إليك أمير المؤمنين يأمرك بالخروج فالله الله أن تستعفي أو تردّ المال.[3]

---

١ ش: عنده. ٢ هـ ،د: هكذا، وفي ش: فتشا. ٣ ورد هذا الخبر بعد ١٤،٧٣ في هـ ، ثم جاء بعده: (أخبرنا إسماعيل ابن أحمد ومحمّد بن عبد الباقي قالا: أخبرنا حمد بن أحمد قال: أخبرنا أبو نُعَيم الحافظ قال: حدثنا أبو بكر بن مالك قال: حدثنا أبو جعفر بن ذَريح العُكبَري قال: طلبتُ أحمد بن حنبل في سَنة ست وثلاثين ومئتين لأسأله عن مسألة) وهو مطلع ٣١،٧٣ إلا أن الخبر جاء بأكمله بعد ١١،٧٣.

We cite Muḥammad ibn Nāṣir, who cites ʿAbd al-Qādir ibn Muḥammad, who cites Ibrāhīm ibn ʿUmar, who cites ʿAlī ibn ʿAbd al-ʿAzīz, who cites ʿAbd al-Raḥmān ibn Abī Ḥātim, who heard Aḥmad ibn Ḥanbal's son Ṣāliḥ report: **73.12**

[Ṣāliḥ:] There was a knock, and my father, who was dressed only in his breechclout, answered the door. The callers read aloud a message from the caliph suggesting that he was harboring a partisan of ʿAlī. He said, "I don't know what he means. I believe that obedience is due him in good times and bad, willingly or not, even if he should favor others over me. I regret not being able to pray with my fellow Muslims, attend Friday prayers, or address the community."[145]

Before he died, Isḥāq had told my father to remain at home and not to come out for Fridays or other group prayers, warning him that if he did, he would suffer what he had suffered under al-Muʿtaṣim.

Ibn al-Kalbī then said: "The Commander of the Faithful has ordered me to ask you to swear that you are not concealing anyone."

"If you want me to swear," he said, "I will."

They made him swear by God, and to swear that he would divorce his wife if he was not telling the truth.

Then Ibn al-Kalbī said, "I want to search your house and your son's"—meaning mine—"as well."

Muẓaffar and Ibn al-Kalbī searched the house while two women who had come with them searched the women. Then they did the same with my house. They even lowered a candle into the well and looked down it. They also sent women into the women's quarters. Finally they left.

Two days later came a letter from ʿAlī ibn al-Jahm saying: "The Commander of the Faithful is reassured of your innocence of the slanderous accusations made against you and praises God, who did not allow your enemies to succeed in their plan. He herewith asks you to come to see him, and calls upon you in the name of God not to plead for exemption or to return the money he sends you."[146]

١٣،٧٣ أخبرنا إسماعيل بن أحمد ومحمّد بن عبد الباقي قالا: أخبرنا حمد بن أحمد قال: أخبرنا أبو نُعَيم الحافظ قال: حدثنا أبو بكر بن مالك قال:

حدثنا أبو جعفر بن ذَرِيح العُكبَري قال: طلبتُ أحمد بن حنبل في سَنة ست وثلاثين ومائتين لأسأله عن مسألة فسألت عنه فقالوا: خرج يصلّي. فجلست حتى جاء فسلّمت عليه فردّ عليّ السلام فدخل الزقاق وأنا أماشيه فلمّا بلغنا آخر الدرب إذا باب يفرج فدفعه وصار خلفه وقال: اذهب عافاك الله.

فثنيت عليه فقال: اذهب عافاك الله!

فخرج رجل فسألته عن تخلّفه عن كلامي فقال: ادُّعي عليه عند السلطان أنّ عنده علوياً فجاء محمّد بن نصر فأحاط بالمحلّة ففُتّشت فلم يوجد فيها شيء ممّا ذُكر فأجم عن كلام العامّة.

١٤،٧٣ أخبرنا ابن ناصر قال: أخبرنا أبو الحسين بن عبد الجبّار قال: أخبرنا أبو بكر محمّد بن عليّ الخيّاط قال: أخبرنا محمّد ابن أبي الفوارس قال: أخبرنا أحمد بن جعفر بن سَلْم[1] قال: حدثنا أحمد بن محمّد بن عبد الخالق قال:

حدثنا أبو بكر المرُّوذي قال: سمعت أبا عبد الله يقول: قد جاءني أبو عليّ بن يحيى[2] ابن خاقان فقال لي: إن كتاباً جاءه فيه إنّ أمير المؤمنين يُقرِئك السلام ويقول لك لو سَلِم أحد من الناس سلمتَ أنت، ها هنا رجل قد رفع عليك وهو في أيدينا محبوس رفع عليك أنّ علوياً قد توجّه من قِبَل خُراسان وقد بعثتَ برجل من أصحابك يتلقّاه وهو ذا محبوس، فإن شئتَ ضربتُه وإن شئتَ حبستُه وإن شئتَ بعثتُ به إليك.

قال: فقلت له: ما أعرف ممّا قال شيئاً، أرى أن يطلقوه ولا يعرضوا[3] له.

فقلت لأبي عبد الله: سفك الله دمه، قد أشاط بدمائكم!

فقال: ما أراد إلا استئصالنا ولكن قلتُ: لعلّ له والدة أو أخوات أو بنات، أرى أن يخلوا سبيله ولا يعرضوا[4] له.

---

١ ش: سالم. ٢ تركي: أبو عليّ يحيى. ٣ ش: تطلقوا ولا تعرضوا. ٤ ش: تخلوا سبيله ولا تعرضوا.

We cite Ismāʿīl ibn Aḥmad and Muḥammad ibn ʿAbd al-Bāqī, who cite Ḥamd ibn Aḥmad, who cites Abū Nuʿaym al-Ḥāfiẓ, who heard Abū Bakr ibn Mālik report that he heard Abū Jaʿfar ibn Dharīḥ al-ʿUkbarī report: 73.13

[Al-ʿUkbarī:] In 236 [850–51], I went to look for Aḥmad ibn Ḥanbal to ask him about a problem. I asked where to find him and was told that he had gone out to pray, so I sat down and waited. Upon his return, I greeted him and he returned my greeting. Then he headed down an alley and I walked along beside him. At the end of the alley was a door. As he pushed it open and went through, he said, "Leave now, with God's blessing!"

I asked my question again, but again he asked me to go. Then another man came out. I asked him why Ibn Ḥanbal was dodging me. He said, "Someone went to the authorities and accused him of harboring a partisan of ʿAlī. So Muḥammad ibn Naṣr came and searched the whole neighborhood without finding anyone. Now Aḥmad won't talk to people who aren't scholars."

We cite Ibn Nāṣir, who cites Abū l-Ḥusayn ibn ʿAbd al-Jabbār, who cites Abū Bakr Muḥammad ibn ʿAlī l-Khayyāṭ, who cites Muḥammad ibn Abī l-Fawāris, who cites Aḥmad ibn Jaʿfar ibn Salm, who heard Aḥmad ibn Muḥammad ibn ʿAbd al-Khāliq report that he heard Abū Bakr al-Marrūdhī report: 73.14

[Al-Marrūdhī:] I heard Aḥmad ibn Ḥanbal say: "I had a visit from Abū ʿAlī ibn Yaḥyā[147] ibn Khāqān, who told me that he had received a letter from the Commander of the Faithful sending me his regards and then saying: 'If anyone should remain safe from harm, it is you. I must nevertheless inform you that a man held here as our prisoner claims that he is an associate of yours and that you sent him to receive a partisan of ʿAlī who recently arrived from Khurasan. If you wish, I can flog this associate of yours, lock him up, or send him to you.'"

Aḥmad said, "I told Abū ʿAlī, 'I don't know what this supposed associate of mine is talking about, so my reply to the letter is: let the man go unharmed!'"

I said, "But why should you care if something happens to him? He's threatened your life!"

"What he's after," said Aḥmad, "is to rip us out, root and branch. But he must have someone—a mother, or brothers, or daughters—who would care if something happens to him. That's why I asked them to let him go."

أخبرنا عبد الملك الكَرُوخي قال: أخبرنا عبد الله بن محمّد الأنصاري قال: أخبرنا أبو يعقوب قال: أخبرنا أبو بكر ١٥،٧٣
محمّد بن عبد الله اللآل[1] قال: أخبرنا محمّد بن إبراهيم الصرّام قال:

أخبرنا إبراهيم بن إسحاق قال: إنّ المتوكّل أخذ العلوي الذي سعى بأبي عبد الله إلى السلطان وأرسله إلى أبي عبد الله ليقول فيه مقالة للسلطان فعفا عنه وقال: لعلّه يكون له صبيان يحزنهم قتله.

سياق قصة خروجه إلى العسكر بعد انقضاء أمر هذه التهمة

أخبرنا محمّد بن أبي منصور قال: أخبرنا عبد القادر بن محمّد قال: أخبرنا إبراهيم بن عمر قال: أخبرنا عليّ بن عبد ١٦،٧٣
العزيز قال: أخبرنا عبد الرحمن بن أبي حاتم قال:

حدثنا صالح بن أحمد بن حنبل قال: ورد كتاب عليّ بن الجَهْم: إنّ أمير المؤمنين قد وجّه إليك يعقوب المعروف بقَوْصَرّة ومعه جائزة ويأمرك بالخروج فاللهَ اللهَ أن تستعفي أو تردّ المال فيتّسع القول لمن يبغضك.

فلمّا كان الغد ورد يعقوب فدخل إليه فقال: يا أبا عبد الله أمير المؤمنين يقرأ عليك السلام ويقول: قد صحّ عندنا نقاء ساحتك وقد أحببتُ أن آنس بقربك وأن أتبرّك بدعائك وقد وجّهتُ إليك عشرة آلاف درهم معونةً على سفرك.

وأخرج بَدْرة فيها صُرّة نحو من مئتي دينار والباقي دراهم صحاح فلم ينظر إليها ثم شدّها يعقوب وقال له: أعود غداً حتى أنظر ما تعزم عليه، وقال له: يا أبا عبد الله الحمد لله الذي لم يُشمت بك أهل البدع. وانصرف.

فجئتُ بإجّانة خضراء فكببتُها على البدرة.

فلمّا كان عند المغرب قال: يا صالح خذ هذا صيِّره عندك!

فصيّرتها عند رأسي فوق البيت.

فلمّا كان سحراً[2] إذا ينادي: يا صالح!

فقمت فصعدت إليه فقال: ما نمت ليلتي هذه.

---

١ د: الدلال. ٢ هـ: سحر

We cite ʿAbd al-Malik al-Karūkhī, who cites ʿAbd Allāh ibn Muḥammad al-Anṣārī, who cites Abū Yaʿqūb, who cites Abū Bakr Muḥammad ibn ʿAbd Allāh al-Laʾʾāl, who cites Muḥammad ibn Ibrāhīm al-Ṣarrām, who cites Ibrāhīm ibn Isḥāq, who reports: 73.15

[Ibrāhīm ibn Isḥāq:] Al-Mutawakkil took the partisan of ʿAlī who denounced Aḥmad to the authorities and sent him to Aḥmad to repeat the accusation. But Aḥmad forgave him, saying, "He might have boys who would mourn if he were killed."

His Journey to Samarra after the Accusation Had Been Cleared Up

We cite Muḥammad ibn Abī Manṣūr, who cites ʿAbd al-Qādir ibn Muḥammad, who cites Ibrāhīm ibn ʿUmar, who cites ʿAlī ibn ʿAbd al-ʿAzīz, who cites ʿAbd al-Raḥmān ibn Abī Ḥātim, who heard Aḥmad ibn Ḥanbal's son Ṣāliḥ report: 73.16

[Ṣāliḥ:] My father received a letter from ʿAlī ibn al-Jahm saying: "The Commander of the Faithful herewith sends you Yaʿqūb, called Qawṣarrah, with a gift for you, and orders you to come to him. He calls upon you in the name of God not to plead for exemption or to return the money he has sent you, for doing so will strengthen the hand of those working against you."

The next day, Yaʿqūb returned and went in to see him. "Abū ʿAbd Allāh," he said, "the Commander of the Faithful conveys his greetings to you and says: 'I am now convinced of your innocence. Desiring, as I do, the comfort of your presence and the blessing of your prayers, I herewith send to you ten thousand dirhams to cover the expenses of your journey.'"

Yaʿqūb then brought out a bag with a knotted pouch containing about two hundred dinars and the rest filled with untrimmed dirhams. My father didn't even look at it. Yaʿqūb tied it back up, saying, "I'll be back tomorrow to find out what you've decided to do." He added, "Praise God, who prevented the innovators from rejoicing in your downfall."

Then he left.

I brought in a green washtub,[148] turned it over, and dropped it on top of the bag. When it was time for the evening prayer, my father said, "Ṣāliḥ, take this and put it in your house."

فقلت: لِمَ يا أبة؟

فجعل يبكي وقال: سلمتُ من هؤلاء حتّى إذا كان في آخر عمري بُليتُ بهم، قد عزمتُ على أن أُفرّق هذا الشيء إذا أصبحتُ.

فقلت: ذلك إليك.

فلمّا أصبح جاءه الحسن البزّاز والمشايخ فقال: جئني يا صالح بميزان! فقال: وجّهوا إلى أبناء المهاجرين والأنصار.

ثم قال: وجِّه إلى فلان حتّى يُفرّق في ناحيته، وإلى فلان.

فلم يزل حتى فرّقها كلّها ونفضتُ الكيس ونحن في حالة الله تعالى بها عليم.

فجاء بُنيّ لي فقال: أعطني يا أبة درهمًا!

فنظر إليّ فأخرجتُ قطعة أعطيته.

وكتب صاحب البريد أنه قد تصدّق بالدراهم من يومه حتّى تصدّق بالكيس.

قال عليّ بن الجهم: ١٧،٧٣

فقلتُ له: يا أمير المؤمنين قد علم الناس أنّه قد قبِل منك،[١] وما يصنع أحمد بالمال، وإنما قوته رغيف؟

قال: فقال لي: صدقتَ يا علي.

قال صالح: ١٨،٧٣

ثم أخرجنا ليلاً معنا حرّاس معهم النفّاطات فلمّا أضاء الفجر قال لي: يا صالح أمعك دراهم؟ قلت: نعم. قال: أعطهم فأعطيتهم درهمًا درهمًا.

فلمّا صرنا إلى الحنّاطين قال يعقوب: قفوا ها هنا.

ثم وجّه إلى المتوكّل يُعلمه بمصيرنا فدخلنا العسكر وأبي منكّس الرأس.

ثم جاء وصيف يريد الدار، فلمّا نظر إلى الناس وجمعهم قال: ما هؤلاء؟

قالوا: هذا أحمد بن حنبل.

فوجّه إليه بعد ما جاز بيحيى بن هَرْثَمة فقال: يقرئك الأمير السلام ويقول الحمدُ

---

١ ش: انه زهد في الدنيا من قبلك.

So I put it on the roof next to where I slept. Early the next morning I heard him calling me so I got up and went over. He told me he hadn't slept. When I asked him why not, he began weeping and said, "Here I thought I'd escaped them, but now they've come to torment me at the end of my life!" He went on, "I've decided to give that thing away as soon as it's morning."

"That's up to you," I said.

In the morning al-Ḥasan al-Bazzāz and the elders came to see him. "Ṣāliḥ," he told me, "bring me a scale." Then he added, "Send for the descendants of the Emigrants and Helpers. And send for So-and-So, and So-and-So, and tell them to distribute the money in their neighborhoods."

So it went, until he had given all the money away and emptied the bag. This was at a time when we were living in a state of deprivation best known to God. At one point one of my little boys came over, looked at me, and said, "Daddy, give me a dirham!" So I got out a coin and gave it to him.

The chief courier reported that my father had given the money away that very day. He even gave away the bag.

'Alī ibn al-Jahm said: **73.17**

I told the caliph that Aḥmad had given the money away. People did see him accept the gift, but they also knew that he had no use for it: "He lives on a loaf of flatbread!"

The caliph said, "You're right, 'Alī."

Sāliḥ said: **73.18**

After my father gave away the money, they escorted us outside. It was nighttime, and there were guardsmen with us carrying torches. When it grew light out, my father asked me if I had any dirhams. I told him I did, and he said, "Give them something." So I gave each guardsman a dirham.[149]

When we reached the grain merchants' district, Ya'qūb said, "Stop here." Then he sent word to al-Mutawakkil that we had arrived. My father kept his eyes on the ground as we entered Samarra.

At that moment Waṣīf came past, heading for the palace. Seeing the mass of people gathered there, he asked, "What's all this?"

"Aḥmad ibn Ḥanbal's here," he was told.

لله الذي لم يشمت بك أهل البدع، قد علمتَ ما كان حال ابن أبي دؤاد فينبغي أن تكلّم بما يحبّ الله عزّ وجلّ.

١٩،٧٣ ثمّ أُنزل دار إيتاخ فجاء عليّ بن الجهم فقال: قد أمر لكم أمير المؤمنين بعشرة آلاف مكانَ التي فرّقها وأمر أن لا يعلم بذلك فيغتمّ.

ثم جاءه أحمد بن مُعاوية فقال: إن أمير المؤمنين يُكثر ذكرك ويشتهي قربك وتُقيم ها هنا تحدّث.

فقال: أنا ضعيف.

ثمّ وضع أصبعه على بعض أسنانه فقال: إنّ بعض أسناني يتحرك وما أخبرت بذلك ولدي.

ثم وجّه إليه: ما تقول في بَهيمتَين انتطحتا فعقرت إحداهما الأخرى فسقطت فذُبحت؟

فقال: إن كان طرف بعينه ومصع بذنبه وسال دمه يؤكل.

٢٠،٧٣ ثمّ صار إليه يحيى بن خاقان فقال: يا أبا عبد الله قد أمرني أمير المؤمنين أن أصير إليك لتركب إلى أبي عبد الله ولده وأمرني أن أقطع لك سوادًا وطَيلَسانًا وقَلَنْسُوَةً فأيّ قلنسوة تلبس[١]؟

فقلت: ما رأيته لبس قلنسوة قطّ.

وقال: إنّ أمير المؤمنين قد أمر أن تصير لك مرتبة في أعلى المراتب ويصير أبو عبد الله في حجرك.

ثمّ قال لي: قد أمر أمير المؤمنين أن يُجرَى عليكم وعلى قراباته أربعة آلاف درهم.

ثمّ عاد يحيى من الغد فقال: يا أبا عبد الله تركب؟

قال: ذاك إليك.

فقال: استخِرِ الله عزّ وجلّ.

فلبس إزاره وخُفّيه وقد كان خفّه قد أتى عليه نحو من خمس عشرة سنة مرقوعًا

١ ش: وطيلسانا وقلنسوة تلبس.

After my father had been checked through by Yaḥyā ibn Harthamah,[150] Waṣīf sent him a message saying, "The Commander of the Faithful conveys his salutations and expresses his gratitude to God for preventing the heretics from rejoicing in your downfall. You are aware of where Ibn Abī Du'ād stood, and must therefore understand how important it is for you to state a position satisfactory to God."[151]

We were given lodgings in Ītākh's palace. My father's first visitor was ʿAlī ibn al-Jahm, who told me that the Commander of the Faithful had sent ten thousand dirhams to replace the money my father had given away. The caliph had also forbidden anyone to tell my father about the gift, which would only upset him. 73.19

The next visitor was Aḥmad ibn Muʿāwiyah, who told my father, "The Commander of the Faithful is always talking about you and wishing you were here close to him. He wants you to live here and teach Hadith."

"I'm not well enough," my father said. He laid his finger on his teeth. "I haven't told my sons," he said, "but some of my teeth are loose."

Later he was sent a question: "Say two beasts fight. If one is gored by the other, falls to the ground, and is slaughtered, may it be eaten?"

He replied: "If it can blink and move its tail, and if it is bleeding, then yes."

The next visitor was Yaḥyā ibn Khāqān, who said, "The Commander of the Faithful has ordered me to escort you to see his son al-Muʿtazz. I need to have a suit, a cowl, and a cap made for you in black, so you'll have to tell me what kind of cap you wear." I said I had never seen him wear a cap. "The Commander of the Faithful is going to grant you one of the higher ranks and place al-Muʿtazz in your care." Then he turned to me. "He's also ordered a stipend of four thousand dirhams for you and the other members of the family." 73.20

The next day Yaḥyā came to see us again. He asked my father, "Will you ride with us?"

"That's up to you," he answered.

"Put it in God's hands, then, and come along."

My father put on his breechclout and his shoes. The shoes were about fifteen years old and had been repaired many times over. Yaḥyā signaled that he should put on a cap.

برقاع عدّة فأشار يحيى إلى أن يلبس قلنسوّة. فقلت: ما له قلنسوّة ولا رأيته يلبس قلنسوة.

فقال: كيف يدخل حاسراً؟

وطلبنا له دابّة يركبها فقال يحيى: مُصَلِّي.

فجلس على التراب وقال: ﴿مِنۡهَا خَلَقۡنَٰكُمۡ وَفِيهَا نُعِيدُكُمۡ﴾.

ثمّ ركب بغل بعض التجار.

فمضينا معه حتّى إذا دخل دار أبي عبد الله أُجلس في بيت في الدّهليز ثم جاء يحيى فأخذ بيده حتّى أدخله ورُفع لنا الستر ونحن ننظره فقعد[١] فقال له: يا أبا عبد الله إنّ أمير المؤمنين جاء بك ليتبرّك بقربك ويصيِّر أبا عبد الله في حجرك.

قال صالح: فأخبرني بعض الخدم أن المتوكّل كان قاعداً وراء ستر فلمّا دخل أبي الدار قال لأمّه: يا أماه قد أنارت الدار.

ثم جاء خادم بمنديل فأخذ يحيى المنديل وأخرج مبطّنة فيها قميص فأدخل يده في جيب القميص والمبطّنة ثمّ أخذ بيده فأقامه حتّى أدخل جيب القميص والمبطّنة في رأسه ثم أدخل يده فأخرج يده اليمنى وكذلك اليسرى وهو لا يحرّك يده. ثمّ أخذ قلنسوّة فوضعها على رأسه وألبسه طيلساناً ولم يجيئوا بخفّ فبقي الخف عليه.

ثم انصرف فلمّا صار إلى الدار نزع الثياب عنه ثم جعل يبكي ثمّ قال: سلمتُ من هؤلاء منذ ستّين سنة حتّى إذا كان في آخر عمري بُليت بهم! ما أحسبني سلمتُ من دخولي على هذا الغلام فكيف بمن يجب عليّ نصحه من وقت أن تقع عيني عليه إلى أن أخرج من عنده؟

ثم قال: يا صالح وجّه هذه الثياب إلى بغداد تُباع ويُتصدّق بثمنها ولا يشتري منكم أحد شيئاً.

فوجهت بها فبيعت وفرّق ثمنها.

---

١ ليس في د.

"He doesn't have one," I said. "I've never seen him wear one."

"He can't go in bareheaded!"

We asked for a mount. Yaḥyā said, "Make it a *muṣallī*."[152]

My father sat down on the ground, reciting, «From the earth We have created you and We will return you thereto.»[153] Then he mounted a mule belonging to a merchant. We joined him as he rode to the heir apparent's palace, where he was given a seat in a room adjoining the entryway. Yaḥyā came to take his arm and escort him inside. There was a partition there, but it was removed so we could see him. My father sat down and Yaḥyā said, "The Commander of the Faithful has brought you here to derive blessing from your presence and to place his son in your care."

One of the staff later told us that al-Mutawakkil had been sitting behind a screen. When my father came in, the caliph had said to his mother, "Look, Mother! He lights up the whole room."[154]

Then a servant appeared carrying a bundle. Yaḥyā took it and pulled out a lined outer garment with a shirt inside it. He put my father's arm into one sleeve, then took him by the arm and lifted him up to get the neck-hole of the garment over his head. After that he reached into the garment and pulled my father's right hand, then his left, out through the sleeves, with my father doing nothing to help him. Finally Yaḥyā took a cap and put it on my father's head and draped a cowl over his shoulders. The one thing they didn't bring was a pair of shoes, so he was left wearing his old ones.

As soon as my father was dismissed and we returned to the place where we were staying, he tore the clothes off, then burst into tears. "I kept myself well away from these people for sixty years, but now at the end of my life they've come to torment me! I don't think I can get out of attending that boy, not to mention all the people I'll have to advise from the moment I lay eyes on them to the moment I leave." Then he said: "Ṣāliḥ, send these clothes to Baghdad, have them sold, and give the money away in alms. I don't want any of you buying anything with it."

I sent the clothes back to be sold, and he gave the money away.

أخبرنا محمّد بن أبي منصور قال: أنبأنا ابن البُسْري عن أبي عبد الله ابن بَطّة قال: أخبرنا الآجُرّي قال: أخبرنا ٢١،٧٣
أبو نصر بن كُردي قال: حدثنا المرُّوذي قال:

سمعت زُهير بن محمّد يقول: أنا أول من تلقّى أبا عبد الله قبل أن يخرج من الحرّاقة. قال: فخرج وعليه الكساء الذي خُلع عليه. قال: فسقط فجعل يجرّه وما سوّاه عليه.

أخبرنا ابن ناصر قال: أخبرنا عبد القادر بن يوسف قال: أخبرنا أبو إسحاق البرمكي قال: أخبرنا ابن مَرْدَك ٢٢،٧٣
قال: حدثنا ابن أبي حاتم قال:

حدثنا صالح بن أحمد قال: ثم أخبرناه أنّ الدار التي هو فيها لإيتاخ[١] فقال: اكتب رُقعة إلى محمّد بن الجرّاح استعفِ لي من هذه الدار.

فكتبنا رقعة فأمر المتوكّل أن يُعفَى منها ووجّه إلى قوم ليخرجوا عن منازلهم فسأل أن يُعفَى من ذلك.

فاكتُريت لنا دار بمئتي درهم فصار إليها وأُجري لنا مائدة وثلج وضُرب الخَيش وفُرش الطَّبَري.

فلمّا رأى الخيش والطبري تنحّى عن ذلك الموضع وألقى نفسه على مُضَرَّبَة له.

واشتكت عينه ثم برئت فقال لي: ألا تعجب؟ كانت عيني تشتكي فتمكث حيناً حتى تبرأ ثم قد برئت في سرعة.

أخبرنا عبد الملك بن أبي القاسم قال: أخبرنا عبد الله بن محمّد الأنصاري قال: أخبرنا محمّد بن المنتصر قال: أخبرنا ٢٣،٧٣
أبو بكر بن أبي الفضل قال: حدثنا محمّد بن إبراهيم الصرّام قال: حدثنا إبراهيم بن إسحاق الغَسِيلي قال:

حدثني أبو بكر المرُّوذي قال: قال لي أحمد بن حنبل ونحن بالعسكر: لي اليوم ثمانٍ منذ لم آكل شيئاً ولم أشرب إلّا أقلّ من ربع سَويق. وكان يمكث ثلاثاً لا يطعم فإذا كانت ليلة الرابعة أضع بين يديه قدر نصف ربع سويق فربّما شربه وربّما ترك بعضه وكان إذا ورد عليه أمر يغمّه لم يطعم ولم يُفطر إلّا على شربة ماء.

---

١ ش: لتياخ.

We cite Muḥammad ibn Abī Manṣūr, who was informed by Ibn al-Busrī, citing Abū 'Abd Allāh ibn Baṭṭah, who cites al-Ājurrī, who cites Abū Naṣr ibn Kurdī, who heard al-Marrūdhī report that he heard Zuhayr ibn Muḥammad say: 73.21

[Zuhayr:] I was the first to meet Aḥmad when he got out of the boat. He disembarked wearing the wrap they had put on him. It slipped off and fell, but instead of putting it back on and adjusting it, he dragged it along after him.

We cite Ibn Nāṣir, who cites 'Abd al-Qādir ibn Yūsuf, who cites Abū Isḥāq al-Barmakī, who cites Ibn Mardak, who heard Ibn Abī Ḥātim report that he heard Aḥmad's son Ṣāliḥ report: 73.22

[Ṣāliḥ:] After we sent the clothes away, we told my father that the house where we were staying belonged to Ītākh.

"Write a note to Muḥammad ibn al-Jarrāḥ," he said, "and ask him to let us stay somewhere else."

After we wrote the note, al-Mutawakkil gave us permission to leave. But the new place he assigned us was available only because he had evicted the people living there, so my father wouldn't go there either. Next the caliph rented a property for two hundred dirhams for us to stay in, with delivery of food and ice. Punkahs[155] were installed and carpets from Ṭabaristān spread out on the floor. When my father saw the punkahs and the carpets, he left the place and threw himself down on a quilt he had with him.

At one point my father had something wrong with his eye, but then it cleared up. "Isn't that something?" he said. "My eye was bothering me for a while, but look how quickly it got better."

We cite 'Abd al-Malik ibn Abī l-Qāsim, who cites 'Abd Allāh ibn Muḥammad al-Anṣārī, who cites Muḥammad ibn al-Muntaṣir, who cites Abū Bakr ibn Abī l-Faḍl, who heard Muḥammad ibn Ibrāhīm al-Ṣarrām report that he heard Ibrāhīm ibn Isḥāq al-Ghasīlī report that he heard Abū Bakr al-Marrūdhī report: 73.23

[Al-Marrūdhī:] When we were in Samarra, Aḥmad told me at one point that he had gone eight nights without eating or drinking anything except some barley water—less than a quarter-measure. He would go three nights without eating. On the fourth, I would put an eighth-measure of barley water in front of him. Sometimes he would finish it and sometimes he'd leave some. If there was anything bothering him, he wouldn't eat at all, and break his fast with only a drink of water.

٢٤،٧٣ أخبرنا ابن ناصر قال: أخبرنا عبد القادر بن يوسف[١] قال: أخبرنا إبراهيم بن عمر قال: أخبرنا ابن مردك قال: حدثنا ابن أبي حاتم قال:

حدثنا صالح بن أحمد قال: جعل أبي يواصل في العسكر يفطر في كل ثلاث على تمر شهريز فمكث بذلك خمسة عشر يوماً يفطر في كل ثلاث ثم جعل بعد ذلك يُفطر ليلةً وليلة لا يفطر إلّا على رغيف وكان إذا جيء بالمائدة تُوضع في الدهليز لكي لا يراها فيأكل مَن حضر.

٢٥،٧٣ وكان إذا أجهده الحرّ تُلقَى له خرقة فيضعها على صدره وفي كل يوم يوجّه المتوكّل بابن ماسَوَيْه ينظر إليه ويقول: يا أبا عبد الله أنا أميل إليك وإلى أصحابك وما بك من علّة إلّا الضعف وقلة الرِزّ وإنّ عبادنا ربّما أمرناهم بأكل دُهن الخَلّ فإنه يلين. وجعل يجيئه بالشيء ليشربه فيصبّه.

٢٦،٧٣ وجعل يعقوب وعَتّاب يصيران إليه فيقولان له: يقول لك أمير المؤمنين: ما تقول في ابن أبي دؤاد وفي ماله؟

فلا يُجيب في ذلك شيئاً وجعلا يُخبرانه بما يحدُث من أمر ابن أبي دؤاد في كلّ يوم ثمّ أُحدر ابنُ أبي دؤاد إلى بغداد بعد ما أُشهد عليه ببيع ضياعه.

٢٧،٧٣ وكان ربّما صار إليه يحيى وهو يُصلّي فيجلس في الدهليز حتى يفرغ ويجيء عليّ ابن الجَهْم فينزع سيفه وقلنسوّته ويدخل عليه.

وأمر المتوكل أن يُشترى لنا دار فقال لي: يا صالح! قلت: لبَّيك.

قال: لئن أقررتَ لهم بشراء دار لتكونَنّ القطيعة بيني وبينك، إنّما يريدون أن يُصيّروا هذا البلد لي مأوى ومسكنا.

فلم يزل يدفع شراء الدار حتى اندفع.

وصار إليّ صاحب النُزل[٢] فقال: أُعطيك كل شهر ثلاثة آلاف درهم مكان المائدة؟

قلت: لا.

---

١ د: عبد القادر بن محمد بن يوسف. ٢ د: المنزل.

We cite Ibn Nāṣir, who cites ʿAbd al-Qādir ibn Yūsuf, who cites Ibrāhīm ibn ʿUmar, who cites Ibn Mardak, who heard Ibn Abī Ḥātim report that he heard Aḥmad's son Ṣāliḥ report: **73.24**

[Ṣāliḥ:] In Samarra my father started fasting for three days at a time and breaking his fast with Shihrīz dates. He did this for fifteeen days, eating every third day. Then he started eating every other night, but only a loaf of flat-bread. Whenever a table was brought in, they set it down in the anteroom where he wouldn't see it and the rest of us would eat.

Whenever the heat got too much for him, he would lay a wet rag on his chest. Every day al-Mutawakkil would send Ibn Māsawayh over to examine him. "Abū ʿAbd Allāh," he would say, "I like you and I like the people you have with you. There's nothing wrong with you except inanition and infrequent bowel movements. You know, we often tell our monks to eat sesame oil to relax the bowels." He started bringing him things to drink but he would pour them out. **73.25**

Among his other visitors were Yaʿqūb and ʿAttāb, who would come to ask him on behalf of the caliph what he thought should be done with Ibn Abī Du'ād and his estate, but he would never answer. They started coming every day to tell him how the case was coming along. Finally it was testified that Ibn Abī Du'ād's estates could be sold off, and he himself was sent down to Baghdad. **73.26**

Yaḥyā would sometimes come to see him, and wait in the anteroom until he was finished praying. When ʿAlī ibn al-Jahm came to see my father, he would remove his sword and cap before coming in. **73.27**

At one point al-Mutawakkil ordered a house to be bought for us. My father called me over and said, "Ṣāliḥ, if you let them buy a house I'll never speak to you again. All they want is to find a way to keep me here for good."

He remained so obstinate that the idea was finally dropped.

At one point the caterer came to me and said, "Would you rather I stopped sending food over and give you the three thousand dirhams a month instead?"

I told him no.

٢٨،٧٣ وجعلت رسل المتوكّل تأتيه يسألونه عن خبره فيصيرون إليه فيقولون له: هو ضعيف، وفي خلال ذلك يقولون: يا أبا عبد الله لا بدّ له من أن يراك، فيسكت.

فإذا خرجوا قال: أما تعجب من قولهم: لا بدّ أن يراك، وما علمهم من أنّه لا بد أن يراني؟

وجاء يعقوب فقال: يا أبا عبد الله أمير المؤمنين مشتاق إليك. ويقول: انظر اليوم الذي تصير إليه فيه أي يوم هو حتّى أعرفه؟

.فقال: ذاك إليكم.

فقال: يوم الأربعاء يوم خالٍ.

ثم خرج يعقوب. فلمّا كان من الغد جاء فقال: البشرى يا أبا عبد الله، أمير المؤمنين يقرأ عليك السلام ويقول لك: قد أعفيتُك عن لبس السواد والركوب إلى ولاة العهد[١] وإلى الدار فإن شئت فالبس القطن وإن شئت فالبس الصوف.

فجعل يحمد الله عزّ وجلّ على ذلك.

ثم قال له يعقوب: إنّ لي ابناً وأنا به معجب وله من قلبي موقع فأحب أن تُحدّثه بأحاديث.

فسكت، فلمّا خرج قال: أتُراه ما يرى ما أنا فيه[٢]؟

٢٩،٧٣ أخبرنا ابن ناصر قال: أنبأنا أبو القاسم بن البُسْري عن أبي عبد الله بن بَطّة قال: أخبرنا الآجُرِي قال: أخبرنا أبو نصر بن كردي قال:

حدثنا المَرُّوذي قال: سمعت يعقوب رسول الخليفة يقول لأبي عبد الله: يجيئك ابني بين المغرب والعشاء فتحدّثه بحديث واحد أو حديثين؟

فقال: لا، لا يجيء.

فلمّا خرج سمعته يقول: ترى لو بلغ أنفه طرف السماء حدثّته؟[٣] أنا أحدّث حتّى يوضع الحبل في عنقي؟

---

١ ش: العهود. ٢ بعدها في ش: وانا معجب به. ٣ د: ترى لو بلغ أنفه الى طرف السماء ما حدثّته.

Al-Mutawakkil's messengers continued coming over to ask after my father and then going back to the caliph and saying that he didn't look well. Meanwhile they would tell my father that the caliph needed to see him. My father would say nothing. After they left, he would say, "Isn't that strange? How would they know whether he needs to see me or not?" 73.28

Then Yaʿqūb came over and said, "The Commander of the Faithful is eager to see you. Think about when you can come see him, and let me know."

"That's up to you," my father replied.

"He has Wednesday free," said Yaʿqūb, and went out.

The next day Yaʿqūb came back and said, "Good news! The Commander of the Faithful sends his regards and informs you that he has excused you from wearing the black, attending the heirs apparent, and coming to the palace. If you prefer to wear cotton or wool, you may do so."

My father praised God for this turn of events.

Then Yaʿqūb said, "I have a son who's dear to my heart. I wonder if you would recite some Hadith for him."

My father said nothing. After Yaʿqūb left, he said to me, "Doesn't he see what I'm going through?"

We cite Ibn Nāṣir, who was informed by Abū l-Qāsim ibn al-Busrī, citing Abū ʿAbd Allāh ibn Baṭṭah, who cites al-Ājurrī, who cites Abū Naṣr ibn Kurdī, who heard al-Marrūdhī report: 73.29

[Al-Marrūdhī:] I heard Yaʿqūb, the caliph's messenger, ask Abū ʿAbd Allāh, "If my son comes here between sunset and evening prayers, would you teach him one or two Hadith?"

"No," said Abū ʿAbd Allāh. "Tell him not to come."

After Yaʿqūb had left, I heard Aḥmad say, "Even if his nose touched the sky I wouldn't teach him. Does he want me to put my own head through a noose?"[156]

أخبرنا ابن ناصر قال: أخبرنا عبد القادر بن محمّد قال: أخبرنا البرمكي قال: حدثنا ابن مردك قال: حدثنا ابن ٣٠،٧٣
أبي حاتم قال:

حدثنا صالح بن أحمد قال: كان أبي يختم من جمعة إلى جمعة فإذا ختم يدعو ونؤمّن فلمّا فرغ جعل يقول: أستخير الله عزّ وجلّ مِراراً.

فجعلتُ أقول: ما تريد؟

فقال: أُعطي الله عهداً إنّ عهده كان مسؤولاً وقال: ﴿يَأَيُّهَا الَّذِينَ آمَنُوا أَوْفُوا بِالْعُقُودِ﴾ أنّي لا أحدّث حديثاً تامّاً أبداً حتّى ألقى الله عزّ وجلّ ولا أَستثني منكم أَحداً.

وجاء عليّ بن الجَهْم فقلنا له فقال: ﴿إِنَّا لله وَإِنَّا إِلَيهِ رَاجِعون﴾ وأخبر المتوكل بذلك.

وقال أبي: يُريدون أن أحدّث فيكون هذا البلد حَبْسِي وإنّما كان سبب الذين أقاموا بهذا البلد أنهم أُعطوا فقبلوا وأُمروا فحدّثوا.

٣١،٧٣ وكان يدخل عليه يحيى ويعقوب وعَتّاب وغيرهم فيتكلّمون وهو مغمّض العين يتعلّل وضعف ضعفاً شديداً فكانوا يُخبرون المتوكّل بضعفه فيتوجّع لذلك ويوجِّه إليه في كل وقت يسأله عن حاله وكان في خلال ذلك يأمرلنا بالمال فيقول: يُوصَل إليهم ولا يعلم شيخهم، ويقول: ما يريد منهم؟ إن كان هو لا يريد الدنيا فلم يمنعهم؟

وقالوا للمتوكّل: إنه لا يأكل من طعامك ولا يجلس على فراشك ويحرّم هذا الشراب الذي تشرب.

فقال: لو نُشر المعتصم وقال لي فيه شيئاً لم أَقبله.

٣٢،٧٣ قرأت على أبي الفضل بن أبي منصور عن أبي القاسم بن البُسْري عن أبي عبد الله بن بطّة قال: أخبرنا أبو بكر الآجُرّي قال: حدثنا محمّد بن كُردي قال:

حدثنا أبو بكر المَرُّوذي قال: سمعتُ أبا عبد الله يقول: أنا منذ كذا وكذا أستخير الله عزّ وجلّ في أن أحلف أن لا أحدّث.

We cite Ibn Nāṣir, who cites ʿAbd al-Qādir ibn Muḥammad, who cites al-Barmakī, who heard Ibn Mardak report that he heard Ibn Abī Ḥātim report that he heard Aḥmad's son Ṣāliḥ report: 73.30

[Ṣāliḥ:] My father would start reading the Qurʾan every Friday and finish it by the following Friday. Whenever he finished a reading, he would make a supplication and we would say, "Amen!" Then he would say, "God, guide me," over and over. Finally I asked him what he was concerned about and he said, "Whether to make a vow to God, knowing that I'll be held accountable for it. «Believers, fulfill your obligations.»[157] I'm considering a vow never to recite a full Hadith report again for the rest of my life—not to anyone, not even all of you."

Then ʿAlī ibn al-Jahm arrived. When we told my father, he said, «We belong to God and to Him we shall return»[158] and ʿAlī reported this back to al-Mutawakkil.

My father told us, "They want me to recite Hadith so they can keep me here. The scholars who ended up staying here were the ones who accepted what they were offered for teaching Hadith, or obeyed when they were ordered to teach."

Meanwhile my father continued to receive visits from Yaḥyā, Yaʿqūb, ʿAttāb, and others. They would talk and he would sit with his eyes closed as if ill. He gradually became very feeble. When his condition was reported to al-Mutawakkil, the stricken caliph sent message after message asking about his health. All the while, he continued to send us money, telling the messengers, "Give it to the family without telling the father. What does he expect of them? He might not care about the things of this world, but why should he stop his family from enjoying them?" 73.31

"He won't eat any of the food you give him," the caliph was told. "He won't sit on your carpets, and he declares what you drink to be forbidden."

"Even if al-Muʿtaṣim himself came back to life and spoke against Aḥmad," said the caliph, "I wouldn't listen."

We read back to Abū l-Faḍl ibn Abī Manṣūr his report, citing Abū l-Qāsim ibn al-Busrī, citing Abū ʿAbd Allāh ibn Baṭṭah, who cites Abū Bakr al-Ājurrī, who heard Muḥammad ibn Kurdī report that he heard Abū Bakr al-Marrūdhī report: 73.32

[Al-Marrūdhī:] I once heard Aḥmad say, "For some time I've been asking God to guide me on whether I should vow not to teach Hadith any more."

وقال: قد تركنا الحديث وليس يتركونا.

٣٣،٧٣ أخبرنا ابن ناصر قال: أخبرنا ابن يوسف قال: أخبرنا البرمكي قال: حدثنا بن مردك قال: حدثنا ابن أبي حاتم قال: حدثنا صالح قال:

ثمّ انحدرت إلى بغداد وخلّفت عبد الله عنده فإذا عبد الله قد قدم وجاء بثيابي التي كانت عنده، فقلت: ما حالك؟

فقال: قال لي: انحدر وقل لصالح لا يخرج فأنتم كنتم آفتي والله لو استقبلتُ من أمري ما استدبرت ما أخرجتُ واحداً منكم معي، ولولا مكانكم لمن كانت تُوضع هذه المائدة، ولمن كان يُفرش هذا الفرش ويُجرى هذا الشيء؟

فكتبتُ أعلمه بما قال عبد الله فكتب بخطّه:

بسم الله الرحمن الرحيم[1]

أحسن الله عاقبتك ودفع عنك كل مكروه ومحذور، الذي حملني على الكتابة إليك والذي قلتُ لعبد الله: لا يأتيني منكم أحد رجاء أن ينقطع ذكري ويَخْمُد، فإنكم إذا كنتم ها هنا فشا ذكري، وكان يجتمع الناس إليك، قوم ينقلون أخبارنا، ولم يكن إلّا خير، واعلم يا بنيّ أنك إن أقمتَ فلم تأتني أنت ولا أخوك فهو رضائي فلا تجعل في نفسك إلا خيراً، والسلام عليك ورحمة الله وبركاته.

٣٤،٧٣ قال أبو الفضل: ثمّ ورد كتاب آخر بخطه إليّ يذكر فيه:

بسم الله الرحمن الرحيم

أحسن الله عاقبتك ودفع عنك السوء برحمته، كتابي إليك وأنا بأنعُم[2] من الله عزّ وجلّ مُتظاهرة[3] أسأله تمامها والعون على أداء شكرها، قد انفكّت عنّا عُقَد، إنّما كان حبسُ مَن كان ها هنا لِما أُعطوا فقبلوا وأُجريَ عليهم فصاروا

١ الرسالة ناقصة في هـ، د واللذين يستأنفان بالتي بعدها. ٢ د: بنعم. ٣ هـ: متضاهرة.

He added, "I've stopped teaching, but they still won't leave me alone."

We cite Ibn Nāṣir, who cites Ibn Yūsuf, who cites al-Barmakī, who heard Ibn Mardak report that he heard Ibn Abī Ḥātim report that he heard Ṣāliḥ report: 73.33

[Ṣāliḥ:] Some time later I went back down to Baghdad and left ʿAbd Allāh there with our father. Not long afterward ʿAbd Allāh appeared, bringing with him the clothes I had left in Samarra. I asked him what was going on.

ʿAbd Allāḥ replied: "He said, 'Go back, and tell Ṣāliḥ not to come back here. All of you are the cause of my troubles. If I could do it all over again, I would have left you in Baghdad and come here by myself. If you hadn't been here, they wouldn't have brought us food or laid down carpets or started sending us you-know-what every month.'"[159]

So I wrote to my father telling him what ʿAbd Allāh had said. He wrote back in his own hand:

> *In the name of God, full of compassion, ever-compassionate*
>
> May God give you a just reward and protect you from all misfortune.
>
> I am writing to tell you the same thing I told ʿAbd Allāh: all of you need to stay away. If you do they may forget that I'm here, but as long as you're with me I'll be the center of attention. We even had people coming to see you so they could report back about what we're doing. That's why I'm asking, not because I'm angry at you. Please understand, son, that if you and your brother stay in Baghdad and stop coming here you'll be doing what I want. So don't worry and don't be upset with me.
>
> Peace be upon you, and the mercy of God, and His blessings.

Then I received another letter in his handwriting addressed to me. It said: 73.34

> *In the name of God, full of compassion, ever-compassionate*
>
> May God give you a just reward and in His mercy protect you from all harm.
>
> I write to you enjoying successive blessings from God, whom I ask to complete them and to aid me in expressing my gratitude for them. I've been released from some of my obligations.[160] Only those who were offered rewards and accepted them remained in confinement here. They were given stipends and ended up where you see them now. They've taught

في الحدّ الذي صاروا إليه وحدّثوا ودخلوا عليهم. فنسأل الله عزّ وجلّ أن يُعيذنا من شرّهم وأن يُخلّصنا فقد كان ينبغي لكم لو فديتموني بأموالكم وأهاليكم لَهانَ ذلك عليكم للذي أنا فيه، ولا يكبر عليكم ما أكتب به إليكم فالزموا بيوتكم لعلّ الله عزّ وجلّ أن يُخلّصنا والسلام عليكم ورحمة الله.

ثم ورد عليّ غير كتاب بخطه بنحو من هذا. فلما خرجنا رُفِعَت المائدة والفُرش وكلّ ما كان أُقيم لنا.

٣٥،٧٣ وأوصى وصيّة:

بسم الله الرحمن الرحيم

هذا ما أوصى به أحمد بن محمّد بن حنبل

أوصى أنه يشهد أنّ لا إله إلا الله وحده لا شريك له وأنّ محمّدا عبده ورسوله، أرسله بالهدى ودين الحقّ ليُظهره على الدين كله ولو كره المشركون.

وأوصى من أطاعه من أهله وقرابته أن يعبدوا الله في العابدين وأن يحمدوه في الحامدين وأن ينصحوا لجماعة المسلمين، وأُوصي أَني رضيتُ بالله عزّ وجل ربّاً وبالإسلام ديناً وبمحمّد صلّى الله عليه وسلّم نبيّاً.

وأُوصي أنّ لعبد الله بن محمّد المعروف بفُوران عليّ نحوًا من خمسين دينارًا وهو مصدَّق فيما قال فيُقْضَى مالَه عليّ من غلة الدار إن شاء الله فإذا استوفى أُعطي ولدُ صالح[1] كلّ ذكر وأنثى عشرة دراهم[2] بعد وفاء مال أبي محمّد.

شهد أبو يوسف وصالح وعبد الله ابنا أحمد بن محمّد بن حنبل.

٣٦،٧٣ أخبرنا عبد الملك بن أبي القاسم قال: أخبرنا عبد الله بن محمّد الأنصاري قال: أخبرنا محمّد بن المنتصر الباهِلي قال: أخبرنا أبو بكر بن أبي الفضل قال: حدثنا إبراهيم بن إسحاق الأنصاري قال:

---

١ تركي: وعبد الله ابني أحمد بن محمّد بن حنبل. ٢ وردت مرة واحدة فقط في ش.

Hadith and consorted with those people. I ask God to protect us from them and to free us from this predicament. If you could see the wretched state I'm in, you would gladly give up your property and your families to free me. But don't let what I'm telling you trouble you. Just stay home; perhaps God will find a way to set me free.

Peace and the blessings of God.

Later I got another letter similar to the one above.

After we left, the food stopped being delivered and the carpets, cushions, and other items put there for us were removed.

Then my father made a will: 73.35

In the name of God, full of compassion, ever-compassionate

This is the testament of Aḥmad ibn Muḥammad ibn Ḥanbal.

He declares that there is no god but God, alone, without partner; and that Muḥammad is His servant and Emissary, bringing right guidance and a true religion that he carried to victory over all other cults and creeds despite the resistance of the polytheists.

All those members of his family willing to heed him he enjoins to partake with the like-minded in worshipping and praising God and in giving good counsel to the Muslim community.

He testifies that he accepts God, mighty and glorious, as his lord; Islam as his religion; and Muḥammad, God bless him and grant him peace, as his prophet.

I declare that I owe ʿAbd Allāh ibn Muḥammad, known as Fūrān, approximately fifty dinars; he is to be believed when he says so.[161] Let him be repaid out of the income from the house, God willing. Once the debt is paid, let ten dirhams be given to each of Ṣāliḥ's children,[162] male and female, after the money due Abū Muḥammad is paid back.

Witnessed by Abū Yūsuf as well as Ṣāliḥ and ʿAbd Allāh, sons of Aḥmad ibn Muḥammad ibn Ḥanbal.

We cite ʿAbd al-Malik ibn Abī l-Qāsim, who cites ʿAbd Allāh ibn Muḥammad al-Anṣārī, who cites Muḥammad ibn al-Muntaṣir al-Bāhilī, who cites Abū Bakr ibn Abī l-Faḍl, who heard Ibrāhīm ibn Isḥāq al-Anṣārī report that he heard Abū Bakr al-Marrūdhī report: 73.36

حدثني أبو بكر المرُّوذي قال: أنبهني أبو عبد الله ذات ليلة وقد كان واصَلَ فإذا هو قاعد فقال: هو ذا يُدار بي من الجوع فأطعِمْني شيئاً.

فجئته بأقلّ من رغيف فأكل ثمّ قال: لولا أني أخاف العون على نفسي ما أكلتُ.

وكان يقوم من فراشه إلى الخروج فيقعد يستريح من الضعف من الجوع حتّى إن كنت لأبلّ له الخرقة فيلقيها على وجهه لترجع إليه نفسه حتّى أوصى وأشهد على وصيته من الضعف من غير مرض.

فسمعته يقول عند وصيته ونحن بالعَسكر:

بسم الله الرحمن الرحيم

هذا ما أوصى به أحمد بن محمد

أوصى أنه يشهد أن لا إله إلا الله وحده لا شريك له وأن محمدا عبده ورسوله، أرسله بالهدى ودين الحق ليُظهره على الدين كله ولو كره المشركون، وأوصى من أطاعه من أهله وقرابته أن يحمدوا الله في الحامدين وأن ينصحوا لجماعة المسلمين.

وأوصى إنّي رضيت بالله ربّاً وبالإسلام ديناً وبمحمّد نبياً وأوصى أن عليه خمسين ديناراً تُؤدّى من الغلّة حتى تُستَوفى.

أخبرنا إسماعيل بن أحمد ومحمّد بن أبي القاسم قالا: أخبرنا حمد بن أحمد قال: أخبرنا أحمد بن عبد الله الحافظ ٣٧،٧٣ قال: حدثنا أبي والحسين بن محمّد قالا: حدثنا أحمد بن محمّد بن عمر قال:

سمعت عبد الله بن أحمد ابن حنبل يقول: مكث أبي بالعسكر عند الخليفة ستّة عشر يوماً ما ذاق شيئاً إلا مقدار ربع سويق في كلّ ليلة، كان يشرب شربة ماء وفي كل ثلاث ليال يستفّ حفنة من السويق فرجع إلى البيت ولم يرجع[1] إليه نفسه إلّا بعد ستّة أشهر ورأيتُ مأقَيه قد دخلا في حَدَقتيه.

---

[1] ش: ترجع.

[Al-Marrūdhī:] One night after he had been fasting continuously, Aḥmad woke me up. He was sitting up and saying, "I'm so hungry that my head's spinning. Find me something to eat!"

I found part of a loaf of flatbread for him and he ate it.

"If I weren't afraid of helping them break my resistance," he said, "I wouldn't eat at all."

He would often get out of bed and try to leave the house but then find himself so weakened by hunger that he would have to sit down and rest. Sometimes I would have to moisten a rag and give it to him to lay on his face in order to revive him. At one point he was so weak—from starvation, not illness—that he made a will and had it witnessed. Here's what I heard him say when making his will in Samarra:

In the name of God, full of compassion, ever-compassionate

This is the testament of Aḥmad ibn Muḥammad.

He declares that there is no god but God, alone, without partner; and that Muḥammad is His servant and Emissary, bringing right guidance and a true religion that he carried to victory over all other cults and creeds despite the resistance of the polytheists.

All those members of his family willing to heed him he enjoins to partake with the like-minded in worshipping God and giving good counsel to the Muslim community.

He testifies that he accepts God, mighty and glorious, as his lord; Islam as his religion; and Muḥammad as his prophet.

He also testified that he owed fifty dinars, to be repaid out of the income of the rental property.

We cite Ismāʿīl ibn Aḥmad and Muḥammad ibn Abī l-Qāsim, who cite Ḥamd ibn Aḥmad, **73.37**
who cites Aḥmad ibn ʿAbd Allāh al-Ḥāfiẓ, who heard his father and al-Ḥusayn ibn Muḥammad report that they heard Aḥmad ibn Muḥammad ibn ʿUmar report that he heard Aḥmad ibn Ḥanbal's son ʿAbd Allāh say:

[ʿAbd Allāh:] My father spent sixteen days at the caliph's palace in Samarra without eating anything but a quarter-measure of barley meal. Every night he would have a drink of water, and every third night eat a handful of meal. Even after he came home it took him six months to recover. The inner corners of his eyes seemed to have receded toward the pupil.[163]

٣٨،٧٣ أخبرنا محمّد بن أبي منصور قال: أخبرنا عبد القادر بن محمّد قال: أنبأنا إبراهيم بن عمر قال: أنبأنا عبد العزيز بن جعفر قال: حدثنا أحمد بن محمد الخلال:

أخبرني محمد بن الحسين أن أبا بكر المَرُّوذي حدثهم قال: كان أبو عبد الله بالعسكر يقول: انظر هل تجد لي ماء الباقلاء؟ فكنت ربّما بللتُ خبزه بالماء فيأكله بالملح، ومنذ دخلنا العسكر إلى أن خرجنا ما ذاق طبيخًا ولا دسمًا.

٣٩،٧٣ أخبرنا محمّد بن ناصر قال: أخبرنا المبارك بن عبد الجبار قال: أخبرنا أبو بكر محمد بن عليّ الخياط قال: أخبرنا ابن أبي الفوارس قال: أخبرنا أحمد بن جعفر بن محمد بن سَلْم قال: حدثنا أحمد بن محمّد بن عبد الخالق قال:

حدثنا أبو بكر المَرُّوذي قال: قال أبو عبد الله أحمد بن حنبل: إني لأتمنّى الموت صباحًا ومساء، أخاف أن أُفتن بالدنيا، لقد تفكّرت البارحة فقلت: هذه محنتان امتحنتُ بالدين وهذه محنة بالدنيا.

وقال لي ونحن بالعسكر: ألا تعجب! كان قوتي فيما مضى أرغفة وقد ذهبت عني شهوة الطعام فما أشتهيه، قد كنت في السجن آكل وذلك عندي زيادة في إيماني وهذا نُقصان.

وقال لنا يومًا ونحن بالعسكر: لي اليوم ثمانٍ لم آكل شيئًا ولم أشرب إلا أقلّ من ربع سويق.

وكان يمكث ثلاثًا لا يطعم وأنا معه فإذا كان الليلة الرابعة أضع بين يديه قدر نصف ربع سويق فربّما شربه و ربّما ترك بعضه، فمكث نحوًا من خمسة عشر يومًا أو أربعة عشر يومًا لم يطعم إلا أقل من ربعين سويقًا، وكان إذا ورد عليه أمر يَغمّه لم يطعم ولم يفطر وواصل إلّا شربة ماء. وكُلّم في أمره وفي الحمل على نفسه فقيل له: لو أمرت بِقدر تُطبخ لك لترجع إليك نفسك؟

فقال: الطبيخ طعام المطمئنّين، مكث أبو ذرّ ثلاثين يومًا ما له طعام إلا ماء زَمزم، وهذا إبراهيم التيّمي كان يمكث في السجن كذا وكذا لا يأكل، وهذا ابن الزُّبير كان يمكث سبعًا.

We cite Muḥammad ibn Abī Manṣūr, who cites ʿAbd al-Qādir ibn Muḥammad, who was informed by Ibrāhīm ibn ʿUmar, who was informed by ʿAbd al-ʿAzīz ibn Jaʿfar, who heard Aḥmad ibn Muḥammad al-Khallāl cite Muḥammad ibn al-Ḥusayn, who heard Abū Bakr al-Marrūdhī report: 73.38

[Al-Marrūdhī:] When we were in Samarra, Aḥmad used to ask me if I could find him some bean broth. Many times I would moisten some bread in water and he would eat it with salt. From the time we entered Samarra to the time we left, he tasted no cooked food or any fat.

We cite Muḥammad ibn Nāṣir, who cites al-Mubārak ibn ʿAbd al-Jabbār, who cites Abū Bakr Muḥammad ibn ʿAlī l-Khayyāṭ, who cites Ibn Abī l-Fawāris, who cites Aḥmad ibn Jaʿfar ibn Muḥammad ibn Salm, who heard Aḥmad ibn Muḥammad ibn ʿAbd al-Khāliq report that he heard Abū Bakr al-Marrūdhī report: 73.39

[Al-Marrūdhī:] Aḥmad ibn Ḥanbal once said to me, "All day long I hope for death. I'm afraid of being tempted by the things of this world. Yesterday I was thinking that it's been two trials. Before, they tested my religion, and this time they're trying me with the things of this world."

Once in Samarra he said, "Isn't it surprising? Before this, I lived on bread, and stopped craving food altogether. When I was in jail, I ate. To me, that meant that my faith had increased. But now it seems to have decreased."

On another occasion he said, "Today makes eight days I've gone without eating or drinking anything except some barley meal—less than a quarter-measure."

He would go three days without eating—and I was with him all the time. On the fourth night I would serve him an eighth-measure of barley meal. Sometimes he would drink it and sometimes he wouldn't. For fourteen or fifteen days, he survived on less than two quarter-measures of barley meal. Whenever he was upset about something he wouldn't eat at all and would drink only water. People tried to make him stop doing what he was doing to himself, suggesting that if he asked for a cooked meal he would feel much better.

"You can enjoy a cooked meal," he replied, "only if you're sure of being saved. Abū Dharr lived for thirty days on nothing but water from the well of Zamzam, Ibrāhīm al-Taymī went for days without eating. Ibn al-Zubayr could go for seven."

٤٠،٧٣ أخبرنا محمّد بن ناصر قال: أخبرني عبد القادر بن محمّد قال: أخبرنا إبراهيم بن عمر قال: حدثنا عليّ بن عبد العزيز قال: حدثنا عبد الرحمن بن أبي حاتم قال:

حدثنا صالح بن أحمد أنّ المتوكّل كان قد اكترى لهم داراً، قال: فسأل أبي أن يحوَّل من الدار التي اكتُريت له فاكترى هو داراً وتحوّل إليها فسأل عنه المتوكّل فقيل له إنه عليل فقال: كنت أحبّ أن يكون في قربي وقد أذنت له، يا عبيد الله احمل إليه ألف دينار يقسمها، وقل لسعيد يهيئ له حَرّاقة يَنحدر فيها.

فجاءه عليّ بن الجهم في جوف الليل ثم جاء عبيد الله ومعه ألف دينار فقال: إنّ أمير المؤمنين قد أذن لك وقد أمر بهذه الألف دينار.

فقال: قد أعفاني أمير المؤمنين ممّا أكره فردّها. وقال: أنا رقيق على البرد والبرّ أرفق بي.

فكُتب له جواز وكتب إلى محمّد بن عبد الله في برّه وتَعاهده فقدم علينا بين الظهر والعصر.

٤١،٧٣ أخبرنا عبد الملك بن أبي القاسم قال: أخبرنا عبد الله بن محمّد الأنصاري قال: أخبرنا أبو يعقوب قال: أخبرنا أحمد بن حَسْنَوَيْه[١] قال: حدثنا محمّد بن عبد الرحمن السامي[٢] قال:

سمعت سليمان بن الأشعث يقول: كتب المتوكّل إلى خليفته أن يحمل أحمد إليه فلمّا قدم أحمد أمر أن يفرغ له قصر ويبسط له فيه ويجرى عليه مائدة،[٣] كل يوم كذا وكذا، وأراد أن يُسمع ولده الحديث فأبى أحمد ولم يجلس على بساطه ولم ينظر إلى مائدته وكان صائماً فإذا كان عند الإفطار أمر رفيقه الذي معه أن يشتري له ماء الباقلاء فيُفطر عليه فبقي أياماً على هذه الحال.

وكان عليّ بن الجهم من أهل السنّة حسن الرأي في أحمد فكلّم أمير المؤمنين فيه وقال: هذا رجل زاهد لا يُنتفع به، فإن رأى أمير المؤمنين أن يأذن له.

ففعل ورجع أحمد إلى منزله.

---

١ مشكلة في ش. ٢ د: الشامي. ٣ ش: على مائدته.

We cite Muḥammad ibn Nāṣir, who cites ʿAbd al-Qādir ibn Muḥammad, who cites Ibrāhīm ibn ʿUmar, who heard ʿAlī ibn ʿAbd al-ʿAzīz report that he heard ʿAbd al-Raḥmān ibn Abī Ḥātim report that he heard Aḥmad's son Ṣāliḥ report: 73.40

[Ṣāliḥ:] Al-Mutawakkil had rented a house for them, but my father asked to move out of it and rented another place himself. When al-Mutawakkil asked how my father was faring, he was told that he was ill. "I had hoped to keep him close, but I grant him leave to go. ʿUbayd Allāh! Give him a thousand dinars to distribute, and tell Saʿīd to prepare a boat to take him back to Baghdad."

Late that night, ʿAlī ibn al-Jahm arrived, followed by ʿUbayd Allāh with the thousand dinars.

"The Commander of the Faithful has exempted me from doing anything I don't want to do," said Aḥmad. "So take the money back." Then he said, "I don't like the cold. It would be more comfortable for me to travel by land."

A document of safe passage was written up for him as well as a letter to Muḥammad ibn ʿAbd Allāh instructing him to take care of him. He arrived back home that afternoon.

We cite ʿAbd al-Malik ibn Abī l-Qāsim, who cites ʿAbd Allāh ibn Muḥammad al-Anṣārī, who cites Abū Yaʿqūb, who cites Aḥmad ibn Ḥasnawayh, who heard Muḥammad ibn ʿAbd al-Raḥmān al-Sāmī report that he heard Sulaymān ibn al-Ashʿath say: 73.41

[Ibn al-Ashʿath:] Al-Mutawakkil wrote to his deputy ordering Aḥmad to be sent to him. When Aḥmad arrived, al-Mutawakkil had a palace vacated and furnished for his use, with food of various kinds delivered every day. He wanted Aḥmad to teach his son Hadith, but Aḥmad refused. He also refused to sit on the carpets or look at the food provided him even though he was fasting. When it came time to break the fast, he told his companion to buy him some bean broth. He went on this way for some days. Then, ʿAlī ibn al-Jahm, who was a Sunni and favorable to Aḥmad, said to the caliph, "A renunciant like him is no good to you. Would you consider giving him permission to leave?"

So the caliph gave his permission, and Aḥmad came home.

أخبرنا محمد بن أبي منصور قال: أنبأنا عليّ بن البُسْري عن أبي عبد الله ابن بَطّة قال: حدثني أبو بكر الآجُرّي قال: حدثنا أبو نصر بن كُردي قال: ٤٢،٧٣

حدثنا أبو بكر المرُّوذي قال: سمعتُ إسحاق بن حنبل ونحن بالعسكر يناشد أبا عبد الله ويسأله الدخول على الخليفة ليأمره وينهاه.

وقال: إنّه يقبل منك هذا، إسحاق بن راهَوَيه يدخل على ابن طاهر فيأمره وينهاه.

فقال أبو عبد الله: تحتجّ عليّ بإسحاق، فأنا غير راضٍ بفعله؟ ما له في رؤيتي خير ولا لي في رؤيته خير، يجب عليّ إذا رأيتُه أن آمره وأنهاه، الدنوّ منهم فتنة والجلوس معهم فتنة ونحن متباعدون منهم ما أرانا نَسْلَم، فكيف لو قربنا منهم؟

قال المرُّوذي: ٤٣،٧٣

وسمعتُ إسماعيل ابن أخت ابن المبارك يناظر أبا عبد الله ويكلّمه في الدخول على الخليفة فقال له أبو عبد الله: قد قال خالك، يعني ابن المبارك، لا تأتِهم فإنْ أتيتهم فاصدُقهم وأنا أخاف أن لا أصدُقهم.

وسمعت أبا عبد الله يقول: لو دخلتُ عليه ما ابتدأته إلّا بأبناء المهاجرين والأنصار.

وفي رواية أنّ عمّ أحمد قال له: لو دخلتَ على الخليفة فإنك تَكْرُم عليه.

فقال: إنّما غمّي من كرامتي عليه.

وبلغني عن أبي الحسين بن المُنادي أنّه قال: ٤٤،٧٣

امتنع أحمد من الحديث قبل أن يموت بثمان سنين أقلّ أو أكثر وذلك أنّ المتوكّل وجّه إليه فيما بلغنا يقرأ عليه السلام ويسأله أن يجعل المُعْتَزّ في حجره ويُعلمه العلم.

فقال للرسول: اقرأ على أمير المؤمنين السلام وأعلمه أنّ عليّ يميناً مُقفلة أنّي لا أُتمّ حديثاً حتى أموت. وقد كان أمير المؤمنين أعفاني ممّا أكره وهذا ممّا أكره.

فقام الرسول من عنده.

We cite Muḥammad ibn Abī Manṣūr, who was informed by ʿAlī ibn al-Busrī, citing Abū ʿAbd Allāh ibn Baṭṭah, who heard Abū Bakr al-Ājurrī report that he heard Abū Naṣr ibn Kurdī report that he heard Abū Bakr al-Marrūdhī report: **73.42**

[Al-Marrūdhī:] While we were in Samarra, I heard Isḥāq ibn Ḥanbal pleading with Aḥmad to go see the caliph so he could command him to do right and forbid him to do wrong.[164]

"He would listen to you," said Isḥāq. "Look at Ibn Rāhawayh: Doesn't he preach to Ibn Ṭāhir?"

"Ibn Rāhawayh is no example because I think what he's doing is wrong. As far as I'm concerned he does no good, and he thinks the same of me. If there's anyone who needs to hear me preach, it's him. Consorting with the high and mighty is a trial. We've tried to steer clear of them, but still they've managed to cause trouble for us. Think how much worse it'll be if we start associating with them."

Al-Marrūdhī also said: **73.43**

I heard Ibn al-Mubārak's nephew Ismāʿīl arguing with Aḥmad and trying to persuade him to go see the caliph.

"Your uncle," said Abū ʿAbd Allāh, "said, 'Keep away from them, and if you can't, speak the truth.' I'm afraid of not speaking the truth."

I also heard Aḥmad say, "If I were to see the caliph, the only subject I'd raise is the Emigrants and the Helpers."[165]

According to another account, Aḥmad's uncle said, "Why don't you go see the caliph? He thinks highly of you."

"That's what worries me," said Aḥmad.

Abū l-Ḥusayn ibn al-Munādī reports: **73.44**

[Ibn al-Munādī:] Eight years or so before he died, Aḥmad stopped teaching Hadith. As far as I know, the reason was that al-Mutawakkil sent him a message conveying his greetings and asking him to take his son al-Muʿtazz as a pupil and teach him Hadith. Aḥmad replied: "Convey my greetings to the Commander of the Faithful and tell him that I have sworn a solemn oath never to recite a complete Hadith again as long as I live. The Commander of the Faithful has exempted me from doing anything I detest, and this is something I detest."

Hearing this, the messenger departed.

سياق ما جرى بينه وبين المتوكّل بعد عوده عن العسكر

٤٥،٧٣ أخبرنا علي أخبرنا محمّد بن أبي منصور قال: أخبرنا عبد القادر بن محمّد قال: أخبرنا إبراهيم بن عمر البرمكي قال: أخبرنا علي ابن عبد العزيز قال: حدثنا أبو محمّد بن أبي حاتم قال:

حدثنا صالح بن أحمد قال: كان يأتيه رسول المتوكل يُبلغه السلام ويسأله عن حاله فنسرّ نحن بذلك وتأخذه نفضة حتّى ندثّره ثمّ يقول: والله لو أنّ نفسي في يدي لأرسلتها.

ويضمّ أصابعه ثمّ يفتحها.

وقدم المتوكّل فنزل الشمّاسيّة يُريد المدائن فقال: يا صالح أُحبّ أن لا تذهب إليهم ولا تُنبههم.

قلت: نعم.

فلمّا كان بعد يوم وأنا قاعد خارجاً وكان يوماً مطيراً إذا يحيى بن خاقان قد جاء والمطر عليه في موكب عظيم فقال: سُبحان الله! لم تَصِرْ إلينا حتّى تُبلغ أمير المؤمنين عن شيخك حتّى وجّه بي.

ثم نزل خارج الزقاق فجهدت به أن يدخل على الدابّة فلم يفعل فجعل يخوض الطين.

فلمّا صار إلى الباب نزع جُرموقاً كان على خُفّه ودخل البيت وأبي في الزاوية قاعد عليه كساء مرقّع وعمامة والستر الذي على باب البيت قطعة خيش.

فسلّم عليه وقبّل جبهته وسأله عن حاله وقال: أمير المؤمنين يقرأ عليك السلام ويقول: كيف أنت في نفسك، وكيف حالك؟ قد أنستُ بقربك. ويسألك أن تدعو الله عزّ وجلّ له.

فقال: ما يأتي عليّ يوم إلّا وأنا أدعو الله عزّ وجلّ له.

ثم قال له: قد وجّه معي ألف دينار تفرّقها على أهل الحاجة.

فقال: يا أبا زكريّا أنا في البيت منقطع عن الناس وقد أعفاني ممّا أكره وهذا ممّا أكره.

More on What Happened between Him and al-Mutawakkil after His Return from Samarra

We cite Muḥammad ibn Abī Manṣūr, who cites ʿAbd al-Qādir ibn Muḥammad, who cites Ibrāhīm ibn ʿUmar al-Barmakī, who cites ʿAlī ibn ʿAbd al-ʿAzīz, who heard Abū Muḥammad ibn Abī Ḥātim report that he heard Aḥmad's son Ṣāliḥ report: **73.45**

[Ṣāliḥ:] My father used to receive visits from messengers conveying al-Mutawakkil's greetings and asking after his health. We were happy to receive the visitors, but my father would shudder so violently that we had to bundle him up in heavy clothes. He would bunch his fingers together and say, "If I had my soul in my hand, I would let it go," then open his hand.

Some time later, al-Mutawakkil and his entourage were passing through al-Shammāsiyyah on their way to al-Madāʾin. My father told me that he didn't want me to go to them or send them word of any kind. I said I wouldn't.

The next day I was sitting outside and there right in front of me—even though it was a rainy day—appeared Yaḥyā ibn Khāqān, who had come, rain and all, with a vast entourage.

"Is this any way to act?" he said, dismounting just outside our alley. "You didn't come and convey your father's greetings to the Commander of the Faithful, so he sent *me* to *you*."

I tried to persuade him to come through the alley on horseback, but he refused and began sloshing his way through the mud instead. When he reached the door, he removed the galoshes he was wearing over his boots and went into the house.

My father was sitting in the corner wearing a patched wrap and a turban. The only curtain across the door was a strip of burlap. Yaḥyā greeted him, kissed him on the forehead, and asked after his health.

"The Commander of the Faithful conveys his greetings and asks, 'How are your spirits and how is your health?' He says that he took comfort in having you close by and asks you to pray for him."

"Not a day passes," says my father, "that I don't pray for him."

"He's sent along a thousand dinars for you to distribute to those in need."

"Abū Zakariyyā," he replied, "I don't leave the house and I don't see anyone. And he's exempted me from doing what I detest, and this is something I detest."

"Abū ʿAbd Allāh! Caliphs will only tolerate so much."

فقال: يا أبا عبد الله الخلفاء لا يحتملون هذا كله.

فقال: يا أبا زكريّا تلطَّفْ في ذلك.

فدعا له ثمّ قام فلمّا صار إلى الدار رجع وقال: هكذا لو وجّه إليك بعض إخوانك كنت تفعل؟

قال: نعم.

قال صالح: فلمّا صرنا إلى الدهليز قال: قد أمرني أمير المؤمنين أن أدفعها إليك تفرّقها في أهل بيتكم. فقلت: تكون عندك حتى تمضي هذه الأيّام. وقلّ يومٌ يمضي إلّا رسول المتوكّل يأتيه.

قال ابن أبي حاتم: ٤٦،٧٣

وأخبرنا عبد الله بن أحمد فيما كتب إليّ قال: سمعت أبي يقول: لقد تمنّيتُ الموت وهذا أمر أشدّ عليّ من ذلك، ذاك فتنة الدين، الضرب والحبس كنت أحتمله في نفسي، وهذه فتنة الدنيا. أو كما قال.

أخبرنا إسماعيل بن أحمد ومحمد بن عبد الباقي قالا: أخبرنا حمد بن أحمد قال: حدثنا أبو نُعَيم الحافظ قال: حدثنا ٤٧،٧٣
أبي قال: حدثنا أحمد بن محمد بن عمر قال:

حدثنا عبد الله بن أحمد بن حنبل قال: سمعتُ أبي يقول: هذا أمر أشدّ عليّ من ذلك، ذاك فتنة الدين، الضرب والحبس كنتُ أحتمله في نفسي، وهذا فتنة الدنيا.

أخبرنا ابن ناصر قال: أنبأنا ابن البُسْري عن أبي عبد الله بن بَطّة قال: حدثنا الآجُرِّي قال: حدثنا أبو نصر بن ٤٨،٧٣
كُردي قال:

حدثنا المَرُّوذي قال: قال لي أبو عبد الله: قد جاء يحيى بن خاقان ومعه شُويّ.

فجعل يقلّله أبو عبد الله.

قلت له: قالوا: إنها ألف دينار.

قال: هكذا.

"Do what you can to handle it discreetly, Abū Zakariyyā."

Yaḥyā wished him well and rose. On the way out he turned around and came back.

"Would you say the same thing if it was one of your associates who was giving you the money?"

"Yes."

When we reached the anteroom, he said, "The Commander of the Faithful has ordered me to give you the money to distribute to your families."

"Keep it with you for now," I said. After that a messenger came from al-Mutawakkil nearly every day.

Ibn Abī Ḥātim also cites what Aḥmad's son ʿAbd Allāh wrote to him: 73.46

[ʿAbd Allāh:] I heard my father say, "All I wish for is death. Living this way is worse than dying. What happened before was a test of faith. Flogging and prison I could stand, since I was the only one who suffered. But now we're being tested by the things of this world," or words to that effect.

We cite Ismāʿīl ibn Aḥmad and Muḥammad ibn ʿAbd al-Bāqī, who cite Ḥamd ibn Aḥmad, 73.47
who heard Abū Nuʿaym al-Ḥāfiẓ report that he heard his father report that he heard Aḥmad ibn Muḥammad ibn ʿUmar report that he heard Aḥmad ibn Ḥanbal's son ʿAbd Allāh report that he heard his father say:

[ʿAbd Allāh:] I heard my father say, "This time it's worse. Flogging and prison I could stand, since I was the only one involved. But now we're being tested by the things of this world."

We cite Ibn Nāṣir, who was informed by Ibn al-Busrī, citing Abū ʿAbd Allāh ibn Baṭṭah, 73.48
who cites al-Ājurrī, who heard Abū Naṣr ibn Kurdī report that he heard al-Marrūdhī report:

[Al-Marrūdhī:] Aḥmad told me, "Yaḥyā ibn Khāqān came bearing that pittance of his," and went on about how meager a sum it was.

"But I heard he brought a thousand dinars," I said.

"That's right," he said. He went on: "I wouldn't take it from him. He got as far as the door and then turned around and asked, 'If one of your associates

قال: فرددتُها عليه فبلغ الباب ثمّ رجع فقال: إن جاءك أحد من أصحابك بشيء تقبله؟ قلت: لا. قال: إنّما أُريد أن أُخبر الخليفة بهذا.

قلت لأبي عبد الله: أي شيء كان عليك لو أخذتها فقسمتها؟

فكلَح وجهه وقال: إذا أنا قسمتها أي شيء كنت أريد، أكون له قهرمانًا؟

أخبرنا المحمّدان: ابن ناصر وابن عبد الباقي قالا: أخبرنا حمد بن أحمد قال: أخبرنا أبو نعيم[1] أحمد بن عبد الله الحافظ قال: حدثنا سليمان بن أحمد قال: حدثنا عبد الله بن أحمد. قال أبو نعيم: وحدثنا محمّد وعلي والحسين[2] قالوا: حدثنا محمّد بن إسماعيل قال: ٤٩،٧٣

حدثنا صالح بن أحمد بن حنبل قال: كتب عبيد الله بن يحيى إلى أبي يخبره إنّ أمير المؤمنين أمرني أن أكتب إليك أسألك عن أمر القرآن لا مسألةَ امتحان ولكن مسألة معرفة وبصيرة.

فأملى عليّ أبي:

إلى عبيد الله بن يحيى:

بسم الله الرحمن الرحيم

أحسن الله عاقبتك يا أبا الحسن في الأمور كلّها ودفع عنك مَكارِه الدنيا والآخرة برحمته. قد كتبتُ إليك، رضي الله عنك، بالذي سأل عنه أمير المؤمنين بما حضرني، وإني أسأل الله أن يُديم توفيق أمير المؤمنين فقد كان الناس في خوض من الباطل واختلاف شديد يغتمسون فيه حتّى أفضت الخلافة إلى أمير المؤمنين فنفى الله بأمير المؤمنين كلّ بدعة وانجلى عن الناس ما كانوا فيه من الذلّ وضيق المحابس فصرف الله ذلك كلّه وذهب به بأمير المؤمنين، وقع ذلك من المسلمين موقعًا عظيمًا ودعوا الله لأمير المؤمنين، فأسأل الله أن يستجيب في أمير المؤمنين صالح الدعاء وأن يتمّ ذلك لأمير المؤمنين وأن يزيد في نيّته ويُعينه على ما هو فيه.

---

١ ما بعدها ناقص في هـ حتى لفظة (وحدثنا محمّد وعلي والحسين.) ٢ هـ: عليّ بن الحسين.

brought you something, would you take it?' I told him I wouldn't. He said he had asked so he would know what to tell the caliph."

"But would it have been so wrong," I asked, "if you had accepted the money and then given it away?"

He glowered at me. "If I did that, what do you think it would mean? Am I supposed to be his housekeeper?"

We cite the two Muḥammads, Ibn Nāṣir and Ibn ʿAbd al-Bāqī, who cite Ḥamd ibn Aḥmad, who cites Abū Nuʿaym Aḥmad ibn ʿAbd Allāh al-Ḥāfiẓ, who heard Sulaymān ibn Aḥmad report that he heard Aḥmad's son ʿAbd Allāh report; and Abū Nuʿaym reports that he heard Muḥammad, ʿAlī, and al-Ḥusayn report that they heard Muḥammad ibn Ismāʿīl report that he heard Aḥmad ibn Ḥanbal's son Ṣāliḥ report: **73.49**

[Ṣāliḥ:] ʿUbayd Allāh ibn Yaḥyā wrote to my father saying, "The Commander of the Faithful has ordered me to write and ask you about the Qur'an—not to test you, but instead to learn from you and benefit from your insight."

In response, Aḥmad dictated the following letter to me, for delivery to ʿUbayd Allāh ibn Yaḥyā:[166]

In the name of God, full of compassion, ever-compassionate

> May God reward you, Abū l-Ḥasan, as you deserve, in all matters; and in His mercy stave off all that is hateful in this world and the next. I am writing to you—may God be pleased with you!—to convey such thoughts as occur to me in response to the question posed by the Commander of the Faithful. I ask God to perpetuate the guidance with which He has favored him, inasmuch as the people had waded deep into the treacherous waters of falsehood and disagreement and were floundering there until the Commander of the Faithful succeeded to the caliphate and God, acting through him, banished every heretical innovation. The wretchedness, suffering, and constraint endured by the community vanished all at once, swept away by a Commander of the Faithful doing God's will; and great was the rejoicing of the Muslims, who pray for his well-being. I pray God answer every righteous prayer for the caliph, strengthen his good intentions, and aid him in his quest.

فقد ذُكر عن ابن عبّاس أنّه قال: لا تضربوا كتاب الله بعضَه ببعضٍ فإنّ ذلك يُوقع الشكّ في قلوبكم. وذُكر عن عبد الله بن عمرو أنّ نفرًا كانوا جُلوسًا بباب النبيّ صلّى الله عليه وسلّم فقال بعضهم: ألم يقُل الله كذا؟ وقال بعضهم: ألم يقل الله كذا؟ فسمع رسولُ الله صلّى الله عليه وسلّم فخرج كأنّما فُقئ في وجهه حبّ الرمان فقال: أَبِهذا أُمِرتُم، أنْ تَضرِبوا كتابَ الله بَعضَهُ ببعضٍ، إنّما ضَلّتِ الأُمَمُ قَبلَكُم في مِثْلِ هذا، إنّكُم لَستُم مِمّا ها هُنا في شيءٍ، انظُروا الذي أُمِرتم بهِ فاعْمَلوا بِهِ وَانظُروا الذي نُهيتُم عَنْهُ فانتَهوا عَنه. ٥٠.٧٣

وذكر أحاديث ثم قال: ٥١.٧٣

وقد قال الله تعالى: ﴿حَتَّىٰ يَسْمَعَ كَلَامَ اللَّهِ﴾ وقال: ﴿أَلَا لَهُ الْخَلْقُ وَالْأَمْرُ﴾ فأخبر أن الأمر غير الخلق -

وذكر آيات وقال:

لستُ بصاحب كلام ولا أرى الكلام في شيء من هذا إلّا ما كان في كتاب الله أو في حديث عن النبيّ صلّى الله عليه وسلّم أو عن أصحابه أو عن التابعين.

الباب الرابع والسبعون في ذكر ما جرى له مع ابن طاهر من طلب استزارته وامتناعه عليه

أخبرنا عبد الله بن عليّ المُقرئ قال: أخبرنا عبد الملك بن أحمد السُيوري قال: أخبرنا عبد العزيز بن عليّ بن أحمد بن الفضل قال: حدثنا عليّ بن عبد العزيز البَرذَعي قال: حدثنا أبو محمّد بن أبي حاتم قال: ١.٧٤

73.50 Of Ibn 'Abbas it is related that he said, "Do not strike one verse of God's Book against another for doing so will cast doubt into your hearts."

Citing 'Abd Allāh ibn 'Amr it is related that a group of people were sitting at the door of the Prophet's house. One said, "Did God not say such-and-such?" Another said, "But did He not also say such-and-such?" Overhearing them, the Prophet came out, looking as if a pomegranate had been split open and spattered his face with bitter juice.

"Is this what you've been told to do?" he asked. "To strike the verses of God's Book one against another? That's how the nations before you went astray. What you're doing has no place here. Look to what you are enjoined to do, and do it; look to what is forbidden you, and forbid yourself to do it!"

73.51 Aḥmad cited additional Hadith reports, then said:

> God—exalted be He—has said «so that he may hear the word of God»[167] and «His is the creation, His the command»[168] thereby conveying that command and creation are two different things.

After citing additional verses, he wrote:

> I am no man for Disputation. I do not approve of speculation regarding any of these matters except what is in the Book of God or in reports of what was believed by the Prophet—may God bless and keep him—his Companions, or their Successors.

Chapter 74: His Refusing Ibn Ṭāhir's Request to Visit Him

74.1 We cite 'Abd Allāh ibn 'Alī l-Muqri', who cites 'Abd al-Malik ibn Aḥmad al-Suyūrī, who cites 'Abd al-'Azīz ibn 'Alī ibn Aḥmad ibn al-Faḍl, who heard 'Alī ibn 'Abd al-'Azīz al-Bardha'ī report that he heard Abū Muḥammad ibn Abī Ḥātim report that he heard Aḥmad's son Ṣāliḥ report:

حدثنا صالح ابن أحمد قال: قدم محمّد بن عبد الله بن طاهر فوجّه إلى أبي: أحبّ أن تصير إليّ وتعلمني اليوم الذي تعزم عليه حتّى لا يكون عندي أحد.

فوجّه إليه: أنا رجل لم أخالط السلطان وقد أعفاني أمير المؤمنين ممّا أكره وهذا ممّا أكره.

فجهد أن يصير إليه فأبى.

فكتب إليّ إسحاق بن راهويه:

> إنّي دخلتُ على طاهر بن عبد الله فقال: يا أبا يعقوب كتب إليّ محمد أنّه وجّه إلى أحمد ليصير إليه فلم يأتِه. فقلتُ: أصلح الله الأمير إنّ أحمد قد حلف أن لا يحدّث فلعلّه كره أن يصير إليه فيسأله أن يحدّثه. فقال: ما تقول؟ قال: فقلتُ: نعم.

قال صالح: فأخبرتُ أبي بذلك فسكت.

قلتُ: وإنّما امتنع أحمد من زيارة ابن طاهر لأنّه كان سُلطاناً وإلّا فقد كان يزور أهل الدين والعلم.

٢،٧٤ أخبرنا محمّد بن أبي منصور قال: أخبرنا المبارك بن عبد الجبّار قال: أخبرنا أبو القاسم عبيد الله بن محمّد بن الحسين ابن الفرّاء قال: أخبرنا القاضي أبو محمّد هُمام بن محمّد بن الحسن الأَيْلي قال: حدثنا أبو بكر أحمد ابن عليّ بن الحسين ابن قَسانِية[1] الخطيب قال: حدثنا أبو عبد الله الحسين ابن بكر الورّاق قال: حدثنا أبو الطّيب محمّد بن جعفر قال:

حدثنا عبد الله بن أحمد بن حنبل قال: لمّا أُطلق أبي من المحنة خشي أن يجيء إليه إسحاق بن راهويه فرحل أبي إليه فلمّا بلغ الريّ دخل إلى مسجد فجاءه مطر كأفواه القِرَب فلمّا كانت العتمة قالوا له: اخرج من المسجد فإنّا نريد أن نغلقه.

فقال لهم: هذا مسجد الله وأنا عبد الله.

فقيل له: أيّما أحبّ إليك، أن تخرج أو تُجرّ برجلك؟

قال أحمد: فقلت: سَلاماً.

---

[1] د: قيسانية.

[Ṣāliḥ:] When Muḥammad ibn ʿAbd Allāh ibn Ṭāhir came to Baghdad, he sent a message to my father saying, "I'd like you to come and see me. Tell me the day you prefer and I'll make sure there's no one else here."

My father replied, "I am a man who has never consorted with rulers. Furthermore, the Commander of the Faithful has exempted me from doing anything I detest. This I detest."

Muḥammad strove to change his mind but to no avail.

I then received a letter from Isḥāq ibn Rāhawayh saying:

> I went to see Ṭāhir ibn ʿAbd Allāh and he told me that Muḥammad had invited Aḥmad to call on him but Aḥmad had refused.
>
> I said, "May God correct the emir! Aḥmad has vowed never to teach Hadith again. Perhaps he was afraid that if he went, he would ask him to teach."
>
> He asked, "Are you serious?"
>
> I said, "I am."

I told my father about this but he said nothing.

[The author:] I think Aḥmad refused to visit Ibn Ṭāhir because he was a ruler. He did visit people so long as they were men of piety and learning.

We cite Muḥammad ibn Abī Manṣūr, who cites al-Mubārak ibn ʿAbd al-Jabbār, who cites Abū l-Qāsim ʿUbayd Allāh ibn Muḥammad ibn al-Ḥusayn ibn al-Farrāʾ, who cites Judge Abū Muḥammad Humām ibn Muḥammad ibn al-Ḥasan al-Aylī, who heard Abū Bakr Aḥmad ibn ʿAlī ibn al-Ḥusayn ibn Qasāniyah al-Khaṭīb report that he heard Abū ʿAbd Allāh al-Ḥusayn ibn Bakr al-Warrāq report that he heard Abū l-Ṭayyib Muḥammad ibn Jaʿfar report that he heard Aḥmad ibn Ḥanbal's son ʿAbd Allāh report: 74.2

[ʿAbd Allāh:] After my father was released by the Inquisition, he was worried that Isḥāq ibn Rāhawayh would come to see him so he decided to go see him first. No sooner had he reached Rey and gone into a mosque when the clouds opened like waterskins. He sheltered there until night fell and he was told to leave the mosque because they wanted to close it.

"This is a house of God," he said, "and I'm a worshipper of God."

"Either leave," they said, "or we'll drag you out by the feet. Your choice."

My father continued the story:

فخرجتُ من المسجد والمطر والرعد والبرق[1] فلا أدري أين أضع رجلي ولا أين أتوجّه فإذا رجل قد خرج من داره فقال لي: يا هذا أين تمرّ في هذا الوقت؟

فقلت: لا أدري أين أمرّ.

فقال لي: ادخل.

فأدخلني دارًا ونزع ثيابي وأعطوني ثيابًا جافّة وتطهّرت للصلاة فدخلتُ إلى بيت فيه كانون فحم ولبود ومائدة منصوبة فقيل لي: كُل. فأكلت معهم.

فقال لي: من أين أنت؟

قلتُ: أنا من بغداد.

فقال لي: تعرف رجلًا يقال له أحمد بن حنبل؟

فقلتُ: أنا أحمد بن حنبل.

فقال لي: وأنا إسحاق بن راهويه.

الباب الخامس والسبعون في ذكر ما جرى له مع ولديه وعمّه حين قبلوا صلة السلطان

١٠٧٥ أخبرنا محمّد بن أبي منصور قال: أخبرنا عبد القادر بن محمّد بن يوسف قال: أخبرنا إبراهيم بن عمر البرمكي؛ وأخبرنا عبد الله بن عليّ المقرئ قال: أخبرنا عبد الملك بن أحمد السُيُوري قال: أخبرنا عبد العزيز بن أحمد بن الفضل قالا: أخبرنا عليّ بن عبد العزيز قال: حدثنا عبد الرحمن بن أبي حاتم قال:

حدثنا صالح بن أحمد قال: لمّا قدم أبي من عند المتوكّل مكث قليلًا ثم قال: يا صالح!

قلتُ: لبّيسك.

---

١ هكذا في جميع النسخ.

"Good-bye,"[169] I said, and went out into the thunderstorm with no idea where to go. Then a man came out of his house and said, "You there! Where are you going at a time like this?"

"I have nowhere to go," I said.

"Come in," he said.

He brought me in, had me undress, and gave me dry clothes to change into. I performed my ablutions and then went into a room where there was a heater full of coals, a blanket of felt on the floor, and a laden table. The members of the family invited me to join them. After we ate, the man said, "Where are you from?"

I told them I was from Baghdad.

"Do you know a man named Aḥmad ibn Ḥanbal?"

"I'm Aḥmad ibn Ḥanbal."

"Well," said the man, "I'm Isḥāq ibn Rāhawayh."[170]

Chapter 75: What Happened When His Two Sons and His Uncle Accepted Gifts from the Authorities

We cite Muḥammad ibn Abī Manṣūr, who cites ʿAbd al-Qādir ibn Muḥammad ibn Yūsuf, who cites Ibrāhīm ibn ʿUmar al-Barmakī; and we cite ʿAbd Allāh ibn ʿAlī l-Muqriʾ, who cites ʿAbd al-Malik ibn Aḥmad al-Suyūrī, who cites ʿAbd al-ʿAzīz ibn Aḥmad ibn al-Faḍl, who along with al-Barmakī cites ʿAlī ibn ʿAbd al-ʿAzīz, who heard ʿAbd al-Raḥmān ibn Abī Ḥātim report that he heard Aḥmad's son Ṣāliḥ report: 75.1

[Ṣāliḥ:] A short while after my father came back from Samarra, he summoned me and said, "Ṣālīh, I want you to give up that stipend. Stop accepting it and don't transfer it to anyone else, either. It's only because of me that you get it at all. When I'm gone you can do as you think best."

I said nothing.

قال: أُحبّ أن تدع هذا الرزق فلا تأخذه ولا توكّل فيه أحداً، قد علمتُ أنّكم إنمّا تأخذون هذا بسببي فإذا أنا متّ فأنتم تعلمون.

فسكتُّ فقال: ما لك؟

فقلت: أكره أن أعطيك شيئاً بلساني وأُخالف إلى غيره فأكون قد كذبتُك ونافقتك، وليس في القوم أكثر عِيالاً منّي ولا أعذر وقد كنت أشكو إليك فتقول: أمرُك منعقد بأمري ولعلّ الله أن يحلّ عنّي هذه العُقدة.

ثم قلتُ: وقد كنت تدعو لي وأرجو أن يكون الله عزّ وجلّ قد استجاب لك.

فقال: لا تفعل؟

فقلت: لا.

فقال: قُم فعل الله بك وفعل!

ثم أمر بسدّ الباب بيني وبينه.

فتلقّاني عبد الله وسألني فأخبرتُه فقال: ما أقول؟ ٢،٧٥

فقلت: ذاك إليك.

فقال له مثل ما قال لي فقال: لا أفعل.

فكان منه نحو ممّا كان منه إليّ.

ولقينا عمّه فقال: لِمَ أردتم أن تقولوا له، وما كان علمه إذا أخذتم شيئاً؟

فدخل عليه فقال: يا أبا عبد الله لستُ آخذ شيئاً من هذا.

فقال: الحمد لله!

فهجرَنا وسدّ الأبواب بيننا وتحامى منازلنا أن يدخل منها إلى منزله شيء وقد كان قديماً قبل أن نأخذ من السلطان يأكل عندنا وربّما وجّهنا بالشيء فيأكل منه.

فلمّا مضى نحو من شهرين كُتب لنا بشيء فجئ به إلينا فأوّل من جاء عمّه فأخذ. ٣،٧٥

فأُخبر فجاء إلى الباب الذي كان سدّه بيني وبينه وقد فتح الصبيان كُوّة فقال: ادعوا إليّ صالحاً!

فجاءني الرسول فقلت له: لستُ أجيء.

"What's wrong?"

I said: "I don't like to tell you one thing to your face and then do something else behind your back, so I'm not going to lie to you or tell you what you want to hear. No one here has more dependents than I do and no one has a better excuse to take that money. When I would come complaining to you, you'd say, 'Your fate is bound up with mine. I wish God would remove that burden from me!' Now it seems He's granted your wish."

"So you're not going to turn down the money?"

"No."

"Get out, damn you!" he said.

After that he had someone block up the door between our houses.

When I ran into my brother ʿAbd Allāh, he asked me what was going on 75.2
and I told him.

"What should I say to him?" he asked me.

"That's up to you."

My father made the same request of him as he had made of me. ʿAbd Allāh also said he wouldn't turn down the stipend, and our father got angry at him too.

Later we saw his uncle, who asked why we had said anything about it at all. "If you took something, how would he know?"

His uncle then went to see him. "Abū ʿAbd Allāh," he said, "I'm not taking any of that money."

"Thank God!" said my father.

With that he stopped talking to us, shut up all the doors between our houses, and said that nothing should come from our homes into his. Before we began accepting stipends from the ruler, he used to eat with us. Often we would send him something and he would eat part of it.

Two months later we received our designated payment, delivered to our 75.3
door, and the first to arrive and claim a share was his uncle.

When he learned what was going on, my father came to the door that had been blocked up and spoke through a hole that the boys had made.

"Call Ṣāliḥ for me!" he said.

Someone brought me the message.

"I'm not coming," I said.

My father sent another message to ask why not.

فوجّه إليّ: لِمَ لا تجيء؟

فقلتُ له: هذا الرزق يَرتزقه جماعة كثيرة وإنّما أنا واحد منهم وليس فيهم أعذر منّي، فإذا كان توبيخ خُصِصْتُ به أنا.

٤،٧٥ فمضى فلمّا نادى عمّه بالأذان خرج فلمّا خرج قيل له: إنه قد خرج إلى المسجد.

فجئتُ حتى صرت في الموضع الذي أسمع كلامه.

فلمّا فرغ من الصلاة التفت إلى عمّه ثم قال له: يا عدوّ الله نافَقتني وكذبتني وكان غيرك أعذر منك! زعمتَ أنّك لا تأخذ من هذا شيئاً ثم أخذتَ فأنت تستغلّ مئتي درهم وعمدتَ إلى طريق المسلمين تستغلّه، إنمّا أُشفق أن تُطوَّق يوم القيامة بسبع أرضين.

ثم هجره وترك الصلاة في المسجد وخرج إلى مسجد خارج[1] يصلّي فيه.

٥،٧٥ أخبرنا إسماعيل بن أحمد ومحمّد بن أبي القاسم قالا: أخبرنا حمد بن أحمد قال: أخبرنا أحمد بن عبد الله الحافظ قال: حدثنا أبو بكر بن مالك قال:

حدثنا أبو جعفر بن ذَرِيح العُكبَري قال: طلبت أحمد بن حنبل في سنة ستّ وثلاثين ومائتين لأسأله عن مسألة فسألت عنه فقالوا إنّه خرج يصلّي خارجاً.

فجلست له على باب الدرب حتّى جاء فقمتُ فسلّمت عليه فردّ عليّ السلام فدخل الزُّقاق وأنا أماشيه فلمّا بلغنا آخر الدرب إذا باب يُفرج فدفعه وصار خلفه وقال: اذهب عافاك الله!

فالتفتّ فإذا مسجد على الباب وشيخ مخضوب قائم يصلّي بالناس فجلست حتى سلّم الإمام فخرج رجل فقلت: هذا الشيخ من هو؟

قال: إسحاق عمّ أحمد بن حنبل.

قلتُ: فما له لا يصلّي خلفه؟

فقال: ليس يكلّم ذا ولا ابنَيه لأنّهم أخذوا جائزة السلطان.

---

١ ش: آخر.

"There are plenty of people who depend on this stipend," I said. "I'm not the only one, but I am the most entitled. If you've chosen me of all people for a scolding, I'm not coming."

A bit later his uncle called everyone to prayer. My father came out of the house and was told that his uncle had gone out to the mosque. I went there too, but stopped and waited in a spot where I could hear what they were saying. As soon as the prayer was over, my father turned to his uncle and said, "You enemy of God! You lied to my face even though other people need the money more than you. You said you wouldn't take any of it and then you did—even though you've got a property that pays you two hundred dirhams and you were hoping to make more by taking over a public road! When the Day of Resurrection comes, I'm afraid we'll find you with seven tracts of land tied around your neck!"[171] 75.4

With that he stopped speaking to him. He also stopped praying in our mosque and started going out to pray in someone else's mosque.

We cite Ismāʿīl ibn Aḥmad, who along with Muḥammad ibn Abī l-Qāsim cites Ḥamd ibn Aḥmad, who heard Aḥmad ibn ʿAbd Allāh al-Ḥāfiẓ report that he heard Abū Bakr ibn Mālik report that he heard Abū Jaʿfar ibn Dharīḥ al-ʿUkbarī report: 75.5

[Al-ʿUkbarī:] In 236 [850–51] I went looking for Aḥmad ibn Ḥanbal so I could ask him about something. I asked for him and they told me he had gone out to pray, so I sat down to wait by the alley gate. When he appeared, I rose and greeted him and he returned the greeting. He went down the alley and I walked beside him all the way to the end, where there was an open door. He pushed it open and went in, saying, "Go away now, and may God spare you!"

As I turned, I saw that the gate opened onto a mosque where an elder with a dyed beard was standing and leading the congregation in prayer. I sat and waited until he spoke the parting salutation. When someone came out, I asked him who the elder was.

"That's Isḥāq, Aḥmad ibn Ḥanbal's uncle," he said.

"Why won't Aḥmad pray behind him?"

"He won't talk to him, or to his own sons, because they accept a stipend from the authorities."

٦،٧٥ أخبرنا محمّد بن أبي منصور قال: أخبرنا عبد القادر بن محمّد قال: أخبرنا إبراهيم بن عمرن قال: أخبرنا عليّ بن مَرْدَك قال: حدثنا أبو محمّد بن أبي حاتم قال:

حدثنا صالح بن أحمد قال: بلغ أبي في زمان هجره لنا أنّه قد كُتب لنا بشيء إلى ما دورنا[1] فجاء إلى الكُوّة التي في الباب فقال: يا صالح انظر ما كان للحسن وأمّ عليّ فاذهب به إلى فُوران حتى يتصدّق به في الموضع الذي أُخذ منه.

فقلت له: ما علم فوران من أي موضع أُخذ؟

فقال: افعل ما أقول لك! فوجّهت ما كان أُضيف إليهما إلى فوران.

وكان إذا بلغه أنا قد قبلنا طوى تلك الليلة فلم يُفطر ثم مكث شهرًا لا أدخل عليه ثمّ فتح الصبيان الباب ودخلوا غير أنّه لا يُدخل إليه شيء من منزلي. ثم وجّهت إليه: يا أبةِ قد طال هذا الأمر وقد اشتقتُ إليك.

فدخلتُ عليه فسكت فأكببتُ عليه وقلت: يا أبة تُدخل على نفسك هذا الغمّ؟

قال: يا بُنيّ ما لا أملكه.

٧،٧٥ ثم مكثنا مدة لم نأخذ شيئًا. ثم كُتب لنا بشيء فقبضناه.

فلمّا بلغه هجرَنا أشهرًا فكلّمه فوران ووجّه إليّ فوران فدخلت فقال له: يا أبا عبد الله، صالح وحُبّكَ له!

فقال: يا أبا محمّد لقد كان أعزّ الخلق عليّ وأيّ شيء أردتُ له إلا ما أردتُه لنفسي؟

فقلت له: يا أبة ومن رأيت أنت ممّن لقيت قوي على ما قويت عليه أنت؟

قال: وتحتجّ عليّ؟

ثم كتب إلى يحيى بن خاقان يسأله ويعزم عليه أن لا يُعيننا على شيء من أرزاقنا ولا يتكلّم فيها.

فلمّا وصل رسوله بالكتاب إلى يحيى أخذه صاحب الخبر فأخذ نسخته ووصلت إلى المتوكل فقال لعُبيد الله: كم من شهر لولد أحمد بن حنبل؟

فقال: عشرة أشهر.

---

١ هكذا في جميع النسخ، وفي تركي: فبلغه.

We cite Muḥammad ibn Abī Manṣūr, who cites ʿAbd al-Qādir ibn Muḥammad, who cites Ibrāhīm ibn ʿUmar, who cites ʿAlī ibn Mardak, who heard Abū Muḥammad ibn Abī Ḥātim report that he heard Aḥmad's son Ṣāliḥ report: 75.6

[Ṣāliḥ:] At some point when my father wasn't speaking to us, he found out that we'd been sent another sum.[172] My father came to the opening in the door and said, "Ṣāliḥ! Find out which parts are for Ḥasan and Umm ʿAlī[173] and take them to Fūrān. Tell him to go to wherever the money came from and give it away as alms."

"How would Fūrān know where it came from?"

"Just do as I say."

So I sent the two portions to Fūrān.

Meanwhile, my father, after he heard that we had accepted the money, went to bed without eating. I didn't see him for a month. Then the boys opened the door and went in. But he still wouldn't let them bring in anything from my house. Finally I sent him a message saying: "This has gone on long enough, and I miss you." Then I went in. He wouldn't speak to me. I bent down and embraced him.

"Dad," I asked, "why are you doing this to yourself?"

"It's something I can't help, son."

After that we didn't accept anything for a while. Then we were granted something more and we took it. When my father found out he stopped talking to us for months. Finally Fūrān had a word with him and I went in. 75.7

"It's Ṣāliḥ," said Fūrān. "Remember how much you care for him."

"Ṣāliḥ was the dearest person in the world to me," said my father. "All I wanted was for him to have what I wanted for myself. What's wrong with that?"

"Dad," I said, "have you ever met anyone who could survive what you put yourself through?"

"So now you're arguing with me?"

Then he wrote to Yaḥyā ibn Khāqān demanding that he stop paying the stipend and never mention it again. No sooner had the message reached Yaḥyā than the chief of intelligence took it and sent a copy to al-Mutawakkil.

"How many months are due to Aḥmad's sons?" the caliph asked.

"Ten."

"Have forty thousand dirhams—whole coins from the treasury—sent to them immediately without telling Aḥmad."

فقال: تحمل إليهم الساعة أربعين ألف درهم من بيت المال صحاح ولا يعلم بها.
فقال يحيى للقيّم: أنا أكتب إلى صالح أُعلمه.
فورد عليّ كتابه فوجّهتُ إلى أبي أعلمته فقال الذي أخبره: سكتَ قليلاً وضرب بذقنه صدره ثمّ رفع رأسه وقال: ما حيلتي إذا أردتُ أمرًا وأراد الله عزّ وجلّ أمرًا.

٨،٧٥ أخبرنا عبد الملك بن أبي القاسم قال: أخبرنا عبد الله بن محمّد الأنصاري قال: أخبرنا أبو يعقوب الحافظ قال: أخبرنا أبو عليّ بن أبي بكر المَرْوَزي قال: حدثنا أبو عبد الله محمّد بن الحسن بن عليّ البُخاري قال:
سمعت محمّد بن إبراهيم البُوشَنْجي يقول: حُكي لنا عن المتوكل أنّه قال إنّ أحمد ليمنعنا من برّ ولده.
وذلك أنّه كان وجّه إلى ولده وإلى ولد ولده وإلى عمّه بمال عظيم فأخذوه دون علم أحمد فلمّا بلغه ذلك أنكر عليهم وتقدّم إليهم بردّه وقال لهم: لِمَ تأخذوه والثُّغور مُعطَّلة غير مشحونة والفَيْء غير مقسوم بين أهله؟
فاعتلّوا بخروج ذلك المال من أيديهم في ديونهم وما كان عليهم.
٩،٧٥ ثم وجّه المتوكّل مالاً آخر وقال: لِيُعْطَ ولده من غير علم أحمد. فأخذوه فبلغ ذلك أحمد فجمعهم وقال لهم: احتججتم في المال الأول بذهابه عنكم وبديونكم، فردّوه!
فأنا شهدت وقد سد باباً كان بينه وبين صالح ابنه وترك مسجده ومُؤذّنه عمّه وإمامه ابن عمير وداره لزنقة المسجد وهجرهم من أجل ذلك المال.
وأنا رأيته يخرج من زقاقه ومن دربه إلى الشارع ويدخل درباً آخر فيه مسجد يقال له مسجد سِدرة يُصلّي فيه الجماعة.
١٠،٧٥ ثمّ لمّا أُشخص إلى العسكر أيّام المتوكّل أُحضر دار الخلافة ليحدّث فيها ولدَ المتوكّل[١] المُعتزّ والمُنتَصر والمؤيَّد وهم وُلاة العهود فجعل يتمارض وإذا سُئل قال: لا أحفظ وكُتبي عني غائبة، حتى أُعفي.
ووقّع المتوكل في بعض ما وقّع: أعفينا أحمد ممّا يكره.

---

١ د: ولده.

"I'll write to Ṣāliḥ and let him know," said Yaḥyā to the official.

When I received Yaḥyā's letter, I sent word to my father.

The one who delivered the message reported: "Aḥmad sat silently for a while staring at the ground. Then he raised his head and said, 'If I want one thing but God decrees another, there's nothing more I can do.'"

We cite ʿAbd al-Malik ibn Abī l-Qāsim, who cites ʿAbd Allāh ibn Muḥammad al-Anṣārī, who cites Abū Yaʿqūb al-Ḥāfiẓ, who cites Abū ʿAlī ibn Abī Bakr al-Marwazī, who heard Abū ʿAbd Allāh Muḥammad ibn al-Ḥasan ibn ʿAlī l-Bukhārī report that he heard Muḥammad ibn Ibrāhīm al-Būshanjī say: 75.8

[Al-Būshanjī:] Someone quoted al-Mutawakkil as saying, "Aḥmad won't let us take care of his family." This was because he had sent vast sums to Aḥmad's children, grandchildren, and uncle, who had taken it without telling him. When Aḥmad realized what had happened, he reproached them and told them to return the money. "How could you take it when the frontier is undefended and no one is distributing the spoils to the Muslims who deserve a share?"[174]

Everyone pleaded that they had already paid the money to their creditors.

Then al-Mutawakkil sent another sum, ordering that it be given to his sons 75.9
without his knowing about it. Again, they accepted it. When Aḥmad found out, he summoned them and said, "With the first amount, you claimed that you had spent it already or used it to pay your debts. This one, though, you can still send back."

I myself saw him block off the door that joined his house to his son Ṣāliḥ's. I also saw him stay away from the mosque that adjoined his house, where the prayer caller was his uncle and the prayer leader was Ibn ʿUmayr. It was because of the money that he stopped talking to them. I saw him walk all the way through the alley, into the lane, onto the main thoroughfare, and then down another lane where there was a mosque called the Sidrah Mosque, big enough for Friday prayers.

When Aḥmad was sent to Samarra during the reign of al-Mutawakkil, 75.10
they took him to the palace to recite Hadith for caliph's children al-Muʿtazz, al-Muntaṣir, and al-Mu'ayyad, his heirs apparent. Aḥmad responded by feigning illness and, if asked about a report, saying, "I don't remember, and I don't have my books here." In the end al-Mutawakkil relented and let him

ولقد جاءته تحفة رُطَب من قبل المتوكّل مختومة فما طعم منها، وبلغني أنّه احتجّ في ذلك اليوم فقال: إنّ أَمير المؤمنين قد أعفاني ممّا أكره.

فإذا جاءه شيء قال: هذا ممّا أكره فَيُعفى فكانت هذه حاله.

١١،٧٥ أخبرنا هِبة الله بن أحمد الحَريري قال: أنبأنا محمّد بن عليّ بن الفتح قال: حدثنا عبد الله بن أحمد بن الصبّاح الكوفي قال: حدثنا جعفر بن محمّد ابن نُصير قال: حدثنا أحمد بن محمّد بن مسروق قال:

قال لي عبد الله بن أحمد بن حنبل: دخل عليّ أبي رحمه الله في مرضي يعودني فقلتُ: يا أبة عندنا شيء قد بقي ممّا كان يبرّنا به المتوكّل أفأحجّ منه؟

قال: نعم.

قلتُ: فإذا كان هذا عندك هكذا فلِمَ لمْ تأخُذ؟[1]

قال: يا بُنيّ ليس هو عندي حرام[2] ولكنّي تنزّهت عنه.

الباب السادس والسبعون في ذكر جماعة من الكبار الذين أجابوا في المحنة

١،٧٦ أجاب من كبار العلماء عليّ بن الجعد، وإسماعيل بن إبراهيم بن عُليّة، وسعيد ابن سليمان الواسطي المعروف بسَعْدُوَيْه، وإسحاق بن أبي إسرائيل، وأبو حَسّان الزِيادي، وبِشْر بن[3] الوَليد، وعُبيد الله بن عمر القَواريري، وعلي بن أبي مُقاتل، والفَضل بن غانم، والحسن بن حَمّاد سَجّادة، وإسماعيل بن أبي مسعود، ومحمّد بن سعد كاتب الواقدي، وأحمد بن إبراهيم الدَّورقي، وإسماعيل بن داوود الجَوْزي،[4]

---

١ د: لا تاخذ. ٢ هـ، د: هكذا، وفي ش: بحرام. ٣ د: بن ابي. ٤ هـ: الخوزي، صححه التركي.

go, signing an order that read as follows: "We herewith excuse Aḥmad from doing anything he detests."

On one occasion Aḥmad received a gift of dates bearing al-Mutawakkil's seal but refused to taste them. To explain himself, he reportedly said, "The Commander of the Faithful has excused me from doing anything I detest." He said the same thing whenever anything was sent to his house, and that became his custom.

We cite Hibat Allāh ibn Aḥmad al-Ḥarīrī, who was informed by Muḥammad ibn ʿAlī ibn al-Fatḥ, who heard ʿAbd Allāh ibn Aḥmad ibn al-Ṣabbāḥ al-Kūfī report that he heard Jaʿfar ibn Muḥammad ibn Nuṣayr report that he heard Aḥmad ibn Muḥammad ibn Masrūq report that Aḥmad ibn Ḥanbal's son ʿAbd Allāh said to him: 75.11

[ʿAbd Allāh:] When I was ill, my father came to check on me.

"Dad," I said, "we still have some of the money al-Mutawakkil gave us. What if I used it to make the pilgrimage?"

"You should," he said.

"But if you don't mind spending it," I asked, "why didn't *you* take it?"

"I don't consider it forbidden, son," he answered. "But I'd rather abstain."

Chapter 76: Some Major Figures Who Capitulated to the Inquisition

Among the prominent men of learning who capitulated were ʿAlī ibn al-Jaʿd; Ismāʿīl ibn Ibrāhīm ibn ʿUlayyah[175]; Saʿīd ibn Sulaymān al-Wāsiṭī, known as Saʿduwayh; Isḥāq ibn Abī Isrāʾīl; Abū Ḥassān al-Ziyādī; Bishr ibn al-Walīd; ʿUbayd Allāh ibn ʿUmar al-Qawārīrī; ʿAlī ibn Abī Muqātil; al-Faḍl ibn Ghānim; al-Ḥasan ibn Ḥammād Sajjadah; Ismāʿīl ibn Abī Masʿūd; Muḥammad ibn Saʿd, scribe to al-Wāqidī; Aḥmad ibn Ibrāhīm al-Dawraqī; Ismāʿīl ibn Dāwūd 76.1

ويحيى بن مَعِين، وعلي بن المَدِيني، وأبو خَيْثَمَة زُهير بن حَرْب، وأبو نَصْر التمّار، وأبو كُرَيب في آخرين.

٢،٧٦ وما صعبت إجابة أحد من هؤلاء على أحمد بن حنبل كما شقّت إجابة أبي نصر التمّار[١] ويحيى بن مَعين وأبي خَيثمة لأنهم كانوا عنده في أعلى مرتبة وما ظنّ بهم الإسراع في الإجابة. فأما أبو نصر التمار فإنّه كان من العبّاد وسمع الحديث من مالك والحمّادين وخلق كثير إلّا أنّه لم يصبر على الامتحان فأجاب، فكان أحمد لا يرى الكتابة عنه،[٢] ولمّا مات لم يصلِّ عليه.

٣،٧٦ وقد أخبرنا عليّ بن عبد الواحد قال: أخبرنا عليّ بن عمر القَزْويني قال: قرأت على يوسف بن عمر قلت له: حدثكم أبو الحسن عليّ بن محمّد بن سعيد المَوْصِلي قال: حدثني محمّد بن حرب قال: سمعتُ عبد الصمد بن محمّد بن مقاتل يقول:

سمعت أبا حَفْص ابن أخت بشر بن الحارث يقول:[٣] قال لي بشر في اليوم الذي أُحضر فيه أبو نصر التمّار إلى دار إسحاق بن إبراهيم: تعرَّفْ لي خبر أبي نصر.

قال: فقلت له: إنّه قد أجاب.

فاسترجع مرارًا ثم قال: ما كان أحسن تلك اللحية لو كانت خُضِبت، يعني بالدم، ولم يُجِبْ حتّى يُقتل.

٤،٧٦ أخبرنا عبد الرحمن بن محمّد قال: أخبرنا أحمد بن عليّ بن ثابت قال: حدثني عبيد الله بن أبي الفتح قال: حدثنا عمر بن إبراهيم المقرئ قال: سمعت أحمد بن عليّ الديباجي يقول:

سمعت عبيد الله بن شريك يقول: كان أبو مَعْمَر القَطيعي من شدّة إدلاله بالسنّة يقول: لو تكلّمت بغلتي لقالت إنها سُنّية.

قال: فأُخذ في المحنة فأجاب فلمّا خرج قال: كفرنا وخرجنا.

١ بعده في هـ : وعلي بن المديني. ٢ بعدها تتكرر الورقة ١٢٩ من الصورة الضوئية لـ ش. ٣ سمعت أبا حَفْص ابن أخت بشر بن الحارث يقول: ليس في ش.

al-Jawzī; Yaḥyā ibn Maʿīn; ʿAlī ibn al-Madīnī; Abū Khaythamah Zuhayr ibn Ḥarb; Abū Naṣr al-Tammār; and Abū Kurayb.

The capitulations that were hardest for Aḥmad ibn Ḥanbal to bear were those of Abū Naṣr al-Tammār, Yaḥyā ibn Maʿīn, and Abū Khaythamah. He had a high opinion of them all and did not expect any of them to give in as quickly as they did. Abū Naṣr al-Tammār was a Worshipper who heard Hadith from Mālik, the two Ḥammāds, and many others, but was unable to withstand the Inquisition and caved in. Aḥmad consequently held that one should not write down the reports he transmitted, and refused to pray over him when he died. 76.2

We cite ʿAlī ibn ʿAbd al-Wāḥid, who cites ʿAlī ibn ʿUmar al-Qazwīnī, who said that he read back to Yūsuf ibn ʿUmar that Abū l-Ḥasan ʿAlī ibn Muḥammad ibn Saʿīd al-Mawṣilī had reported to him that Muḥammad ibn Ḥarb had reported to him that he heard ʿAbd al-Ṣamad ibn Muḥammad ibn Muqātil say that he heard Abū Ḥafṣ, who was the nephew of Bishr ibn al-Ḥārith, say: 76.3

[Abū Ḥafṣ:] The day Abū Naṣr al-Tammār was taken in for questioning by Isḥāq ibn Ibrāhīm, Bishr asked me to find out what happened. When I told him that al-Tammār had capitulated, he recited «We are of God, and to Him we return!»[176] several times, then said, "How beautiful that beard of his would have been if he had dyed it"—meaning with blood—"and resisted until death."

We cite ʿAbd al-Raḥmān ibn Muḥammad, who cites Aḥmad ibn ʿAlī ibn Thābit, who heard ʿUbayd Allāh ibn ʿAlī l-Fatḥ report that he heard ʿUmar ibn Ibrāhīm al-Muqriʾ report that he heard Aḥmad ibn ʿAlī l-Dībājī (maker of brocade?) say that he heard ʿUbayd Allāh ibn Sharīk say: 76.4

[ʿUbayd Allāh:] Abū Maʿmar al-Qaṭīʿī was such a fervent adherent of the *sunnah* that he used to say, "If my mule could talk, she'd say she was a Sunni."

But then when he was put to the test, he gave in. After he was released he said, "We denied our faith and they let us go."

٥،٧٦ أخبرنا عبد الرحمن بن محمّد قال: أخبرنا أحمد بن عليّ قال: قرأت على البَرقاني عن أبي إسحاق المُزَكّي[١] قال: أخبرنا محمّد بن إسحاق السرّاج قال:

سمعت ابن عسكر يقول: لما دُعي سَعْدُوَيه للمحنة رأيته حين خرج من دار الأمير فقال: يا غُلام قدّمْ الحمار فإنّ مولاك قد كفر.

قلت: سعدويه هو سعيد بن سليمان أبو عثمان الواسطي يُعرف بسَعدويه وقد حدّث عن الليث بن سعد وغيره وحجّ ستين حجة.

٦،٧٦ أخبرنا عبد الرحمن بن محمّد قال: أخبرنا أحمد بن عليّ قال: أخبرنا محمّد بن عبد الواحد قال: أخبرنا الوليد بن بكر قال: حدثنا عليّ بن أحمد ابن زكريّا قال: حدثنا صالح بن أحمد العِجْلي قال:

حدثني أبي قال: قيل لسعدويه بعد ما انصرف من المحنة: ما فعلتم؟

قال: كفرنا ورجعنا.

الباب السابع والسبعون في ذكر كلامه فيمن أجاب في المحنة

١،٧٧ أخبرنا أبو منصور القزاز قال: أخبرنا أبو بكر أحمد بن عليّ بن ثابت قال: أخبرنا البَرقاني قال: أخبرنا يعقوب بن موسى الأَرْدَبيلي[٢] قال: حدثنا أحمد بن طاهر بن النَّجْم قال: حدثنا سعيد بن عَمْرو البَرْدَعي قال:

سمعتُ أبا زُرْعة وهو الرازي يقول: كان أحمد بن حنبل لا يرى الكتابة عن أبي نصر التمّار ولا يحيى بن مَعين ولا أحد ممّن امتُحن فأجاب.

٢،٧٧ قال البَرقاني: وأخبرنا الحسين بن عليّ التميمي قال: حدثنا أبو عَوَانة يعقوب بن إسحاق الإسفَرايني قال:

---

١ د: البرمكي. ٢ هـ: الأردنيلي، ش: الأرذلي.

We cite ʿAbd al-Raḥmān ibn Muḥammad, who cites Aḥmad ibn ʿAlī, who read back to al-Barqānī his report citing Abū Isḥāq al-Muzakkī, who cites Muḥammad ibn Isḥāq al-Sarrāj, who reports he heard Ibn ʿAskar say: 76.5

[Ibn ʿAskar:] After Saʿduwayh was called in, I saw him come out of the emir's residence and say, "Boy, bring the donkey. Your master has denied his faith!"

[The author:] I say: Saʿduwayh is Saʿīd ibn Sulaymān Abū ʿUthmān al-Wāsiṭī, known as Saʿduwayh. He recited Hadith citing Ibn Saʿd and others and performed the pilgrimage sixty times.

We cite ʿAbd al-Raḥmān ibn Muḥammad, who cites Aḥmad ibn ʿAlī, who cites Muḥammad ibn ʿAbd al-Wāḥid, who cites al-Walīd ibn Bakr, who heard ʿAlī ibn Aḥmad ibn Zakariyyā report that he heard Ṣāliḥ ibn Aḥmad al-ʿIjlī report that he heard his father say: 76.6

[Al-ʿIjlī:] After his interrogation, Saʿduwayh was asked what he had done. "We denied our faith and they let us go," he said.

Chapter 77: His Comments on Those Who Capitulated

We cite Abū Manṣūr al-Qazzāz, who cites Abū Bakr Aḥmad ibn ʿAlī ibn Thābit, who cites al-Barqānī, who cites Yaʿqūb ibn Mūsā l-Ardabīlī, who heard Aḥmad ibn Ṭāhir ibn al-Najm report that he heard Saʿīd ibn ʿAmr al-Bardaʿī report that he heard Abū Zurʿah—that is, al-Rāzī—say: 77.1

[Abū Zurʿah:] Aḥmad held that one should not write down reports transmitted by Abū Naṣr al-Tammār, Yaḥyā ibn Maʿīn, or anyone else who capitulated to the Inquisition.

Al-Barqānī also cited al-Ḥusayn ibn ʿAlī l-Tamīmī, who heard Abū ʿAwānah Yaʿqūb ibn Isḥāq al-Isfarāyīnī, who heard al-Maymūnī say: 77.2

سمعت الميموني يقول: صحّ عندي أنّه لم يحضر أبا نصر التمّار حين مات - يعني أحمد بن حنبل - فحسبتُ أنّ ذلك لما كان أجاب في المحنة.

٣،٧٧ أخبرنا عبد الملك بن أبي القاسم قال: أخبرنا عبد الله بن محمّد قال: أخبرني محمّد بن محمّد بن محمود قال: أخبرنا أحمد ابن محمّد العَنْجاري[١] قال: أخبرنا محمّد بن العباس العُصْمي قال: أخبرنا أحمد بن محمّد بن ياسين قال: أخبرنا أحمد بن محمود بن مُقاتِل قال: سمعت زكريّا بن يحيى السِّجْزي يقول:

سمعتُ حَجّاج بن الشاعر يقول: سمعت أحمد بن حنبل يقول: لو حدّثت عن أحد ممّن أجاب لحدّثت عن اثنين: أبي مَعْمَر وأبي كُرَيْب.

قلت: أبو معمر اسمه إسماعيل بن إبراهيم الهُذَلي، أجاب كرهاً ثمّ نَدم وأخذ يذمّ نفسه على إجابته ويمدح من لم يُجِبْ ويغبطهم وأمّا أبو كريب فاسمه محمّد بن العَلاء وكانوا قد أجرَوْا له بعد أن أجاب دينارين فعلم أنهم إنما أجروها لإجابته فتركهما وهو مُحتاج إليهما.

٤،٧٧ أخبرنا عبد الملك بن أبي القاسم قال: أخبرنا عبد الله بن محمّد قال: أخبرني محمّد بن المنتصر قال: أخبرنا أبو بكر ابن أبي الفضل قال: حدثنا أبو إسحاق الأنصاري قال:

حدثنا صالح بن أحمد قال: جاء الحِزامي إلى أبي، وقد كان ذهب إلى ابن أبي دُؤاد، فلمّا خرج إليه ورآه أغلق الباب في وجهه ودخل.

قلت: وكذلك فعل بأبي خَيْثَمة فإنّه جاء فطرق عليه الباب فلمّا خرج فرآه أغلق الباب ورجع[٢] مغضباً يتكلم هو ونفسه بكلمات سمعها أبو خيثمة فلم يعد إليه، وعاده يحيى بن مَعِين في مرضه فولّاه ظهره وأمسك عن كلامه حتى قام عنه وهو يتأفّف ويقول: بعد الصحبة الطويلة لا أُكلَّم.

---

١ مشكلة في ش، ومشطوبة في د، وتركي: الغُنْجاري. ٢ ليس في د، وفي ش: خرج.

[Al-Maymūnī:] I have it on good authority that he—meaning Aḥmad ibn Ḥanbal—did not attend the funeral of Abū Naṣr al-Tammār. I believe the reason was al-Tammār's capitulation to the Inquisition.

We cite ʿAbd al-Malik ibn Abī l-Qāsim, who cites ʿAbd Allāh ibn Muḥammad, who cites Muḥammad ibn Muḥammad ibn Maḥmūd, who cites Aḥmad ibn Muḥammad al-ʿAnjārī, who cites Muḥammad ibn al-ʿAbbās al-ʿUṣmī, who cites Aḥmad ibn Muḥammad ibn Yāsīn, who cites Aḥmad ibn Maḥmūd ibn Muqātil, who heard Zakariyyā ibn Yaḥyā l-Sijzī say that he heard Ḥajjāj ibn al-Shāʿir: 77.3

[Ḥajjāj ibn al-Shāʿir:] I heard Aḥmad ibn Ḥanbal say, "If I were to transmit Hadith from anyone who gave in, I'd transmit from Abū Maʿmar and Abū Kurayb."

[The author:] Abū Maʿmar's full name is Ismāʿīl ibn Ibrāhīm al-Hudhalī and he capitulated under duress. He later regretted doing so, reproaching himself and expressing envious admiration of those who resisted. As for Abū Kurayb, his real name is Muḥammad ibn Abū l-ʿAlāʾ. After his capitulation he was given a stipend of two dinars. When he discovered that they were rewarding him for giving in, he renounced the stipend even though he needed it.

We cite ʿAbd al-Malik ibn Abī l-Qāsim, who cites ʿAbd Allāh ibn Muḥammad, who cites Muḥammad ibn al-Muntaṣir, who cites Abū Bakr ibn Abī l-Faḍl, who heard Abū Isḥāq al-Anṣārī report that he heard Aḥmad's son Ṣāliḥ report: 77.4

[Ṣāliḥ:] Al-Ḥizāmī came to see us after having been to see Ibn Abī Duʾād. As soon as my father went out and saw him there, he shut the door in his face and went back inside.

[The author:] He did the same with Abū Khaythamah, who came and knocked on the door. When Aḥmad came out and saw him there he shut the door and went back inside muttering angrily to himself. Abū Khaythamah, who could hear whatever it was that Aḥmad was saying, never came back.

When Aḥmad fell ill, Yaḥyā ibn Maʿīn came to see him; but Aḥmad turned his back on him and refused to say a word. Finally Yaḥyā got up and left, grumbling, "After all that time together he won't even speak to me!"

٥،٧٧ أخبرنا محمد بن ناصر قال: أنبأنا أبو عليّ الحسن بن أحمد قال: أنبأنا إبراهيم بن عمر البرمكي قال: وجدت بخط أبي: أخبرنا أبو القاسم عبد العزيز بن أحمد بن يعقوب الحربي قال: سمعت أبا الفَرَج الهِندِبائي يقول:

سمعتُ أبا بكر المَرُّوذي يقول: جاء يحيى بن مَعِين فدخل على أحمد بن حنبل وهو مريض فسلّم فلم يردَّ عليه السلام وكان أحمد قد حلف بالعهد لا يكلّم أحداً ممّن أجاب حتى يلقى الله عزّ وجلّ.

فما زال يحيى يعتذر ويقول: حديث عمّار، وقال الله تعالى: ﴿إلاَّ مَنْ أُكْرِهَ وَقَلْبُهُ مُطْمَئِنٌّ بالإيمَانِ﴾.

فقلب أحمد وجهه إلى الجانب الآخر.

فقال يحيى: أُفّ! وقام وقال: لا يقبل لنا عذراً.

فخرجتُ بعده وهو جالس على الباب فقال: أيّ شيء قال أحمد بعدي؟

قلتُ: يحتجُّ بحديث عمّار- وحديث عمار: مَررتُ[١] وهم يَسبّونَك فَنهَيتُهم فَضَربوني -وأنتم قيل لكم: نريد أن نضربكم.

فسمعت يحيى يقول: مُر يا أحمد، غفر الله لك! فما رأيتُ والله تحت أديم سماء الله أفقه في دين الله منك.

فصل

٦،٧٧ فإن قال قائل: إذا ثبت أنّ القوم أجابوا مُكرَهين فقد استعملوا الجائز فلمَ هجرهم أحمد؟ فالجواب من ثلاثة أوجه:

أحدها أنّ القوم تُوعِّدوا ولم يُضربوا فأجابوا والتواعد ليس بإكراه وقد بان هذا بما ذكرناه من حديث يحيى بن مَعِين.

والثاني أنّه هجرهم على وجه التأديب ليعلم العَوامّ تعظيم القول الذي أجابوا عليه فيكون ذلك حفظاً لهم من الزّيغ.

---

١ هـ: مررت بهم.

We cite Muḥammad ibn Nāṣir, who was informed by Abū ʿAlī l-Ḥasan ibn Aḥmad, who was informed by Ibrāhīm ibn ʿUmar al-Barmakī, who reports finding a document in his father's handwriting, citing Abū l-Qāsim ʿAbd al-ʿAzīz ibn Aḥmad ibn Yaʿqūb al-Ḥarbī, who reports that he heard Abū l-Faraj al-Hindibāʾī (the endive merchant?) say that he heard Abū Bakr al-Marrūdhī say: 77.5

[Al-Marrūdhī:] When Aḥmad ibn Ḥanbal fell ill, Yaḥyā ibn Maʿīn came to visit him. But Aḥmad, who had vowed never to speak to anyone who had capitulated, did not return his greeting. Yaḥyā began offering excuses, including the Hadith of ʿAmmār, and the verse «with the exception of one who is forced to do it, while his heart rests securely in faith.»[177] Aḥmad's only response was to turn his head away. Finally Yaḥyā said, "I give up!" and got to his feet, muttering "It's no use explaining anything to him."

I followed him out and found him sitting by the door.

"Did Aḥmad say anything after I left?" he asked.

"He said, 'I can't believe he's citing the Hadith of ʿAmmār! (The Ḥadīth of ʿAmmār runs as follows: "As I passed them, I heard them cursing you; and when I told them not to, they beat me."[178]) All they did was *threaten* to beat you.'"

Finally I heard Yaḥyā say, "Go on, then, Aḥmad, and may God forgive you! Never on God's green earth have I met anyone who knew His Law better than you."

Addendum

Someone might well ask why, if it can be shown that certain individuals capitulated under duress, which the Law allows, did Aḥmad end his relationship with them? There are three possible responses: 77.6

1. The persons in question were threatened but not beaten before they capitulated. Threats do not count as coercion, as is evident from the aforementioned report about Yaḥyā ibn Maʿīn.

2. Aḥmad may have ended his relationship with them in order to make a point: to show the common people what a heinous doctrine it was that the offenders had assented to and thus help the mass of believers stay on the right path.

والثالث أنّ معظم القوم لمّا أجابوا قبلوا الأموال وتردّدوا إلى القوم وتقرّبوا إليهم ففعلوا ما لا يجوز فلهذا استحقّوا الذمّ والهجر.

٧،٧٧ أخبرنا محمّد بن أبي منصور قال: أخبرنا عبد القادر بن محمّد قال: أنبأنا إبراهيم بن عمر قال: أنبأنا عبد العزيز بن جعفر قال: حدثنا أبو بكر أحمد بن محمّد الخلاّل قال:

أخبرني محمّد بن الحسين أنّ أبا بكر المَرُّوذي حدثهم قال: دخلنا العسكر إلى أن خرجنا ما ذاق أبو عبد الله طبيخًا ولا دسمًا وقال: كم تمتّع أُولئك، يعني ابن أبي شَيْبَة وابن المَدِيني وعَبد الأعلى، إني لأعجب من حرصهم على الدنيا، فكيف يطوفون على أبوابهم؟

ومن أقبح ما نُقل عن ابن المَديني أنه روى لابن أبي دُؤاد حديثًا عن الوَليد ابن مسلم كان الوليد أخطأ في لفظة منه فذكره لهم على الخطإ ليَقوى به احتجاجهم فكان ذلك مما أنكره عليه أحمد.

٨،٧٧ أخبرنا عبد الرحمن بن محمّد القزاز قال: أخبرنا أحمد بن عليّ بن ثابت قال: أخبرنا أبو طالب عمر بن إبراهيم الفقيه قال: أخبرنا عيسى بن حامد القاضي قال: حدثنا أبو بكر أحمد بن محمّد الصَّيدلاني قال:

حدثنا أبو بكر المَرُّوذي قال: قلت لأبي عبد الله أحمد بن حنبل إن عليّ بن المديني يحدّث عن الوليد بن مسلم عن الأوزاعي عن الزُّهري عن أَنَس عن عُمر: كِلُوه إلى خالِقه.

فقال أبو عبد الله: كذب، حدّثنا الوليد بن مسلم ما هو هكذا إنّما هو: كِلُوهُ إلى عالِمه. وقال أحمد: قد علم عليّ بن المديني أنّ الوليد أخطأ فيه فلمَ أراد أن يحدّثهم به، يعطيهم الخطأ؟

فكذّبه أبو عبد الله.

٩،٧٧ أخبرنا عبد الرحمن بن محمّد القزاز[١] قال: أخبرنا أحمد بن عليّ بن ثابت قال: أخبرني الحسين بن عليّ الصَّيمَري

---

١ ابن محمّد القزّاز: ليس في هـ، د.

3. Upon giving their assent, most of the offenders accepted payments and began associating with members of the regime. In doing so they went beyond what the Law allows and thus deserved ostracism and condemnation.

We cite Muḥammad ibn Abī Manṣūr, who cites ʿAbd al-Qādir ibn Muḥammad, who was informed by Ibrāhīm ibn ʿUmar, who was informed by ʿAbd al-ʿAzīz ibn Jaʿfar, who heard Abū Bakr Aḥmad ibn Muḥammad al-Khallāl cite Muḥammad ibn al-Ḥusayn, who heard Abū Bakr al-Marrūdhī report: 77.7

[Al-Marrūdhī:] From the time we entered Samarra to the time we left, Aḥmad tasted no cooked food or any fat. At one point he said, "That lot"—meaning Ibn Abī Shaybah, Ibn al-Madīnī, and ʿAbd al-Aʿlā—"have certainly been enjoying themselves. I had no idea they were so attached to this world. How can they bring themselves to hang about palace doors like that?"

[The author:] One of the most damning things reported about Ibn al-Madīnī was that he recited a report transmitted by al-Walīd ibn Muslim, including a verbal error that al-Walīd had made, to Ibn Abī Duʾād in order to help his side argue for its point of view. This was one of the things that Aḥmad held against him.

We cite ʿAbd al-Raḥmān ibn Muḥammad al-Qazzāz, who cites Aḥmad ibn ʿAlī ibn Thābit, who cites Abū Ṭālib ʿUmar ibn Ibrāhīm al-Faqīh, who cites Judge ʿĪsā ibn Ḥāmid, who heard Abū Bakr Aḥmad ibn Muḥammad al-Ṣaydalānī report that he heard Abū Bakr al-Marrūdhī report: 77.8

[Al-Marrūdhī:] I told Aḥmad that ʿAlī l-Madīnī was reciting a report transmitted by al-Walīd ibn Muslim, citing al-Awzāʿī, citing al-Zuhrī, citing Anas citing ʿUmar, saying: "Leave it to its Creator."[179]

"He's a liar!" said Aḥmad. "Al-Walīd ibn Muslim's report says 'Leave it to its Maker.'" He added: "Al-Madīnī knows that al-Walīd made an error when he transmitted it. So why would he recite it for those people? Why give them a wrong report?"

He thus declared al-Madīnī to be a liar.

We cite ʿAbd al-Raḥmān ibn Muḥammad al-Qazzāz, who cites Aḥmad ibn ʿAlī ibn Thābit, who cites al-Ḥusayn ibn ʿAlī l-Ṣaymarī, who heard Muḥammad ibn ʿImrān al-Marzubānī 77.9

قال: حدثنا محمد بن عمران المَرْزُبَاني قال: حدثنا محمد بن يحيى قال: حدثنا الحسين بن فَهْم قال:

حدثنا أبي قال: قال ابن أبي دُؤاد للمعتصم: يا أمير المؤمنين هذا يزعم - يعني أحمد بن حنبل - أنّ الله تعالى يُرَى في الآخرة، والعين لا تقع إلا على محدود.

فقال له المعتصم: ما عندك في هذا؟

فقال يا أمير المؤمنين عندي ما قاله رسول الله صلّى الله عليه وسلّم.

قال: وما قال عليه السلام؟

قال: حدثنا محمّد بن جعفر غُنْدر قال: حدثنا شعبة عن إسماعيل بن أبي خالد عن قَيْس بن أبي حازم عن جَرِير بن عبد الله البَجَلي قال: كُنَّا مع النبيّ صلّى الله عليه وسلّم في ليلة أربع عشرة من الشهر فنظر إلى البدر فقال: أَما إِنَّكُم سَتَرَوْنَ ربَّكُم كما تَرَوْنَ هذا البَدْرَ لا تُضامونَ في رُؤيته.

فقال لأحمد بن أبي دؤاد: ما عندك في هذا؟

فقال: أَنظر في إسناد هذا الحديث.

وكان هذا في أوّل يوم.

ثمّ انصرف فوجّه ابنُ أبي دؤاد إلى عليّ بن المَديني وهو ببغداد مُملِق لا يقدر على درهم فأحضره فما كلّمه بشيء حتّى وصله بعشرة آلاف درهم وقال له: هذه وَصَلَك بها أمير المؤمنين.

وأمر أن يدفع إليه جميع ما استحق من أرزاقه وكان له رزق سنتين ثم قال له: يا أبا الحسن حديث جرير بن عبد الله في الرّؤية ما هو؟

قال: صحيح.

قال: فهل عندك فيه شيء؟

قال: يُعفيني القاضي من هذا.

فقال: يا أبا الحسن هو حاجة الدهر.

ثم أمر له بثياب وطيب ومركب بسرجه ولجامه ولم يزل حتى قال له: في هذا الإسناد من لا يُعتمد عليه ولا على ما يرويه وهو قَيسُ بن أبي حازم إنّما كان

report that he heard Muḥammad ibn Yaḥyā report that he heard al-Ḥusayn ibn Qahm report that he heard his father report:

[Qahm:] Ibn Abī Du'ād told al-Mu'taṣim that Aḥmad ibn Ḥanbal claimed that God will be visible in the afterlife even though the eye can perceive only finite objects. When al-Mu'taṣim asked Aḥmad to explain himself, he replied that he was citing the Emissary of God.

"And what did the Emissary say?"

"I heard Muḥammad ibn Ja'far Ghundar report," said Aḥmad, "that he heard Shu'bah report, citing Ismā'īl ibn Abī Khālid, citing Qays ibn Abī Ḥāzim, citing Jarīr ibn 'Abd Allāh al-Bajalī: 'We were once with the Prophet on the fourteenth night of the month when he looked at the full moon and said, "You will most certainly see your Lord as clearly as you see the moon; you will not be cheated of seeing him."'" Then he turned to Ibn Abī Du'ād. "What do you say to that?"

"I'll have to look into the chain of transmitters," he replied.

This exchange took place on the first day of Aḥmad's trial. After the session ended, Ibn Abī Du'ād sent for 'Alī ibn al-Madīnī, who was then living in Baghdad without a dirham to his name. No sooner had al-Madīnī arrived than Ibn Abī Du'ād, without further ado, gave him ten thousand dirhams. Then he said, "That's a gift from the Commander of the Faithful." By his command, al-Madīnī also received the two years' worth of stipends that were owed him. Then Ibn Abī Du'ād asked him about the Hadith of Jarīr ibn 'Abd Allāh regarding the visibility of God.

"It's authentic," said al-Madīnī.

"Do you have any criticism of it at all?"

"I ask His Honor the Judge for permission not to discuss this."

"'Alī," he said, "this is the most serious question you'll ever be asked."

After regaling him with new clothes, bottles of scent, and a riding animal complete with saddle, bridle, and reins, Ibn Abī Du'ād continued to press his question until al-Madīnī finally said, "One of the transmitters is unreliable. It's Qays ibn Abī Ḥāzim, who was no more than a desert Arab who used to piss on his own heels."

Ibn Abī Du'ād rose and embraced him.

The next day, when the trial had resumed, Ibn Abī Du'ād said, "Commander of the Faithful, Aḥmad cited the Hadith of Jarīr and named Qays ibn

أعرابيًا بوّالًا على عقبيه.

فقام ابن أبي دؤاد إلى عليّ بن المديني فاعتنقه.

فلمّا كان من الغد وحضروا قال ابن أبي دؤاد: يا أمير المؤمنين يحتجّ في الرؤية بحديث جرير وإنّما رواه عنه قيس ابن أبي حازم وهو أعرابي بوّال على عقبيه.

قال: فقال أحمد بن حنبل: فعلمت أنه من عمل عليّ بن المديني.

١٠،٧٧ قلت: وهذا إن صحّ عن ابن المديني فهو أمر عظيم لأنّه إقدام منه على ما يعلم خلافه فإن قيس بن أبي حازم من كبار التابعين وليس في التابعين كلّهم من أدرك العشرة المقدمين وروى عنهم غيره كذلك يقول أكثر أهل العلم، وقال أبو داوود سُليمان بن أشعث: روى عن تسعة من العَشرة ولم يروِ عن عبد الرحمن بن عوف وقد روى عن خلق كثير من الصحابة ولم يَعِبْه أحد بشيء ومَن فعل مثل هذا يستحقّ الهجر.[١]

١١،٧٧ أخبرنا عبد الرحمن بن محمّد قال: أنبأنا أحمد بن عليّ بن ثابت قال: أخبرنا أحمد بن عليّ الرزّاز قال: حدثنا محمّد بن عبد الله الشافعي قال: قيل لإبراهيم الحربي: لم لا تحدّث عن عليّ ابن المَديني؟

فقال: لِقيته يومًا وبيده نعله وثيابه في فمه فقلتُ: إلى أين؟

فقال: ألحقُ الصلاة خلف أبي عبد الله.

فظننتُ أنّه يعني أحمد بن حنبل فقلت: من أبو عبد الله؟

فقال: أبو عبد الله ابن أبي دُؤاد.

فقلتُ: والله لا حدّثتُ عنك بحرف.

١٢،٧٧ أخبرنا عبد الرحمن قال: أخبرنا أحمد بن عليّ قال: أخبرنا العَتيقي قال: حدثنا محمّد بن العبّاس قال: حدثنا سليمان ابن إسحاق الجلّاب قال:

قال إبراهيم الحربي: كان عليّ بن المديني إذا رأى في كتاب حديثًا عن أحمد قال: اضرب على ذا — ليرضى به ابن أبي دؤاد.

---

١ هـ : الهجرة.

Abī Ḥāzim as a transmitter, but Qays was no more than a desert Arab who used to piss on his own heels."

Aḥmad later said that he realized immediately that this was the work of ʿAlī l-Madīnī.

[The author:] If this story is true, Ibn al-Madīnī is guilty of a terrible crime: volunteering an assessment he knew to be false. Qays ibn Abī Ḥāzim was one of the leading Successors and the only one to have met all ten of the foremost Companions and transmitted reports on their authority. This is the view of most men of learning, though Abū Dāwūd Sulaymān ibn al-Ashʿath says that he transmitted from only nine of the ten, the missing one being ʿAbd al-Raḥmān ibn ʿAwf. In any event, Qays did transmit from a great many Companions and was never criticized for any reason. Anyone who does what al-Madīnī reportedly did therefore deserves to be ostracized. 77.10

We cite ʿAbd al-Raḥmān ibn Muḥammad, who was informed by Aḥmad ibn ʿAlī ibn Thābit, who cites Aḥmad ibn ʿAlī l-Razzāz, who heard Muḥammad ibn ʿAbd Allāh al-Shāfiʿī report: 77.11

[Muḥammad ibn ʿAbd Allāh al-Shāfiʿī:] Ibrāhīm al-Ḥarbī was asked why he didn't transmit reports transmitted by ʿAlī ibn al-Madīnī. He replied, "One day I saw him walking along with his sandals in his hand and the hem of his garment between his teeth.[180]

"'Where are you off to?' I asked.

"'I need to get to Abū ʿAbd Allāh's in time to pray behind him.'

"I thought he meant Aḥmad ibn Ḥanbal, but when I asked him he said he meant Ibn Abī Du'ād.

"'By God,' I said, 'I'm never citing another word I heard from you.'"

We cite ʿAbd al-Raḥmān, who cites by Aḥmad ibn ʿAlī, who cites al-ʿAtīqī, who heard Muḥammad ibn al-ʿAbbās report that he heard Sulaymān ibn Isḥāq al-Jallāb report that Ibrāhīm al-Ḥarbī said: 77.12

[Ibrāhīm al-Ḥarbī:] Whenever ʿAlī ibn al-Madīnī came across a Hadith transmitted by Aḥmad in a document, he would say, "Cross it out," to please Ibn Abī Du'ād.

١٣،٧٧ أخبرنا المحمّدان: ابن أبي منصور وابن عبد الباقي قالا: أخبرنا حمد بن أحمد قال: أخبرنا أحمد بن عبد الله الحافظ قال: حدثنا أحمد بن جعفر بن سَلْمٍ[1] قال: حدثنا أحمد بن عليّ الأبّار قال:

حدثنا يحيى بن عثمان الحربي قال: سمعتُ بشر بن الحارث يقول: وددت أنّ رؤوسهم خُضِبت بدمائهم وأنهم لم يُجيبوا.

الباب الثامن والسبعون في ذكر جماعة ممّن لم يُجِبْ في المحنة

١،٧٨ أخبرنا أبو منصور القزّاز قال: أخبرنا أبو بكر أحمد بن عليّ بن ثابت قال: أخبرنا محمّد بن عليّ بن يعقوب قال: أخبرنا محمّد بن نُعَيم الضَّبّي قال: سمعتُ أبا العباس السَّيّاري يقول:

سمعت أبا العبّاس بن سعيد المَرْوَزي يقول: لم يصبر في المحنة إلّا أربعة كلّهم من مَرْو: أحمد بن حنبل وأحمد بن نصر ومحمّد بن نوح ونُعيم بن حمّاد.

قال أبو الحسين بن المُنادي: وممّن لم يُجب: أبو نُعيم الفضل بن دُكَيْن وعفّان والبُوَيطي وإسماعيل بن أبي أُوَيس وأبو مُصْعَب المَدَنِيّان يحيى الحِمّاني.[2]

سياق أخبار المشتهرين بالذكر منهم

عفّان بن مُسلم

٢،٧٨ أخبرنا عبد الرحمن بن محمّد القزّاز قال: أخبرنا أحمد بن عليّ بن ثابت قال: أخبرنا محمّد بن أحمد بن رِزْق قال: أخبرنا عثمان بن أحمد الدقّاق قال:

حدثنا حنبل بن إسحاق قال: حضرت عند عفّان بعد ما دعاه إسحاق بن إبراهيم للمحنة وكان أول من امتُحِن من الناس عفّان، فسأله يحيى بن مَعين من الغد بعد

---

١ قال حدثنا أحمد بن جعفر بن سلم: ليس في ش. ٢ د: الحمامي.

We cite the two Muḥammads, Ibn Abī Manṣūr and Ibn ʿAbd al-Bāqī, who cite Ḥamd ibn Aḥmad, who cites Aḥmad ibn ʿAbd Allāh al-Ḥāfiẓ, who heard Aḥmad ibn Jaʿfar ibn Salm report that he heard Aḥmad ibn ʿAlī l-Abbār report that he heard Yaḥyā ibn ʿUthmān al-Ḥarbī report: 77.13

[Yaḥyā ibn ʿUthmān:] I heard Bishr ibn al-Ḥārith say: "I would rather have seen their hair dyed with blood than see them give in."

Chapter 78: Those Who Defied the Inquisition

We cite Abū Manṣūr al-Qazzāz, who cites Abū Bakr Aḥmad ibn ʿAlī ibn Thābit, who cites Muḥammad ibn ʿAlī ibn Yaʿqūb, who cites Muḥammad ibn Nuʿaym al-Ḍabbī, who heard Abū l-ʿAbbās al-Sayyārī say that he heard Abū l-ʿAbbās ibn Saʿīd al-Marwazī say: 78.1

[Al-Marwazī:] Only four men, all of them from Marv, remained steadfast throughout the Inquisition: Aḥmad ibn Ḥanbal, Aḥmad ibn Naṣr, Muḥammad ibn Nūḥ, and Nuʿaym ibn Ḥammād.

Abū l-Ḥusayn ibn al-Munādī mentions the following men as having remained steadfast as well: Abū Nuʿaym al-Faḍl ibn Dukayn, ʿAffān, al-Buwayṭī, Ismāʿīl ibn Abī Uways al-Madanī, Abū Muṣʿab al-Madanī, and Yaḥyā l-Ḥimmānī.

Reports Concerning the Prominent Dissenters

ʿAffān ibn Muslim

We cite ʿAbd al-Raḥmān ibn Muḥammad al-Qazzāz, who cites Aḥmad ibn ʿAlī ibn Thābit, who cites Muḥammad ibn Aḥmad ibn Rizq, who cites ʿUthmān ibn Aḥmad al-Daqqāq, who heard Ḥanbal ibn Isḥāq report: 78.2

[Ḥanbal ibn Isḥāq:] The first to be called for interrogation was ʿAffān. The next day, after his return, I was there, as were all of us, including Aḥmad ibn

ما امتحن وأبو عبد الله أحمد بن حنبل حاضر ونحن معه فقال له يحيى: يا أبا عثمان أَخبِرنا بما قال لك إسحاق بن إبراهيم وما رددت عليه.

فقال عفّان ليحيى: يا أبا زكريّا لم أُسوّد وجهك ولا وجوه أصحابك، يعني بذلك إنّي لم أُجب.

فقال له: فكيف كان؟

قال: دعاني إسحاق بن إبراهيم فلمّا دخلت عليه قرأ عليّ الكتاب الذي كتب به المأمون من أرض الجزيرة إلى الرقّة فإذا فيه: امتحِنْ عفّان[1] وادعُه إلى أن يقول: القرآن كذا وكذا فإن قال ذلك فأقرّه على أمره وإن لم يُجبك إلى ما كتبت به إليك فاقطع عنه الذي يُجرى عليه.

وكان المأمون يُجري على عفّان خمس مائة درهم كلّ شهر.

قال عفّان: فلمّا قرأ عليّ الكتاب قال لي إسحاق بن إبراهيم: ما تقول؟ فقرأتُ عليه: ﴿قُل هُوَ اللهُ أَحَد ۞ اللهُ الصَّمَد﴾ حتى ختمتُها فقلت: أمخلوق هذا؟

فقال لي إسحاق: يا شيخ إنّ أمير المؤمنين يقول: إن لم تُجبه إلى الذي يدعوك إليه يقطع عنك ما يجرى عليك وإن قطع عنك أمير المؤمنين قطعنا عنك نحن أيضاً.

فقلت له: يقول الله تعالى: ﴿وَفِي السَّمَاءِ رِزْقُكُمْ وما تُوعَدُون﴾ فسكت عني إسحاق وانصرفت. فسُرّ بذلك أبو عبد الله ومن حضر من أصحابنا.

٣،٧٨ أخبرنا عبد الرحمن بن محمّد قال: أخبرنا أحمد بن عليّ بن ثابت قال: أخبرنا أبو منصور بن محمّد بن عيسى بن عبد العزيز البزّاز قال: حدثنا أبو الفضل صالح بن أحمد التميمي قال: سمعتُ القاسم بن أبي صالح قال:

سمعت إبراهيم، يعني ابن الحسين بن دَيْزيل، يقول: لمّا دُعي عفّان للمحنة كنت آخذ بلجام حماره فلمّا حضر عرض عليه القول فامتنع أن يجيب فقيل له: يُحبس عطاؤك قال، وكان يُعطى في كل شهر ألف درهم، فقال: ﴿وَفِي السَّمَاءِ رِزْقُكُمْ وَمَا تُوعَدونَ﴾ .

[1] ش: عثمان.

Ḥanbal. Yaḥyā ibn Maʿīn asked ʿAffān to tell us what Isḥāq had said to him and how he had answered.

"I did nothing to dishonor you or your associates," he said, meaning that he had not said what Isḥāq wanted him to say.

"So what was it like?"

"Isḥāq ibn Ibrāhīm called me in. When I got there, he read out the letter that al-Ma'mūn had sent to al-Raqqah from northern Iraq. In the letter it said, 'Test ʿAffān, and call on him to say that the Qur'an is such-and-such. If he does so, confirm him in his position. If he refuses, cut off his stipend.'"

Al-Ma'mūn had been paying ʿAffān five hundred dirhams a month.

"When the letter had been read out, Isḥāq asked me to state my position. By way of reply, I recited «Say, He is God, the One, the *ṣamad*»[181] through to the end, then asked, 'Is that created?'

"Isḥāq said, 'Listen, elder, the Commander of the Faithful says he'll cut off your stipend, and if he does I will too.'

"I told him that God says «In heaven is your sustenance, and also that which you are promised.»[182] He had no reply to that and let me go."

Aḥmad and those of our associates who were there were heartened by this report.

We cite ʿAbd al-Raḥmān ibn Muḥammad, who cites Aḥmad ibn ʿAlī ibn Thābit, who cites Abū Manṣūr ibn Muḥammad ibn ʿĪsā ibn ʿAbd al-ʿAzīz al-Bazzāz, who heard Abū l-Faḍl Ṣāliḥ ibn Aḥmad al-Tamīmī report that he heard al-Qāsim ibn Abī Ṣāliḥ report that he heard Ibrāhīm—meaning Ibn al-Ḥusayn ibn Dayzīl—say: 78.3

[Ibrāhīm ibn al-Ḥusayn:] I was working for ʿAffān, holding the reins of his mule, when he was called in for trial. When he went in, he was asked to agree to what they said but he wouldn't. They told him they would keep back his stipend, which came to a thousand dinars a month, but he said, «In heaven is your sustenance, and also that which you are promised.»[183]

قال: فلمّا رجع إلى داره عذله نساؤه ومن في داره. قال: وكان في داره نحو أربعين إنساناً. قال: فدقّ عليه داقّ الباب فدخل عليه رجل شَبّهتُه بسمّان أو زيّات ومعه كيس فيه ألف درهم فقال: يا أبا عثمان ثبّتك الله كما ثبّت الدين وهذا لك في كلّ شهر.

أبو نُعَيم الفَضل بن دُكَين

أخبرنا أبو البَرَكات بن عليّ البزّاز قال: أخبرنا أحمد بن عليّ الطُّرَيْثيثي قال: أخبرنا هِبَة الله بن الحسن الطَّبَري قال: ٤،٧٨
ذكر عبد الرحمن بن أبي حاتم قال: حدثنا محمّد بن أحمد بن عمر[1] بن عيسى قال:

سمعتُ أبي يقول: ما رأيت مجلساً يجتمع فيه المشايخ أنبل من مشايخ اجتمعوا في مسجد جامع الكوفة في وقت الامتحان فقُرئ عليهم الكتاب الذي فيه المحنة فقال أبو نعيم: أدركت ثمان مائة شيخ ونيفاً وسبعين شيخاً منهم الأعمش فمن دونه فما رأيت خلقاً يقول بهذه المقالة، يعني بخلق القرآن، ولا تكلّم أحد بهذه المقالة إلا رُمي بالزندقة.

فقام أحمد بن يونس فقبّل رأس أبي نعيم وقال: جزاك الله عن الإسلام خيراً.

أخبرنا عبد الرحمن بن محمّد القزاز قال: أخبرنا أحمد بن عليّ بن ثابت قال: قرأت على البَرقاني عن أبي إسحاق ٥،٧٨
المُزَكّي قال: أخبرنا محمّد بن إسحاق الثقفي قال:

سمعت محمّد بن يونس قال: لمّا أُدخل أبو نعيم على الوالي ليمتحنه قال: أدركتُ الكوفة وبها أكثر من سبع مائة شيخ، الأعمش فَمَن دونه، يقولون القُرآن كلام الله وعُنقي أهون عندي من زِرّي هذا.

فقام إليه أحمد بن يونس فقبّل رأسه وكان بينهما شحناء، وقال: جزاك الله من شيخ خيراً.

---

[1] هـ: عمرو.

When we got back, the women of the house, and everyone else there, started berating him. There were about forty people living in that house. Then we heard a knock on the door. In came a man who looked to me like a seller of ghee or oil carrying a thousand dirhams in a bag. "You've supported the faith," he said to ʿAffān, "and may God support you! You'll be getting a bag like this every month."

Abū Nuʿaym al-Faḍl ibn Dukayn

We cite Abū l-Barakāt ibn ʿAlī l-Bazzāz, who cites Aḥmad ibn ʿAlī l-Ṭuraythīthī, who cites **78.4**
Hibat Allāh ibn al-Ḥasan al-Ṭabarī, who said that ʿAbd al-Raḥmān ibn Abī Ḥātim recalled hearing Muḥammad ibn Aḥmad ibn ʿUmar ibn ʿĪsā report that he heard his father say:

[Aḥmad ibn ʿUmar:] Of all the elders' gatherings I've seen, the greatest was the one I saw in Kufa during the Inquisition. After the letter with the doctrine in it was read aloud, Abū Nuʿaym spoke up and said, "I've heard reports from 870-some teachers, from al-Aʿmash on down, but I never met anyone who held that view"—that the Qur'an is a created thing—"nor saw anyone espouse it without being accused of heresy."

Hearing this, Aḥmad ibn Yūnus rose and kissed Abū Nuʿaym's head, saying, "May God reward you on behalf of Islam!"

We cite ʿAbd al-Raḥmān ibn Muḥammad al-Qazzāz, who cites Aḥmad ibn ʿAlī ibn **78.5**
Thābit, who read back to al-Barqānī his report citing Abū Isḥāq al-Muzakkī, who cites Muḥammad ibn Isḥāq al-Thaqafī, who heard Muḥammad ibn Yūnus report:

[Muḥammad ibn Yūnus:] When Abū Nuʿaym was taken in to the governor, he said, "I've seen all the elders in Kufa—that's more than seven hundred, from al-Aʿmash on down—say that the Qur'an is the speech of God, and my neck means as little to me as this button."

At that, Aḥmad ibn Yūnus rose and kissed him on the head even though there had been bad blood between them and said, "May God reward you for the great elder you are!"

٦،٧٨ أخبرنا عبد الرحمن بن محمد قال: أخبرنا أحمد بن عليّ قال: أخبرنا محمّد بن أحمد بن أبي طاهر قال: أخبرنا أبو بكر أحمد بن سليمان النجّاد قال: حدثنا محمّد بن يونس الكُدَيْمي قال:

سمعت أبا بكر بن أبي شَيْبة يقول: لمّا أن جاءت المحنة إلى الكوفة قال لي أحمد بن يونس: الْقَ أبا نعيم فقل له. فلقيتُ أبا نعيم فقلت له فقال: إنّما هو ضرب الأسياط وأخذ زِرّه فقطعه وقال: رأسي أهون عليّ من زرّي.

٧،٧٨ أخبرنا عبد الرحمن بن محمد قال: أخبرنا أحمد بن عليّ قال: أخبرنا بن رزق قال: أخبرنا عثمان بن أحمد قال:

حدثنا حنبل بن إسحاق قال: سمعتُ أبا عبد الله، يعني أحمد بن حنبل، يقول: شيخان قاما لله بأمر لم يقُم به أحد، أو كثير أحد، مثل ما قاما به، عفّان وأبو نُعيم – يعني امتناعهما من الإجابة.

نُعيم بن حمّاد

٨،٧٨ أخبرنا عبد الرحمن بن محمّد القزاز قال: أخبرنا أحمد بن عليّ بن ثابت قال: أخبرني الأزهري قال: حدثنا محمّد بن العبّاس قال: حدثنا أحمد بن معروف الخشّاب قال: حدثنا الحسين بن فَهْم قال:

حدثنا محمّد بن سعد قال: نُعَيم بن حمّاد كان من أهل مَرْو، طلب الحديث طلباً كثيرًا بالعراق والحجاز ثم نزل مصر فلم يزل بها حتى أُشخص منها في خلافة أبي إسحاق ابن هارون وسُئل عن القرآن فأبى أن يجيب فيه بشيء ممّا أرادوه عليه فحُبس بسامرا فلم يزل محبوساً بها حتى مات في السجن سنة ثمان وعشرين ومائتين.

٩،٧٨ أخبرنا عبد الرحمن بن محمد قال: أخبرنا أحمد بن عليّ بن ثابت قال: أخبرني الأزهري قال: أخبرنا أحمد بن إبراهيم قال:

أخبرنا إبراهيم بن محمد بن عرفة قال: سنة تسع وعشرين ومائتين فيها مات نعيم ابن حمّاد وكان مقيّدًا محبوساً لامتناعه من القول بخلق القرآن فجُرّ بأقياده فأُلقي في

We cite ʿAbd al-Raḥmān ibn Muḥammad, who cites Aḥmad ibn ʿAlī, who cites Muḥammad ibn Aḥmad ibn Abī Ṭāhir, who cites Abū Bakr Aḥmad ibn Sulaymān al-Najjād, who heard Muḥammad ibn Yūnus al-Kudaymī report that he heard Abū Bakr ibn Abī Shaybah say: **78.6**

[Ibn Abī Shaybah:] When the Inquisition came to Kufa, Aḥmad ibn Yūnus told me to go find Abū Nuʿaym and let him know. When I found him and told him, he said, "It's just a flogging." Then he tore a button off his garment. "My head means less to me than this button."

We cite ʿAbd al-Raḥmān ibn Muḥammad, who cites Aḥmad ibn ʿAlī, who cites Ibn Rizq, who cites ʿUthmān ibn Aḥmad, who heard Ḥanbal ibn Isḥāq report: **78.7**

[Ḥanbal ibn Isḥāq:] I heard Abū ʿAbd Allāh—meaning Aḥmad ibn Ḥanbal—say, "Two elders stood up for God better than anyone else"—or "nearly everyone else"—"ever has: ʿAffān and Abū Nuʿaym."

He was referring to their refusal to capitulate.

Nuʿaym ibn Ḥammād

We cite ʿAbd al-Raḥmān ibn Muḥammad al-Qazzāz, who cites Aḥmad ibn ʿAlī ibn Thābit, who cites al-Azharī, who heard Muḥammad ibn al-ʿAbbās report that he heard Aḥmad ibn Maʿrūf al-Khashshāb report that he heard al-Ḥusayn ibn Qahm report that he heard Muḥammad ibn Saʿd report: **78.8**

[Muḥammad ibn Saʿd:] Nuʿaym ibn Ḥammād was from Marv. He pursued Hadith extensively in Iraq and western Arabia before settling in Egypt, where he stayed until he was summoned to Iraq during the caliphate of al-Muʿtaṣim. He was questioned regarding the Qur'an but refused assent to what was demanded of him. He was then jailed in Samarra, where he died, still in prison, in 228 [842–43].

We cite ʿAbd al-Raḥmān ibn Muḥammad, who cites Aḥmad ibn ʿAlī ibn Thābit, who cites al-Azharī, who cites Aḥmad ibn Ibrāhīm, who cites Ibrāhīm ibn Muḥammad ibn ʿArafah, who reports: **78.9**

[Ibrāhīm ibn Muḥammad ibn ʿArafah:] Among those who died in 228 [842–43] was Nuʿaym ibn Ḥammād, who perished in chains in a dungeon because he refused to say that the Qur'an was a created thing. He was dragged by his chains and thrown into a pit, and died without being wrapped

حفرة ولم يُكفّن ولم يُصلّ عليه، فعل ذلك به صاحب ابن أبي دُؤاد.

أبو يعقوب يوسف بن يحيى البُوَيطي

١٠،٧٨ حُمل في أيّام المحنة وأُريد على القول بخلق القرآن فامتنع فحُبس ببغداد ولم يزل في الحبس إلى أن مات فيه وكان فقيهاً زاهداً.

أخبرنا عبد الرحمن بن محمّد قال: أخبرنا أحمد بن عليّ الحافظ قال: أخبرنا أبو منصور محمّد بن عيسى بن عبد العزيز البزّاز قال: حدثنا عبد الرحمن بن أحمد الأَنْماطي قال: حدثنا محمّد بن حمدان الطَّرائفي قال:

حدثنا الرَّبيع بن سُليمان قال: رأيت البُوَيطي على بغل في عنقه غُلّ وفي رجليه قيد وبين الغلّ والقيد سلسلة حديد فيها طوبة وزنها أربعون رطلاً وهو يقول: إنّما خلق اللهُ الخلق بكُنْ فإذا كانت كُنْ مخلوقة فكأنّ مخلوقاً خلق مخلوقاً والله لأموتنّ في حديد هذا حتّى يأتي من بعدي قوم يعلمون أنّه قد مات في هذا الشأن قوم في حديدهم ولئن أُدخلتُ عليه لأصدُقنّه - يعني الواثق.

١١،٧٨ أخبرنا عبد الرحمن بن محمّد قال: أخبرنا أبو بكر الخطيب قال: أخبرنا العَتيقي قال:

أخبرنا عليّ بن عبد الرحمن بن أحمد المصري قال: حدثنا أبي قال: كان البُوَيطي متقشّفاً حُمل من مصر أيّام المحنة إلى العراق وأرادوه على المحنة فامتنع فسُجن ببغداد وقُيّد فتوفِّي في السجن والقيد سنة اثنتين وثلاثين ومائتين.

أحمد بن نَصر بن مالك بن الهَيثَم الخُزاعي يُكنى أبا عبد الله

١٢،٧٨ وسُوَيقة نصر ببغداد منسوبة إلى أبيه، ومالك بن الهيثم جدّه كان أحد نُقباء بني العبّاس في ابتداء الدولة، وكان أحمد من أهل الدين والصلاح والأمّارين بالمعروف، وسمع الحديث من مالك بن أنَس وحمّاد بن زيد وهُشَيم في آخرين، وقد

in a shroud or having anyone pray over his body. This was the doing of Ibn Abī Du'ād's man.[184]

Abū Ya'qūb Yūsuf ibn Yaḥyā l-Buwayṭī

He was taken away during the Inquisition and pressured to espouse the claim that the Qur'an is a created thing. When he refused, he was jailed in Baghdad and died in prison. He was a renunciant and a man who understood the Law. 78.10

We cite 'Abd al-Raḥmān ibn Muḥammad, who cites Aḥmad ibn 'Alī l-Ḥāfiẓ, who cites Abū Manṣūr Muḥammad ibn 'Īsā ibn 'Abd al-'Azīz al-Bazzāz, who heard 'Abd al-Raḥmān ibn Aḥmad al-Anmāṭī report that he heard Muḥammad ibn Ḥamdān al-Ṭarā'ifī report that he heard al-Rabī' ibn Sulaymān report:

[Al-Rabī' ibn Sulaymān:] I saw al-Buwayṭī mounted on a mule with a manacle around his neck and a fetter on his legs. The manacle and the fetter were joined by an iron chain. Suspended from the chain was a brick weighing thirty-five pounds.[185] He was saying, "God created the world by saying 'Be.' If 'be' is created, then one created thing brought another created thing into being." He went on: "By God, I'll die with this very chain still on me, so that when I'm gone, people will know that men died in irons for this cause. If they put me before him"—meaning al-Wāthiq—"I'll speak my mind."

We cite 'Abd al-Raḥmān ibn Muḥammad, who cites Abū Bakr al-Khaṭīb, who cites al-'Atīqī, 78.11
who cites 'Alī ibn 'Abd al-Raḥmān ibn Aḥmad al-Miṣrī, who heard his father report:

['Abd al-Raḥmān ibn Aḥmad:] Al-Buwayṭī lived a life of pious self-denial. During the Inquisition, he was taken from Egypt to Iraq, where he refused to capitulate and was clapped into irons and thrown in jail. He died, in prison and in fetters, in 232 [846–47].

Aḥmad ibn Naṣr ibn Mālik ibn al-Haytham al-Khuzā'ī, called Abū 'Abd Allāh

The Little Market of Naṣr in Baghdad is named after his father. His grand- 78.12
father, Mālik ibn al-Haytham, was one of the leaders of the Abbasid revolutionary movement. Ibn Naṣr himself was a man of piety and rectitude who called upon others to do right. He heard Hadith from Mālik ibn Anas,

روى عنه يحيى بن مَعين وغيره.

١٣،٧٨ وكان قد اتُّهم بأنّه يريد الخلافة فأُخذ وحمل إلى الواثق فقال له: دَع ما أُخذت له، ما تقول في القرآن؟

قال: كلام الله.

قال: أفمخلوق هو؟

قال: هو كلام الله.

قال: أفترى ربّك في القِيامة؟

قال: كذا جاءت الرواية.

فقال: ويحك يُرى كما يُرى المحدود المجسّم؟

ودعا بالسيف وأمر بالنطع فأُجلس عليه وهو مقيّد وأمر بشدّ رأسه بحبل وأمرهم أن يمدّوه ومشى إليه حتّى ضرب عنقه. وأمر بحمل رأسه إلى بغداد فنُصب في الجانب الشرقي أيّاماً وفي الجانب الغربي أيّاماً.

١٤،٧٨ أخبرنا عبد الرحمن بن محمّد قال: أخبرنا أحمد بن عليّ بن ثابت قال: أخبرنا عليّ بن محمّد بن عبد الله الحذّاء قال: حدثنا أحمد بن جعفر بن سَلْم قال: حدثنا أبو بكر أحمد بن محمّد بن عبد الخالق قال:

حدثنا أبو بكر المَرُّوذي قال: سمعتُ أبا عبد الله أحمد بن حنبل، وذكر أحمد بن نصر، فقال: رحمه الله، ما كان أسخاه، لقد جاد بنفسه.

١٥،٧٨ أخبرنا أبو منصور القزاز قال: أخبرنا أبو بكر أحمد بن عليّ الخطيب قال: حدثنا أبو نصر إبراهيم بن هِبة الله الجَرْبَاذْقاني قال: حدثنا معمر بن أحمد الأصبهاني قال: أخبرني أبو عمرو عثمان بن محمّد العثماني إجازةً قال: حدثني عليّ بن محمّد بن إبراهيم قال:

حدثنا إبراهيم بن إسماعيل بن خَلَف قال: كان أحمد بن نصر خِلّي فلمّا قُتل في المحنة وصُلب رأسه أُخبرت أنّ الرأس يقرأ القرآن.

فمضيت فبتّ بقرب من الرأس مشرفاً عليه وكان عنده رجالة وفُرسان يحفظونه.

Ḥammād ibn Zayd, and Hushaym, among others. Yaḥyā ibn Maʿīn and others transmitted on his authority.

Ibn Naṣr was accused of seeking the caliphate, but when he was arrested and brought before al-Wāthiq, the latter said, "Never mind what you were arrested for. What do you have to say about the Qur'an?" 78.13

"It's the word of God," said Ibn Naṣr.

"But is it a created thing?"

"It's the word of God."

"Well then: Can you see God on the Day of Resurrection?"

"That's what the reports say."

"Hah!" said al-Wāthiq. "You mean He'll be visible as if he were a finite object with a body?"

Al-Wāthiq then called for the sword and the leather mat. At his command, Ibn Naṣr, still in chains, was sat upon. Next a rope was put around his neck and he was stretched out. Finally al-Wāthiq marched up to him and hacked off his head. At his command, the severed head was sent to Baghdad and displayed for several days on the East Side and then on the West.

We cite ʿAbd al-Raḥmān ibn Muḥammad, who cites Aḥmad ibn ʿAlī ibn Thābit, who cites ʿAlī ibn Muḥammad ibn ʿAbd Allāh al-Ḥadhdhāʾ, who heard Aḥmad ibn Jaʿfar ibn Salm report that he heard Abū Bakr Aḥmad ibn Muḥammad ibn ʿAbd al-Khāliq report that he heard Abū Bakr al-Marrūdhī report: 78.14

[Al-Marrūdhī:] At the mention of Aḥmad ibn Naṣr, I heard Aḥmad ibn Ḥanbal say, "God have mercy on him! How generous he was: he gave up his life!"

We cite Abū Manṣūr al-Qazzāz, who cites Abū Bakr Aḥmad ibn ʿAlī l-Khaṭīb, who heard Abū Naṣr Ibrāhīm ibn Hibat Allāh al-Jarbādhqānī report that he heard Maʿmar ibn Aḥmad al-Iṣfahānī cite, with his permission, Abū ʿAmr ʿUthmān ibn Muḥammad al-ʿUthmānī, who heard ʿAlī ibn Muḥammad ibn Ibrāhīm report that he heard Ibrāhīm ibn Ismāʿīl ibn Khalaf report: 78.15

[Ismāʿīl ibn Khalaf:] Aḥmad ibn Naṣr was my friend. After the Inquisition killed him and displayed his head, I heard that the head was reciting the Qur'an. So I went and spent the night in a spot overlooking the head, which was guarded by men on horse and men on foot. As soon as everyone had

فلمّا هدأت العيون سمعت الرأس يقرأ: ﴿الٓمٓ ☆ أَحَسِبَ النَّاسُ أَن يُتْرَكُوا أَن يَقُولُوا آمَنَّا وَهُمْ لا يُفْتَنُونَ﴾. فاقشعرّ جلدي.

ثمّ رأيتُه بعد ذلك في المنام وعليه السُّنْدُس والإسْتَبْرَق وعلى رأسه تاج فقلت: ما فعل الله بك يا أخي؟

قال: غفر لي وأدخلني الجنّة إلّا أني كنت مغموماً ثلاثة أيّام.

قلتُ: ولِمَ؟

قال: كان رسول الله صلّى الله عليه وسلّم مرّ بي فلمّا بَلَغ خشبتي حوّل وجهه فقلت له بعد ذلك: يا رسول الله قُتلت على الحقّ أو على الباطل؟

فقال لي: أنت على الحقّ ولكن قتلك رجل من أهل بيتي فإذا بلغتُ إليك أستحيي منك.

١٦،٧٨ أخبرنا القزّاز قال: أخبرنا أبو بكر الخطيب قال: قرأتُ على أبي بكر البَرْقاني عن أبي إسحاق إبراهيم بن محمّد[1] المُزَكّي قال: أخبرنا محمّد بن إسحاق السرّاج قال: سمعت عبد الله بن محمّد يقول:

حدثنا إبراهيم بن الحسن قال: رأى بعض أصحابنا أحمد بن نصر في النوم بعد ما قُتل فقال له: ما فعل بك ربّك؟

قال: ما كانت إلّا غفوة حتّى لقيتُ الله فضحك إليّ.

١٧،٧٨ قال الخطيب: لم يزل رأس أحمد بن نصر منصوباً ببغداد وجسده مصلوباً بسُرَّ مَنْ رَأَى ستّ سنين إلى أن حُطّ وجُمع بين رأسه وبدنه ودُفن بالجانب الشرقي في المقبرة المعروفة بالمالِكية ودفن في شوّال سنة سبع وثلاثين.

١٨،٧٨ وممّن أُخذ في المحنة الحارث بن مِسْكين أبو عَمْرو المصري

وكان قد سمع من سُفْيان بن عُيَيْنة وغيره وكان فقيهاً على مذهب مالك ثَبْتاً في الحديث فحمله المأمون إلى بغداد في أيّام المحنة وسجنه لأنّه لم يُجب إلى القول بخلق

---

١ ابن محمّد: ليس في ش.

dozed off, I heard the head reciting «Do people think that once they say, "We believe," they will be left alone and not be put to the test?»[186] When I heard it, I shuddered.

Later I dreamed of seeing him draped in fine silk and heavy brocade[187] with a crown on his head. "Brother," I asked him, "how have you fared?"

"God has forgiven me," he answered, "and admitted me to the Garden. But I did spend three unhappy days first."

"Why?"

"The Emissary of God came to visit me, but when he passed the stake where my head was he averted his eyes. Finally I asked him whether I had died for the truth or for a falsehood.

"'For truth,' he said. 'But it was a member of my family who killed you, so whenever I pass you I feel ashamed.'"

We cite al-Qazzāz, who cites Abū Bakr al-Khaṭīb, who read back to Abū Bakr al-Barqānī 78.16
his report citing Abū Isḥāq Ibrāhīm ibn Muḥammad al-Muzakkī, who cites Muḥammad ibn Isḥāq al-Sarrāj, who heard ʿAbd Allāh ibn Muḥammad say that he heard Ibrāhīm ibn al-Ḥasan report:

[Ibrāhīm ibn al-Ḥasan:] The night after Aḥmad ibn Naṣr was killed, one of my associates saw him in a dream. He asked him how God had judged him.

"It felt as if I had dozed off for a moment," he replied, "and then I saw God smiling at me."

Al-Khaṭīb reports: Ibn Naṣr's head remained on display in Baghdad, and 78.17
his body crucified in Samarra, for six years before his remains were finally taken down. The head and body were brought back together in Shawwāl of '37 [851–52] and buried in al-Mālikiyyah, a cemetery on the East Side.

Those arrested during the Inquisition include al-Ḥārith ibn Miskīn, Abū 78.18
ʿAmr al-Miṣrī.

He heard reports from Sufyān ibn ʿUyaynah and others, and followed Mālik in his judgments of the Law. He was a reliable transmitter of Ḥadith. During the Inquisition, he was taken to Baghdad by order of al-Maʾmūn, who jailed him when he refused to espouse the creed of the created Qurʾan.

القرآن فلم يزل محبوساً إلى أن ولي المتوكّل فأطلقه وأطلق جميع من كان في السجن.

١٩،٧٨ وممّن امتُحن عبد الأعلى بن مُسهِر أبو مُسهر الدمشقي الغَسّاني، أُشخص إلى المأمون بالرّقة.

فأخبرنا أبو منصور القزاز قال: أخبرنا أبو بكر أحمد بن عليّ قال: أخبرنا الأزهري قال: حدثنا محمّد بن العبّاس قال: حدثنا أحمد بن معروف الخشّاب قال: حدثنا الحسين بن فهم قال:

حدثنا محمّد بن سعد قال: أُشخص أبو مُسهر الغسّاني من دمشق إلى عبد الله بن هارون وهو البرقّة فسأله عن القرآن فقال: القُرآن كلام الله وأبى أن يقول: مخلوق.

فدعا له بالسيف والنطع ليضرب عُنقه فلمّا رأى ذلك قال: مخلوق.

فتركه من القتل وقال: أمّا إنّك لو قلت ذلك قبل أن أدعو بالسيف لقبلتُ منك ورددتك إلى بلادك وأهلك ولكنّك تخرج الآن فتقول: قلتُ ذلك فَرَقاً من القتل، أَشخِصوه إلى بغداد فاحبسوه بها حتى يموت.

فأُشخص من الرقّة إلى بغداد في شهر ربيع الآخر من سنة ثمان عشرة ومائتين فحُبس فلم يلبث إلا يسيراً حتى مات في الحبس في غُرّة رجب سنة ثمان عشرة فأُخرج ليُدفن فشهده قوم كثير من أهل بغداد.

٢٠،٧٨ قلت: وعُموم هؤلاء الذين لم يجيبوا أُهمل منهم قوم وحُبس منهم قوم فلم يُلتفت إليهم وإنّما كان المقصود أحمد بن حنبل لجلالة قَدْره وعِظَم موقعه.

He remained in jail until the accession of al-Mutawakkil, who released all the detainees.

Another victim of the Inquisition was ʿAbd al-Aʿlā ibn Mushir, Abū Mushir, al-Dimashqī l-Ghassānī, who was sent to al-Maʾmūn in al-Raqqah. 78.19

We cite Abū Manṣūr al-Qazzāz, who cites Abū Bakr Aḥmad ibn ʿAlī, who cites al-Azharī, who heard Muḥammad ibn al-ʿAbbās report that he heard Aḥmad ibn Maʿrūf al-Khashshāb report that he heard al-Ḥusayn ibn Qahm report that he heard Muḥammad ibn Saʿd report:

[Muḥammad ibn Saʿd:] Abū Mushir al-Ghassānī was sent from Damascus to al-Raqqah to meet with ʿAbd Allāh [al-Maʾmūn] ibn Hārūn, who asked him about the Qurʾan.

"It's the speech of God," he said, refusing to say it was created.

Al-Maʾmūn called for the sword and the mat. Seeing that he was going to be beheaded, Abū Mushir said, "It's created!"

Al-Maʾmūn spared his life but said, "If you had said that before I called for the sword, I would have sent you back home to your family. But if I let you go now you'll say you were coerced. Take him to Baghdad and lock him up until he dies!"

Abū Mushir was accordingly sent from al-Raqqah to Baghdad in Rabīʿ II 218 [April–May 833], and remained in jail only a short time before he died on the first day of Rajab '18 [July 23, 833]. A great many people in Baghdad witnessed the removal of his body for burial.

[The author:] Of those who refused to capitulate, some were overlooked or ignored while others were imprisoned and forgotten. None received as much attention as Aḥmad ibn Ḥanbal, a man of standing whose story was especially memorable. 78.20

الباب التاسع والسبعون في ذكر مرضه

أخبرنا عبد الملك بن أبي القاسم قال: أخبرنا عبد الله بن محمد الأنصاري قال: أخبرنا أبو يعقوب قال: أخبرنا الحسن بن محمّد بن الحسن بن نصر قال: حدثنا يعقوب بن إسحاق قال: ١،٧٩

حدثنا عبد الله بن أحمد بن حنبل قال: سمعتُ أبي يقول: استكملتُ سبعاً وسبعين سنة ودخلت في ثمان وسبعين. فحُمّ من ليلته ومات يوم العاشر سنة إحدى وأربعين.

أخبرنا محمّد بن ناصر قال: أخبرنا عبد القادر بن محمّد قال: أنبأنا إبراهيم بن عمر قال: أنبأنا ابن بطة قال: أخبرنا ابن مخلد قال: ٢،٧٩

حدثنا محمّد بن يوسف الجوهري قال: دخلتُ على أبي عبد الله أحمد بن حنبل في الحبس وعنده أبو سعيد الحدّاد فقال له: كيف تجدك يا أبا عبد الله؟

فقال: بخير في عافية والحمد لله.

فقال له أبو سعيد: حُمت البارحة؟

قال: إذا قلتُ لك أنا في عافية فحسبك، لا تخرجني إلى ما أكره.

أخبرنا ابن ناصر قال: أخبرنا عبد القادر بن محمّد بن يوسف قال: أخبرنا أبو إسحاق البرمكي قال: أخبرنا عليّ بن عبد العزيز قال: أخبرنا عبد الرحمن بن أبي حاتم قال: ٣،٧٩

حدثنا صالح بن أحمد بن حنبل قال: لمّا كان في أول يوم من شهر ربيع الأول من سنة إحدى وأربعين ومائتين حُمّ أبي ليلة الأربعاء فدخلتُ عليه يوم الأربعاء وهو محموم يتنفّس تنفُّساً شديداً وكنتُ قد عرفت علّته وكنت أمرّضه إذا اعتلّ فقلت له: يا أبَةِ علامَ أفطرت البارحة؟

قال: على ماء باقلاّء.

ثم أراد القيام فقال: خُذ بيدي.

Chapter 79: His Final Illness

We cite ʿAbd al-Malik ibn Abī l-Qāsim, who cites ʿAbd Allāh ibn Muḥammad al-Anṣārī, **79.1**
who cites Abū Yaʿqūb, who cites al-Ḥasan ibn Muḥammad ibn al-Ḥasan ibn Naṣr, who heard Yaʿqūb ibn Isḥāq report that he heard Aḥmad ibn Ḥanbal's son ʿAbd Allāh report:

[ʿAbd Allāh:] My father told me: "I've lived seventy-seven years and started my seventy-eighth."

That same night he took fever. He died on the tenth, in '41 [855].

We cite Muḥammad ibn Nāṣir, who cites ʿAbd al-Qādir ibn Muḥammad, who was **79.2**
informed by Ibrāhīm ibn ʿUmar, who was informed by Ibn Baṭṭah, who cites Ibn Makhlad, who heard Muḥammad ibn Yūsuf al-Jawharī report:

[Al-Jawharī:] I went to visit Ibn Ḥanbal in jail and found Abū Saʿīd al-Ḥaddād there with him. Abū Saʿīd asked him how he was feeling.

"Well," he answered. "In good health, praise God!"

"Did you have any fever last night?"

"If I say I'm in good health," said Aḥmad, "don't ask any more questions. I don't want to talk about anything detestable."

We cite Ibn Nāṣir, who cites ʿAbd al-Qādir ibn Muḥammad ibn Yūsuf, who cites Abū **79.3**
Isḥāq al-Barmakī, who cites ʿAlī ibn ʿAbd al-ʿAzīz, who cites ʿAbd al-Raḥmān ibn Abī Ḥātim, who heard Aḥmad ibn Ḥanbal's son Ṣāliḥ report:

[Ṣāliḥ:] On the first day of Rabīʿ I 241, on a Tuesday night,[188] my father took fever. The next day I went to see him. He was feverish and he was breathing only with great effort. I knew how his illnesses went and I was the one who nursed him whenever he was unwell.

"What did you eat last night, Dad?" I asked him.

"Bean broth," he said.

Then he tried to get up.

"Take my hand," he said.

فأخذتُ بيده فلمّا صار إلى الخلاء ضعفت رجلاه حتى توكأ عليّ.

وكان يختلف إليه غير متطبب كلّهم مسلمون فوصف له مُتطبب يقال له عبد الرحمن قَرعة تُشوى ويُسق ماءها. وهذا يوم الثلاثاء، وتُوفّي يوم الجُمعة.

فقال: يا صالحّ!

قلتُ: لبّيك.

قال: لا تُشوى في منزلك ولا في منزل عبد الله أخيك.

وصار الفَتح بن سهل إلى الباب ليعوده فجبتُه وأتى علي[1] بن الجَعد فجبتُه. ٤،٧٩

وكثُر الناس فقلتُ: يا أبة قد كثر الناس.

قال: فأَيّ شيء ترى؟

قلتُ: تأذنُ لهم فيدعون لك.

قال: استخِرِ[2] الله!

فجعلوا يدخلون عليه أفواجاً حتّى تمتلئ الدار فيسألونه ويدعون له ثمّ يخرجون ويدخل فوج آخر وكثُر الناس وامتلأ الشارع وأغلقنا باب الزقاق.

وجاء رجل من جيراننا قد خضب فدخل عليه فقال: إنّي لأرى الرجل يُحيي ٥،٧٩ شيئاً من السنّة فأفرح به، فدخل فجعل يدعو له فجعل يقول: له ولجميع المسلمين.

وجاء رجل فقال: تلطّفْ لي بالإذن عليه فإنّي قد حضرت ضربه يوم الدار وأريد أن أستحلّه.

فقلتُ له فأمسك فلم أزل به حتّى قال: أدخله.

فأدخلته فقام بين يديه وجعل يبكي وقال: يا أبا عبد الله أنا كنت ممّن حضر ضربك يوم الدار وقد أتيتك فإنْ أحببتَ القصاص فأنا بين يديك وإن رأيتَ أن تُحلّني فعلت.

فقال: على أن لا تعود لمثل ذلك.

قال: نعم.

---

١ تركي: ابن علي. ٢ ش: استخير.

I took it. When he reached the privy his legs gave way and he had to lean on me.

He was attended by several physicians, all of them Muslims. One of them, a man called ʿAbd al-Raḥmān, advised him to roast a gourd and drink the juice. That was on the Tuesday before the Friday when he died.

"Ṣāliḥ," he said.

"Yes."

"Don't roast it in your house or ʿAbd Allāh's either."

Al-Fatḥ ibn Sahl came to check on him but I didn't let him in. Then ʿAlī 79.4
ibn al-Jaʿd[189] came but I didn't let him in either. But as people kept arriving, I finally told my father he had visitors.

"What do you think we should do?" he asked me.

"Let them in to pray for you."

He agreed, and in they came, pouring into the house until it was full, asking him how he was feeling and calling on God to cure him. As soon as one group went out, another would come crowding in. As more and more arrived, the street filled up and we had to close the alley gate.

Among the callers was a neighbor of ours who had just dyed his beard. As soon as my father saw him, he said, "Now there's a man who's keeping some *sunnah* alive. That makes me happy." The man went in and began praying for my father, who kept adding, "And for him, and for all Muslims."

Another man came and said, "Find some way to get me in to see him. I was there the day they flogged him at the palace and I want him to forgive me."

When I told my father, he said nothing. But I kept at him until he relented. 79.5
When I let the man in, he stood there weeping. "Abū ʿAbd Allāh," he said, "I was there the day they flogged you at the palace. Now here I am before you. If you want revenge, take it. If you can forgive me, forgive me."

"On one condition," said my father. "Don't do anything like it again."

قال: قد جعلتك في حلّ.

فخرج يبكي وبكى من حضر من الناس.

٦،٧٩ وكان له في خُرَيقة قُطيعات فإذا أراد الشيء أعطينا من يشتري له فقال لي يوم الثلاثاء وأنا عنده: انظر[١] في خريقتي شيء؟

فنظرت فإذا فيها درهم فقال: وجِّه فاقْتَضِ بعض السكان. فوجّهت فأُعطيت شيئاً. فقال: وجِّه فاشترِ تمراً وكفِّرعني كفارة يمين.

فوجّهتُ فاشتريت وكفّرت عنه كفارة يمين وبقي ثلاثة دراهم أو نحو ذلك فأخبرتُه فقال: الحمدُ لله.

وقال: اقرأ عليّ الوصيّة.

فقرأتها عليه فأقرّها.

قلتُ: قد ذكرنا وصيّته في قصّة المحنة فغنينا عن الإعادة.

٧،٧٩ أخبرنا محمد بن أبي منصور قال: أخبرنا عبد القادر بن محمد قال: أنبأنا أبو إسحاق البرمكي قال: أنبأنا عبد العزيز ابن جعفر قال: حدثنا أحمد بن محمد الخلّال قال:

حدثنا أبو بكر المَرُّوذي قال: مرض أبو عبد الله ليلة الأربعاء لليلتين خلتا من شهر ربيع الأوّل سنة إحدى وأربعين ومائتين ومرض تسعة أيّام. فلمّا اشتدّت علّته وتسامع الناس أقبلوا لعيادته فكثروا ولزموا الباب الليل والنهار يبيتون، وسمع السلطان بكثرة الناس فوكّل السلطان ببابه وباب الزقاق الرابطة وأصحاب الأخبار.

وكان أبو عبد الله ربّما أذن للناس فيدخلون عليه أفواجاً أفواجاً يسلّمون عليه فيردّ عليهم بيده. فلمّا جاءت الرابطة مُنع الناس من ذلك وأُغلق باب الزقاق فكان الناس في الشوارع والمساجد حتى تعطّل بعض الباعة وحيل بينهم وبين البيع والشراء.

وكان الرجل إذا أراد أن يدخل عليه ربّما أُدخل من بعض الدور وطُرُز الحاكة وربما تسلّق.

---

١ ش: انه.

"I won't," said the man.

"I forgive you."

The man went out in tears and all those present wept as well.

My father kept some scraps of coin in a bit of rag. Whenever he needed anything, we would give some of the money to whoever was doing the shopping for him. On that Tuesday, he asked me if there was anything in the rag. I looked and found a dirham. 79.6

"Find one of the tenants to run an errand," he said. So I sent word and one of the women was given some money.[190]

"Send out and get me some dates so I can expiate a broken oath," he said. I sent out for the dates, bought them, and expiated his oath.[191] After that there were about three dirhams left. When I told him, he said, "Praise God!" Then he said, "Read out my will."

I read it out to him and he affirmed that it was his.

[The author:] We have already cited his will in our account of the Inquisition and will therefore refrain from citing it again.

We cite Muḥammad ibn Abī Manṣūr, who cites ʿAbd al-Qādir ibn Muḥammad, who was informed by Abū Isḥāq al-Barmakī, who was informed by ʿAbd al-ʿAzīz ibn Jaʿfar, who heard Aḥmad ibn Muḥammad al-Khallāl report that he heard Abū Bakr al-Marrūdhī report: 79.7

[Al-Marrūdhī:] Aḥmad fell ill on Tuesday night, two nights into Rabīʿ I 241, and remained unwell for nine days. As word spread that he was growing worse, crowds of visitors appeared at the gate and remained there through the night. When the authorities learned that a crowd had gathered, they posted watchers and horse-troopers at the door of the house and the gateway into the alley. Up to that point Aḥmad had been allowing people in to see him. They would crowd into the house calling out greetings, and he would respond by lifting his hand. That ended with the arrival of the mounted troops, who stopped people from going in and shut the alley gate. But so many people had crowded into the streets and mosques that some of the vendors could no longer do business. The only way to see Ibn Ḥanbal was

وجاء أصحاب الأخبار فقعدوا على الباب من قبل إبراهيم بن عطاء وكان ابن عطاء[1] يتعاهده بالغداة والعشي وربّما لم يجتمعا وأصحاب الأخبار من قِبَل ابن طاهر يسألون عن خبره.

وقال أبو عبد الله: جاءني[2] حاجب ابن طاهر فقال: إن الأمير يُقرئك السلام وهو يشتهي أن يراك.

قال: فقلتُ له: هذا ممّا أكرهُ وأمير المؤمنين قد أعفاني ممّا أكره.

وجاء حاجب ابن طاهر بالليل فسأل من يختلف إليه من المتطبّبين وأصحاب الأخبار يكتبون بخبره إلى العسكر والبُرُد تختلف[3] كلّ يوم.

وجاء بنو هاشم فدخلوا عليه وجعلوا يبكون عليه.

وجاء قوم من القضاة وغيرهم فلم يؤذن لهم.

وجاء غلام لأبي يوسف عمّه ليروحه فأشار إليه بيده أن لا يفعل لأنه كان اشتراه من الشيء الذي يكره، وقال: لا تبرح، قد تغيرتُ.

فقلت: لا أبرح.

٨،٧٩ فكان إذا أراد الشيء ممّا يتعالج أخرج خُريقة فيها قُطيعات فيعطيني منها فأشتري له. وكان قد كتب وصيّته بالعسكر وأشهدنا عليه فبلغني أنّه قال: أقرؤوها فقُرئت عليه.

ثم أمر بكفارة يمين فاشترينا له تمرًا فبقي عليه منه دانق ونصف أو أرجح، فلمّا جئت قال: ما صنعتم؟

قلت: أخذنا التمر وقد بعثنا به.

فأشار برأسه إلى السماء وجعل يحمد الله.

وجاء عبد الوهاب فلمّا استأذنوا له قال أبو عبد الله: عزّ عليّ بمجيئه في الحرّ.

فلمّا دخل عليه أكبّ عليه فأخذ بيده فلم تزل يده في يده حتّى قام.

---

١ وكان ابن عطاء: ليس في ش، د. ٢ ما يليها في هـ إلى (بن احمد هل عقل أبوك) في الورقة ١٨٥ على غير ترتيب.

٣ د: والبريد يختلف.

to find a way in through the adjoining houses or the weavers' tenements, or to climb over a wall. After sending men to take up positions near the gate and report back to him, Ibrāhīm ibn ʿAṭāʾ came twice a day—once in the morning and once in the evening—to ask after Ibn Ḥanbal but as often as not went away without seeing him. Meanwhile, watchers acting on behalf of Ibn Ṭāhir were making inquiries as well.

Aḥmad told me, "Ibn Ṭāhir's chamberlain came to see me and reported, 'The caliph sends his salutations; he wishes to see you.' I told him that was something I would detest doing, and the Commander of the Faithful had exempted me from doing what I detest."

Ibn Ṭāhir's chamberlain came back at night and asked questions of the doctors who were attending my father. Meanwhile, the watchers were sending reports back to Samarra, and the courier horses came and went every day. The members of the clan of Hāshim came to see him and wept. A number of judges and other officials arrived but were not admitted. A boy belonging to his uncle Yūsuf was sent to fan him, but my father waved him away because he had been purchased with funds he disapproved of.

"Stay with me," he said. "It won't be long now."

"I'm right here," I told him.

Whenever he needed to buy anything for his health, he would take out a 79.8
bit of rag containing some scraps of coin and give them to me and I would buy what he needed.

He had us witness his will, which he had written in Samarra. I heard that he said, "Read it out," and it was read aloud for him. Then he asked us to buy some dates to expiate an oath. Afterward he was left with a *dāniq* and a half, more or less. When I came in he asked how it had gone, and I told him that we had taken the dates and sent them. He turned his face to the heavens and began praising God.

He also had a visit from ʿAbd al-Wahhāb. "It means a lot to me," said Aḥmad when he was admitted, "that he came here in this heat." ʿAbd al-Wahhāb bent over him and took his hand. The two sat hand in hand until it was time for ʿAbd al-Wahhāb to leave.

ودخل عليه جماعة فيهم شيخ مخضوب فنظر إليه فقال: إنّي لأسرّ أن أرى الشيخ قد خضب، أو نحو هذا من الكلام.

وقال له رجل ممّن دخل عليه: أعطاك الله ما كنت تريده لأهل الإسلام.

فقال: استجاب الله لك.

وجعلوا يخصُّونه بالدعاء فجعل يقول: قولوا ولجميع المسلمين.

وربّما دخل عليه الرجل الذي في قلبه عليه الشيء فإذا رآه غمض عينه كالمعرض وربمّا سلّم عليه الرجل منهم فلا يردّ عليه.

ودخل عليه شيخ فكلّمه وقال: اذكر وقوفك بين يدي الله.

فشهق أبو عبد الله وسالت الدموع على خدّيه.

٩،٧٩ فلمّا كان قبل وفاته بيوم أو يومين قال: ادعوا الصبيان، بلسان ثقيل، يعني الصغار.

فجعلوا ينضمّون إليه وجعل يشمّهم ويمسح بيده على رؤوسهم وعينه تدمع، فقال له رجل: لا تغتمّ لهم يا أبا عبد الله!

فأشار بيده فظننّا أنّ معناه إنّي لم أُرد هذا المعنى.

وكان يصلّي قاعداً ويصلّي وهو مضطجع ولا يكاد يفتر ويرفع يديه في إيماء الركوع.

وأدخلتُ الطّست تحته فرأيت بوله دماً عبيطاً ليس فيه بول فقلت للطبيب فقال: هذا الرجل قد فتّت الحزن والغمّ جوفه.

واشتدّت به العلّة يوم الخميس ووضّأته فقال: خَلِّل الأصابع.

فلمّا كانت ليلة الجمعة ثقُل فظننتُ أنه قد قُبض وأردنا أن نمدّده فجعل يقبض قدميه وهو موجِّه وجعلنا نلقّنه فنقول لا إله إلا الله ونردّد ذلك عليه وهو يهلّل وتوجَّه إلى القبلة واستقبلها بقدميه.

فلمّا كان يوم الجمعة اجتمع الناس حتى ملؤوا السكك والشوارع فلمّا كان صدر النهار قُبض رحمه الله.

At one point a group of people came in, one of them an elder with a dyed beard. Aḥmad said, "It makes me happy to see that he's dyed his beard," or words to that effect.

One of his visitors said, "May God give you what you asked Him to give all of us." "May God grant your prayer!" replied Aḥmad. As his visitors began naming him in their prayers, he kept saying, "For all Muslims too!"

Several of his visitors were people he disapproved of for one reason or another. Whenever such a person entered, Aḥmad would close his eyes as if to dismiss him. Often he would refuse to return his greeting.

One elder came to see him and said to him, "Be mindful of the moment when you'll stand before God!" At that, Aḥmad gave a sob and the tears streamed down his cheeks.

A day or two before he died, he slurred out the words, "Call the boys," 79.9
meaning the little ones. As the children gathered around him one by one, he held them close to inhale their scent and, tears in his eyes, ran his hand over their heads. Someone said, "Don't worry, Abū ʿAbd Allāh: they'll be fine." But Aḥmad made a gesture as if to say, "That's not what I was thinking."

When he could only sit, he would pray from that position; and when he couldn't rise he would pray lying down, tirelessly, by lifting his hands as if performing a cycle of prostrations.

When I put a basin under him I saw that his urine was nothing but bright red blood with no other fluid in it at all. I mentioned this to the doctor, who said that anyone who spent that much time in suffering and sorrow might well shred his own innards.

On Thursday he grew worse. I washed him so he could pray. "Get the water between my fingers," he said.

On Thursday night he stopped moving. Thinking he was dead, we were trying to stretch him out when he began to bend his knees with his face turned toward Mecca. We began saying "There is no god but God" for him to repeat but he had already started saying it. He on his side to face Mecca.

On Friday, throngs of people began to gather, filling the streets and alleys. At noon he was taken from us. A great cry arose and people began to weep so loudly that it felt as if the earth were shaking. When everyone sat down, we realized that we might miss Friday prayers, so I found a place where I

فصاح الناس وعلَتِ الأصوات بالبكاء حتى كأنّ الدنيا قد ارتجّت وقعد الناس فخفنا أن ندع الجمعة فأشرفتُ عليهم فأخبرتهم إنّا نُخرجه بعد صلاة الجمعة.

١٠،٧٩ أخبرنا محمّد بن أبي منصور قال: أخبرنا أبو الغنائم محمّد بن محمّد بن المهتدي قال: أنبأنا عبد العزيز بن عليّ الأَزَجي قال: أنبأنا عبد العزيز بن جعفر قال: أخبرنا أبو بكر أحمد بن محمّد الخلّال قال: أخبرني عِصْمة بن عِصام قال:

حدثنا حنبل قال: أعطى بعض ولد الفضل بن الرّبيع أبا عبد الله وهو في الحبس ثلاث شَعرات فقال: هذا من شعر النبيّ صلّى الله عليه وسلّم.

فأوصى أبو عبد الله عند موته أن يُجعل على كلّ عين شعرة وشعرة على لسانه ففُعل به ذلك عند موته.

١١،٧٩ أخبرنا محمّد بن ناصر قال: أخبرنا عبد القادر بن محمّد قال: أخبرنا أبو إسحاق البرمكي قال: أخبرنا عليّ بن عبد العزيز بن مردك قال: حدثنا عبد الرحمن بن أبي حاتم قال:

حدثنا صالح بن أحمد قال: لم يزل أبي يصلّي في مرضه قائماً أُمسكه فيركع ويسجد وأرفعه في ركوعه وسُجوده.

ودخل عليه مُجاهد بن موسى فقال: يا أبا عبد الله قد جاءتك البُشرى، هذا الخلق يشهدون لك، ما تُبالي لو وردت على الله عزّ وجلّ الساعة.

وجعل يُقبل يده ويبكي وجعل يقول: أوصِني يا أبا عبد الله! فأشار إلى لسانه. ودخل سَوّار القاضي فجعل يبشّره ويُخبره بالرُّخص وذكر له عن معتمر أنّه قال: قال[١] أبي عند موته: حدّثني بالرخص.

١٢،٧٩ واجتمعت عليه أوجاع الحصر وغير ذلك ولم يزل عقله ثابتاً وهو في خلال ذلك يقول: كم اليوم في الشهر؟ فأُخبره.

وكنتُ أنام بالليل إلى جنبه فإذا أراد حاجة حركني فأناوله، وقال لي: جئني بالكتاب الذي فيه حديث ابن إدريس عن ليث عن طاووس أنه كان يكره الأنين. فقرأته عليه فلم يئِنّ إلّا في الليلة التي تُوفّي فيها.

١ د: قال لي.

could look out over the crowd and announced that we would bring him out after the prayer.

We cite Muḥammad ibn Abī Manṣūr, who cites Abū l-Ghanā'im Muḥammad ibn Muḥammad ibn al-Muhtadī, who was informed by 'Abd al-'Azīz ibn 'Alī l-Azajī, who was informed by 'Abd al-'Azīz ibn Ja'far, who cites Abū Bakr Aḥmad ibn Muḥammad al-Khallāl, who cites 'Iṣmah ibn 'Iṣām, who heard Ḥanbal report: 79.10

[Ḥanbal:] While Ibn Ḥanbal was in jail, one of al-Faḍl ibn al-Rabī''s sons gave him three hairs, saying that they belonged to the Prophet.[192] As he lay dying, Aḥmad asked that one hair be put over each of his eyes and the third on his tongue. This we did for him when he died.

We cite Muḥammad ibn Nāṣir, who cites 'Abd al-Qādir ibn Muḥammad, who cites Abū Isḥāq al-Barmakī, who cites 'Alī ibn 'Abd al-'Azīz ibn Mardak, who heard 'Abd al-Raḥmān ibn Abī Ḥātim report that he heard Aḥmad's son Ṣāliḥ report: 79.11

[Ṣāliḥ:] During his illness my father prayed by having me hold him upright so he could bow and prostrate himself, which he did by having me lift him.

At one point Mujāhid ibn Mūsā came in, saying, "No need to be afraid, Abū 'Abd Allāh! With all these people to testify on your behalf, there's nothing to fear when you meet God!" He began kissing my father's hand and weeping. When he asked for his counsel, my father pointed to his tongue.

Another visitor was Judge Sawwār, who reassured him that God would not hold him to the strictest accounting, citing the report transmitted by Mu'tamir to the effect that his father had said to him as he lay dying, "Tell me about God's lenience."[193]

He began to suffer from retention of urine and other pains but his mind remained clear. All the while he would ask what day of the month it was and I would tell him. At night I slept beside him. If he wanted anything he would shake me and I would hand it to him. Once he asked me to bring him the notes where he'd written that Ibn Idrīs cites Layth ibn Ṭāwūs as saying he hated to moan. I read the report for him and he never moaned after that except on the night he died. 79.12

١٣،٧٩ أخبرنا إسماعيل بن أحمد ومحمّد بن أبي القاسم قالا: أخبرنا حمد بن أحمد قال: حدثنا أبو نعيم الحافظ قال: حدثنا أبي قال: حدثنا أحمد بن محمّد بن عمر قال:

حدثنا عبد الله بن أحمد بن حنبل قال: قال لي أبي في مرضه الذي توفّي فيه: أخرجْ كتاب عبد الله بن إدريس. فأخرجتُ الكتاب فقال: أخرج أحاديث ليث بن أبي سُليم. فأخرجت أحاديث ليث فقال: اقرأ عليّ حديث ليث قال: قلت لطَلْحة إنّ طاووساً كان يكره الأنين في المرض فما سُمع له أنين حتى مات رحمه الله. فقرأت الحديث على أبي فما سمعت أبي يئنّ في مرضه ذلك إلى أن توفّي رحمه الله.

سِياقُ ذكر حاله عند احتضاره

١٤،٧٩ أخبرنا المحمّدان ابن عبد الملك وابن ناصر قالا: أخبرنا أحمد بن الحسن المعدّل قال: أخبرنا أبو عليّ بن شاذان، وأخبرنا إسماعيل بن أحمد ومحمّد بن أبي القاسم قالا: أخبرنا حَمْد بن أحمد قال: أخبرنا أبو نُعَيم الحافظ قال: حدثنا عمر بن أحمد بن عثمان قالا: حدثنا محمّد بن عبد الله بن عَمْرُوَيه ويُعرف بابن عَلَمَ قال:

سمعتُ عبد الله بن أحمد بن حنبل قال: لمّا حضرت أبي الوفاة جلست عنده وبيدي الخرقة لأشدّ بها لِحْيَيْه فجعل يغرق ثم يُفيق ثم يفتح عينيه ويقول بيده هكذا لا بَعْدُ، لا بعد، لا بَعْدُ، ثلاث مرات، ففعل هذا مرة وثانية فلمّا كان في الثالثة قلت له: يا أبة أيّ شيء هذا، قد لهجت به في هذا الوقت؟ تغرق حتى نقول قد قضيْتَ ثم تعود فتقول لا بَعْدُ، لا بعد!

فقال لي: يا بنيّ ما تدري؟

فقلت: لا.

فقال إبليس لعنه الله قائم حذائي عاضّ على أنامله يقول لي: يا أحمد فُتَّني وأنا أقول له: لا بَعْدُ حتّى أموت.

١٥،٧٩ أخبرنا إسماعيل بن أحمد ومحمّد بن عبد الباقي قالا: أخبرنا حمد بن أحمد قال: أخبرنا أحمد بن عبد الله الحافظ قال: حدثنا أبي قال:

We cite Ismāʿīl ibn Aḥmad, who along with Muḥammad ibn Abī l-Qāsim cites Ḥamd ibn Aḥmad, who heard Abū Nuʿaym al-Ḥāfiẓ report that he heard his father report that he heard Aḥmad ibn Muḥammad ibn ʿUmar report that he heard Aḥmad ibn Ḥanbal's son ʿAbd Allāh report: 79.13

[ʿAbd Allāh:] During his final illness, my father asked me to find where he had written the reports transmitted by ʿAbd Allāh ibn Idrīs. When I found the book for him, he asked me to find the report related by Layth and read it to him. The report ran: "I told Ṭalḥah that Ṭāwūs disapproved of moaning when ill, and did not moan until he died." After I read this to my father, I didn't hear him moan until he died, God have mercy on him.

More on His Final Moments

We cite the two Muḥammads, Ibn ʿAbd al-Malik and Ibn Nāṣir, who cite Aḥmad ibn al-Ḥasan al-Muʿaddal, who cites Abū ʿAlī ibn Shadhān; and we cite Ismāʿīl ibn Aḥmad, who along with Muḥammad ibn Abī l-Qāsim cites Ḥamd ibn Aḥmad, who cites Abū Nuʿaym al-Ḥāfiẓ, who heard ʿUmar ibn Aḥmad ibn ʿUthmān, who along with Abū ʿAlī ibn Shadhān heard Muḥammad ibn ʿAbd Allāh ibn ʿAmruwayh—also known as Ibn ʿAlam—report that he heard Aḥmad ibn Ḥanbal's son ʿAbd Allāh report: 79.14

[ʿAbd Allāh:] As my father lay dying, I sat beside him holding the rag I would use to tie his mouth closed. He was slipping in and out of consciousness and gesturing with his hand three times, like this, as if to say, "Not yet!" After the third time, I asked him, "Dad, what are you trying to say? You pass out and we think you're gone, and then you come back and say 'Not yet.'"

"Don't you understand, son?"

"No."

"The Devil, damn him, is standing in front of me biting his fingers in frustration and saying 'Aḥmad, you've escaped me,' and I keep telling him 'Not yet I haven't—not till I'm dead.'"[194]

We cite Ismāʿīl ibn Aḥmad, who along with Muḥammad ibn ʿAbd al-Bāqī cites Ḥamd ibn Aḥmad, who cites Aḥmad ibn ʿAbd Allāh al-Ḥāfiẓ, who heard his father report that he heard Aḥmad ibn Muḥammad ibn ʿUmar report: 79.15

حدثنا أحمد بن محمّد بن عمر قال: سُئِل عبد الله بن[١] أحمد: هل عقَل أبوك عند المعاينة؟

قال: نعم، كنا نُوضّئه فجعل يشير بيده فقال لي صالح[٢]: أيّ شيء يقول؟ فقلتُ: هو ذا يقول: خلِّلوا أصابعي. فخلّلنا أصابعه فترك الإشارة فمات من ساعته.

أخبرنا ابن ناصر قال: أخبرنا عبد القادر بن محمّد قال: أخبرنا إبراهيم ابن عمر قال: أخبرنا ابن مردك قال: حدثنا ابن أبي حاتم قال: ١٦،٧٩

حدثنا صالح بن أحمد قال: جعل أبي يحرّك لسانه إلى أن توفّي رحمه الله.[٣]

الباب الثمانون في تاريخ موته ومبلغ سنه

أخبرنا عبد الرحمن بن محمّد القزّاز قال: أخبرنا أحمد بن عليّ بن ثابت قال: أخبرنا ابن رزق قال: أخبرنا عثمان ابن أحمد الدقاق قال: ١،٨٠

حدثنا حنبل بن إسحاق قال: مات أبو عبد الله في يوم الجمعة في شهر ربيع الأول سنة إحدى وأربعين ومائتين وهو ابنُ سبع وسبعين سنة.

أخبرنا إسماعيل بن أحمد[٤] قال: أخبرنا عمر بن عبيد الله البقّال قال: أخبرنا أبو الحسين بن بِشْران قال: حدثنا عثمان بن أحمد قال: ٢،٨٠

حدثنا حنبل قال: مات أبو عبد الله أحمد بن حنبل في سنة إحدى وأربعين ومائتين في يوم الجمعة في ربيع الأوّل وهو ابن[٥] سبع وسبعين سنة.

---

١ ما قبلها إلى (حاجب ابن طاهر فقال) ورد بعد الورقة ١٨٤ على غير ترتيب في الصورة الضوئية من هـ.

٢ هـ، ش: يا صالح. ٣ رحمه الله: ليس في ش. ٤ من ها هنا إلى ٩٢،٧ ناقص في د. ٥ هـ: في.

[Aḥmad ibn Muḥammad ibn ʿUmar:] ʿAbd Allāh ibn Aḥmad was asked whether his father was conscious when he saw the Angel of Death.

"He was. We were washing him so he could pray and he started gesturing. Ṣāliḥ asked me what he was trying to say, and I told him that he wanted us to spread his fingers and wash between them. When we did that, he stopped gesturing. A little later he died."

We cite Ibn Nāṣir, who cites ʿAbd al-Qādir ibn Muḥammad, who cites Ibrāhīm ibn ʿUmar, who cites Ibn Mardak, who heard Ibn Abī Ḥātim report that he heard Aḥmad's son Ṣāliḥ report: **79.16**

[Ṣāliḥ:] My father's tongue kept moving until he died.

Chapter 80: His Date of Death and His Age When He Died

We cite ʿAbd al-Raḥmān ibn Muḥammad al-Qazzāz, who cites Aḥmad ibn ʿAlī ibn Thābit, who cites Ibn Rizq, who cites ʿUthmān ibn Aḥmad al-Daqqāq, who heard Ḥanbal ibn Isḥāq report: **80.1**

[Ḥanbal:] Aḥmad died on a Friday in Rabīʿ I 241 [July or August 855], at the age of seventy-seven.

We cite Ismāʿīl ibn Aḥmad, who cites ʿUmar ibn ʿUbayd Allāh al-Baqqāl, who cites Abū l-Ḥusayn ibn Bishrān, who heard ʿUthmān ibn Aḥmad report that he heard Ḥanbal report: **80.2**

[Ḥanbal:] Aḥmad ibn Ḥanbal died in 241, on a Friday in Rabīʿ I, at the age of seventy-seven.

٣،٨٠ أخبرنا عبد الرحمن بن محمّد قال: أخبرنا أحمد بن عليّ قال: أخبرنا محمّد بن الحسين بن الفضل القطان قال: أخبرنا جعفر بن محمّد الخُلْدِي قال:

حدثنا محمّد بن عبد الله بن سليمان الحَضْرَمي قال: مات أحمد بن حنبل لاثنتي عشرة خَلَتْ من شهر ربيع الأول سنة إحدى وأربعين ومائتين.

٤،٨٠ أخبرنا إسماعيل بن أحمد ومحمّد بن أبي القاسم قالا: أخبرنا حمد بن أحمد قال: أخبرنا أحمد بن عبد الله الحافظ قال: حدثنا سليمان بن أحمد قال:

سمعت عبد الله بن أحمد يقول: توفّي أبي في يوم الجمعة ضَحوةً ودفنّاه بعد العصر لاثنتي عشرة ليلة خلت من شهر ربيع الأوّل سنة إحدى وأربعين.

٥،٨٠ أخبرنا ابن ناصر أخبرنا عبد القادر بن محمّد قال: أخبرنا البَرْمَكي قال: أخبرنا ابن مَرْدَك قال: حدثنا ابن أبي حاتم قال:

حدثنا صالح بن أحمد قال: لمّا كان يوم الجمعة لاثنتي عشرة خلت من شهر ربيع الأوّل لساعتين من النهار أو أكثر أو أقل تُوفّي أبي رحمه الله.

٦،٨٠ أخبرنا ابن ناصر قال: أخبرنا عبد القادر بن محمّد[١] قال: أنبأنا البرمكي قال: أنبأنا عبد العزيز بن جعفر قال: حدثنا الخلال قال:

حدثنا المَرُّوذي قال: توفّي أبو عبد الله يوم الجمعة لاثنتي عشرة ليلة خلت من شهر ربيع الأول سنة إحدى وأربعين ومائتين[٢] وأُخرجت جنازته بعد مُنصَرف الناس من جُمعتهم.

٧،٨٠ أخبرنا عبد الملك بن أبي القاسم قال: أخبرنا عبد الله بن محمّد الأنصاري قال: أخبرنا إسحاق بن إبراهيم المعدّل قال: أخبرنا العباس بن محمّد القُرَشي قال:

١ ابن محمّد: ليس في هـ. ٢ ليس في هـ.

We cite ʿAbd al-Raḥmān ibn Muḥammad, who cites Aḥmad ibn ʿAlī, who cites Muḥammad ibn al-Ḥusayn ibn al-Faḍl al-Qaṭṭān, who cites Jaʿfar ibn Muḥammad al-Khuldī, who heard Muḥammad ibn ʿAbd Allāh ibn Sulaymān al-Ḥaḍramī report: 80.3

[Al-Ḥaḍramī:] Aḥmad ibn Ḥanbal died twelve nights into Rabīʿ I 241.

We cite Ismāʿīl ibn Aḥmad and Muḥammad ibn Abī l-Qāsim, who cite Ḥamd ibn Aḥmad, who cites Aḥmad ibn ʿAbd Allāh al-Ḥāfiẓ, who heard Sulaymān ibn Aḥmad report that he heard Aḥmad's son ʿAbd Allāh say: 80.4

[ʿAbd Allāh:] My father died before noon on Friday, and we buried him after praying the afternoon prayer, twelve nights into Rabīʿ I 241.[195]

We cite Ibn Nāṣir, who cites ʿAbd al-Qādir ibn Muḥammad, who cites al-Barmakī, who cites Ibn Mardak, who heard Ibn Abī Ḥātim report that he heard Aḥmad's son Ṣāliḥ report: 80.5

[Ṣāliḥ:] It was on Friday, twelve nights into Rabīʿ I, about two hours after dawn, that my father died—God have mercy on him!

We cite Ibn Nāṣir, who cites ʿAbd al-Qādir ibn Muḥammad, who was informed by al-Barmakī, who was informed by ʿAbd al-ʿAzīz ibn Jaʿfar, who heard al-Khallāl report that he heard al-Marrūdhī report: 80.6

[Al-Marrūdhī:] Aḥmad died on Friday, twelve nights into Rabīʿ I 241, and his funeral procession took place after Friday prayers had ended.

We cite ʿAbd al-Malik ibn Abī l-Qāsim, who cites ʿAbd Allāh ibn Muḥammad al-Anṣārī, who cites Isḥāq ibn Ibrāhīm al-Muʿaddal, who cites al-ʿAbbās ibn Muḥammad al-Qurashī, who heard Muḥammad ibn Abī Jaʿfar al-Mundhirī report, citing Aḥmad ibn Dāwūd al-Aḥmasī, who said: 80.7

حدثنا محمّد بن أبي جعفر المُنذري عن أحمد بن داوود الأَحْمَسِي قال: مات أحمد ابن حنبل في سنة إحدى وأربعين ومائتين يوم الجمعة مع طلوع الشمس ورفعنا جنازته مع العصر ودفنّاه مع غروب الشمس.

٨،٨٠ أخبرنا عبد الملك قال: أخبرنا عبد الله بن محمّد قال: أخبرنا أحمد بن محمّد بن إسماعيل السِّيرْجاني[١] قال: أخبرنا أحمد بن عليّ السليماني الحافظ قال: سمعت الحسن بن إسماعيل الفارسي قال:

سمعت محمّد بن إبراهيم البُوشَنْجي يقول: مات أحمد بن حنبل سنة إحدى وأربعين ومائتين.

٩،٨٠ أخبرنا عبد الملك قال: أخبرنا عبد الله بن محمّد قال: أخبرنا أبو يعقوب ومحمّد بن المنتصر قالا: أخبرنا أبو بكر بن أبي الفضل قال: أخبرنا محمّد بن إبراهيم الصرّام قال: حدثنا إبراهيم بن إسحاق الأنصاري قال:

سمعتُ صالح بن أحمد بن حنبل يقول: توفّي أبي وله سبع وسبعون سنة.

فصل: ومن فضل الإمام أحمد موته في يوم الجمعة

١٠،٨٠ فقد أخبرنا ابن الحُصَين قال: أخبرنا ابن المُذْهب قال: أخبرنا أحمد بن جعفر قال: حدثنا عبد الله بن أحمد قال: حدثني أبي قال:

حدثنا أبو عامر قال: حدثنا هشام، يعني ابن سعد، عن سعيد بن أبي هِلال عن ربيعة بن سيف عن عبد الله بن عمر عن النبيّ صلّى الله عليه وسلّم قال: ما مِن مُسلِمٍ يموتُ يَوْمَ الجُمُعَةِ إلّا وَقاهُ اللهُ عزّ وجلّ فِتْنَةَ القَبْرِ.

وقد تُوفّي يوم الجمعة خلق كثير من السادات، فقُتل عثمان بن عفّان يوم الجمعة وضُرب عليّ عليه السلام يوم الجمعة إلا أنّه مات ليلة الأحد وقُتل الحسين بن عليّ يوم الجمعة وتوفّي العبّاس بن عبد المُطّلِب يوم الجمعة وتوفّي الحسن البصري وابن سِيرين في يوم الجمعة، وخلق كثير يطول ذكرهم.

---

١ هـ: الشيرجاني، صححه التركي.

[Al-Aḥmasī:] Aḥmad ibn Ḥanbal died in 241, at sunrise on a Friday. We lifted the body in the afternoon and buried him at sunset.

We cite ʿAbd al-Malik, who cites ʿAbd Allāh ibn Muḥammad, who cites Aḥmad ibn Muḥammad ibn Ismāʿīl al-Sīrjānī, who cites Aḥmad ibn ʿAlī l-Sulaymānī l-Ḥāfiẓ, who heard al-Ḥasan ibn Ismāʿīl al-Fārisī say that he heard Muḥammad ibn Ibrāhīm al-Būshanjī say: 80.8

[Al-Būshanjī:] Aḥmad ibn Ḥanbal died in 241.

We cite ʿAbd al-Malik, who cites ʿAbd Allāh ibn Muḥammad, who cites Abū Yaʿqūb and Muḥammad ibn al-Muntaṣir, who cite Abū Bakr ibn Abī l-Faḍl, who cites Muḥammad ibn Ibrāhīm al-Ṣarrām, who heard Ibrāhim ibn Isḥāq al-Anṣārī report that he heard Aḥmad ibn Ḥanbal's son Ṣāliḥ say: 80.9

[Ṣāliḥ:] My father died at the age of seventy-seven.

Addendum. The Virtue Manifested in His Dying on a Friday

We cite Ibn al-Ḥuṣayn, who cites Ibn al-Mudhhib, who cites Aḥmad ibn Jaʿfar, who heard Aḥmad's son ʿAbd Allāh report that he heard his father report that he heard Abū ʿĀmir report that he heard Hishām—meaning Ibn Saʿd—report, citing Saʿīd ibn Abī Hilāl, citing Rabīʿah ibn Sayf, citing ʿAbd Allāh ibn ʿĀmir, that the Prophet—God bless and keep him—said: 80.10

[The Prophet:] "If a Muslim dies on a Friday, God mighty and glorious spares him the ordeal of the tomb."

A great number of preeminent Muslims died on a Friday. It was on a Friday, for example, that ʿUthmān ibn ʿAffān was assassinated and ʿAlī ibn Abī Ṭālib struck down, though he expired on the Sunday; and on a Friday that al-Ḥusayn was killed. Al-ʿAbbās ibn ʿAbd al-Muṭṭalib, al-Ḥasan al-Baṣrī, Ibn Sīrīn, and others too numerous to mention also died on a Friday.

الباب الحادي والثمانون في ذكر غسله وكَفَنه

١٠٨١ أخبرنا محمّد بن أبي منصور قال: أخبرنا عبد القادر بن محمّد قال: أخبرنا إبراهيم بن عمر قال: أخبرنا عليّ بن عبد العزيز قال: أخبرنا عبد الرحمن بن أبي حاتم قال:

حدثنا صالح بن أحمد قال: لما توفِّي أبي واجتمع الناس في الشوارع وجّهت إليهم أُعلمهم بوفاته وأنّي أُخرجه بعد العصر.

ووجّه ابن طاهر بحاجبه مُظفَّر معهم مَناديل فيها ثياب وطيب فقالوا: الأمير يُقرِئك السلام ويقول: قد فعلتُ ما لو كان أمير المؤمنين حاضرَه كان يفعل ذلك له.

فقلت له: أَقْرِئه السلام وقل له: إنّ أمير المؤمنين قد كان أعفاه في حياته ممّا كان يكره ولا أُحبّ أن أُتبِعَه بعد موته بما كان يكرهه في حياته.

فعاد وقال: يكون شِعارَه ولا يكون دِثاره.

فأعدتُ عليه مثل ذلك.

وقد كان غزلت له الجارية ثوباً عُشارياً قُوِّم بثمانية وعشرين درهماً ليقطع منه قميصين فقطعنا له لُفافتين وأخذنا من فُوران لفافة أخرى فأدرجناه في ثلاث لفائف، واشترينا له حَنُوطاً.

وقد كان بعض أصحابنا من العطّارين سألني أن يوجّه بِحَنوط فلم أفعل.

وصُبَّ في حُبّ لنا ماء فقلت: قولوا لأبي محمّد يشتري راوية ويصبّ الماء في الحُبّ الذي كان يشرب منه فإنّه كان يكره أن يدخل في منازلنا إليه شيء.

وفُرِغ من غسله وكفنّاه وحضر نحو من مائة من بني هاشم ونحن نُكفّنه وجعلوا يُقبلون جبهته حين رفعناه على السرير.

٢٠٨١ أخبرنا محمّد بن أبي منصور قال: أخبرنا عبد القادر بن يوسف قال: أنبأنا إبراهيم بن عمر قال: أنبأنا عبد العزيز ابن جعفر قال: حدثنا أحمد بن محمد الخلّال قال:

Chapter 81: How His Body Was Washed and Shrouded

We cite Muḥammad ibn Abī Manṣūr, who cites ʿAbd al-Qādir ibn Muḥammad, who cites Ibrāhīm ibn ʿUmar, who cites ʿAlī ibn ʿAbd al-ʿAzīz, who cites ʿAbd al-Raḥmān ibn Abī Ḥātim, who heard Aḥmad's son Ṣāliḥ report: 81.1

[Ṣāliḥ:] When my father died the streets filled with mourners. I sent word that I would bring his body out when the afternoon prayer was over.

Ibn Ṭāhir sent us his chamberlain Muẓaffar with bundles of cloth, perfumes, and a message: "The emir conveys his greetings and says, 'I am doing what the Commander of the Faithful would do if he were here.'"

I said, "Return the greeting and tell him that while Aḥmad was alive, he was exempt from doing anything he detested. I'm not going to inflict anything detestable on him now that he's dead."

"Wrap him in this cloth," he replied, "and put something else over it."

I repeated what I had said.

My father's slave woman had spun a ten-cubit length of cloth worth twenty-eight dirhams to be used to make two shirts. From it we cut two strips to wrap him in. Taking another strip from Fūrān, we had three layers of cloth to wrap the body.[196] We bought the aromatics ourselves. An associate of ours who was a perfumer asked if he could send us some of his but I wouldn't let him.

Meanwhile, someone had taken a jar of ours and poured water into it. I told them to tell Fūrān to buy a waterskin and fill the jar my father used to drink from, since he would never take anything from our houses.

When the body had been washed we wrapped it in the shrouds with some hundred members of the clan of Hāshim looking on. As soon as we got the body onto the bier they began kissing him on the forehead.

We cite Muḥammad ibn Abī Manṣūr, who cites ʿAbd al-Qādir ibn Yūsuf, who was informed by Ibrāhīm ibn ʿUmar, who was informed by ʿAbd al-ʿAzīz ibn Jaʿfar, who heard Aḥmad ibn Muḥammad al-Khallāl report that he heard Abū Bakr al-Marrūdhī report: 81.2

حدثنا أبو بكر المَرُّوذي قال: لمّا أردتُ غسله جاء بنو هاشم فاجتمعوا في الدار خلقًا كثيرًا فأدخلناه البيت وأرخينا الستر وجلّلته بثوب حتّى فرغنا من أمره ولم يحضره أحد من الغُرباء ونحن نغسله.

فلمّا فرغنا من غسله وأردنا أن نكفنه غلبنَا عليه بنو هاشم وجعلوا يبكون عليه ويأتون بأولادهم فيكبّونهم عليه ويقبّلونه، فوضعناه على سريره وشددناه بالعمائم.

وأرسل ابن طاهر بأكفان فرددتُها وقال عمّه للرسول: هو لم يدعْ غلامي يروّحه.

وقال له رجل: قد أوصى أن يكفن في ثيابه.

فكفناه في ثوب كان له مَرَوِيّ أراد أن يقطعه فزدنا فيه وصيّرناه ثلاث لفائف.

الباب الثاني والثمانون في ذكر المتقدم للصلاة عليه

أخبرنا إسماعيل بن أحمد ومحمّد بن أبي القاسم قالا: أخبرنا حَمْد بن أحمد قال: أخبرنا أبو نُعَيم أحمد بن عبد الله ١،٨٢
قال: حدثنا سليمان بن أحمد قال:

سمعت عبد الله بن أحمد بن حنبل يقول: توفّي أبي يوم الجمعة ضحوةً وصلّى عليه محمّد بن عبد الله بن طاهر غلبنَا على الصلاة عليه وقد كنّا صلّينا عليه نحن والهاشميون داخل الدار ودفنّاه بعد العصر.

أخبرنا محمّد بن أبي منصور قال: أخبرنا عبد القادر بن محمّد قال: أخبرنا أبو إسحاق البرمكي قال: حدثنا عليّ بن ٢،٨٢
عبد العزيز قال: حدثنا عبد الرحمن بن أبي حاتم قال:

حدثنا صالح بن أحمد قال: لمّا توفي أبي وجّه إليّ ابن طاهر: مَن يصلّي عليه؟ قلتُ: أنا.

[Al-Marrūdhī:] As I was preparing to wash him, enough tribesmen of Hāshim arrived to fill the house. So we took him into his set of rooms, let down the door curtain, and covered him with a cloth while we worked. No outsiders were present for the washing of the corpse. When that was done, we prepared to shroud him, but the Hāshimīs pushed us aside, weeping, pushing their children forward over the body, and kissing it. Finally we got him onto the bier and bound him to it using strips of turban cloth. Ibn Ṭāhir had sent some shrouds but I sent them back. His uncle told the messenger, "He wouldn't even let my slave fan him." Someone else said, "He asked to be shrouded in his own clothes."

In the end we shrouded him in a piece of Marawī fabric that he had been planning to make some clothes from. We added another piece to it and so wrapped him in three layers of cloth.

Chapter 82: On Who Sought to Pray over Him

We cite Ismāʿīl ibn Aḥmad and Muḥammad ibn Abī l-Qāsim, who cite Ḥamd ibn Aḥmad, who cites Abū Nuʿaym ibn ʿAbd Allāh, who heard Sulaymān ibn Aḥmad report that he heard Aḥmad ibn Ḥanbal's son ʿAbd Allāh say: **82.1**

[ʿAbd Allāh:] My father died before noon on a Friday. Muḥammad ibn ʿAbd Allāh ibn Ṭāhir pushed us aside and performed the funeral prayer for him, though we and the tribesmen of Hāshim prayed over the body while it was still in the house. We buried him after the afternoon prayer.

We cite Muḥammad ibn Abī Manṣūr, who cites ʿAbd al-Qādir ibn Muḥammad, who cites Abū Isḥāq al-Barmakī, who heard ʿAlī ibn ʿAbd al-ʿAzīz report that he heard ʿAbd al-Raḥmān ibn Abī Ḥātim report that he heard Aḥmad's son Ṣāliḥ report: **82.2**

[Ṣāliḥ:] When my father died, Ibn Ṭāhir sent a message asking who was going to pray for him. I told him I was.

فلمّا صرنا إلى الصحراء إذا ابن طاهر واقف، فخَطا إلينا خطوات وعزّانا، ووُضع السَّرير. فلمّا انتظرتُ هُنيّةً تقدّمتُ وجعلت أُسوِّي الناس فجاءني ابن طالوت ومحمّد بن نصر فقبض هذا على يدي وهذا على يدي وقالوا[1]: الأمير!

فمانعتهم فنحّياني فصلّى، ولم يعلم الناس بذلك.

فلمّا كان من الغد علم الناس فجعلوا يجيئون ويصلّون[2] على القبر ومكث الناس ما شاء الله يأتون فيصلون على القبر.

٣،٨٢ أخبرنا محمّد بن أبي منصور قال: أخبرنا أبو الحسين بن عبد الجبار قال: أخبرنا محمّد بن عبد الواحد الحريري قال: أخبرنا أبو عُمر بن حَيُّويه قال: أخبرنا أبو مُزاحم الخاقاني قال: حدثني أبو يحيى بن أبي عليّ عمّي قال: سمعت أبي يقول:

حدثني أخي عُبيد الله بن يحيى أبو الحسن قال: سَمعتُ المتوكل يقول لمحمّد بن عبد الله: طوبى لك يا محمّد صلّيتَ على أحمد بن حنبل.

الباب الثالث والثمانون في ذكر كثرة الجمع الذين صلّوا عليه

١،٨٣ أخبرنا عبد الملك بن أبي القاسم الكَرُوخي قال: أخبرنا عبد الله بن محمّد الأنصاري قال: أخبرنا محمّد بن أحمد الجارودي، أو محمّد بن محمّد عنه، قال: حدثنا محمّد بن جعفر بن مَطَر قال:

حدثنا الهيثم بن خَلَف قال: دفنّا أحمد بن حنبل يوم الجمعة بعد العصر سنة إحدى وأربعين، وما رأيت جمعاً قط أكثر من ذلك.

١ ش: وقال. ٢ ش: يصلون عليه.

When we reached the desert, we found Ibn Ṭāhir standing there waiting for us. He approached us and offered his condolences. The bier was lowered to the ground. I waited a bit, then stepped forward and began lining everyone up. Then Ibn Ṭālūt and Muḥammad ibn Naṣr came forward and, each seizing one of my arms, said, "Make way for the emir!" I tried to stop them but they took me aside and Ibn Ṭāhir ended up performing the prayer. The mourners didn't realize what had happened. The next day, when they found out, they began praying at the gravesite. That went on for a good while: people coming and praying at the grave.

We cite Muḥammad ibn Abī Manṣūr, who cites Abū l-Ḥusayn ibn ʿAbd al-Jabbār, who cites Muḥammad ibn ʿAbd al-Wāḥid al-Ḥarīrī, who cites Abū ʿUmar ibn Ḥayyuwayh, who cites Abū Muzāḥim al-Khāqānī, who heard his uncle Abū Yaḥyā ibn Abī ʿAlī report that he heard his father say that his brother ʿUbayd Allāh ibn Yaḥyā Abū l-Ḥasan reported: 82.3

[ʿUbayd Allāh:] I heard al-Mutawakkil say to Ibn Ṭāhir: "What a blessing for you: praying over Aḥmad ibn Ḥanbal!"

Chapter 83: The Number of People Who Prayed over Him

We cite ʿAbd al-Malik ibn Abī l-Qāsim al-Karūkhī, who cites ʿAbd Allāh ibn Muḥammad al-Anṣārī, who cites Muḥammad ibn Aḥmad al-Jārūdī—or Muḥammad ibn Muḥammad citing him—who heard Muḥammad ibn Jaʿfar ibn Maṭar report that he heard al-Haytham ibn Khalaf report: 83.1

[Al-Haytham ibn Khalaf:] We buried Aḥmad ibn Ḥanbal in 241, after the afternoon prayer. I never saw so many people in one place.

٢،٨٣ أخبرنا محمّد بن أبي منصور قال: أخبرنا عبد القادر بن محمد قال: أنبأنا إبراهيم بن عمر البرمكي[١] قال: أنبأنا عبد العزيز بن جعفر قال:

حدثنا أحمد بن محمد الخلّال قال: سمعت ابن أبي صالح القَنْطَري يقول: شهدتُ الموسم أربعين عاماً، ما رأيت جمعاً قط مثل هذا.

٣،٨٣ قال الخلّال:

وسمعت عبد الوهاب الورّاق يقول: ما بلغَنا أنّ جمعاً كان في الجاهلية والإسلام مثله حتى بلغنا أنّ الموضع مُسح وحُزر على التصحيح فإذا هو نحو من ألف ألف، وحزرنا على السور نحواً من ستّين ألف امرأة، وفتح الناس أبواب المنازل في الشوارع والدروب يُنادون من أراد الوضوء وكثُر ما اشترى الناس من الماء فسُقُوه.

٤،٨٣ أخبرنا عبد الرحمن بن محمّد القزّاز قال: أخبرنا أحمد بن عليّ بن ثابت قال: أخبرنا الحسن بن أبي بكر قال:

ذكر عبد الله بن إسحاق البَغَوي عن بُنان بن أحمد القَصَبَاني أخبرهم أنّه حضر جنازة أحمد بن حنبل مع من حضر.

قال: فكانت الصفوف من الميدان إلى قنطرة باب القطيعة وحُزر من حضرها من الرجال ثمان مائة ألف ومن النساء ستون ألف امرأة.

٥،٨٣ أخبرنا عبد الملك قال: أخبرنا عبد الله بن محمّد قال: أخبرنا أبو يعقوب قال: أخبرنا جدّي قال: أخبرنا أحمد بن محمّد بن ياسين قال:

سمعت موسى بن هارون يقول: يقال إنّ أحمد بن حنبل لمّا مات مُسحت الأمكنة المبسوطة التي وقف الناس عليها للصلاة عليه فحُزر مقادير الناس بالمساحة على التقدير ستّ مائة ألف وأكثر سوى ما كان في الأطراف والحوالي والسطوح والمواضع المتفرّقة أكثر من ألف ألف.

---

١ ليس في ش.

We cite Muḥammad ibn Abī Manṣūr, who cites ʿAbd al-Qādir ibn Muḥammad, who was informed by Ibrāhīm ibn ʿUmar, who was informed by ʿAbd al-ʿAzīz ibn Jaʿfar, who heard Aḥmad ibn Muḥammad al-Khallāl report that he heard Ibn Abī Ṣāliḥ al-Qanṭarī say: 83.2

[Al-Qanṭarī:] I've seen forty pilgrimages but never so many people as I did then.

Al-Khallāl said: I heard ʿAbd al-Wahhāb al-Warrāq say: 83.3

[Al-Warrāq:] We've never heard of more people gathering in one place, whether in the Age of Ignorance or in the Age of Islam. We've even heard that the place was surveyed and a proper estimate made of the number of people there. It came to about a million, plus the sixty thousand or so women I counted looking on from the walls. People had opened the gates of the houses all along the streets and alleys to anyone who wanted to come in and do their ablutions. People also bought great quantities of drinking water.

We cite ʿAbd al-Raḥmān ibn Muḥammad al-Qazzāz, who cites Aḥmad ibn ʿAlī ibn Thabit, who cites al-Ḥasan ibn Abī Bakr, who said that ʿAbd Allāh ibn Isḥāq al-Baghawī mentioned: 83.4

[Al-Baghawī:] Bunān ibn Aḥmad al-Qaṣabānī told us that he was present for the funeral of Aḥmad ibn Ḥanbal.

"There were people lined up from the square as far as the bridge at Bāb al-Qaṭīʿah. The estimates I heard were of eight hundred thousand men and sixty thousand women."

We cite ʿAbd al-Malik, who cites ʿAbd Allāh ibn Muḥammad, who cites Abū Yaʿqūb, who cites his grandfather, who cites Aḥmad ibn Muḥammad ibn Yāsīn, who heard Mūsā ibn Hārūn say: 83.5

[Mūsā ibn Hārūn:] The flat tracts of land where people stood after Aḥmad ibn Ḥanbal died were surveyed and the number of people present was calculated to have been more than six hundred thousand, not counting the ones off to the side, around the edges, on the roofs, and scattered around, who if counted would have brought the total to more than a million.

٦،٨٣ أخبرنا أبو منصور القزّاز قال: أخبرنا أبو بكر أحمد بن عليّ قال: أخبرنا محمّد بن عيسى بن عبد العزيز وعلي ابن أبي عليّ قالا: أخبرنا أبو بكر محمّد بن عبيد الله بن الشِّخّير قال: حدثنا أبو بكر محمّد بن أحمد بن النحّاس قال:

سمعت عبد الوهاب الورّاق يقول: ما بلغنا أنّه كان للمسلمين جمع أكثر منهم على جنازة أحمد بن حنبل إلّا جنازة[1] في بني إسرائيل.

٧،٨٣ أخبرنا إسماعيل بن أحمد ومحمّد بن عبد الباقي قالا: أخبرنا حمد بن أحمد قال: أخبرنا أبو نعيم الحافظ قال: سمعت ظَفَر بن أحمد يقول: حدثنا أبو سهل بشر بن أحمد الإِسْفَرَاييني قال: سمعت محمّد بن خُشْنَام بن سعد يقول:

أخبرني الفتح بن الحجّاج أو غيره قال: بعث أمير المؤمنين عشرين حازرًا ليحزروا كم صلّى على أحمد بن حنبل فحزروا ألف ألف وثلاث مائة ألف سوى من كان في السفن.

٨،٨٣ أخبرنا ابن ناصر قال: أخبرنا عبد القادر بن محمّد قال: أخبرنا البرمكي قال: أخبرنا ابن مردك قال: حدثنا ابن أبي حاتم قال:

سمعتُ أبا زُرْعة يقول: بلغني أن المتوكّل أمر أن يُمسح الموضع الذي وقف عليه الناس حيث صُلِّي على أحمد بن حنبل فبلغ مقام ألفي ألف وخمس مائة ألف.

٩،٨٣ أنبأنا يحيى بن أبي عليّ بن البنّا قال: أنبأنا محمّد بن الحسين بن خَلَف قال: أخبرنا أبو الحسن عليّ بن محمّد الحِنّائي قال: أخبرنا أبو محمّد الطَّرَسُوسي قال: حدثنا أبو العبّاس البَرْدَعي قال: حدثني أحمد بن الحسن المَقّانعي قال:

قال أبي: كنت ببغداد وأنا في بستان لصديق لي وأنا وحدي، فإذا بشيخ وشابّ وعليهما طِمْران من شعر فسلّمت عليهما وقلتُ لهما: أراكما من غير هذا البلد!

قالا: نعم، نحن من جبل اللّكام، حضرنا جنازة أحمد بن حنبل وما بقي أحد من الأولياء إلّا شاهد هذا المكان.

---

١ ش: جنازة كانت.

We cite Abū Manṣūr al-Qazzāz, who cites Abū Bakr Aḥmad ibn ʿAlī, who cites Muḥammad ibn ʿĪsā ibn ʿAbd al-ʿAzīz and ʿAlī ibn Abī ʿAlī, who cite Abū Bakr Muḥammad ibn ʿUbayd Allāh ibn al-Shikhkhīr, who heard Abū Bakr Muḥammad ibn Aḥmad ibn al-Naḥḥās say that he heard ʿAbd al-Wahhāb al-Warrāq say: 83.6

[Al-Warrāq:] Not counting a certain funeral that took place among the Children of Israel, we have never heard of there being more Muslims gathered in one place than there were for Ibn Ḥanbal's funeral procession.

We cite Ismāʿīl ibn Aḥmad and Muḥammad ibn ʿAbd al-Bāqī, who cite Ḥamd ibn Aḥmad, who cites Abū Nuʿaym al-Ḥāfiẓ, who heard Ẓafar ibn Aḥmad say that he heard Abū Sahl Bishr ibn Aḥmad al-Isfarāyīnī report that he heard Muḥammad ibn Khushnām ibn Saʿd say that al-Fatḥ ibn al-Ḥajjāj—or someone else—said: 83.7

[Al-Fatḥ ibn al-Ḥajjāj?:] The Commander of the Faithful sent twenty men to estimate how many people prayed over Aḥmad ibn Ḥanbal. They counted 1,300,000, plus the people who were on boats.

We cite Ibn Nāṣir, who cites ʿAbd al-Qādir ibn Muḥammad, who cites al-Barmakī, who cites Ibn Mardak, who heard Ibn Abī Ḥātim report that he heard Abū Zurʿah say: 83.8

[Abū Zurʿah:] I heard that al-Mutawakkil ordered a survey of the area where people were standing while the funeral prayer was said for Aḥmad. It turned out there was room for 2,500,000 people.

We were informed by Yaḥyā ibn Abī ʿAlī ibn al-Bannā, who was informed by Muḥammad ibn al-Ḥusayn ibn Khalaf, who cites Abū l-Ḥasan ʿAlī ibn Muḥammad al-Ḥinnāʾī, who cites Abū Muḥammad al-Ṭarasūsī, who heard Abū l-ʿAbbās al-Bardhaʿī report that he heard Aḥmad ibn al-Ḥasan al-Maqāniʿī (maker and seller of veils) report that his father said: 83.9

[Al-Ḥasan al-Maqāniʿī:] I was in Baghdad, alone in an orchard belonging to a friend, when I saw two men—one old, one young—dressed in ragged hair shirts. I greeted them and said, "You look like strangers here."

"We are," they said. "We're from the Lukkām Mountains[197] and we're here for Aḥmad ibn Ḥanbal's funeral. Every one of God's friends has come to see it."

أخبرنا محمد بن عبد الباقي قال: أنبأنا رزق الله بن عبد الوهاب قال: ١٠،٨٣

أنبأنا أبو عبد الرحمن السُّلَمي قال: حضرت جنازة أبي الفتح القوّاس الزاهد مع أبي الحسن الدَّارَقُطْني فلمّا نظر إلى الجمع قال: سمعت أبا سَهْل بن زِياد القطّان يقول: سمعتُ عبد الله بن أحمد بن حنبل يقول: سمعت أبي يقول: قُولوا لأهل البدع بيننا وبينكم يوم الجنائز.

الباب الرابع والثمانون في ذكر ما جرى عند حمل جنازته من مدح السنة وذمّ أهل البدعة

أخبرنا عبد الملك بن أبي القاسم قال: أخبرنا عبد الله بن محمد الأنصاري قال: أخبرنا أحمد بن محمد بن إسماعيل ١،٨٤ السِّيرجاني قال: أخبرنا أحمد بن عليّ السليماني قال: سمعت الحسن بن إسماعيل الفارسي قال:

سمعتُ محمد بن إبراهيم البُوشَنْجي يقول: صلّوا على أحمد بن حنبل في المصلّى وظهر اللعن على الكَرابيسي، فأخبر بذلك المتوكّل فقال: مَن الكَرابيسي؟ فقيل إنّه رجل أحدث قولاً لم يتقدّمه أحد فأمره بلزوم بيته حتّى مات.

أخبرنا عبد الملك قال: أخبرنا الأنصاري قال: أخبرنا أبو يعقوب قال: أخبرنا جدّي قال: حدثنا يحيى بن عبد ٢،٨٤ الله الهَمَذاني قال:

سمعتُ جعفر بن محمد النَّسَوِي يقول: شهدت جنازة أحمد بن حنبل وفيها بشر كثير والكرابيسي يُلعن لعناً كثيراً بأصوات عالية، والمَرِيسي أيضاً.

We cite Muḥammad ibn ʿAbd al-Bāqī, who was informed by Rizq Allāh ibn ʿAbd al-Wahhāb, who was informed by Abū ʿAbd al-Raḥmān al-Sulamī, who said: **83.10**

[Al-Sulamī:] Abū l-Ḥasan al-Dāraquṭnī and I attended the funeral of Abū l-Fatḥ al-Qawwās the renunciant. Seeing the crowd, al-Dāraquṭnī said, "I've heard Abū Sahl ibn Ziyād al-Qaṭṭān say that he heard ʿAbd Allāh, son of Aḥmad ibn Ḥanbal, say that he heard his father say: 'Tell the innovators that if we compare funerals, we win.'"

Chapter 84: The Praising of the *Sunnah* and the Decrying of Innovation That Took Place during His Funeral Procession

We cite ʿAbd al-Malik ibn Abī l-Qāsim, who cites ʿAbd Allāh ibn Muḥammad al-Anṣārī, who cites Aḥmad ibn Muḥammad ibn Ismāʿīl al-Sīrjānī, who cites Aḥmad ibn ʿAlī l-Sulaymānī, who heard al-Ḥasan ibn Ismāʿīl al-Fārisī say that he heard Muḥammad ibn Ibrāhīm al-Būshanjī say: **84.1**

[Al-Būshanjī:] During the funeral prayers for Aḥmad ibn Ḥanbal, some of the mourners cursed al-Karābīsī openly. The cursing was reported to al-Mutawakkil, who asked who he was. Told that al-Karābīsī had invented a doctrine previously unknown, he ordered him confined to his house until he died.

We cite ʿAbd al-Malik, who cites al-Anṣārī, who cites Abū Yaʿqūb, who cites his grandfather, who heard Yaḥyā ibn ʿAbd Allāh al-Hamadhānī report that he heard Jaʿfar ibn Muḥammad al-Nasawī say: **84.2**

[Al-Nasawī:] I attended Aḥmad ibn Ḥanbal's funeral. It was very crowded. Al-Karābīsī was cursed loud and long, as was al-Marīsī.

أخبرنا محمّد بن أبي منصور قال: أخبرنا عبد القادر بن محمّد قال: أنبأنا إبراهيم بن عمر قال: أنبأنا عبد العزيز بن جعفر قال: حدثنا أحمد بن محمد الخلّال قال: ٣،٨٤

سمعتُ عبد الوهّاب الورّاق يقول: أظهر الناس في جنازة أحمد بن حنبل السنّة والطعن على أهل البدع فسرّ الله المسلمين بذلك على ما عندهم من المصيبة لِما رأوا من العزّ وعُلوّ الإسلام وكبت الله أَهلَ البدع والزَّيغ والضلالة، ولزم بعض الناس القبر وباتوا عنده وجعل النساء يأتين، فأرسل السلطان أصحاب المَسالح فلزموا ذلك الموضع حتّى منعوهم مخافة الفتنة.

قال الخلال: وحدثني أبو بكر المَرُّوذي قال: سمعت عليّ بن مَهْرُوَيْه يقول: ٤،٨٤

سمعتُ خالتي وهي امرأة حارث المُحَاسِبي قالت: ما صلّوا ببغداد في مسجد العصر يوم مات أحمد بن حنبل إلّا في مسجد حارث.

الباب الخامس والثمانون في ذكر ازدحام الناس على قبره بعد دفنه

أنبأنا أحمد بن الحسن بن البنّا قال: أخبرني أبي قال: ١،٨٥

حدث أبو الحسن التَّميمي عن أبيه عن جدّه أنّه حضر جنازة أحمد بن حنبل قال: فمكثتُ طول الأسبوع رجاءَ أَن أَصِل إلى قبره فلم أصل من ازدحام الناس فلمّا كان بعد أسبوع وصلتُ إلى القبر.

We cite Muḥammad ibn Abī Manṣūr, who cites ʿAbd al-Qādir ibn Muḥammad, who was informed by Ibrāhīm ibn ʿUmar, who was informed by ʿAbd al-ʿAzīz ibn Jaʿfar, who heard Aḥmad ibn Muḥammad al-Khallāl report that he heard ʿAbd al-Wahhāb al-Warrāq say: 84.3

[Al-Warrāq:] At Aḥmad ibn Ḥanbal's funeral, the mourners made an open display of adherence to the *sunnah* and cursed the purveyors of reprehensible innovation. By showing them the ascendancy and might of Islam as well as the suppression of errant guides, dissenters, and reprehensible innovators, God consoled the Muslims for the calamity they had suffered. Some mourners camped out at the gravesite, and women began to visit as well. The authorities accordingly sent patrolmen to clear the area and restore order.

Al-Khallāl heard Abū Bakr al-Marrūdhī report that he heard ʿAlī ibn Mahruwayh say that he heard his aunt—the wife of Ḥārith al-Muḥāsibī—say: 84.4

[ʿAlī ibn Mahruwayh's aunt:] On the day Ibn Ḥanbal died, the only place in Baghdad where the afternoon prayer was performed was Ḥārith's mosque.

Chapter 85: The Crowds That Gathered around His Grave

We were informed by Aḥmad ibn al-Ḥasan ibn al-Bannā, who cites his father: 85.1

[Al-Ḥasan ibn al-Bannā:] Abū Ḥasan al-Tamīmī cites his father as saying that his grandfather attended the funeral of Aḥmad ibn Ḥanbal and reported, "I stayed for an entire week hoping to reach the grave but there were too many people there. It took a week for me to get through."

الباب السادس والثمانون في ذكر ما خلّف من التّرِكة[1]

١٠٨٦ أخبرنا محمّد بن أبي منصور قال: أخبرنا عبد القادر بن محمّد قال: أنبأنا إبراهيم بن عمر قال: أنبأنا عبد العزيز بن جعفر قال: أخبرنا أحمد بن محمّد الخلّال قال:

أخبرني محمّد بن أبي هارون أن إسحاق حدثهم قال: مات أحمد بن حنبل رحمه الله وما خلّف إلّا ستّ قطع أو سبع قطع كانت في خرقته - خرقة كان يمسح بها وجهه قدر دانِقَين.

الباب السابع والثمانون في ذكر تأثير موته عند جميع الناس

١٠٨٧ أخبرنا أبو منصور عبد الرحمن بن محمّد القزّاز قال: أخبرنا أبو بكر أحمد بن عليّ بن ثابت الخطيب، وأخبرنا محمّد ابن ناصر قال: أخبرنا عبد القادر بن محمّد بن يوسف قالا: أخبرنا إبراهيم بن عمر البرمكي، وأخبرنا عبد الله بن عليّ المقرئ قال: أخبرنا عبد الملك بن أحمد السُّيوري قال: أخبرنا عبد العزيز بن عليّ بن أحمد بن الفضل قالا: أخبرنا عليّ بن عبد العزيز بن مَرْدَك، وأخبرنا إسماعيل بن أحمد ومحمّد بن عبد الباقي قالا: أخبرنا حمد[2] بن أحمد قال: أخبرنا أحمد بن عبد الله الحافظ أبو نعيم قال: سمعت ظفر بن أحمد يقول: حدثني الحسين بن عليّ قال: حدثني أحمد الورّاق قال: حدثنا أبو محمّد عبد الرحمن بن أبي حاتم الرازي قال: حدثني أبي قال: حدثني أبو بكر محمّد بن عياش قال:

سمعتُ الوَرْكاني جار أحمد بن حنبل يقول: يوم مات أحمد بن حنبل وقع المأتم والنوح في أربعة أصناف من الناس: المسلمين واليهود والنصارى والمجوس، وأسلم يوم

---

١ هـ: البركة. ٢ هـ: احمد.

Chapter 86: His Estate

We cite Muḥammad ibn Abī Manṣūr, who cites ʿAbd al-Qādir ibn Muḥammad, who was informed by Ibrahīm ibn ʿUmar, who was informed by ʿAbd al-ʿAzīz ibn Jaʿfar, who cites Aḥmad ibn Muḥammad al-Khallāl, who cites Muḥammad ibn Abī Hārūn to the effect that Isḥāq reported to them: 86.1

[Isḥāq:] When Aḥmad ibn Ḥanbal died, he left six or seven coins in a rag, worth two *dāniq*s, that he used to use to wipe his face.

Chapter 87: Reactions to His Death

We cite Abū Manṣūr ʿAbd al-Raḥmān ibn Muḥammad al-Qazzāz, who cites Abū Bakr Aḥmad ibn ʿAlī ibn Thābit al-Khaṭīb; and we cite Muḥammad ibn Nāṣir, who cites ʿAbd al-Qādir ibn Muḥammad ibn Yūsuf, who cites Ibrāhīm ibn ʿUmar al-Barmakī; and we cite ʿAbd Allāh ibn ʿAlī l-Muqriʾ, who cites ʿAbd al-Malik ibn Aḥmad al-Suyūrī, who cites ʿAbd al-ʿAzīz ibn ʿAlī ibn Aḥmad ibn al-Faḍl, who along with al-Barmakī cites ʿAlī ibn ʿAbd al-ʿAzīz ibn Mardak; and we cite Ismāʿīl ibn Aḥmad and Muḥammad ibn ʿAbd al-Bāqī, who cite Ḥamd ibn Aḥmad, who cites Aḥmad ibn ʿAbd Allāh al-Ḥāfiẓ Abū Nuʿaym, who heard Ẓafar ibn Aḥmad say that he heard al-Ḥusayn ibn ʿAlī report that he heard Aḥmad al-Warrāq report that he heard Abū Muḥammad ʿAbd al-Raḥmān ibn Abī Ḥātim al-Rāzī report that he heard his father report that he heard Abū Bakr Muḥammad ibn ʿAyyāsh report that he heard al-Warkānī, a neighbor of Aḥmad ibn Ḥanbal's, say: 87.1

The day Aḥmad ibn Ḥanbal died, there was an outpouring of grief from four communities: the Muslims, the Jews, the Christians, and the Magians;

مات عشرون ألفاً من اليهود والنصارى والمجوس. وفي رواية أبي نُعَيم عَشرة آلاف.

أخبرنا محمّد بن أبي منصور قال: أخبرنا عبد القادر بن محمّد قال: أنبأنا إبراهيم بن عمر قال: أنبأنا عبد العزيز بن ٢،٨٧
جعفر قال: أخبرنا أحمد بن محمّد الخلال قال: حدثنا محمّد بن حَمْدان القاضي قال: سمعت هارون بن عبد الله يقول:

سمعتُ عليّ بن حُرَيْث يقول: ما من أهل بيت لم يدخل عليهم[١] يوم موت أحمد ابن حنبل يوم مات إلّا بيت سوء.[٢]

الباب الثامن والثمانون في ذكر تأثير موته عند الجنّ

أخبرنا عبد الملك بن أبي القاسم الكَرُوخي قال: أخبرنا عبد الله بن محمّد الأنصاري قال: أخبرنا إسحاق بن إبراهيم ١،٨٨
الحافظ قال: أخبرنا محمّد بن عبد الله اللآل قال: حدثنا محمّد بن إبراهيم بن عبد الله المكّي قال: حدثنا عبد الله
ابن إبراهيم الأَزْدي قال: حدثنا أبو بكر المَرُّوذي قال:

قال رجل بطَرَسوس: أنا من اليمن وكانت لي بنت مُصابة فجئت بالعزّامين فعزموا عليها ففارقها الجنّي على أن لا يعاود فعاود بعد سنة فقلتُ: أليس قد فارقت على أن لا تُعاود؟

قال: بلى، ولكن مات اليوم رجل بالعراق يقال له أحمد بن حنبل فذهبت الجنّ كلّها تصلّي عليه إلا المَرَدة وأنا منهم ولست أعود بعد يومي هذا. فما عاد.

وقد رُويت لنا هذه الحكاية على وجه آخر.

أخبرنا محمّد بن أبي منصور قال: أخبرنا عبد القادر بن محمّد قال: أنبأنا إبراهيم بن عمر قال: أنبأنا عبد العزيز بن ٢،٨٨

---

١ تركي: عليهم الحزن. ٢ هكذا في هـ، ش.

and of the latter three, twenty thousand—or, as reported by Abū Nuʿaym, ten thousand—embraced Islam.[198]

We cite Muḥammad ibn Abī Manṣūr, who cites ʿAbd al-Qādir ibn Muḥammad, who was informed by Ibrāhīm ibn ʿUmar, who was informed by ʿAbd al-ʿAzīz ibn Jaʿfar, who cites Aḥmad ibn Muḥammad al-Khallāl, who heard Muḥammad ibn Ḥamdān al-Qāḍī report that he heard Hārūn ibn ʿAbd Allāh say that he heard ʿAlī ibn Ḥurayth say: 87.2

[Ibn Ḥurayth:] The day Aḥmad died, the news spread swiftly to every household except where sinners dwelt.[199]

Chapter 88: Reaction to His Death on the Part of the Jinns

We cite ʿAbd al-Malik ibn Abī l-Qāsim al-Karūkhī, who cites ʿAbd Allāh ibn Muḥammad al-Anṣārī, who cites Isḥāq ibn Ibrāhīm al-Ḥāfiẓ, who cites Muḥammad ibn ʿAbd Allāh al-Laʾʾāl, who heard Muḥammad ibn Ibrāhīm ibn ʿAbd Allāh al-Makkī report that he heard ʿAbd Allāh ibn Ibrāhīm al-Azdī report that he heard Abū Bakr al-Marrūdhī report: 88.1

[Al-Marrūdhī:] I heard this from a man in Tarsus.

"I'm from Yemen, and I have a daughter who was possessed. I brought in some exorcists who drove out her jinni and made it promise not to return. But then a year later it came back.

"'Didn't you promise not to come back?' I asked.

"'I did,' said the jinni. 'But a man named Aḥmad ibn Ḥanbal has died in Iraq and all the jinns—except for the demons, like me—have gone to pray over him. But I won't be back again.'

"He never returned."

This story has also come down to us in another telling.

We cite Muḥammad ibn Abī Manṣūr, who cites ʿAbd al-Qādir ibn Muḥammad, who was informed by Ibrāhīm ibn ʿUmar, who was informed by ʿAbd al-ʿAzīz ibn Jaʿfar, who cites 88.2

جعفر قال: أخبرنا أحمد بن محمد الخلال قال: حدثنا محمد بن الحسين قال: حدثنا أبو بكر المَرُّوذي قال:

حدثني أبو محمد اليَماني بطرسوس قال: كنتُ باليمن فقال لي رجل: إنّ ابنتي قد عرض لها عارض فمضيت معه إلى عزّام عندنا باليمن فعزم عليها فأخذ على الذي عزم عليه أن لا يعرِض لها فمكث نحوًا من ستة أشهر ثم جاءني أبوها فقال: قد عاد إليها.

قال: قلتُ: فاذهب إلى العزّام فذهب إليه فعزم عليه فكلّمه الجِنّي فقال: ويلك، أليس قد أخذتُ عليك أن لا تقربها؟

قال: فقال: إنه ورد علينا موت أحمد بن حنبل فلم يبقَ أحد من صالحي الجنّ إلّا حضره إلّا المَرَدة فإنّي تخلّفت معهم.

٣٠٨٨ أخبرنا محمد بن أبي منصور قال: أخبرنا عبد القادر بن محمد قال: أخبرنا إبراهيم بن عمر قال: أنبأنا عبد العزيز بن جعفر قال: أخبرنا أحمد بن محمد الخلّال قال:

حدثني أحمد بن محمد بن محمود قال: كنت في البحر مُقبلاً من ناحية السِّند فقمتُ في الليل فإذا هاتف من ناحية البحر يقول: مات العبد الصالح أحمد بن حنبل!

فقلتُ لبعض من كان معنا: من هذا؟

فقال: هذا من صالحي الجنّ.

ومات أحمد تلك الليلة.

وبلغني عن أبي زُرعة أنه قال: كان يُقال عندنا بخُراسان إنّ الجنّ نَعَتْ أحمد ابن حنبل قبل موته بأربعين صباحًا.

وبلغني عن صالح بن أحمد بن حنبل قال: كان أهلنا يذكرون أنّهم كانوا يسمعون رنّة لا تُشبه رنّة الإنس من دار أبي عبد الله إذا هدأت العيون بعد وفاته بأربعين صباحًا.

Aḥmad ibn Muḥammad al-Khallāl, who heard Muḥammad ibn al-Ḥusayn report that he heard Abū Bakr al-Marrūdhī report that he heard Abū Muḥammad al-Yamānī report in Tarsus:

[Abū Muḥammad al-Yamānī:] When I was in Yemen, a man told me that his daughter had been possessed by a demon. So I took him to one of our Yemeni exorcists, who drove out her jinni and made it promise not to return. But then about six months later her father came to me and said the demon had returned.

"Go back to the exorcist," I said.

So he went back. The exorcist drew out the jinni and got it talking.

"Shame on you!" said the exorcist. "Didn't you promise to leave her alone?"

"I did," said the jinni. "But we've heard that Aḥmad ibn Ḥanbal is dead. All the righteous jinns have gone to mourn him, and the demons like me are tagging along behind."

We cite Muḥammad ibn Abī Manṣūr, who cites ʿAbd al-Qādir ibn Muḥammad, who cites Ibrāhīm ibn ʿUmar, who was informed by ʿAbd al-ʿAzīz ibn Jaʿfar, who cites Aḥmad ibn Muḥammad al-Khallāl: **88.3**

[Al-Khallāl:] Aḥmad ibn Muḥammad ibn Maḥmūd told me the following:

I was on my way back from Sind on board ship. At one point I woke up in the night and heard a voice calling from the sea, "Aḥmad ibn Ḥanbal, the faithful servant of God, is dead!"

"What was that?" I asked one of the others on board.

"That was a righteous jinni."

We later learned that Aḥmad had died that night.

[Al-Khallāl:] I also heard that Abū Zurʿah said that where he was from in Khurasan, the jinns announced Aḥmad's death forty days before it happened.

I also heard Aḥmad's son Ṣāliḥ say, "Forty days after my father died, after everyone had gone to bed, my family said they heard a sobbing, unlike any sound a human would make, coming from my father's house."

الباب التاسع والثمانون في ذكر التعازي به

١،٨٩ قد ذكر أولاد أحمد رضي الله عنه أنّ خلقاً كثيراً عزّوْهم عنه وأنّ جماعة من الصالحين لم يُعرفوا جاءوا للتعزية فلم أطِل بذكر ذلك وإنّما ذكرتُ نبذة من مشهور ذلك.

٢،٨٩ أخبرنا ابن أبي منصور قال: أخبرنا عبد القادر بن محمّد قال: أخبرنا إبراهيم بن عمر قال: أخبرنا عليّ بن عبد العزيز قال: حدثنا عبد الرحمن بن أبي حاتم قال:

حدثنا صالح بن أحمد قال: جاء كتاب المتوكّل بعد أيّام من موت أبي إلى محمّد بن عبد الله بن طاهر يأمره بتعزيتنا ويأمر بحمل الكتب.

فحملتها وقلت: إنّها لنا سماع فتكون في أيدينا وتُنسخ عندنا.

فقال: أقول لأمير المؤمنين.

فلم يزل يدافع الأمر ولم تخرج عن أيدينا والحمد لله ربّ العالمين.

٣،٨٩ قرأتُ على محمّد بن أبي منصور عن أبي القاسم بن البُسري عن أبي عبد الله بن بَطّة قال: حدثنا عبد العزيز بن جعفر قال: حدثنا أبو بكر الخلّال قال: حدثنا محمّد بن عليّ قال:

حدثنا صالح بن أحمد قال: كتب إليّ أخ لي يعزّيني عن أبي:

بسم الله الرحمن الرحيم

أما بعد فإنّ الله عز وجل حتم الموت على عباده حتماً عدلاً على بريّته كافّة قضاء فصلاً حتى يأتي ذلك على جميع من ذرأ وبرأ. وكان ممّن أتى عليه حتم الله وقضاؤه أبو عبد الله رحمة الله عليه، دعاه الله إليه فأجابه رَضيّاً مرضيّاً نَقيّاً من الدّنس والعيب، طاهر الثوب غير مبتدع ولا ضالّ ولا مُضلّ ولا زائغ عن هدىً ولا مائل إلى هوى، لم يُرهبه وعيد إلى أن نقله الله عزّ وجلّ

Chapter 89: On the Condolences Offered to His Family

89.1 Aḥmad's children reported that many people, including certain righteous men who had kept their identities a secret, came to offer their condolences. Without spending too much time on the subject, I will present a few of the more famous accounts.

89.2 We cite Ibn Abī Manṣūr, who cites ʿAbd al-Qādir ibn Muḥammad, who cites Ibrāhīm ibn ʿUmar, who cites ʿAlī ibn ʿAbd al-ʿAzīz, who heard ʿAbd al-Raḥmān ibn Abī Ḥātim report:

[Ibn Abī Ḥātim:] We heard Aḥmad's son Ṣāliḥ report:

A few days after my father died, Muḥammad ibn ʿAbd Allāh ibn Ṭāhir received a letter from al-Mutawakkil ordering him to pay us a visit of condolence and to carry off the books. But I gathered up the books first and told him, "All of the reports we've ever heard are in here. If you want them, stay here and copy them."[200]

"I'll tell the caliph," he said.

[Ibn Abī Ḥātim:] Ṣāliḥ kept putting him off and the books stayed in our hands, thank God!

89.3 I read aloud to Muḥammad ibn Abī Manṣūr his report citing Abū l-Qāsim ibn al-Busrī, citing Abū ʿAbd Allāh ibn Baṭṭah, who heard ʿAbd al-ʿAzīz ibn Jaʿfar report that he heard Abū Bakr al-Khallāl report that he heard Muḥammad ibn ʿAlī report that he heard Aḥmad's son Ṣāliḥ report:

[Ṣāliḥ:] One of my friends wrote me this letter of condolence:

> *In the name of God, full of compassion, ever-compassionate*
>
> God, mighty and glorious, has decreed that death deal impartially with humankind, dooming His creatures to a finite span until fate comes to claim them all. Bowing now to God's decree is Abū ʿAbd Allāh—may God have mercy on him!—whom He has summoned to Himself. Accepting God's welcome with a willing heart, he came faultless as always, unsullied, and immaculate, firm in tradition, inerrant, and guiding aright, unswerving from the path of good guidance, unswayed by caprice, and dauntless in adversity, until God drew him close to Himself. Let all aspire to the grace

إلى جواره. فلمثل ما صار إليه من كرامة الله فليعمل العاملون، وعلى أنّ المصيبة به قد مضّت وأرمَضت وأبلغت من القلوب، وأنا أُعزّيك وعامّة المسلمين ممّن يقرأ كتابنا هذا بما أمر الله به تنجّزاً لما وعد من صلواته ورحمته، وهداه لمن احتسب وصبر وسلّم ورضي بحكم الله النافذ على جميع خلقه، فقد مضى على أحسن حالاته وأحسن قصده وهديه، ثابتاً على حزمه وعزمه. أرادته الدنيا ولم يُردها، ولم تأخذه في الله لومَة لائم، فقدكَلَم وثلم في الإسلام فَقدُه. وأنا أسأل الله الذي يجود بالجزيل ويعطي الكثير أن يصلّي على محمّد عبده ورسوله وأن يُعطي أبا عبد الله أفضل ما أعطى أحداً من أوليائه الذين خلقهم لطاعته وأن يُعلي درجته ويرفع ركنه ويجعل مجلسه مع النبيين والصدّيقين والشهداء والصالحين، وحسُن أُولئك رَفيقاً، وأنْ يهب لك صبراً يُبلغك ما وعد الصابرين ويَقيناً يوجب لك ثواب المحسنين، فإنه وليّ النّعم وبيده الخير وهو على كُلّ شيء قدير.

٤،٨٩ أخبرنا إسماعيل بن أحمد ومحمّد بن عبد الباقي قالا: أخبرنا حمد بن أحمد قال: أخبرنا أحمد بن عبد الله الحافظ قال: حدثنا أبي قال: حدثنا أحمد بن محمّد بن أبان قال:

حدثنا أبو العباس أحمد بن إبراهيم الصوفي قال: قال لي رجل من أهل العلم، وكان خيراً فاضلاً يُكنى بأبي جعفر، في العَشية التي دفنّا فيها أبا عبد الله: تَدري من دفنّا اليوم؟

قلتُ: من؟

قال: سادس خمسة.

قلتُ: من؟

قال: أبو بكر الصدّيق وعمر بن الخطّاب وعُثمان بن عفّان وعليّ بن أبي طالب وعمر بن عبد العزيز وأحمدُ بن حنبل.

قال: فاستحسنتُ ذلك منه وعنى بذلك أن كلّ واحد في زمانه.

that he has gained; and though losing him brings a wrenching grief that bites deep into the heart, and I console you and any other Muslim who reads this letter by reminding you of God's promised blessings, mercies, and signs vouchsafed to those who ponder well, suffer long, and submit with good grace to the fate God has decreed for all things He has made. I remind you that he left us in the best possible way: present in mind, confident of God's guidance, and unshaken in his courage and resolve. The world pursued him but he spurned it, and he brooked no rebuke when he stood up for God; his passing leaves a ragged scar on the heart of Islam.

I pray to God, who gives freely of His bounty, to bless Muḥammad, His servant and Emissary; and to grant Aḥmad no lesser reward than that He grants to any of the allies He has created to serve Him. May He raise him in rank, exalt him in standing, and seat him among the prophets, the truth-tellers, the martyrs, and the saints—goodly companions all! I ask God to give you strength, and the reward promised to the strong; and grant you that certainty that confers the reward promised to those who live out their faith. I ask Him, for He is the fount of all blessing, the dispenser of all good things, and the One for whom nothing is impossible.

We cite Ismāʿīl ibn Aḥmad and Muḥammad ibn ʿAbd al-Bāqī, who cite Ḥamd ibn Aḥmad, 89.4
who cites Aḥmad ibn ʿAbd Allāh al-Ḥāfiẓ, who heard his father report that he heard Aḥmad ibn Muḥammad ibn Abān report that he heard Abū l-ʿAbbās Aḥmad ibn Ibrāhīm al-Ṣūfī report:

[Al-Ṣūfī:] The night we buried Abū ʿAbd Allāh, one of our scholars—a kindly, learned man named Abū Jaʿfar—asked me, "Do you know who was buried today?"

"Who?"

"The sixth of five."

"What do you mean?"

"The first is Abū Bakr al-Ṣiddīq," he said. "The second was ʿUmar ibn al-Khaṭṭāb. ʿUthmān ibn ʿAffān was the third, ʿAlī ibn Abī Ṭālib the fourth, ʿUmar ibn ʿAbd al-ʿAzīz the fifth, and now we have a sixth: Aḥmad ibn Ḥanbal."

I appreciated his saying that. What he meant was that each man was the greatest in his own time.

الباب التسعون في ذكر المنتخب من الأشعار التي مُدح بها في حياته ورُثي بها بعد وفاته

أخبرنا عبد الملك بن أبي القاسم قال: أخبرنا عبد الله بن محمد الأنصاري قال: أخبرنا محمد بن المنتصر القتيبي[1] ‎١،٩٠
قال: أخبرنا أبو بكر بن أبي الفضل المزكّي قال: أخبرنا محمد بن إبراهيم السنّي قال: حدثنا إبراهيم بن إسحاق الأنصاري قال:

أنشدني عبد الله بن أحمد بن حنبل لأبي سعيد اليَخامُري في أبي عبد الله رحمه الله:

فَأَنْتَ أبا عبدِ الإلهِ مُسَدَّدٌ ... بتَسْديدِ ذي العَرْشِ الرَّفيعِ الدَّعائِمِ
لَكَ الفَضْلُ في الدُّنْيا على عُلَمائِنا ... وزُهّادِنا يا بنَ القُرونِ[2] الأَكارِمِ
وَقَوْلُكَ مَقْبولٌ وَرَأْيُكَ فاضِلٌ ... وأَمرُكَ مَحْمودُ القُوى والعَزائِمِ
وكلُّ امْرِئٍ وَثَّقْتَه في حَديثِهِ ... شَدَدْتَ له أَركانَه بدَعائِمِ
حَللتَ من الإسلامِ والبِرِّ والتُّقى ... بمرتبةٍ لا تُرتَقى بسَلالِمِ
حويتَ بحُورَ العِلم من كلِّ بَلدةٍ ... ففزتَ بغُنْمٍ من جَزيلِ الغنائِمِ

أخبرنا عبد الملك قال: أخبرنا عبد الله بن محمد قال: أخبرنا أبو يعقوب الحافظ قال: أخبرنا محمد بن عبد الله اللّال ‎٢،٩٠
قال: أخبرنا محمد بن إبراهيم الصرّام قال:

أخبرنا إبراهيم بن إسحاق الغَسيلي قال: أخذت هذه القصيدة من أبي بكر المرُّوذي وذكر أنّ إسماعيل بن فُلان التِّرمذي قالها وأنشدها أحمد بن حنبل وهو في سِجن المحنة:

تَبارَكَ مَن لا يَعلَمُ الغيبَ غيرُه ... ومَن لم يَزَلْ يُثْنَى عَلَيْهِ ويُذكَرُ
عَلا في السَّماواتِ العُلَى فَوقَ عَرْشِهِ ... إلى خَلْقِهِ في البَرِّ والبَحْرِ يَنظُرُ

---

١ ش: القتيني. ٢ تركي: القروم.

Chapter 90: A Selection of the Verses Spoken in Praise of Him in Life and in Commemoration of Him in Death

We cite ʿAbd al-Malik ibn Abī l-Qāsim, who cites ʿAbd Allāh ibn Muḥammad al-Anṣārī, who cites Muḥammad ibn al-Muntaṣir al-Qutaybī, who cites Abū Bakr ibn Abī l-Faḍl al-Muzakkī, who cites Muḥammad ibn Ibrāhīm al-Sunnī, who heard Ibrāhīm ibn Isḥāq al-Anṣārī report: 90.1

[Al-Anṣārī:] Aḥmad ibn Ḥanbal's son ʿAbd Allāh recited these verses about his father, by Saʿīd al-Yakhāmurī:

Our tow'ring God, from high on pillared seat
  Doth you, his servant Aḥmad, guide aright.
Our learnèd men and pious poor alike
  Call you their chieftain, you their noblest lord;
Tis you they follow, you whose words they heed,
  And you they trust to judge a man's report.
All strive, but none attains a place so high
  As yours on Islam's scale of what is right;
From lands afar you learning sought, and then
  Returned to us, the brimming sea your prize.[201]

We cite ʿAbd al-Malik, who cites ʿAbd Allāh ibn Muḥammad, who cites Abū Yaʿqūb al-Ḥāfiẓ, who cites Muḥammad ibn ʿAbd Allāh al-Laʾʾāl, who cites Muḥammad ibn Ibrāhīm al-Ṣarrām, who cites Ibrāhīm ibn Isḥāq al-Ghasīlī, who said: 90.2

[Al-Ghasīlī:] I got this poem from Abū Bakr al-Marrūdhī, who said that Ismāʿīl ibn So-and-So composed it and recited it to Aḥmad ibn Ḥanbal, who at the time was in the dungeons of the Inquisition.

All praise is due to Him alone who knows
  What we do not. We extol and laud the One
Who soars aloft above His throne in Heav'n,
  And gazes down on land and sea below.

سَميعٌ بَصيرٌ لا نَشُكُّ مُدبِّرٌ ومَن دونَهُ عَبدٌ ذَليلٌ مُدبَّرُ
يَدا رَبِّنا مَبسوطَتانِ كِلاهُما تَسحّانِ والأَيدي مِنَ الخَلقِ تَقتُرُ
إذا فيهِ فَكَّرنا استَحالَت عُقولُنا فَأُبنا[1] حَيارى واضمَحَلَّ التَّفكُّرُ
وإن نَقَّرَ المَخلوقُ عَن عِلمِ ذاتِهِ وعَن كَيفَ كانَ الأَمرُ ضَلَّ المُنَقِّرُ
فَلَو وَصَفَ النّاسُ البَعوضَةَ وَحدَها بِعِلمِهِمُ لَم يُحكِموها وقَصَّروا
فَكَيفَ بِمَن لا يَقدِرُ الخَلقُ قَدرَه ومَن هُوَ لا يَبلى ولا يَتَغَيَّرُ
نُهينا عَنِ التَّفتيشِ والبَحثِ رَحمَةً لَنا وطَريقُ البَحثِ يُردي ويُخسِرُ
وقالوا لَنا قولوا ولا تَتَعَمَّقوا بِذلكَ أَوصانا النَّبيُّ المُعَزَّرُ
فَقُلنا وقَلَّدنا ولَم نَأتِ بِدعَةً وفي البِدعَةِ الخُسرانُ والحَقُّ أَنوَرُ
ولَم نَرَ[2] كالتَّسليمِ حِرزًا ومَوئِلاً لِمَن كانَ يَرجو أَن يُثابَ ويَحذَرُ
شَهِدنا بِأَنَّ اللهَ لا رَبَّ غَيرُه وأَحمَدَ مَبعوثٌ إلى الخَلقِ مُنذِرُ
وأَنَّ كِتابَ اللهِ فينا كَلامُهُ وإن شَكَّ فيهِ المُلحِدونَ وأَنكَروا
شَهِدنا بِأَنَّ اللهَ كَلَّمَ عَبدَه ولَم يَكُ غَيرُ اللهِ عَنهُ يُعَبِّرُ
غَداةَ رَأى نارًا فَقالَ لِأَهلِهِ سَآتي بِنارٍ أَو عَنِ النّارِ أُخبِرُ
فَناداهُ يا موسى أَنا اللهُ لا تَخَف وأَرسَلَهُ بِالحَقِّ يَدعو ويُنذِرُ
وَقالَ انطَلِق إِنّي سَميعٌ لِكُلِّ ما يَجيءُ بِهِ فِرعَونُ ذو الكُفرِ مُبصِرُ
وكَلَّمَهُ أَيضًا عَلى الطّورِ رَبُّهُ وقُرِّبَ والتَّوراةُ في اللَّوحِ تُسطَرُ
كَذلكَ قالَ اللهُ في مُحكَمِ الهُدى وإِسنادُهُ الرُّوحُ الأَمينُ المُطَهَّرُ

١ هـ: ترك. ٢ هـ: لم ار.

He hears and sees, we doubt it not, and all
His creatures need His guiding hand.
His bounty pours unstinting forth, while we,
His creatures, give but grudging mete.
In vain we strive to compass Him with thought
But thought before that vastness shrinks away.
Let creatures flail in search of hidden truth:
They wander, lost; His secret self remains.
Or let them take a flea and then describe
Its workings; all their words will not avail.
How then to grasp with feeble mortal mind
The One who neither changes nor decays?
Out of mercy did He bid us not inquire,
For vain dispute brings only strife and death.
We follow the Law the Prophet brought
And seek, as he bid us, no more to know.
And thus do we all innovation shun
Lest we be damned! We have the truth:
And if we hold that truth without a doubt
Then and then alone shall we be saved.
We proclaim that God our Lord is One
And Aḥmad[202] did He send to warn the earth;
His Book is His own spoken Word, despite
The doubts of all who scoff and disbelieve.
We proclaim that God to Moses spoke
And the words He spoke were His alone
When His servant glimpsed that fiery glow and went
To see the fire and fetch it back; but then
A voice he heard: "Fear not, but go and tell
The truth, and warn of Me, for I am God;
And all that Pharaoh does I see and hear."
And then, as God engraved His holy Law
Atop the Mount, He brought His servant near.
So says the Lord, His guiding Book vouchsafed
To a pure and trusty Spirit, then to us.
From it we know that all His friends, once dead

وإنَّ وَلِيَّ اللهِ في دارِ خُلْدِهِ   إلى رَبِّهِ ذي الكِبْرِياءِ سَيَنْظُرُ
ولم نَرَ[1] في أَهلِ الخُصوماتِ كلِّها   رَكِينًا[2] ولا ذا خَشْيةٍ يتوقَّرُ
وَلَمْ يَحْمَدِ اللهُ الجِدالَ وأَهْلَهُ   وَكانَ رَسولُ اللهِ عَنْ ذاكَ يَزْجُرُ
وسُنَّتُنا تَرْكُ الكَلامِ وأَهلِهِ   وَمَنْ دِينُه تَشْديقُهُ والتَّقَعُّرُ
وَكلِّ كَلامِيٍّ قَليلٍ خُشوعُهُ   لَهُ بيعٌ فيهِ وسوقٌ وَمَتجَرُ[3]
تَفَرَّغَ قَوْمٌ لِلجِدالِ وأَغفَلوا   طَريقَ التُّقَى حتّى غَلا المُتَهوِّرُ
وقاسوا بآراءِ ضِعافٍ وفرَّطوا   وَرأيُ الذي لا يَتبعُ الحَقَّ أَبتَرُ
جَزَى اللهُ رَبُّ الناسِ عنّا ابنَ حنبل   وصاحبَه خيرًا إذا الناسُ أُحضِروا
سَمِيَّ نَبِيِّ اللهِ أَعني محمّدا   فَقُلْ في ابنِ نوحٍ والمقالةُ تَقْصُرُ
سَقَى اللهُ قَبرًا حلَّه ما ثوى بهِ   مِنَ الغَيثِ وَسْمِيًّا يَروحُ ويَبكُرُ
هُما صَبَرا للحقِّ عندَ امتحانِهم   وقاما بنَصرِ اللهِ والسَّيفُ يَقطُرُ
وأَربعةٌ جاؤوا من الشامِ سادَةٌ   عليهم كُبولٌ بالحديدِ تُسمَّرُ
دُعوا فأَبَوْا إلا اعتِصامًا بدينِهم   فأُجلوا عَنِ الأَهلينَ طُرًّا وسُيِّروا
إلى البَلَدِ المَشحونِ مِن كُلِّ فِتنةٍ   وفي السِّجنِ كالسُّرّاقِ أُلقوا وصُيِّروا
فَما زادَهُمْ إلّا رِضًا وتَمَسُّكًا   بِدينِهمُ واللهُ بالخَلقِ أَبصَرُ
إذا مُيِّزَ الأَشياخُ يومًا وحُصِّلوا   فأَحمدُ مِنْ بَينِ المَشايخِ جَوهَرُ
رَقيقُ أديمِ الوَجهِ حُلوٌ مُهذَّبٌ   إلى كُلِّ ذي تَقوى وَقورٌ مُوَقَّرُ
أَبيٌّ إذا ما خافَ ضَيمٌ مُؤمَّرٌ   ومُرٌّ إذا ما خاشَنوهُ مُذكَّرُ

[1] هـ: فانا. [2] ش: قل. [3] تركي: زكينا.

Will gaze for aye upon their glorious Lord.
Behold the squabblers! I cannot discern
A single one who boasts of piety and wit.
Did God command debate on higher things?
And did the Prophet ever urge it on?
Our creed is not polemical; we walk away;
Our foes may huff and bellow as they like.
Instead of pious fear, they feel but greed
And lust of pelf and squalid clink of coin.
With naught to do but play at idle games
They lost their way and wandered far from faith.
With feeble minds they strove, but only made
Absurdity and fruitless lies their creed.
For our sake, Lord, requite our Aḥmad and his friend
As they deserve, when Judgment Day is come.
Muḥammad was a namesake of our Prophet,
And of "Noah's son" one can never say enough.[203]
May God send rain, come early spring, to greet
His grave at morn and evening time.
When put to the test they stood their ground
For God, despite the blades that ran with blood.
Reward, o God, the four who came in chains,
From Syria, with fetters clamped upon their limbs.
Called to perfidy, they clung to perfect faith
And, taken from their families and homes,
Were brought to a land of storm and strife
And cast amid the thieves in dungeons deep.
And yet—as God all-knowing knew they would—
Their pains did make them love Him all the more.
But if one day the elders choose their best
'Tis Aḥmad who will seem the crowning jewel.
Kind is he, plain-faced, belov'd of all who fear their Lord;
But if some peril should come, a haughty prince
Is he, and truculent, bitter if provoked.
No man, I swear, could wish him harm, unless
He be unsound in mind or evil in his heart.

لَعَمرِكَ ما يَهوى لأحمدَ نكبةً *** مِنَ النّاسِ إلا ناقِصُ العَقلِ مُعْوِرُ

هُوَ المِحنةُ اليَومَ الذي يُبتَلى بِهِ *** فَيَعتَبِرُ السُّنِّيُّ فينا ويُسْبَرُ

شَجىً في حُلوقِ المُلحِدينَ وَقُرَّةٌ *** لأَعيُنِ أهلِ النُّسكِ عَفٌّ مُشَمِّرُ

فَقا أَعيُنَ المُرّاقِ فعلُ[1] ابنِ حَنبَلٍ *** وأَخرَسَ من يَبغي العُيوبَ ويحقِرُ

جَرى سابقاً في حَلبةِ الصِّدقِ والتُّقى *** كما سَبقَ الطِّرفُ الجَوادُ المُضَمَّرُ

وبَلَّدَ عَنْ إدراكِهِ كُلُّ كَوْدَنٍ *** قَطوفٍ إذا ما حاولَ السَّبقَ يَعثُرُ

إذا افتَخرَ الأقوامُ يوماً بسيِّدٍ *** فَفيهِ لنا والحمدُ للهِ مَفخَرُ

فَقُل للأُلى يَشنَونَه لصَلاحِه *** وصِحّتِهِ واللهُ بالعُذرِ يَعذِرُ

جُعِلتم فِداءً أجمعينَ لنَعلِهِ *** فإنّكُمُ مِنها أذَلُّ وأحقَرُ

أَرَيحانةَ القُرّاءِ تَبغُونَ عَثْرةً *** وكُلُّكُمُ مِن جيفةِ الكَلبِ أقذَرُ

فَيا أَيُّها الساعي لِتُدرِكَ شَأوَهُ *** رُوَيدَكَ عَن إدراكِهِ سَتُقَصِّرُ

تَمسَّكَ بالعِلمِ الذي كانَ قَدْ وَعى *** ولَم يُلهِهِ عنه الخَبيصُ المُزَعفَرُ

ولا بَغلةٌ هِمْلاجَةٌ مَغرِبيّةٌ *** ولا حُلّةٌ تُطوى مِراراً وتُنشَرُ

ولا مَنزِلٌ بالساجِ والكِلسِ مُتقَنٌ *** يُنَقَّشُ فيه جِصُّه ويُصَوَّرُ

ولا أَمَةٌ بَرّاقةُ الجيدِ بَضَّةٌ *** بِمَنطِقِها يُصبى الحَليمُ ويُسحَرُ

حَمى نَفسَه الدُّنيا وَقد سَنَحَت لَهُ *** فَمَنزِلُهُ إلّا مِنَ القُوتِ مُقفِرُ

فإن يَكُ في الدُّنيا مُقِلّاً فإنّه *** مِنَ الأَدَبِ المَحمودِ والعِلمِ مُكثِرُ

وقُل للأُلي حادُوا مَعاً عَن طَريقِه *** ولَم يَمكثوا حتّى أجابوا وغَيَّروا

---

١ ليس في هـ.

The trial we face today is one to test
The strength of all who bear the Sunni name;
The heretics will see us win, and choke;
The poor, the chaste, the ragged will rejoice.
Let deviants see what Aḥmad does: for all
Who wish him ill shall lose their eyes and tongues.
And if sincere and pious deeds were like a track,
A lean and flashing stallion would he be;
The nags would strain to match his breathless pace
But flag, or stumble gasping to the ground.
Convoke the nations! Let each vaunt its chief;
In Aḥmad have we pride enough for all.
Tell those who hate him for being good
Hear us out, and seek forgiveness from the Lord:
The lot of you at once we'd ne'er accept
In barter for a shoe that Aḥmad's worn;
He is the basil of the pious and you wish him ill:
You, who stink like carcasses of dogs?
And should you strive our Aḥmad to outrace,
Slow down, because you never will.
Could you, like Aḥmad, study without let,
Unswayed by thoughts of tasty saffron sweets,
Or trotting mules Morocco-bred, or gowns
That fold and drape, or house of teak and lime,
With ornamented plaster on the walls?
Or chattel-girls a-glitter at the neck
Who speak and rob a man of all good sense?
All of that he might have made his own,
But look: at home he keeps but meager food.
Penurious he is and yet his share
Of learning and of uprightness is profuse.
Go tell the ones who bolted off the path
And waited not a moment to give in:
Your choice was wrong, for all it seemed not so
And soon enough your punishment will come.
How soon did you forget your learned ways

فلا تأمنوا عُقبَى الذي قد أتيتُمُ   فإنَّ الذي جئتُم ضلالٌ مُزوَّرُ
فيا عُلماءَ السوءِ أينَ عُقولكم   وأينَ الحديثُ المُسنَدُ المتخيَّرُ
ألا إنني أرجو النجاةَ ببُغضِكم   وكل امرئٍ يَشْنى الضَّلالةَ يؤجرُ[1]
تأسّى بكم قومٌ كثيرٌ فأصبحوا   لكُم ولَهم في كل مِصرٍ مُعيِّرُ
ويا تسعةً كانوا كتسعةِ صالحٍ   نبيّ الهُدَى إذ ناقةُ اللهِ تُعقَرُ[2]
نكصتُم على الأعقابِ حينَ امتُحنتُمُ   ولم يَكُ فيكم [من لـ] ذلك منكِرُ[3]
كَتَبْتُم بأيديكم حُتوفَ نُفوسِكم   فيا سوءتا ممّا يَخُطُّ المُقدِّرُ
وأشمتّم أعداءَ دين مُحمّدٍ   ولم تُضربِ الأعناقُ منكُم وتُنشَرُ
فَسبحانَ مَن يُعصَى فيعفو ويَغفِرُ   ويُظهِرُ إحسانَ المُسيءِ ويَستُرُ

٣،٩٠ أخبرنا محمد بن عبد الملك بن أبي القاسم قال: أخبرنا عبد الله بن محمد الأنصاري قال: أخبرنا أبو يعقوب قال: أخبرنا محمد ابن عبد الله اللآل قال: أخبرنا محمد بن إبراهيم الصرام قال: أخبرنا إبراهيم بن إسحاق الغَسيلي قال:

أنشدني الهَيثم بن أحمد لأبيه يرثي أحمد بن حنبل فذكر قصيدة انتخبتُ منها:

يا ناعيَ العِلم بيومِ أحمدا   نَعيتَ بحراً كانَ يجري مُزبِدا
ومَكرُماتٍ وتُقًى وسُودَدا   صلابةً في دينِهِ تجرَّدا
إذا غدا قُلتَ الرَّبيعُ قد غدا   يا أحمدَ الخيرِ الذي تحمَّدا
أشبهتَ سُفيانَ الذي تعبَّدا   ومِسعَرًا دانيتَهُ ومِعضَدا
أشبهتَهُم قناعةً ومُهتدَى   وعِفّةً بنتَ بها ومقتدَى
وكنتَ في هذا وذاكَ أوحدا   سُمّيتَ في هذا وذاكَ المُفرَدا

١ ليس في هـ. ٢ ليس في هـ. ٣ ليس في هـ، وما بين القوسين أضافه التركي لتستقيم البيت.

And all the Prophet's well-preserved reports!
And by hating you, I hope to be saved
For man is rewarded for his choice of foe.
Because of you did many fall away
And now in every town are you decried.
O you nine who first betrayed the cause,
Like the nine who Ṣāliḥ's camel slew,[204]
No sooner tested did you break and run.
Did none among you say that it was wrong?
With your own hands you wrote the fateful words
That doomed you to a wretched end indeed;
And gave Muḥammad's foes a cause for joy
Although your necks were never shown a blade!
Praise Him who is disobeyed but still forgives,
Revealing the good and hiding away the sin.[205]

We cite ʿAbd al-Malik ibn Abī l-Qāsim, who cites ʿAbd Allāh ibn Muḥammad al-Anṣārī, who cites Abū Yaʿqūb, who cites Muḥammad ibn ʿAbd Allāh al-Laʾʾāl, who cites Muḥammad ibn Ibrāhīm al-Ṣarrām, who cites Ibrāhīm ibn Isḥāq al-Ghasīlī, who said that he heard al-Hayḍam ibn Aḥmad recite an elegy his father composed for Aḥmad ibn Ḥanbal. From it I have selected the following: **90.3**

[Al-Hayḍam's father:]

When now you told of learning and of Aḥmad gone
You might have said the foaming sea was dry.
Of a gen'rous heart, of piety and lordly sway,
Of one so firm in faith are we bereft.
At his approach, you felt the breath of spring;
As befits his name, all spoke of him to praise.[206]
Most like Sufyān in piety was he
Nor did Misʿar or Miʿḍad leave him far behind.
Like them, he little sought, and guided right,
Denied himself, and showed us how to live.
In all these things was his alone the prize,
In all these things did we him call unmatched.

قد زُلزِلَتْ أَرضُ العِراقِ كَمدا والشامُ حُزنًا والحِجازُ أَرعَدا
يا أحمدَ بنَ حنبلٍ لا تبعُدا شَيَّدتَ للدِّينِ بِناءً مِرفَدا
إذ كُنتَ في الدين لَهُ مشيَّدًا ولَم تُرِدْ[1] قَصرًا بِها[2] مُمرَّدا
ولا حِصانًا كالعُقابِ أَجرَدا ولا إماءً كالسَّعالي نُهَّدا
أُلبِسْنَ ريطًا وحُلينَ عَسجَدًا فَقُمنَ يُشبِهنَ غُصونًا مُيَّدا
إنَّ المَنيّاتِ تَوافي المَوعِدا تَنزِلُ بالنازِلِ دُنياه الرَّدى
وحَظُّهُ مِنها الذي تَزَوَّدا

قال: وأنشدني الهَيضَم لأبيه فذكر قصيدة انتخبتُ منها: ٩٠.٤

لِتَبكِ عُيونٌ مُسبِلاتٌ بوَلها على زينةِ الدُّنيا وعالمِ أَهلِها
قليلٌ عليه فاستَقِلّا بُكاكُما على مُستَقِلٍّ بالخُطوبِ مُقِلِّها
إمامٌ لأَهلِ العِلمِ تَفري مَطيُّهم إليه الفَلا بينَ السَّديسِ وبُزلِها[3]
فَبانَ بيَومٍ كانَ مِقدارَ يومِهِ وصارَ إلى دارِ البِلَى ومَحَلِّها
فَتِلكَ المَطايا قد أُرِحنَ مِنَ السُّرى ومِن شَدِّ أَنساعِ الرِّحالِ وحَلِّها
لِمُهلَكِ ثاوٍ كانَ مأوى رِحالِهِم إذا ما أُنيخَتْ كُلُّ عيسٍ بِرَحلِها
لِيُروَ رَميمٌ تَحتَ رَدمٍ مِنَ الثَّرى تَصوبُ عليه البارِقاتُ بهَطلِها
سَتَحدُثُ أَحداثٌ يُقالُ لِمِثلِها ألا مِثلُهُ في مِثلِها عِندَ مِثلِها

قال: وأَنشدني الهَيضَم لأبيه فيه: ٩٠.٥

للزّاهِدينَ مَعَ الدُّموعِ دُموعُ والعابِدينَ لَهُم عَلَيكَ خُشوعُ
يَبكونَ فَقدَكَ والجُفونُ شِفاؤها هَمَلانُها ورُقادُها مَمنوعُ

١ هـ: قصرانها، ش: تر. ٢ هـ: قصرانها. ٣ ش: نزلها.

Come back! Your hands an edifice of faith
Did build, not a palace to inhabit in this world.
You craved no eagle-footed steed,
Nor shapely slave, bewitching as the jinn,
In finery bedecked, and golden weave,
Swaying like a cane-brake when she walks.
But to each must come that fateful hour when death
Arrives, the tenants of the world to lead away;
And from this world can they but one thing take:
The deeds they stored away while yet they could.[207]

Al-Hayḍam recited another poem by his father, of which I have selected the following: **90.4**

Let all eyes weep and mourn the loss
Of earth's bright crown, and her leading light;
Although no tears you cry could e'er suffice
To mourn the one who bore such sore travail.
Through deserts did the learnèd guide their mounts—
Their camels eight years old and nine—to him.
But then did end his destined span of years
And gone he was, to the way-place of decay.
No more need camels march by night, no more
Need girthing-ropes be pulled and loosed again:
The one whose courts were once their kneeling place
Has gone to lie beneath them underground.
Upon his grave, where earth is mounded high
Let thunderclouds loose their sheets of rain.
In days to come, those left will say, "Is there
For us no one like him in times like these?"[208]

Al-Hayḍam also recited a poem by his father, including these lines: **90.5**

To the tears that world-renouncers weep, add tears;
And let the ones who fear their Lord behold
And fear the more. They mourn for you, their eyes
Bereft of sleep, their only comfort tears.

يا أَحْمدَ الخيْرَ الذي وارى الثَّرى وبهِ الشَّتاتُ مِن الجَميعِ جَميعُ
أَرْوَى مَحلَّتَكَ السَّماءُ وَجادَها دِيَمُ الخَريفِ وصَيِّفٌ ورَبيعُ

٦،٩٠ أنبأنا عليّ بن عُبيد الله قال: أخبرنا عبد الواحد بن عليّ العلاّف قال: أخبرنا محمّد بن أحمد بن محمّد بن سهل قال: أخبرنا أبو بكر أحمد بن جعفر بن سَلْم قال: حدثنا محمّد بن السري أبو بكر قال:[١] حدثنا محمّد بن إسماعيل بن الحجّاج النّيسابوري قال: سمعت أحمد بن المبارك يقول:

سمعتُ عليّ بن حُجْر يقول ونَعى إليه أحمدَ بن حنبل رجلٌ يُقال له إبراهيم فقال عليّ بن حُجر:

نَعى لي إبراهيمُ أوْرَعَ عالِمٍ سَمِعتُ بهِ مِن مُعدِمٍ ومُخوَّلِ
إماماً على قَصْدِ السَّبيل وسُنَّةِ النَّبيّ أمينَ اللهِ آخرِ مُرسَلِ
فقلتُ وفاضَ الدَّمعُ منّي بأرْبعٍ على النَّحْرِ فَيضاً كالجُمانِ المُفَصَّلِ
سَلامٌ عَديدُ القَطْرِ والنَّجمِ والثَّرى على أحْمدِ البرِّ التَّقي ابنَ حَنبلِ
ألا فَتأهَّبْ للمَنايا فإنَّما الْـ ـبَقاءُ قليلٌ بَعْدَهُ لكَ أيْ علي

٧،٩٠ أنبأنا يحيى بن الحسن بن البنّا قال: أنبأنا محمّد بن الحسين قال: أنشدنا عُبيد الله بن أحمد قال: أنشدنا أبو أحمد عبد السلام بن عليّ قال:

أنشدنا أبو مُزاحِم الخاقاني:

جَزى اللهُ ابنَ حَنبلٍ التَّقيّا عنِ الإسلام إحْسانًا هَنيّا
فَقدْ أَعطاهُ إذ صَبَرَ احتِساباً على الأَسواطِ إيماناً قَويّا
هُو الورِعُ الذي امتَحنُوه قِدْماً فألفَوْهُ عَليماً لا غَبيّا

١ قال حدثنا محمّد بن السري أبو بكر: ليس في ش.

Embraced by earth good Aḥmad lies, as far
From us as anyone can be. May clouds refresh
His grave with rain as days turn into years![209]

We were informed by ʿAlī ibn ʿUbayd Allāh, who cites ʿAbd al-Wāḥid ibn ʿAlī l-ʿAllāf, who cites Muḥammad ibn Aḥmad ibn Muḥammad ibn Sahl, who cites Abū Bakr Aḥmad ibn Jaʿfar ibn Salm, who heard Abū Bakr Muḥammad ibn al-Sarī report that he heard Muḥammad ibn Ismāʿīl ibn al-Ḥajjāj al-Naysābūrī report that he heard Aḥmad ibn al-Mubārak say: **90.6**

[Ibn al-Mubārak:] I heard ʿAlī ibn Ḥujr say, when a man named Ibrāhīm broke the news of Aḥmad ibn Ḥanbal's death:

Of all the learnèd men I know, the one who most
Denied himself, the poorest of them all, whom God
Did trust, is gone: or so says Ibrāhīm.
A guide he was to all who walk the path behind
The Prophet, God's trustee, the last He sent.
My tears well up and pool like silver beads about
My neck. I bid him "Peace!" as many times as stars
There are, or drops of rain, or sand; a man he was
Who feared his God and loved his fellow man.
And now we too prepare for death: if none like him
On earth are left, pray why should we remain?[210]

We were informed by Yaḥyā ibn al-Ḥasan ibn al-Bannā, who was informed by Muḥammad ibn al-Ḥusayn, who heard it recited by ʿUbayd Allāh ibn Aḥmad, who heard it recited by Abū Aḥmad ʿAbd al-Salām ibn ʿAlī: **90.7**

[Abū Aḥmad:] We heard Abū Muzāḥim al-Khāqānī recite:

For all that Aḥmad did, may God on our behalf
Bountifully requite him;
Did He not give him faith and strength to face
The flogging when they tried him?
And when they put his learning to the test
Did he not confound them?

وجاءَ بصادِقِ الآثارِ حتّى أقامَ بذلكَ الدّينَ الرّضيّا
حَبا المتوكّلُ السنِيُّ بَدْءاً وعودًا أحمدَ المالَ السنيّا
فآثرَ أحمدُ الإقلالَ زُهداً على الدنيا وكانَ بها سَخيّا
فأحمدُ جامعٌ وَرَعًا وزُهداً وعِلمًا نافِعًا حَبْرًا تقيّا
وأحمدُ كانَ للفتوى إماماً رِضًا للمسلمين معًا وفيّا
وأحمدُ محنةٌ للناسِ طُراً نَميزُ به المُعوَّجَ والسّويّا

٨،٩٠ أخبرنا ابن ناصر قال: أخبرنا محمّد بن عبد الملك بن عبد القاهر قال: أنبأنا عُبيد الله بن أحمد بن عُثمان قال: أنشدنا عبد السلام بن عليّ قال:

أنشدنا أبو مُزاحم الخاقاني له:

لَقدْ صارَ في الآفاقِ أحمدُ مِحنَةً وأَمْرُ الوَرى فيها فَليسَ بمُشكِلِ
تَرى ذا الهوى جهلاً لِأَحْمدَ مُبغِضاً وتَعرِفُ ذا التَّقوى بحُبِّ ابنِ حَنبلِ

٩،٩٠ أخبرنا محمّد بن أبي منصور قال: أخبرنا عبد القادر بن محمّد بن يوسف قال: أخبرنا إبراهيم بن عمر البرمكي قال: أخبرنا عبيد الله بن عبد الرحمن الزُّهري قال:

أخبرنا أبو بكر محمّد بن هارون بن حُمَيد المُجَدَّر[1] قال: لمّا دفنّا أحمد بن حنبل أنشدَنا ابنُ الخبّازة فيه:

وَمَن أَفْضَتِ الدنيا إليهِ فعافَها وقالَ هَبلتِ الدينُ أَنبلَ مُشكِلِ

---

١ هـ: المحله

A mighty witness did he bear, and restore
The faith of all around him.
The rueful caliph, now of Sunni creed,
With goodly gifts did ply him;
But Aḥmad took them not, nor could the wealth
He hated ever try him.
He lived to learn, and shunned the world;
No doubtful act could sway him;
And when he told us how to live the Law
We Muslims would obey him.
He is the test: if we but ask a man
Whom he seeks to guide him,
And if he tells us "Aḥmad," then we know
It's safe to pray beside him.[211]

We cite Ibn Nāṣir, who cites Muḥammad ibn ʿAbd al-Malik ibn ʿAbd al-Qāhir, who was informed by ʿUbayd Allāh ibn Aḥmad ibn ʿUthmān, who heard it recited by ʿAbd al-Salām ibn ʿAlī: 90.8

[ʿAbd al-Salām:] We heard Abū Muzāḥim al-Khāqānī recite from his own work:

For all the world, for all mankind is he
The test of faith, the measure, and the rod;
To hate him means to turn away from truth;
To love him means to know the fear of God.[212]

We cite Muḥammad ibn Abī Manṣūr, who cites ʿAbd al-Qādir ibn Muḥammad ibn Yūsuf, who cites Ibrāhīm ibn ʿUmar al-Barmakī, who cites ʿUbayd Allāh ibn ʿAbd al-Raḥmān al-Zuhrī, who cites Abū Bakr Muḥammad ibn Hārūn ibn Ḥumayd al-Mujaddar, who said: 90.9

[Al-Mujaddar:] After we buried Aḥmad ibn Ḥanbal, Ibn al-Khabbāzah recited:

He scorned the world that gave itself to him
But faith is worthier to call itself bereaved;

وَمَن رامَ إبليسُ اسْتِمالةَ قَلبِهِ   فألفاهُ كالقِدحِ الذي لم يُميَّلِ[1]
ومَن لم يزَلْ في سُنّةِ اللهِ صابرًا   على الضَّرْبِ والأَنكالِ والسّجنِ مُذْ بُلي[2]
كأَنّي أَرى الجلاّدَ يثني سِياطَه   على بَدنٍ بالٍ من الصَّومِ مُنْحَلِ
وأَعْضاؤه تجْري الدماءَ كأنّها   عيونٌ إذا ما السوط منكبه عَلي
وقد وَهنَتْ من شدّةِ الضَّربِ نَفسُهُ   وحَسَّ دَبيبَ الموْتِ في كلِّ مَفْصِلِ
وقال له الجُهّالُ يا مُبتَلى أَجِبْ   فإنَّكَ إن تأْبَ الإجابةَ تُقْتَلِ
فقال: على البَرِّ الرَّحيمِ توكُّلي   أَعوذُ بِربِّي من مَقالةِ مُبطِلِ
ويا مَنْ يُعافي من يَشاءُ ويَبْتَلي   أَغِثْني بِصَبْرٍ مِنكَ غيرِ مُؤجَّلِ
وإنْ كنتَ في ذا الحالِ قَدّرتَ مِيتَتي   أَمِتْني سَليمَ الدينِ غيرَ مبدِّلِ
فما حَجَبَ البرُّ الرحيمُ سُؤالَه   لقد خصّهُ منه بِصَبْرٍ مُعجّلِ
فَنجّاه منهُ كاملَ الدينِ سالمًا   بلا بِدْعةٍ من سُنّةٍ لم يُحوَّلِ[3]
فعاشَ حَميدًا ثمّ ماتَ مُفْرَدًا   بِهِ أَحَدٌ من دَهْرِهِ لم يمثَّلِ
فَبُورِكَ مَوْلودًا وبُورِكَ ناشِئًا   وبورِكَ كَهْلاً من أَمينٍ معدَّلِ
وبُورِكَ مَقْبوضًا وبورِك مُلْحَدًا   وبورِكَ مَبعوثًا إلى خَيرِ مَنْزِلِ
أُرجّي له الحُسْنَى بإظْهارِهِ التُّقَى   وما يَشإِ العَلاّمُ بالسِّرِّ يَفْعَلِ[4]
وبَعْدُ فإنَّ السُنّةَ اليَوْمَ أَصْبحَتْ   مُعَزَّزةً حَتّى كأَنْ لَمْ تُذلَّلِ
تَصولُ وتَسْطو[5] إذ أُقيمَ مَنارها   وحُطَّ مَنارُ الإفْكِ والزّورِ من عَلِ
وَوَلّى أَخو الإبداعِ في الدين هارِبًا   إلى النارِ يهوي مُدْبِرًا غيرَ مُقْبِلِ

[1] ش: تزهو. [2] ش: سقى. [3] ش: يُمْثَلِ، تركي: يمثّلِ. [4] هـ: مذيل، ش: مُذيلي، وما أثبتناه هوما أورده التركي.
[5] ليس في ش.

The Devil wished his heart to win but found
His heart was hard as flint, and never bent.
He bore it all—the whip, the stock, the jail—
But stood his ground for God. I see him now,
His body, worn by fasting, and the lash,
And wounds like gaping wells of blood.
So savage were the blows, his soul did quail,
And death lay its creeping fingers on his limbs;
That witless lot all cried, "You wretch! Give up,
For if you don't, we'll slay you here and now!"
"I put my trust," he said, "in God alone,
And God forbid I speak a lying creed!
O You, who smite or cure as You see fit,
I ask but for the strength to bear the pain.
And if by Your decree today I die,
Know that firm in faith I died unbowed."
Straight up to God did Aḥmad's prayer go,
And God without delay increased his strength,
And brought him forth, his creed untinged by lies.
In honor thus he lived; and when he died
He left no man his age to call him peer.
Blest he was at birth, and as he grew,
A man he was who earned the trust of all:
Now blest is he, his spirit taken up,
His body in the grave, but on the way to peace.
I pray that God, the One he feared, will give
A just reward: but only He can know.
The *sunnah*, though, one morn arose and found
Her strength restored, as if she'd never known
Defeat; while all about, the keep of lies
In ruins lay, its tower in a heap;
And wrong belief in terror has fled to Hell
Its face turned back, not knowing where it goes.
It flees from our new caliph, Mutawakkil,
Who by grace of God has brought the *sunnah* back,
Convoked the men of learning, once dispersed,

شَفَى[1] اللهُ منه بالخليفةِ جعفرٍ خليفتِنا ذي السُّنّةِ المُتوكّلِ
وجامعِ أهلِ الدّينِ بعد تشتُّتٍ وفاري رؤوسِ المارقينَ بمِقْصَلِ
أطالَ لنا ربُّ العبادِ بقاءَه سليمًا مِنَ الأهواءِ غيرَ مُبدّلِ
وبوّأه بالنّصرِ للدّينِ جنّةً يُجاوِرُ في روضاتِها خيرَ مُرسَلِ

أنشدنا محمد بن ناصر قال: ١٠،٩٠

أنشدنا جعفر بن أحمد السرّاج لنفسه في الإمام أبي عبد الله أحمد بن حنبل:

سَقَى اللهُ قبرًا حلَّ فيه ابنُ حنبلٍ مِنَ الغيثِ وَسْميًّا على إثره وَلي
على أنَّ دَمْعي فيه ريٌّ عِظامِه إذا فاضَ ما لَمْ يَبْلَ مِنها وما بَلي
فَلِلّهِ ربِّ النّاسِ مَذْهَبُ أحمدٍ فإنَّ عليهِ ما حَييتُ مُعوَّلي
دَعَوْه إلى خلقِ القُرآنِ كما دَعَوْا سِواه فلَمْ يَسْمَعْ ولم يتأوَّلِ
ولا ردَّهُ ضربُ السِّياطِ وسجنُه عَنِ السُّنّةِ الغرّاءِ والمذهبِ الجَلي
ولمّا يَرِدْهُم والسّياطُ تَنُوشُه فَشَلَّتْ يمينُ الضاربِ المُتبتّلِ
على قولِه القُرآنُ وليَشْهدِ الوَرى كلامُكَ يا ربّ الوَرى كيفَما تُلي
فمن مُبلغٌ أصحابَه أنّني به أُفاخِرُ أهلَ العِلْمِ في كلِّ مَحْفِلِ
وألقى به الزُّهّادَ كلَّ مُطلِّقٍ مِنَ الخوفِ دُنياه طلاقَ التبتُّلِ
مناقِبُه إنْ لم تكُنْ عالِمًا بها فكَشِّفْ طُروسَ القومِ عنهنَّ واسْألِ
لَقَدْ عاشَ في الدنيا حميدًا مُوفّقًا وصارَ إلى لأخرى إلى خيرِ منزلِ
وإنّي لَراجٍ أن يكونَ شفيعَ مَنْ تولّاه من شيخٍ ومن مُتكهِّلِ
ومن حَدَثٍ قد نوَّرَ اللهُ قلبَه إذا سألوا عن أصلِه قالَ حَنْبلي

---

[1] ش: وما العلام بالستر يفعل.

And with his blade lopped off the liars' heads.
May God, the Lord of all, prolong his life,
And keep him safe from ev'ry erring creed;
And may he gain, as his reward, a place
In the Garden, with the Prophet at his side.[213]

Muḥammad ibn Nāṣir recited for us verses recited to him, and composed, by Jaʿfar ibn Aḥmad al-Sarrāj, on the exemplar Aḥmad ibn Ḥanbal: **90.10**

The rains of spring, then winter rain, may God
Upon the tomb where Aḥmad lies let pour!
Although my flowing tears alone suffice
To wet his bones, or what of them remains.
I praise to God the path that Aḥmad took,
And vow the same to take, so long I live!
They bid him call the Book create, but he
And he alone refused, nor made excuse;
No lash or jail of theirs could make him leave
The *sunnah*'s shining road and well-marked path;
And though the whips had bitten through his flesh,
And the lictors had to rest their wearied arms,
He would add no word to this: "The Book of God
In all its forms is His: bear witness, all!"
So take this message to his friends: I go
To boast of him to ev'ry learnèd man,
And ev'ry shunner of the world, now free
As any monk from fear of things below.
And if you have not heard of what he did
Then go and read the scrolls his people keep!
Right-guided in this world, and much beloved,
He leaves us for another, better place,
To intercede—I pray—for all of us,
The young, the old, and all those in between,
Who say, when asked which path is theirs, reply,
"By grace of God, the one that Aḥmad took!"[214]

أخبرنا عبد الملك بن أبي القاسم الكَرُوخي قال: ١١،٩٠

أنشدنا أبو إسماعيل عبد الله بن محمّد الأَنصاري في مَدْح أحمد بن حنبل:

وإمامي القوّامُ للهِ الذي   دفنُوا حميدَ الشأنِ في بَغْدَانِ
جَمَعَ التُّقى والزُّهْدَ في دُنياهمُ   والعِلْمَ بَعْدَ طَهارةِ الأَرْدانِ
خَصِمُ النَّبيِّ وصَيْرَفيُّ حديثِهِ   ومُفلّقٍ أغرافِها بِمَعانِ
حبْرُ العراقِ ومِحْنةٌ لذوي الهوَى   يُدْرَى بِبغضتِهِ[1] ذَوُو الأَضْغانِ
عَرَفَ الهُدَى فاجْتابَ ثَوْبَيْ نُصْرةٍ   وسَخا بمُهْجَتِهِ علَى عِرفانِ
عُرِضَتْ له الدنيا فأَعْرَضَ سالمًا   عَنْها كَفِعْلِ الراهِبِ الخُمْصانِ
هانَتْ عَلَيْهِ نَفْسُه في دينِه   فَفَدَى الإمامُ الدينَ بالجُثْمانِ
للهِ ما لَقِيَ ابنُ حنبل صابرًا   عزمًا وينصره بلا أَعْوانِ
أنا حَنبليٌّ ما حَيِيتُ فإنْ أَمُتْ   فَوَصِيّتي ذاكُم إلى إِخْواني

قلت: وقد نقلت مدائح كثيرة ومَراثٍ كثيرة اقتصرت على ما انتخبت منها والله الموفّق.

١ هـ: بعصمته.

We cite ʿAbd al-Malik ibn Abī l-Qāsim al-Karūkhī: 90.11

[Al-Karūkhī:] We heard Abū Ismāʿīl ʿAbd Allāh ibn Muḥammad al-Anṣārī recite in praise of Aḥmad ibn Ḥanbal:

Our leader lies at rest in Baghdad now,
Who stood and fought for God. He feared his Lord,
and shunned the world, and blameless lived to learn.
To aid the Prophet up he sprang. He told
The true reports from false, and made us learn
Everything they meant, in words that split the peaks.
The sage of all Iraq he was, of wrongful creeds
The test: to hate him was to leave Islam.
Rightly guided, clad in fighting dress,
His soul in willing combat did he spend.
He might have had the world, but like a monk,
He, though starving, spurned it and was saved.
For him, a life was given him to lose
For God, his body but a shield for the faith;
And when he stood, none stood with him, nor could
Another match his strength against the foe.
A Ḥanbalī am I, until the death,
And these verses are my testament to you.[215]

[The author:] I have copied many of the praise poems and elegies composed for him but confined myself here to a few selections. May God guide me aright!

الباب الحادي والتسعون في ذكر المنامات التي رآها أحمد بن حنبل

١،٩١ أخبرنا عبد الملك بن أبي القاسم قال: أخبرنا عبد الله بن محمد الأنصاري قال: أخبرنا محمد بن عبد الجليل بن أحمد قال: أخبرنا محمد بن أحمد بن إبراهيم، وأخبرنا ابن ناصر قال: أنبأنا أبو عليّ الحسن بن أحمد قال: أخبرنا أبو محمد الخلّال قال: أخبرنا عبيد الله بن عبد الرحمن الزهري قالا: حدثنا أحمد بن محمد بن مِقْسَم قال: سمعتُ عبد العزيز بن أحمد النَّهاوَنْدي قال:

سمعتُ عبد الله بن أحمد بن حنبل قال: سمعتُ أبي يقول: رأيتُ ربّ العزّة عزّ وجلّ في المَنام فقلت: يا ربّ ما أفضل ما تقرّب به المتقربون إليك؟

فقال: كلامي يا أحمد.

قال: قلت: يا ربّ بفهم أو بغير فهم؟

قال: بفهم وبغير فهم.

٢،٩١ أخبرنا عبد الملك بن أبي القاسم قال: أخبرنا عبد الله بن محمد الأنصاري قال: أخبرنا أبو يعقوب الحافظ قال: حدثنا محمد بن عبد الله بن خَمِيرَوَيْهِ قال: حدثنا عمر بن أحمد بن عليّ الجَوهري قال: حدثنا أبو إسحاق إبراهيم ابن يزيد بن عبد المَجيد قال:

حدثنا الحسن بن بكر بن عبد الرحمن عن صَدَقة بن الفَضْل قال: أقبلت من الكوفة أريد بغداد وليست معي نَفَقة، فلمّا بلغت نهر صَرْصَر اشتدّ بي الجوع فدخلتُ مسجدًا هناك فِنِمْت فإذا رجل يحرّكني برجله فانتبهتُ فإذا أحمد بن حنبل ومعه حمّال معه خُبز فقال: إني أُتيت البارحة في المنام فقيل لي: صديقك صَدَقة ابن الفضل أَقبل من الكوفة وهو بحال فأدْرِكْه.

Chapter 91: His Dreams

91.1 We cite ʿAbd al-Malik ibn Abī l-Qāsim, who cites ʿAbd Allāh ibn Muḥammad al-Anṣārī, who cites Muḥammad ibn ʿAbd al-Jalīl ibn Aḥmad, who cites Muḥammad ibn Aḥmad ibn Ibrāhīm; and we cite Ibn Nāṣir, who was informed by Abū ʿAlī l-Ḥasan ibn Aḥmad, who cites Abū Muḥammad ibn Khallāl, who cites ʿUbayd Allāh ibn ʿAbd al-Raḥmān al-Zuhrī, who like Muḥammad ibn Aḥmad ibn Ibrāhīm heard Aḥmad ibn Muḥammad ibn Miqsam report that he heard ʿAbd al-ʿAzīz ibn Aḥmad al-Nihāwandī say that he heard Aḥmad ibn Ḥanbal's son ʿAbd Allāh say:

[ʿAbd Allāh:] I heard my father say, "The Lord of Glory appeared to me in a dream and I asked Him how best to draw nearer to Him.

"'Through my Speech, Aḥmad,' He said.

"'Do we have to understand it?' I asked.

"He said, 'It works whether you understand it or not.'"

91.2 We cite ʿAbd al-Malik ibn Abī l-Qāsim, who cites ʿAbd Allāh ibn Muḥammad al-Anṣārī, who cites Abū Yaʿqūb al-Ḥāfiẓ, who heard Muḥammad ibn ʿAbd Allāh ibn Khamīruwayh report that he heard ʿUmar ibn Aḥmad ibn ʿAlī l-Jawharī report that he heard Abū Isḥāq Ibrāhīm ibn Yazīd ibn ʿAbd al-Majīd report that he heard al-Ḥasan ibn Bakr ibn ʿAbd al-Raḥmān report, citing Ṣadaqah ibn al-Faḍl, who said:

[Ṣadaqah ibn al-Faḍl:] I was traveling from Kufa to Baghdad without any money to spend. By the time I reached the Ṣarṣar Canal I was starving. I went into a mosque there and fell asleep. I woke up to find a man joggling me with his foot. It was Aḥmad ibn Ḥanbal. With him was a porter carrying bread.

"Last night I had a dream," he said. "A voice said, 'Your friend Ṣadaqah ibn al-Faḍl has arrived from Kufa in a bad way so go help him.'"

الباب الثاني والتسعون في ذكر المنامات التي رُئي فيها أحمد بن حنبل

١،٩٢ أخبرنا محمّد بن أبي منصور قال: أخبرنا عبد القادر بن محمّد بن يوسف قال: أخبرنا إبراهيم بن عمر البرمكي قال: أخبرنا عليّ بن عبد العزيز قال: أخبرنا عبد الرحمن بن أبي حاتم قال: حدثنا أبو زُرْعَة قال:

سمعت محمّد بن مِهْران الجمّال يقول: رأيتُ أحمد بن حنبل في المنام كأنّ عليه بُردًا مخطّطًا أو مُعيّنًا وكأنّه بالرّيّ يُريد المصير إلى الجامع يوم الجمعة. فاستعبرت بعض أهل التعبير فقال: هذا يشتهر بالخير.

قال: فما أتى عليه إلّا قريب حتى ورد ما ورد من خبره في أمر المحنة.

٢،٩٢ قال عبد الرحمن: وسمعت أبي يقول: رأيتُ أحمد بن حنبل في المنام فرأيته أضخم[1] ما كان وأحسن وجهاً فجعلت أسأله الحديث وأُذاكره.

٣،٩٢ أخبرنا المحمّدان ابن ناصر وابن عبد الباقي قالا: أخبرنا حمد بن أحمد قال: أخبرنا أحمد بن عبد الله الحافظ قال: حدثنا أبي قال: حدثنا أحمد بن محمّد بن عمر قال: حدثني نصر بن خُزَيمة قال: حدثني محمّد بن مَخْلَد قال: حدثنا أحمد بن محمّد بن عبد الحميد الكوفي قال:

سمعت إبراهيم بن خُرَّزاذ قال: رأى جارٌ لنا كأنّ ملكًا نزل من السماء ومعه سبعة تيجان فأوّل من تُوّج من الدنيا أحمد بن حنبل.

٤،٩٢ أخبرنا محمّد بن ناصر قال: أخبرنا المبارك بن عبد الجبال قال: أخبرنا عليّ بن عمر القزويني قال: أخبرنا أبو عمر بن حَيُّوَيْه قال: حدثنا أبو الحسن عليّ بن إبراهيم بن الحسين الشافعي قال: حدثنا أبو بكر محمّد بن الحسين بن محمّد قال: حدثنا عَزْرة بن عبد الله وطالوت بن لُقمان قالا:

---

١ ليس في هـ.

Chapter 92: Dreams in Which He Appeared to Others

We cite Muḥammad ibn Abī Manṣūr, who cites ʿAbd al-Qādir ibn Muḥammad ibn Yūsuf, who cites Ibrāhīm ibn ʿUmar al-Barmakī, who cites ʿAlī ibn ʿAbd al-ʿAzīz, who cites ʿAbd al-Raḥmān ibn Abī Ḥātim, who heard Abū Zurʿah report that he heard Muḥammad ibn Mihrān al-Jammāl say: 92.1

[Muḥammad ibn Mihrān al-Jammāl:] Aḥmad Ibn Ḥanbal appeared to me in a dream wearing a striped mantle, or one with lozenges. He seemed to be in Rey, trying to get to Friday prayer. I asked a dream interpreter what it meant. He said Aḥmad would become renowned for some great deed. It wasn't long after that we heard about what he had done during the Inquisition.

ʿAbd al-Raḥmān added: I heard my father say, "Aḥmad ibn Ḥanbal appeared to me in a dream. He looked larger than life and had very beautiful features. I began asking him about Hadith and comparing reports." 92.2

We cite the two Muḥammads, Ibn Nāṣir and Ibn ʿAbd al-Bāqī, who cite Ḥamd ibn Aḥmad, who cites Aḥmad ibn ʿAbd Allāh al-Ḥāfiẓ, who heard his father report that he heard Aḥmad ibn Muḥammad ibn ʿUmar report that he heard Naṣr ibn Khuzaymah report that he heard Muḥammad ibn Makhlad, who heard Aḥmad ibn Muḥammad ibn ʿAbd al-Ḥumayd al-Kūfī report that he heard Ibrāhīm ibn Khurrazādh say: 92.3

[Ibn Khurrazādh:] A neighbor of ours had a dream where an angel came down from the heavens carrying seven crowns. The first person on earth to receive one was Aḥmad ibn Ḥanbal.

We cite Muḥammad ibn Nāṣir, who cites al-Mubārak ibn ʿAbd al-Jabbār, who cites ʿAlī ibn ʿUmar al-Qazwīnī, who cites Abū ʿUmar ibn Ḥayyuwayh, who heard Abū l-Ḥasan ʿAlī ibn Ibrāhīm ibn al-Ḥusayn al-Shāfiʿī report that he heard Abū Bakr Muḥammad ibn al-Ḥusayn ibn Muḥammad, who heard ʿAzrah ibn ʿAbd Allāh and Ṭālūt ibn Luqmān, who both heard Abū Yaḥyā Zakariyyā ibn Yaḥyā l-Simsār say: 92.4

سمعنا أبا يحيى زكريّا بن يحيى السِّمْسار يقول: رأيت أحمد بن حنبل رحمه الله في المنام على رأسه تاج مرصَّع بالجوهر في رجليه نَعْلاَن وهو يَخْطِر بهما.

قال: قلتُ: أبا عبد الله، ماذا فعل الله بك؟

قال: غفر لي وأدناني من نفسه وتوّجني بيده بهذا التاج وقال لي: هذا بقولك القرآن كلام الله غير مخلوق.

قلت: فما هذه الخَطْرة التي لم أعرفها لك في دار الدنيا؟

قال: هذه مِشْيَة الخُدّام في دار السلام.

٥،٩٢ أخبرنا عبد الملك بن أبي القاسم قال: أخبرنا عبد الله بن محمّد الأنصاري قال: أخبرنا عبد الصمد بن محمّد بن محمّد ابن صالح قال: أخبرنا أبي قال: أخبرنا محمّد بن حيّان قال: حدثنا أحمد بن محمّد بن سعيد المَرْوَزي قال: حدثنا محمّد بن الحسن السُّلَمي قال: سمعت طالوت ابن لقمان قال:

سمعت أبا يحيى السمسار البغدادي يقول: رأيت أحمد بن حنبل في المنام وعلى رأسه تاج مرصّع بالجوهر وإذا هو يخطر خطرة لم أعرفها له في دار الدنيا فقلتُ له: يا أبا عبد الله ما فعل الله بك؟

قال: غفر لي وأدناني وتوّجني التاج فقال: هذا بقولك القرآن كلام الله غير مخلوق، وهذه مشية الخدّام في دار السلام.

٦،٩٢ أخبرنا المحمّدان: ابن ناصر وابن عبد الباقي قالا: أخبرنا حمد بن أحمد قال: أخبرنا أبو نُعَيم الحافظ قال: حدثنا عبد الله بن محمّد بن جعفر قال: قرأت على مُسبِح[1] بن حاتم العُكْلي قال:

حدثنا إبراهيم بن جعفر المَرْوَزي قال: رأيت أحمد بن حنبل في المنام يمشي مشية يختال فيها فقلتُ: ما هذه المشية يا أبا عبد الله؟

قال: هذه مشية الخدّام في دار السلام.

---

[1] ش: تر.

[Zakariyyā ibn Yaḥyā l-Simsār:] Aḥmad ibn Ḥanbal—God have mercy on him— appeared to me in a dream with a jeweled crown on his head and sandals on his feet, strutting around. I asked him how God had judged him.

"He forgave me," he said, "brought me near Him, and placed this crown on my head with His own hands, saying that He was rewarding me for saying that the Qur'an was His uncreated speech."

I remarked that I had never seen him strut on earth.

"This is how servants walk in Paradise," he said.

We cite ʿAbd al-Malik ibn Abī l-Qāsim, who cites ʿAbd Allāh ibn Muḥammad al-Anṣārī, who cites ʿAbd al-Ṣamad ibn Muḥammad ibn Muḥammad ibn Ṣāliḥ, who cites his father, who cites Muḥammad ibn Ḥayyān, who heard Aḥmad ibn Muḥammad ibn Saʿīd al-Marwazī, who heard Muḥammad ibn al-Ḥasan al-Sulamī, who heard Ṭālūt ibn Luqmān say that he heard Abū Yaḥyā l-Simsār al-Baghdādī say: **92.5**

[Abū Yaḥyā l-Simsār al-Baghdādī:] Aḥmad ibn Ḥanbal—God have mercy on him!—appeared to me in a dream with a jeweled crown on his head, strutting around in a way he never had on earth. I asked him how God had judged him.

"He forgave me," he said, "brought me near Him, and placed this crown on my head, saying that He was rewarding me for saying that the Qur'an was His uncreated speech. And this is how servants walk in Paradise."

We cite the two Muḥammads, Ibn Nāṣir and Ibn ʿAbd al-Bāqī, who cite Ḥamd ibn Aḥmad, who cites Abū Nuʿaym al-Ḥāfiẓ, who heard ʿAbd Allāh ibn Muḥammad ibn Jaʿfar, who read aloud to Musabbiḥ ibn Ḥātim al-ʿUklī his report that he heard Ibrāhīm ibn Jaʿfar al-Marwazī report: **92.6**

[Al-Marwazī:] Aḥmad ibn Ḥanbal appeared to me in a dream walking with a swagger. I asked him why he was walking that way and he said, "This is how servants walk in Paradise."

أخبرنا المحمّدان: ابن عبد الملك وابن ناصر قالا: أخبرنا أحمد بن الحسن الشاهد، وأخبرنا عليّ بن محمّد بن حَسُّون ٧٩٢
قال: أخبرنا المبارك بن عبد الجبّار قالا: أخبرنا عبد العزيز بن عليّ الطحّان قال: حدثنا محمّد بن أحمد الحافظ قال: حدثنا محمّد بن الحسين الحارثي قال:

حدثنا أبو[1] بكر المَرُّوذي قال: رأيتُ أحمد بن حنبل في النوم كأنّه في روضة وعليه حُلّتان خضراوان وعلى رأسه تاج من النور وإذا هو يمشي مشية لم أكن أعرفها.

فقلتُ: يا أحمد ما هذه المشية التي لا أعرفها لك؟

فقال: هذه[2] مشية الخدام في دار السلام.

فقلت له: ما هذا التاج الذي أراه على رأسك؟

فقال: إن ربّي عزّ وجلّ وقفني فحاسبني حساباً يسيراً وكساني وحَباني وقرّبني وأباحني النظر إليه وتوّجني بهذا التاج وقال لي: يا أحمد هذا تاج الوقار توّجتك به كما قلت القرآن كلامي غير مخلوق.

أخبرنا المحمّدان: ابن ناصر وابن عبد الباقي قالا: أخبرنا أبو الفضل الحداد قال: أخبرنا أبو نُعَيم الحافظ قال: حدثنا ٨٩٢
أبو نصر الحنبلي قال: حدثنا عبد الله بن محمّد النَّهْرَواني قال: حدثنا أبو القاسم عبد الله بن القاسم القُرَشي قال:

سمعت المَرُّوذي يقول: رأيت أحمد بن حنبل في المنام وعليه حُلّتان خضراوان وفي رجليه نعلان من الذهب الأحمر شِراكهما من الزمرّد الأخضر وعلى رأسه تاج من النور مُرصّع بالجوهر فإذا هو يخطر في مشيته فقلت له: حبيبي يا أبا عبد الله ما هذه المشية التي لا أعرفها لك في دار الدنيا؟

قال: هذه مشية الخدام في دار السلام.

فقلت له: حبيبي ما هذا التاج الذي أراه على رأسك؟

قال: إنَّ الله عزّ وجلّ غفر لي وأدخلني الجنّة وحباني وكساني وتوّجني بيده وأباحني النظر إليه وقال لي: يا أحمد فعلتُ بك هذا لقولك القرآن كلامي غير مخلوق.

---

[1] من ها هنا تستأنف الصورة الضوئية من د. [2] ليس في هـ.

We cite the two Muḥammads, Ibn ʿAbd al-Malik and Ibn Nāṣir, who cite Aḥmad ibn al-Ḥasan al-Shāhid; and we cite ʿAlī ibn Muḥammad ibn Ḥassūn, who cites al-Mubārak ibn ʿAbd al-Jabbār, who, like Aḥmad ibn al-Ḥasan al-Shāhid, cites ʿAbd al-ʿAzīz ibn ʿAlī l-Ṭaḥḥān, who heard Muḥammad ibn Aḥmad al-Ḥāfiẓ report that he heard Muḥammad ibn al-Ḥusayn al-Ḥārithī report that he heard Abū Bakr al-Marrūdhī report: **92.7**

[Al-Marrūdhi:] I dreamed I saw Aḥmad ibn Ḥanbal in a garden. He was dressed in green with a crown of light on his head and walking in a way I had never seen him walking before.

"Aḥmad," I said, "what's this new stride of yours?"

"This is how servants walk in Paradise," he said.

"What's the crown I see on your head?"

"My Lord, mighty and glorious, stood me before Him, judged me lightly, dressed me in these clothes, honored me, drew me near, let me gaze upon Him, and crowned me with this crown, saying, 'Aḥmad, this is the crown of glory that you earned by saying that the Qur'an is My uncreated speech.'"

We cite the two Muḥammads, Ibn Nāṣir and Ibn ʿAbd al-Bāqī, who cite Abū l-Faḍl al-Ḥaddād, who cites Abū Nuʿaym al-Ḥāfiẓ, who heard Abū Naṣr al-Ḥanbalī report that he heard ʿAbd Allāh ibn Muḥammad al-Nahrawānī report that he heard Abū l-Qāsim ʿAbd Allāh ibn al-Qāsim al-Qurashī report that he heard al-Marrūdhī say: **92.8**

[Al-Marrūdhī:] Aḥmad ibn Ḥanbal appeared to me in a dream wearing two green garments, sandals of red gold with straps of emerald, and a crown of light studded with gems, strutting as he walked.

"Dear Abū ʿAbd Allāh!" I said. "I never saw you walking that way here on earth."

"This is how servants walk in Paradise," he said.

"What about the crown on your head?"

"God, mighty and glorious, has forgiven me, admitted me to the Garden, honored me, dressed me, crowned me with His own hand, and allowed me to gaze upon Him, saying, 'Aḥmad, this is your reward for saying that the Qur'an is My uncreated speech.'"

٩٠٩٢ أخبرنا المحمّدان: ابن ناصر وابن عبد الباقي قالا: أخبرنا حمد بن أحمد قال: أخبرنا أبو نُعَيم الحافظ قال: أخبرني محمّد بن عبد الله الرازي في كتابه قال: سمعت أبا القاسم أحمد بن محمد السائح قال:

حدثني أبو عبد الله محمّد بن خُزَيْمة بالإسكندرية قال: لمّا مات أحمد بن حنبل اغتممت غمّاً شديداً فبتّ من ليلتي فرأيته في المنام وهو يتبختر في مشيته فقلتُ له: يا أبا عبد الله أي مشية هذه؟

فقال: مشية الخدام في دار السلام.

فقلتُ: ما فعل الله بك؟

قال: غفر لي وتوّجني وألبسني نعلَين من ذهب وقال لي: يا أحمد هذا بقولك القرآن كلامي.

ثم قال لي: يا أحمد ادْعُني بتلك الدعوات التي بلغَتْك عن سفيان الثوري كنْتَ تدعو بهن في دار الدنيا.

فقلت: يا ربّ كل شيء بقدرتك على كلّ شيء، لا تسألني عن شيء واغفر لي كلّ شيء.

فقال لي: يا أحمد هذه الجنة فقم ادخل إليها.

فدخلت فإذا أنا بسُفيان الثوري وله جَناحان أخضران يطير بهما من نخلة إلى نخلة وهو يقول: ﴿الحَمْدُ لله الَّذِي صَدَقَنَا وَعْدَهُ وَأَوْرَثَنَا الأَرْضَ نَتَبَوَّأُ مِنَ الجَنَّةِ حَيْثُ نَشَاءُ فَنِعْمَ أَجْرُ العَامِلِينَ﴾.

قال: فقلتُ: ما فعل عبد الوهاب الورّاق؟

فقال: تركتُه في بحر من نور في زلال من نور يزور ربّه الملك الغفور.

فقلت له: ما فعل بِشْر؟

فقال لي: بَخٍ بَخٍ ومَن مثل بشر؟ تركته بين يدي الجليل وبين يديه مائدة من الطعام والجليل جلّ جلاله مُقبل عليه يقول له: كُلْ يا مَنْ لم يأكل واشرب يا من لم يشرب وانعم يا من لم ينعم،[1] أو كما قال.

---

[1] د: يتنعم.

We cite the two Muḥammads, Ibn Nāṣir and Ibn ʿAbd al-Bāqī, who cite Ḥamd ibn Aḥmad, who cites Abū Nuʿaym al-Ḥāfiẓ, who cites the document of Muḥammad ibn ʿAbd Allāh al-Rāzī, who heard Abū l-Qāsim Aḥmad ibn Muḥammad al-Sāʾiḥ say that Abū ʿAbd Allāh Muḥammad ibn Khuzaymah reported in Alexandria: **92.9**

[Ibn Khuzaymah:] When Aḥmad ibn Ḥanbal died I was grief-stricken. That night he appeared to me in a dream. He was swaggering as he walked. I asked him why he was walking that way and he said, "This is how servants walk in Paradise."

"And how did you fare?"

"God forgave me, crowned me, and gave me sandals of gold, saying, 'Aḥmad, this is your reward for saying that the Qurʾan is My speech.'

"Then He said, 'Aḥmad, call upon Me with those prayers you learned from Sufyān al-Thawrī and[216] used to recite on earth.'

"So I said, 'Lord of all things! By your power over all things, hold me accountable for nothing, and forgive me for everything.'

"'Aḥmad, this is the Garden. Rise, and enter.'

"I went into the Garden, and there was Sufyān al-Thawrī. He had wings and he was flying from one palm tree to another, saying, «Praise be to God who has fulfilled His promise to us and made us the inheritors of this land, letting us settle in the Garden wherever we want. How excellent is the reward of those who labor!»"[217]

I[218] asked him how ʿAbd al-Wahhāb al-Warrāq had fared.

"I left him swimming in a sea of light, in pure water made of light, visiting his Lord."

"What about Bishr?"

"Fortunate Bishr!" said Sufyān. "Who could match him? I left him in the presence of the Glorious One, sitting at a laden table, with the Glorious One addressing him directly, saying 'Eat, you who never ate; drink, you who never drank; revel, you who never did,' or words to that effect."

١٠،٩٢ أخبرنا محمد بن ناصر قال: أنبأنا المؤتمن بن أحمد قال: أخبرنا محمد بن عليّ بن محمد الفقيه قال: أخبرنا أبو إسماعيل محمد بن عبد الرحمن الحداد قال: حدثنا أبو عبد الله محمد بن خُفيف الصوفي قال: حدثنا أبو القاسم القصري قال: سمعتُ ابن خُزيمة بالإسكندرية يقول: لمّا مات أحمد بن حنبل اغتممتُ غمّاً شديداً فبتّ من ليلتي فرأيته في النوم وهو يتبختر في مشيته فقلتُ: يا أبا عبد الله ما هذه المشية؟

قال: مشية الخدام في دار السلام.

فقلت له: ما فعل الله بك؟

فقال: غفر لي وتوّجني وألبسني نعلَين من ذهب وقال لي: يا أحمد هذا بقولك القرآن كلامي.

ثم قال لي: يا أحمد لِمَ كتبتَ عن جرير بن عثمان؟

فقلتُ: يارب كان ثِقة.

فقال: صدقت ولكنه كان يُبغض علياً أَبغضه الله.

ثم قال لي: يا أحمد ادعني بتلكَ الدعوات التي بلغتكَ عن سُفيان الثوري كنتَ تدعو بها[١] في دار الدنيا.

فقلت: ياربّ كل شيء.

فقال: هيه!

فقلت: بقدرتك على كل شيء.

فقال: صدقت.

فقلت: لا تسألني عن شيء واغفر لي كل شيء.

فقال: يا أحمد هذه الجنّة فادخل إليها.

فدخلتُ فإذا أنا بسفيان الثوري وله جناحان أخضران يطير بهما من نخلة إلى نخلة وهو يقول: ﴿الحمدُ لله الّذي صَدَقنا وَعْدَهُ وأَوْرثَنا الأَرضَ نَتَبوَّأُ من الجنَّة حيثُ نَشَاءُ فَنِعْمَ أَجْرُ العاملينَ﴾.

---

١ كنتَ تدعو بها: ليس في هـ.

We cite Muḥammad ibn Nāṣir, who was informed by al-Mu'taman ibn Aḥmad, who cites Muḥammad ibn 'Alī ibn Muḥammad al-Faqīh, who cites Abū Ismā'īl Muḥammad ibn 'Abd al-Raḥmān al-Ḥaddād, who heard Abū 'Abd Allāh Muḥammad ibn Khufayf al-Ṣūfī report that he heard Abū l-Qāsim al-Qaṣrī say that he heard Ibn Khuzaymah say in Alexandria: **92.10**

[Ibn Khuzaymah:] When Aḥmad ibn Ḥanbal died I was grief-stricken. That night he appeared to me in a dream. He was swaggering as he walked. I asked him why he was walking that way and he said, "This is how servants walk in Paradise."

"And how did you fare?"

"God forgave me, crowned me, and gave me sandals of gold, saying, 'Aḥmad, this is your reward for saying that the Qur'an is My speech.' Then He asked, 'Aḥmad, why did you write down reports via Jarīr ibn 'Uthmān?' I said he was trustworthy. 'True,' said God, 'but he hated 'Alī, God curse him!'[219]

"Then He said, 'Aḥmad, pray to me using those prayers you learned from Sufyān al-Thawrī and used to recite on earth.'

"So I said, 'Lord of all things!'

"'Go on.'

"'By Your power over all things.'

"'Go on.'

"'Hold me accountable for nothing, and forgive me for everything.'

"'Aḥmad, this is the Garden. Rise, and enter.'

"I went into the Garden, and there was Sufyān al-Thawrī. He had wings and he was flying from one palm tree to another, saying, «Praise be to God who has fulfilled His promise to us and made us the inheritors of this land, letting us settle in the Garden wherever we want. How excellent is the reward of those who labor!»"[220]

فقلت له: فما فعل عبد الوهّاب الورّاق؟

فقال: تركتُه في بحر من نور في زلال من نور يرى ربّه الملك الغفور.

فقلت له: فما فعل بشر، يعني الحافي.

فقال لي: بخ بخ ومن مثل بشر؟ تركته بين يدي الجليل وبين يديه مائدة من الطعام والجليل مُقبل عليه وهو يقول: كُلْ يا من لم يأكل واشرب يا من لم يشرب وانعم يا من لم ينعم.

قال: فأصبحت فتصدقت بعشرة آلاف درهم، أو كما قال.

قلت: وقد رُويت لنا هذه القصة من طريق آخر. ١١،٩٢

فأخبرنا المبارك بن عليّ قال: أخبرنا سعد الله بن عليّ بن أيّوب قال: أخبرنا هنّاد بن إبراهيم قال: أخبرنا أحمد ابن عمر بن الحسن قال: حدثنا أحمد بن الحسن بن أحمد التِكْريتي قال: حدثنا أبو بكر التيمي قال:

حدثنا عبد الله بن عُبَيد الله بن بَهْرام قال: رأيتُ أبا عبد الله أحمد بن حنبل في المنام وعليه نعلان من ذهب شراكهما من اللؤلؤ وهو يخطر فقلت: ما هذا المشية يا أبا عبد الله؟

قال: هذه مشية الخدّام في دار السلام.

فقلت: ما فعل الله بك؟

فقال: غفر لي وقال لي: ادخل الجنة بقولك القرآن كلامي غير مخلوق. ثم قال لي: يا أحمد ادعُني ومجّدْني بالدعوات التي بلغتك عن سُفيان الثوري.

فقلتُ: يا ربّ كلّ شيء ويا من عنده كلّ شيء ويا من بيده كلّ شيء هَبْ لي كل شيء ولا تسألني عن شيء.

فدخلتُ الجنّة فرأيتُ سُفيان الثوري وله جناحان أخضران وهو يطير من هذه النخلة إلى هذه النخلة ويأكل الرطب ويقرأ هذه الآية: ﴿الحمدُ لله الذي صَدَقنا وَعْدَهُ وأَورثَنا الأَرضَ نَتَبوّأُ من الجنّة حيثُ نَشَاءُ فَنِعمَ أَجْرُ العاملينَ﴾.

فقلت له: ما فعل بشر الحافي؟

I asked him how ʿAbd al-Wahhāb al-Warrāq had fared.

"I left him swimming in a sea of light, in pure water made of light, visiting his merciful King and Lord."

"What about Bishr?" I asked, meaning Bishr the Barefoot.

"Fortunate Bishr!' he replied. "Who could match him? I left him in the presence of the Glorious One, sitting at a laden table, with the Glorious One addressing him directly, saying 'Eat, you who never ate; drink, you who never drank; revel, you who never did.'"

Then I woke up and gave away ten thousand dirhams—or some such amount—in charity.

[The author:] I have heard this story from another set of authorities, as follows. **92.11**

We cite al-Mubārak ibn ʿAlī, who cites Saʿd Allāh ibn ʿAlī ibn Ayyūb, who cites Hannād ibn Ibrāhīm, who cites Aḥmad ibn ʿUmar ibn al-Ḥasan, who heard Aḥmad ibn al-Ḥasan ibn Aḥmad al-Tikrītī report that he heard Abū Bakr al-Tamīmī report that he heard ʿAbd Allāh ibn ʿUbayd Allāh ibn Bahrām say:

[ʿAbd Allāh ibn ʿUbayd Allāh ibn Bahrām:]

Aḥmad ibn Ḥanbal appeared to me in a dream dressed in green, wearing sandals of gold with straps of pearl, and strutting as he walked.

"What's this stride of yours?"

"This is how servants walk in Paradise," he said.

"And how did you fare?"

"God forgave me and admitted me to the Garden for saying that the Qur'an is His uncreated speech. Then He said, 'Aḥmad, call upon Me and glorify Me with those prayers you learned from Sufyān al-Thawrī.'

"So I said, 'Lord of all things! By Your power over all things, hold me accountable for nothing, and forgive me for everything.'

"Then I went into the Garden and there was Sufyān al-Thawrī. He had green wings and he was flying from one palm tree to another eating fresh dates and reciting, «Praise be to God who has fulfilled His promise to us and made us the inheritors of this land, letting us settle in the Garden wherever we want. How excellent is the reward of those who labor!»"[221]

I asked him how Bishr had fared.

قال لي : بَخٍ بخ من مثل بشر ؟ تركته بين يدي الله وبين يديه مائدة وهو يقول له: كل يا من لم يأكل واشرب يا من لم يشرب وانعم يا من لم ينعم .

١٢،٩٢ قلت: وقد رُويت من طريق آخر .

أخبرنا محمد بن ناصر قال: أنبأنا أبو عليّ الحسن بن أحمد الفقيه قال: أخبرنا أبو إسحاق إبراهيم بن عمر بن أحمد البرمكي قال: وجدت في كتاب أبي بخطّ يده: أخبرنا أبو بكر بن شاذان قال: أخبرنا أبو عيسى يحيى بن سهل العُكبَري[1] إجازةً قال: حدثنا أبو بكر السامَرّي القاسم بن الحسن قال: حدثنا عليّ بن محمد القَصْري قال:

حدثنا عبد الله بن عبد الرحمن قال: رأيت أحمد بن حنبل في المنام وعليه ثياب بيض وعلى رأسه تاج من الدرّ مُكلّل بالياقوت وفي رجليه نعلان من الذهب شراكهما من الزَّبَرْجَد فقلت: يا أحمد ما فعل الله بك؟ قال: خيرًا، كساني وجلاني[2] وقال هذا بقولك في القرآن كلامي.

قال: ثم قال لي: يا أحمد!

قلت: لبّيك.

قال: ادعُني بتلك الدعوات التي كان يدعوني بها سُفيان الثوري.

قلت: يا ربّ كل شيء.

فقال: صدقت.

قلتُ: بقدرتك على كل شيء اغفر لي كل شيء.

قال: قد غفرتُ لك.

قلت: ولا تسألني عن شيء.

قال: هذه الجنّة فادخل فاسرح فيها.

قال: فدخلت الجنة فرأيت سفيان الثوري له جناحان أخضران وهو يطير من نخلة إلى نخلة وهو يقول: ﴿الحمدُ لله الذي صَدَقنا وَعْدَهُ وأَورثَنا الأَرضَ نَتَبوَّأُ من الجنَّة حيثُ نَشَاءُ فَنِعْمَ أَجْرُ العاملينَ﴾ .

فقلت: يا أبا عبد الله ما فعل عبد الوهّاب الورّاق؟

---

١ هـ: العذري. ٢ ش، د: حلاني.

"Fortunate Bishr!" he replied. "Who could match him? I left him in the presence of God, sitting at a laden table, with God telling him 'Eat, you who never ate; drink, you who never drank; revel, you who never did.'"

I also have it according to another set of transmitters, as follows. **92.12**

We cite Muḥammad ibn Nāṣir, who was informed by Abū ʿAlī l-Ḥasan ibn Aḥmad al-Faqīh, who cites Abū Isḥāq Ibrāhīm ibn ʿUmar ibn Aḥmad al-Barmakī, who found written in his father's handwriting that he cites Abū Bakr ibn Shādhān, who cites—with his permission—Abū ʿĪsā Yaḥyā ibn Sahl al-ʿUkbarī, who heard Abū Bakr al-Sāmarrī l-Qāsim ibn al-Ḥasan report hearing ʿAlī ibn Muḥammad al-Qaṣrī report hearing ʿAbd Allāh ibn ʿAbd al-Raḥmān say:

[ʿAbd Allāh ibn ʿAbd al-Raḥmān:] Aḥmad ibn Ḥanbal appeared to me in a dream. He was dressed in white. On his head was a crown of pearls circled with rubies, and on his feet golden sandals with straps of emerald. I asked him how God had treated him.

"Well," he said. "He dressed me and adorned me, saying, 'This is your reward for saying what you said about My speech, the Qurʾan.' Then he said, 'Aḥmad!'

"'Here I am,' I answered.

"'Pray to Me with the same prayers that Sufyān al-Thawrī used to use.'

"'I said, "O Lord of all things!"'

"'Well spoken!' he said.

"'By Your power over all things,' I said, 'forgive me for everything. . .'

"'I forgive you!'

"'. . . and hold me accountable for nothing.'

"'This is the Garden,' He said. 'Enter, and roam as you will!'

"I entered the Garden and saw Sufyān al-Thawrī. He had green wings and was flying from one palm tree to another saying, «Praise be to God who has fulfilled His promise to us and made us the inheritors of this land, letting us settle in the Garden wherever we want. How excellent is the reward of those who labor!»"[222]

I asked him how ʿAbd al-Wahhāb al-Warrāq had fared.

قال: تركته في زلال من نور يسير في رحل الكافور إلى الملك الغفور.

قلت: ما فعل بشر بن الحارث؟

قال: تركته بين يدي الجليل وبين يديه مائدة يُراح ويغدي عليه بأطايب الطعام والجليل مقبل عليه يقول: كُلْ يا من لم يأكل واشرب يا من لم يشرب وانعم يا من لم ينعم.

قلت: ما فعلت مسكينة الطُّفاوِيّة؟

فإذا هي من ورائي تقول: هيهات هيهات، ذهبت المسكنة اليوم وجاء الغني.

أنبأنا محمد بن أبي منصور عن أبي نصر الساجي قال: سمعتُ أبا إسماعيل الأنصاري يقول: ١٣،٩٢

سمعتُ بعض أهل باخَرْز، وهي في نواحي نيسابور، يقول: رأيتُ كأنّ القيامة قد قامت وإذا برجل على فرس به من الحُسن ما الله به عليم ومُنادٍ ينادي: ألا لا يتقدّمَنَّ اليوم أحد! فقلتُ: من هذا؟ فقالوا: أحمد بن حنبل رحمه الله.

أخبرنا عبد الملك الكَرُوخي قال: أخبرنا عبد الله بن محمّد الأنصاري قال: أخبرنا الفضل بن أبي الفضل قال: ١٤،٩٢ حدثنا محمّد بن يعقوب الضَّبَعي قال: سمعتُ إبراهيم بن محمّد بن عبد المجيد[١] قال:

سمعتُ عبد الله بن أحمد بن حنبل يقول: رأيت أبي في المنام فقلت له: يا أبَةِ ما فعل الله بك؟

قال: وَقفني بين يديه وقال لي: يا أحمد بِسببي ضُربتَ وامتُحنتَ من أجلي، ها وجهي فقد أبحتك النظر إليّ.

أخبرنا ابن ناصر قال: أنبأنا الحسن بن أحمد الفقيه قال: أخبرنا هلال بن محمّد[٢] قال: حدثنا عثمان بن أحمد السمّاك ١٥،٩٢ قال: حدثنا محمد بن أحمد بن المهدي قال:

حدثنا أحمد بن محمّد الكندي قال: رأيتُ أحمد ابن حنبل في المنام فقلت: يا أبا عبد الله ما صنع الله بك؟

---

١ هـ: عبد الحميد. ٢ هـ: احمد.

“I left him in a pure torrent of light, riding on a saddle of camphor toward his merciful Lord.”

“What about Bishr ibn al-Ḥārith?”

“I left him in the presence of the Glorious One, sitting before a table where the tastiest of foods appear morning and evening. The Glorious One was telling him ‘Eat, you who never ate; drink, you who never drank; revel, you who never did.’”

“What about Miskīnah of Ṭūfāwah?” I asked. Then I saw her behind me.

“If only you knew!” she said. “There’s no wretchedness here, only riches.”[223]

We were informed by Muḥammad ibn Abī Manṣūr, citing Abū Naṣr al-Sājī, who heard Abū Ismāʿīl al-Anṣārī say: **92.13**

[Al-Anṣārī:] A man from Bākharz, which is in the region of Nishapur, told me, “I dreamed that it was Resurrection Day. I saw a man on a splendid horse and heard a crier calling out: ‘Let no one precede him this day!’

“I asked who the rider was and they told me it was Aḥmad ibn Ḥanbal.”

We cite ʿAbd al-Malik al-Karūkhī, who cites ʿAbd Allāh ibn Muḥammad al-Anṣārī, who cites al-Faḍl ibn Abī l-Faḍl, who heard Muḥammad ibn Muḥammad ibn Yaʿqūb al-Ḍubaʿī report that he heard Ibrāhīm ibn Muḥammad ibn ʿAbd al-Majīd say that he heard Aḥmad ibn Ḥanbal’s son ʿAbd Allāh say: **92.14**

[ʿAbd Allāh:] I dreamed I saw my father. I asked him how God had judged him.

“He stood me before Him and said, ‘Aḥmad, for My sake were you tried and flogged. Here: behold My countenance, which I grant you leave to see.’”

We cite Ibn Nāṣir, who was informed by al-Ḥasan ibn Aḥmad al-Faqīh, who cites Hilāl ibn Muḥammad, who heard ʿUthmān ibn Aḥmad al-Sammāk report that he heard Muḥammad ibn Aḥmad ibn al-Mahdī report that he heard Aḥmad ibn Muḥammad al-Kindī report: **92.15**

[Al-Kindī:] Aḥmad ibn Ḥanbal appeared to me in a dream and I asked him how God had judged him.

قال: غفر لي وقال لي: يا أحمد ضُربتَ فيّ؟
قال: قلت: نعم يا ربّ.
قال: هذا وجهي فانظر إليه فقد أبَحتُكَ النظر إليه.

١٦،٩٢ أخبرنا عبد الرحمن بن محمّد القزاز قال: أخبرنا أحمد بن عليّ بن ثابت قال: أخبرنا عليّ بن أحمد الرزّاز[١] قال: أخبرنا عثمان بن أحمد الدّقاق قال: حدثنا محمّد بن أحمد بن المهدي قال:

حدثنا أحمد بن محمّد الكندي قال: رأيتُ أحمد بن حنبل في المنام فقلت: يا أبا عبد الله ما صنع الله بك؟

قال: غفر لي ثم قال لي: يا أحمد ضُربت فيّ؟

قال: فقلت: نعم يا رب فقال: يا أحمد هذا وجهي فانظر إليه فقد أبحتُك النظر إليه.

١٧،٩٢ أخبرنا عبد الملك بن أبي القاسم قال: أخبرنا عبد الله بن محمّد الأنصاري قال: أخبرنا أبو يعقوب قال: أخبرنا الحسن بن حفص الأَنْدَلُسي قال: حدثنا أبو محمّد الحسين[٢] بن أحمد التُّسْتَري قال: حدثنا أبو محمّد[٣] بن الحسن ابن سهل قال: حدثنا أبو القاسم عبيد الله بن يعقوب المفسّر قال: حدثنا يعقوب بن يوسف الأنصاري قال: حدثنا أبي قال:

سمعت عليّ بن الموفّق يقول: رأيت كأنّي أُدخلت الجنّة فإذا أنا بثلاثة نفر: رجل قاعد على مائدة قد وكّل الله به ملكين فملكٌ يطعمه وملك يسقيه، وآخر واقف على باب الجنّة ينظر إلى وُجوه قوم فيُدخلهم الجنّة، وآخر واقف في وسط الجنّة شاخص ببصره إلى العرش ينظر إلى الربّ.

فجئت إلى رضوان فقلت: من هؤلاء؟

فقال: أمّا الأول فبشر الحافي، خرج من الدنيا وهو جائع عطشان، وأمّا الواقف في وسط الجنّة فمعروف الكرْخي، عبَد الله شوقًا منه للنظر فقد أُعطي، وأمّا الواقف

---

١ هـ: القزاز. ٢ د: ابن الحسين. ٣ هـ: أبو بكر.

"He forgave me," he said, "and asked me if it was for His sake that I had been flogged. I told Him it was, and He said, 'Here: behold My countenance, which I grant you leave to see.'"

We cite ʿAbd al-Raḥmān ibn Muḥammad al-Qazzāz, who cites Aḥmad ibn ʿAlī ibn Thābit, who cites ʿAlī ibn Aḥmad al-Razzāz, who cites ʿUthmān ibn Aḥmad al-Daqqāq, who heard Muḥammad ibn Aḥmad ibn al-Mahdī report that he heard Aḥmad ibn Muḥammad al-Kindī report: **92.16**

[Al-Kindī:] Aḥmad ibn Ḥanbal appeared to me in a dream and I asked him how God had judged him.

"He forgave me," he said, "and asked me if it was for His sake that I had been flogged. I told Him it was, and He said, 'Here: behold My countenance, which I grant you leave to see.'"

We cite ʿAbd al-Malik ibn Abī l-Qāsim, who cites ʿAbd Allāh ibn Muḥammad al-Anṣārī, who cites Abū Yaʿqūb, who cites al-Ḥasan ibn Ḥafṣ al-Andalūsī, who heard Abū Muḥammad al-Ḥusayn ibn Aḥmad al-Tustarī, who heard Abū Muḥammad ibn al-Ḥasan ibn Sahl report that he heard Abū l-Qāsim ʿUbayd Allāh ibn Yaʿqūb al-Mufassir report that he heard Yaʿqūb ibn Yūsuf al-Anṣārī report that he heard his father report that he heard ʿAlī ibn al-Muwaffaq say: **92.17**

[ʿAlī ibn al-Muwaffaq:] I dreamed I entered the Garden and there saw three men. The first was sitting at a table where God had assigned one angel to serve him food and another to pour him drink. The second was standing at the gate of the Garden with some other people, looking into their faces and letting them inside. And the third was standing in the middle of the Garden gazing at the Throne and looking at the Lord.

I went to Riḍwān and asked, "Who are those three?"

"The first one," he said, "is Bishr the Barefoot, who came here parched and starving. The one standing in the middle of the Garden is Maʿrūf al-Karkhī, who worshipped God because he desired to see Him, and now he can. And

على باب الجنّة فأحمد بن حنبل، قد أمره الجبّار أن ينظر إلى وجوه أَهل السنّة فيأخذ بأيديهم فيُدْخلهم الجنّة.

١٨،٩٢ أخبرنا عبد الملك بن أبي القاسم قال: أخبرنا عبد الله بن محمّد الأنصاري قال: أخبرنا عبد الرحمن بن محمّد بن محمّد ابن إبراهيم قال: أخبرنا عليّ بن القاسم الخَطّابي قال: حدثنا أبو نصر محمّد بن حَمْدُويه المُطّوِعي قال: حدثنا عبد الرحمن بن الحسين بن عليّ الفارسي قال: حدثنا الأسود بن يحيى البَرْدَعي قال:

أخبرنا أبو بكر أحمد بن محمد الرَمْلي قاضي دمشق قال: دخلت العراق فكتبت كتب أهلها وأهل الحجاز فمن كثرة خلافهما لم أدرِ بأيهما آخذ. فلمّا كان جوف الليل قمت فتوضّأت وصلّيت ركعتين وقلت: اللّهمّ اهدِني إلى ما تحبّ.

ثم أويتُ إلى فراشي فرأيت النبيّ صلّى الله عليه وسلّم فيما يرى النائم دخل من باب بني شَيْبَة وأسند ظهره إلى الكعبة فرأيت الشافعي وأحمد بن حنبل على يمين النبيّ صلّى الله عليه وسلّم والنبيّ يتبسّم إليهما وبشر المرِيسي من ناحية فقلت: يا رسول الله من كثرة اختلافهما لا أدري بأيّهما آخذ.

فأومأ إلى الشافعي وأحمد رضي الله عنهما فقال: ﴿أُولَئِكَ الذين آتَيْنَاهُمُ الكِتَابَ والْحُكْمَ والنُّبُوَّةَ﴾ ثم أومأ إلى بشر فقال: ﴿فإن يَكْفُرْ بِهَا هؤلاءِ فَقد وكَّلْنَا بِهَا قومًا ليسوا بها بكافرِينَ * أُولئك الذين هَدى الله فَبِهُدَاهم اقْتَدِه﴾.

١٩،٩٢ أخبرنا أبو منصور عبد الرحمن بن محمّد القزاز قال: أخبرنا أحمد بن عليّ بن ثابت قال: أخبرنا أحمد بن محمّد بن عبد الله الكاتب قال: أخبرنا أبو القاسم عبد الله بن الحسن بن سليمان المقرئ قال: حدثني خالي محمّد بن[1] أحمد قال: حدثنا هارون بن موسى بن زياد قال: حدثني محمد بن أبي الوَرْد قال:

سمعت يحيى الجلاء[2] أو عليّ بن الموفّق قال: ناظرتُ قومًا من الواقِفة أيّام المحنة فنالوني بما أكره وصرت إلى منزلي وأنا مغموم بذلك فقدّمت إليّ امرأتي عشاء فقلت

---

١ خالي محمّد بن: ليس في د. ٢ هـ: الخلال.

the one standing at the gate is Aḥmad ibn Ḥanbal. God has commanded him to look into the faces of the Sunnis, take them by the hand, and bring them inside."

We cite ʿAbd al-Malik ibn Abī l-Qāsim, who cites ʿAbd Allāh ibn Muḥammad al-Anṣārī, who cites ʿAbd al-Raḥmān ibn Muḥammad ibn Muḥammad ibn Ibrāhīm, who cites ʿAlī ibn al-Qāsim al-Khaṭṭābī, who heard Abū Naṣr Muḥammad ibn Ḥamduwayh al-Muṭṭawwiʿī report that he heard ʿAbd al-Raḥmān ibn al-Ḥusayn ibn ʿAlī l-Fārisī report that he heard al-Aswad ibn Yaḥyā l-Bardaʿī report that he heard the judge of Damascus, Abū Bakr Aḥmad ibn Muḥammad al-Ramlī, say: **92.18**

[Al-Ramlī:] I traveled to Iraq and copied what the Iraqis and the Hijazis had written, but found their views so different that I couldn't choose which school to follow. Late one night, I got up, performed my ablutions, prayed two cycles, and asked God to guide me as He wished. Then I went to bed and dreamed of the Prophet. I saw him march through the Gate of the Banū Shaybah and sit down with his back resting on the Kaʿbah. He was smiling at al-Shāfiʿī and Aḥmad ibn Ḥanbal, who were on his right. Off to the other side was al-Marīsī.

I said, "Emissary of God! They're so divergent I don't know which to follow."

Pointing to al-Shāfiʿī and Aḥmad, he recited «Those are the ones to whom We gave the Scripture, wisdom, and prophethood.»[224] Then, gesturing at al-Marīsī, he recited «If these people reject it, We shall entrust it to a people who will never refuse to acknowledge it. Those were the people whom God guided, so follow their guidance.»[225]

We cite Abū Manṣūr ʿAbd al-Raḥmān ibn Muḥammad al-Qazzāz, who cites Aḥmad ibn ʿAlī ibn Thābit, who cites Aḥmad ibn Muḥammad ibn ʿAbd Allāh al-Kātib, who cites Abū l-Qāsim ʿAbd Allāh ibn al-Ḥasan ibn Sulaymān al-Muqriʾ, who heard his maternal uncle Muḥammad ibn Aḥmad report that he heard Hārūn ibn Mūsā ibn Ziyād, who heard Muḥammad ibn Abī l-Ward report that he heard Yaḥyā l-Jallāʾ or ʿAlī ibn al-Muwaffaq say: **92.19**

[Yaḥyā l-Jallāʾ or ʿAlī ibn al-Muwaffaq:] At one point during the Inquisition, I debated a group of Stoppers, who trounced me. I went home heartsick. My wife put out some dinner, but I told her I wasn't eating, and she took it away. Then I went to bed and dreamed I saw the Prophet coming into

لها: لست آكل، فرفعته. ونمت فرأيت النبيّ صلّى الله عليه وسلّم في النوم داخل المسجد وفي المسجد حلقتان إحداهما فيها أحمد بن حنبل وأصحابه والأُخرى فيها ابنُ أبي دُؤاد وأصحابه فوقف بين الحلقتين وأشار بيده وقال: ﴿فإن يَكفُر بها هَوُلاءِ﴾ وأشار على حلقة ابن أبي دؤاد ﴿فقد وَكّلْنا بها قوماً ليسوا بها بِكافرين﴾ وأشار إلى الحلقة التي فيها أحمد بن حنبل.

٢٠،٩٢ أخبرنا إسماعيل بن أحمد ومحمد بن عبد الباقي قالا: أخبرنا حمد بن أحمد قال: أخبرنا أبو نُعيم أحمد بن عبد الله قال: حدثنا الحسين بن محمّد قال: حدثنا عمر بن الحسن القاضي قال: حدثني هارون بن يوسف قال: حدثنا حَبَش بن أبي الوَرْد العابد قال:

سمعتُ يحيى الجلاّء وكان من أفاضل الناس قال: رأيت النبيّ صلّى الله عليه وسلّم في المنام واقفاً في صينيّة الكرخ وابن أبي دؤاد جالس عن يسرته وأحمد بن حنبل جالس عن يمينه فالتفت النبيّ صلى الله عليه وسلم وأشار إلى ابن أبي دؤاد فقال: ﴿فإنْ يَكفُر بها هؤلاءِ فَقد وَكّلنا بها قوماً لَيسوا بها بكافرين﴾ وأشار إلى أحمد بن حنبل.

قلت: حبش لقب لمحمّد بن أبي الورد.

٢١،٩٢ أخبرنا إسماعيل بن أحمد ومحمد بن أبي القاسم قالا: أخبرنا حمد بن أحمد قال: أخبرنا أحمد بن عبد الله الحافظ قال: حدثنا ظفر بن أحمد قال: حدثنا عبد الله بن أحمد بن حَمْدُوَيه قال: حدثنا عبد الله بن القاسم القُرَشي قال: حدثنا محمّد بن إسحاق القاشاني قال:

حدثنا إسحاق بن حكيم قال: رأيتُ أحمد بن حنبل في المنام فإذا بين كتفَيه سطران مكتوبان من نور كأنّهما بحبر: ﴿فَسَيَكْفِيكَهُمُ الله وَهو السَّميعُ العَليم﴾.

٢٢،٩٢ أنبأنا محمّد بن أبي منصور الحافظ قال: أخبرنا المبارك بن عبد الجبّار قال: أخبرنا عبيد الله بن عمر بن شاهين قال: حدثني أبي قال: حدثنا أحمد بن محمّد بن يوسف الأصبهاني قال: حدثنا أحمد بن كثير القَزويني قال:

the mosque. There were two circles there: in one, Aḥmad ibn Ḥanbal and his associates had gathered, and in the other Ibn Abī Du'ād and his cronies. Standing between the two, the Prophet gestured toward Ibn Abī Duʿād and his circle and recited «If these people reject it. . . » and then, pointing to the circle of Aḥmad ibn Ḥanbal, recited «. . . We shall entrust it to a people who will never refuse to acknowledge it.»[226]

We cite Ismāʿīl ibn Aḥmad and Muḥammad ibn ʿAbd al-Bāqī, who cite Ḥamd ibn Aḥmad, who cites Abū Nuʿaym Aḥmad ibn ʿAbd Allāh, who heard al-Ḥusayn ibn Muḥammad report that he heard ʿUmar ibn al-Ḥasan al-Qāḍī report that he heard Hārūn ibn Yūsuf report that he heard Ḥabash ibn Abī l-Ward al-ʿĀbid report: **92.20**

[Ḥabash:] Yaḥyā l-Jallā', who was among the finest of men, said that the Prophet came to him in a dream standing in Ṣīnīyyat al-Karkh[227] with Ibn Abī Du'ād sitting on his left and Aḥmad ibn Ḥanbal on his right. Turning toward Ibn Abī Du'ād, the Prophet recited «If these people reject it. . . » Then, turning to Aḥmad ibn Ḥanbal, he recited «. . . We shall entrust it to a people who will never refuse to acknowledge it.»[228]

[The author:] Ḥabash was Muḥammad ibn Abī l-Ward's nickname.

We cite Ismāʿīl ibn Aḥmad and Muḥammad ibn Abī l-Qāsim, who cite Ḥamd ibn Aḥmad, who cites Aḥmad ibn ʿAbd Allāh al-Ḥāfiẓ, who heard Ẓafar ibn Aḥmad report that he heard ʿAbd Allāh ibn Aḥmad ibn Ḥamduwayh report that he heard ʿAbd Allāh ibn al-Qāsim al-Qurashī report that he heard Muḥammad ibn Isḥāq al-Qāshānī report that he heard Isḥāq ibn Ḥakīm report: **92.21**

[Isḥāq ibn Ḥakīm:] Aḥmad ibn Ḥanbal appeared to me in a dream. Written on his back, in light instead of ink, were the words «God will surely suffice to defend you against them, for He is All Hearing, All Knowing.»[229]

We were informed by Muḥammad ibn Abī Manṣūr al-Ḥāfiẓ who cites al-Mubārak ibn ʿAbd al-Jabbār, who cites ʿUbayd Allāh ibn ʿUmar ibn Shāhīn, who heard his father report **92.22**

سمعتُ عبد الله بن حُبَيق الأَنطاكي يقول: قدم علينا رجل من أهل العراق يُقال إنّه من أفضلهم فقال يوماً: رأيت رُؤيا وقد احتجتُ إلى أن تدلّني على رجل حسن العبارة، رأيت النبيّ صلى الله عليه وسلم في فضاء من الأرض وعنده نفر، فقلت لبعضهم: من هذا؟ قال: هذا محمّد صلى الله عليه وسلم.

فقلت: ما يصنع ها هنا؟

قال: ينتظر أمتّه أن يوافوا.

فقلت في منامي: لأَقعدنّ حتّى أنظر ما يكون من حاله في أُمته.

فبينا أنا كذلك واجتمع الناس وإذا مع رجل منهم قناة فظننتُ أنّه يريد أن يبعث بَعثاً فنظر صلى الله عليه وسلم فرأى قناة أطول من تلك القُنِيّ كُلّها فقال: من صاحب هذه القناة؟

قالوا: أحمد بن حنبل.

قال: فقال النبيّ صلى الله عليه وسلم: ائتوني به.

قال: فجيء به والقناة في يده فأخذها النبيّ صلى الله عليه وسلم فهزّها ثم ناولها إياه وقال له: اذهب فأنت أمير القوم.

ثمّ قال للناس: اتبعوه فهذا أميركم فاسمعوا له وأطيعوا.

قال عبد الله بن حُبيق: فقلتُ: هذه الرؤيا لا تحتاج إلى تعبير.

٢٣،٩٢ أخبرنا إسماعيل بن أحمد ومحمّد بن عبد الباقي قالا: أخبرنا أبو الفضل ابن أحمد الحداد قال: أخبرنا أحمد بن عبد الله الحافظ قال: حدثنا محمّد بن عليّ بن حُبيش قال: حدثنا عبد الله بن أبي داوود قال:

حدثنا عليّ بن إسماعيل السِّجِسْتاني قال: رأيت كأنّ القيامة قد قامت وكأنّ الناس جاؤوا إلى موضع عنده قنطرة لا يترك أحد يجوز حتى يجيء بخاتم ورجل ناحية[١] يختم للناس ويعطيهم فمن جاء بخاتم جاز، فقلتُ: من هذا الذي يعطي الناس الخواتيم؟ فقالوا: هذا أحمد بن حنبل.

---

١ هكذا في جميع النسخ.

that he heard Aḥmad ibn Muḥammad ibn Yūsuf al-Iṣfahānī report that he heard Aḥmad ibn Kathīr al-Qazwīnī report that he heard ʿAbd Allāh ibn Ḥubayq al-Anṭākī say:

[Al-Anṭākī:] We had a visit from an Iraqi who was reputed to be one of the most learned in that region. One day he asked me to direct him to a good interpreter who could explain a dream he had had.

"I saw the Prophet," he explained, "standing on a plain with some other people. I asked one of them who he was and he said, 'That's Muḥammad.'

"'What's he doing here?'

"'Waiting for his community to arrive.'

"In the dream I thought to myself, 'I'll stay here and see what happens.'

"After the people had gathered around, I noticed that one of them was carrying a spear, as if intending to dispatch an expedition. The Prophet looked out and saw a spear taller than any of the others and asked whose it was.[230]

"'It belongs to Aḥmad ibn Ḥanbal.'

"'Bring him to me!'

"Aḥmad came forward, spear in hand. The Prophet took the spear, brandished it, and gave it back, saying, 'Go forth and lead these people!' Then he called out to the people, 'This is your leader. Follow him, heed him, and obey him!'"

"Your dream," I said to the man, "needs no explanation."

92.23 We cite Ismaʿīl ibn Aḥmad and Muḥammad ibn ʿAbd al-Bāqī, who cite Abū l-Faḍl ibn Aḥmad al-Ḥaddād, who cites Aḥmad ibn ʿAbd Allāh al-Ḥāfiẓ, who heard Muḥammad ibn ʿAlī ibn Ḥubaysh report that he heard ʿAbd Allāh ibn Abī Dāwūd report that he heard ʿAlī ibn Ismāʿīl al-Sijistānī report:

[Al-Sijistānī:] I dreamed it was Resurrection Day. The people were lined up at a bridge that no one could cross unless he had a stamp. Off to one side was a man making stamps with his seal-ring and handing them out. Whoever got one could cross the bridge. I asked who was making the stamps and they told me it was Aḥmad ibn Ḥanbal.

٢٤،٩٢ أخبرنا محمّد بن ناصر قال: أنبأنا الحسن بن أحمد وأنبأنا أحمد بن الحسن ابن البنّا قال: أخبرنا أبي قال: أخبرنا هلال بن محمّد الحفّار قال: حدثنا أبو القاسم عبد الله بن عبد الوهّاب الخُوارِزْمي قال:

سمعت عبد الرحمن بن يُونُس يقول: رأيت في المنام لما توفّي أحمد بن حنبل كأنّي قد دخلت الجنّة فقيل لي: أنت في جنة عدن.

فاستقبلني ثلاثة فوارس وبين أيديهم فارس بيده لواء فقلت: من هؤلاء؟

فقيل لي: الذي عن يمينه جبرائيل وعن يساره ميكائيل والأوسط أحمد بن حنبل وصاحب اللواء إسرافيل وإن الله تعالى أعطاه هذا اللواء وولّاه جنّة عدن لا يدخلها إلّا من أحبّه.

٢٥،٩٢ أخبرنا المحمّدان: ابن ناصر وابن عبد الباقي قالا: أخبرنا حمد بن أحمد قال: أخبرنا أحمد عبد الله الحافظ قال: حدثنا الحسين بن محمّد قال: حدثنا محمّد بن أحمد بن مَحْمُوَيْه قال: حدثنا أحمد بن عليّ بن سعيد القاضي قال: حدثنا أبو بكر بن أبي خَيْثَمَة قال:

حدثنا يحيى بن أَيُّوب المَقْدِسي قال: رأيت كأنّ النبيّ صلى الله عليه وسلم نائم وعليه ثوب مُغطى وأحمد ويحيى يَذُبّان عنه.

٢٦،٩٢ أخبرنا محمّد بن أبي منصور قال: أخبرنا أبو الحسين بن عبد الجبّار قال: أخبرنا محمّد بن عبد الواحد بن جعفر الحَرِيري قال: أخبرنا أبو عمر[1] بن حَيُّويه قال: حدثنا عبد الله بن محمّد بن إسحاق المروزي قال: سمعت أحمد بن منصور الرَّمادي يقول:

حدثني بعض أصحابنا، ولم يُسَمِّه، عن سهل بن أبي حليمة قال: كنّا على باب إسماعيل ابن عُلَيّة فرأيت أحمد بن حنبل في النوم يجرّ ثوبه فأوّلتُ ذلك العلمَ.

٢٧،٩٢ أخبرنا ابن ناصر قال: أخبرنا عبد القادر بن محمّد قال: أنبأنا البرمكي قال: أنبأنا عبد العزيز بن جعفر قال: حدثنا الخلّال قال: حدثنا محمّد بن أبي هارون قال:

---

١ د: أبو عمرو.

We cite Muḥammad ibn Nāṣir, who was informed by al-Ḥasan ibn Aḥmad, who was informed by Aḥmad ibn al-Ḥasan ibn al-Bannā, who cites his father, who cites Hilāl ibn Muḥammad al-Ḥaffār, who heard Abū l-Qāsim ʿAbd Allāh ibn ʿAbd al-Wahhāb al-Khuwārizmī report that he heard ʿAbd al-Raḥmān ibn Yūnus say: **92.24**

[Ibn Yūnus:] After Aḥmad ibn Ḥanbal died, I dreamed I was in the Garden. A voice said, "You're in the Garden of Eden." Then I saw three horsemen in front of me, with a fourth horsemen riding ahead with a banner. I asked who they were.

"The one on the right is Gabriel and the one on the left is Michael. The one in the middle is Aḥmad ibn Ḥanbal. The one with the banner is Isrāfīl. God has given him that banner and ordered him to admit to Eden only those who love Ibn Ḥanbal."[231]

We cite the two Muḥammads, Ibn Nāṣir and Ibn ʿAbd al-Bāqī, who cite Ḥamd ibn Aḥmad, who cites Aḥmad ʿAbd Allāh al-Ḥāfiẓ, who heard al-Ḥusayn ibn Muḥammad report that he heard Muḥammad ibn Aḥmad ibn Maḥmuwayh report that he heard the judge Aḥmad ibn ʿAlī ibn Saʿīd report that he heard Abū Bakr ibn Abī Khaythamah report that he heard Yaḥyā ibn Ayyūb al-Maqdisī report: **92.25**

[Al-Maqdisī:] In a dream I saw the Prophet lying asleep under a garment with Aḥmad and Yaḥyā[232] whisking the flies away from him.

We cite Muḥammad ibn Abī Manṣūr, who cites Abū l-Ḥusayn ibn ʿAbd al-Jabbār, who cites Muḥammad ibn ʿAbd al-Wāḥid ibn Jaʿfar al-Ḥarīrī, who cites Abū ʿUmar ibn Ḥayyuwayh, who heard ʿAbd Allāh ibn Muḥammad ibn Isḥāq al-Marwazī report that he heard Aḥmad ibn Manṣūr al-Ramādī say that one of his associates—whom he did not name—reported hearing Sahl ibn Abī Ḥalīmah say: **92.26**

[Sahl ibn Abī Ḥalīmah:] We were camped out at Ismāʿīl ibn ʿUlayyah's gate when Aḥmad ibn Ḥanbal appeared to me in a dream, dragging his robe. I took the robe to mean knowledge.

We cite Ibn Nāṣir, who cites ʿAbd al-Qādir ibn Muḥammad, who was informed by al-Barmakī, who was informed by ʿAbd al-ʿAzīz ibn Jaʿfar, who heard al-Khallāl report that he heard Muḥammad ibn Abī Hārūn report that he heard Aḥmad ibn al-Ḥusayn ibn Muḥammad al-Shaybānī report: **92.27**

حدثنا أحمد بن الحسين بن محمد الشَّيْباني قال: كنتُ بعَسْقلان فرأيت كأنّي دخلت طرسوس فدخلت المسجد الجامع فنظرت عن يمين المحراب فإذا النبيّ صلى الله عليه وسلم جالس وأبو بكر عن يمينه وعمر عن يساره وبِلال واقف بين يديه عليهم ثياب خضر وعلى رؤوسهم مَناديل أحسن ما يكون. فقلت: السلام عليك يا رسول الله.

فقال لي: وعليك السلام يا بنيّ.

قلت: يا رسول الله حديثُ أبي الزُبير عن عبد الله بن عمرو أنّك قلت: يَكونُ في أُمّتي قَذفٌ ومَسخٌ.

قال: نعم وذلك في القَدَرية.

قلت: يا رسول الله لمن نُقلّد هذا الدين؟

قال: لهذا الرجل.

فأنظر عن يمين أبي بكر فإذا رجل مُستلقٍ على قفاه وقد مُدّ عليه ثوب أبيض فكشفت عن وجهه فإذا رجل جيد الجثّة عريض اللّحية أحمر الخدّين فلم أعرفه فقلتُ: يا رسول الله من هذا الرجل؟

قال: أما تعرفه؟

قلت: لا.

قال: هذا أبو عبد الله أحمد بن حنبل.

٢٨،٩٢ أخبرنا محمّد بن ناصر قال: أخبرنا الحسن بن أحمد بن البنّا، وأنبأنا أحمد ابن الحسن البنا قال أخبرنا أبي قال: أخبرنا إبراهيم بن عمر الفقيه قال: حدثنا محمّد بن إسماعيل الورّاق قال: حدثني أبو بكر محمّد بن عيسى بن عبد الكريم الطَرَسوسي قال: حدثنا أبو الحسن عليّ بن يعقوب[١] السندي البغدادي قال: حدثنا محمّد بن الحسن بن معاوية قال: حدثنا أبو شعيب صالح بن عمران الأنصاري قال:

---

١ في هـ فقط.

[Al-Shaybānī:] In Ascalon I dreamed I was in Tarsus. I went into the Friday mosque. I looked to the right of the niche and saw the Prophet sitting there with Abū Bakr on his right, ʿUmar on his left, and Bilāl in front, all in green, with beautiful cloths covering their heads.

"Peace be upon you, Emissary of God!" I said.

"And upon you be peace, my son."

"Emissary of God, in the Hadith of Abū l-Zubayr citing ʿAbd Allāh ibn ʿAmr, you said 'My community will be pelted and disfigured.'"[233]

"Yes. That refers to the proponents of free will."

"Emissary of God, to whom can we entrust this religion?"

"To this man here," he replied.

I looked to the right of Abū Bakr and saw a man lying on his back covered in a white garment. I lifted it away from his face and saw a well-built man with a wide beard and rosy cheeks. Not recognizing him, I asked, "Emissary of God, who is he?"

"Don't you recognize him?"

"No."

"That's Aḥmad ibn Ḥanbal."

We cite Muḥammad ibn Nāṣir, who cites al-Ḥasan ibn Aḥmad ibn al-Bannā; and we were **92.28**
informed by Aḥmad ibn al-Ḥasan al-Bannā, who cites his father, who cites Ibrāhīm ibn ʿUmar al-Faqīh, who heard Muḥammad ibn Ismāʿīl al-Warrāq report that he heard Abū Bakr Muḥammad ibn ʿĪsā ibn ʿAbd al-Karīm al-Ṭarasūsī report that he heard Abū l-Ḥasan ʿAlī ibn Yaʿqūb al-Sindī l-Baghdādī report that he heard Muḥammad ibn al-Ḥasan ibn Muʿāwiyah report that he heard Abū Shuʿayb Ṣāliḥ ibn ʿImrān al-Anṣārī report that he heard Maʿrūf's nephew Yaʿqūb report, citing Muḥammad ibn Isḥāq:

حدثني يعقوب ابن أخي معروف عن محمّد بن إسحاق قال: رأيت[1] القيامة قد قامت ورأيت ربّ العزّة عزّ وجلّ، أَسمعُ الكلام وأرى النور، فقال: ما تقول في القرآن؟

فقلت: كلامُك يا ربّ العالمين.

قال: من أخبرك؟

فقلت: أحمد بن حنبل.

فقال: الحمد لله. فدُعي أحمد فقال له: ما تقول في القرآن؟

فقال: كلامك يا رب العالمين.

قال: ومن أين علمت؟

قال: فصفح أحمد ورقتين فإذا في إحدى[2] الورقتين شُعْبة عن المُغِيرة وفي الأُخرى عَطاء عن ابن عبّاس، فدُعي شعبة فقال الله تعالى: ما تقول في القرآن؟

فقال: كلامك يا رب العالمين.

فقال: من أين علمت؟

قال: أخبرنا عطاء عن ابن عباس. فلم يُدعَ عطاء ودُعي ابن عباس فقال: ما تقول في القرآن؟

فقال: كلامك يا رب العالمين.

قال: من أين علمت؟

قال: أخبرنا محمّد رسول الله.

قال: فدعي النبيّ صلّى الله عليه وسلّم فقال الله عزّ وجلّ له: ما تقول في القرآن؟

قال: كلامك يا رب العالمين.

قال: ومن أخبرك؟

قال: جبريل عنك.

قال: صدقتَ وصدقوا.

---

١ تركي: رأيت كأن. ٢ في ش فقط.

[Muḥammad ibn Isḥāq:] I dreamed that Resurrection Day had come. I saw the Lord of Glory and I could hear Him speak and see His light. He asked me, "What do you believe about the Qur'an?"

"It is Your speech, o Lord of the Universe."

"Who told you so?"

"Aḥmad ibn Ḥanbal."

God praised Himself and summoned Aḥmad.

"What do you believe about the Qur'an?"

"It is Your speech, o Lord of the Universe."

"How do you know?"

Aḥmad turned over two sheets of paper. On one it said "Shuʿbah citing al-Mughīrah," and on the other "ʿAṭāʾ citing Ibn ʿAbbās."

God then summoned Shuʿbah and asked, "What do you believe about the Qur'an?"

"It is Your speech, o Lord of the Universe."

"How do you know?"

"We cite ʿAṭāʾ citing Ibn ʿAbbās."

ʿAṭāʾ was not summoned but Ibn ʿAbbās was.

"What do you believe about the Qur'an?"

"It is Your speech, o Lord of the Universe."

"How do you know?"

"We cite Muḥammad, the Emissary of God."

So the Prophet was summoned.

"What do you believe about the Qur'an?"

"It is Your speech, o Lord of the Universe."

"Who told you?"

"Gabriel, on Your authority."

"You have spoken the truth," said God, "and so have all of them."

أخبرنا عبد الملك بن أبي القاسم قال: أخبرنا عبد الله بن محمّد الأنصاري قال: أخبرنا غالب بن عليّ وأحمد بن حَمْزة ومنصور بن العباس قالوا: حدثنا محمّد بن الحسين قال: سمعت يعقوب بن أحمد بن يوسف الأَبْهَري قال: ٢٩،٩٢

سمعتُ أبا عبد الله الزُّبَيْري يقول: جاءني رجل من أهل البصرة يقال له أبو محمّد القرشي من أهل العلم والستر والصلاح فقال لي: يا أبا عبد الله أُخبرك برؤيا تُسرّ بها: رأيت النبيّ صلّى الله عليه وسلّم في النوم وعنده أبو بكر وعمر وعثمان وعلي إذ جاءه أربعة نفر فقرّبهم فتعجبتُ من تقريبه لهم.

فسألتُ بعض من يحضره عن النفر[1] فقال لي: هذا مالك وأحمد وإسحاق والشافعي.

فرأيت كأنّ النبيّ صلى الله عليه وسلم أخذ بيد مالك فأجلسه إلى جنب أبي بكر وأخذ بيد أحمد فأجلسه إلى جنب عمر وأخذ بيد إسحاق فأجلسه إلى جنب عثمان وأخذ بيد الشافعي فأجلسه إلى جنب علي.

قال الزبيري: فسألتُ بعض العلماء بالتعبير عن ذلك فقال: منزلة مالك من العلماء كمنزلة أبي بكر في الصحابة لم يختلف فيه أحد، ومنزلة أحمد كمنزلة عمر في صلابته وجلادته وأنّه لم تأخذه في الله لومة لائم كذلك كان أحمد بن حنبل احتمل الشدائد ولم يتكلم في القرآن إلّا بحقّ ولم يَضعف في المحن، ومنزلة إسحاق كمنزلة عثمان لقي إسحاق في بلدته[2] من أهل الإرجاء ما لقي حتّى فارق بلدته، ومنزلة الشافعي كمنزلة عليّ فإنّه كان أقضاهم كذلك كان الشافعي أعلم بالفقه والقضايا.

أخبرنا محمّد بن أبي منصور قال: أخبرنا عبد القادر بن محمّد بن يوسف قال: أخبرنا إبراهيم بن عمر البرمكي قال: أخبرنا عبيد الله بن عبد الرحمن الزُّهري قال: حدثنا عبد الله بن إسحاق المَدائني[3] قال: حدثنا أبو الفضل الورّاق قال: ٣٠،٩٢

حدثني أحمد بن هانئ عن صَدَقة المَقْبُري قال: كان في نفسي شيء على أحمد ابن حنبل. قال: فرأيت في النوم كأنّ النبيّ صلى الله عليه وسلم يمشي في طريق

---

١ عن النفر: ليس في د. ٢ في بلدته: ليس في هـ. ٣ د: المديني.

We cite ʿAbd al-Malik ibn Abī l-Qāsim, who cites ʿAbd Allāh ibn Muḥammad al-Anṣārī, who cites Ghālib ibn ʿAlī and Aḥmad ibn Ḥamzah and Manṣūr ibn al-ʿAbbās, all of whom heard Muḥammad ibn al-Ḥusayn report that he heard Yaʿqūb ibn Aḥmad ibn Yūsuf al-Abharī report that he heard Abū ʿAbd Allāh al-Zubayrī say: **92.29**

[Abū ʿAbd Allāh al-Zubayrī:] A man from Basra named Abū Muḥammad al-Qurashī, who was a man of learning, untarnished reputation, and rectitude, came to me and said, "I had a dream you'll enjoy hearing about; let me tell you. I saw the Prophet. With him were Abū Bakr, ʿUmar, ʿUthmān, and ʿAlī. Then four more people came up to him and he invited them to come closer. I was surprised, and so I asked someone who was there who they were.

"ʿMālik, Aḥmad, Isḥāq,[234] and al-Shāfiʿī.'

"Then I saw the Prophet take Mālik's hand and seat him next to Abū Bakr, take Aḥmad's hand and seat him next to ʿUmar, take Isḥāq's hand and seat him next to ʿUthmān, and take al-Shāfiʿī's hand and seat him next to ʿAlī."

I asked a dream interpreter about this and he told me: "Mālik has the same standing among men of learning that Abū Bakr does among the Companions: no one disputes his rank.

"Aḥmad has the same standing as ʿUmar: he's famous for being tough and unflinching and brooking no opposition when doing God's work. That's because Aḥmad never wavered from the truth about the Qurʾan and never succumbed to the Inquisition despite the brutality he had to endure.

"Isḥāq is like ʿUthmān: the Postponers caused him so much suffering that he had to leave his home town.

"And al-Shāfiʿī is like ʿAlī. Of them all, ʿAlī was the best judge; and al-Shāfiʿī was the most learned in the derivation of law and the judging of legal matters."

We cite Muḥammad ibn Abī Manṣūr, who cites ʿAbd al-Qādir ibn Muḥammad ibn Yūsuf, who cites Ibrāhīm ibn ʿUmar al-Barmakī, who cites ʿUbayd Allāh ibn ʿAbd al-Raḥmān al-Zuhrī, who heard ʿAbd Allāh ibn Isḥāq al-Madāʾinī report that he heard Abū l-Faḍl al-Warrāq report that he heard Aḥmad ibn Hāniʾ report, citing Ṣadaqah al-Maqburī: **92.30**

[Ṣadaqah:] I had always resented Aḥmad ibn Ḥanbal. Then I had a dream where I saw the Prophet walking down a road holding his hand in perfect amity. I tried to catch up to them but couldn't. When I woke up the resentment was gone. Then I dreamed I was among crowds of people at pilgrimage

وهو آخذ بيد أحمد بن حنبل وهما يمشيان على تُؤَدة و رفق وأنا خلفهما أُجهد نفسي أن ألحق بهما فما أقدر فلمّا استيقظت ذهب ما كان في نفسي ثم رأيت بعد كأنني في الموسم وكأنّ الناس مجتمعون فنادى منادٍ: الصلاة جامعة، فاجتمع الناس فنادى مناد: ليؤمّكم أحمد بن حنبل فإذا أحمد بن حنبل فصلّى بهم.

فكنت بعدُ إذا سُئِلت عن شيء قلت: عليكم بالإمام أحمد رحمه الله.

٣١،٩٢ أخبرنا إسماعيل بن أحمد ومحمّد بن عبد الباقي قالا: أخبرنا حمد بن أحمد قال: حدثنا أحمد بن عبد الله قال: حدثنا إبراهيم بن عبد الله قال: حدثنا محمّد بن إسحاق الثّقفي قال: سمعت يعقوب بن يوسف يقول: سمعت محمّد ابن عُبيد يقول:

قال صَدَقة: رأيتُ في النوم كأنّا بعَرَفة وكأنّ الناس ينتظرون الصلاة فقلت: ما لهم لا يصلّون؟ قال: ينتظرون الإمام. فجاء أحمد بن حنبل فصلّى بالناس.

قال محمّد: وكان صدقة يذهب إلى رأي الكوفيّين فكان بعد ذلك إذا سُئل عن شيء قال: سَلوا الإمام.

٣٢،٩٢ أخبرنا المحمّدان: ابن ناصر وابن عبد الباقي قالا: أخبرنا أبو الفضل الحدّاد قال: أخبرنا أبو نُعَيم الحافظ قال: حدثنا عمر بن أحمد بن عثمان قال: حدثنا حَمْزة بن الحسن قال:

حدثنا أحمد بن مَخْلَد الدعّاء قال: كان اليوم الذي مات فيه أحمد بن حنبل يوم الجمعة فانصرفت فلمّا أردت أن أنام قلت: اللّهمّ أرِنيه هذه الليلة في منامي. فرأيته كأنّه بين السماء والأرض على نجيب من نور وبيده خطام من نور فضربتُ بيدي إلى الخطام فأخذه وقال لي: ليس الخبر كالمعاينة، ليس الخبر كالمعاينة. فانتبهتُ.

٣٣،٩٢ أخبرنا محمّد بن أبي منصور قال: أخبرنا عبد القادر بن محمّد قال: أنبأنا إبراهيم بن عمر قال: أنبأنا عبد العزيز بن جعفر قال: أخبرنا أحمد بن محمد الخَلاّل[1] قال:

---

١ د: مكان (الخلال) في د: بن ابراهيم بن عمر.

time. Prayer was announced and everyone lined up. "Let Aḥmad lead the prayer!" said a voice. Then Aḥmad appeared and led the prayer. After that, whenever I was asked about anything, I would say, "Ask my exemplar Aḥmad ibn Ḥanbal."

We cite Ismāʿīl ibn Aḥmad and Muḥammad ibn ʿAbd al-Bāqī, who cite Ḥamd ibn Aḥmad, who heard Aḥmad ibn ʿAbd Allāh report that he heard Ibrāhīm ibn ʿAbd Allāh report that he heard Muḥammad ibn Isḥāq al-Thaqafī report that he heard Yaʿqūb ibn Yūsuf say that he heard Muḥammad ibn ʿUbayd say: **92.31**

[Muḥammad ibn ʿUbayd:] Ṣadaqah said, "I dreamed we were at ʿArafah. Everyone was waiting for the ritual prayer to start. I asked what they were waiting for and someone said, 'They're waiting for the prayer leader.' Then Aḥmad ibn Ḥanbal arrived and led the prayer."

This Ṣadaqah was inclined to the opinion of the Kufans,[235] but after the dream, whenever he was asked a question, he would say, "Ask the exemplar."

We cite the two Muḥammads, Ibn Nāṣir and Ibn ʿAbd al-Bāqī, who cite Abū l-Faḍl al-Ḥaddād, who cites Abū Nuʿaym al-Ḥāfiẓ, who heard ʿUmar ibn Aḥmad ibn ʿUthmān report that he heard Ḥamzah ibn al-Ḥasan report that he heard Aḥmad ibn Makhlad al-Daʿʿāʾ report: **92.32**

[Al-Daʿʿāʾ:] Ibn Ḥanbal died on a Friday. That night, I asked God to show him to me in a dream. Then I slept and dreamed of seeing him perched on a steed of light that hung between the heavens and the earth. He was holding it by a halter that was also made of light. I reached for the halter but he pulled it away, saying, "Hearing is one thing but seeing is another." He said it twice. Then I woke up.

We cite Muḥammad ibn Abī Manṣūr, who cites ʿAbd al-Qādir ibn Muḥammad, who was informed by Ibrāhīm ibn ʿUmar, who was informed by ʿAbd al-ʿAzīz ibn Jaʿfar, who cites Aḥmad ibn Muḥammad al-Khallāl, who heard Aḥmad ibn Ḥanbal's son ʿAbd Allāh report: **92.33**

حدثنا عبد الله بن أحمد بن حنبل قال: خرجت أريد العسكر فنزلت الخان الذي نزله أبي لمّا خرج إلى العسكر فجعلت أنظر إلى أثره فيه، وبتُّ في الخان فرأيته في النوم فقلت: خرجتُ في كذا وكذا فتراه يتمّ؟ فسكت هُنَيْهة فأعدت عليه. قال: لا.

فخرجت فأقمت شهرين فلم يتمّ، ثمّ قدمت وخرجت بعد السنة فنزلت في ذلك الخان وبتّ فيه فرأيته في المنام فقلت: يا أَبَةِ خرجت في كذا وكذا فتراه يتمّ؟

فسكت هنيهة ثمّ قال: نعم، أو أشار إليّ بنعم.

فخرجتُ فتمّ لنا ذلك الأمر.

قال الخلّال: وحدثنا محمّد قال: حدثني أبو نصر قال: ٣٤،٩٢

حدثني عليّ بن عبد الله الطبري[1] قال: رأيت أحمد بن حنبل في النوم وكأنّي أقول له: يا أبا عبد الله ألا ترى إلى ما نحن فيه من الاختلاف؟

فقال أحمد: إذا كان الله معك فلا يضرّك شيء.

أخبرنا ابن ناصر قال: أخبرنا أبو الغنائم محمّد بن محمّد بن المُهتدي بالله قال: أنبأنا عبد العزيز بن عليّ الأَزَجي قال: ٣٥،٩٢
أنبأنا عبد العزيز بن جعفر قال: حدثنا أبو بكر الخلال قال:

حدثنا عبد الله[2] بن هارون العُكْبَري قال: رأيتُ أحمد بن حنبل في النوم وحوله ناس كأنّها حلقة فقلتُ: يا أبا عبد الله احتجمتُ فما آكل؟

قال: كُل الرّمّان.

أخبرنا محمّد بن ناصر قال: أخبرنا أبو الحسين بن عبد الجبّار وأبو طالب بن محمّد قالا: أخبرنا إبراهيم بن عمر البرمكي ٣٦،٩٢
قال: أخبرنا أبو عبد الله ابن بَطّة قال: أخبرنا أبو بكر محمّد بن أيّوب بن المُعافَى العُكْبَري قال:

سمعتُ إبراهيم الحَرْبي يقول: رأيتُ أحمد بن حنبل في المنام قائمًا وعليه مُبطّنة حاسِرًا فقال لي: يا أبا إسحاق بلغني أنّك خرّجت فضائل النبيّ صلّى الله عليه وسلّم.

فقلت له: نعم.

---

١ هـ: الطبراني. ٢ هـ: عبد العزيز.

[ʿAbd Allāh:] I was on my way to Samarra and stayed at the inn where my father had stayed on his way to Samarra. I spent some time looking for traces of his presence. That night, he came to me in a dream. I told him that I was going to Samarra to accomplish something and asked if I would succeed. When he said nothing, I asked again, and he said "No." I ended up spending two months in Samarra but came home empty-handed.

A year later, I went again, and stayed at the same inn. Again I saw my father in a dream, and I asked him the same question. After a moment he said, "Yes," or made a gesture that meant yes. This time I got what I wanted.

Al-Khallāl said: we heard Muḥammad report that he heard Abū Naṣr report that he heard ʿAlī ibn ʿAbd Allāh al-Ṭabarī report: **92.34**

[Al-Ṭabarī:] I dreamed of seeing Aḥmad ibn Ḥanbal and telling him, "Have you seen how no one agrees with anyone any more?"

"So long as God is on your side," he said, "nothing can harm you."

We cite Ibn Nāṣir, who cites Abū l-Ghanāʾim Muḥammad ibn Muḥammad ibn al-Muhtadī bi-Lāh, who was informed by ʿAbd al-ʿAzīz ibn ʿAlī l-Azajī, who was informed by ʿAbd al-ʿAzīz ibn Jaʿfar, who heard Abū Bakr al-Khallāl report that he heard ʿAbd Allāh ibn Hārūn al-ʿUkbarī report: **92.35**

[Al-ʿUkbarī:] Aḥmad ibn Ḥanbal appeared to me in a dream with people around him as if it were a study circle.

"I just had a cupping," I told him. "What should I eat?"

"Pomegranates," he said.

We cite Muḥammad ibn Nāṣir, who cites Abū l-Ḥusayn ibn ʿAbd al-Jabbār and Abū Ṭālib ibn Muḥammad, who cite Ibrāhīm ibn ʿUmar al-Barmakī, who cites Abū ʿAbd Allāh ibn Baṭṭah, who cites Abū Bakr Muḥammad ibn Ayyūb ibn al-Muʿāfā l-ʿUkbarī, who heard Ibrāhīm al-Ḥarbī report: **92.36**

[Al-Ḥarbī:] Aḥmad appeared to me in a dream standing there wearing a lined outer garment but nothing on his head.

"I hear you've edited a work on the virtues of the Prophet," he said.

"I have."

فقال لي: أحسنتَ.

فقلت له: كيف لا أخرج فضائله ولولا هو لكُنَّا مجوساً؟ إنّما وُلدنا بين العجم ولم نُولد بين العرب.

قال: فقال لي: مجوس مجوس مجوس! ثم وقع على الحائط مغشياً عليه.

قلتُ: وقد رُويت لنا هذه الحكاية على وجه آخر على أنها يحتمل أن تكون غيرها فيكونا مَنامَيْن.

٣٧،٩٢ فأخبرنا محمّد بن أبي منصور قال: أخبرنا المبارك بن عبد الجبّار قال: أخبرنا عبيد الله بن عمر بن شاهين قال: حدثنا أبي قال: سمعت أبا بكر محمّد بن عبد الله الشافعي يقول:

سمعتُ إبراهيم الحَرْبي يقول: رأيت أحمد بن حنبل في النوم فقال لي: يا أبا إسحاق أيّ شيءٍ تصنّف؟

فقلت: دَلائل النبوة.

فقال: لولا هذا النبيّ لكنّا مجوساً.

٣٨،٩٢ أخبرنا محمّد بن أبي منصور قال: أخبرنا عبد القادر بن محمّد قال: أنبأنا إبراهيم بن عمر قال: أنبأنا عبد العزيز بن جعفر قال: أخبرنا أحمد بن محمّد الخلّال قال: حدثنا عبد الرحيم بن محمّد المُخَرِّمي[١] قال:

سمعتُ إسحاق بن إبراهيم لُولُو يقول: رأيت أحمد بن حنبل في النوم فقلت: يا أبا عبد الله أليس قد متَّ؟

قال: بلى.

قلتُ: فما فعل الله بك؟

قال: غفر لي ولكلّ من صلّى عليّ.

قلت: يا أبا عبد الله فقد كان فيهم أصحاب بِدع.

قال: أُولئك أُخِّروا.

---

١ هـ: المخزومي.

"Well done!" he said.

"How could I do otherwise? If not for him we'd be Magians. After all, we were born among non-Arabs, not Arabs."

"Magians!" he cried. "Magians! Magians!" Then he fell against the wall in a faint.

[The author:] I have encountered this story in another source, though it may actually be a different story, meaning that there were two different dreams.

We cite Muḥammad ibn Abī Manṣūr, who cites al-Mubārak ibn ʿAbd al-Jabbār, who cites **92.37**
ʿUbayd Allāh ibn ʿUmar ibn Shāhīn, who heard his father report that he heard Abū Bakr Muḥammad ibn ʿAbd Allāh al-Shāfiʿī report that he heard Ibrāhīm al-Ḥarbī say:

[Al-Ḥarbī:] I saw Aḥmad in a dream and he asked me what I was writing.

"*Proofs of Prophethood,*" I told him.

"If not for that Prophet," he said, "we'd be Magians."

We cite Muḥammad ibn Abī Manṣūr, who cites ʿAbd al-Qādir ibn Muḥammad, who **92.38**
was informed by Ibrāhīm ibn ʿUmar, who was informed by ʿAbd al-ʿAzīz ibn Jaʿfar, who cites Aḥmad ibn Muḥammad al-Khallāl, who heard ʿAbd al-Raḥīm ibn Muḥammad al-Mukharrimī report that he heard Isḥāq ibn Ibrāhīm Lūlū say:

[Lūlū:] Aḥmad appeared to me in a dream and I asked him, "Aren't you dead?"

"I am."

"How did God deal with you?"

"He's forgiven me and everyone who prayed over me."

"But some of them were innovators!"

"They were left till the end."

أخبرنا ابن ناصر قال: أنبأنا الحسن بن أحمد الفقيه قال: أخبرنا أبو إسحاق إبراهيم بن عمر البرمكي قال: ٣٩،٩٢
وجدتُ في كتاب أبي بخطّ يده: حدثنا أبو بكر بن شاذان قال: حدثنا أبو عيسى يحيى بن عبد الوهّاب بن أبي عصمة قال: حدثنا أبو الحسن عليّ بن الحسين قال:

سمعتُ بُنداراً محمّد[١] بن بشّار العَبْدي يقول: رأيتُ أحمد بن حنبل في المنام شبيه المُغضَب فقلتُ: يا أبا عبد الله أراك مُغضباً.

فقال: وكيف لا أغضب وجاءني مُنكر ونَكير يَسألان: من ربّك؟

فقلت لهما: ولمثلي يُقال من ربّك؟ فقالا لي: صدقتَ يا أبا عبد الله ولكن بهذا أُمرنا فاعذرنا.

أنبأنا ابن ناصر قال: أخبرنا يحيى بن عبد الوهّاب بن مَندة قال: أخبرنا عمّي قال: أخبرنا عليّ بن محمّد بن عليّ قال: ٤٠،٩٢
سمعت أبا الفرج الهِندِبائي يقول:

سمعت عبد الله بن أحمد يقول: رأيت أبي في المنام فقلت: ما فعل الله بك؟

قال: غفر لي.

قلت: جاءك منكر ونكير؟

قال: نعم، قالا لي: من ربك؟ قلت: سبحان الله، أما تستحيان مني؟

فقالا لي: يا أبا عبد الله اعذرنا بهذا أُمرنا.[٢]

أخبرنا محمّد بن أبي منصور قال: أخبرنا عبد القادر بن محمّد قال: أخبرنا إبراهيم بن عمر البرمكي قال: أخبرنا عبيد الله[٣] بن عبد الرحمن الزهري قال: ٤١،٩٢

حدثني بعض الشيوخ عن ابن الطَّلَمَوري قال: رأيت أبا عبد الله أحمد بن حنبل في النوم فقال لي: ألّا أدلّك على شيء ينفعك؟

قال: فقلت: نعم يا أبا عبد الله. فقال لي: من المحراب إلى القبر.

قال شيخنا عليّ بن عبيد الله الزاغوني: ٤٢،٩٢

---

١ د: بندار بن محمد. ٢ الخبر في ش فقط. ٣ هـ: عبد الله.

We cite Ibn Nāṣir, who was informed by al-Ḥasan ibn Aḥmad al-Faqīh, who cites Abū Isḥāq Ibrāhīm ibn ʿUmar al-Barmakī, who found in a book in his father's hand that he had heard Abū Bakr ibn Shādhān report that he heard Abū ʿIsā Yaḥyā ibn ʿAbd al-Wahhāb ibn Abī ʿIṣmah report that he heard Abū l-Ḥasan ʿAlī ibn al-Ḥusayn report that he heard Bundār Muḥammad ibn Bashshār al-ʿAbdī say: **92.39**

[Bundār:] Aḥmad appeared to me in a dream looking angry. I asked him why.

"How could I not be angry," he replied, "when Munkar and Nakīr came and asked me to name my Lord. 'Do you know who you're talking to?' I asked them.

"'We know,' they said. 'But it's our duty to ask, so forgive us!'"

We were informed by Ibn Nāṣir, who cites Yaḥyā ibn ʿAbd al-Wahhāb ibn Mandah, who cites his uncle, who cites ʿAlī ibn Muḥammad ibn ʿAlī, who heard Abū l-Faraj al-Hindibāʾī say that he heard Aḥmad's son ʿAbd Allāh say: **92.40**

[ʿAbd Allāh:] My father appeared to me in a dream and I asked how God had judged him.

"He forgave me," he said.

"What about Munkar and Nakīr?"

"They came and asked me to name my Lord. I said, 'Good heavens, aren't you ashamed to ask me that?' They said, 'Forgive us! It's our duty to ask.'"

We cite Muḥammad ibn Abī Manṣūr, who cites ʿAbd al-Qādir ibn Muḥammad, who cites Ibrāhīm ibn ʿUmar al-Barmakī, who cites ʿUbayd Allāh ibn ʿAbd al-Raḥmān al-Zuhrī, who heard an elder report, citing Ibn al-Ṭalmakhūrī: **92.41**

[Al-Ṭalmakhūrī:] Aḥmad ibn Ḥanbal appeared to me in a dream.

"May I tell you something useful?" he asked.

"Yes!"

He said: "From the niche to the grave."[236]

My teacher ʿAlī ibn ʿUbayd al-Zāghūnī said: **92.42**

رأيت في المنام كأنّي أمضي إلى قبر الإمام أحمد وإذا به جالس على قبره وهو شيخ كبير السنّ فقال لي: يا فلان قلّ[1] أنصارنا ومات أصحابنا. ثمّ قال لي: إذا أردتَ أن تُنصَر فإذا دعوت فقلْ: يا عظيم يا عظيمَ كلِّ عظيم، وادعُ بما شئت تُنصر.

٤٣،٩٢ حدثني أبو بكر بن مكارم بن أبي يَعْلَى الحَرْبي وكان شيخًا صالحًا قال: كان قد جاء في بعض السنين مطر كثير جداً قبل دخول رمضان بأيّام فنمتُ ليلة في رمضان فأريتُ[2] في منامي كأنّي قد جئت على عادتي إلى قبر الإمام أحمد بن حنبل أزوره فرأيت قبره قد التصق بالأرض حتى بقي بينه وبين الأرض مقدار ساق أو ساقين فقلت: إنّما تمّ هذا على قبر الإمام أحمد من كثرة الغيث.

فسمعته من القبر وهو يقول: لا بل هذا من هيبة الحقّ عزّ وجلّ لأنّه عزّ وجلّ قد زارني فسألته عن سرّ زيارته إياي في كلّ عام فقال عزّ وجلّ: يا أحمد لأنّك نَصرت كلامي فهو يُنشر ويُتلى في المحاريب.

فأقبلت على لحده أقبّله ثمّ قلت: يا سيّدي ما السرّ في أنّه لا يُقبَّل قبر إلا قبرك؟

فقال لي: يا بُنيّ ليس هذا كرامة لي ولكن هذا كرامة لرسول الله صلّى الله عليه وسلّم لأنّ معي شعرات من شعره صلّى الله عليه وسلّم، ألا ومن يحبّني لِمَ لا يزورني في شهر رمضان؟ ألا ومن يحبّني لِمَ لا يزورني في شهر رمضان؟[3]

---

١ هـ: قتل. ٢ هـ: رايت. ٣ بدل الثانية في د: قال ذلك مرتين.

[Al-Zāghūnī:] I dreamed of going to Aḥmad's tomb and seeing him sitting there on top of it. He looked like a very old man.

"Our friends are dead," he said, "and our allies few." Then he said, "Whenever you need help, say, 'Great One! Great One, greater than all who think themselves great!' Do that, and your prayers will be answered."

Abū Bakr ibn Makārim ibn Abī Yaʿlā l-Ḥarbī, who was a worthy elder, told me: **92.43**

[Abū Bakr:] One year, a few days before Ramadan, we had heavy rains. Later, during Ramadan, I went to sleep one night and dreamed I had gone as usual to visit Aḥmad ibn Ḥanbal's tomb. But it had sunk so deep into the ground that only a *sāq*[237] or two was left above ground.

"It must be the rain that did this," I thought.

"No," said Aḥmad from inside the tomb. "It was the terrifying presence of the One True God, mighty and glorious, who came to visit me. I asked Him why He came every year, and He said, 'Because you stood up for My speech, which is read aloud from every niche.'"

I bent toward his grave-shaft to kiss it, then asked him, "Why is yours the only grave that one can kiss?"

"Son," he said, "it's not out of respect for me, but for the Emissary of God. I have some of his hairs with me. Why don't those who care for me come visit me in Ramadan?"

He asked the question twice.

الباب الثالث والتسعون في ذكر المنامات التي رُئيت له

١،٠٩٣ أخبرنا عبد الملك بن أبي القاسم قال: أخبرنا عبد الله بن محمّد الأنصاري قال: أخبرنا غالب بن عليّ قال: أخبرنا محمّد بن الحسين قال: حدثنا محمّد بن عبد الله بن شاذان قال: سمعتُ أبا القاسم بن صَدَقة يقول: سمعتُ عليّ ابن عبد العزيز الطَّلْحي قال:

قال لي الرَّبيع: قال لي الشافعي: يا ربيع خُذ كتابي وامضِ به وسلِّمْه إلى أبي عبد الله أحمد بن حنبل وأْتني بالجَواب.

قال الربيع: فدخلت بغداد ومعي الكتاب فلِقيت أحمد بن حنبل صلاةَ الصبح فصلّيت معه الفجر فلمّا انفتل من المحراب[1] سلمتُ إليه الكتاب وقلت له: هذا كتاب أخيك الشافعي من مصر. فقال أحمد: نظرتَ فيه؟

قلتُ: لا.

فكسر أحمد الخاتم وقرأ الكتاب فتغرغرت عيناه بالدموع فقلتُ له: أي شيء فيه يا أبا عبد الله؟

فقال: يذكر أنّه رأى النبيّ صلّى الله عليه وسلّم في المنام فقال له: اكتُب إلى أبي عبد الله أحمد بن حنبل واقرأ عليه مني السلام وقُل: إنّك ستُمتحن وتُدعى إلى خلق القرآن فلا تُجبْهم يرفعْ الله لك عَلَماً إلى يوم القيامة.

قال الربيع: فقلتُ: البشارة.

فخلع قميصه الذي يلي جلده فدفعه إليّ فأخذته وخرجت إلى مصر وأخذت جواب الكتاب وسلّمته إلى الشافعي فقال لي: يا ربيع أي شيء الذي[2] دفع إليك؟

قلت: القميص الذي يلي جلده.

فقال لي الشافعي: ليس[3] نفجعك به ولكن بُلّه وادفع إلينا الماء حتّى أشركك فيه.

---

١ هـ: من صلاته. ٢ ليس في ش. ٣ هـ: لا.

Chapter 93: Dreams in Which He Was Mentioned

We cite ʿAbd al-Malik ibn Abī l-Qāsim, who cites ʿAbd Allāh ibn Muḥammad al-Anṣārī, who cites Ghālib ibn ʿAlī, who cites Muḥammad ibn al-Ḥusayn, who heard Muḥammad ibn ʿAbd Allāh ibn Shādhān report that he heard Abū l-Qāsim ibn Ṣadaqah say that he heard ʿAlī ibn ʿAbd al-ʿAzīz al-Ṭalḥī say that al-Rabīʿ told him: **93.1**

[Al-Rabīʿ:] Al-Shāfiʿī told me to take a letter he had written, deliver it to Aḥmad ibn Ḥanbal, and bring back his reply. When I reached Baghdad, I found Ibn Ḥanbal praying the dawn prayer and I joined him. As soon as he finished I handed him the letter, saying, "This is from your brother al-Shāfiʿī in Egypt."

"Have you read it?"

"No."

He broke the seal and read the letter, tears welling up in his eyes.

"What is it?"

"He says the Prophet came to him in a dream and told him to write to me and convey his greetings. I'm going to be tested and asked to call the Qur'an created, but if I don't give in, God will raise a banner in my honor that will fly until the Day of Resurrection."

"That's good news, then," I said. "What's my reward?"

Aḥmad removed the shirt he was wearing next to his skin and handed it to me. I took it, and his reply, and returned to Egypt. When I handed the letter to al-Shāfiʿī he asked what Aḥmad had given me.

"The shirt off his back," I said.

"I won't take it away from you," he said, "but soak it and give me the water so I can share in the blessing."

٢،٩٣ أخبرنا محمّد بن ناصر قال: أنبأنا أبو الحسن بن أحمد[١] قال: أخبرنا إبراهيم بن عمر[٢] البرمكي قال: وجدت في كتاب أبي قال: حدثنا أبو بكر أحمد بن شاذان قال: حدثنا أبو عيسى يحيى بن سهل العُكبري إجازة قال البرمكي: وكتبت من مَدرجة أبي إسحاق بن شَاقلا وقدم علينا فاستجزتُ منه، قالا: حدثنا أبو القاسم حمزة بن الحسن الهاشمي الشافعي وكان ثقة قال: حدثنا أبو بكر عبد الله بن محمّد النَّيسابوري قال:

حدثنا الربيع بن سليمان قال: كتب على يدي الشافعي كتاباً إلى أبي عبد الله أحمد ابن حنبل ثمّ قال لي: يا أبا سليمان انحدر بكتابي هذا إلى العراق ولا تقرأه.

فأخذتُ الكتاب وخرجت من مصر حتى قدمت العراق فوافيت مسجد أحمد بن حنبل فصادفته يصلّي الفجر فصلّيت معه وكنتُ لم أركع السنّة فقمتُ أركع عقيب الصلاة فجعل ينظر إليّ مليّاً حتى عرفني.

فلمّا سلّمت من صلاتي سلّمتُ عليه وأوصلت الكتاب إليه فجعل يسألني عن الشافعي طويلاً قبل أن ينظر في الكتاب ثم فضّه وقرأه حتى إذا بلغ موضعاً منه بكى وقال: أرجو الله تعالى أن يحقّق ما قاله الشافعي.

قلت: يا أبا عبد الله أي شيء قد كتب؟

قال: إنه يذكر في كتابه أنه رأى النبيّ صلى الله عليه وسلم في نومه وهو يقول له: يا ابن إدريس بشِّر هذا الفتى أبا عبد الله أحمد بن حنبل أنّه سيُمتحن في دين الله ويُدعى إلى أن يقول القرآن مخلوق فلا يفعلْ وأنّه سيُضرب بالسياط وأنّ الله عز وجل ينشر له بذلك عَلَماً لا ينطوي إلى يوم القيامة.

فقلتُ: بشارة، فأيّ شيء جائزتي عليها؟

وكان عليه ثوبان فنزع أحدهما فدفعه إليّ وكان ممّا يلي جلده وأعطاني جواب الكتاب فخرجتُ حتى قدمت على الشافعي فأخبرته بما جرى.

قال: فأين الثوب؟

قلتُ: هو ذا.

فقال: لا نبتاعه منك ولا نستهديك ولكن اغسِلْه وجئنا بمائه.

---

١ هـ: ابو عليّ الخلال. ٢ هـ: علي.

We cite Muḥammad ibn Nāṣir, who was informed by Abū ʿAlī l-Ḥasan ibn Aḥmad, who cites Ibrāhīm ibn ʿUmar al-Barmakī, who found in his father's notes that his father heard Abū Bakr Aḥmad ibn Shādhān report that he heard Abū ʿĪsā Yaḥyā ibn Sahl al-ʿUkbarī report, and repeat with his permission, that al-Barmakī said; and I copied from the folded strips of notes of Abū Isḥāq ibn Shāqlā—who came to us, and whose permission I asked—that he heard Abū l-Qāsim Ḥamzah ibn al-Ḥasan al-Hāshimī, who was reliable, say that he heard Abū Bakr ʿAbd Allāh ibn Muḥammad al-Naysābūrī report that he heard al-Rabīʿ ibn Sulaymān say: **93.2**

[Al-Rabīʿ:] Al-Shāfiʿī asked me to deliver a letter he had written to Aḥmad ibn Ḥanbal, saying, "Sulaymān, take this letter down to Iraq and don't read it."

I took the letter and left Egypt for Iraq. When I reached Ibn Ḥanbal's mosque, I found him praying the dawn prayer and I joined him. I hadn't prayed the usual number of cycles, so I continued praying after he had finished. It took him a moment to recognize me but he did. When I finished praying, I greeted him and handed him the letter. He spent a long time asking about al-Shāfiʿī before he even looked at the letter. Finally he broke the seal and began reading. At one point he burst into tears, saying, "I pray to God to do what al-Shāfiʿī says!"

"What did he say?" I asked.

"He says the Prophet came to him in a dream and said, 'Tell that young man Aḥmad ibn Ḥanbal that he'll be tried on account of God's religion and asked to say that the Qur'an is created. He should refuse. He'll be flogged, but God will unfurl a banner for him that will fly until the Day of Resurrection.'"

"That's good news, then," I said. "What's my reward?"

He was wearing two garments, one on top of the other. He took the under-garment off and handed it to me, then handed me a reply to the letter. I went back and told al-Shāfiʿī what had happened.

"Where's the garment?" he said.

"Right here."

"I won't try to buy it from you," he said, "or ask for it as a gift. But wash it and give me the water."

قال: فغسلتُه فحملت ماءه إليه فتركه في قِنّينة وكنت أراه في كلّ يوم يأخذ منه فيمسح على وجهه تبرّكًا بأحمد بن حنبل.

أخبرنا محمّد بن عبد الباقي قال: أخبرنا حمد بن أحمد قال: أخبرنا أبو نُعيم الحافظ قال: حدثنا أحمد بن جعفر بن حمدان قال: حدثنا عبد الله بن أحمد بن حنبل قال: ٣،٩٣

حدثني أبو جعفر محمّد بن الفرج قال: لمّا نزل بأحمد بن حنبل من الحبس والضرب ما نزل دخلتْ عليّ من ذلك مصيبة.

فأُتيت في منامي فقيل لي: أمّا ترضى أن يكون عند الله عزّ وجلّ بمنزلة أبي السوّار العدوي؟

فأتيتُ أبا عبد الله فأخبرته فاسترجع.

أخبرنا المحمّدان: ابن ناصر وابن عبد الباقي قالا: أخبرنا حمد بن أحمد قال: أخبرنا أحمد بن عبد الله الحافظ قال: حدثنا سليمان بن أحمد قال: حدثنا محمّد بن عَبْدوس بن كامل قال: ٤،٩٣

حدثنا محمّد بن الفرج أبو جَعْفَر جار أحمد بن حنبل قال: لمّا نزل بأحمد بن حنبل ما نزل من الحبس والضرب دخلتْ عليّ من ذلك مصيبة فأُتيت في منام فقيل لي: أما ترضى أن يكون أحمد بن حنبل عند الله تعالى بمنزلة أبي سوار العدوي أو لست تروي خبر أبي السوّار؟

قلت: بلى.

قيل: فإنه عند الله تعالى بتلك المنزلة.

قال أبو جعفر محمّد بن الفَرَج: ٥،٩٣

وحدثنا عليّ بن عاصم عن بِسْطام بن مسلم عن الحسن بن أبي الحسن قال: دعا بعض مُترفي هذه الأُمّة أبا السوّار العَدَوي فسأله عن شيء من أمر دينه فأجابه بما يعلم فلم يوافقه ذلك فقال: وإلا فأنت بريء من الإسلام.

قال: فإلى أي دين أفرّ؟

So I washed it and brought him the water. He put it in a bottle, and every day I'd see him take a little bit and dab it onto his face so he could share in Ibn Ḥanbal's blessing.

We cite Muḥammad ibn ʿAbd al-Bāqī, who cites Ḥamd ibn Aḥmad, who cites Abū Nuʿaym al-Ḥāfiẓ, who heard Aḥmad ibn Jaʿfar ibn Ḥamdān report that he heard ʿAbd Allāh ibn Aḥmad ibn Ḥanbal report that he heard Abū Jaʿfar Muḥammad ibn al-Faraj report: 93.3

[Ibn al-Faraj:] Ibn Ḥanbal's imprisonment and beating had a devastating effect on me. But then I dreamed I heard a voice say, "Aren't you glad that he'll have the same standing with God as Abū l-Sawwār al-ʿAdawī?"[238]

I found Aḥmad and told him about this. He protested: «We are of God, and to Him we return!»[239]

We cite the two Muḥammads, Ibn Nāṣir and Ibn ʿAbd al-Bāqī, who cite Ḥamd ibn Aḥmad, who cites Aḥmad ibn ʿAbd Allāh al-Ḥāfiẓ, who heard Sulaymān ibn Aḥmad report that he heard Muḥammad ibn ʿAbdūs ibn Kāmil report that he heard Aḥmad ibn Ḥanbal's neighbor Abū Jaʿfar Muḥammad ibn al-Faraj report: 93.4

[Ibn al-Faraj:] Ibn Ḥanbal's imprisonment and beating had a devastating effect on me. But then I dreamed I heard a voice say, "Aren't you glad to see Ibn Ḥanbal reach the same high standing with God as Abū Sawwār al-ʿAdawī, or don't you tell that story?"

"Of course I do!"

"Well, Aḥmad is there too."

Abū Jaʿfar Muḥammad ibn al-Faraj said that he heard ʿAlī ibn ʿĀṣim report, citing Bisṭām ibn Muslim, citing al-Ḥasan ibn Abī l-Ḥasan: 93.5

A dissolute member of the Muslim community summoned Abū l-Sawwār al-ʿAdawī and asked him a question about a religious matter.[240] Abū l-Sawwār gave the answer he thought was right, but the other man didn't like it, and said: "If you insist on that opinion, I declare you quit of Islam!"

"Which religion should I go to, then?"

قال: وإلا فامرأته طالق.

قال: فإلى من آوي في الليل؟

فضربه أربعين سوطاً.

قال أبو جعفر: فأتيت أبا عبد الله فأخبرته بذلك فسرّ به.

قلت: أبو السوّار العدوي اسمه حسّان بن حُريت، يَروي عن عليّ بن أبي طالب وعِمران بن حُصين وكان من العلماء الزهّاد وقد وافق أحمد في الصبر على الضرب.

٦،٩٣ أخبرنا إسماعيل بن أحمد قال: أخبرنا عمر بن عُبيد الله البقّال قال: أخبرنا أبو الحسين بن بِشْران قال: أخبرنا عثمان بن أحمد الدقاق قال: حدثنا حنبل بن إسحاق قال: حدثني أبو عبد الله أحمد بن حنبل قال: حدثنا عفان قال:

حدثنا حمّاد بن زيد عن هشام قال: كان أبو السوّار العدوي يعرض له الرجل فيشتمه فيقول: إن كنتُ كما قلتَ إني إذاً لرجل سوء.

٧،٩٣ أخبرنا عبد الملك قال: أخبرنا عبد الله بن محمد قال: أخبرنا الحسن بن محمّد بن أحمد المقرئ قال: أخبرنا أبي قال: حدثنا منصور بن أحمد بن جعفر الجَرْمي[١] قال: حدثنا أحمد بن محمّد بن سَلْم الكاتب، وأخبرنا عبد الملك قال: أخبرنا عبد الله بن محمد قال أخبرنا اسحاق بن إبراهيم قال أخبرنا محمّد بن أحمد بن بشر قال: حدثنا أبو زُرْعة أحمد ابن الحسين قال: حدثنا غُنْدَر، وأخبرنا أبو منصور القزاز قال: أخبرنا أحمد بن عليّ بن ثابت، وأخبرنا المحمّدان: ابن عبد الملك وابن ناصر قالا: أخبرنا أحمد بن الحسن بن خَيرون قال: أخبرنا البَرْقاني قال: حدثنا إسحاق النِّعالي، وأخبرنا إسماعيل بن أحمد ومحمّد بن عبد الباقي قالا: أخبرنا حَمْد قال: حدثنا أبو نُعَيم الحافظ قال: حدثنا محمّد بن عليّ بن حُبَيْش قالوا: حدثنا عبد الله بن إسحاق المَدائِني[٢] قال:

حدثنا أبي قال: رأيت في المنام كأنّ الحجر الأسود تصدّع وخرج منه لواء، فقلت: ما هذا؟

فقيل: أحمد بن حنبل قد بايع الله عز وجل.

قال أبو نُعيم: وقيل إنّه كان في اليوم الذي ضُرب فيه.

---

١ هـ: الحَرمي. ٢ د: المديني.

"Well then, consider your wife divorced!"

"So where I am I supposed to go at night?"

At that the man struck him forty lashes.

Abū Ja'far added: I visited Aḥmad and told him this story, and he was happy to hear it.

[The author:] Abū l-Sawwār al-'Adawī's name was Ḥassān ibn Ḥurayth. He transmitted Hadith via 'Alī ibn Abī Ṭālib and 'Imrān ibn Ḥuṣayn. He was a scholarly renunciant, and he matched Aḥmad in the endurance he displayed while being flogged.

We cite Ismā'īl ibn Aḥmad, who cites 'Umar ibn 'Ubayd Allāh al-Baqqāl, who cites Abū l-Husayn ibn Bishrān, who cites 'Uthmān ibn Aḥmad al-Daqqāq, who heard Ḥanbal ibn Isḥāq report that he heard Abū 'Abd Allāh Aḥmad ibn Ḥanbal report that he heard 'Affān report that he heard Ḥammād ibn Zayd report, on the authority of Hishām: 93.6

[Hishām:] Whenever someone would insult Abū l-Sawwār al-'Adawī, he would say, "If I'm what you say I am, I suppose I'm a bad man."

We cite 'Abd al-Malik, who cites 'Abd Allāh ibn Muḥammad, who cites al-Ḥasan ibn Muḥammad ibn Aḥmad al-Muqri', who cites his father, who heard Manṣūr ibn Aḥmad ibn Ja'far al-Jarmī report that he heard Aḥmad ibn Muḥammad ibn Salm al-Kātib report; and we cite 'Abd al-Malik, who cites 'Abd Allāh ibn Muḥammad, who cites Isḥāq ibn Ibrāhīm, who cites Muḥammad ibn Aḥmad ibn Bishr, who heard Abū Zur'ah Aḥmad ibn al-Ḥusayn report that he heard Ghundar report; and we cite Abū Manṣūr al-Qazzāz, who cites Aḥmad ibn 'Alī ibn Thābit; and we cite the two Muḥammads, Ibn 'Abd al-Malik and Ibn Nāṣir, who cite Aḥmad ibn al-Ḥasan ibn Khayrūn, who cites al-Barqānī, who heard Isḥāq al-Ni'ālī (maker and seller of sandals) report; and we cite Ismā'īl ibn Aḥmad and Muḥammad ibn 'Abd al-Bāqī, who cite Ḥamd, who heard Abū Nu'aym al-Ḥāfiẓ report that he heard Muḥammad ibn 'Alī ibn Ḥubaysh report that he heard 'Abd Allāh ibn Isḥāq al-Madā'inī report that he heard his father say: 93.7

[Isḥāq al-Madā'inī:] I dreamed that the Black Stone cracked open and from it a banner emerged.

"What's going on?" I asked.

"Aḥmad ibn Ḥanbal has sworn allegiance to God."[241]

This was on the day he was flogged.

٨،٩٣ أخبرنا محمّد بن ناصر قال: أخبرنا المبارك بن عبد الجبّار قال: أخبرنا محمّد بن عبد الواحد الحَرِيري قال: أخبرنا محمّد ابن العباس بن حَيُّويه قال: حدثنا عبد الله بن محمّد بن إسحاق[١] المَرْوَزي قال: حدثنا محمّد بن أحمد بن الحسين المَرْوَزي قال:

سمعتُ سَلَمة بن شَبيب يقول: كنّا مع أحمد بن حنبل جُلوساً إذا جاءه رجل فقال: من منكم أحمد بن حنبل؟

فسكتنا فلم نقلْ شيئاً فقال: أنا أحمد بن حنبل، ما حاجتك؟

قال: ضربتُ إليك من أربع مائة فرسخ بَرّها وبحرها، جاءني الخَضِر ليلةَ الجمعة وقال لي: لِمَ لا تخرج إلى أحمد بن حنبل؟ فقلت: لا أعرفه فقال: تأتي بغداد وتسأل عنه وقلْ له إنّ ساكنَ السماء الذي على عرشه راضٍ عنك وسائر الملائكة راضون عنك بما صبّرت نفسك لله عزّ وجلّ.

٩،٩٣ أخبرنا عبد الملك بن أبي القاسم قال: أخبرنا عبد الله بن محمّد قال: أخبرنا أحمد بن محمّد بن إبراهيم قال: أخبرنا أحمد بن محمّد بن شاذان قال: حدثنا محمّد بن إبراهيم بن نافع قال: حدثنا الحسن بن إدريس السِّجِسْتاني قال:

حدثنا سَلمة بن شَبيب قال: كنتُ مع أحمد بن حنبل في مسجده ببغداد ونحن جماعة وقد صلّينا الصبح إذ دخل رجل فقال: من منكم أحمد بن حنبل؟ فسكتنا نحن هيبة لأحمد فقال أحمد: أنا أحمد، ما حاجتك؟

قال: جئتُ برّاً وبحرًا أربع مائة فرسخ أتاني آتٍ في ليلة جمعة فقال: أنا الخَضِر، اخرج إلى بغداد فسلْ عن أحمد بن حنبل فقل له: إنّ ساكنَ العرش والملائكة راضون عنك بما صبّرت نفسك.

فقال أحمد: الأعمال بالخواتيم.

فلمّا أراد القيام قال أحمد للرجل: ألك حاجة سوى الذي جئت له؟

قال: لا. ورجع.

---

١ محمّد بن العباس بن حَيُّويه: ليس في هـ.

We cite Muḥammad ibn Nāṣir, who cites al-Mubārak ibn ʿAbd al-Jabbār, who cites Muḥammad ibn ʿAbd al-Wāḥid al-Ḥarīrī, who cites Muḥammad ibn al-ʿAbbās ibn Ḥayyuwayh, who heard ʿAbd Allāh ibn Muḥammad ibn Isḥāq al-Marwazī report that he heard Muḥammad ibn Aḥmad ibn al-Ḥusayn al-Marwazī report that he heard Salamah ibn Shabīb say: 93.8

[Salamah ibn Shabīb:] We were once sitting with Aḥmad when a man appeared and asked, "Which of you is Aḥmad ibn Ḥanbal?"

None of us spoke up, but Aḥmad said, "I'm Aḥmad. What do you need?"

"I've crossed four hundred leagues of land and sea to find you. I had a visit from al-Khaḍir on a Friday night.[242] He said, 'Why don't you go visit Aḥmad ibn Ḥanbal?' I said I didn't know you but he said, 'Go to Baghdad and ask. Tell him that the Lord of Heaven on His throne is pleased with you, and all the angels too, because of your endurance for the sake of God.'"

We cite ʿAbd al-Malik ibn Abī l-Qāsim, who heard ʿAbd Allāh ibn Muḥammad, who cites Aḥmad ibn Muḥammad ibn Ibrāhīm, who cites Aḥmad ibn Muḥammad ibn Shādhān, who heard Muḥammad ibn Ibrāhīm ibn Nāfiʿ report that he heard al-Ḥasan ibn Idrīs al-Sijistānī report that he heard Salamah ibn Shabīb report: 93.9

[Salamah ibn Shabīb:] I was once with Aḥmad in his mosque in Baghdad. There were several others there too. We had just finished the morning prayer when a man came in and asked, "Which of you is Aḥmad ibn Ḥanbal?"

Out of deference to Aḥmad, no one said anything. Then he himself said, "I'm Aḥmad. What do you need?"

"I've crossed four hundred leagues of land and sea to find you. I had a visitor on a Friday who said he was al-Khaḍir. He told me to go to Baghdad and ask for you, and tell you that the Lord of Heaven on His throne is pleased with you, and all the angels too, because of your endurance."

"Count no one meritorious before his work is done," said Aḥmad.

When the man rose to go, Aḥmad asked him if there was anything else he could do for him. The man said no and went out.

١٠،٩٣ أخبرنا عبد الرحمن بن محمد القزاز قال: أخبرنا أحمد بن عليّ بن ثابت قال: حدثنا محمد بن أحمد بن أبي الفَوارس قال: حدثنا محمد بن العباس الخزاز قال: حدثنا محمد بن حَفص أبو عبد الله الخصيب قال: حدثنا أبو بكر محمد بن أحمد بن داوود المؤدّب قال:

حدثنا سَلَمة بن شَبيب قال: كنّا عند أحمد بن حنبل فجاءه رجل فدقّ الباب وكنّا قد دخلنا عليه مُستخفين فظننّا أنّه قد غُمز بنا فدقّ ثانية وثالثة فقال أحمد: ادخل.

فدخل فسلّم وقال: أيّكم أحمد؟

فأشار بعضنا إليه فقال: جئتُ من البحر مسيرة أربع مائة فرسخ، أتاني آتٍ في منامي فقال: أئتِ أحمد بن حنبل وسَلْ عنه فإنّك تُدَلّ عليه وقل له: إنّ الله عز وجل عنك راضٍ وملائكة[١] سماواته عنك راضون وملائكة أرضه عنك راضون.

قال: ثم خرج فما سأله عن حديث ولا مسألة.

١١،٩٣ أخبرنا إسماعيل بن أحمد ومحمد بن أبي القاسم قالا: أخبرنا أبو الفضل ابن أحمد الحدّاد قال: أخبرنا أبو نعيم الحافظ قال: حدثنا عبد الله بن محمد قال: حدثنا محمد بن الحسن بن عليّ بن بحر قال:

حدثنا سَلَمة بن شَبيب قال: كنّا في أيّام المعتصم يوماً جلوساً عند أحمد بن حنبل فدخل رجل فقال: من منكم أحمد بن حنبل؟

فَسَكتنا فلم نقل شيئاً فقال أحمد: ها أنذا أحمد فما حاجتك؟

قال: جئتك من أربع مائة فرسخ برّاً وبحراً كنت ليلة جمعة نائماً[٢] فأتاني آتٍ فقال لي: تعرف أحمد بن حنبل؟ قلت: لا. قال: فَأْتِ بغداد وسلْ عنه فإذا رأيته فقل له: إن الخَضِر يُقرِئك السلام ويقول: إن ساكنَ السماء الذي على عرشه راضٍ عنك والملائكة راضون عنك بما صبّرت نفسك لله.

فقال له أحمد: ما شاء الله لا قوة إلّا بالله، ألك حاجة غير هذه؟

قال: ما جئتك إلّا لهذا. وانصرف.

---

١ هـ: سبع. ٢ ليس في د.

We cite ʿAbd al-Raḥmān ibn Muḥammad al-Qazzāz, who cites Aḥmad ibn ʿAli ibn Thābit, who heard Muḥammad ibn Aḥmad ibn Abī l-Fawāris report that he heard Muḥammad ibn al-ʿAbbās al-Khazzāz report that he heard Muḥammad ibn Ḥafṣ Abū ʿAbd Allāh al-Khaṣīb report that he heard Abū Bakr Muḥammad ibn Aḥmad ibn Dāwūd al-Muʾaddib report that he heard Salamah ibn Shabīb report: **93.10**

[Salamah ibn Shabīb:] We were once at Aḥmad's when a man came and knocked on the door. We had gathered secretly in defiance of the authorities and thought that someone must have denounced us. The man knocked again, and then a third time, until Aḥmad finally told him to come in. The man came in, greeted us, and asked which of us was Aḥmad ibn Ḥanbal. When Aḥmad was pointed out, the man said, "I've traveled four hundred leagues by sea to find you. I had a dream where someone told me to find you and tell you, 'The Lord of Heaven on His throne is pleased with you, and all the angels in Heaven and on Earth as well.'"

Then, without asking about a Hadith or a point of law, the man departed.

We cite Ismāʿīl ibn Aḥmad and Muḥammad ibn Abī l-Qāsim, who cite Abū l-Faḍl ibn Aḥmad al-Ḥaddād, who cites Abū Nuʿaym al-Ḥāfiẓ, who heard ʿAbd Allāh ibn Muḥammad report that he heard Muḥammad ibn al-Ḥasan ibn ʿAlī ibn Baḥr report that he heard Salamah ibn Shabīb report: **93.11**

[Salamah ibn Shabīb:] Once, during the reign of al-Muʿtaṣim, we were sitting with Aḥmad when a man appeared and asked, "Which of you is Aḥmad ibn Ḥanbal?"

None of us spoke up, but Aḥmad said, "I'm Aḥmad. What do you need?"

"I've crossed four hundred leagues of land and sea to find you. One Friday I was sleeping and dreamed someone was asking me if I knew you. I said no. He said, 'Go to Baghdad and ask. When you find him, convey greetings from al-Khaḍir and tell him that the Lord of Heaven on His throne is pleased with him, and all the angels too, because of his endurance for the sake of God.'"

"Praise God!" said Aḥmad. "There is no power save in Him. Is there anything I can do for you?"

"I came only to deliver that message," said the man, and departed.

١٢،٩٣ أنبأنا أبو بكر محمد بن عبد الباقي قال: أخبرنا هَنّاد بن إبراهيم النَّسَفي قال: سمعت أبا الحُسين بن بِشْران يقول: سمعتُ أبا عمرو بن السمّاك يقول سمعتُ حنبل بن إسحاق يقول:

سمعت سَلَمة بن شَبيب النيسابوري يقول: كنت عند أبي عبد الله فإذا رجل قد جاء فقال: أيّما هو أحمد بن حنبل؟

قالوا له: هذا.

فقال: أنا رجل قد جئت من موضع كذا وكذا، وذكر بلدة بعيدة، وضربت برّها وبحرها ولولا أنّه قيل لي في النوم أن آتيك فأُخبرك[1] ما جئت، قد قيل لي: قل له إنّ الله عز وجل قد باهى بضربك الملائكة.

١٣،٩٣ أخبرنا محمّد بن ناصر قال: أنبأنا الحسن بن أحمد بن البنا قال: أخبرنا أبو محمّد الحسن[2] بن محمّد الحافظ قال: حدثنا عبد الواحد بن عليّ بن الحسين الفامي[3] قال: حدثنا أبو الحسن عليّ بن موسى بن عيسى البزّاز قال:

حدثني أحمد بن محمّد بن الحجّاج المرُّوذي قال: كنتُ يوماً قاعداً على قَنْطَرة التَّبّانين فإذا أنا برجلَين يقدمان رجلاً بدوياً على قَعُود له إذ وقفوا عليّ وقالوا: هو ذا، هو جالس.

فقال لي البدوي: أنت أحمد بن حنبل؟

فقلت له: لا، أنا صاحبه، اذكرْ حاجتك.

فقال: أريده.

قلت: أدلّك عليه؟

قال: إي والله.

فمضيتُ بين يديه حتّى أتيت باب أبي عبد الله فدققت الباب فقالوا: من هذا؟

فقلت: أنا المرُّوذي.

قالوا: ادخُل.

قلت: أنا ومن معي؟

---

١ ليس في د. ٢ د: ابن الحسن. ٣ د: القاضي.

We were informed by Abū Bakr Muḥammad ibn ʿAbd al-Bāqī, who cites Hannād ibn Ibrāhīm al-Nasafī, who heard Abū l-Ḥusayn ibn Bishrān say that he heard Abū ʿAmr ibn al-Sammāk say that he heard Ḥanbal ibn Isḥāq say that he heard Salamah ibn Shabīb al-Naysābūrī say: **93.12**

[Salamah ibn Shabīb:] I was once sitting with Aḥmad when a man appeared and asked, "Which of you is Aḥmad ibn Ḥanbal?"

Aḥmad was pointed out, and the man said, "I've come from Such-and-Such a place"—he mentioned a distant town—"across land and sea to find you. I was told in a dream to come find you and deliver a message; otherwise I wouldn't be here. I was told to tell you that God boasts of your flogging to the angels."

We cite Muḥammad ibn Nāṣir, who was informed by al-Ḥasan ibn Aḥmad ibn al-Bannā, who cites Abū Muḥammad al-Ḥasan ibn Muḥammad al-Ḥāfiẓ, who heard ʿAbd al-Wāḥid ibn ʿAlī ibn al-Ḥusayn al-Fāmī report that he heard Abū l-Ḥasan ʿAlī ibn Mūsā ibn ʿĪsā l-Bazzāz report that he heard Aḥmad ibn Muḥammad ibn al-Ḥajjāj al-Marrūdhī report: **93.13**

[Al-Marrūdhī:] One day I was sitting on the Straw-Sellers' Bridge when I saw two men clearing the way for a Bedouin on camelback. They stopped in front of me and told the Bedouin, "That's him: the one sitting there."

"Are you Aḥmad ibn Ḥanbal?" the Bedouin asked.

"No," I said. "But I know him. What do you want him for?"

"I have to see him."

"Shall I take you?"

"Aye."

I led the way to Aḥmad's place and knocked on the door.

"Who is it?"

"Al-Marrūdhī."

"Come in."

"I have someone with me."

قالوا: أنت ومن معك.

فأناخ الأعرابي ناقته وعقَلها ودخلتُ ودخل معي[1] فلمّا رأى أبا عبد الله قال الأعرابي: إي والله، ثلاث مرات، فسلّم عليه فقال له: ما حاجتك؟

فقال: أنا رسول رسول الله إليك.

قال: ويحك ما تقول؟

قال: إنّي رجل بدوي بين حَيّي والمدينة أربعون ميلاً أوفدني أهلي المدينة أمتار لهم بُرًّا وتمرًا فأتيت المدينة فابتعتُ ما عهدوا إليّ من ذلك وجَنّني المساء فصلّيتُ في مسجد النبيّ صلّى الله عليه وسلّم عشاء الآخرة واضطجعتُ فبَيْنا أنا نائم إذ أتاني محرّك فحرّكني وقال لي: أتمضي لرسول الله في حاجة؟

فقلتُ: إي والله. فقبض بيده اليمنى على ساعدي اليسرى وأتى بي حائط قبر النبي صلى الله عليه وسلم فوقفني عند رأسه وقال: يا رسول الله! فسمعتُ من وراء الحائط قائلاً يقول: أتمضي لنا في حاجة؟

فقلت: إي والله إي والله إي والله ثلاثًا.

فقال: تمضي حتى تأتي بغداد أو الزَّوْراء - الشكُّ من المرُّوذي - فإذا أتيت بغداد فسلْ عن منزل أحمد بن حنبل فإذا لقيته فقل: النبيّ يقرأ عليك السلام ويقول لك إنّ الله مُبتليك ببليّة ومُمتحِنك بمحنة وقد سألتُه لك الصبر عليها فلا تجزع.

قال المرُّوذي: وكان إذا قال له رجل: وحَمَلك يا أبا عبد الله في السوط! يقول: قد تقدمت المسألة.

قال أبو بَكر: وكان بين مُنصرَف الأعرابي وبين المحنة خمسة وعشرون يوماً.

أخبرنا عبد الملك بن أبي القاسم قال: أخبرنا عبد الله بن محمّد قال: أخبرنا الحسن بن محمّد بن أحمد المقرئ قال: ١٤،٩٣ أخبرنا أبي قال: أخبرنا منصور بن أحمد بن جعفر بالرَّمْلة قال: حدثنا محمّد بن عَبْدون الضرّاب قال: حدثنا أبو بكر الناقد قال:

---

[1] فأناخ الأعرابي ناقته وعقَلها ودخلتُ ودخل معي: ليس في هـ.

"Bring them too."

The Bedouin knelt his camel and tethered her, and we went inside. When he saw Aḥmad, he said, "Aye, by God," three times, and greeted him.

"What do you need?"

"I'm an emissary sent by God's Emissary."

"What on earth do you mean?"

"I'm a Bedouin, with quarters forty miles outside Medina. My family needed some wheat and some dates, so I went to Medina and bought what they wanted. Then it got dark. I prayed the last evening prayer of the day in the Prophet's mosque and lay down to sleep. Then I felt someone shaking me, and a voice said, 'Will you run an errand for the Emissary of God?'

"I said I would. He put his right hand on my left arm, walked me over to the wall of the Prophet's tomb, and placed me by his head.

"'Emissary of God!' he called out.

"From behind the wall a voice said, 'Will you do an errand for me?'

"'Aye, by God,' I said, three times.

"'Go to Baghdad'—or 'Crooked Town'[243]—al-Marrūdhī couldn't remember which he said, 'and ask for the house of Aḥmad ibn Ḥanbal. When you find him, tell him: "The Prophet sends his greetings, and a warning that God is preparing to subject you to a grievous ordeal; but I have asked Him to give you the strength to bear it, so fear not."'"

After that, whenever anyone marveled at his endurance during the flogging, he would say, "I knew it was coming."

Twenty-five days after the Bedouin departed, the Inquisition began.

We cite ʿAbd al-Malik ibn Abī l-Qāsim, who cites ʿAbd Allāh ibn Muḥammad, who cites al-Ḥasan ibn Muḥammad ibn Aḥmad al-Muqriʾ, who cites his father, who cites Manṣūr ibn Aḥmad ibn Jaʿfar in Ramlah, who heard Muḥammad ibn ʿAbdūn al-Ḍarrāb (the coiner?) report that he heard Abū Bakr al-Nāqid report: 93.14

قال سَريّ السَّقَطي: رأيت كأني أُدخلت جنّة الفردوس فجعلت أدور فيها إذ أشرفتُ على غرفة فإذا جارية فقلتُ: لمن أنت؟

قالت: لأحمد بن حنبل.

قال أبو بكر: فرأيت سَريًّا بعد وفاته في المنام فقلتُ: ما فعل أحمد وبشر؟

قال: الساعة دخلا جنّة عدن يأكلان منها.

١٥،٩٣ أخبرنا المحمّدان: ابن ناصر وابن عبد الباقي قالا: أخبرنا حمد بن أحمد قال: أخبرنا أحمد بن عبد الله قال: حدثنا سليمان بن أحمد قال: حدثنا أحمد بن عليّ الأَبّار قال:

حدثنا حُبَيْش بن أبي الوَرْد قال: رأيتُ النبيّ صلّى الله عليه وسلّم في المنام فقلتُ: يا نبيّ الله ما بال أحمد بن حنبل؟

فقال: سَيأتيك موسى عليه السلام فسَلْه.

فإذا أنا بموسى عليه السلام فقلتُ: يا نبيّ الله ما بالُ أحمد بن حنبل؟

فقال: أحمد بن حنبل بُلي في السرّاء والضراء فوُجد صادقاً فأُلحق بالصدّيقين.

١٦،٩٣ أخبرنا محمّد بن ناصر قال: أنبأنا أبو عليّ الحسن بن أحمد الفقيه قال: حدثنا أبو محمّد الحسن بن محمّد السرّاج قال: حدثنا يوسف بن عمر الزاهد قال: حدثنا أبو بكر محمّد بن جعفر الكتّاني قال: حدثنا أبو أحمد سليمان بن محمّد بن سَلَمة قال: حدثنا المرُّوذي قال: حدثنا أبو العبّاس الخُرَيمي قال:

حدثني فَتْح بن شَخْرَف أبو نصر قال: رأيت النبيّ صلّى الله عليه وسلّم في المنام كأنّه يُصلّي وأنا أصلّي بصلاته.

فلمّا انفتل قلتُ: بأبي أنت يا رسول الله، رجل من أُمّتك أريد أن أسألك عنه.

فقال: من هو؟

فقلت: أحمد بن حنبل.

فقال: سَل عنه أخي موسى.

فانتبهتُ ثمّ غلبتْني عيني فإذا أنا بموسى عليه السلام فقلتُ: يا كليم الله رأيتُ النبيّ صلّى الله عليه وسلّم في منامي فسألته عن رجل من أُمّته فقال لي: سَل أخي موسى.

[Abū Bakr al-Nāqid:] Sarī l-Saqaṭī said, "I dreamed I had been admitted to the Garden of Paradise. As I was wandering through it, I found myself looking down into a room and seeing a slave. I asked her whose she was and she said, 'Aḥmad ibn Ḥanbal's.'"

Abū Bakr added: I myself saw Sarī in a dream after he died. I asked him what had become of Aḥmad and Bishr.

"They've just entered the Garden of Eden," he said, "and they're eating."

We cite the two Muḥammads, Ibn Nāṣir and Ibn ʿAbd al-Bāqī, who cite Ḥamd ibn Aḥmad, who cites Aḥmad ibn ʿAbd Allāh, who heard Sulaymān ibn Aḥmad report that he heard Aḥmad ibn ʿAlī l-Abbār report that he heard Ḥubaysh ibn Abī l-Ward report: **93.15**

[Ḥubaysh:] The Prophet appeared to me in a dream. I asked him what had become of Aḥmad ibn Ḥanbal.

"Moses will be along," he said. "Ask him."

When Moses appeared, I asked him and he said, "Aḥmad ibn Ḥanbal was put to the test in good times and bad. He proved himself sincere and has joined the truth-tellers."

We cite Muḥammad ibn Nāṣir, who was informed by Abū ʿAlī l-Ḥasan ibn Aḥmad al-Faqīh, who heard Abū Muḥammad al-Ḥasan ibn Muḥammad al-Sarrāj report that he heard Yūsuf ibn ʿUmar al-Zāhid report that he heard Abū Bakr Muḥammad ibn Jaʿfar al-Kattānī report that he heard Abū Aḥmad Sulaymān ibn Muḥammad ibn Salamah report that he heard al-Marrūdhī report that he heard Abū l-ʿAbbās al-Khuraymī report that he heard Fatḥ ibn Shakhraf Abū Naṣr report: **93.16**

[Abū Naṣr:] I dreamed I was praying along with the Prophet. When he finished I said, "May my father redeem you, Emissary of God![244] There's a member of your community I want to ask you about."

"Who?"

"Aḥmad ibn Ḥanbal."

"Ask my brother Moses."

I woke up. Then I dozed off again, and there was Moses.

"O Addressee of God![245] The Prophet came to me in a dream and I asked him about a member of his community but he said to ask you."

"Is it Aḥmad ibn Ḥanbal you want to know about?"

فقال: أحمد بن حنبل تريد؟

قلت: نعم.

قال: ذاكَ رجل ابتُلي بالسرّاء والضّراء فصبر وهو في عِليّين.

١٧،٩٣ أخبرنا محمّد بن أبي منصور قال: أخبرنا عبد القادر بن محمد قال: أنبأنا إبراهيم بن عمر قال: أنبأنا عبد العزيز بن جعفر قال: حدثنا أحمد بن محمّد الخلال قال: حدثنا عبد الله بن إسماعيل قال: حدثنا أبو عبد الله محمّد بن يعقوب المُقرئ قال: حدثنا الحسين بن عليّ الأَذْرمِي قال:

حدثنا بُنْدار بن يَسَار[١] قال: رأيت سفيان الثوري في المنام فقلت: إلى ما صرتَ؟

قال: صرتُ إلى أكثر ممّا أملت.

فقلت: ما هذا في كُمّك؟

قال: دُرّ وياقوت وجوهر، قَدِمَتْ علينا روح أحمد بن حنبل فأمر الله أن يُنثَر عليها الدرّ والياقوت والجوهر فهذا نصيبي.

١٨،٩٣ أخبرنا عبد الرحمن بن محمّد القزّاز قال: أخبرنا أحمد بن عليّ بن ثابت قال: أخبرنا محمّد بن أحمد بن رزق قال: حدثنا سلام[٢] بن سليمان البَاجَدّائي قال: حدثنا محمّد بن أبي شيخ قال: حدثنا عليّ بن الحسين التيمي قال:

حدثنا بُنْدار قال: قلتُ لعبد الرحمن بن مهدي: صِف لي الثوري.

قال: فوصفه لي فسألتُ الله أن يُرِينيه في مَنامي فلمّا أن مات عبد الرحمن رأيته في منامي في الصورة التي وصفها عبد الرحمن فقلت: ما فعل الله بك؟

قال: غفر لي.

قال: وإذا في كُمّه شيء، فقلت: أي شيء في كُمّك؟

قال: اعلم أنه قُدّم بروح أحمد بن حنبل فأمر الله عزّ وجلّ جبريل عليه السلام أن ينثر عليها الدرّ والجوهر الزَّبَرْجَد وهذا نصيبي منه.

---

١ د: بشار. ٢ تركي: سلامة.

"Yes."

"He was put to the test in good times and bad but endured it all, and now he's in ʿIlliyyīn."[246]

93.17 We cite Muḥammad ibn Abī Manṣūr, who cites ʿAbd al-Qādir ibn Muḥammad, who was informed by Ibrāhīm ibn ʿUmar, who was informed by ʿAbd al-ʿAzīz ibn Jaʿfar, who heard Aḥmad ibn Muḥammad al-Khallāl report that he heard ʿAbd Allāh ibn Ismāʿīl report that he heard Abū ʿAbd Allāh Muḥammad ibn Yaʿqūb al-Muqriʾ report that he heard al-Ḥusayn ibn ʿAlī l-Adhramī report that he heard Bundār ibn Yasār report:

[Bundār:] Sufyān al-Thawrī came to me in a dream and I asked him how he had fared.

"Better than I expected," he said.

"What's that in your sleeve?"

"Pearls, rubies, and gems," he said. "When Aḥmad ibn Ḥanbal's spirit joined us, God greeted him with a shower of precious stones. This is my share."

93.18 We cite ʿAbd al-Raḥmān ibn Muḥammad al-Qazzāz, who cites Aḥmad ibn ʿAlī ibn Thābit, who cites Muḥammad ibn Aḥmad ibn Rizq, who heard Salām ibn Sulaymān al-Bājaddāʾī report that he heard Muḥammad ibn Abī Shaykh report that he heard ʿAlī ibn al-Ḥusayn al-Tamīmī report that he heard Bundār report:

[Bundār:] I asked ʿAbd al-Raḥmān ibn Mahdī to describe al-Thawrī for me, and he did. Then I asked God to show him to me in a dream. No sooner had ʿAbd al-Raḥmān[247] died than I dreamed of Sufyān, who matched the description ʿAbd al-Raḥmān had given me. I asked what God had done with him.

"He's forgiven me," he said.

I noticed that he was carrying something in his sleeve and I asked him what it was.

"Aḥmad ibn Ḥanbal's spirit has been brought here, and God commanded Gabriel to shower it with pearls, gems, and chrysolite. This is my share."

قال الخطيب: يُشبه أن يكون هذا المنام رآه بُندار عند موت أحمد بن حنبل والله أعلم.

أخبرنا ابن ناصر قال: أخبرنا عبد القادر بن محمّد قال: أنبأنا إبراهيم بن عمر قال: أنبأنا عبد العزيز بن جعفر قال: حدثنا أبو بكر الخلّال قال: حدثنا العباس القَراطيسي قال: ١٩،٩٣

حدثنا إسماعيل بن عبد الأعلى قال: رأيتُ أحمد بن عمرو في المنام فقلت: أحمد، أحمد!

ورأيت يده مضمومة هكذا فقلتُ: ما صنع الله بك؟

قال: غفر لي.

قلت: يدك مضمومة؟

قال: قدم علينا أحمد بن حنبل الجنّة فهذا من نِثاره.

قال الخلّال: ورأيت[١] في كتابي بخطّي عن أبي بكر المرّوذي قال: سمعت أحمد بن يعقوب البُخاري يقول: ٢٠،٩٣

قال أبو عبد الله المحاربي: رأيت عبد الله بن الصبّاح في المنام قاعداً في القِبلة فسلّمت عليه فقلت: إلى ما صرت؟

فقال: إلى خير، وعليكم بابن حنبل وعليكم بابن حنبل وعليكم بابن حنبل!

قال: ورأى الفضل بن زياد في المنام في منزل قد وصفه.

قال: فقلتُ: بمَ انتفعتَ به؟

قال: بالسنّة.

قال: فقلتُ: فما حال أحمد بن حنبل؟

قال: حالَت بيننا وبينه الحُجُب.

أخبرنا عبد الملك بن أبي القاسم الكَرُوخي قال: أخبرنا عبد الله بن محمّد الأنصاري قال: أخبرنا إسحاق بن إبراهيم المعدّل قال: أخبرنا أحمد بن أبي عمران قال: حدثنا محمّد بن أحمد بن الفضل قال: حدثنا عليّ بن أحمد بن عيسى ٢١،٩٣

---

١ هـ: قرات.

Al-Khaṭīb added: Bundār would seem to have had this dream upon the death of Aḥmad ibn Ḥanbal, but God alone knows the truth.

We cite Ibn Nāṣir, who cites ʿAbd al-Qādir ibn Muḥammad, who was informed by Ibrāhīm ibn ʿUmar, who was informed by ʿAbd al-ʿAzīz ibn Jaʿfar, who heard Abū Bakr al-Khallāl report that he heard al-ʿAbbās al-Qarāṭīsī report that he heard Ismāʿīl ibn ʿAbd al-Aʿlā report: **93.19**

[Ibn ʿAbd al-Aʿlā:] Aḥmad ibn ʿAmr came to me in a dream and said, "Aḥmad, Aḥmad!" I saw that his fist was clenched—like this. I asked him what God had done with him.

"He's forgiven me."

"What's in your hand?"

"Aḥmad ibn Ḥanbal just joined us here in the Garden and this is my share of the gifts that were showered on us."

Al-Khallāl cited, from a document he found in his own handwriting, Abū Bakr al-Marrūdhī, who heard Aḥmad ibn Yaʿqūb al-Bukhārī say: **93.20**

[Al-Bukhārī:] Al-Muḥāribī said that he dreamed of seeing ʿAbd Allāh ibn al-Ṣabbāḥ sitting by the niche in the mosque. He greeted him and asked how he had fared.

"Well," he said. "Follow Ibn Ḥanbal! Follow him! Follow him!"[248]

He also dreamed of seeing al-Faḍl ibn Ziyād. He described the dwelling where he saw al-Faḍl, and then said that he asked him what he had done to earn it.

"'Follow the *sunnah*,' said al-Faḍl.

"'What about Aḥmad ibn Ḥanbal?'

"'He's on the other side of something we can't see through.'"

We cite ʿAbd al-Malik ibn Abī l-Qāsim al-Karūkhī, who cites ʿAbd Allāh ibn Muḥammad al-Anṣārī, who cites Isḥāq ibn Ibrahīm al-Muʿaddal, who cites Aḥmad ibn Abī ʿImrān, who heard Muḥammad ibn Aḥmad ibn al-Faḍl report that he heard ʿAlī ibn Aḥmad ibn **93.21**

قال: حدثنا إسحاق بن إبراهيم الصفّار قال:

حدثنا إبراهيم الحربي قال: رأيت بشر بن الحارث كأنّه خارج من مسجد الرّصافة وفي كمّه شيء يتحرك فقلتُ: ما فعل الله بك؟

قال: غفر لي وأكرمني.

قلتُ: فما هذا الذي في كمّك؟

قال: قدم علينا البارحة روح أحمد بن حنبل ونُثر عليه الدرّ والياقوت فهذا ما التقطتُ.

قلت: فما فعل يحيى بن مَعين وأحمد بن حنبل؟

قال: تركتُهما وقد زارا ربّ العالمين ووُضعت لهما الموائد.

٢٢،٩٣ أخبرنا محمّد بن ناصر قال: أخبرنا أبو الحسين بن الطُّيُوري قال: أخبرنا أبو محمّد الحسن بن محمّد الخلّال قال: حدثنا أحمد بن إبراهيم بن شاذان قال: حدثنا عبد الله بن محمّد بن سعيد الجمّال قال: حدثنا أبو جعفر أحمد بن سهل البُنْدار قال:

سمعت أسود بن سالم يقول: بينا أنا نائم إذا رأيتُ كأنّ آتياً أتاني فقال: يا أسود إنّ الله يقرأُ عليك السلام ويقول لك: هذا أحمد بن حنبل يردّ الأُمة عن الضلالة فما أنت فاعل؟ اتبعْه وإلّا هلكتَ.

٢٣،٩٣ أنبأنا يحيى بن الحسن قال: أنبأنا محمّد بن الحسين الحاكم عن أبي الفَرَج محمّد بن فارس الغُوري عن أبيه قال: سمعت أبا محمّد بن[١] عبد الله بن بَدْر الأَنْماطي يقول:

سمعت أبا عليّ الحسن بن الحسين الصوّاف يقول: رأيتُ ربّ العِزّة في المنام فقال لي: يا حسن من خالف ابن حنبل عُذِّب.

٢٤،٩٣ أخبرنا المحمّدان: ابن ناصر وابن عبد الباقي قالا: أخبرنا أبو الفضل بن أحمد الحداد قال: أخبرنا أحمد بن عبد الله الحافظ قال: حدثنا أبي قال: حدثنا أحمد بن محمّد بن عمر قال: حدثني نصر بن خُزيمة قال:

---

١ ليس في د.

ʿĪsā report that he heard Isḥāq ibn Ibrāhīm al-Ṣaffār report that he heard Ibrāhīm al-Ḥarbī report:

[Al-Ḥarbī:] Bishr ibn al-Ḥārith appeared to me in a dream. He was coming out of the Ruṣāfah mosque with something swinging around inside his sleeve.

"What did God do with you?"

"He's forgiven me and honored me."

"What's that in your sleeve?"

"Yesterday Aḥmad ibn Ḥanbal's spirit joined us and we were showered with pearls and rubies. This is what I picked up."

"So what happened to Yaḥyā ibn Maʿīn? And to Aḥmad?"

"When I left them, they had gone to visit the Lord of the Worlds, and tables had been laid for them."

We cite Muḥammad ibn Nāṣir, who cites Abū l-Ḥusayn ibn al-Ṭuyūrī, who cites Abū Muḥammad al-Ḥasan ibn Muḥammad al-Khallāl, who heard Aḥmad ibn Ibrāhīm ibn Shādhān report that he heard ʿAbd Allāh ibn Muḥammad ibn Saʿīd al-Ḥammāl report that he heard Abū Jaʿfar Aḥmad ibn Sahl al-Bundār report that he heard Aswad ibn Sālim say: **93.22**

[Aswad ibn Sālim:] Once in my sleep I sensed a presence that spoke to me and said, "Aswad! God sends His greetings and says, 'Aḥmad ibn Ḥanbal is bringing this community back to the right path, so be sure to follow him. If you don't, you'll perish.'"

We were informed by Yaḥyā ibn al-Ḥasan, who was informed by Muḥammad ibn al-Ḥusayn al-Ḥākim, on the authority of Abī l-Faraj Muḥammad ibn Fāris al-Ghūrī, on the authority of his father, who heard Abū Muḥammad ibn ʿAbd Allāh ibn Badr al-Anmāṭī say that he heard Abū ʿAlī l-Ḥasan ibn al-Ḥusayn al-Ṣawwāf say: **93.23**

[Al-Ḥasan al-Ṣawwāf:] The Lord of Glory appeared to me in a dream and said, "Ḥasan, anyone who disagrees with Ibn Ḥanbal will be tormented."

We cite the two Muḥammads, Ibn Nāṣir and Ibn ʿAbd al-Bāqī, who cite Abū l-Faḍl ibn Aḥmad al-Ḥaddād, who cites Aḥmad ibn ʿAbd Allāh al-Ḥāfiẓ, who heard his father report that he heard Aḥmad ibn Muḥammad ibn ʿUmar report that he heard Naṣr ibn Khuzaymah report that Ibn Mijmaʿ ibn Muslim mentioned: **93.24**

ذكر ابن مُجَمِّع بن مسلم قال: كان لنا جار قُتل بقزوين فلمّا كانت الليلة التي مات فيها أحمد بن حنبل خرج إلينا أخوه في صبيحتها فقال: إنّي رأيت رؤيا عجيبة، رأيت أخي الليلة في أحسن صورة راكبًا على فرس فقلتُ له: يا أخي أليس قد قُتلت فما جاء بك؟

قال: إنّ الله عزّ وجلّ أمر الشهداء وأهل السماوات أن يحضروا جنازة أحمد بن حنبل فكنت فيمن أمر بالحضور.

فأرّخنا تلك الليلة فإذا أحمد بن حنبل مات فيها.

٢٥،٩٣ أخبرنا محمّد بن أبي منصور قال: أخبرنا عبد القادر بن محمّد قال: أخبرنا إبراهيم بن عمر البرمكي قال: أخبرنا عليّ ابن عبد العزيز قال: حدثنا عبد الرحمن بن أبي حاتم قال: حدثنا محمّد بن مسلم قال:

حدثنا أبو عبد الله الطِّهْراني عن الحسن بن عيسى عن أخي أبي عَقيل القَزْويني ثمّ لقيتُ أخا أبي عقيل فسمعتُ منه قال: رأيت شابًّا توفّي بقزوين في النوم فقلتُ: ما فعل بك ربّك؟

قال: غفر لي.

قلت: غفر لك؟

قال: نعم، وتعجب! ولفلان وفلان.

قلت: فما لي أراك مُستعجلًا؟

قال: لأنّ أهل السماوات من السماء السابعة إلى السماء الدنيا قد اشتغلوا بعقد الألْوِية لاستقبال أحمد بن حنبل وأنا أُريد استقباله.

وكان توفّي أحمد في تلك الأيّام.

٢٦،٩٣ أخبرنا المحمّدان: ابن ناصر وابن عبد الباقي قالا: أخبرنا أبو الفضل بن أحمد قال: حدثنا أبو نعيم قال: حدثنا أبي قال: حدثنا أحمد بن محمّد بن عمر قال: حدثنا نصر بن خُزيمة قال: ذكر ابن مُجَمِّع عن أبي القاسم الأَحْوَل قال:

[Ibn Mijma':] We had a neighbor who was killed in Qazwīn. The morning after Aḥmad ibn Ḥanbal died, the neighbor's brother came over and said, "I had the strangest dream last night! I saw my brother, looking better than he ever did, riding on a horse. I said, 'Brother, weren't you killed? What are you doing here?'

"He said, 'God commanded all the martyrs and the blessed in Heaven to attend Aḥmad ibn Ḥanbal's funeral, so here I am.'"

Later we checked the date and it was the same day Aḥmad died.

We cite Muḥammad ibn Abī Manṣūr, who cites 'Abd al-Qādir ibn Muḥammad, who cites Ibrāhīm ibn 'Umar al-Barmakī, who cites 'Alī ibn 'Abd al-'Azīz, who heard 'Abd al-Raḥmān ibn Abī Ḥātim report that he heard Muḥammad ibn Muslim report that he heard Abū 'Abd Allāh al-Ṭihrānī report, on the authority of al-Ḥasan ibn 'Īsā, citing the brother of Abū 'Aqīl al-Qazwīnī: **93.25**

[Abū 'Aqīl's brother:] A young man who died in Qazwīn came to me in a dream. I asked him what God had done with him.

"He forgave me."

"He did?"

"You sound surprised! Well, he also forgave So-and-So, and So-and-So."

"You seem to be in a hurry."

"Everyone in Heaven—from the seventh Heaven on down—is busy tying banners to receive Aḥmad ibn Ḥanbal. I want to go too."

I had this dream around the same time that Aḥmad passed away.

We cite the two Muḥammads, Ibn Nāṣir and Ibn 'Abd al-Bāqī, who cite Abū l-Faḍl ibn Aḥmad, who heard Abū Nu'aym report that he heard his father report that he heard Aḥmad ibn Muḥammad ibn 'Umar report that he heard Naṣr ibn Khuzaymah report that Ibn Mijma' mentioned, citing Abū l-Qāsim al-Aḥwal, that Ya'qūb ibn 'Abd Allāh reported: **93.26**

حدثنا يعقوب بن عبد الله قال: رأيت سَرِيّاً السَّقَطي في النوم فقلتُ: ما فعل الله بك؟

قال: أباحني النظر إلى وجهه.

قلت: فما فعل أحمد بن حنبل وأحمد بن نصر؟ فقال: شُغلا بأكل الثمار في الجنّة.

٢٧،٩٣ قال نَصر: وحدثني محمّد بن مخلد قال: حدثنا محمّد بن الحسين بن عبد الرحمن عن أحمد بن عمر بن يونس قال:

حدثنا أبو عبد الله السِّجِستاني قال: رأيت رسول الله صلى الله عليه وسلم في المنام فقلت: يا رسول الله من تركتَ لنا في عصرنا هذا من أمّتك نقتدي به في ديننا؟

قال: عليكم بأحمد بن حنبل.

٢٨،٩٣ أخبرنا ابن ناصر قال: أنبأنا الحسن بن أحمد الفقيه قال: حدثنا محمّد بن أحمد الحافظ قال: حدثنا عمر بن جعفر بن سَلْمٍ قال: حدثنا عمر بن محمّد الجوهري قال: حدثنا أبو أحمد محمّد بن جعفر قال: حدثنا أحمد بن محمّد الأنماطي قال:

حدثني أحمد بن نصر قال: رأيت النبي صلى الله عليه وسلم في النوم فقلت: يا رسول الله من تركتَ لنا في عصرنا هذا من أمّتك نقتدي به؟

فقال: عليك بأحمد بن حنبل.

٢٩،٩٣ أنبأنا يحيى بن الحسن قال: أنبأنا محمّد بن الحسين بن خلف قال: أنبأنا أبو الحسن عليّ بن محمّد الحِنّائي قال: أخبرنا أبو محمّد الطرسوسي قال: حدثنا أبو بكر محمّد بن عيسى قال:

سمعت هِبة الله بن السَريّ يقول: رأيتُ النبيّ صلى الله عليه وسلم في المنام فقلتُ: يا رسول الله قد اختلف علينا الفُقهاء فما ندري بقول من نقول!

فقال النبيّ صلى الله عليه وسلم: القول قول أحمد بن حنبل.

[Yaʿqūb ibn ʿAbd Allāh:] Sarī l-Saqaṭī came to me in a dream and I asked him how he had fared. He said that God had permitted him to gaze upon His countenance.

"What about Aḥmad ibn Ḥanbal and Aḥmad ibn Naṣr?"

"They're busy eating fruit in the Garden."

Naṣr said: We heard Muḥammad ibn Makhlad report that he heard Muḥammad ibn al-Ḥusayn ibn ʿAbd al-Raḥmān report, citing Aḥmad ibn ʿUmar ibn Yūnus, that he heard Abū ʿAbd Allāh al-Sijistānī report: 93.27

[Al-Sijistānī:] The Emissary of God came to me in a dream. I asked him who he'd left in our time for members of his community to emulate in their religion.

"Aḥmad ibn Ḥanbal."

We cite Ibn Nāṣir, who was informed by al-Ḥasan ibn Aḥmad al-Faqīh, who heard Muḥammad ibn Aḥmad al-Ḥāfiẓ report that he heard ʿUmar ibn Jaʿfar ibn Salm report that he heard ʿUmar ibn Muḥammad al-Jawharī report that he heard Abū Aḥmad Muḥammad ibn Jaʿfar report that he heard Aḥmad ibn Muḥammad al-Anmāṭī report that he heard Aḥmad ibn Naṣr report: 93.28

[Aḥmad ibn Naṣr:] I saw the Emissary of God in a dream and asked him who he'd left in our time for members of his community to emulate in their religion.

"Aḥmad ibn Ḥanbal."

We were informed by Yaḥyā ibn al-Ḥasan, who was informed by Muḥammad ibn al-Ḥusayn ibn Khalaf, who was informed by Abū l-Ḥasan ʿAlī ibn Muḥammad al-Ḥinnāʾī, who cites Abū Muḥammad al-Ṭarasūsī, who heard Abū Bakr Muḥammad ibn ʿĪsā report that he heard Hibat Allāh ibn al-Sarī say: 93.29

[Hibat Allāh ibn al-Sarī:] I saw the Emissary of God in a dream and said, "Emissary of God! Our thinkers all disagree and we don't know whose view to follow."

"Follow Aḥmad ibn Ḥanbal's," he replied.

أخبرنا محمّد بن أبي منصور قال: أخبرنا عبد القادر بن محمّد قال: أنبأنا إبراهيم بن عمر قال: أنبأنا عبد العزيز بن جعفر قال: أخبرنا أبو بكر أحمد بن محمّد الخلّال قال: ٣٠،٩٣

حدثنا أبو داوود السِّجستاني قال: رأيتُ في المنام سنة ثمان وعشرين ومائتين كأنّي في المسجد الجامع فأقبل رجل شبه الخَصِيّ من ناحية المقصورة وهو يقول: قال رسول الله صلى الله عليه وسلم: اقتدوا باللَّذَيْن من بعدي أحمد بن حنبل وفُلان، قال أبو داوود: لا أحفظ اسمه.

فجعلتُ أقول في نفسي هذا حديث غريب ففسَّرته على رجل فقال: الخصي مَلَك.

قال الخلّال: وحدثنا عبد الله بن إسماعيل قال: حدثنا عبد الله بن صالح بن الضحّاك قال: ٣١،٩٣

حدثنا عبد المؤمن أبو الهيثم المَرْوَزي قال: رأيتُ في المنام كأني عند قبر أحمد ابن حنبل إذ رأيت غبرة قد أقبلت وإذا فيها شيخ راكب على دابّة فقالوا: قد جاء الأمير، قد جاء الأمير![1]

قال: فنزل إلى القبر فقلتُ: من هذا؟ فقالوا: عبد الله بن عمر بن الخطّاب.

قال الخلّال: وحدثنا أبو يحيى الناقد قال: ٣٢،٩٣

سمعت حجّاج بن الشاعر يقول: رأيت عمّا لي في المنام بعدما مات كان قد كتب عن هُشيم فسألته عن أحمد بن حنبل فقال: ذاك من أصحاب عمر بن الخطّاب.

قال الخلال: وحدثنا عبد الله بن محمّد: ٣٣،٩٣

حدثني عبد الله بن أبي قُرّة قال: رأيت في المنام كأنّي دخلت الجنّة وإذا قصر من فضّة فانفتح باب القصر فخرج أحمد بن حنبل وعليه رِداء من نور متّزر به ورِداء من نور متّشح به فأسرعتُ المشي فصرت إليه فقال لي: قد جئت؟

قلت: نعم.

فلم يزل يردد عليّ حتى انتبهتُ.

---

١ قد جاء الأمير: ليس في د.

We cite Muḥammad ibn Abī Manṣūr, who cites ʿAbd al-Qādir ibn Muḥammad, who was informed by Ibrāhīm ibn ʿUmar, who was informed by ʿAbd al-ʿAzīz ibn Jaʿfar, who cites Abū Bakr Aḥmad ibn Muḥammad al-Khallāl, who heard Abū Dāwūd al-Sijistānī report: **93.30**

[Al-Sijistānī:] I had a dream in 228 [842–43] where I was in the Friday mosque and a man who looked like a eunuch came out of the enclosure toward me saying, "The Emissary of God has said, 'After I'm gone, follow Aḥmad ibn Ḥanbal and. . . '" someone else whose name I can't remember.

I thought, "What a strange report!" When I asked someone to interpret the dream, he said, "The one who looked like a eunuch was an angel."

Al-Khallāl said: We heard ʿAbd Allāh ibn Ismāʿīl report that he heard ʿAbd Allāh ibn Ṣāliḥ ibn al-Ḍaḥḥāk report that he heard ʿAbd al-Muʾmin Abū l-Haytham al-Marwazī report: **93.31**

[Al-Marwazī:] I dreamed I was by Aḥmad's tomb. A cloud of dust appeared, and out of it an elder came riding.

"The prince is here!" came the cry.

The man dismounted by the tomb. I asked who he was and they told me, "ʿAbd Allāh ibn ʿUmar ibn al-Khaṭṭāb."[249]

Al-Khallāl said: we heard Abū Yaḥyā l-Nāqid report that he heard Ḥajjāj ibn al-Shāʿir say: **93.32**

[Ḥajjāj:] An uncle of mine who had written down reports heard from Hushaym appeared to me in a dream. I asked him about Aḥmad ibn Ḥanbal and he said, "He's an associate of ʿUmar ibn al-Khaṭṭāb."

Al-Khallāl said that ʿAbd Allāh ibn Muḥammad reported to him that ʿAbd Allāh ibn Abī Qurrah reported: **93.33**

[Ibn Abī Qurrah:] I dreamed that I had gone into the Garden. There I saw a palace made of silver. The door opened and out came Aḥmad ibn Ḥanbal wearing one garment of light as a breechclout and another as a sash. I raced up to him and he said, "Are you here already?"

"Yes," I said.

He kept asking the question until I woke up.

قال ابن أبي قُرة: ورأيت في المنام أنّي مررت بمِصْراعين من ذهب فإذا جبال المِسْك والناس مجتمعون وهم يقولون: قد جاء الغازي، قد جاء الغازي!

فدخل أحمد بن حنبل متقلّدًا السيف ومعه رمح فقال: هذه الجنّة.

قال ابن أبي قرة: وقالت لي أُختي فاطمة بنت أبي قرة إنها رأت في المنام ليلة الجمعة قرافير من نور نزلت من السماء ثم صُعد بها.

فقلت: ما هذا؟

فقيل لي: روح أحمد بن حنبل يُصْعَد بها إلى الله عز وجل.

قال الخلال: وحدثنا محمّد بن موسى الورّاق قال: ٣٤،٩٣

سمعت عبيد الله[١] بن العبّاس يقول: رأيت في المنام كأنّا ننتظر جنازة أبي عبد الله أحمد أن يُخرَج بها ثمّ نظرت فإذا هي قد أُخرجت وكأنها تُرفع إلى السماء فما زالت تُرفع حتى غابت في السماء.

قال الخلّال: وحدثنا عبد الله بن إسماعيل قال: حدثنا محمّد بن رجاء قال: حدثنا منصور بن عِمْران النَّيْسابوري قال: ٣٥،٩٣

حدثنا مَجْزَأَة عن عبد الوهّاب الورّاق قال: رأيت النبيّ صلّى الله عليه وسلّم أقبل فقال لي: ما لي أراك محزونًا؟

قال: قلت: وكيف لا أكون محزونًا وقد حلّ بأُمّتك ما قد ترى؟

قال: فقال لي: لينتهِيَنَّ الناس إلى مذهب أحمد بن حنبل، لينتهيَنّ الناس إلى مذهب أحمد بن حنبل.

أنبأنا يحيى بن الحسن قال: أنبأنا محمّد بن الحسين الفقيه قال: أخبرنا الحسن بن حامد الورّاق قال: حدثنا أبو الحسن الطَّرَسُوسي قال: حدثنا محمّد بن الحسن بن أبان القُرشي قال: ٣٦،٩٣

---

١ في هـ فقط.

I also dreamed of walking through a gate whose doors were made of gold. On the other side were mountains of musk and people saying, "The warrior is here!"

Then Aḥmad ibn Ḥanbal came in wearing a sword and carrying a spear. "This is the Garden," he said.

My sister Fāṭimah bint Abī Qurrah told me that one Friday she dreamed of seeing birds made of light coming down from Heaven and people using them to fly up.

"I asked what the light was and they said, 'It's Aḥmad ibn Ḥanbal's spirit, and it takes you up to God.'"

Al-Khallāl said: We heard Muḥammad ibn Mūsā l-Warrāq report that he heard 'Ubayd Allāh ibn al-'Abbās say: **93.34**

[Ibn al-'Abbās:] I dreamed we were waiting for Aḥmad's funeral procession to come out. When it appeared, I looked and saw that it was rising into the sky. It kept on rising until it disappeared.

Al-Khallāl said that 'Abd Allāh ibn Ismā'īl reported that he heard Muḥammad ibn Rajā' report that he heard Manṣūr ibn 'Imrān al-Naysābūrī report that he heard Majza'ah report, citing 'Abd al-Wahhāb al-Warrāq, who said: **93.35**

[Al-Warrāq:] The Prophet came to me in a dream and asked me, "Why do you look so sad?"

"How could I not look sad," I answered, "when your community has fallen on such hard times?"

"Tell everyone to cleave to the path of Aḥmad ibn Ḥanbal," he said, twice.

We were informed by Yaḥyā ibn al-Ḥasan, who was informed by Muḥammad ibn al-Ḥusayn al-Faqīh, who cites al-Ḥasan ibn Ḥāmid al-Warrāq, who heard Abū l-Ḥasan al-Ṭarasūsī report that he heard Muḥammad ibn al-Ḥasan ibn Abān al-Qurashī report that he heard 'Abd al-Ṣamad al-Quhunduzī report, on the authority of Abū Zur'ah, who said: **93.36**

حدثنا عبد الصمد القُهُنْدُزي عن أبي زُرْعة قال: رأيت النبيّ صلىّ الله عليه وسلّم في النوم فشكوتُ ما نَلقى من الجَهْمية فقال: لا تحزن فإنّ أحمد بن حنبل قد سدّ عليهم الأُفق.

أخبرنا محمّد بن أبي منصور قال: أنبأنا أبو عليّ الحسن بن أحمد قال: أخبرنا أبو محمّد الخلال قال: وجدتُ بخط أبي الفتح ابن أبي الفوارس[1] قال: حدثنا صَدَقة بن هُبَيرة المَوْصِلي قال: حدثنا محمّد بن عبد الله الواسطي قال: ٣٧،٩٣

قال عبد الله بن المبارك الزَّمِن: رأيتُ زبيدة في المنام فقلت: ما فعل الله بك؟

قالت: غفر لي في أول مِعْوَل ضُرب في طريق مكّة.

قلتُ: فما هذه الصفرة في وجهك؟

قالت: دُفن في ظهرانينا رجل يُقال له: بِشْر المَرِيسي زَفرت عليه جهنّم زفرةً فاقشعرّ لها جلدي فهذه الصفرة من تلك الزفرة.

قلت: فما فعل أحمد بن حنبل؟

قالت: الساعة فارقني أحمد بن حنبل في طيّار من دُرّة بيضاء في لُجّة حمراء يريد زيارة الجبّار عزّ وجلّ.

قلت: بِمَ نال ذلك؟

قالت: بقوله القرآن كلام الله غير مخلوق.

أنبأنا أبو بكر محمّد بن عبد الباقي قال: أخبرنا هنّاد بن إبراهيم قال: أخبرنا عليّ بن محمّد بن عبد الله قال[2]: حدثنا عثمان بن أحمد قال: ٣٨،٩٣

حدثنا حنبل قال: حدثني بعض من أثق به أنّ امرأة رأوها في النوم وقد شاب صدغها فقيل لها: ما هذا الشيب؟

قالت: لما ضُرب أحمد بن حنبل زفرت جهنم زفرة لم يبقَ منّا أحد إلّا شاب.

أنبأنا يحيى بن الحسن قال: أنبأنا محمّد بن الحسين بن خلف قال: أخبرنا عبد الله بن أحمد قال: أخبرنا أبو عمر ٣٩،٩٣

---

١ د: القواس، اعتمده التركي.   ٢ : أخبرنا عليّ بن محمّد بن عبد الله قال: ليس في د.

[Abū Zurʿah:] I saw the Prophet in a dream and complained to him about the trouble we were having with the followers of Jahm.

"Have no fear," he said. "Aḥmad ibn Ḥanbal stands in their way."

We cite Muḥammad ibn Abī Manṣūr, who was informed by Abū ʿAlī l-Ḥasan ibn Aḥmad, who cites Abū Muḥammad al-Khallāl, who found in the handwriting of Abū l-Fatḥ ibn Abī al-Qawwās that he heard Ṣadaqah ibn Hubayrah al-Mawṣilī report that he heard Muḥammad ibn ʿAbd Allāh al-Wāsiṭī report that he heard ʿAbd Allāh ibn al-Mubārak al-Zamin say: 93.37

[Ibn al-Mubārak al-Zamin:] I saw Zubaydah in a dream and asked her how God had judged her.

"The moment we broke ground for the Mecca road, He forgave me."

"But why do you look jaundiced?"

"A man called Bishr al-Marīsī was buried among us. Hell wanted him so badly it gave a groan that made my skin crawl and turned my face yellow."

"What happened to Aḥmad ibn Ḥanbal?"

"He just passed me in a boat of white pearl that sails on a fathomless red sea, on his way to visit the Merciful One."

"What did he do to deserve his reward?"

"Saying that the Qur'an is the speech of God and not created."

We were informed by Abū Bakr Muḥammad ibn ʿAbd al-Bāqī, who cites Hannād ibn Ibrāhīm, who cites ʿAlī ibn Muḥammad ibn ʿAbd Allāh, who heard ʿUthmān ibn Aḥmad report that he heard Ḥanbal report: 93.38

[Ḥanbal:] Someone I trust told me that he dreamed of a woman whose hair had turned white at the temples. When he asked her about it, she said, "When Aḥmad was flogged, Hell breathed such a sigh that all of us went grey."

We were informed by Yaḥyā ibn al-Ḥasan, who was informed by Muḥammad ibn al-Ḥusayn ibn Khalaf, who cites ʿAbd Allāh ibn Aḥmad, who cites Abū ʿUmar ibn 93.39

بن حَيُّويه أنّ ابن مخلد أخبرهم قال: أخبرنا أبو خالد يزيد بن خالد بن طَهْمان قال:

حدثنا عبيد الله بن عمر القَواريري قال: بلغني عن رجل له حال أنه رأى رؤيا فأحببتُ أن أسمعها منه فجاء فخلا بي فسمعتُ صبية لي تقول: على وجهه النور.

فقال: رأيتُ النبيّ صلّى الله عليه وسلّم قاعدًا ومعه أحمد بن نصر فقال: على أبي فُلان لعنة الله، ثلاث مرات، وعلى فُلان وفلان لعنة الله، ثلاث مرات، فإنّهما يكيدان الإسلام وأهله ويكيدان أحمد بن حنبل والقَواريري وليس يصلان إلى شيء منهما إن شاء الله. ثمّ قال لي: أَقْرِئ أحمد والقَواريري السلام وقل لهما: جزاكما الله عنّي خيرًا وعن أُمّتي.

أخبرنا محمّد بن أبي منصور قال: أخبرنا عبد القادر بن محمّد بن يوسف قال: أخبرنا إبراهيم بن عمر البرمكي قال: ٤٠،٩٣
أخبرنا عبيد الله بن عبد الرحمن قال:

حدثني ابن المَحامِلي عن أبيه قال: رأيت أبا سعيد النَّهرَتيري في النوم بعد وفاته وكان رجلاً من أهل القرآن والعلم والفقه، قال: وكأنّه قد تلقّاني بباب دار قطن.

فقلت: أي شيء خبرك؟

فأومأ إليّ أنه تخلّص بعد شدّة.

قلت: أي شيء خبر الناس؟

قال: فقال لي: ليس غير القرآن والعلم.

قلت: فمجلسنا هذا؟

قال: ما أنتم عليه فهو الحقّ. وعنى مذهب الشافعي.

قلت: فأحمد بن حنبل؟

فأوما إلى أنه في منزلة جليلة.[1]

أخبرنا عمر بن ظفر قال: أخبرنا جعفر بن أحمد قال: أخبرنا عبد العزيز بن عليّ قال: أخبرنا عليّ بن عبد الله بن ٤١،٩٣
جهضم قال: حدثنا يوسف بن أحمد بن محمّد الدُّوري قال: حدثني أحمد بن أبي شجاع الصوفي أبو العباس قال:

---

١ د: مقام جليلة.

Ḥayyuwayh to the effect that Ibn Makhlad told them that Abū Khālid Yazīd ibn Khālid ibn Ṭahmān heard ʿUbayd Allāh ibn ʿUmar al-Qawārīrī report:

[Al-Qawārīrī:] A certain man of spiritual standing was said to have had a dream vision and I wanted to hear about it from him. He came and we sat alone for a while. Later my little girl said, "He had light coming from his face."

He told me that he had seen the Prophet sitting with Aḥmad ibn Naṣr.

"The Prophet said, 'God's curse on So-and-So,' three times, 'and So-and-So and So-and-So! They're plotting against Aḥmad ibn Ḥanbal and al-Qawārīrī, but they won't get anywhere, God willing!' Then he said to me, 'Greet Aḥmad and al-Qawārīrī and tell them that I pray to God to reward them on my behalf and on behalf of my community.'"[250]

We cite Muḥammad ibn Abī Manṣūr, who cites ʿAbd al-Qādir ibn Muḥammad ibn Yūsuf, who cites Ibrāhīm ibn ʿUmar al-Barmakī, who cites ʿUbayd Allāh ibn ʿAbd al-Raḥmān, who heard Ibn al-Maḥāmilī (maker of camel-litters) report, citing his father, who said: 93.40

[Al-Maḥāmilī:] Abū Saʿīd al-Nahratīrī was a man of Qur'an, Hadith-learning, and religious understanding. After he died, he came to me in a dream, as if he were meeting me at the gate of Cotton House.[251]

"What happened to you?" I asked him. Using gestures, he conveyed that he had suffered an ordeal but gained salvation in the end.

"What about us here?"

"Only two things matter," he said. "The Qur'an and Hadith-knowledge."

"What about our study circle?"

"The way you've taken"—meaning the legal school of al-Shāfiʿī—"is right."

"What about Aḥmad ibn Ḥanbal?"

He conveyed with a gesture that Aḥmad had attained a lofty rank.

We cite ʿUmar ibn Ẓafar, who cites Jaʿfar ibn Aḥmad, who cites ʿAbd al-ʿAzīz ibn ʿAlī, who cites ʿAlī ibn ʿAbd Allāh ibn Jahḍam, who heard Yūsuf ibn Aḥmad ibn Muḥammad al-Dūrī report that he heard Aḥmad ibn Abī Shujāʿ al-Ṣūfī Abū l-ʿAbbās report that he heard Abū Bakr Aḥmad ibn Muḥammad ibn al-Ḥajjāj report: 93.41

حدثني أبو بكر أحمد بن محمّد بن الحجّاج قال: حدثني رجل من أهل طَرَسُوس قال: كنتُ أدعو الله أن يريني أهل القُبور فأسألهم عن أحمد بن حنبل ما فعل.

قال: فرأيت بعد موته بعشر سنين كأنّ أهل القبور قيام على قبورهم فبادروني بالكلام وقالوا: يا هذا كم تدعو الله أن يُريك إيّانا؟ تسألنا عن رجل منذ فارقكم تَحْلوه الملائكة بالحِلْي تحت شجرة طوبى!

٤٢،٩٣ أخبرنا عبد الملك بن أبي القاسم قال: أخبرنا عبد الله بن محمّد الأنصاري قال: أخبرنا إسحاق بن إبراهيم المعدّل قال: أخبرنا محمّد بن عبد الله بن محمّد بن زكريا قال: حدثنا أبو عبد الله محمّد بن إبراهيم قال: سمعت عبد الله بن إبراهيم الأزدي قال: حدثنا زياد بن أبي يزيد القصري قال:

سمعتُ يحيى بن عبد الحميد الحِمّاني يقول: رأيت في المنام كأنّي في صُفّة لي جالس إذ جاء النبيّ صلى الله عليه وسلم فأخذ بعضادتَي الباب ثمّ أذّن فأقام فقال: نجا الناجُون وهلك الهالكون!

فقلتُ يا رسول الله من الناجون؟

قال: أحمد بن حنبل وأصحابه.

٤٣،٩٣ أخبرنا أبو منصور القزّاز قال: أخبرنا أبو بكر أحمد بن عليّ بن ثابت قال: أخبرنا عليّ بن أحمد الرزّاز قال: حدثنا محمّد بن الحسن بن زياد النقّاش قال: حدثنا أبو سعيد محمّد بن يحيى البغدادي قال:

حدثنا عُبيد بن محمّد الورّاق قال: كان بالرَّمْلة رجل يُقال له عَمّار يقولون إنّه من الأبدال فاشتكى فذهبتُ إليه أعوده وقد بلغني عنه رؤيا رآها فقلت له: رؤيا حكَوها عنك.

فقال لي: نعم، رأيت النبيّ صلى الله عليه وسلم في النوم فقلت: يا رسول الله ادعُ الله لي بالمغفرة.

فدعا لي ثمّ رأيت الخضر بعد ذلك فقلت له: ما تقول في القرآن؟

قال: كلام الله ليس بمخلوق.

قلت: فما تقول في بشر بن الحارث؟

[Abū Bakr:] A man from Tarsus told me this story.

"I used to pray to God to show me dead people in their graves so I could ask them what had happened to Aḥmad ibn Ḥanbal. Ten years after his death, I dreamed that the dead were standing on their graves and calling out to me.

"'You there! How much longer will you ask God to show us to you? Ever since he left you, the one you've been asking about has been under the Ṭūbā tree,[252] with angels piling him with finery.'"

We cite ʿAbd al-Malik ibn Abī l-Qāsim, who cites ʿAbd Allāh ibn Muḥammad al-Anṣārī, who cites Isḥāq ibn Ibrāhīm al-Muʿaddal, who cites Muḥammad ibn ʿAbd Allāh ibn Muḥammad ibn Zakariyyā, who heard Abū ʿAbd Allāh Muḥammad ibn Ibrāhīm, who heard ʿAbd Allāh ibn Ibrāhīm al-Azdī say that he heard Ziyād ibn Abī Yazīd al-Qaṣrī report that he heard Yaḥyā ibn ʿAbd al-Ḥamīd al-Ḥimmānī say: **93.42**

[Al-Ḥimmānī:] I dreamed I was sitting under a portico at home when the Prophet appeared. He stood in the doorway with his hands on the jambs, called to prayer, and announced that prayer had begun. Then he said, "The saved are saved and the damned damned."

"Emissary of God," I said. "Who are the saved?"

"Aḥmad ibn Ḥanbal and his followers."

We cite Abū Manṣūr al-Qazzāz, who cites Abū Bakr Aḥmad ibn ʿAlī ibn Thabit, who cites ʿAlī ibn Aḥmad al-Razzāz, who heard Muḥammad ibn al-Ḥasan ibn Ziyād al-Naqqāsh report that he heard Abū Saʿīd Muḥammad ibn Yaḥyā l-Baghdādī report that he heard ʿUbayd ibn Muḥammad al-Warrāq report: **93.43**

[Al-Warrāq:] In Ramla there lived a man named ʿAmmar who people claimed was one of the Substitutes. He fell ill and I went to see him. I had heard about a vision he'd had, and so I asked him about it.

"It's true," he said. "I saw the Prophet in a dream and I asked him to pray to God to forgive me, and so he did. Later I saw al-Khaḍir and asked him, 'What do you say about the Qur'an?'

"He said, 'It's God's speech, and not created.'

"'What do you say about Bishr ibn al-Ḥārith?'

فقال: مات بشر يوم مات وما على ظهر الأرض أتقى لله منه.

قلت: فأحمد بن حنبل؟

فقال: صديق.

قلت: فالحسين الكرابيسي؟

فَغلّظ في أمره. فقلت: ما تقول في أمّي؟

فقال: تمرض وتعيش سبعة أيّام ثمّ تموت. فكان كما قال.

أخبرنا عبد الملك قال: أخبرنا عبد الله بن محمّد قال: أخبرنا محمّد بن محمّد بن محمود، ثم أخبرنا أبو يعقوب عنه قال: ٤٤،٩٣
أخبرنا عبد الرحمن بن أحمد بن حَمْدُوَيه المؤَذّن قال: حدثنا إسحاق بن إبراهيم بن الخليل قال: حدثنا عمر بن محمّد النَّسائي قال:

حدثنا أبو عمار الدهّان وكان من خِيار المسلمين قال: رأيتُ الخضر في المنام فقلت له: أنت الذي كنت مع موسى؟

قال: نعم. قلت: فما تقول في أحمد بن حنبل؟

قال: صِدّيق.

أخبرنا عبد الوهّاب بن المبارَك ويحيى بن عليّ قالا: أخبرنا أبو محمّد الصَّرِيفِيني قال: أخبرنا أبو بكر بن عَبدان قال: ٤٥،٩٣
أخبرنا أبو أحمد بن المهتدي قال: حدثنا حسين بن الخصيب قال:

حدثني أبو بكر بن حماد قال: رأيت النبيّ صلى الله عليه وسلم في النوم وكأنّي في مسجد الخَيْف فقلت: يا رسول الله كيف بشر عندكم؟

قال: أُنزل في وَسط الجنّة.

قلتُ: فأحمد بن حنبل؟

قال: أمّا بلغك أن الله تعالى إذا أدخل أهل الذكر[1] الجنّة ضحك إليهم عز وجل؟

أخبرنا يحيى بن عليّ المَدِيني قال: أخبرنا أبو بكر محمّد بن عليّ الخيّاط قال: أخبرنا الحسن بن الحسين بن حَمكان ٤٦،٩٣

---

١ ش: اهل الجنة.

"'The day he died, he left behind him no one more fearful of God.'

"'What about Aḥmad ibn Ḥanbal?'

"'He was a truth-teller.'

"'What about al-Ḥusayn al-Karābīsī?'

"In response he vilified him. Then I asked, 'What's going to happen to my mother?'

"He said, 'She'll fall ill and live for seven days before she dies,' and that's what happened."

We cite ʿAbd al-Malik, who cites ʿAbd Allāh ibn Muḥammad, who cites Muḥammad ibn Muḥammad ibn Maḥmūd—whom Abū Yaʿqūb also cited to me later as his source—who cites ʿAbd al-Raḥmān ibn Aḥmad ibn Ḥamduwayh al-Muʾadhdhin, who heard Isḥāq ibn Ibrāhīm ibn al-Khalīl report that he heard ʿUmar ibn Muḥammad al-Nasāʾī report that he heard Abū ʿAmmār al-Dahhān (maker or seller of grease), who was a good Muslim say: 93.44

[Al-Dahhān:] I saw al-Khaḍir in a dream and asked him if he was the one who was with Moses.[253]

He said he was. Then I asked him what he thought of Aḥmad ibn Ḥanbal.

"He's a truth-teller."

We cite ʿAbd al-Wahhāb ibn al-Mubārak and Yaḥyā ibn ʿAlī, who cite Abū Muḥammad al-Ṣarīfīnī, who cites Abū Bakr ibn ʿAbdān, who cites Abū Aḥmad ibn al-Muhtadī, who heard Ḥusayn ibn al-Khaṣīb report that he heard Abū Bakr ibn Ḥammād report: 93.45

[Abū Bakr:] I dreamed I was in the mosque of al-Khayf and there I saw the Prophet. I asked, "How is Bishr doing with you?"

"He was given a place in the middle of the Garden."

"What about Aḥmad ibn Ḥanbal?"

"Haven't you heard that when God admits the people of remembrance[254] to the Garden, he smiles at them?"

We cite Yaḥyā ibn ʿAlī l-Madīnī, who cites Abū Bakr Muḥammad ibn ʿAlī l-Khayyāṭ, who cites al-Ḥasan ibn al-Ḥusayn ibn Ḥamakān, who cites Abū Bakr Muḥammad ibn al-Ḥasan 93.46

قال: أخبرنا أبو بكر محمّد بن الحسن النقّاش: حدثنا محمّد بن إسحاق السراج قال:

سمعتُ أحمد بن الفتح يقول: رأيت بشر بن الحارث في منامي وهو قاعد في بستان وبين يديه مائدة وهو يأكل منها فقلت له: يا أبا نصر ما فعل الله بك؟

قال: رحمني وغفر لي وأباحني الجنّة بأسرها.

فقلتُ: فأين أخوك أحمد بن حنبل؟

فقال: هو قائم على باب الجنّة يشفع لأهل السنّة ممّن يقول إنّ القُرآن كلام الله غير مخلوق.

٤٧،٩٣ أخبرنا عليّ بن عبد الواحد المُوَحّد قال: أخبرنا هناد بن إبراهيم النسفي قال: أخبرنا عبد الواحد بن عبد الله بن السَّري قال: حدثنا محمّد بن العباس بن أحمد الطبري قال: حدثنا أبو الحسن عَقيل بن سمير قال: حدثنا عيسى ابن عبد الله قال: حدثنا جعفر بن محمد المروزي قال:

قال عليّ بن الموفق: كان لي وِرْد من الليل أقومه فقمتُ ليلة الجمعة ثم أخذت مضجعي فرأيت كأنّي أُدخلت الجنة فرأيت ثلاثة نفر من الناس أحدهم قاعد وبين يديه مائدة وعلى رأسه مَلَكان ملكٌ يطعمه الطعام وملكٌ يسقيه الشراب، ورأيت رجلاً في وسط الجنّة شاخصاً ببصره إلى الله عز وجل لا يطرف، ورجل آخر يخرج من الجنّة فيتعلّق بالناس فيُدخلهم الجنّة.

فقلت لرضوان: من هؤلاء الثلاثة الذين قد أُعطوا في الجنّة هذا الخير كله؟

قال: هؤلاء إخوانكم الذين ماتوا ولا ذنب عليهم.

قلتُ: صِف لي.

قال: أما الأوّل فإنّه بشر الحافي منذ عقل عقله ما شبع من الطعام ولا روي من الماء مخافة الله تعالى فقد وكّل الله به اليوم هذين المَلَكين ملك يُطعمه وملك يسقيه، وأما الآخر الشاخص ببصره نحو العرش فهو معروف الكرخي عبَد الله لا خوفاً من النار ولا شوقاً إلى الجنة ذلك عبَد الله شوقاً إلى الله فقد مَكّنه من النظر ينظر إليه كما شاء، وأما الثالث فهو الصادق في قوله الورع في دينه أبو عبد الله أحمد بن

al-Naqqāsh, who heard Muḥammad ibn Isḥāq al-Sarrāj report that he heard Aḥmad ibn al-Fatḥ say:

[Ibn al-Fatḥ:] Bishr ibn al-Ḥārith came to me in a dream, sitting and eating at a table laid for him in an orchard. I asked him how God had judged him.

"He took pity on me and forgave me, and opened the whole Garden to me."

"And where's your friend Aḥmad ibn Ḥanbal?"

"Standing at the gate to intercede for Sunnis who declare the Qur'an to be the uncreated speech of God."

We cite ʿAlī ibn ʿAbd al-Wāḥid al-Muwaḥḥid, who cites Hannād ibn Ibrāhīm al-Nasafī, who cites ʿAbd al-Wāḥid ibn ʿAbd Allāh ibn al-Sarī, who heard Muḥammad ibn al-ʿAbbās ibn Aḥmad al-Ṭabarī report that he heard Abū l-Ḥasan ʿAqīl ibn Samīr report that he heard ʿĪsā ibn ʿAbd Allāh report that he heard Jaʿfar ibn Muḥammad al-Marwazī report that ʿAlī ibn al-Muwaffaq said: **93.47**

[ʿAlī ibn al-Muwaffaq:] I had some personal devotions to do at night, so I stayed up from Thursday night until Friday morning then went to bed. I dreamed that I had entered the Garden. There I saw three men. The first was sitting at a table with one angel serving him food and another pouring him drink. The second was standing in the middle of the Garden gazing at God, Mighty and Glorious, without blinking. The third would leave the Garden, take hold of people, and bring them inside.

I asked Riḍwān, "Who are those three who've been so well rewarded?"

"Your brothers who died sinless."

"Tell me more."

"The first one," he said, "is Bishr the Barefoot, who from the time he reached the age of reason never once ate his fill or drank as much water as he wanted, all for fear of God, who has assigned him two angels: one to feed him and one to pour for him. The second man—the one gazing at the throne—is Maʿrūf al-Karkhī, who worshipped God because he longed for Him, not for fear of the Fire or in hope of the Garden; and now God has allowed him to gaze at Him all he wants. And the third one is Aḥmad ibn Ḥanbal, who was

حنبل أمره الجبّار أن يتصفّح وجوه أهل السُنّة فيُدخلهم الجنّة.[1]

٤٨،٩٣ أخبرنا محمّد بن ناصر قال: أنبأنا أبو عليّ الحسن بن أحمد قال: أخبرنا أبو الفتح هلال بن محمّد قال: حدثنا عثمان بن أحمد السماك إملاءً قال: حدثنا محمّد بن أحمد بن البراء قال:

حدثنا محمّد بن المثنى قال: رأيت بشر بن الحارث في المنام فقلت له: يا أبا نصر ما فعل الله بك؟

قال: غفر لي.

قال: قلت: يا أبا نصر ما فعل أحمد بن حنبل وعبد الوهّاب الوراق؟

قال: أُولئك في الفِردَوس، أو في الجنّة، يأكلون ويَشربون.

٤٩،٩٣ أخبرنا عبد الملك بن أبي القاسم قال: أخبرنا عبد الملك بن محمّد الأنصاري قال: أخبرنا إسماعيل بن إبراهيم قال: أخبرنا محمّد بن عبد الله البيّع قال: حدثني أبو عبد الله بن إبراهيم المؤذّن قال: أخبرني محمّد بن أحمد بن زكريا عن سعيد بن جمعة قال: سمعت أبا زُرعَة المكّي يقول:

سمعتُ عثمان بن جُرّزاذ[2] الأَنطاكي يقول: رأيتُ كأنّ القيامة قد قامت ومناديًا من بطنان العرش ينادي: ألا أدخِلوا أبا عبد الله وأبا عبد الله وأبا عبد الله وأبا عبد الله الجنّة. فقلت لملك بجنبي: من هؤلاء؟ قال: أوّلهم مالك والثاني الثوري والثالث محمّد بن إدريس ورابعهم أحمد بن حنبل.

وفي رواية أُخرى: هؤلاء أئمة أمّة محمّد وقد سُبق بهم إلى الجنّة.

٥٠،٩٣ أخبرنا عبد الملك قال: أخبرنا عبد الله بن محمّد الأَنصاري قال: أخبرنا أبو يعقوب قال: حدثنا أَسد بن رستم قال: أخبرنا الحسين بن أحمد البَيهقي قال:

حدثنا الحسين بن إسماعيل المَحامِلي قال: رأيت القاشاني فيما يرى النائم. فقلتُ: ما تقول في أحمد بن حنبل؟

قال: غفر الله له.

---

١ الخبر في ش فقط. ٢ ف: حرب.

truthful in his speech and scrupulous in his religion. God has commanded him to look into the faces of the Sunnis and bring them into the Garden."

We cite Muḥammad ibn Nāṣir, who was informed by Abū ʿAlī l-Ḥasan ibn Aḥmad, who cites Abū l-Fatḥ Hilāl ibn Muḥammad, who heard ʿUthmān ibn Aḥmad al-Sammāk dictate that he heard Muḥammad ibn Aḥmad ibn al-Barrāʾ report that he heard Muḥammad ibn al-Muthannā report: **93.48**

[Ibn al-Muthannā:] I saw Bishr ibn al-Ḥārith in a dream and asked him how God had judged him.

"He's forgiven me."

"What about Aḥmad ibn Ḥanbal and ʿAbd al-Wahhāb al-Warrāq?"

"They're in Paradise"—or "in the Garden"—"eating and drinking."

We cite ʿAbd al-Malik ibn Abī l-Qāsim, who cites ʿAbd Allāh ibn Muḥammad al-Anṣārī, who cites Ismāʿīl ibn Ibrāhīm, who cites Muḥammad ibn ʿAbd Allāh al-Bayyiʿ, who heard Abū ʿAbd Allāh ibn Ibrāhīm al-Muʾadhdhin cite Muḥammad ibn Aḥmad ibn Zakariyyā report on the authority of Saʿīd ibn Jumʿah, who heard Abū Zurʿah al-Makkī say that he heard ʿUthmān ibn Khurrazādh al-Anṭākī say: **93.49**

[Al-Anṭākī:] I dreamed it was the Day of Resurrection. From inside the Throne a herald called out, "Bring Abū ʿAbd Allāh, Abū ʿAbd Allāh, Abū ʿAbd Allāh, and Abū ʿAbd Allāh into the Garden!"

I asked an angel next to me, "Who are they?"

"Mālik, al-Thawrī, Muḥammad ibn Idrīs, and Aḥmad ibn Ḥanbal."

In another telling he added: "Those four are the exemplars of Muḥammad's community, and they were brought to the Garden ahead of everyone else."

We cite ʿAbd al-Malik, who cites ʿAbd Allāh ibn Muḥammad al-Anṣārī, who cites Abū Yaʿqūb, who heard Asad ibn Rustam report that he cites al-Ḥusayn ibn Aḥmad al-Bayhaqī, who heard al-Ḥusayn ibn Ismāʿīl al-Maḥāmilī report: **93.50**

[Al-Maḥāmilī:] Al-Qāshānī came to me in a dream and I asked what he knew about Aḥmad ibn Ḥanbal.

"God forgave him," he said.

٥١،٩٣ أخبرنا إسماعيل بن أحمد ومحمّد بن عبد الباقي قالا: أخبرنا حَمْد بن أحمد قال: أخبرنا أحمد بن عبد الله الحافظ قال: حدثنا عثمان بن أحمد قال: حدثنا عبد الله بن أحمد بن حنبل قال:

حدثني ثابت بن أحمد بن شَبُّويه المَرْوَزي قال: كان يخيل إليّ أن لأبي أحمد ابن شَبُّويه فضيلة على أحمد بن حنبل للجهاد وفكاك الأَسارى ولزوم الثغور فسألتُ أخي عبد الله بن أحمد: أيّهما أرجح في نفسك؟

فقال: أبو عبد الله أحمد بن حنبل.

فلم أقنع بقوله وأبيتُ إلا العجب بأبي أحمد بن شَبُّويه.

فأريت بعد سنة في منامي كأنّ شيخًا حوله الناس يسمعون منه فقعدتُ إليه فلمّا قام تبعته فقلت: أخبِرْني أحمد بن حنبل وأحمد بن شبويه أيّهما عندك أعْلَى وأفضل[١]؟

فقال: سُبحان الله! إنّ أحمد بن حنبل ابتُلي فصبر وإن أحمد بن شَبُّويه عوفي، المبتلى الصابر كالمعافَى؟ هيهات، ما أبعد ما بينهما!

٥٢،٩٣ أنبأنا يحيى بن الحسن قال: أنبأنا محمّد بن الحسين بن خلف قال: أخبرنا أبو الحسن عليّ بن محمّد الحنائيّ قال: أخبرنا أبو محمّد الطرسوسي قال: حدثنا أبو العبّاس البَرْدَعي قال: سمعتُ أَبا الفضل العباس بن عبد الرحمن يقول:

سمعتُ أبا حفص الجلّاء يقول: قال لي صديق لي[٢]: رأيت النبيّ صلّى الله عليه وسلّم في النوم وسألته عن أشياء وعمّا اختلف الفقهاء فقال لي النبيّ صلى الله عليه وسلم: كلّ يُخطئ ويُصيب وأحمد بن حنبل مؤيَّد قليل الخطأ، استمسِكْ به واحتجّ به فإنّك في زمان لا ترى مثله أبدًا.

٥٣،٩٣ أخبرنا عمر بن ظَفَر قال: أخبرنا جعفر بن أحمد قال: أخبرنا عبد العزيز بن عليّ الأَزَجي قال: أخبرنا عليّ بن عبد الله بن جَهْضَم قال:

---

١ د: أعلى فضيلة. ٢ ليس في د.

We cite Ismāʿīl ibn Aḥmad and Muḥammad ibn ʿAbd al-Bāqī, who cite Ḥamd ibn Aḥmad, who cites Aḥmad ibn ʿAbd Allāh al-Ḥāfiẓ, who heard ʿUthmān ibn Aḥmad report that he heard ʿAbd Allāh ibn Aḥmad ibn Ḥanbal report that he heard Thābit ibn Aḥmad ibn Shabbuwayh al-Marwazī report: **93.51**

[Thābit al-Marwazī:] I used to think that Ibn Shabbuwayh, who fought in the jihad, ransomed prisoners, and lived on the frontier, had more merit than Aḥmad. I asked my brother ʿAbd Allāh ibn Aḥmad which of the two he preferred.

"Aḥmad ibn Ḥanbal."

I wasn't convinced, and couldn't bring myself to admire anyone but Ibn Shabbuwayh.

A year later, I had a dream where an elder was speaking to a group of people gathered around him. When he rose to go I followed him and said, "Tell me who has more merit and a higher rank: Aḥmad ibn Ḥanbal or Aḥmad ibn Shabbuwayh?"

"What a question!" he replied. "Aḥmad ibn Ḥanbal was put to the test and stood firm while Aḥmad ibn Shabbuwayh was spared. How can you compare someone who survived an ordeal to one who never went through it? I can't! There's a world of difference between them."

We were informed by Yaḥyā ibn al-Ḥasan, who was informed by Muḥammad ibn al-Ḥusayn ibn Khalaf, who cites Abū l-Ḥasan ʿAlī ibn Muḥammad al-Ḥinnāʾī, who cites Abū Muḥammad al-Ṭarasūsī, who heard Abū l-ʿAbbās al-Bardaʿī report that he heard Abū l-Faḍl al-ʿAbbās ibn ʿAbd al-Raḥmān say that he heard Ḥafṣ al-Jallāʾ say: **93.52**

[Al-Jallāʾ:] A friend told me that he saw the Prophet in a dream and asked him about some of the issues that jurists disagree on. The Prophet told him, "All jurists are right about some things and wrong about others. Aḥmad ibn Ḥanbal has God's help, and makes fewer errors, so cleave to his example and cite him when you make an argument. You live in an age that will see no other like him."

We cite ʿUmar ibn Ẓafar, who cites Jaʿfar ibn Aḥmad, who cites ʿAbd al-ʿAzīz ibn ʿAlī l-Azajī, who cites ʿAlī ibn ʿAbd Allāh ibn Jahḍam, who heard Muḥammad ibn al-ʿAbbās ibn Fuḍayl report: **93.53**

حدثنا محمّد بن العبّاس بن فُضيل قال: حدثني الخيّاط صاحب بشر قال: جاء رجل إلى بشر بن الحارث وكان بشر مؤاخياً له فقال له: يا أبا نصر رأيت في منامي ليلة عيد فطر أو أضحى كأنّ القيامة قد قامت والناس في كرب وشدّة حتى رأيت الناس دموعهم تجري دماً إذ خرج منادٍ ينادي أين بشر وأين أحمد بن حنبل؟

فأخذوكما فأدخلوكما على الله عز وجل فقال أهل الموقف: إن حوسب هؤلاء هلكنا! إذ خرج علينا ملك من الملائكة فقلنا: ما فعل بشر وأحمد؟

فقال: يُحاسبون بقيام الشكر بما مَنّ عليهم من سترهم.

فقال بشر: أمّا أحد الاثنين فالتقصير قرينه وأمّا الآخر فتشهد له الحقائق بقيامه بالشكر.

أخبرنا عبد الملك بن أبي القاسم قال: أخبرنا عبد الله بن محمّد الأنصاري قال: سمعت إسماعيل بن إبراهيم يقول: ٩٣،٥٤

سمعت محمّد بن عبد الله الحافظ يقول: رأيتُ أبا الحسن بن عَبْدوس في المنام فإذا عليه أثواب بيض فقلتُ له: أرأيت أبا عبد الله الشافعي؟

فقال: بحر لا ينزف عنده مجمع القوم.

فقلت: مالك بن أنس؟

فقال: فوقهم بدرجات.

قلت: فأبو عبد الله أحمد بن حنبل؟

قال: أقربهم إلى الله وسيلة.

أخبرنا إسماعيل بن أحمد ومحمّد بن عبد الباقي قالا: أخبرنا أبو الفضل ابن أحمد قال: أخبرنا أحمد بن عبد الله قال: حدثنا محمّد بن عليّ بن حُبيش قال: حدثنا عبد الله بن إسحاق المدائني قال: حدثنا محمّد بن حرب قال: حدثنا عبيد بن محمّد قال: ٩٣،٥٥

حدثنا عَمّار قال: رأيت الخضر عليه السلام في المنام فقلت له: أَخبرني عن أحمد بن محمّد بن حنبل.

قال: صِدّيق.

[Muḥammad ibn al-ʿAbbās:] Bishr's associate al-Khayyāṭ told me that a man who was an intimate of Bishr ibn al-Ḥārith once came to Bishr and said, "On one of the festival days I dreamed that it was the end of the world. Everyone was so terrified that I saw people weeping tears of blood. A herald came forward and called out, 'Where is Bishr and where is Aḥmad ibn Ḥanbal?'

"They took the two of you and brought you into God's presence.

"'If those two are found wanting,' said the people waiting to be judged, 'then we're all doomed.'

"Then an angel appeared. 'What happened to Bishr and Aḥmad?' we asked.

"'They're being judged on how well they showed their gratitude to God for blessing them with untarnished reputations.'"

Hearing this story, Bishr said, "One of the two can never do enough. As for the other, experience shows how grateful he is."

We cite ʿAbd al-Malik ibn Abī l-Qāsim, who cites ʿAbd Allāh ibn Muḥammad al-Anṣārī, who heard Ismāʿīl ibn Ibrāhīm say that he heard Muḥammad ibn ʿAbd Allāh al-Ḥāfiẓ say: 93.54

[Muḥammad ibn ʿAbd Allāh:] I saw Abū l-Ḥasan ibn ʿAbdūs in a dream. He was dressed in white. I said, "Have you seen al-Shāfiʿī?"

"He's a sea that never runs dry," he said, "and the community should gather around him."

"What about Mālik ibn Anas?"

"Head and shoulders above the others."

"What about Aḥmad ibn Ḥanbal?"

"His is the closest approach to God."

We cite Ismāʿīl ibn Aḥmad and Muḥammad ibn ʿAbd al-Bāqī, who cite Abū l-Faḍl ibn Aḥmad, who cites Aḥmad ibn ʿAbd Allāh, who heard Muḥammad ibn ʿAlī ibn Ḥubaysh report that he heard ʿAbd Allāh ibn Isḥāq al-Madāʾinī report that he heard Muḥammad ibn Ḥarb report that he heard ʿUbayd ibn Muḥammad report that he heard ʿAmmār report: 93.55

[ʿAmmār:] Al-Khaḍir came to me in a dream and I asked him to tell me about Aḥmad ibn Ḥanbal.

"A truth-teller," he said.

أخبرنا ابن ناصر قال: أخبرنا عبد القادر بن محمّد قال: أخبرنا إبراهيم ابن عمر البرمكي قال: أخبرنا أبو عبد الله بن بَطّة قال: حدثني أبي قال: قال لنا ابن ذَريح: ٥٦،٩٣

قال بِلال الخوّاص: رأيت الخضر عليه السلام في النوم فسألته عن بشر بن الحارث فقال: لم يُخلّف بعده مثله.

وسألته عن أحمد بن حنبل فقال: صِدّيق.

أخبرنا إسماعيل ومحمّد قالا: أخبرنا حَمْد بن أحمد قال: أخبرنا أحمد بن عبد الله قال: حدثنا ظَفَر بن أحمد قال: حدثنا عبد الله بن إبراهيم الحريري[١] قال: قال أبو جعفر محمّد بن صالح بن ذريح: ٥٧،٩٣

قال بلال الخوّاص: رأيت الخضر في النوم فقلت له: ما تقول في بشر؟

قال: لم يُخلف بعده مثله.

قلت: ما تقول في أحمد بن حنبل؟

قال: صِدّيق.

قلت: بأي وسيلة رأيتك؟

قال: ببرّك لأمّك.

قلت: وقد روي لنا أن بلالاً رأى الخضر في اليقظة وقد ذكرنا ذلك فيما تقدم من كتابنا في ذكر ثناء الخضر على أحمد.

أخبرنا محمّد بن أبي منصور قال: أخبرنا عبد القادر بن محمّد قال: أنبأنا إبراهيم بن عمر قال: أنبأنا عبد العزيز بن جعفر قال: حدثنا أبو بكر الخلال قال: حدثنا محمّد بن موسى قال: ٥٨،٩٣

قال هَيْذام: رأى رجل في النوم كأنّ قائلاً يقول: يكون في الناس من يدفع الله بهم البلاء - أو كذا - وأنّ أحمد بن حنبل منهم.

أخبرنا عمر بن ظفر قال: أخبرنا جعفر بن أحمد قال: أخبرنا عبد العزيز بن عليّ قال: أخبرنا أبو الحسن بن جَهْضَم قال: حدثنا أحمد بن محمّد بن عيسى قال: حدثنا محمّد بن الحسن قال: حدثني أبو بكر المَرُّوذي قال: ٥٩،٩٣

---

١ د: الحربي.

We cite Ibn Nāṣir, who cites ʿAbd al-Qādir ibn Muḥammad, who cites Ibrāhīm ibn ʿUmar al-Barmakī, who cites Abū ʿAbd Allāh ibn Baṭṭah, who heard his father report that Ibn Dharīḥ told them that Bilāl al-Khawwāṣ said: **93.56**

[Bilāl al-Khawwāṣ:] Al-Khaḍir came to me in a dream and I asked him about Bishr ibn al-Ḥārith.

"He was the last of his kind," he said.

Then I asked about Aḥmad ibn Ḥanbal.

"A truth-teller," he said.

We cite Ismāʿīl and Muḥammad, who cite Ḥamd ibn Aḥmad, who cites Aḥmad ibn ʿAbd Allāh, who heard Ẓafar ibn Aḥmad report that he heard ʿAbd Allāh ibn Ibrāhīm al-Ḥarīrī report that Abū Jaʿfar Muḥammad ibn Ṣāliḥ ibn Dharīḥ said that Bilāl al-Khawwāṣ said: **93.57**

[Bilāl al-Khawwāṣ:] Al-Khaḍir came to me in a dream and I asked him about Bishr ibn al-Ḥārith.

"He was the last of his kind," he said.

Then I asked about Aḥmad ibn Ḥanbal.

"A truth-teller," he said.

"How is it that I'm able to see you?"

"It's because of your kindness to your mother."

[The author:] It has also been reported that Bilāl saw al-Khaḍir while awake. The story appears in our chapter on al-Khaḍir's praise of Aḥmad.

We cite Muḥammad ibn Abī Manṣūr, who cites ʿAbd al-Qādir ibn Muḥammad, who was informed by Ibrāhīm ibn ʿUmar, who was informed by ʿAbd al-ʿAzīz ibn Jaʿfar, who heard Abū Bakr al-Khallāl report that he heard Muḥammad ibn Mūsā report that Haydhām said: **93.58**

[Haydhām:] A man dreamed he heard someone saying, "God has chosen certain persons among you to protect you from disaster—or words to that effect—and Aḥmad ibn Ḥanbal is one of them."

We cite ʿUmar ibn Ẓafar, who cites Jaʿfar ibn Aḥmad, who cites ʿAbd al-ʿAzīz ibn ʿAlī, who cites Abū l-Ḥasan ibn Jahḍam, who heard Aḥmad ibn Muḥammad ibn ʿĪsā report that he heard Muḥammad ibn al-Ḥasan report that he heard Abū Bakr al-Marrūdhī report that he heard a man of Ṭarsūs report: **93.59**

حدثني رجل بطرسوس قال: فكرت ليلة في أحمد بن حنبل وصبره على ضرب السوط وكيف قوي على ذلك مع ضعف بدنه فبكيتُ فرأيت في منامي كأن قائلاً يقول: فكيف لو رأيتَ الملائكة في السماوات وهو يُضرب وهي تُباهي به.

قال: فقلتُ: وعلمت الملائكة بضرب أحمد؟

فقال: ما بقي في السماوات ملك إلّا وأَشرف عليه وهو يُضرَب.

٦٠،٩٣ أخبرنا المحمّدان: ابن ناصر وابن عبد الباقي قالا: أخبرنا حمد بن أحمد قال: أخبرنا أحمد بن عبد الله قال: حدثنا سليمان بن أحمد قال: حدثنا أحمد بن عليّ الأَبّار قال:

حدثني يعقوب بن يوسف ابن أخي معروف الكَرْخي قال: بينما أنا نائم في أيّام المحنة إِذ دخل عليّ رجل عليه جُبّة صوف بلا كُمّين فقلتُ: من أنت؟

فقال: أنا موسى بن عِمْران.

فقلتُ: أنت موسى بن عمران الذي كلّمك الله عز وجل وما بينك وبينه ترجمان؟

قال: أنا موسى الذي كلّمني الله عز وجل وما بيني وبينه ترجمان.

فبينا أنا كذلك إذ هبط علينا رجل من السقف عليه حُلّتان جَعد الشعر فقلتُ: من هذا؟

قال: هذا عيسى ابن مريم.

ثمّ قال لي موسى: أنا موسى الذي كلّمني الله وما بيني وبينه ترجمان وهذا عيسى ابن مريم ونبيّكم صلى الله عليه وسلم وأحمد بن حنبل وحَمَلةُ العرش وجميعُ الملائكة يشهدون أنّ القُرآن كلام الله غير مخلوق.

٦١،٩٣ أخبرنا محمّد بن أبي منصور قال: أخبرنا عبد القادر بن محمّد قال: أخبرنا إبراهيم بن عمر قال: أخبرنا عليّ بن عبد العزيز قال: أخبرنا عبد الرحمن بن أبي حاتم قال:

سمعتُ عبد الله بن الحسن بن موسى يقول رأيت رجلاً من أَهل الحديث توفي فقلتُ له: ما فعل الله بك؟ فقال: غفر لي.

فقلت: بالله؟

One night I fell to thinking about Aḥmad ibn Ḥanbal and how he survived being flogged despite how frail he was. I was moved to tears. That night I dreamed of a voice that said, "If only you could have seen how proud the angels in Heaven were as they saw him being beaten!"

"What?" I asked. "The angels knew about Aḥmad's flogging?"

"There wasn't a single one who wasn't looking down."

We cite the two Muḥammads, Ibn Nāṣir and Ibn ʿAbd al-Bāqī, who cite Ḥamd ibn Aḥmad, who cites Aḥmad ibn ʿAbd Allāh, who heard Sulaymān ibn Aḥmad report that he heard Aḥmad ibn ʿAlī l-Abbār report that he heard Yaʿqūb ibn Yūsuf, the nephew of Maʿrūf al-Karkhī, report: 93.60

[Yaʿqūb ibn Yūsuf:] One night during the Inquisition, I was sleeping when a man wearing a sleeveless woolen cloak came into the room.

"Who are you?" I asked.

"Moses, son of ʿImrān."

"You're the Moses who had God speak to him directly, without an interpreter?"

"That's right."

It was at that moment that a second man, this one curly-haired and dressed in two robes, fell from the ceiling.

"Who's that?" I asked.

"Jesus, the son of Mary."

Then Moses spoke again. "I, the Moses who had God speak to him directly, without an interpreter, and Jesus the son of Mary, and your Prophet, and Aḥmad ibn Ḥanbal, and the Carriers of the Throne, and all the angels bear witness that the Qur'an is the speech of God and not created."

We cite Muḥammad ibn Abī Manṣūr, who cites ʿAbd al-Qādir ibn Muḥammad, who cites Ibrāhīm ibn ʿUmar, who cites ʿAlī ibn ʿAbd al-ʿAzīz, who cites ʿAbd al-Raḥmān ibn Abī Ḥātim, who heard ʿAbd Allāh ibn al-Ḥasan ibn Mūsā say: 93.61

[ʿAbd Allāh ibn al-Ḥasan:] In a dream I saw a Hadith-man who had just died. I asked him how God had judged him and he said, "He's forgiven me."

"Really?"

فقال: بالله إنّه غفر الله عز وجل لي.

فقلتُ: فبماذا غفر الله لك؟

قال: بمحبّتي لأحمد بن حنبل.

فقلت: فأنت في راحة؟

فتبسّم وقال: أنا في راحة وفي فرح.

٦٢،٩٣ أخبرنا المحمّدان: ابن ناصر وابن عبد الباقي قالا: أخبرنا حمد بن أحمد، وأخبرنا عبد الرحمن بن محمّد قال: أخبرنا أحمد بن عليّ بن ثابت قالا: أخبرنا أبو نُعَيم الحافظ قال: حدثنا الحسين بن محمّد الزَّعْفَراني قال: حدثنا أحمد بن محمّد بن عمر قال: حدثنا أبو بكر بن بحر قال:

حدثنا محمّد بن الهيثم الفَسَوي قال: لما قدم حَمْدون البَرْذَعي على أبي زُرْعَة لكتابة الحديث دخل فرأى في داره أواني وفُرشاً كثيرة وكان ذلك لأخيه فهمّ أن يرجع ولا يكتب عنه فلمّا كان من الليل رأى كأنّه على شطّ بِرْكة ورأى ظلّ شخص في الماء فقال: أنت الذي زهدت في أبي زرعة؟ أَعَلِمْتَ أن أحمد بن حنبل كان من الأبدال فلمّا مات أحمد بن حنبل أبدل الله مكانه أبا زرعة؟

الباب الرابع والتسعُون في فضيلة زيارة قبره

١،٩٤ أخبرنا عبد الرحمن بن محمّد القزاز قال: أخبرنا أحمد بن عليّ بن ثابت قال: أخبرنا أحمد بن أبي جعفر قال: سمعت عبد العزيز غلام الزجّاج يقول:

سمعتُ أبا الفرج الهِنْدِبائي يقول: كنت أزور قبر أحمد بن حنبل فتركته مدّة فرأيت في المنام قائلاً يقول لي: تركتَ زيارة قبر إمام السنّة.

"I swear to God He's forgiven me!"

"Why?"

"Because I loved Aḥmad ibn Ḥanbal."

"And are you comfortable?"

He smiled. "Comfortable and happy."

We cite the two Muḥammads, Ibn Nāṣir and Ibn ʿAbd al-Bāqī, who cite Ḥamd ibn Aḥmad; **93.62**
and we cite ʿAbd al-Raḥmān ibn Muḥammad, who cites Aḥmad ibn ʿAlī ibn Thābit, who like Ḥamd cites Abū Nuʿaym al-Ḥāfiẓ, who heard al-Ḥusayn ibn Muḥammad al-Zaʿfarānī report that he heard Aḥmad ibn Muḥammad ibn ʿUmar report that he heard Abū Bakr ibn Baḥr report that he heard Muḥammad ibn al-Haytham al-Fasawī report:

[Al-Fasawī:] When Ḥamdūn al-Bardhaʿī came to Abū Zurʿah to study Hadith, he saw that the house was full of utensils, carpets, and the like—which, as it happened, belonged to Abū Zurʿah's brother. Ḥamdūn was on the verge of leaving without copying any Hadith. That night, however, he dreamed that he was standing on the shore of a lake. He saw a man's shadow reflected in the water and heard a voice say, "Are you the one who thinks Abū Zurʿah needs to be more of a renunciant?" The voice continued: "You should know that Aḥmad ibn Ḥanbal was one of the Substitutes, and when he died, God sent Abū Zurʿah to take his place."

Chapter 94: The Benefit of Visiting His Grave

We cite ʿAbd al-Raḥmān ibn Muḥammad al-Qazzāz, who cites Aḥmad ibn ʿAlī ibn Thābit, **94.1**
who cites Aḥmad ibn Abī Jaʿfar, who heard ʿAbd al-ʿAzīz, al-Zajjāj's young manservant, say that he heard Abū l-Faraj al-Hindibāʾī say:

[Al-Hindibāʾī:] I used to visit Aḥmad ibn Ḥanbal's grave but then stopped. After some time had passed, I had a dream where a voice said, "You've stopped visiting the exemplar of the *sunnah*."

٢،٩٤ أخبرنا محمّد بن ناصر الحافظ قال: أنبأنا أحمد بن الحسن بن البنّا، وأنبأنا أحمد بن الحسن قال: أخبرنا أبي قال:

قال لي الشيخ أبو طاهر مَيْمون: يا بُنيّ رأيت رجلاً بجامع الرُّصافة في شهر ربيع الآخر من سنة ستّ وستين وأربع مائة فسألته فقال: قد جئت من ستّ مائة فرسخ.

فقلت: في أيّ حاجة؟

قال: رأيت وأنا ببلدي في ليلة جمعة كأني في صحراء أو في فضاء عظيم والخلق قيام وأَبواب السماء قد فُتحت وملائكة تنزل من السماء تلبس أقواماً ثياباً خضراً وتطير بهم في الهواء فقلت: من هؤلاء الذين قد اختصّوا بهذا؟

فقالوا لي: هؤلاء الذين يزورون أحمد بن حنبل.

فانتبهت ولم ألبث أن أصلحت أمري وجئت إلى هذا البلد وزُرته دفعات وأنا عائد إلى بلدي إن شاء الله.

٣،٩٤ أنبأنا محمّد بن ناصر الحافظ قال: أخبرنا يحيى بن عبد الوهّاب بن مَنْده قال: حُدثت عن أبي الحسن عليّ بن محمّد ابن فُورَك قال: سمعتُ أبا بكر محمّد بن القاسم العَدْل قال:

سمعت أبا بكر بن أبرويه يقول: رأيت رسول الله صلى الله عليه وسلم ومعه أحمد بن حنبل فقلت: يا رسول الله من هذا؟

قال: هذا أحمد بن حنبل وليُّ الله ووليُّ رسول الله يا أبا بكر إنّ الله عز وجل ينظر كلّ يوم سبعين ألف نظرة في تُربة أحمد بن حنبل ومن يزوره يغفر الله له.

قال: فانتبهتُ فاغتسلت وصلّيت ركعتين شكرًا لله عز وجل وخلعت ثيابي فتصدّقت بها على الفقراء وحججتُ فزُرت قبر أحمد بن حنبل وأقمت عنده أسبوعاً.[١]

٤،٩٤ أنبأنا ابن ناصر قال: أخبرنا أبو الحسن أحمد بن عبد القادر بن يوف قال: سمعت الشيخ الصالح أبا الحسن عليّ ابن الحسين العُكْبَري يقول: سمعتُ ابن بَطّة يقول:

---

١ الخبر في ش فقط.

We cite Muḥammad ibn Nāṣir al-Ḥāfiẓ, who was informed by Aḥmad ibn al-Ḥasan ibn al-Bannā; and we were informed by Aḥmad ibn al-Ḥasan: **94.2**

[Aḥmad ibn al-Ḥasan:] My father cited Abū Ṭāhir al-Maymūn as saying, "Son, I met a man in the Ruṣāfah mosque—this was in Rabīʿ II 466 [December 1073]—who told me when I asked him that he had traveled six hundred leagues to be there.

"'Why?'

"'One Friday night back home,' he said, 'I dreamed I was in the desert, or in a great wilderness. All the people in creation were standing there, the gates of Heaven were open, and angels were coming down. The angels were dressing certain people in green and flying back up with them. I asked who the special ones were.'

"'The ones who visited Aḥmad ibn Ḥanbal.'

"As soon as I woke up, I put my affairs in order and came here. I've visited him several times and now I'm going home, God willing."

We were informed by Muḥammad ibn Nāṣir al-Ḥāfiẓ, who cites Yaḥyā ibn ʿAbd al-Wahhāb ibn Mandah, who said that it was reported to him regarding Abū l-Ḥasan ʿAlī ibn Muḥammad ibn Fūrak that he heard Abū Bakr Muḥammad ibn al-Qāsim al-ʿAdl say that he heard Abū Bakr ibn Abruwayh say: **94.3**

[Abū Bakr ibn Abruwayh:] The Emissary of God and Aḥmad ibn Ḥanbal appeared to me in a dream.

"Emissary of God," I asked, "who's that?"

"This is Aḥmad ibn Ḥanbal, God's ally and the ally of His Emissary. Listen, Abū Bakr! Every day God looks over at Aḥmad's grave seventy thousand times and forgives anyone he sees there."

I woke up, washed, and prayed two cycles in gratitude to God. Then I took off my clothes, gave them away to the poor, and set off on the pilgrimage. After that I visited Aḥmad's tomb and spent a week there.

We were informed by Ibn Nāsir, who cites Abū l-Ḥasan Aḥmad ibn ʿAbd al-Qādir ibn Yūsuf, who heard the righteous elder Abū l-Ḥasan ʿAlī ibn al-Ḥusayn al-ʿUkbarī say that he heard Ibn Baṭṭah say that Abū Bakr al-Najjād told them: **94.4**

قال لنا أبو بكر النجّاد: بلغني أنّ من كانت به إضاقة فزار قبر أحمد بن حنبل يوم الأربعاء ودعا رزقه الله سَعةً فوجدتُ إضاقة فزُرته يوم الأربعاء ثم عدت وأنا متفكّر فنادتني عجوز من بعض المقابر: يا أحمد!

قلتُ: ما حاجتك؟

- إنّ أُمّك أودعتني كيساً وقالت: إذا رأيت ابني أحمد في إضاقة فادفعيه له، فأنت مضيق؟

قلت: نعم.

فأَخذته وإذا فيه كذا — سقط من أصلح الشيخ[١] المبلغ.[٢]

قال أبو الحسن العكبري وهو ابن جَدَا:

٥،٩٤ انحدرتُ من عكبرا إلى بغداد وأنا صبي ولم يكن معي شيء من النفقة فبقيت في جامع المدينة أيّاماً - أحسب قال: لم أطعم.

قال: فخرجتُ إلى قبر أحمد يوم الأربعاء لأزوره وإذا برجل عند قبره فسلّم عليّ وكانت عليّ[٣] ثياب جميلة وقال لي: أنت جائع؟

فسكتُّ فدفع إليّ خبزًا وذهباً أنفقته مدّة وكان يَفتقدني زمانًا.[٤]

الباب الخامس والتسعون في فضيلة[٥] مجاورته

١،٩٥ أخبرنا أبو منصور عبد الرحمن بن محمّد القزاز قال: أخبرنا أبو بكر أحمد بن عليّ بن ثابت قال: حدثني الحسن بن أبي طالب قال: حدثنا يوسف بن عمر القوّاس قال: حدثنا أبو مُقاتل محمّد بن شُجاع، وأخبرنا محمّد بن ناصر قال:

---

١ هكذا في ش ولعل الصحيح (سقط من الشيخ المبلغ أصلحه الله). ٢ الخبر في ش فقط. ٣ هكذا في ش ولعل الصحيح (عليه). ٤ الخبر في ش فقط. ٥ د: فضل.

[Abū Bakr al-Najjād:] I had heard that anyone in need who visits Aḥmad's grave on a Wednesday and prays there will receive generous sustenance from God. So once when I was in need, I visited the grave on a Wednesday. I was on my way back in a dismal frame of mind when an old woman called out to me from one of the cemeteries.

"Abū Bakr!" she said.

"What is it?"

"Your mother left a bag with me and told me that if I saw you looking needy I should give it to you. Do you need it?"

"Yes," I said, and took it. In it was—

The amount is missing, may God care for the worthy elder who transmitted the story!

Abū l-Ḥasan al-ʿUkbarī—also known as Ibn Jadā—said:

[Abū l-Ḥasan al-ʿUkbarī:] When I was a boy I traveled from ʿUkbarā down to Baghdad without any money to spend. I stayed in the mosque inside the Round City for several days ["without eating," he may have added]. On Wednesday I went to visit Aḥmad's tomb. There I found a man who greeted me—I was wearing fine clothes[255]—and asked me if I was hungry. When I said nothing, he gave me some bread and enough gold to live on for a while. For a while he continued to check on me. 94.5

Chapter 95: The Benefit of Being Buried Near Him

We cite Abū Manṣūr ʿAbd al-Raḥmān ibn Muḥammad al-Qazzāz, who cites Abū Bakr Aḥmad ibn ʿAlī ibn Thābit, who heard al-Ḥasan ibn Abī Ṭālib say that he heard Yūsuf ibn ʿUmar al-Qawwās report that he heard Abū Muqātil Muḥammad ibn Shujāʿ report; and we cite Muḥammad ibn Nāṣir, who cites al-Mubārak ibn ʿAbd al-Jabbār, who cites Muḥammad ibn ʿAbd al-Wāḥid al-Ḥarīrī, who cites Abū ʿUmar ibn Ḥayyuwayh, who 95.1

أخبرنا المبارك بن عبد الجبّار قال: أخبرنا محمد بن عبد الواحد الحريري قال: أخبرنا أبو عمر بن حَيُّوَيْه قال: حدثنا عبد الله بن محمد بن إسحاق المروزي قالا: حدثنا أبو بكر بن أبي الدنيا قال:

حدثني أبو يوسف بن بُخْتان وكان من خيار المسلمين قال: لمّا مات أحمد بن حنبل رأى رجل في منامه كأنّ على كلّ قبر قنديلاً فقال: ما هذا؟

فقيل له: أمّا علمتَ أنّه نُوّر لأهل القبور قبورهم بنزول هذا الرجل بين أظهُرهم وقد كان فيهم من يُعذَّب فَرُحم؟

٢،٩٥ أخبرنا محمّد بن أبي منصور قال: أخبرنا عبد القادر بن محمّد قال: أنبأنا أبو إسحاق البرمكي قال: أنبأنا عبد العزيز ابن جعفر قال: حدثنا أبو بكر الخلّال قال: حدثني محمد بن العباس قال:

سمعتُ عُبيد بن شَريك يقول: مات رجل مُخنَّث فَرُئِيَ في النوم فقال: قد غُفر لي، دُفن عندنا أحمد بن حنبل فغُفر لأهل القبور.

٣،٩٥ أنبأنا محمّد بن أبي منصور:

عن أبي عليّ الحسن بن أحمد الفقيه قال: لمّا ماتت أُمّ القَطِيعي دفنها في جوار أحمد بن حنبل فرآها بعد ليالٍ فقال: ما فعل الله بك؟

فقالت: يا بنيّ، رضي الله عنك، فلقد دفنتني في جوار رجل ينزل على قبره في كلّ ليلة - أو قالت: في كلّ ليلة جمعة - رحمة تعمّ جميع أهل المقبرة وأنا منهم.

٤،٩٥ قال أبو علي:

وحكى أبو طاهر الجمال، شيخ صالح، قال: قرأتُ ليلة وأنا في مقبرة أحمد بن حنبل قوله تعالى: ﴿فَمِنۡهُمۡ شَقِيّٞ وَسَعِيدٞ﴾. ثمّ حملتني عيني فسمعت قائلاً يقول: ما فينا شقي والحمد لله ببركة أحمد بن حنبل.

heard 'Abd Allāh ibn Muḥammad ibn Isḥāq al-Marwazī, who like Abū Muqātil heard Abū Bakr ibn Abī l-Dunyā report:

[Ibn Abī l-Dunyā:] I heard Abū Yūsuf ibn Bukhtān—who was a good Muslim—report that when Aḥmad ibn Ḥanbal died, someone had a dream where he saw a lamp on every grave. When he asked why, he was told, "Don't you see? As soon as that man was put in among them, the tombs of all the dead were illuminated. Some of the dead who were being tormented were forgiven."

We cite Muḥammad ibn Abī Manṣūr, who cites 'Abd al-Qādir ibn Muḥammad, who was informed by Abū Isḥāq al-Barmakī, who was informed by 'Abd al-'Azīz ibn Ja'far, who heard Abū Bakr al-Khallāl report that he heard Muḥammad ibn al-'Abbās report that he heard 'Ubayd ibn Sharīk say: **95.2**

['Ubayd ibn Sharīk:] A drag queen[256] who died was seen in a dream saying, "I've been forgiven: as soon as Aḥmad was placed among us, everyone dead and buried was forgiven."

We were informed by Muḥammad ibn Abī Manṣūr, citing Abū 'Alī l-Ḥasan ibn Aḥmad al-Faqīh: **95.3**

[Al-Ḥasan ibn Aḥmad:] When al-Qaṭī'ī's mother died, he had her buried near Aḥmad ibn Ḥanbal. A few nights later she appeared to him in a dream. He asked her how she had fared and she said, "God bless you, my son! Every night"—or "Every Friday night"—"a wave of mercy descends on the grave of the man you buried me near, and it covers all of us buried here, including me."

Abū 'Alī also said that Abū Ṭāhir al-Jammāl, a righteous elder, told him the following story: **95.4**

[Al-Jammāl:] One night, in the cemetery where Aḥmad is buried, I recited the verse «Among those some shall be damned, and others shall be blessed.»[257] Then I nodded off and heard a voice say, "Because of Aḥmad's presence, no one here is damned, thank God!"

قلت: وبلغني عن بعض السلف القدماء قال: ٥،٩٥

كانت عندنا عجوز من المتعبّدات قد خلتْ بالعبادة خمسين سنة فأصبحت ذات يوم مذعورة فقالت: جاءني بعض الجنّ في منامي فقال: إنّي قرينك من الجنّ وإنّ الجنّ استرقت السمع بتعزية الملائكة بعضها بعضاً بموت رجل صالح يقال له أحمد ابن حنبل، وتُربته في موضع كذا وإن الله يغفر لمن جاوره فإن استطعتِ أن تجاوريه في وقت وفاتك فافعلي فإنّي لك ناصح، وإنّك ميّتة بعده بليلة.

فماتت كذلك فعلمنا أنّه منام حق.[١]

أنبأنا محمّد بن ناصر الحافظ قال: ٦،٩٥

حدثني أبو البركات طلحة بن أحمد بن طلحة القاضي قال: كان لي صديق اسمه ثابت وكان رجلا صالحًا يقرأ القرآن ويأمر بالمعروف وينهي عن المنكر فتوفّي فلم أصلِ عليه لعذر منعني فرأيته في المنام فسلّمت عليه فلم يرد عليّ السلام وأعرض عنّي فقلت: يا ثابت ما تكلّمني وأنت صديقي وبيني وبينك مودّة؟

فقال: أنت صديقي ولم تصلّ عليّ!

فاعتذرتُ إليه.

ثم قال له: حدثني كيف أنت بمقبرة أحمد بن حنبل لأنّه دفن هناك.

فقال لي: ليس في مقبرة أحمد أحد يعذَّب بالنار.

فقلت له: ما تقول في مقابر قريش؟

فقال: لا أعلم ما ثَمّ، ما عندنا حدّثتُك به.

فقلت: إذا قدم أحد عليكم تزورونه وتستخبرونه؟

فقال: إذا قدم علينا أحد زُرناه واستخبرناه عن الأحياء.

---

١ الخبر في ش فقط.

[The author:] One of the early Muslims is said to have told the following story. 95.5

Where I lived there was an old woman, a Worshipper, who had spent fifty years serving God. One day she woke up in terror.

"Last night a jinni came to me," she said. "He said he was my male counterpart.[258] He told me that the jinns had overheard the angels offering each other condolences on the imminent death of a righteous man named Aḥmad ibn Ḥanbal who would be buried in Such-and-Such a place. God will forgive anyone who takes up residence nearby, so if you can go there when you feel death coming on, do it. Please believe me: I'm telling you this for your own good. You'll die the night after he does."

And that's what happened, so we knew it was a truthful dream.

We cite Muḥammad ibn Nāṣir al-Ḥāfiẓ, who heard the judge Abū l-Barakāt Ṭalḥah ibn Aḥmad ibn Ṭalḥah report: 95.6

[Abū l-Barakāt:] I had a friend named Thābit: a righteous man who read the Qur'an, called on people to do good, and forbade them to do ill. When he died, I didn't pray over him because something happened to prevent me. Then he came to me in a dream. When I greeted him, he didn't answer, and turned aside.

"Thābit!" I said. "How can you ignore me when we've been such good friends?"

"So if we're friends, why didn't you pray over me?"

I apologized to him then asked him to tell me how things were in Aḥmad's burial ground, since he'd been buried there.

"No one here feels the Fire," he said.

"What about the burial ground of Quraysh?"

"I don't know about that," he said. "I've told you as much as I know."

"When someone new comes to join you, do you visit them and ask them questions?"

"We visit and ask about the living people they've left behind."

٧،٩٥ قال: قرأت بخطّ شيخنا أبي الحسن عليّ بن عبيد الله بن الزاغوني قال: كُشف قبر إمامنا أحمد بن حنبل حين دُفن الشريف أبو جعفر ابن أبي موسى إلى جانبه وجثّته لم تتغيّر وكفنه صحيح لم يَبْلَ.

قلتُ: بين وفاة الإمام أحمد بن حنبل ووفاة الشريف أبي جعفر مائتا سنة وتسع وعشرون.

الباب السّادس والتسعون في ذكر عقوبة مَن آذاه

١،٩٦ أخبرنا عبد الملك بن أبي القاسم قال: أخبرنا عبد الله بن محمد الأنصاري قال: سمعتُ أبا يعقوب الحافظ يقول: سمعت عليّ بن محمّد بن أحمد بن رِزْق قال: سمعتُ محمّد بن إبراهيم يقول: سمعت أُخَيْد بن جَرير الجَوْهَري قال:

سمعتُ محمّد بن فُضَيل يقول: تناولت مرة أحمد بن حنبل فوجدتُ في لساني ألمًا لم أجد القرار فنمت ليلة فأتاني آتٍ فقال: هذا بتناوُلك الرجل الصالح، هذا بتناولك الرجل الصالح.

فانتبهتُ فلم أزل أتوب إلى الله تعالى حتّى سكن.

٢،٩٦ أخبرنا محمّد بن ناصر قال: أنبأنا أحمد بن عليّ بن خَلَف قال: أخبرنا أبو عبد الله محمّد بن عبد الله الحاكم قال: حدثنا أبو أحمد بكر بن محمد الصوفي قال: حدثنا أبو بكر أُخَيْد بن جرير اللؤلؤي قال:

سمعت محمّد بن فُضَيل البَلْخي يقول: كنت أتناول أحمد بن حنبل فوجدت في لساني ألمًا فاغتممت ثم وضعت رأسي فنمت فأتاني آتٍ فقال: هذا الذي وجدت في لسانك بتناولك الرجل الصالح.

قال: فانتبهت فجعلت أقول: أستغفر الله، وأقول: لا أعود إلى شيء من هذا.

قال: فذهب ذلك الألم.

[The author:] I read something my teacher Abū l-Ḥasan ʿAlī ibn ʿUbayd Allāh ibn al-Zāghūnī wrote in his own hand, as follows: "When the Prophet's descendant Abū Jaʿfar ibn Abī Mūsā was buried next to him, Aḥmad ibn Ḥanbal's tomb was exposed. His corpse had not putrified and the shroud was still whole and undecayed." 95.7

Abū Jaʿfar died 129 years after Ibn Ḥanbal.

Chapter 96: The Punishments That Befall Anyone Who Attacks Him

We cite ʿAbd al-Malik ibn Abī l-Qāsim, who cites ʿAbd Allāh ibn Muḥammad al-Anṣārī, who heard Abū Yaʿqūb al-Ḥāfiẓ say that he heard ʿAlī ibn Muḥammad ibn Aḥmad ibn Rizq say that he heard Muḥammad ibn Ibrāhīm say that he heard Aḥyad ibn Jarīr al-Jawharī say that he heard Muḥammad ibn Fuḍayl say: 96.1

[Muḥammad ibn Fuḍayl:] I made some remarks critical of Aḥmad ibn Ḥanbal after which my tongue started to hurt and wouldn't stop. One night I heard a voice in my sleep saying, "It's because of what you said about that good man," over and over. When I woke up, I expressed contrition to God until the pain went away.

We cite Muḥammad ibn Nāṣir, who was informed by Aḥmad ibn ʿAlī ibn Khalaf, who cites Abū ʿAbd Allāh Muḥammad ibn ʿAbd Allāh al-Ḥākim, who heard Abū Aḥmad Bakr ibn Muḥammad al-Ṣūfī report that he heard Abū Bakr Aḥyad ibn Jarīr al-Luʾluʾī report that he heard Muḥammad ibn Fuḍayl al-Balkhī say: 96.2

[Muḥammad ibn Fuḍayl:] Once as I was criticizing Aḥmad ibn Ḥanbal my tongue started to hurt. Upset, I went to bed, and heard a voice saying, "Your tongue hurts because of what you said about that good man."

When I woke up, I said, "I seek God's forgiveness!" and "I won't do it again!" until the pain went away.

أخبرنا عبد الملك بن أبي القاسم قال: أخبرنا عبد الله بن محمد الأنصاري قال: أخبرنا أبو يعقوب إملاءً قال: ٣،٩٦
أخبرنا أبو العباس أحمد بن محمّد بن الحسين الرازي[١] قال: حدثنا أبو الحسين أحمد بن محمد بن الحسين بن معاوية الرازي قال: حدثنا بكر بن عبد الله بن حبيب أبو محمّد قال:

سمعتُ مِسْعَرَ بن محمّد بن وَهْب يحدّث أبي قال: كنتُ مؤدّباً للمُتَوَكِّل قبل أن يلي الخلافة فلمّا ولي الخلافة أنزلني حجرة من حجر الخاصّة.

فربّما كانت تعرض في فكرته مسألة في الدّين فيوجّه إليّ فيسألني عنها، وكان إذا جلس للخاصّة أقوم على رأسه فإنّ افتقدني دعاني حتى أقف موقفي لا يُخلّيني منه ليلاً ولا نهاراً إلاّ في وقت خلوته.

وأنّه جلس للخاصّة ذات يوم في مجلسه الذي كان يسمّى الوَديع ثمّ قام منه حتى دخل بيتاً له من قوارير سقفه وحيطانه وأرضه وقد أُجري له الماء فيه فالماء يعلو على البيت وأسفله وحيطانه يتقلب فيه يرى من هو داخله كأنّه في جوف الماء جالس وقد فُرش له فراش من قباطي مصر وسائدها ومَخادّها الأُرجوان.

فجلس في مجلسه وجلس عن يمينه الفَتْح بن خاقان وعُبَيد الله بن خاقان وعن يساره بُغا الكبير ووَصيف وأنا واقف في زاوية البيت اليمنى ممّا يليه وخادم آخذ بعضادة الباب واقف، إذ ضحك المتوكل فأرمّ القوم وسكتوا فقال: ألا تسألوني ممّ ضحكت؟

فقالوا: ممّ ضحك أَمير المؤمنين أضحك الله سِنّه؟

فقال: أضحكني أنّي ذات يوم واقف على رأس الواثق وقد قعد للخاصّة في مجلسي الذي كنت فيه جالساً وأنا واقف على رأسه إذ قام من مجلسه فجاء حتّى دخل هذا البيت الذي دخلته فجلس في مجلسي هذا، ورُمتُ الدخول فمُنعت ووقفتُ حيث الخادم واقف. ٤،٩٦

وجلس ابن أبي دُؤاد في مجلسك يا فتح، وجلس محمّد بن عبد الملك بن الزيات في مجلسك يا عُبيد الله، وجلس إسحاق بن إبراهيم في مجلسك يا بُغا، وجلس نَجاح

١ ليس في د.

We cite ʿAbd al-Malik ibn Abī l-Qāsim, who cites ʿAbd Allāh ibn Muḥammad al-Anṣārī, who cites from the dictation of Abū Yaʿqūb, who cites Abū l-ʿAbbās Aḥmad ibn Muḥammad ibn al-Ḥusayn al-Rāzī, who heard Abū l-Ḥusayn Aḥmad ibn Muḥammad ibn al-Ḥusayn ibn Muʿāwiyah al-Razī report that he heard Bakr ibn ʿAbd Allāh ibn Ḥabīb Abū Muḥammad report that he heard Misʿar ibn Muḥammad ibn Wahb tell my father: 96.3

[Misʿar ibn Muḥammad ibn Wahb:] Before al-Mutawakkil became caliph, I was his tutor. When he became caliph, he gave me a room in the section reserved for his intimates. Whenever he had a question about religion he would send for me. During his intimate audiences, I would stand next to him. Whenever he needed me for any reason, he would summon me and I would take up my usual post. He kept me by his side day and night except when he wanted to be alone.

One day, after holding an intimate audience in the hall called The Serene, he moved into another room he had where the ceiling, walls, and floor were made of glass tiles. Water could be piped in and sent flowing in any direction across the top of the room, along the floor, and down the walls, and anyone sitting inside looked as if he were sitting underwater. The room was fitted out with Coptic textiles and pillows and cushions of Tyrian purple. Al-Mutawakkil was sitting with al-Fatḥ ibn Khāqān and ʿUbayd Allāh ibn Khāqān on his right and Bughā the Elder and Waṣīf on his left. I was standing in the corner of the room to his right and a servant stood in the doorway with his hand on the jamb. Suddenly al-Mutawakkil laughed out loud and everyone fell silent.

"Aren't you going to ask me why I laughed?" he said.

"Why did the Commander of the Faithful laugh?" they asked. "May God keep him smiling!"

"I remembered one day when I was attending al-Wāthiq. He had been holding an intimate audience in the hall where we were sitting before, and I was standing next to him. Suddenly he rose and went into the room where we are now, and sat where I'm sitting. I tried to follow him in but I was stopped, so I stood where the servant is standing now. Ibn Abī Du'ād was sitting where Fatḥ is now, Muḥammad ibn ʿAbd al-Malik ibn al-Zayyāt was sitting where ʿUbayd Allāh is, Isḥāq ibn Ibrāhīm was sitting where Bughā is, and Najāḥ was sitting where Waṣīf is now. 96.4

في مجلسك يا وَصيف، إذ قال الواثق: والله لقد فكّرت فيما دعوت الناس إليه من أنّ القرآن مخلوق وسُرعة إجابة من أجابنا وشدّة خلاف من خالفنا حتّى حملنا من خالَفنا على السّوط والسيف والضرب الشديد والحبس الطويل ولا يردعه ذلك ولا يردّه إلى قولنا. فوجدت من أجابنا رغب فيما في أيدينا فأسرع إلى إجابتنا رغبة منه فيما عندنا ووجدتُ من خالَفنا منعه دين وورع عن إجابتنا وصبر على ما يناله من القتل والضرب والحبس.

فوالله لقد دخل قلبي من ذلك أمر شككت فيما نحن فيه وفي محنة من نمتحنه وعذاب من نُعذّبه في ذلك حتى هممتُ بترك ذاك والكلام والخَوْض فيه ولقد هممتُ أن آمر بالنداء في ذلك وأكفّ الناس بعضهم عن بعض.

فبدأ ابن أبي دُؤاد فقال: الله الله يا أمير المؤمنين أنْ تُميت سُنّة قد أَحييتَها ٥،٩٦
وأن تُبطل ديناً قد أقمْتَه! ولقد جهد الأسلاف فما بلغوا فيه ما بلغت فجزاك الله عن الإسلام والدين خير ما جزى وَليّاً عن أوليائه.

ثمّ أطرقوا رؤوسهم ساعة يفكرون في ذلك إذ بدأ ابن أبي دؤاد، وخاف أَن يكون من الواثق في ذلك أمر ينقض عليه قوله ويفسد عليه مذهبه، فقال: والله يا أمير المؤمنين إنّ هذا القول الذي نحن عليه، ندعو إليه الناس، لهو الدين الذي ارتضاه الله لأنبيائه ورسله وبعث به نبيّه محمّدا صلّى الله عليه وسلّم ولكن الناس عَمُوا عن قبوله.

فقال الواثق: فإنّي أريد أن تُباهلوني على ذلك.

فقال ابن أبي دؤاد ضَربه الله بالفالج في دار الدنيا قبل الآخرة إن لم يكن ما يقول أمير المؤمنين حقّاً من أن القرآن مَخلوق.

وقال محمّد بن عبد الملك الزيات وهو[١] فسمّر الله يديه بمسامير من حديد في دار الدنيا قبل الآخرة إن لم يكن ما يقول أمير المؤمنين حقاً من أن القرآن مخلوق.

فقال إسحاق بن إبراهيم وهو فأنْتَنَ الله ريحه في دار الدنيا قبل الآخرة حتى

---

١ هكذا في جميع النسخ.

"Then al-Wāthiq said: 'I've been thinking about how I've demanded everyone's assent to the doctrine that the Qur'an is created. I've noticed how quickly some people adopted the belief and how stubbornly the others are resisting it. With the ones who resist, I've tried flogging, beheading, beating, and imprisonment, but none of it seems to have any effect. Not only that: the ones who've obeyed me did so because they wanted something from me, and so adopted my creed immediately hoping for a reward. The dissenters, on the other hand, have no motive except pious scruple, which sustains them even when they're killed or beaten or thrown in jail. All of this started me thinking, and I'm beginning to doubt whether what we're doing is right. Should we really be putting people on trial and torturing them over this? I've reached the point where I'm ready to stop the Inquisition and give up Disputation altogether, and I'm ready to send out some heralds to announce my decision and put a stop to all this fighting among ourselves.'

"The first to respond was Ibn Abī Du'ād. He said: 'Have a care, Com- 96.5
mander of the Faithful! You've revived a precedent and restored an element of the faith, so think twice before you annul it and kill it off. Try as they did, your predecessors never achieved as much as you have. May God reward you as generously as he awards any of His allies on behalf of Islam and true religion!'

"The others sat silently, their heads bowed in thought, for a time. Then Ibn Abī Du'ād, who was afraid that al-Wāthiq would say something to contradict him and undo the work he had done to promote his creed, again took the initiative and said: 'The creed that we've adopted and that we're asking people to espouse is the one God chose for His prophets and emissaries and the one he sent Muḥammad to propagate. It's just that people have become too blind to accept it.'

"'Well then,' said al-Wāthiq, 'I want you to swear an oath of good faith.'

"Ibn Abī Du'ād promptly called on God to strike him down with paralysis in this world, not to mention the torments of the next, if the caliph was wrong about the Qur'an being created. Muḥammad ibn 'Abd al-Malik al-Zayyāt called on God to drive iron spikes through his hands in this world, not to mention the torments of the next, if the caliph was wrong about the Qur'an

يهرب منه حميم وقريب إن لم يكن ما يقول أمير المؤمنين حقًّا بأن القرآن مخلوق.

وقال نَجاح: وهو فقتله الله في أضيَق محبس إن لم يكن ما يقول أمير المؤمنين حقًّا من أن القرآن مَخلوق. ودخل عليهم إيتاخ وهم في ذلك فأخذوه على البديهة وسألوه عن ذلك فقال: وهو، فغرقه الله في البحر إن لم يكن ما يقول أمير المؤمنين حقًّا من أَن القرآن مخلوق.

فقال الواثق وهو فأحرق الله بدنه بالنار في دار الدنيا قبل الآخرة إن لم يكن ما يقول أمير المؤمنين حقًّا من أَن القرآن مخلوق.

٦،٩٦ فأضحكُ أنّه لم يَدعُ أحد منهم يومئذ بدعوة على نفسه إلّا استُجيبت. أمّا ابن أبي دُؤاد فقد رأيتُ ما نزل به وما ضربه الله به من الفالج، وأما ابن الزيات فأنا أقعدته في تنور من حديد وسَمرتُ يديه بمسامير من حديد، وأمّا إسحاق بن إبراهيم فإنّه مرض مرضه الذي مات فيه فأقبل يعرق عرقاً مُنتناً حتى هرب منه الحميم والقريب وكان يُلقى عليه كل يوم عشرون غِلالة فتؤخذ منه وهي مثل الجيفة فيرمى بها في دجلة لا ينتفع بها تتقطع من شدة النتن والعرق، وأمّا نجاح فأنا بنيتُ عليه بيتاً ذراعاً في ذراعين حتى مات فيه، وأمّا إيتاخ فأنا كتبت إلى إسحاق بن إبراهيم وقد رجع من الحجّ كَبّلهُ بالحديد وغرّقه.

٧،٩٦ وأما الواثق فإنّه كان يُحبّ النساء وكثرة الجماع فوجّه ذات يوم إلى ميخائيل الطبيب فدُعي له فدخل عليه وهو نائم في مَشرقة وعليه قطيفة خزّ فوقف بين يديه فقال: يا ميخائيل ابغِني دواء للباه.

فقال: يا أمير المؤمنين بدنَك فلا تهدّه فإنّ كثرة الجماع تهدّ البدن ولا سيّما إذا تكلّف الرجل ذلك فاتّقِ الله في بدنك وأبقِ عليه[1] فليس لك من بدنك عِوض.

فقال له: لا بدّ منه.

ثم رفع القطيفة عنه فإذا بين فخذيه وصيفة قد ضمّها إليه ذكر من جمالها وهيئتها أمراً عجباً فقال: من يصبر عن مثل هذه؟

---

١ د: عليك.

being created. Isḥāq ibn Ibrāhīm called on God to make him stink so badly in this world that his friends and relatives would flee from him, not to mention the torments of the next, if the caliph was wrong about the Qur'an being created. And Najāḥ called on God to kill him by confining him in the smallest of prison cells if the caliph was wrong about the Qur'an being created.

"While this was going on, Ītākh came in and they challenged him to come up with his own oath. He called on God to drown him in the sea if the caliph was wrong about the Qur'an being created. Finally, al-Wāthiq himself called on God to set him on fire if he was wrong about the Qur'an being created.

"And now I'm laughing because every one of the things they proposed 96.6
came true. Ibn Abī Du'ād was stricken with paralysis, as I saw with my own eyes. I myself put Ibn al-Zayyāt into a brazen bull and drove steel spikes through his hands. During his final illness, Isḥāq ibn Ibrāhīm gave off a stinking sweat that drove everyone away. Twenty times a day they changed the gown he was wearing and threw the old one into the Tigris because it smelled like carrion and stank too much to be used again. For Najāḥ, I built a cell one cubit by two and kept him there until he died. Ītākh was executed by Isḥāq ibn Ibrāhīm at my command: when he returned from the pilgrimage he was weighed down with chains and dropped in the water.

"Now about al-Wāthiq. He had a great love for women and sex. One day 96.7
he sent for Mikhā'īl the physician, who was called in to see him and found him in a sunroom lying under a silken sheet.

"'Mikhā'īl,' said al-Wāthiq, 'I need you to get me an aphrodisiac.'

"'Commander of the Faithful,' said the physician, 'I don't approve of putting stress on the body. Too much sex wears the body down, especially if a man has to force it. Respect the body God has given you and take care of it, since it's the only one you have!'

"'No,' said al-Wāthiq, 'I must have something.' He lifted up the sheet and clamped there between his legs was a concubine whom Mikhā'īl later described as extraordinarily beautiful and shapely. 'Who could resist someone like this?'

"'Well then, if you must have it, then what you need is lion meat. Have them prepare four hundred grams and boil it seven times in aged wine

قال: فإن كان ولا بدّ فعليك بلحم السبع، فَأْمُرْ أن يؤخذ لك منه رطل فيُغلى سبع غليات بخلّ خمر عتيق فإذا جلستَ على شربك أمرت أن يوزن لك منه ثلاث دراهم فانتقلت به على شربك في ثلاث ليالٍ فإنّك تجد فيه بُغيتك واتّقِ الله في نفسك ولا تُسرف فيها ولا تجاوز ما أمرتك به.

فلها عنه أيّاما فبينا هو ذات ليلة جالس على شرابه إذ ذكره فقال: عليّ بلحم السبع الساعة!

فأُخرج له سبع من الجُبّ وذُبح من ساعته فأمر فكُبب له منه ثم أمر فأغلي له منه بالخلّ ثم قدد له منه فأَخذ ينتقل به على شرابه.

٨،٩٦ وأتت عليه الأيّام والليالي فسُقي بطنه فجُمع له الأطبّاء فأجمع رأيهم على أنّه لا دواء له إلا أن يُسجر له تنّور بحطب الزيتون ويُشحن حتى يَمتلئ جمرًا فإذا امتلأ كُسح ما في جوفه فألقي على ظَهره ثم حُشي جوفه بالرطبة ويقعد فيه ثلاث ساعات من النهار فإن استسقى ماء لم يُسق فإذا مضت ثلاث ساعات كوامل أُخرج منها وأُجلس جلسة منتصبة على نحو ما أمروا به فإذا أصابه الروح وجد لذلك وجعًا شديدًا وطلب أن يُردّ إلى التنّور فيُترك على حاله تلك ولا يرد إلى التنور حتى تمضي ساعتان من النهار فإنه إذا مضت ساعتان من النهار جرى ذلك الماء وخرج من مخارج البول وإن سُقي ماء أو ردّ إلى التنور كان تلفُه فيه.

فأمر بتنّور فاتُّخذ له وسجر له بحطب الزيتون حتى إذا امتلأ جمرًا أُخرج ما فيه وجُعل على ظهره ثم حُشي بالرطبة وعُرّي وأُجلس فيه وأقبل يصيح ويستغيث ويقول: أحرقتموني، اسقوني ماء!

وقد وُكل به مَن يمنعه الماءَ ولا يدعه أن يقوم من موضعه الذي قد أُقعد فيه ولا يتحرّك فتنفّط بدنه كلّه فصارت فيه نُفاخات مثل أكبر البطيخ وأعظمه فتُرك على حالته حتى مضت له ثلاث ساعات من النهار ثم أُخرج وقد كاد يحترق أو يقول القائل في رأي العين قد احترق، فأجلسه المتطببون فلمّا وجد روح الهواء اشتدّ به الوجع والألم وأقبل يصيح ويخور خوار الثور ويقول: رُدّوني إلى التنور فإنّي إن لم أُردّ مِتُّ!

vinegar. When you sit down to drink, have them weigh out three dirhams' worth. Take one dirham's worth with wine for three nights running and you'll get the results you want. But be careful not to take too much. Whatever you do, don't exceed the dosage I've prescribed.'

"For several days al-Wāthiq neglected to pursue the matter, but then one day as he was sitting and drinking he remembered the prescription.

"'Bring me lion meat right away!' he cried.

"A lion was brought up out of the pit and slaughtered on the spot, and the meat put on the grill. At his orders, it was then boiled in vinegar, cut into strips, and dried. He began taking some of it as an accompaniment to wine.

"After some time he began to suffer from a dropsy of the belly. The physi- 96.8
cians were summoned and agreed that the only remedy was to light an open-topped oven, stoke it with olive branches until it was full of coals, then sweep out the coals, turn it over, fill it with green clover, and have al-Wāthiq sit inside it for three hours.[259] If he asked for water he was not to have it. After three full hours had passed, he was to be taken out and made to sit upright in the manner they prescribed. He was likely to feel severe pain if exposed to a breeze, but if he asked to be put back into the oven he must instead be kept as he was for two hours. At that point, the water in his belly should come out as urine. If he were to take water or go back into the oven before the two hours had passed, he would expire.

"The oven was accordingly lit, stoked, emptied, turned over, and filled with clover, and al-Wāthiq was stripped and put inside. He began shouting, 'I'm burning up! Bring me water!'

"But there were people there assigned to prevent anyone from giving him water, and to stop him from getting out of the place where he'd been put, or moving around. Even after his whole body broke out in blisters and parts of it swelled up as big as the largest melon, he was kept where he was until the three hours had passed. Then he was taken out. He was nearly burned to death—and those who saw him thought he had been. The doctors put him into a seated position. Whenever there was a breeze, it hurt him, and he would bellow like a bull.

"'Put me back in the oven!' he would say. 'If you don't I'll die!'

فاجتمع نساؤه وخواصّه لمّا رأوا به من شدّة الألم والوجع وكثرة الصياح فرجَوا أن يكون فَرَجُه[1] في أن يُرَدّ إلى التنور فردّوه إلى التنّور ثانية فلمّا وجد مسّ النار سكن صياحه وتفطّرت النفاخات التي كانت خرجت ببدنه وخمدت وبرد في جوف التنّور، فأُخرج من التنور وقد احترق وصار أسود كالفحم فلم تمضِ به ساعة حتى قضى.

فأضحك[2] أنّه لم يدعُ أحد منهم على نفسه في تلك الساعة بدعاء إلّا استجاب الله له في نفسه.

قلت: وقد رُويت لنا هذه الحكاية على وجه آخر. ٩،٩٦

أخبرنا أبو منصور القزاز قال: أخبرنا أحمد بن عليّ بن ثابت قال: أخبرنا محمّد بن عليّ بن يعقوب قال: أخبرنا محمّد بن نُعيم الضَبّي قال: سمعتُ أبا العباس السيّاري يقول:

سمعتُ أبا العباس بن سعيد المَرْوَزي قال: لمّا جلس المتوكّل دخل عليه عبد العزيز ابن يحيى المكّي فقال: يا أمير المؤمنين ما رُئي أعجب من أمر الواثق، قتل أحمد بن نصر وكان لسانه يقرأ القرآن إلى أن دُفن.

قال: فوجد المتوكّل من ذلك وساءه[3] ما سمعه في أخيه[4] إذ دخل عليه محمّد بن عبد الملك الزيّات فقال له: يا ابن عبد الملك في قلبي من قتل أحمد بن نصر.

فقال: يا أمير المؤمنين أحرقني الله بالنار إنْ قتله أمير المؤمنين الواثق إلّا كافرًا.

قال: ودخل عليه هَرْثَمة فقال: يا هرثمة في نفسي من قتل أحمد بن نصر.

فقال: يا أمير المؤمنين قطعني الله إربًا إربًا إن قتله أمير المؤمنين الواثق إلا كافرًا.

قال: ودخل عليه أحمد بن أبي دؤاد فقال: يا أحمد في قلبي من قتل أحمد بن نصر.

فقال: يا أمير المؤمنين ضربني الله بالفالج إن قتله أمير المؤمنين الواثق إلّا كافرًا.

قال المتوكّل: فأمّا الزيّات فأنا أحرقتُه بالنار وأما هرثمة فإنّه هرب فأخذه قوم من العرب فقالوا: هذا الذي قتل ابن عمّكم فقطعوه إربًا إربًا، وأمّا ابن أبي دؤاد فقد سجنه الله في جلده.

---

١ ش: ان يكون له فرجة. ٢ ش: فانا اضحك. ٣ ش: فوجد المتوكل وساءه. ٤ هـ: ابيه.

"Seeing him in agony, and hearing his cries, his intimates and the women of his family gathered and begged them to put him back in the oven in the hope that it would give him some relief. So they put him back inside. As soon as he felt the heat, he stopped shouting, and the swellings on his body burst and subsided. After the inside of the oven had cooled, he was taken out. This time he had been burnt black as coal. Within an hour he died.

"So," said al-Mutawakkil, "I'm laughing because God answered the prayers of every one of them by inflicting the punishment he had called down on himself."

[The author:] I've also heard a different telling of the story. 96.9

We cite Abū Manṣūr al-Qazzāz, who cites Aḥmad ibn ʿAlī ibn Thābit, who cites Muḥammad ibn ʿAlī ibn Yaʿqūb, who cites Muḥammad ibn Nuʿaym al-Ḍabbī, who heard Abū l-ʿAbbās al-Sayyārī say that he heard Abū l-ʿAbbās ibn Saʿīd al-Marwazī say:

[Al-Marwazī:] No sooner had al-Mutawakkil become caliph than ʿAbd al-ʿAzīz ibn Yaḥyā l-Makkī appeared before him and said, "Commander of the Faithful, something extraordinary happened when al-Wāthiq executed Aḥmad ibn Naṣr: Aḥmad's head continued reciting the Qur'an until it was buried!"

Al-Mutawakkil found this news upsetting, especially because of what it implied for his brother. When Muḥammad ibn ʿAbd al-Malik ibn al-Zayyāt appeared, al-Mutawakkil told him he was upset about Aḥmad ibn Naṣr.

"May God burn me alive," said Muḥammad, "if Aḥmad ibn Naṣr didn't die an Ingrate."

Then Harthamah appeared and al-Mutawakkil said the same thing.

"May God chop me into pieces," said Harthamah, "if Aḥmad ibn Naṣr didn't die an Ingrate."

Then Ibn Abī Du'ād appeared and al-Mutawakkil said the same thing.

"May God strike me with paralysis," said Ibn Abī Du'ād, "if Aḥmad ibn Naṣr didn't die an Ingrate."

Later al-Mutawakkil was to say, "Al-Zayyāt ended up burned to death at my command. Harthamah fled and was captured by some Arabs who blamed him for killing their cousin and chopped him to pieces.[260] And Ibn Abī Du'ad was imprisoned in his own skin."

قلت: وقد كان أحمد بن أبي دؤاد يَلي قضاء القُضاة للمعتصم ثم وليه للواثق وحملهما على امتحان الناس بخلق القرآن فضربه الفالج.

فأخبرنا أبو منصور القزاز قال: أخبرنا أبو بكر أحمد بن عليّ الخطيب قال: أخبرني محمد بن أحمد بن يعقوب قال: ١٠،٩٦ أخبرني محمد بن نعيم الضبّي قال: سمعتُ أبا الحسين بن أبي القاسم يقول: سمعتُ أبي يقول: سمعتُ أبا الحسين ابن الفضل يقول:

سمعتُ عبد العزيز بن يحيى المكّي يقول: دخلتُ على أحمد بن أبي دؤاد وهو مفلوج فقلتُ: إنّي لم آتِك عائداً ولكن جئتُ لأحمد الله على أنه سجنك في جلدك.

أخبرنا أبو منصور القزاز قال: أخبرنا أبو بكر الخطيب قال: أخبرنا أبو الحسين بن بِشْران قال: حدثنا عثمان بن ١١،٩٦ أحمد الدقّاق قال: حدثنا إسحاق ابن إبراهيم الخُتّلي قال:

حدثني أبو يوسف يعقوب بن موسى بن الفَيْرُزان ابن أخي معروف الكَرْخي قال: رأيتُ في المنام كأنّي وخالي نمرُّ على نهر عيسى فبينا نحن نمشي إذا امرأة تقول: ما تدري ما حدث الليلة؟ أهلك الله ابن أبي دُؤاد.

فقلتُ لها: وما كان سبب هلاكه؟

قالت: أَغضب الله فغضب عليه من فوق سبع سموات.

قال يعقوب: وأخبرني بعض أصحابنا قال: كنت عند سفيان بن وَكيع فقال: تدرون ما رأَيتُ الليلة؟ - وكانت الليلة التي رأوا فيها النار ببغداد وغيرها - رأيتُ كأنّ جهنّم زفرت فخرج منها اللّهب، أو نحو هذا الكلام.

فقلت: ما هذا؟ قال: أُعدّت لابن أبي دؤاد.

أخبرنا القزاز قال: أخبرنا الخطيب قال: قرأتُ على محمد بن الحسين القطان عن دَعْلَج قال: أخبرنا أحمد بن عليّ ١٢،٩٦ الأبّار قال: حدثنا الحسن بن الصبّاح قال:

سمعتُ خالد بن خِدَاش قال: رأيت في المنام قائلاً يقول: مُسِخ ابن أبي دؤاد ومُسِخ شُعَيب وأصاب ابن سماعة فالج وأصاب آخر الذُّبَحة ولم يُسمِّ.

[The author:] Ibn Abī Du'ād served as chief judge under al-Mu'taṣim and al-Wāthiq and urged both caliphs to try people regarding the createdness of the Qur'an. As a result, God struck him with paralysis.

We cite Abū Manṣūr al-Qazzāz, who cites Abū Bakr Aḥmad ibn 'Alī l-Khaṭīb, who cites **96.10**
Muḥammad ibn Aḥmad ibn Ya'qūb, who cites Muḥammad ibn Nu'aym al-Ḍabbī, who heard Abū l-Ḥusayn ibn Abī l-Qāsim say that he heard his father say that he heard Abū l-Ḥusayn ibn l-Faḍl say that he heard 'Abd al-'Azīz ibn Yaḥyā l-Makkī say:

[Al-Makkī:] I went to see Ibn Abī Du'ād after he had his stroke.

"I didn't come to check on you," I said, "but to thank God for imprisoning you in your own skin."

We cite Abū Manṣūr al-Qazzāz, who cites Abū Bakr al-Khaṭīb, who cites Abū l-Ḥusayn **96.11**
ibn Bishrān, who heard 'Uthmān ibn Aḥmad al-Daqqāq report that he heard Isḥāq ibn Ibrāhīm al-Khuttalī report that he heard Ma'rūf al-Karkhī's nephew Abū Yūsuf Ya'qūb ibn Mūsā ibn Fayruzān report:

[Abū Yūsuf Ya'qūb:] I dreamed that my uncle and I were walking along the 'Īsā Canal and heard a woman say, "Don't you know what happened tonight? God has taken Ibn Abī Du'ād."

"How did he die?" I asked.

"He made God angry, and God sent his anger down from seven heavens high."

One of my associates told me that he was at Sufyān ibn Wakī''s place the morning after fires had been sighted in Baghdad and elsewhere.

Sufyān asked, "Do you know what I dreamed last night? I dreamed that Hell gave a sigh and a flame rose up," or words to that effect. "I asked what was happening and someone said, 'They're preparing to receive Ibn Abī Du'ād.'"

We cite al-Qazzāz, who cites al-Khaṭīb, who read aloud to Muḥammad ibn al-Ḥusayn **96.12**
al-Qaṭṭān his report citing Da'laj, who cites Aḥmad ibn 'Alī l-Abbār, who heard al-Ḥasan ibn al-Ṣabbāḥ report that he heard Khālid ibn Khidāsh say:

[Khālid ibn Khidāsh:] I dreamed I heard a voice say, "Ibn Abī Du'ād and Shu'ayb have been transformed into animals, Ibn Samā'ah has suffered a stroke, and So-and-So"—he didn't say who—"has choked on his own blood."

قلت: شُعيب هو ابن سَهْل القاضي، كان جَهْمِيًّا. ومات ابن أبي دؤاد منكوبًا، أخذ ماله وفلج وهلك في سنة أربعين ومائتين.

أخبرنا عبد الملك قال: أخبرنا عبد الله بن محمّد قال: حدثنا محمّد بن أحمد الجارودي قال: أخبرنا أبو الحسن أحمد ابن جعفر بن أبي تَوْبة قال: حدثني أبو المُثَنَّى أحمد بن إبراهيم قال: حدثنا سَلَمة بن شبيب قال: حدثنا الوليد ابن الوليد الدِّمشقي قال: حدثنا ابن ثوبان عن عِكْرِمة عن ابن عباس قال: ١٣،٩٦

قال رسول الله صلى الله عليه وسلم: مَن مَشَى إلَى سُلطانِ الله عزّ وجلّ في الأَرْضِ لِيُذِلَّهُ أَذَلَّهُ اللهُ وقَمَعَهُ قَبلَ يوْمِ القيامة مع ما يَدّخِرُ له في الآخِرةِ من الخِزْيِ والنَّكال.

وسُلطان الله في الأرض كِتابه وسُنّته.

أخبرنا عبد الملك قال: أخبرنا عبد الله بن محمّد قال: أخبرنا عليّ بن بشرى[1] قال: أخبرنا محمّد بن إسحاق بن محمّد ابن مَنْدَة قال: أخبرنا عليّ بن عباس بن أبي عَياش المغربي قال: حدثنا محمّد بن عبد الوهّاب العَسْقَلاني قال: حدثنا زكريا بن نافع قال: ١٤،٩٦

حدثنا عبد العزيز يعني ابن الحُصين عن رَوْح بن القاسم عن عبد الله بن حَنَش عن عِكْرِمة عن ابن عبّاس عن النبي صلى الله عليه وسلم قال: سُلْطانُ اللهِ في الأَرْضِ كِتابُ الله وسُنَّةُ نَبيّه.

أخبرنا عبد الملك قال: أخبرنا عبد الله بن محمّد قال: أخبرنا أبو يعقوب قال: أخبرنا جدي قال: حدثنا يعقوب ابن إسحاق قال: ١٥،٩٦

حدثنا أبو بكر محمّد بن عليّ بن شُعيب الطوسي قال: كتب خالد بن خِداش إلى أبي في اليوم الذي ضُرب فيه أحمد بن حنبل: وأُخبرك أنّ رجلًا بلغه ما صُنع بأحمد فدخل المسجد ليُصلّي شكرًا فخسف به إلى صدره فاستغاث الناسَ فأغاثوه.

---

١ د: السري.

[The author:] The Shuʿayb mentioned here is Ibn Sahl, the judge; he was a follower of Jahm. Ibn Abī Du'ād suffered a stroke, had his property confiscated, and in the year 240 [854–55] perished in disgrace.

We cite ʿAbd al-Malik, who cites ʿAbd Allāh ibn Muḥammad, who heard Muḥammad ibn Aḥmad al-Jārūdī report that he cites Abū l-Ḥasan Aḥmad ibn Jaʿfar ibn Abī Tawbah, who heard Abū l-Muthannā Aḥmad ibn Ibrāhīm report that he heard Salamah ibn Shabīb report that he heard al-Walīd ibn al-Walīd al-Dimashqī report that he heard Ibn Thawbān report, citing ʿIkrimah, citing Ibn ʿAbbās, who quotes the Prophet: 96.13

[The Prophet:] Anyone who challenges God's authorities on earth with the intention of demeaning them will suffer crushing humiliation in this world, apart from the shame and disgrace that await him in the next.

[The author:] "God's authorities on earth" means the Book and the *sunnah* of the Prophet.

We cite ʿAbd al-Malik, who cites ʿAbd Allāh ibn Muḥammad, who cites ʿAlī ibn Bushrā, who cites Muḥammad ibn Isḥāq ibn Muḥammad ibn Mandah, who cites ʿAlī ibn ʿAbbās ibn Abī Ayyāsh al-Maghribī, who heard Muḥammad ibn ʿAbd al-Wahhāb al-ʿAsqalānī report that he heard Zakariyyā ibn Nāfiʿ report that he heard ʿAbd al-ʿAzīz—meaning Ibn al-Ḥuṣayn—report, citing Rawḥ ibn al-Qāsim, citing ʿAbd Allāh ibn Ḥanash, citing ʿIkrimah, citing Ibn ʿAbbās, who quotes the Prophet: 96.14

[The Prophet:] "God's authorities on earth" means His Book and the *sunnah* of His Prophet.

We cite ʿAbd al-Malik, who cites ʿAbd Allāh ibn Muḥammad, who cites Abū Yaʿqūb, who cites his grandfather, who heard Yaʿqūb ibn Isḥāq report that he heard Abū Bakr Muḥammad ibn ʿAlī ibn Shuʿayb al-Ṭūsī report: 96.15

[Al-Ṭūsī:] The day Aḥmad ibn Ḥanbal was flogged, Khālid ibn Khidāsh wrote to my father to let him know that when the news came of what had been done to Aḥmad, a certain man went into a mosque to offer a prayer of thanksgiving but the earth gave way under him and he sunk chest-deep into the ground. When he cried out for help some people came and pulled him out.

أخبرنا ابن ناصر قال: أخبرنا أبو الحسين بن عبد الجبّار قال: أخبرنا أبو محمّد الخلّال قال: حدثنا أحمد بن إبراهيم ١٦،٩٦
ابن شاذان قال: حدثنا محمّد بن عليّ بن هارون المقرئ قال: حدثنا إبراهيم بن جعفر بن جابر قال: حدثنا أحمد
ابن منصور الرّمادي قال:

حدثنا خالد بن خِدَاش: أن رجلاً فرِح بضرب أحمد بن حنبل فخسف الله به.

بلغني عن أبي بكر أحمد بن سليمان النجّاد أنّه قال: ١٧،٩٦

حدثني شيخ كنّا نتردد معه في طلب[1] الحديث ونتأدّب به قال: قصدتُ قبر أحمد ابن حنبل وحوله من القبور قبور يسيرة إذ ذاك فجاء قوم ممّن يرمي بالبُنْدُق فقال بعضُهم لبعض: أيما هو قبر أحمد بن حنبل؟

قالوا له: ذاك. فرماه ببُندقة وكنت أعرفه فرأيته بعد ذلك وقد جفّت يده.

أنبأنا أبو بكر محمّد بن عبد الباقي قال: أخبرنا هنّاد بن إبراهيم قال: أخبرنا عليّ بن محمّد قال: حدثنا عثمان بن أحمد ١٨،٩٦
قال: حدثنا حنبل بن إسحاق قال:

حدثني عمران بن موسى قال: دخلتُ على أبي العروق الجلاّد الذي ضرب أحمد لأنظر إليه فمكث خمسةً وأربعين يوماً ينبح كما ينبح الكلب.

الباب السابع والتسعون في ذكر ما قيل فيمن يتنقّصه

أنبأنا عبد الملك بن أبي القاسم قال: أخبرنا عبد الله بن محمّد الأنصاري قال: سمعتُ أحمد بن الحسن السنّي يقول: ١،٩٧
سمعتُ أبا زيد الاصبهاني يقول: سمعتُ أحمد بن محمّد بن سليل قال: سمعتُ ابن أبي حاتم قال:

١ ليس في هـ.

We cite Ibn Nāṣir, who cites Abū l-Ḥusayn ibn ʿAbd al-Jabbār, who cites Abū Muḥammad al-Khallāl, who heard Aḥmad ibn Ibrāhīm ibn Shādhān report that he heard Muḥammad ibn ʿAlī ibn Hārūn al-Muqriʾ report that he heard Ibrāhīm ibn Jaʿfar ibn Jābir report that he heard Aḥmad ibn Manṣūr al-Ramādī report that he heard Khālid ibn Khidāsh report: **96.16**

[Khālid ibn Khidāsh:] A certain man was rejoicing over the flogging of Aḥmad ibn Ḥanbal when the ground he was standing on suddenly gave way.

I was told that Abū Bakr Aḥmad ibn Sulaymān al-Najjād said: **96.17**

[Al-Najjād:] An elder who used to tutor us and study Hadith with us told me that he once went to visit the grave of Aḥmad ibn Ḥanbal.

"There were only a few other graves around it at the time," he said. "Some people had gathered nearby to shoot pellets. One of them asked which was Aḥmad's grave. When it was pointed out to him, he shot a pellet at it. I knew him, and I saw him some time later. His hand had shriveled up."

We were informed by Abū Bakr Muḥammad ibn ʿAbd al-Bāqī, who cites Hannād ibn Ibrāhīm, who cites ʿAlī ibn Muḥammad, who heard ʿUthmān ibn Aḥmad report that he heard Ḥanbal ibn Isḥāq report that he heard ʿImrān ibn Mūsā report: **96.18**

[ʿImrān ibn Mūsā:] I went to visit Abū l-ʿUrūq, the lictor who had flogged Aḥmad, just to get a look at him. For forty-five days, he could only bark like a dog.

Chapter 97: What to Think about Anyone Who Speaks Ill of Him

We were informed by ʿAbd al-Malik ibn Abī l-Qāsim, who cites ʿAbd Allāh ibn Muḥammad al-Anṣārī, who heard Aḥmad ibn al-Ḥasan al-Sunnī say that he heard Abū Zayd al-Iṣfahānī say that he heard Aḥmad ibn Muḥammad ibn Salīl say that he heard Ibn Abī Ḥātim say that he heard Abū Jaʿfar Muḥammad ibn Hārūn al-Mukharrimī say: **97.1**

سمعتُ أبا جعفر محمّد بن هارون المخرّمي يقول: إذا رأيتَ الرجل يقع في أحمد ابن حنبل فاعلم أنّه مبتدع.

٢،٩٧ أخبرنا عبد الرحمن بن محمّد القزاز قال: أخبرنا أحمد بن عليّ بن ثابت قال: أخبرني محمّد بن أحمد بن رزق قال: حدثنا جعفر بن محمّد بن نُصَيْر قال: حدثنا أبو محمّد عبد الله بن جابر قال: سمعتُ أبا بكر محمّد بن يزيد المُستَمْلي يقول:

سمعتُ نُعَيْم بن حمّاد يقول: إذا رأيتَ العراقي يتكلّم في أحمد بن حنبل فاتّهمه في دينه، وإذا رأيتَ الخُراساني يتكلّم في إسحاق بن راهويه فاتّهمه في دينه.

٣،٩٧ أخبرنا محمّد بن أبي منصور قال: أخبرنا المبارك بن عبد الجبّار قال: أخبرنا محمّد بن عليّ الصوري قال: حدثنا أبو بكر بن أبي الخصيب قال: سمعتُ أحمد بن صالح يقول:

سمعتُ أبا زُرْعة الرازي يقول: إذا رأيتَ الكوفي يطعن على سُفيان الثَّوْري وزائدة فلا تشكّ في أنّه رافضيّ وإذا رأيتَ الشامي يطعن على مكحول والأَوْزاعي فلا تشكّ في أنّه ناصِبيّ وإذا رأيتَ البصري يطعن على أَيُّوب السَّخْتياني وابن عَوْن فلا تشكّ في أنّه قَدَري وإذا رأيتَ الخُراساني يطعن على عبد الله بن المبارَك فلا تشك أنه مرجئي، واعلم أنّ هذه الطوائف كلها مُجْمِعة على بغض أحمد بن حنبل لأنّه ما منهم أحد إلّا وفي قلبه منه سهم لا بُرْءَ له.

٤،٩٧ أخبرنا عبد الرحمن بن محمّد قال: أخبرنا أحمد بن عليّ بن ثابت قال: أخبرني أبو القاسم الأزهري قال: حدثنا محمّد بن المظفَّر قال: حدثنا عبد الله بن محمّد بن جعفر القاضي قال:

سمعتُ أبا بكر الصاغاني يقول: أول ما تبيّنتُ من إسحاق بن أبي إسرائيل أنّ الله يضعه أنّي سمعته يقول: ها هنا قوم قد اختُصّوا يدّعون أنّهم سمعوا من إبراهيم بن سعد - يعرّض بأحمد بن حنبل فكان ذاك أنّ الله وضعه ورفع أحمد بن حنبل.

[Al-Mukharrimī:] If you hear a man slander Aḥmad ibn Ḥanbal, you know he's an innovator.

We cite ʿAbd al-Raḥmān ibn Muḥammad al-Qazzāz, who cites Aḥmad ibn ʿAlī ibn Thābit, who cites Muḥammad ibn Aḥmad ibn Rizq, who heard Jaʿfar ibn Muḥammad ibn Nuṣayr report that he heard Abū Muḥammad ʿAbd Allāh ibn Jābir report that he heard Abū Bakr Muḥammad ibn Yazīd al-Mustamlī say that he heard Nuʿaym ibn Ḥammād say: 97.2

[Nuʿaym ibn Ḥammād:] If you hear an Iraqi criticize Aḥmad ibn Ḥanbal, doubt his religion, and do the same if you hear a Khurasani criticize Isḥāq ibn Rāhāwayh.

We cite Muḥammad ibn Abī Manṣūr, who cites al-Mubārak ibn ʿAbd al-Jabbār, who cites Muḥammad ibn ʿAlī l-Ṣūrī, who heard Abū Bakr ibn Abī l-Khaṣīb report that he heard Aḥmad ibn Ṣāliḥ say that he heard Abū Zurʿah al-Rāzī say: 97.3

[Abū Zurʿah:] If you hear a Kufan attack Sufyān al-Thawrī or Zāʾidah, you can be sure he's a Rejectionist. If you hear a Syrian attack Makḥūl or al-Awzāʿī, you can be sure he's an ʿAlī-hater. If you hear a Basran attack Ayyūb al-Sakhtiyānī or Ibn ʿAwn, you can be sure he's an advocate of free will. If you hear a Khurasani attack ʿAbd Allāh ibn al-Mubārak, you can be sure he's a Postponer. And you should also know that all those sects have one thing in common: they hate Aḥmad ibn Ḥanbal because he's inflicted mortal wounds on them all.

We cite ʿAbd al-Raḥmān ibn Muḥammad, who cites Aḥmad ibn ʿAlī ibn Thābit, who cites Abū l-Qāsim al-Azharī, who heard Muḥammad ibn al-Muẓaffar report that he heard ʿAbd Allāh ibn Muḥammad ibn Jaʿfar al-Qāḍī report that he heard Abū Bakr al-Ṣāghānī say: 97.4

[Al-Ṣāghānī:] The first time I realized that God no longer favored Isḥāq ibn Abī Isrāʾīl was when I heard him refer to "some people who claim to be special because they've heard reports from Ibrāhīm ibn Saʿd," alluding to Aḥmad ibn Ḥanbal. The reason for his resentment was that God had left him in obscurity while making Ibn Ḥanbal famous.

٥،٩٧ أخبرنا عبد الرحمن قال: أخبرنا أحمد بن عليّ قال: أخبرنا أبو عبد الرحمن محمّد بن يوسف النيسابوري قال: أخبرنا محمّد بن حمزة الدمشقي قال: حدثنا يوسف بن القاسم القاضي قال: سمعت أبا يعلى التميمي يقول:

سمعتُ أحمد بن إبراهيم يعنى الدَّوْرَقي يقول: من سمعتموه يذكر أحمد بن حنبل بسوء فاتّهموه على الإسلام.

٦،٩٧ أخبرنا عبد الرحمن قال: أخبرنا أحمد بن عليّ قال: أخبرنا الحسين بن شُجاع الصوفي قال: حدثنا عمر بن جعفر ابن محمّد بن سَلْمٍ[١] قال: حدثنا أحمد بن عليّ الأَبَّار قال:

سمعتُ سفيان بن وَكيع يقول: أحمد عندنا محنة، من عاب أحمد عندنا فهو فاسق.

٧،٩٧ أخبرنا عبد الرحمن قال: اخبرنا أحمد بن علي قال: أخبرنا عبد العزيز ابن أبي الحسن القِرْميسيني قال: حدثنا يوسف بن عمر بن مسرور القوّاس قال: حدثنا أبو الحسن عليّ بن محمد المطيري[٢] قال:

سمعتُ أبا الحسن الهَمَذاني يقول: أحمدُ بن حنبل مِحنة، به يُعرف المسلم من الزِّنْديق.

٨،٩٧ أنبأنا محمّد بن أبي منصور قال: أخبرنا المبارك بن عبد الجبار قال: حدثنا عُبَيْد الله بن عمر بن شاهين قال: حدثني أبي قال: حدثني محمّد بن إبراهيم الحَرْبي قال: قال محمّد بن عليّ بن شُعَيْب:

سمعتُ مَرْدُوَيْه الصائغ يقول: إذا جاءني من لا أعرفه من أصحاب الحديث أجريتُ ذكر أحمد بن حنبل فإن رأيته يسارع فيه أمنته وإن رأيته يسكت اتَّهمته.

٩،٩٧ أخبرنا عبد الرحمن بن محمّد قال: أخبرنا أحمد بن عليّ قال: حدثني الحسن بن أبي طالب قال: حدثنا أحمد بن إبراهيم بن شاذان قال: حدثنا محمّد بن عليّ المُقرئ قال: أنشدنا أبو جعفر محمّد بن بَدينا الموصلي قال:

أنشدني ابنُ أعين في أحمد بن حنبل:

---

١ د: سلمة. ٢ ش: المطري، د: الطبري.

We cite ʿAbd al-Raḥmān, who cites Aḥmad ibn ʿAlī, who cites Abū ʿAbd al-Raḥmān Muḥammad ibn Yūsuf al-Naysābūrī, who cites Muḥammad ibn Ḥamzah al-Dimashqī, who heard Yūsuf ibn al-Qāsim al-Qāḍī report that he heard Abū Yaʿlā l-Tamīmī say that he heard Aḥmad ibn Ibrāhīm—meaning al-Dawraqī—say: 97.5

[Al-Dawraqī:] If you hear anyone speak ill of Aḥmad ibn Ḥanbal, doubt his Islam.

We cite ʿAbd al-Raḥmān, who cites Aḥmad ibn ʿAlī, who cites al-Ḥusayn ibn Shujāʿ al-Ṣūfī, who heard ʿUmar ibn Jaʿfar ibn Muḥammad ibn Salm report that he heard Aḥmad ibn ʿAlī l-Abbār report that he heard Sufyān ibn Wakīʿ say: 97.6

[Sufyān ibn Wakīʿ:] We think of Aḥmad as the standard: anyone who finds fault with him is a sinner to us.

We cite ʿAbd al-Raḥmān, who cites Aḥmad ibn ʿAlī, who cites ʿAbd al-ʿAzīz ibn Abī l-Ḥasan al-Qirmīsīnī, who heard Yūsuf ibn ʿUmar ibn Masrūr al-Qawwās report that he heard Abū l-Ḥasan ʿAlī ibn Muḥammad al-Maṭīrī report that he heard Abū l-Ḥasan al-Hamadhānī say: 97.7

[Al-Hamadhānī:] Aḥmad is the test that separates Muslims from heretics.

We were informed by Muḥammad ibn Abī Manṣūr, who cites al-Mubārak ibn ʿAbd al-Jabbār, who heard ʿUbayd Allāh ibn ʿUmar ibn Shāhīn report that he heard his father report that he heard Muḥammad ibn Ibrāhīm al-Ḥarbī report that he heard Muḥammad ibn ʿAlī ibn Shuʿayb say that he heard Marduwayh al-Ṣāʾigh say: 97.8

[Al-Ṣāʾigh:] Whenever I meet a Hadith-man I don't know I make sure to bring up Aḥmad ibn Ḥanbal. If the man speaks of him with enthusiasm I know he's all right. If he says nothing I know he's no good.

We cite ʿAbd al-Raḥmān ibn Muḥammad, who cites Aḥmad ibn ʿAlī, who heard al-Ḥasan ibn Abī Ṭālib report that he heard Aḥmad ibn Ibrāhim ibn Shādhān report that he heard Muḥammad ibn ʿAlī l-Muqriʾ report that Abū Jaʿfar Muḥammad ibn Badīnā l-Mawṣilī said: 97.9

[Abū Jaʿfar:] Ibn Aʿyan recited these verses about Aḥmad ibn Ḥanbal:

أَضْحَى ابنُ حَنبلٍ مِحْنَةً مَأمونةً   وبِحُبِّ أحمدَ يُعرَفُ المُتَنَسِّكُ
وإذا رأيتَ لأحمدٍ مُتَنَقِّصًا   فاعْلَمْ بأَنَّ سُتورَه سَتُهتَّكُ

١٠،٩٧ أخبرنا إسماعيل بن أحمد قال: أخبرنا حَمْد بن أحمد قال: حدثنا أحمد بن[١] عبد الله الحافظ قال: حدثنا الحسين ابن محمّد قال: حدثنا عمر بن الحسن القاضي قال: حدثنا أبو جعفر أحمد بن القاسم المقرئ قال: سمعتُ الحُسين الكَرَابيسي يقول: مَثَل الذين يذكرون أحمد بن حنبل مثل قوم يجيئون إلى أبي قُبَيس يريدون أن يهدموه بنعالهم.

الباب الثامن والتسعون في سبب اختيارنا لمذهبه على مذهب غيره

١،٩٨ اعلم، وفقك الله، أنه إنّما يتبيّن[٢] الصواب في الأمور المشتبهة لمن أعرض عن الهوى والتفت عن العصبيّة وقصد الحقّ بطريقه ولم ينظر في أسماء الرجال ولا في صيتهم فذلك الذي ينجلي له غامض المشتبه، فأمّا من مال به الهوى فعسير تقويمه.

٢،٩٨ واعلم أنّا نظرنا في أدلّة الشرع وأصول الفقه وسبرنا أحوال الأعلام المجتهدين فرأينا هذا الرجل أوفرهم حظًّا من تلك العلوم.

٣،٩٨ فإنّه كان من الحافظين لكتاب الله عزّ وجلّ.

---

١ حدثنا أحمد بن: ليس في هـ.   ٢ د: يبين.

To know who holds religion firm
  One test is the key:
A man who speaks of Aḥmad ill
  Admits to heresy.[261]

We cite Ismāʿīl ibn Aḥmad, who cites Ḥamd ibn Aḥmad, who heard Aḥmad ibn ʿAbd al-Ḥāfiẓ report that he heard al-Ḥusayn ibn Muḥammad report that he heard Judge ʿUmar ibn al-Ḥusayn report that he heard Abū Jaʿfar Aḥmad ibn al-Qāsim al-Muqriʾ report that he heard al-Ḥusayn al-Karābīsī say: 97.10

[Al-Karābīsī:] People who go after Aḥmad ibn Ḥanbal might as well go up to Mount Abū Qubays and try to knock it down with their sandals.

Chapter 98: Why We Chose His Legal School over the Others

Recall—may God lead you aright!—that when faced with a difficult choice, 98.1
the only way to discern the right course of action is to put personal feelings and partisanship aside and search systematically for the truth, without undue deference to the names and reputations of those involved. If you do this, the fog of perplexity will dissipate. If, on the other hand, you allow yourself to be led astray by your inclinations, it will be difficult to find your way back to the straight and narrow.

Note, then, that after examining the evidentiary basis of the Law and the 98.2
foundations of jurisprudence, and delving into the biographies of those who exercised their faculties on behalf of the Law, I find our man to have been the most knowledgeable in those fields.

To begin with, he was active in the preservation and transmission of the 98.3
Book of God.

قال أبو بكر بن حمدان القطيعي: ٤،٩٨

قرأتُ على عبد الله بن أحمد بن حنبل قال: لقّنني أبي أحمد بن حنبل القُرآن كلّه باختياره.

وقرأ أحمد بن حنبل على يحيى بن آدم وعُبَيد[1] بن الصبّاح وإسماعيل بن جعفر وغيرهم بإسنادهم وكان أحمد لا يُميل شيئاً في القرآن ويروي الحديث: أُنزِلَ مُفخَّماً ففَخِّموه وكان لا يُدغم شيئاً في القرآن إلّا (اتّخذتم) وبابه كأبي بكر ويمدُّ مَدّاً متوسّطاً.

وكان رضي الله عنه من المصنِّفين في فنون علوم القرآن من التفسير والناسخ والمنسوخ والمقدَّم والمؤخَّر إلى غير ذلك ممّا أشرنا إليه في باب ذكر تصانيفه.

٥،٩٨ وأمّا النَّقل فقد سلّمَ الكلّ له انفراده[2] فيه بما لم ينفرد به سواه من الأئمّة من كثرة محفوظه منه ومعرفة صحيحه من سقيمه وفنون علومه وقد ثبت أنّه ليس في الأئمّة الأعلام قبله من له حظّ في الحديث لحظّ مالك. ومن أراد معرفة مقام أحمد في ذلك من مقام مالك فلينظر فرق ما بين المسند والموطأ.

وقد كان أحمد رضي الله عنه يذكر الجَرح والتعديل والعِلَل من حفظه إذا سُئل كما يقرأ الفاتحة ومن نظر في كتاب العلل لأبي بكر الخلّال عرف ذلك ولم يكن هذا لأحد منهم كذلك انفراده في علم النقل بفتاوى الصحابة وفضائلهم وإجماعهم واختلافهم لا ينازَع في ذلك.

٦،٩٨ وأما علم العربية فقد قال أحمد: كتبتُ من العربية أكثر مما كتب أبو عمرو الشَّيباني.

٧،٩٨ وأما القياس فله من الاستنباط ما يطول شرحه وقد أشرنا إلى بعض ذلك في باب قوّة فهمه.

٨،٩٨ ثمّ إنّه ضمّ إلى العلوم ما عجز عنه القوم من الزهد في الدنيا وقوة الوَرَع ولم يُنقل عن أحد من الأئمّة أنّه امتنع من أرفاق السلطان وهدايا الإخوان كامتناعه ولولا

---

١ د: عبيد الله. ٢ د: بانفراده.

Abū Bakr ibn Ḥamdān al-Qaṭīʿī said: I read back to Aḥmad ibn Ḥanbal's son ʿAbd Allāh his report: 98.4

[ʿAbd Allāh:] My father Aḥmad ibn Ḥanbal taught me the entire Qurʾan by his own choice.[262]

Aḥmad himself read the text with Yaḥyā ibn Ādam, ʿUbayd ibn al-Ṣabbāḥ, Ismāʿīl ibn Jaʿfar, and others—omitting here the list of their authorities. When reading, he would not let the pronunciation of *a* approximate that of *i*, citing the Hadith: "The Qurʾan was revealed with *a* pronounced closer to *u* than to *i*, so recite it that way." He would not assimilate adjacent letters except in the word *ittakhadhtum* ("you have taken")[263] and the like, as did Abū Bakr. And he would extend long vowels to a moderate extent.[264]

He also compiled works on the Qurʾanic sciences, including exegesis, abrogation, transposition, and the like, as we have noted in the chapter on his writings.

Turning to Hadith, there is universal agreement that he was unique even 98.5 among his fellow exemplars in the sheer amount he memorized as well as his ability to distinguish the authentic from the dubious. Among earlier men of learning, Mālik knew more Hadith than anyone who came before him. To see that Aḥmad in turn outdid Mālik, one need only compare Aḥmad's *Authenticated Reports* with Mālik's *Well-Trodden Path*.

If asked, furthermore, about the reputations of Hadith transmitters, Aḥmad could list their virtues and defects from memory whenever he was asked as easily as he might recite the opening chapter of the Qurʾan. Anyone who looks at the *Defects* compiled by Abū Bakr al-Khallāl will see this immediately. None of his colleagues could match him in this respect, nor could any contest his mastery of the legal opinions, special virtues, points of agreement, and differences of opinion attributed to the Companions of the Prophet.

As for the study of the Arabic language, Aḥmad himself used to say, "I've 98.6 written more Arabic than Abū ʿAmr al-Shaybānī."

As for ruling on legal questions on the basis of analogy, Aḥmad has more 98.7 feats of deductive reasoning to his credit than we have room for, but several examples may be found in the chapter on his powers of intellect.

In addition to all of these scholarly attainments, he had the force of char- 98.8 acter to renounce the world and impose on himself a scrupulousness that none of his fellows could match. No other scholar is described as declining with such unremitting severity the gifts offered by his friends as well as the emoluments dangled by the authorities. Were I willing to risk the danger to

خَدْش وجوه فضائلهم رضي الله عنهم لذكرنا عنهم ما قبلوه وترخصوا بأخذه، وقد سبق في كتابنا هذا من زُهده في المباحات ما يكفي ويشفي. ثمّ إنّه ضمّ إلى ذلك الصبر على الامتحان وبذل المهجة في نُصرة الحقّ ولم يكن ذلك لغيره.

وقد أخبرنا المحمّدان ابن ناصر وابن عبد الباقي قالا: أخبرنا حمد بن أحمد قال: حدثنا أبو نعيم الحافظ قال: حدثنا ٩،٩٨
محمّد بن عبد الرحمن بن سهل قال: أخبرني محمّد بن يحيى بن آدم الجوهري قال: حدثنا محمّد بن عبد الله بن عبد الحكَم قال:

سمعت الشافعي يقول: قال لي محمّد بن الحسن: صاحبنا أعلم أم صاحبكم؟

قلت: تريد المكابرة أو الإنصاف؟

قال: بل الإنصاف.

قال: قلتُ: فما الحُجّة عندكم؟

قال: الكتاب والإجماع والسنّة والقِياس.

قال: قلتُ: أنشدك الله، أصاحبنا أعلم بكتاب الله أم صاحبكم؟

قال: إذ أنشدتني بالله فصاحبكم.

قلت: فصاحبنا أعلم بسنّة رسول الله أم صاحبكم؟

قال: صاحبكم.

قلت: فصاحبنا أعلم بأقاويل أصحاب رسول الله أم صاحبكم؟

قال: صاحبكم.

قلت: فبقي شيء غير القياس؟

قال: لا.

قلت: فنحن ندّعي القياس أكثر ممّا تدّعونه وإنّما يُقاس على الأُصول فيعرف القياس.

قال: ويريد بصاحبه مالِك بن أَنَس.

their reputations, I could cite examples of gifts accepted by the other major figures and describe their willingness to relax their standards in such cases. Aḥmad, conversely, renounced even permitted things, as this book has shown in more than sufficient detail.

In addition to all of the above, Aḥmad proved himself capable of suffering great and terrible ordeals in the service of truth, a feat unmatched among his comrades.

We cite the two Muḥammads, Ibn Nāṣir and Ibn ʿAbd al-Bāqī, who cite Ḥamd ibn Aḥmad, **98.9**
who heard Abū Nuʿaym al-Ḥāfiẓ report that the heard Muḥammad ibn ʿAbd al-Raḥmān ibn Sahl report that he cites Muḥammad ibn Yaḥyā ibn Ādam al-Jawharī, who heard Muḥammad ibn ʿAbd Allāh ibn ʿAbd al-Ḥakam report that he heard al-Shāfiʿī say:

[Al-Shāfiʿī:] Muḥammad ibn al-Ḥasan asked me who was better: his exemplar or mine?[265] I asked him if he wanted to give each man his due or merely have a boasting match. He replied that he wanted a fair comparison.

"In that case," I said, "tell me where your man excels."

"In the Book, consensus, *sunnah*, and analogy."

"Tell the truth now, with God as your witness! Who knows the Book of God better: our man or yours?"

"Well, if I'm under oath, then it's your man."

"What about the *sunnah* of the Prophet?"

"Your man again."

"And the opinions of the Companions?"

"Your man again."

"So what have you got left besides analogy?"

"Nothing."

"And even there, we have better claim to using analogy than you. The difference is that we draw analogies on the basis of revealed texts so that the reasoning is clear."

The comparison here is between Abū Ḥanīfah and Mālik ibn Anas.

قلت: فقد كفانا الشافعي رضي الله عنه بهذه الحكاية المناظرة لأصحاب أبي حَنيفة وقد عُرف فضل صاحبنا على مالك فإنّه حصّل ما حصّله مالك وزاد عليه كثيرًا وقد ذكرنا شاهد هذا باعتبار المسند والموطّأ. وقد كان الشافعي رضي الله عنه عالمًا بفنون العلم إلّا أنّه سلّم لأحمد علم النقل الذي عليه مَدار الفقه. ١٠،٩٨

فأخبرنا عبد الملك بن أبي القاسم الكَرُوخي قال: أخبرنا عبد الله بن محمد الأنصاري قال: أخبرنا محمد بن أحمد الجارودي قال: قال القَطيعي: سمعت عبد الله بن أحمد بن حنبل يقول: سمعت أبي يقول: ١١،٩٨

سمعتُ الشافعي يقول: أنتم أعلم بالحديث منّا فإذا صحّ الحديث فقولوا لنا حتّى نذهب إليه.

أخبرنا محمّد بن ناصر قال: أخبرنا أبو سهل بن سعدويه قال: أخبرنا أبو الفضل محمّد بن الفضل القرشي[١] قال: أخبرنا أبو بكر بن مَرْدُوَيْه قال: حدثنا سليمان بن أحمد قال: ١٢،٩٨

حدثنا عبد الله بن أحمد بن حنبل قال: سمعت أبي يقول: قال محمّد بن إدريس الشافعي: يا أبا عبد الله إذا صحّ عندكم الخبر عن رسول الله صلّى الله عليه وسلّم فأخبرونا به نرجع إليه.

أخبرنا إسماعيل بن أحمد ومحمّد بن عبد الباقي قالا: أخبرنا حمد بن أحمد قال: أخبرنا أحمد بن عبد الله أبو نعيم الحافظ قال: حدثنا سليمان بن أحمد قال: ١٣،٩٨

سمعتُ عبد الله بن أحمد يقول: سمعت أبي يقول: قال لي محمد بن إدريس الشافعي: يا أبا عبد الله أنت أعلم بالأخبار الصحاح منّا فإذا كان خبر صحيح فأعلمني حتّى أذهب إليه كوفيًا كان أو بَصريًا أو شاميًا.

قال عبد الله: جميع ما حدّث به الشافعي في كتابه فقال حدثّني الثقة أَو أخبرني الثقة فهو أبي رحمه الله.

---

١ هـ: الفضل بن محمّد القرشي.

By reporting this exchange, al-Shāfiʿī saves us the trouble of debating with the partisans of Abū Ḥanīfah. Aḥmad's superiority to Mālik is acknowledged, Aḥmad having learned everything Mālik knew and then added to it, as attested by any comparison of the *Well-Trodden Path* and the *Authenticated Reports*. Al-Shāfiʿī, for his part, was well versed in the various fields of learning but conceded Hadith transmission to Aḥmad; and Hadith is the pivot upon which legal reasoning turns. 98.10

We cite ʿAbd al-Malik ibn Abī l-Qāsim al-Karūkhī, who cites ʿAbd Allāh ibn Muḥammad al-Anṣārī, who cites Muḥammad ibn Aḥmad al-Jārūdī, who said that al-Qaṭīʿī said that he heard Aḥmad ibn Ḥanbal's son ʿAbd Allāh report that he heard his father say: 98.11

[Aḥmad:] Al-Shāfiʿī told me, "You know Hadith better than I do. Whenever a Hadith turns out to be sound, let me know so I can adopt it."

We cite Muḥammad ibn Nāṣir, who cites Abū Sahl ibn Saʿduwayh, who cites Abū l-Faḍl Muḥammad ibn al-Faḍl al-Qurashī, who cites Abū Bakr ibn Marduwayh, who heard Sulaymān ibn Aḥmad report that he heard Aḥmad ibn Ḥanbal's son ʿAbd Allāh report: 98.12

[ʿAbd Allāh:] I heard my father say, "Al-Shāfiʿī once said to me, 'Aḥmad, whenever a report about the Emissary of God proves to be sound, let me know so I can use it.'"

We cite Ismāʿīl ibn Aḥmad and Muḥammad ibn ʿAbd al-Bāqī, who cite Ḥamd ibn Aḥmad, who cites Aḥmad ibn ʿAbd Allāh Abū Nuʿaym al-Ḥāfiẓ, who heard Sulaymān ibn Aḥmad report that he heard ʿAbd Allāh ibn Aḥmad say that he heard his father say: 98.13

[ʿAbd Allāh:] I heard my father say, "Muḥammad ibn Idrīs al-Shāfiʿī once said to me, 'Aḥmad, you know better than I which reports are sound. Whenever you find a sound one, whether from Kufa, Basra, or Syria, let me know so I can adopt it.'"

Whenever in his book al-Shāfiʿī says, "I cite a trustworthy source" or "I heard a trustworthy source report," he means my father.

وكتابه الذي صنّفه ببغداد أعدل من الكتاب الذي صنّفه بمصر وذاك أنّه حيث كان ها هنا كان يسأل الشيخ فيغيّر عليه، ولم يكن بمصر يغيّر عليه إذا ذهب إلى خبر ضعيف. وسمعت أبي يقول: استفاد منّا الشافعي ما لم نستفِدْ منه.

قال سليمان بن أحمد: ١٤،٩٨

وحدثنا محمّد بن إسحاق بن راهويه قال: سمعتُ أبي يقول: ما رأى الشافعي مثل أحمد بن حنبل.

أنبأنا محمّد بن أبي منصور قال: أخبرنا المبارك بن عبد الجبّار قال: أخبرنا عبيد الله بن عمر بن شاهين قال: ١٥،٩٨

حدثنا أحمد بن كامل القاضي قال: حدثني عدة من أصحاب أحمد قالوا: كان يقول: انتفع بنا الشافعي أكثر ممّا انتفعنا به.

أخبرنا محمّد بن أبي منصور قال: أخبرنا عبد القادر بن محمد قال: أخبرنا إبراهيم بن عمر البَرْمكي، وأخبرنا عبد الله ١٦،٩٨
ابن عليّ المقرئ قال: أخبرنا عبد الملك بن محمّد السُيُوري قال: أخبرنا عبد العزيز بن عليّ بن أحمد بن الفضل قالا: أخبرنا عليّ بن عبد العزيز بن مَرْدَك قال:

حدثنا عبد الرحمن بن أبي حاتم الرازي قال: سمعت أبي يقول: أحمد بن حنبل أكثر من الشافعي تعلم الشافعي أشياء من معرفة الحديث من أحمد وكان الشافعي فَقيهاً ولم يكن له معرفة بالحديث فربّما قال لأحمد: هذا الحديث قوي محفوظ؟ فإذا قال أحمد: نعم. جعله أصلاً وبنى عليه.

أخبرنا محمّد بن ناصر قال: أخبرنا أبو سهل بن سَعْدُوَيْه قال: أخبرنا محمّد بن الفضل القرشي قال: حدثنا أبو بكر ١٧،٩٨
ابن مَرْدُوَيْه قال: حدثني أحمد بن إسحاق قال: حدثنا إبراهيم بن محمد الفايَزاني قال:

سمعت أبا بكر الأَثْرَم يقول: كنّا في مجلي البُوَيْطي فقرأ علينا عن الشافعي أن التيمّم ضَربتان. فقلت له: وروبت حديث عمّار بن ياسر عن النبيّ صلّى الله عليه وسلّم

This is why the book al-Shāfiʿī wrote in Baghdad is better argued than the one he wrote in Egypt.[266] When he was here, he would ask my father, who would correct him; but in Egypt there was no one to catch him when he used a weak report. I heard my father say, "Al-Shāfiʿī learned more from me than I did from him."

Sulaymān ibn Aḥmad reports that he heard Muḥammad ibn Isḥāq ibn Rāhawayh report that he heard his father say: **98.14**

[Muḥammad ibn Isḥāq ibn Rāhawayh:] I heard my father say, "Al-Shāfiʿī never met anyone like Aḥmad ibn Ḥanbal."

We were informed by Muḥammad ibn Abī Manṣūr, who cites al-Mubārak ibn ʿAbd al-Jabbār, who cites ʿUbayd Allāh ibn ʿUmar al-Shāhīn, who heard Judge Aḥmad ibn Kāmil report: **98.15**

[Aḥmad ibn Kāmil:] Several of Aḥmad's associates told me that he used to say, "Al-Shāfiʿī learned more from us than we did from him."

We cite Muḥammad ibn Abī Manṣūr, who cites ʿAbd al-Qādir ibn Muḥammad, who cites Ibrāhīm ibn ʿUmar al-Barmakī, who cites ʿAbd Allāh ibn ʿAlī l-Muqri', who cites ʿAbd al-Malik ibn Muḥammad al-Suyūrī, who cites ʿAbd al-ʿAzīz ibn ʿAlī ibn Aḥmad ibn al-Faḍl, who like ʿAbd al-Malik ibn Muḥammad al-Suyūrī cites ʿAlī ibn ʿAbd al-ʿAzīz ibn Mardak, who heard ʿAbd al-Raḥmān ibn Abī Ḥātim al-Rāzī say that he heard his father say: **98.16**

[Abū Ḥātim:] I'd give Aḥmad ibn Ḥanbal precedence over al-Shāfiʿī. Being a jurist and not a Hadith expert, al-Shāfiʿī learned about Hadith from Aḥmad. He would often ask him, "Is this report strong? Do people know it?" If Aḥmad said it was, he would take it and build on it.

We cite Muḥammad ibn Nāṣir, who cites Abū Sahl ibn Saʿduwayh, who cites Muḥammad ibn al-Faḍl al-Qurashī, who heard Abū Bakr ibn Marduwayh report that he heard Aḥmad ibn Isḥāq report that he heard Ibrāhīm ibn Muḥammad al-Fāyazānī report that he heard Abū Bakr al-Athram say: **98.17**

[Al-Athram:] Once when we were in al-Buwayṭī's circle, he read to us, citing al-Shāfiʿī, that ablution with sand consists of two passes.[267] But when I recited the Hadith where ʿAmmār quotes the Prophet as saying, "Ablution

إنّ التيمُّم ضَرْبَةٌ واحِدة فحكّ من كتابه ضَربتين وصيّره ضَربة على حديث عمّار.

وقال: قال الشافعي: إذا رأيتم عن رسول الله الثّبْت فاضربوا على قولي وارجعوا إلى الحديث وخُذوا به فإنّه قولي.

١٨،٩٨ أخبرنا عبد الملك بن أبي القاسم الكَرُوخي قال: أخبرنا عبد الله بن محمد الأنصاري قال: أخبرنا أبو يعقوب قال: أخبرنا منصور بن عبد الله بن خالد قال: حدثنا محمد بن الحسن بن عليّ البخاري قال:

سمعتُ محمّد بن إبراهيم البُوشَنْجي وذكر أحمد بن حنبل فقال: هو عندي أفضل وأفقه من سُفْيان الثَّوْري وذلك أنّ سفيان لم يُمتحن من الشدّة والبلوى بمثل ما امتُحن أحمد بن حنبل ولا عِلْم سفيان ومن تقدّم من فُقهاء الأمصار كعِلْم أحمد بن حنبل لأنّه كان أجمع لها وأبصر بمُتْقِنهم وغالطهم وصدوقهم وكذوبهم منه.

١٩،٩٨ قلت: فهذا بيان لقوة علمه وفضله الذي حثّ على اتباعه عامّة المتّبعين فأمّا المجتهد من أصحابه فإنّه يتبع دليله من غير تقليد له ولهذا يميل إلى إحدى الروايتين عنه دون الأخرى وربّما اختار ما ليس في المذهب أصلاً لأنّه تابع للدليل وإنّما يُنسب هذا إلى مذهب أحمد لميله إلى عموم أقواله.

فصل

٢٠،٩٨ فإن قال أصحاب أبي حَنيفة إنّ أبا حنيفة قد لقي الصحابة. فالجواب من وجهين أحدهما أنّ الدارَقُطْني قال: لم يلقَ أبو حنيفة أحدًا من الصحابة. وقال أبو بكر الخطيب: رأى أَنَس بن مالك. والثاني أنّه لقي الصحابة سعيد بن المسيَّب وغيره ولم يقدّموهم عليه.

with sand consists of one pass,"[268] he rubbed "two passes" out of his book and changed it to "one pass," as in the report of ʿAmmār.

He also said, "Whenever you find a reliable account of the Prophet, prefer it to whatever I might have said. Adopt the Hadith and use it as if it had come from me."

We cite ʿAbd al-Malik ibn Abī l-Qāsim al-Karūkhī, who cites ʿAbd Allāh ibn Muḥammad al-Anṣārī, who cites Abū Yaʿqūb, who cites Manṣūr ibn ʿAbd Allāh ibn Khālid, who heard Muḥammad ibn al-Ḥasan ibn ʿAlī l-Bukhārī report that he heard Muḥammad ibn Ibrāhīm al-Būshanjī say, at the mention of Aḥmad ibn Ḥanbal: **98.18**

[Al-Būshanjī:] I think of Aḥmad as more learned and more insightful than Sufyān al-Thawrī. After all, Sufyān never had to suffer an ordeal as terrible as the one Aḥmad went through. Also, Sufyān and the other local scholars of his time cannot have known as much as Aḥmad did, since Aḥmad knew what all of them knew put together. He also had a clearer sense of which of them transmitted accurately and which ones made mistakes, not to mention which were honest and which ones lied.

[The author:] The foregoing should give a clear idea of the scholarly pre-eminence that has persuaded so many to join Aḥmad's interpretive tradition. Those of his associates who strive to know the Law do not merely imitate him. Rather, they act in accordance with the implication of his rulings. In doing so, they may favor one report of his view over another, and even choose a position that was never adopted by the original jurists of the school so long as it is consistent with the implication of his rulings. The position may thus be attributed to Aḥmad's school only in the sense that it conforms to the general spirit of his statements. **98.19**

Addendum

What if partisans of Abū Ḥanifah boast that their exemplar knew some of the Companions? **98.20**

There are two rebuttals. The first is to cite al-Dāraquṭnī, who said, "Abū Ḥanīfah never met any of the Companions"; and Abū Bakr al-Khaṭīb, who said, "He saw Anas ibn Mālik." The second is to say that by that reasoning they should grant Saʿīd ibn al-Musayyab and others who did meet the Companions precedence over Abū Ḥanīfah.[269]

٢١،٩٨ فإن قال أصحاب مالك إنّه لقي التابعين، بطل بالتابعين الذين لقيهم فإنّهم قد لقوا الصحابة وهو مقدّم عليهم عندهم فإن قالوا هو عالم دار الهجرة فسلّمٌ إلّا أنّ صاحبنا ضمّ علمه إلى غيره.

٢٢،٩٨ فإن قال أصحاب الشافعي له نسب يُلاصق نسب النبيّ صلّى الله عليه وسلّم وقد قال عليه السلام: قَدِّموا قُريشاً ولا تَقَدَّموها وتَعلَّموا من قُرَيْشٍ وَلا تُعالموها قلنا: قربُ نسبه لا يوجب تقديمه في العلم على غيره فإنّ عموم علماء التابعين كانوا من الموالي كالحسن وابن سِيرين وعَطاء وطاووس وعِكرِمة ومَكحول وغيرهم وتقدّموا على خلق كثير من أهل الشرف بالنسب لأنّ تقدُّمهم كان بكثرة العلم لا بقرب النسب، وقد أخذ الناس بقول ابن مسعود وزيد ما لم[١] يأخذوا بقول ابن عبّاس.

فأما قوله قَدِّموا قُريشاً فقال إبراهيم الحَرْبي: سُئل أحمد عن ذلك فقال: يعني في الخلافة، ولا تعالموها محمول على النبيّ صلّى الله عليه وسلّم.

٢٣،٩٨ فإن قالوا: كان الشافعي فصيحاً فسلّمٌ وذلك لا يعطي التقدُّم على غيره لأنّ التقدّم بكثرة العلم، على أنّه قد أُخذ عليه كلمات. فقالوا: قد قال ماء مالح وإنّما يُقال مِلْح. وقال ﴿ألاّ تَعولوا﴾ يكثر عيالكم، ومعناه عند اللغويّين أنْ لا تميلوا. وقال إذا أَشْلَي كلباً يريد أَغراه، وإنّما الإشلاء عند العرب الاستدعاء. وقال: ثوب يَسوى كذا والعرب تقول: يُساوي.

وقال أبو بكر المَرُّوذي: كان أحمد بن حنبل لا يلحن في الكلام.

٢٤،٩٨ فإن قالوا: فقد روى عنه. قلنا: لأنّه كان أكبر سنّاً منه، وقد روى الشافعي عن مالك وهو مُقدَّم عندكم عليه على أنّه قد روى الشافعي عن أحمد أَيضاً على ما

[١] د: ولم.

What if partisans of Mālik boast that their exemplar knew the Successors? 98.21
This claim is invalidated by reference to the Successors whom he met. Those Successors had known the Companions, and yet gave Mālik precedence over them.[270]

If they say, "Mālik is the repository of the knowledge of Medina," then concede the point, but then say that our exemplar Aḥmad acquired everything Mālik knew and added to it.

What if partisans of al-Shāfiʿī boast that his lineage strikes close to that of 98.22
the Prophet, who said, "Put Quraysh first and do not step out ahead of them; learn from them and do not presume to teach them"?

To this we reply that kinship does not entail giving him precedence over others in learning. Among the Successors, almost all the learned men were non-Arab affiliates of the tribes. These include al-Ḥasan al-Baṣrī, Ibn Sīrīn, ʿAṭāʾ, Ṭāwūs, ʿIkrimah, Makḥūl, and others. By virtue of their great learning, they were perceived as having outdone those of their contemporaries whose nobility depended only on lineage. People accepted what Ibn Masʿūd and Zayd told them and rejected the same claim when it came from Ibn ʿAbbās.[271]

As for "Put Quraysh first," I refer you to Ibn al-Ḥarbī, who reports that Aḥmad was asked what it meant and said, "It means first in line for the caliphate. The phrase 'do not presume to teach them' is understood to refer to the Prophet."

Should they say that al-Shāfiʿī was faultless in his Arabic and therefore 98.23
beyond reproach, concede the point, but then say that that does not give him precedence over others because precedence arises from how much one knows. Then again, he was caught making mistakes: saying, for example, "salty water" when the expression is "salt water"; or saying that *allā taʿūlū*[272] means "that you not have many dependents" whereas specialists in language say it means "that you not incline"; or saying "if you call a dog" when he meant "if you sic a dog," as the Arabs use the verb *ashlā* to mean only "call"; or saying "a robe that's *x*," even though the Arabs say "a robe that costs *x*." According to al-Marrūdhī, on the other hand, Aḥmad ibn Ḥanbal never made mistakes when he spoke.

Should anyone say, "It's been reported that Aḥmad recited Hadith on 98.24
al-Shāfiʿī's authority," point out that al-Shāfiʿī was older. Not only that: al-Shāfiʿī himself would cite Mālik, who, according to al-Shāfiʿī's partisans,

قد سبق بيانه.

قال البُوَيطي: سمعتُ الشافعي يقول: كلّ شيء في كتبي[1]. وقال بعض أهل العلم: فهو أحمد بن حنبل.

هذا قدر الانتصار لاختيارنا ورحمة الله على الكلّ وللناس فيما يعشقون مذاهب.

الباب التاسع والتسعون في فضل أصحابه وأتباعه

أخبرنا ابن ناصر قال: أنبأنا أبو عليّ الحسن بن أحمد قال: أخبرنا أبو الفتح بن أبي الفوارس قال: أخبرنا عمر بن جعفر بن سَلْم قال: حدثنا أحمد بن عليّ الأَبّار قال: ١،٩٩

قال عبد الوهّاب الورّاق: إذا تكلّم الرجل في أصحاب أحمد فاتَّهِمْه فإنّ له خَبيئة، ليس هو بصاحب سُنّة.

أنبأنا أبو القاسم الحريري عن أبي إسحاق البرمكي عن عبد العزيز بن جعفر قال: أخبرنا أبو بكر الخلّال قال: حدثنا محمّد بن عليّ السِّمْسار قال: حدثنا أبو داوود قال: ٢،٩٩

سمعت أبا بكر أحمد بن محمّد الأَثْرَم يقول: ربّما يترك أصحاب أحمد بن حنبل أشياء ليس لها تَبِعة عند الله مخافة أن يُعيروا بأحمد بن حنبل.

أخبرنا ابن ناصر قال: أنبأنا أبو عليّ الحسن بن أحمد قال: أخبرنا محمّد بن الحسين بن خَلَف قال: أخبرنا أبو الحسن ٣،٩٩

١ هكذا في جميع النسخ فقد أضاف التركي: حدثني الثقة فهو أحمد بن حنبل.

should have deferred to him. What's more, al-Shāfiʿī reported Hadith citing Aḥmad, as we have seen.

Al-Buwayṭī said that he heard al-Shāfiʿī say, "Everything is in my books," and a certain scholar explained that it came from Aḥmad ibn Ḥanbal.[273]

The foregoing will, I hope, suffice to make our case. Let God be merciful to all, and to each his own.

Chapter 99: On the Excellence of His Associates and Successors

We cite Ibn Nāṣir, who was informed by Abū ʿAlī l-Ḥasan ibn Aḥmad, who cites Abū l-Fatḥ ibn Abī l-Fawāris, who cites ʿUmar ibn Jaʿfar ibn Salm, who heard Aḥmad ibn ʿAlī l-Abbār report that ʿAbd al-Wahhāb al-Warrāq said: 99.1

[Al-Warrāq:] To criticize Aḥmad's associates is to attack Aḥmad himself. Anyone who does that must be harboring a grudge of some kind and is no Sunni.

We were informed by Abū l-Qāsim al-Ḥarīrī, on the authority of Abū Isḥāq al-Barmakī, on the authority of ʿAbd al-ʿAzīz ibn Jaʿfar, who cites Abū Bakr al-Khallāl, who heard Muḥammad ibn ʿAlī l-Simsār report that he heard Abū Dāwūd report that he heard Abū Bakr Aḥmad ibn Muḥammad al-Athram say: 99.2

[Al-Athram:] Aḥmad ibn Ḥanbal's associates sometimes decide to give up matters that have no consequence as far as God is concerned in order to avoid provoking any criticism of Aḥmad.

We cite Ibn Nāṣir, who was informed by Abū ʿAlī l-Ḥasan ibn Aḥmad, who cites Muḥammad ibn al-Ḥusayn ibn Khalaf, who cites Abū l-Ḥasan ʿAlī ibn Muḥammad al-Ḥinnāʾī, who cites Abū Muḥammad ʿAbd Allāh al-Ṭarasūsī, who heard Abū l-ʿAbbās 99.3

عليّ بن محمد الحِنائي قال: أخبرنا أبو محمّد عبد الله الطَّرسوسي قال: حدثنا أبو العباس البَرْدَعي قال: حدثنا أحمد ابن طاهر قال: حدثنا العبّاس قال:

سمعتُ أبا الفضل يقول:

بلغني أنه ذُكر عند المتوكّل بعد موت أحمد أنّ أصحاب أحمد يكون بينهم وبين أهل البدع الشرّ فقال المتوكّل لصاحب الخبر: لا ترفع إليّ من أخبارهم شيئاً وشُدَّ على أيديهم فإنّهم وصاحبهم من سادة أُمّة محمّد وقد عرف الله لأحمد صبره وبلاءه ورفع عَلَمه أيّام حياته وبعد موته، أصحابُه أجلّ الأصحاب. وأنا أظنّ أنّ الله تعالى يُعطي أحمد ثواب الصدّيقين.

أخبرنا محمّد بن أبي منصور قال: أخبرنا عبد القادر بن محمّد قال: أنبأنا إبراهيم بن عمر قال: أنبأنا عبد العزيز بن جعفر قال: حدثنا أبو بكر الخلال قال: حدثنا المرُّوذي قال: ٤،٩٩

قال لي ابن سُحت خَتَن ابن حباب الجوهري: رأيتُ في المنام جماعة ورجلاً عليه ثياب بيض يقول: غفر الله لأحمد بن حنبل ولكل من ذَبّ عنه.

سمعت أبا بكر بن عبد الباقي البزّاز يقول: سمعت أبا المظفَّر هنّاد بن إبراهيم النَّسَفي يقول: ٥،٩٩

سمعتُ أبا القاسم عبد الواحد بن عبد السلام بن الواثق يقول: سمعتُ بعض الصالحين يقول: رُئِيَ بعض الصالحين في النوم فقيل له: ما فعل الله بك؟

فقال: غفر لي.

قيل: من وجدت أكثر أهل الجنّة؟

قال: أصحاب الشافعي.

قال: فأين أصحاب أحمد بن حنبل؟

قال: سألتني عن أكثر أهل الجنّة، ما سألتني عن أعلَى أهل الجنّة، أصحاب أحمد أعلى أهل الجنّة وأصحاب الشافعي أكثر أهل الجنّة.

al-Bardaʿī report that he heard Aḥmad ibn Ṭāhir report that he heard al-ʿAbbās report that he heard Abū l-Faḍl say:

[Abū l-Faḍl:] I heard that after Aḥmad's death, someone mentioned to al-Mutawakkil that unpleasantness was liable to break out between his partisans and the innovators.

"Don't tell me anything more about them," al-Mutawakkil told the informant. "Instead, take their side. Aḥmad and his people are the lords of Muḥammad's community. God knows well enough the ordeal Aḥmad suffered, since He raised him to fame during his life and after his death; and his partisans are the best he could wish for. I daresay that God will give Aḥmad the reward He gives to the truth-tellers."

We cite Muḥammad ibn Abī Manṣūr, who cites ʿAbd al-Qādir ibn Muḥammad, who was informed by Ibrāhim ibn ʿUmar, who was informed by ʿAbd al-ʿAzīz ibn Jaʿfar, who heard Abū Bakr al-Khallāl report that he heard al-Marrūdhī report: **99.4**

[Al-Marrūdhī:] Ibn Suḥt, who was Ibn Ḥubāb al-Jawharī's relation by marriage, said, "I dreamed I saw some people, and a man in white saying, 'God has forgiven Aḥmad ibn Ḥanbal and all who defend him.'"

I heard Abū Bakr ibn ʿAbd al-Bāqī l-Bazzāz say that he heard Abū l-Muẓaffar Hannād ibn Ibrāhīm al-Nasafī say that he heard Abū l-Qāsim ʿAbd al-Wāḥid ibn ʿAbd al-Salām ibn al-Wāthiq say: **99.5**

[Abū l-Qāsim:] I heard a righteous man relate that one of his fellows appeared in a dream and was asked how God had judged him.

"He forgave me," was the reply.

"So who are the majority of people in the Garden?"

"Followers of al-Shāfiʿī."

"What about Aḥmad ibn Ḥanbal?"

"You asked me who the majority were, not who the highest ones were. Al-Shāfiʿī has the greater number, but Aḥmad's people have the higher rank."

أنبأنا أحمد بن الحسن بن البنّا قال: أنبأنا أبي قال: قال أبو حَفص عمر بن المسلم العُكبَري: حدثنا أبو محمّد يحيى[١] ٦،٩٩
ابن محمّد بن سَهل الثقفي قال: حدثنا أبو بكر قال: حدثنا يحيى بن أحمد الخوّاص قال: حدثنا أبو محمّد عبد الله بن
إبراهيم قال: حدثنا يزيد بن أبي يزيد قال:

حدثنا يحيى الجِمّاني قال: رأيت في المنام كأنّي في صُفّة لي إذ جاء النبيّ صلّى الله عليه وسلّم فأخذ بعضادتَي الباب ثم أذّن وأقام وقال: نجا الناجون وهلك الهالكون.

فقلت: يا رسول الله من الناجون؟

قال: أحمدُ بن حنبل وأصحابه.

أنبأنا أحمد بن الحسن قال: أخبرنا أبي قال: حكى أبو الحسن عليّ بن عبد الواحد قال: ٧،٩٩

حدثني أبو عبد الله الحسين بن أحمد الحربي قال: رأيت في النوم كأنّي في جماعة وكأنّا قد اعتُقلنا جماعتنا وكأنّي مكروب من الاعتقال فإذا بقائل يقول: أي شيء أنتم؟

فقلت: حَنابِلة. فقال: قوموا فإنّ الحنابلة لا يُعتقلون. وكأنّ قائلاً يقول: ما من أحد اشتمل على هذا المذهب فحوسِب.

٨،٩٩ وكان ابن عَقيل رضي الله عنه يقول: هذا المذهب إنّما ظلمه أصحابه لأنّ أصحاب أبي حنيفة والشافعي إذا برع أحد منهم في العلم تولّى القضاء وغيره من الولايات، فكانت الولاية سبباً لتدريسه واشتغاله بالعلم، فأمّا أصحاب أحمد فإنّه قلّ فيهم من تعلّق بطرف من العلم إلّا ويخرجه ذلك إلى التعبُّد والتزهُّد لغلبة الخير على القوم فينقطعون عن التشاغل بالعلم.

١ هـ، د: ابو محمد بن يحيى.

We were informed by Aḥmad ibn al-Ḥasan ibn al-Bannā, who was informed by his father that Abū Ḥafṣ ʿUmar ibn al-Muslim al-ʿUkbarī said that he heard Abū Muḥammad Yaḥyā ibn Muḥammad ibn Sahl al-Thaqafī report that he heard Abū Bakr report that he heard Yaḥyā ibn Aḥmad al-Khawwāṣ report that he heard Abū Muḥammad ʿAbd Allāh ibn Ibrāhīm report that he heard Yazīd ibn Abī Yazīd report that he heard Yaḥyā l-Ḥimmānī report: 99.6

[Al-Ḥimmānī:] I dreamed I was sitting under a portico at home when the Prophet appeared. He stood in the doorway with his hands resting on the jamb, issued the call to prayer, and announced that prayer had begun. Then he said, "The saved are saved and the damned damned."

"Emissary of God," I asked, "who are the saved?"

"Aḥmad ibn Ḥanbal and his followers."

We were informed by Aḥmad ibn al-Ḥasan, who cites his father, who said that Abū l-Ḥasan ʿAlī ibn ʿAbd al-Wāḥid related that he heard Abū ʿAbd Allāh al-Ḥusayn ibn Aḥmad al-Ḥarbī report: 99.7

[Al-Ḥarbī:] I dreamed I was in a group and we were being held against our will and I was unhappy about it. Then a voice asked, "What are you?"

I said, "Followers of Ibn Ḥanbal."

"Go, then; Ḥanbalīs aren't to be confined."

Then it felt as if a voice said, "No adherent of the Ḥanbalī school has ever been held accountable for his sins."

Ibn ʿAqīl—God have mercy on him!—used to say: 99.8

"The problem with our school is our own members. If a Ḥanafī or a Shāfiʿī excels in his studies, he's appointed to a judgeship or some other position and as a result of his appointment can devote himself to teaching and research. Aḥmad's people, on the other hand, can hardly study anything without deciding to devote themselves to pious exercises and renounce the world, given how godly the group tends to be. As a result, they stop being scholars."

الباب المائة في ذكر أعيان أصحابه واتباعه من زمانه إلى زماننا

١،١٠٠ أمّا من صحب أحمد وتبع مذهبه من العلماء والأخيار في زمانه خَلقٌ كثير وكذلك من تبع مذهبه بعد وفاته إلى زماننا هذا عدد يفوت الإحصاء وإنّما أذكر من كبار الأعيان المشتهرين بالذكر وقد جعلتهم تسع طبقات والله الموفّق.

ذكر المختارين من الطبقة الأولى وهم الذين صحبوا أحمد ونقلوا عنه

٢،١٠٠ أحمد بن إبراهيم الدَّوْرَقي وقد سمع من إسماعيل بن عُلَيّة ويزيد بن زُرَيع وهُشَيم.

أحمد بن أصرم بن خُزَيمة المُزَني وقد سمع من عبد الأعلى بن حمّاد وغيره.

أحمد بن جعفر الوَكيعي وقد سمع من وكيع وأبي معاوية.

أحمد بن حُمَيد أبو طالب المُشْكاني وكان فقيرًا صالحًا.

أحمد بن أبي خَيْثَمة زُهَير بن حرب وقد سمع من عفّان وأبي نُعيم وكان من كبار العلماء المصنّفين.

أحمد بن سعيد الدّارِمي.

أحمد بن سعيد[1] بن إبراهيم الزُّهْري.

أحمد بن صالح المصري وكان من كبار الحُفّاظ.

أحمد بن الفُرات أبو مسعود الضَّبِّي وقد سمع من يزيد بن هارون.

٣،١٠٠ أحمد بن محمّد بن الحجّاج أبو بكر المَرُّوذي كان وَرعًا صالحًا خَصيصًا بخدمة أحمد، كان يبعثه في حوائجه ويقول: كُلّ ما قلتَ فهو على لساني وأنا قلتُه. وكان

---

[1] هـ، د: سعد.

Chapter 100: His Most Prominent Associates and Their Successors from His Time to Our Own

The number of Aḥmad's associates, and of those learned scholars and good men who, during the years that have elapsed between his death and our own time, have followed his path is too large to count. Here I will mention only the most prominent, arranged in nine generations. May God ensure success! 100.1

Selected Members of the First Generation: Those Who Associated with Aḥmad and Transmitted Directly from Him

Aḥmad ibn Ibrāhīm al-Dawraqī. Heard reports from Ismāʿīl ibn ʿUlayyah, Yazīd ibn Zurayʿ, and Hushaym. 100.2

Aḥmad ibn Aṣram ibn Khuzaymah al-Muzanī. Heard reports from ʿAbd al-Aʿlā ibn Ḥammād and others.

Aḥmad ibn Jaʿfar al-Wakīʿī. Heard reports from Wakīʿ and Abū Muʿāwiyah.

Aḥmad ibn Ḥumayd, Abū Ṭālib al-Mushkānī. Lived in poverty and righteousness.

Aḥmad ibn Abī Khaythamah Zuhayr ibn Ḥarb. Heard reports from ʿAffān and Abū Nuʿaym, and was a major compiler of scholarly works.

Aḥmad ibn Saʿīd al-Dārimī.

Aḥmad ibn Saʿīd ibn Ibrāhīm al-Zuhrī.

Aḥmad ibn Ṣāliḥ al-Miṣrī. A major repository of Hadith.

Aḥmad ibn al-Furāt, Abū Masʿūd al-Ḍabbī. Heard reports from Yazīd ibn Hārūn.

Aḥmad ibn Muḥammad ibn al-Ḥajjāj, Abū Bakr al-Marrūdhī. A scrupulous and righteous man. He was devoted to serving Aḥmad, who would send him out on errands. Aḥmad used to tell him: "Anything you say counts as if I 100.3

أحمد يقدّمه ويأكل من تحت يده. ولمّا قدم أحمد من العسكر كان يقول: جزى الله أبا بكر المرّوذي خيرًا. وهو الذي تولّى إغماض أحمد لمّا مات وغسله وروى عنه أحاديث ومسائل كثيرة.

أنبأنا هبة الله بن أحمد الحريري قال: أنبأنا إبراهيم بن عمر البرمكي عن عبد العزيز بن جعفر قال: ٤،١٠٠

سمعت أبا بكر الخلّال يقول: خرج أبو بكر المرّوذي إلى الغزو فشيّعه الناس إلى سامَرّا فجعل يَردّهم فلا يرجعون.

قال: فحُزِروا فإذا هم بسامَرّا سوى من رجع نحو من خمسين ألف إنسان. فقيل له: يا أبا بكر احمدِ الله فهذا عَلَم قد نُشر لك.

قال: فبكى ثمّ قال: ليس هذا العَلَم لي وإنّما هذا علم أحمد بن حنبل.

قال الخلال: ٥،١٠٠

وأخبرنا العباس بن نصر قال: مضيت أُصلّي على قبر المرُّوذي فرأيت مشايخ عند القبر وسمعتُ بعضهم يقول لبعض: كان فلان ها هنا أمس فنام وانتبه من نومه فزعًا فقلت: أي شيء القصّة؟ فقال: رأيت أحمد بن حنبل راكبًا فقلت: إلى أين يا أبا عبد الله؟

فقال: إلى شجرة طوبى نلحق أبا بكر المرّوذي.

توفّي المرُّوذي لستٍّ خلوْن من جمادى الأُولى سنة خمس وسبعين ومائتين ودفن قريبًا من قبر أحمد وتولّى الصلاة عليه هارون بن العبّاس الهاشمي.

٦،١٠٠ أحمد بن محمّد بن خالد أبو العبّاس البَراثي وقد سمع من عليّ بن الجَعْد.

أحمد بن محمّد بن هانئ أبو بكر الأَثْرَم وكان من حُفّاظ الحديث. قال فيه يحيى بن مَعِين: كان أحد أبويه جنّيّ. وقد سمع من عفّان وأبي نُعيم وتشاغل بمسائل أحمد وصنّفها.

أحمد بن منصور الرَّمادي نقل عن أحمد وقد روى عن عبد الرزّاق.

أحمد بن مُلاعِب بن حيّان وقد سمع من عَفّان وأبي نُعيم.

said it myself." He treated al-Marrūdhī with special consideration and would eat what he gave him.[274] After he returned from Samarra, he would often say, "God reward al-Marrūdhī!" It was al-Marrūdhī who closed Aḥmad's eyes and washed him after he died. He also transmitted many of his reports and discussions of legal issues.

We were informed by Hibat Allāh ibn Aḥmad al-Ḥarīrī, who was informed by Ibrāhīm ibn ʿUmar al-Barmakī, citing ʿAbd al-ʿAzīz ibn Jaʿfar, who heard Abū Bakr al-Khallāl say: 100.4

When Abū Bakr al-Marrūdhī left for the frontier, a crowd of people marched with him as far as Samarra. He kept telling them to turn back but they wouldn't. The size of the crowd was estimated at fifty thousand, not counting the ones who turned back before reaching Samarra.

"Be grateful to God," someone said to him, "that so many people admire you."

He burst into tears then said, "It's not me they admire, it's Aḥmad ibn Ḥanbal."

Al-Khallāl cited al-ʿAbbās ibn Naṣr: 100.5

[Al-ʿAbbās ibn Naṣr:] I went to pray at al-Marrūdhī's grave and saw some old men there. One of them was telling another, "So-and-So slept here last night and woke up scared. I asked him what happened, and he said, 'I dreamed I saw Aḥmad ibn Ḥanbal riding along. I asked him where we were going, and he said, "To the Tree of Ṭūbā to catch up with Abū Bakr al-Marrūdhī."'"

Al-Marrūdhī died the sixth of Jumādā I 275 [September 16, 888] and was buried near Aḥmad's grave. His funeral prayer was led by Hārūn ibn al-ʿAbbās al-Hāshimī.

Aḥmad ibn Muḥammad ibn Khālid, Abū l-ʿAbbās al-Barāthī. He heard reports from ʿAlī ibn al-Jaʿd. 100.6

Aḥmad ibn Muḥammad ibn Ḥāni', Abū Bakr al-Athram. A great memorizer of Hadith. Yaḥyā ibn Maʿīn said of him that one of his parents must have been a jinni. He heard reports from ʿAffān and Abū Nuʿaym. He busied himself with compiling Aḥmad's discussions of legal issues.

Aḥmad ibn Manṣūr al-Ramādī. Transmitted reports from Aḥmad as well as ʿAbd al-Razzāq.

Aḥmad ibn Mulāʿib ibn Ḥayyān. Heard reports from ʿAffān and Abū Nuʿaym.

أحمد بن نَصْر الخُزاعي جالس أحمد واستفاد منه وقد سمع من مالك وهُشَيم.

أحمد بن يحيى ثعلب وكان يقال: ما يرد القيامة أعلم بالنحو من ثعلب وكان صدوقاً ديّناً وكان له مال خلف نحواً من ثمانية آلاف دينار.

٧،١٠٠ إبراهيم بن إسحاق الحربي ولد سنة ثمان وتسعين ومائة وسمع أبا نُعيم الفضل ابن دُكَين وعفّان بن مسلم وعبد الله بن صالح العِجْلي وموسى بن إسماعيل التَّبُوذكي ومُسَدَّداً وخلقاً كثيراً. وكان إماماً في جميع العلوم مُتقناً ومصنّفاً محسناً وعابداً زاهداً ونقل عن أحمد مسائل حساناً.

قال الدَّارَقُطْني: كان إبراهيم الحربي يُقاس بأحمد بن حنبل في زُهده وعلمه وورعه.

٨،١٠٠ أخبرنا عبد الرحمن بن محمّد القزاز قال: أخبرنا أحمد بن عليّ بن ثابت قال: حدثني الأزهري قال: سمعتُ أبا سعد عبد الرحمن بن محمّد الاستِراباذي يقول: سمعتُ أبا أحمد بن عَديّ يقول:

سمعتُ أبا عِمْران الأشْيَب يقول: قال رجل لإبراهيم الحربي: كيف قويتَ على جَمْع هذه الكتب؟

فغضب وقال: بلحمي ودمي، بلحمي ودمي.

٩،١٠٠ أخبرنا عبد الرحمن بن محمّد قال: أخبرنا أحمد بن عليّ قال: حدثني محمّد بن عليّ الصُّوري قال: أخبرنا عبد الرحمن بن محمّد التُّجِيبي قال: حدثنا محمّد بن إسحاق المُلْحَمي قال:

سمعت عبد الله بن أحمد يقول كان أبي يقول لي: امضِ إلى إبراهيم الحربي حتى يُلقي[1] عليك الفرائض.

١٠،١٠٠ أخبرنا عبد الرحمن بن محمّد قال: أخبرنا أحمد بن عليّ قال: حدثني عبد العزيز بن أبي طاهر الصوفي: حدثني عبد الوهاب بن جعفر المَيْداني قال: حدثنا أبو سُليمان محمّد بن عبد الله بن أحمد بن زيد قال:

حدثني أبي قال: قال أبو عليّ الحُسين بن قهم وذكر إبراهيم الحربي: والله يا أبا محمّد لا ترى عيناك مثل أبي إسحاق أيّام الدنيا، لقد رأيتُ وجالستُ الناس من صنوف

[1] ش: يقرأ.

Aḥmad ibn Nāṣr al-Khuzāʿī. Sat with Aḥmad and learned from him. Also heard reports from Mālik and Hushaym.

Aḥmad ibn Yaḥyā, called Thaʿlab. It was said of him that even on the Day of Resurrection there will be no one present more learned in grammar. He was trustworthy and religiously observant. He was also wealthy: his estate came to some eight thousand dinars.

Ibrāhīm ibn Isḥāq al-Ḥarbī. Born in 198 [813–14], heard reports from Abū Nuʿaym al-Faḍl ibn Dukayn, ʿAffān ibn Muslim, ʿAbd Allāh ibn Ṣāliḥ al-ʿIjlī, Mūsā ibn Ismāʿīl al-Tabūdhakī, Musaddad, and many others. He was an exemplar in all fields of learning, a good compiler, and a worshipful renunciant who transmitted from Aḥmad some good discussions of legal problems. 100.7

Al-Dāraquṭnī said, "Ibrāhīm al-Ḥarbī was on a par with Aḥmad ibn Ḥanbal in renunciation, learning, and scrupulosity."

We cite ʿAbd al-Raḥmān ibn Muḥammad al-Qazzāz, who cites Aḥmad ibn ʿAlī ibn Thābit, who heard al-Azharī report that he heard Abū Saʿd ʿAbd al-Raḥmān ibn Muḥammad al-Astirābādhī say that he heard Abū Aḥmad ibn ʿAdī say that he heard Abū ʿImrān al-Ashyab say: 100.8

[Al-Ashyab:] A man once said to Ibrāhīm al-Ḥarbī, "How did you manage to collect all these books?"

"With blood and toil!" Ibrāhīm replied angrily. "Blood and toil!"

We cite ʿAbd al-Raḥmān ibn Muḥammad, who cites Aḥmad ibn ʿAlī, who heard Muḥammad ibn ʿAlī l-Ṣūrī report that he cites ʿAbd al-Raḥmān ibn Muḥammad al-Tujībī, who heard Muḥammad ibn Isḥāq al-Mulḥamī report that he heard Aḥmad's son ʿAbd Allāh say: 100.9

[ʿAbd Allāh:] My father used to tell me, "Go to Ibrāhīm al-Ḥarbī and have him dictate the *Book of Dividing Inheritances* for you."

We cite ʿAbd al-Raḥmān ibn Muḥammad, who cites Aḥmad ibn ʿAlī, who heard ʿAbd al-ʿAzīz ibn Abī Ṭāhir al-Ṣūfī report that he heard ʿAbd al-Wahhāb ibn Jaʿfar al-Maydānī report that he heard Abū Sulaymān Muḥammad ibn ʿAbd Allāh ibn Aḥmad ibn Zayd report that he heard his father report: 100.10

[ʿAbd Allāh ibn Aḥmad ibn Zayd:] Abū ʿAlī l-Ḥusayn ibn Qahm once said to me, at the mention of Ibrāhim al-Ḥarbī, "By God, Abū Muḥammad, you'll never see another like him, at least not in this world. I've met people

أهل العلم والحذق من كلّ فنّ فما رأيت رجلا أكمل في ذلك كلّه من أبي إسحاق.

١١،١٠٠ أخبرنا عبد الرحمن بن محمّد قال: أخبرنا أحمد بن عليّ قال: حدثني الحسن بن محمّد الخلّال قال: حدثنا أحمد ابن محمّد بن عِمْران قال:

حدثنا عبد الله بن جعفر بن دُرُسْتُوَيْه قال: اجتمع[1] إبراهيم الحربي وأحمد بن يحيى ثَعْلَب فقال ثعلب لإبراهيم: متى يستغني الرجل عن مُلاقاة العلماء؟

فقال له إبراهيم: إذا علم ما قالوا وإلى أي شيء ذهبوا فيما قالوا.

توفّي إبراهيم الحربي ببغداد سنة خمس وثمانين ومائتين وصلّى عليه يوسف بن يعقوب القاضي وكان الجمع كثيرًا جدًّا ودُفن في بيته وقبره اليوم ظاهر يُتبرّك به.

١٢،١٠٠ إبراهيم بن إسحاق النَّيسابوري وكان أحمد ينبسط في منزله ويُفطر عنده.

إبراهيم بن الحارث بن مُصْعَب الطَّرَسُوسي كان أحمد يعظّمه ويبسطه فربّما توقّف أحمد عن جواب المسألة فيجيب هو فيقول له أحمد: جزاك الله خيرًا يا أبا إسحاق.

إبراهيم بن هانئ النيسابوري وكان من العلماء العُبّاد وفي بيته اختفى أحمد في أيّام الواثق.

إسماعيل بن إسحاق السرّاج وقد سمع من يحيى بن يحيى وإسحاق بن راهَوَيْه ونقل عن أحمد.

إسماعيل بن يوسف الدَّيْلَمي وجمع بين[2] حفظ العلم والتعبّد وله كرامات قد ذكرناها في كتاب صفة الصفوة.

إسحاق بن منصور الكَوْسَج سمع سُفيان بن عُيَيْنَة ويحيى بن سعيد وعبد الرحمن ابن مَهدي ووَكيعًا في آخرين وروى عن أحمد وأخرج عنه البخاري ومسلم.

١٣،١٠٠ بِشْر بن موسى الأَسَدي وقد سمع من رَوح بن عُبادة وغيره.

---

١ ليس في هـ. ٢ د: من.

of learning and ability in every field, and studied with them, but never saw anyone as accomplished in all of them as he was."

We cite ʿAbd al-Raḥmān ibn Muḥammad, who cites Aḥmad ibn ʿAlī, who heard al-Ḥasan ibn Muḥammad al-Khallāl report that he heard Aḥmad ibn Muḥammad ibn ʿImrān report that he heard ʿAbd Allāh ibn Jaʿfar ibn Durustuwayh report: 100.11

[Ibn Durustuwayh:] Ibrāhīm al-Ḥarbī and Aḥmad ibn Yaḥyā Thaʿlab once met, and Thaʿlab said to Ibrāhīm, "When is it all right to do without meeting other scholars?"

"When one knows what they've said," answered Ibrāhīm, "and what positions they've supported."

Ibrāhīm al-Ḥarbī died in Baghdad in 285 [898–99]. Yūsuf ibn Yaʿqūb al-Qāḍī prayed over him, and a great number of people attended the funeral. He was buried in his house, and his grave is known today and visited for blessings.

Ibrāhīm ibn Isḥāq al-Naysābūrī. Aḥmad felt at ease in his house and would break his fasts there. 100.12

Ibrāhīm ibn al-Ḥārith ibn Muṣʿab al-Ṭarasūsī. Aḥmad showed great respect for him and treated him as an intimate. He often stopped short when answering a question and Ibrāhīm would finish it. "May God reward you, Abū Isḥāq!" he would say.

Ibrāhīm ibn Hāniʾ al-Naysābūrī. A learned man and a Worshipper. Ibn Ḥanbal hid in his house during the reign of al-Wāthiq.

Ismāʿīl ibn Isḥāq al-Sarrāj. Heard reports from Yaḥyā ibn Yaḥyā and Isḥāq ibn Rāhawayh, and transmitted from Aḥmad.

Ismāʿīl ibn Yūsuf al-Daylamī. Combined Hadith scholarship with pious devotion. Displayed manifestations of grace, which I have described in my book *An Account of the Elite.*

Isḥāq ibn Manṣūr al-Kawsaj. Heard reports from Sufyan ibn ʿUyaynah, Yaḥyā ibn Saʿīd, ʿAbd al-Raḥmān ibn Mahdī, and Wakīʿ, among others. He transmitted reports from Aḥmad. Al-Bukhārī and Muslim cite him as an authority.

Bishr ibn Mūsā l-Asadī. Heard reports from Rawḥ ibn ʿUbādah and others. 100.13

بَدْر بن أبي بـدْر أبو بكر المَغازلي واسمه أحمد إنّما لُقب ببدر فغلب عليه، واسم أبي بدر المُنْذِر وكان الإمام أحمد يقدّمه ويُكرِمه ويقول: من مثل بدر قد ملك لسانه؟ وكان صبوراً على الفقر والزهد.

جعفـر بن محمّـد النَّســائي كان أحمد يكرمه ويأنس به.

١٤،١٠٠ زكريّا بن يحيى النـاقد يُكنى أبا يحيى كان عابداً وكان أحمد يقول عنه: هذا رجل صالح وكان يقول: اشتريتُ من الله تعالى حَوْراء بأربعة آلاف خَتْمة فلمّا كان آخر ختمة سمعتُ الخطاب من الحوراء وهي تقول: وفيتَ بعهدك أنا التي اشتريتني. فيُقال: إنه مات عن قريب.

١٥،١٠٠ عبـد الله بن محمّـد بن أبي الدنيـا روى عن أحمد أنه سأله متى يُصلَّي على السَّقط. فقال: إذا كان لأربعة أشهر. وقد روى عن رجل عن أحمد في مواضع من تصانيفه.

١٦،١٠٠ عبـد الله بن محمّـد بن المهـاجـر أبو محمّـد المعـروف بفُوران وقد حدّث عن شُعيب بن حرب ووكيع وأبي معاوية وغيرهم وكان أحمد يُجلّه ويأنس إليه ويستقرض منه.

١٧،١٠٠ عبـد الوهـاب الورّاق جمع بين العلم والتقى وقيل لأحمد: من نسأل بعدك؟ فقال: سَلوا عبد الوهّاب فإنّه رجل صالح مثله يوفّق لإصابة الحق. وتوفِّي عبد الوهاب سنة إحدى وخمسين ومائتين.

عبـد الملك بن عبـد الحُمَيـد المَيْموني وقد سمع من ابن عُلَيّة ويَزيد بن هارون وكان أحمد يكرمه.

عبّـاس بن محمّـد الدُّوري وقد سمع من شَبابه بن سَوَّار وهاشم بن القاسم وعَفّان.

عَبْدوس بن مـالك أبو محمّـد العَطّار حدّث عن شبابة وأحمد ويحيى بن مَعين وكانت له منزلة من أحمد.

Badr ibn Abī Badr, Abū Bakr al-Maghāzilī. His name is Aḥmad, but he was nicknamed Badr and mostly known by that name. His father's name was al-Mundhir. Aḥmad would show consideration and respect for him, saying, "Who has mastered his tongue as well as Badr?" He suffered poverty and austerity without complaint.

Ja'far ibn Muḥammad al-Nasā'ī. Aḥmad respected him and felt at ease in his company.

Zakariyyā ibn Yaḥyā l-Nāqid, called Abū Yaḥyā. A Worshipper of whom Aḥmad used to say, "There's a righteous man." He himself used to say, "I've bought a houri from God for the price of four thousand readings of the Qur'an. When I finished the last reading, I heard the houri herself speak, saying, 'You've fulfilled your obligation, and I'm the one you bought.'" It is said that he died soon thereafter. 100.14

'Abd Allāh ibn Muḥammad ibn Abī l-Dunyā. He reported having asked Aḥmad when one should pray over a miscarried infant. "If it is at least four months old," said Aḥmad. In some of his compilations, he cites Aḥmad through one intermediate transmitter. 100.15

'Abd Allāh ibn Muḥammad ibn al-Muhājir, Abū Muḥammad, called Fūrān. Transmitted reports from Shu'ayb ibn Ḥarb, Wakī', Abū Mu'āwiyah, and others. Aḥmad held him in great esteem, felt at ease with him, and would borrow money from him. 100.16

'Abd al-Wahhāb al-Warrāq. Combined learning and fear of God. Asked who could answer questions after he died, Aḥmad said, "Ask 'Abd al-Wahhāb; he's an upright man, and upright men will manage to hit on the right answer." He died in 251 [865–66]. 100.17

'Abd al-Malik ibn 'Abd al-Ḥumayd al-Maymūnī. Heard reports from Ibn 'Ulayyah and Yazīd ibn Hārūn. Aḥmad treated him with respect.

'Abbās ibn Muḥammad al-Dūrī. Heard reports from Shabābah ibn Sawwār, Hāshim ibn al-Qāsim, and 'Affān.

'Abdūs ibn Mālik, Abū Muḥammad al-'Aṭṭār. Transmitted reports from Shabābah, Aḥmad, and Yaḥyā ibn Ma'īn. Respected by Aḥmad.

الفضل بن زياد القطّان كان يصلّي بأحمد وروى عنه كثيرًا.
محمّد بن موسى بن مُشَيْش كان جار أحمد وصاحبه وكان أحمد يقدّمه.
مُثنى بن جامع الأنباري ويقال: إنّه كان مُجاب الدعوة.
مُهنّأ بن يحيى الشامي وقد روى عن يَزيد بن هارون وعبد الرزّاق وهو من كبار أصحاب أحمد وكان أحمد يُكرمه ويعرف له حقّ الصحبة وكان يسأل أحمد حتى يضجره وهو يحتمل. قال الدَّارَقُطْني: مُهنَّأ ثِقة نَبيل. ١٠٠،١٨

تسمية المختارين من الطبقة الثانية

أحمد بن جعفر بن المنادي سمع جده محمدا وعباساً الدُّوري وأبا داوود السِّجستاني في خلق كثير وكان دَيّناً ثبتاً راسخاً في العلم حُجّة صنّف نحواً من أربع مائة مصنَّف[1] وتوفّي في محرم سنة ستٍ وثلاثين وثلاث مائة ودُفن في مقبرة الخَيْزُران. ١٠٠،١٩

أحمد بن جَعْفَر بن حَمْدان القَطِيعي سمع بشر بن موسى والكُدَيمي وروى المُسْنَد عن عبد الله بن أحمد وكان صاحب سنّة وتوفّي في ذي الحجّة سنة ثمان وستين وثلاث مائة ودُفن بقرب الإمام أحمد. ١٠٠،٢٠

أحمد بن سُلَيمان أبو بَكْر النَّجّاد جمع العلم والزهد وكانت له حلقة بجامع المنصور يُفتي قبل الصلاة ويُملي الحديث بعدها وصنّف كتاب الخِلاف نحو مئتي جُزء وقد سمع من أبي داوود السِّجِسْتاني وغيره وكان يصوم الدهر ويُفطر كل ليلة على رغيف، وتُوفّي في ذي القعدة سنة ثمان وأربعين وثلاث مائة ودُفن قريباً من بشر الحافي. ١٠٠،٢١

[1] ش: مجلد.

Al-Faḍl ibn Ziyād al-Qaṭṭān. Often led Aḥmad in prayer. Transmitted many of his reports.

Muḥammad ibn Mūsā ibn Mushaysh. Aḥmad's neighbor and associate. Aḥmad showed him special consideration.

Muthannā ibn Jāmiʿ al-Anbārī. It is said that his prayers were always answered.

Muhannaʾ ibn Yaḥyā l-Shāmī. Related Hadith citing Yazīd ibn Hārūn and 100.18
ʿAbd al-Razzāq. A major figure among Aḥmad's associates. Aḥmad respected him and gave him the consideration due him as a student of long standing. He would tire him out with his incessant questions, but Aḥmad would bear it patiently. Al-Dāraquṭnī called him a trustworthy and upstanding authority.

Selected Members of the Second Generation

Aḥmad ibn Jaʿfar ibn al-Munādī. Heard reports from his grandfather 100.19
Muḥammad and from ʿAbbās al-Dūrī, Abū Dāwūd al-Sijistānī, and many others. He was observant, firm in his religion, deeply learned, and authoritative in his knowledge. He compiled more than four hundred works. He died in Muḥarram 336 [July–August 947] and was buried in the Cemetery of al-Khayzurān.

Aḥmad ibn Jaʿfar ibn Ḥamdān al-Qaṭīʿī. Heard reports from Bishr ibn Mūsā 100.20
and al-Kudaymī. Transmitted the *Authenticated Reports* citing Aḥmad's son ʿAbd Allāh. He was a man of the *sunnah.* He died in Dhu l-Hijjah 368 [June–July 979] and was buried near Imam Aḥmad.

Aḥmad ibn Sulaymān Abū Bakr al-Najjād. Combined learning and renun- 100.21
ciation. He led a study circle in the mosque of al-Manṣūr, where he would give legal opinions before the prayer and dictate Hadith afterward. He composed *Disputed Points,* which is some two hundred quires long. He heard Hadith from Abū Dāwūd al-Sijistānī and others. He would fast continuously, breaking his fast on nothing more than some bread at night. He died in Dhu l-Qaʿdah 348 [January–February 960] and was buried next to Bishr al-Ḥāfī.

١٠٠،٢٢ أحمد بن محمّد بن هارون أبو بكر الخَلَّال صرف عنايته إلى جمع علوم أحمد ابن حنبل وسافر لأجلها وكتبها عاليةً ونازلةً وصنّفها كتباً منها كتاب الجامع نحو من مئتي جزء ولم يقاربه أحد من أصحاب أحمد في ذلك وكانت حلقته بجامع المهدي.

تُوفّي يوم الجمعة قبل الصلاة ليومين خلوْن من ربيع الأوّل سنة إحدى عشرة وثلاث مائة ودُفن يوم السبت إلى جانب المَرُّوذي.

١٠٠،٢٣ الحسن بن عليّ بن خلَف أبو محمّد البَرْبَهاري جمع العلم والزهد وصحب المَرُّوذي وسهلاً التُّسْتَري وتنزّه عن ميراث أبيه لأمر كرهه عن سبعين ألف درهم.

وكان البَرْبَهاري شديداً على أهل البدع فما زالوا يُثقلون قلب السلطان عليه وكان ينزل بباب محوّل فانتقل إلى الجانب الشرقي واستتر عند أُخت توزون فبقى نحواً من شهر ثمّ أخذه قيام الدم فمات، فقالت المرأة لخادمها: انظر من يغسله.

وغلقت الأبواب حتى لا يعلم أحد فجاء الغاسل فغسله ووقف يصلّي عليه وحده فاطّلعت فإذا الدار ممتلئة رجالاً بثياب بيض وخضر فاستدعت الخادم وقالت: ما الذي فعلت؟

فقال: يا سيّدتي رأيتِ ما رأيتُ؟

قالت: نعم.

قال: هذه مفاتيح الباب وهو مُغلق.

فقالت: ادفنوه في بيتي وإذا متُّ فادفنوني عنده.

فدفنوه في دارها وماتت بعده فدُفنت هنالك والمكان بقرب دار المملكة بالمخرَّم.

وقرأت بخط شيخنا أبي الحسن ابن الزّاغوني قال: كشف قبر أبي محمّد البَرْبَهاري وهو صحيح لم يَرِمّ وظهر من قبره روائح الطيب حتى ملأت مدينة السلام.

١٠٠،٢٤ الحُسين بن عبد الله الخِرَقي أبو عليّ والد أبي القاسم كان يُدعى خليفة المَرُّوذي وكان أكثر صحبته له، توفّي في شوّال سنة تسع وتسعين ومائتين.

Aḥmad ibn Muḥammad ibn Hārūn Abū Bakr al-Khallāl. Dedicated himself to collecting the knowledge transmitted by Aḥmad ibn Ḥanbal. Traveling for that purpose, he documented Aḥmad's teachings both with few intermediaries and with many intermediaries,[275] and compiled a number of works, including his *Compendium* in some two hundred quires. None of Aḥmad's other associates accomplished anything on that scale. His study circle was in the mosque of al-Mahdī. He died before the Friday prayer on the third of Rabīʿ I 311 [June 20, 923]. 100.22

Al-Ḥasan ibn ʿAlī ibn Khalaf, Abū Muḥammad al-Barbahārī. Combined learning and renunciation. Was an associate of al-Marrūdhī and Sahl al-Tustarī. He renounced seventy thousand dirhams left him by his father on account of misgivings he had about its permissibility. He was severe in his denunciations of innovators, who eventually managed to turn the authorities against him. He moved from Muḥawwal Gate, where he had been staying, to the East Side, where Tūzūn's sister hid him in her house. After he had been there a month, he died of a hemorrhage.[276] The woman sent her servant to find someone to wash his corpse, then locked all the doors so no one would know the body was there. The corpse-washer arrived, washed the corpse, and stood praying alone over the body. Suddenly the woman looked up and saw that the house was full of men dressed in green and white. Summoning the servant, she asked, "Did you let them in?" 100.23

"My lady," he replied, "did you see what I saw?"

"I did!"

"Well, here are the keys; the door is still locked."

Hearing this, she told them to bury al-Barbahārī in the house. "When I die," she added, "bury me near him."

He was accordingly buried in the house, and when she died she was buried there as well. The place is in al-Mukharrim, near the royal palace.

I read a report in the handwriting of my teacher Abū l-Ḥasan al-Zāghūnī saying, "The grave of Abū Muḥammad al-Barbahārī was opened and his body found whole and undecayed. From the grave came a scent of perfume that filled the City of Salvation."[277]

Al-Ḥusayn ibn ʿAbd Allāh al-Khiraqī, Abū ʿAlī. Father of Abū l-Qāsim. Called the successor of al-Marrūdhī, who was his closest associate. He died in Shawwāl 399 [May–June 1009]. 100.24

٢٥،١٠٠ سُلَيْمان بن أحمد الطَّبَرَاني كان من الحُفَّاظ والأشِدَّاء في دين الله تعالى وله التصانيف، وتوفّي بأصبهان سنة ستين وثلاث مائة ودفن بباب مدينة أصبهان بجنب قبر حُمَمَة الدَّوسي صاحب رسول الله صلّى الله عليه وسلّم .

٢٦،١٠٠ عبد الله بن أبي داوود السِّجِسْتاني طاف به أبوه شرقًا وغربًا وأسْمعه الحديث الكثير وله الحفظ الوافر والتصانيف المشهورة وحدّث عن عليّ بن خَشْرَم وسَلَمة ابن شَبِيب وغيرهما، وتوفّي في ذي الحجّة سنة ست عشرة وثلاث مائة وقيل: صلّى عليه أكثر من ثلاث مائة ألف وصلّوا عليه ثمانين مرة.

٢٧،١٠٠ عبد الرحمن بن أبي حاتم الرازي ذو علم غزير وتصنيف كثير وروى عن أبيه وصالح بن أحمد وغيرهما وتوفّي سنة سبع وعشرين وثلاث مائة .

٢٨،١٠٠ عمر بن محمّد بن رَجاء أبو حَفْص العُكْبري جمع العلم والزهد، حدّث عن عبد الله بن أحمد وروى عنه ابن بَطّة .

وكان ابن رَجاء إذا مات بعُكْبَرا رافضيّ فبلغه أن بَزّازًا باع له كفنًا أو غاسلًا غَسله أو حمّالًا حمله هجره على ذلك.

٢٩،١٠٠ عثمان بن أحمد الدقاق المعروف بابن السَّمّاك سمع محمّد بن عُبيد الله المُنَادي وحنبل بن إسحاق وكان ثقة ثبتًا صالحًا. وتوفّي يوم الجمعة بعد الصلاة ودُفن يوم السبت لثلاث ليالٍ بقين من ربيع الأول سنة أربع وأربعين وثلاث مائة بمقبرة باب الدَّيْر .

٣٠،١٠٠ علي بن محمّد بن بَشّار أبو الحسن العالم الزاهد روى عن أبي بكر المَرُّوذي وصالح بن أحمد وكان المشايخ كالبَرْبَهاري والخَلّال يُعظّمونه ويقصدونه وكانت له كرامات.

وكان يُذكِّر الناس فيفتتح كلامه فيقول: ﴿وإنَّكَ لَتَعْلَمُ ما نُريدُ﴾ فسأله رجل: ما الذي تريد؟

فقال: هو يعلم أنّي ما أريد من الدنيا والآخرة سواه.

Sulaymān ibn Aḥmad al-Ṭabarānī. A repository of knowledge, an unbending advocate of God's religion, and the compiler of several works. He died in Isfahan in 360 [970–71] and was buried at the city gate next to the grave of Ḥumamah al-Dawsī, a Companion of the Emissary of God. 100.25

'Abd Allāh ibn Abī Dāwūd al-Sijistānī. His father took him along on his travels east and west and had him listen to a good deal of Hadith. He memorized many reports and compiled some well-known works. He transmitted citing 'Alī ibn Khashram, Salamah ibn Shabīb, and others. He died in Dhu l-Hijjah 316 [January–February 929]. It is said that more than three hundred thousand people prayed over him and that they prayed eighty times. 100.26

'Abd al-Raḥmān ibn Abī Ḥatim al-Rāzī. A man of great learning and a prolific compiler. He transmitted reports from his father, from Aḥmad's son Ṣāliḥ, and others. He died in 327 [938–39]. 100.27

'Umar ibn Muḥammad ibn Rajā' Abū Ḥafṣ al-'Ukbarī. Combined learning and renunciation. Transmitted reports citing Aḥmad's son 'Abd Allāh, and had Ibn Baṭṭah transmit in turn from him. Whenever a Shi'i would die in 'Ukbarā, Ibn Rajā' would cut off all contact with the milliner who had sold him a shroud, the corpse-washer who had washed him, and the porter who had carried him, when he found out who they were. 100.28

'Uthmān ibn Aḥmad al-Daqqāq, called Ibn al-Sammāk. Heard Hadith from Muḥammad ibn 'Abd Allāh al-Munādī and Ḥanbal ibn Isḥāq. He was a trustworthy and righteous man, firm in his religion. He died after Friday prayers and was buried on Saturday, the twenty-seventh day of Rabī' I 344 [July 21, 955] in the Monastery Gate Cemetery. 100.29

'Alī ibn Muḥammad ibn Bashshār, Abū l-Ḥasan. A learned renunciant who transmitted citing Abū Bakr al-Marrūdhī and Aḥmad's son Ṣāliḥ. Senior figures such as al-Barbahārī and al-Khallāl revered him and would seek him out. He displayed manifestations of grace. When he led people in the remembrance of God, he would recite «You know very well what we are seeking.»[278] A man once asked him, "So what *are* you seeking?" 100.30

"God knows," he replied, "that I want nothing in this world or the next except Him."

وكان يقول: من قال لكم من أهل الأرض إنّه يعرف مطعم ابن بشّار منذ اربعين سنة فقد كذب، ومن قال لكم إنّ لابن بشّار حاجة إلى مخلوق منذ أربعين سنة فقد كذب، أو إنّ ابن بشّار سأل مخلوقاً حاجة منذ أربعين سنة فقد كذب.

وكان يقول: أعرف رجلاً منذ ثلاثين سنة ما تكلّم بكلمة يعتذر منها وأعرف رجلاً منذ ثلاثين سنة يشتهي أن يشتهي ليترك ما يشتهي فما يجد شيئاً يشتهي.

توفّي في سنة ثلاث عشرة وثلاث مائة.

١٠٠، ٣١ محمّد بن أحمد بن الحسن بن الصوّاف أبو عليّ سمع عبد الله بن أحمد في آخرين. قال الدّارَقُطني: ما رأت عيناي مثل أبي عليّ بن الصوّاف.

محمّد بن الحُسين بن عبد الله أبو بكر الآجُرّي جمع العلم والزهد وصنّف تصانيف كثيرة وسكن مكّة حتى توفّي بها.

١٠٠، ٣٢ محمّد بن عبد الواحد أبو عُمَر اللُّغَوي الزاهد المعروف بغُلام ثَعْلَب كان حافظاً للغة مُتَصَوّنًا في نفسه، توفّي سنة خمس وأربعين وثلاث مائة.

أخبرنا أبو منصور القزاز قال: أخبرنا أبو بكر أحمد بن عليّ قال:

أخبرنا عليّ بن أبي عليّ عن أبيه قال: أملى أبو عُمر غُلام ثَعْلَب من حفظه ثلاثين ألف ورقة لغة فيما بلغني.

١٠٠، ٣٣ محمّد بن القاسم بن محمّد بن بَشّار أبو بكر الأنباري[١] كان من أعلم الناس بالنحو والأدب وأكثرهم حفظاً له وسمع الحديث من إسماعيل بن إسحاق القاضي والكُدَيمي وثَعْلَب وغيرهم وصنف كتباً كثيرة كان يمليها من حفظه وكان صدوقاً خيّراً من أهل السنّة.

أخبرنا القزاز قال: أخبرنا الخطيب قال: أخبرنا أبو العلاء الواسطي قال: قال محمّد بن جعفر التميمي:

حدّثني أبو الحسن العَرُوضي: قلتُ لأبي بكر بن الأنباري: كم تحفظ؟

قال: أحفظُ ثلاثة عشر صندوقاً.

وتوفّي ليلة النحر من ذي الحجّة سنة ثمان وعشرين وثلاث مائة.

---

١ هـ: ابن الأنباري.

He used to say: "If any creature on earth tells you that he knows what I've been eating over the past forty years, or that I've needed help from anyone, or that I've asked for anything from anyone during that time, he's lying."

He also used to say, "I know a man who in thirty years has never uttered a word he later regretted. And I know a man who for thirty years has wished he could wish for something so that he could give it up, but who finds nothing to wish for."

He died in 313 [925–26].

Muḥammad ibn Aḥmad ibn al-Hasan ibn al-Ṣawwāf, Abū ʿAlī. He heard reports from Aḥmad's son ʿAbd Allāh and others. Al-Dāraquṭnī said, "I've never seen anyone like Abū ʿAlī ibn al-Ṣawwāf." 100.31

Muḥammad ibn al-Ḥusayn ibn ʿAbd Allāh, Abū Bakr al-Ājurrī. Combined learning and renunciation, and compiled many works. Lived in Mecca until his death.

Muḥammad ibn ʿAbd al-Wāḥid, Abū ʿUmar al-Lughawī, the renunciant, known as the Disciple of Thaʿlab. A repository of linguistic knowledge who guarded himself from transgression. Died 345 [956–57]. 100.32

We cite Abū Mansūr al-Qazzāz, who cites Abū Bakr Aḥmad ibn ʿAlī, who cites ʿAlī ibn Abī ʿAlī, citing his father, who said:

[Abū ʿAlī:] I heard that the Disciple of Thaʿlab, Abū ʿUmar, dictated from memory thirty thousand pages on language.

Muḥammad ibn al-Qāsim ibn Muḥammad ibn Bashshār, Abū Bakr al-Anbārī. Among the most learned authorities in grammar and the language arts, knowing more of this material by heart than most others. He heard reports from Ismāʿīl ibn Isḥāq the judge, al-Kudaymī, Thaʿlab, and others. He compiled many works, dictating them from memory. He was trustworthy, kind, and a Sunni. 100.33

We cite al-Qazzāz, who cites al-Khaṭīb, who cites Abū l-ʿAlāʾ al-Wāsiṭī, who said that Muḥammad ibn Jaʿfar al-Tamīmī said that Abū l-Ḥasan al-ʿArūḍī reported:

[Al-ʿArūḍī:] I asked Abū Bakr ibn al-Anbārī how much he had memorized. He said, "Thirteen boxes' worth."

He died on the eve of ʿĪd al-Aḍḥā, the tenth of Dhu l-Hijjah 328 [September 16, 940].

ذكر المختارين من الطبقة الثالثة

١٠٠،٣٤ أحمد بن إبراهيم بن إسماعيل البَرْمَكي صحب أصحاب أحمد واختصّ بصُحبة أبي الحسن بن بشّار.

عمر بن الحُسين أبو القاسم الخِرَقي قرأ على أصحاب المرُّوذي وكانت له مصنَّفات لم تنتشر عنه لأنّه خرج من بغداد لمّا ظهر سَبّ السلَف وأودع كتبه في دار سليمان فاحترقت الدار والكتب. وتوفّي بدمشق سنة أربع وثلاثين وثلاث مائة.

١٠٠،٣٥ عبد العزيز بن جعفر بن أحمد أبو بكر غُلام الخلّال حدّث عن محمّد بن عثمان ابن أبي شَيْبَة وموسى بن هارون وقاسم المُطرِّز وأبي القاسم البَغَوي في خلق كثير وله المصنَّفات الحِسان الكبار. وتوفّي في شوّال سنة ثلاث وستّين وثلاث مائة.

أنبأنا يحيى بن الحسن بن البنا قال:

أنبأنا أبو يَعْلى محمّد بن الحسين قال: بلغني أنّ عبد العزيز بن جعفر قال في عِلّته: أنا عندكم إلى يوم الجمعة. فقيل له: يُعافيك الله. فقال: سمعت أبا بكر الخلّال يقول: سمعتُ أبا بكر المرُّوذي يقول: عاش أحمد بن حنبل ثمان وسبعين ومات يومَ الجمعة ودُفن بعد الصلاة، وعاش أبو بكر المرُّوذي ثمان وسبعين سنة ومات يوم الجمعة ودفن بعد الصلاة، وعاش أبو بكر الخلّال ثمان وسبعين سنة ومات يوم الجمعة ودُفن بعد الصلاة، وأنا عندكم إلى يوم الجمعة ولي ثمان وسبعون سنة.

فلمّا كان يوم الجمعة مات ودُفن بعد الصلاة.

١٠٠،٣٦ أبو إسحاق إبراهيم بن أحمد بن عمر بن شاقْلا كبير القَدْر سمع من أبي بكر الشافعي ودَعْلَج وابن الصوّاف.

عبد العزيز بن الحارث بن أَسَد أبو الحَسَن التَّميمي حدث عن أبي بكر النيسابوري ونِفْطَوَيْه والقاضي المَحامِلي[1] وصحب أبا القاسم الخِرَقي وأبا بكر عبد العزيز.

[1] هـ: الحماملي.

Selected Members of the Third Generation

Aḥmad ibn Ibrāhīm ibn Ismāʿīl al-Barmakī. He frequented with Aḥmad's associates, especially Abū l-Ḥasan ibn Bashshār. 100.34

ʿUmar ibn al-Ḥusayn, Abū l-Qāsim al-Khiraqī. Studied with the associates of al-Marrūdhī. He put together compilations which were not passed on: when the cursing of the early Muslims began,[279] he left Baghdad, depositing his writings at the home of Sulaymān,[280] which burned down, taking the books with it. He died in Damascus in 334 [945–46].

ʿAbd al-ʿAzīz ibn Jaʿfar ibn Aḥmad, Abū Bakr, the Disciple of al-Khallāl. 100.35
Recited Hadith citing Muḥammad ibn ʿUthmān ibn Abī Shaybah, Mūsā ibn Hārūn, Qāsim al-Muṭarriz, and Abū l-Qāsim al-Baghawī, among many others. He is the author of several large and well-executed compilations. He died in Shawwāl 363 [June–July 974].

We were informed by Yaḥyā ibn al-Ḥasan ibn al-Bannā, who was informed by Abū Yaʿlā Muḥammad ibn al-Ḥusayn, who said:

[Abū Yaʿlā:] I have heard that during his final illness, ʿAbd al-ʿAzīz ibn Jaʿfar said, "I'll be here with you until Friday."

Those around him wished him a speedy recovery, but he replied: "I heard Abū Bakr al-Khallāl say that he heard Abū Bakr al-Marrūdhī say, 'Aḥmad ibn Ḥanbal lived seventy-eight years, died on a Friday, and was buried after the ritual prayer.' Abū Bakr al-Marrūdhī himself lived seventy-eight years, died on a Friday, and was buried after the ritual prayer. And Abū Bakr al-Khallāl lived seventy-eight years, died on a Friday, and was buried after the ritual prayer. Now I'm seventy-eight, and I'll be here with you until Friday."

When Friday came he died. He was buried after the ritual prayer.

Abū Isḥāq Ibrāhīm ibn Aḥmad ibn ʿUmar ibn Shāqlā. Of great stature. Heard reports from Abū Bakr al-Shāfiʿī, Daʿlaj, and Ibn al-Ṣawwāf. 100.36

ʿAbd al-ʿAzīz ibn al-Ḥārith ibn Asad, Abū l-Ḥasan al-Tamīmī. Recited reports citing Abū Bakr al-Naysābūrī, Nifṭawayh, and al-Qāḍī l-Maḥāmilī. He was an associate of Abū l-Qāsim al-Khiraqī and Abū Bakr ʿAbd al-ʿAzīz.

إبراهيم بن محمّد بن جعفر أبو القاسم الساجي سمع إسماعيل الصفّار وأبا عمرو بن السماك وتخصّص بصحبة عبد العزيز بن جعفر.

الحسن بن عبد الله أبو عليّ النجّاد كان إماماً في الفقه وصحب ابن بشّار والبَرْبَهاري.

يوسف بن عُمَر بن مسرور أبو الفتح القوّاس سمع البَغَوي وابن صاعد ويُقال إنّه كان من الأبدال.

عُبيد الله بن محمّد بن محمّد بن حَمدان أبو عبد الله بن بَطّة العُكبَري سمع البغوي وابن صاعد وخلقاً كثيرًا وسافر طويلاً في طلب العلم وكان له الحظّ الوافر من العلم والعبادة. ٣٧،١٠٠

أخبرنا أبو منصور عبد الرحمن بن محمّد القزاز قال: أخبرنا أحمد بن عليّ بن ثابت قال:

حدثني القاضي أبو حامد أحمد بن محمّد اللُؤلُؤي قال: لما رجع أبو عبد الله بن بطّة من الرحلة لازَمَ بيته أربعين سنة فلم يُرَ يوماً منها في سوق ولا رُئي مفطرًا إلّا في يوم الأضحى والفطر وكان أمّارًا بالمعروف ولم يبلغه خبر منكَر إلّا غيّره، أو كما قال.

أخبرنا عبد الرحمن قال: أخبرنا أحمد بن عليّ قال:

أخبرنا العَتيقي قال: توفّي أبو عبد الله بن بَطّة في المحرّم سنة سبع وثمانين وثلاث مائة وكان شيخاً صالحاً مستجاب الدعوة.

أخبرنا عبد الرحمن قال:

أخبرنا أحمد بن عليّ قال: سألت عبد الواحد بن عليّ العُكبَري عن وفاة ابن بطّة فقال: دفنّاه يوم عاشوراء.

عمر بن أحمد بن إبراهيم أبو حَفص البَرمَكي كان فقيهاً مصنّفاً. ٣٨،١٠٠

محمّد بن أحمد أبو الحُسين بن سَمْعون كان واحد دهره في الكلام بلسان التذكير وله حظّ وافر من العلم والعمل والكرامات وقد ذكرت من أخباره في صفة الصفوة وأخبار جمهور المذكورين في هذا الباب وأنا أكره الإعادة في التصانيف

Ibrāhīm ibn Muḥammad ibn Jaʿfar, Abū l-Qāsim al-Sājī. Heard reports from Ismāʿīl al-Ṣaffār and Abū ʿAmr ibn al-Sammāk. He was especially close to ʿAbd al-ʿAzīz ibn Jaʿfar.

Al-Ḥasan ibn ʿAbd Allāh, Abū ʿAlī l-Najjād. An exemplar in legal reasoning and an associate of Ibn Bashshār and al-Barbahārī.

Yūsuf ibn ʿUmar ibn Masrūr Abū l-Fatḥ al-Qawwās. Heard reports from al-Baghawī and Ibn Ṣāʿid. It is said that he was one of the Substitutes.

ʿUbayd Allāh ibn Muḥammad ibn Muḥammad ibn Ḥamdān, Abū ʿAbd 100.37
Allāh ibn Baṭṭah al-ʿUkbarī. Heard reports from al-Baghawī, Ibn Ṣāʿid, and many others. He traveled extensively in search of Hadith. He was gifted with a generous share of learning and piety.

We cite Abū Manṣūr ʿAbd al-Raḥmān ibn Muḥammad al-Qazzāz, who cites Aḥmad ibn ʿAlī ibn Thābit, who heard al-Qāḍī Abū Ḥāmid Aḥmad ibn Muḥammad al-Luʾluʾī report, in these words, or others to this effect:

[Al-Luʾluʾī:] After Abū ʿAbd Allāh ibn Baṭṭah returned from his travels, he remained at home for forty years, during which he was never once seen at a market, nor ever seen to break his fast except on the Festival of Sacrifice and the Festival of Fast-Breaking. He constantly exhorted others to right action. Whenever he was told anything bad about anyone, he would change the story before repeating it.

We cite ʿAbd al-Raḥmān, who cites Aḥmad ibn ʿAlī, who cites al-ʿAtīqī, who said:

[Al-ʿAtīqī:] Abū ʿAbd Allāh ibn Baṭṭah died in Muḥarram 387 [January–February 997]. He was a righteous elder whose prayers were answered.

We cite ʿAbd al-Raḥmān, who cites Aḥmad ibn ʿAlī, who asked ʿAbd al-Wāḥid ibn ʿAlī l-ʿUkbarī about the death of Ibn Baṭṭah and was told:

[Al-ʿUkbarī:] We buried him on ʿĀshūrāʾ [Muḥarram 10, 387/January 23, 997].

ʿUmar ibn Aḥmad ibn Ibrāhīm, Abū Ḥafṣ al-Barmakī. A jurisprudent and compiler. 100.38

Muḥammad ibn Aḥmad Abū l-Ḥusayn ibn Samʿūn. Unique in his day in his leading others to the remembrance of God. Generous in his gifts of learning, practice, and manifestations of grace. I have collected reports about him, and most of the others in this chapter, in my *Account of the Elite*. As I dislike

والمقصود ها هنا الإشارة لا البسط.

محمّد بن الحسن بن قُشَيْش كان فقيهاً صَدوقاً.

محمّد بن سِيما بن الفتح أبو بكر الحَنْبَلي سمع البَغَوي وابن صاعد وكان صَدوقاً.

عمر بن إبراهيم بن عبد الله أبو حَفص العُكْبَري سمع من أبي عليّ بن الصوّاف وأبي بكر النجّاد ودَعْلَج وصحب أبا بكر عبد العزيز وله التصانيف الكثيرة.

محمّد بن إسحاق بن محمّد بن مَنْدَة الاصفهاني ومندة لقب واسمه إبراهيم ٣٩،١٠٠
سمع من أبي العباس الأصمّ وخلق كثير وكان يقول: كتبت عن ألف وسبع مائة شيخ وطُفت الشرق والغرب مرّتين ولم أسمع من مُبتدع شيئاً.

أحمد بن عبد الله بن الخَضِر أبو الحُسين السُّوسَنْجِرْدي سمع أبا عمرو السمّاك والنجّاد في خلق كثير وكان ثقة دَيِّناً.

عثمان بن عيسى أبو عمرو الباقلاوي[1] كان أحد المتعبّدين ولمّا مات رُئي في المنام بعضُ جيرانه من الموتى فقيل له: كيف فرحُكم بجوار عثمان؟ فقال: وأين عثمان؟ لمّا جيء به سمعنا قائلاً يقول: الفِردوس!

الحسن بن حامد أبو عبد الله انتهى إليه المذهب وله التصانيف الواسعة ٤٠،١٠٠
الكثيرة، وتُوفّي بطريق مكّة بقرب واقِصَة بعد رجوعه من الحجّ سنة ثلاث وأربع مائة، وكان قد استند إلى حجر قبل موته فجاءه رجل بقليل ماء وقد أشفى على التَلَف فقال: من أين هذا؟

فقال له: ما هذا وقته.

فقال: بلى هذا وقته عند لقاء الله تعالى.

الحسين بن أحمد بن جعفر أبو عبد الله البغدادي كان عالماً عابداً لا ينام ٤١،١٠٠
إلّا عن غَلبة ويأكل خُبز الشعير.

---

[1] هكذا في د، ومبيَّنة في هامش هـ، وفي ش: الباقلاني.

repeating myself when I write, I will not provide complete biographies here, only short comments.

Muḥammad ibn al-Ḥasan ibn Qushaysh. A trustworthy jurisprudent.

Muḥammad ibn Sīmā ibn al-Fatḥ, Abū Bakr al-Ḥanbalī. Heard reports from al-Baghawī and Ibn Ṣāʿid. He was trustworthy.

ʿUmar ibn Ibrāhīm ibn ʿAbd Allāh, Abū Ḥafṣ al-ʿUkbarī. Heard reports from Abū ʿAlī ibn al-Ṣawwāf, Abū Bakr al-Najjād, and Daʿlaj. He was an associate of Abū Bakr ʿAbd al-ʿAzīz and authored many compilations.

Muḥammad ibn Isḥāq ibn Muḥammad ibn Mandah al-Iṣfahānī. Mandah 100.39
is a nickname; his great-grandfather's name was Ibrāhīm. He heard reports from Abū l-ʿAbbās al-Aṣamm and many others. He used to say, "I've copied reports from 1,700 teachers and crossed from East to West twice without ever listening to an innovator."

Aḥmad ibn ʿAbd Allāh ibn al-Khaḍir, Abū l-Ḥusayn al-Sūsanjirdī. Heard reports from ʿAmr al-Sammāk and al-Najjād, among many others. He was reliable in transmission and observant in religion.

ʿUthmān ibn ʿĪsā, Abū ʿAmr al-Bāqillāwī. A Worshipper. When he died, one of his neighbors who had died before him appeared in a dream and was asked, "Are you happy to see ʿUthmān?" He replied, "We haven't seen him! When he was brought here, all we heard was the cry, 'Paradise! Paradise!'"[281]

Al-Ḥasan ibn Ḥāmid Abū ʿAbd Allāh. The leader of those who followed 100.40
Aḥmad's way in this generation, and the author of many large-scale compilations. He died on the Mecca road near Wāqiṣah after his return from the pilgrimage of 403 [ca. June 1013]. Shortly before his death, he was leaning against some rocks and a man approached him with some water. Though about to expire, al-Ḥasan asked, "Where did you get this?"[282]

"This is hardly the time to ask," said the man.

"On the contrary," said al-Ḥasan. "What better time than before I face God?"

Al-Ḥusayn ibn Aḥmad ibn Jaʿfar, Abū ʿAbd Allāh al-Baghdādī. A learned 100.41
and worshipful man. He would sleep only against his will and eat only barley bread.

عبد الواحد بن عبد العزيز بن الحارث أبو الفضل التَّمِيمي حدث عن أبي بكر النجّاد وأبي بكر الشافعي في آخرين وكانت له يد في علوم كثيرة. وتوفّي في سنة عشر وأربع مائة ودُفن إلى جنب قبر أحمد.

أحمد بن موسى بن عبد الله الروشنائي[1] سمع أبا بكر القَطِيعي وغيره وكان عالمًا عابدًا.

ذكر المختارين من الطبقة الرابعة

عبد السلام بن الفَرَج أبو القاسم المَزْرَفي صاحب ابن حامد له تصانيف. ١٠٠،٤٢

الحُسين بن محمّد بن موسى أبو عبد الله الفُقّاعي فقيه مُناظر وكانت حلقته بجامع المدينة.

عبد الوهاب بن عبد العزيز بن الحارث أبو الفَرَج التَّميمي سمع الحديث ورواه وكانت له حلقة في جامع المنصور للفتوى والوعظ، وتوفّي سنة خمس وعشرين وأربع مائة ودُفن عند قبر أحمد.

محمّد بن أحمد بن أبي موسى أبو عليّ الهاشمي القاضي سمع الحديث من محمّد بن المُظفّر وغيره وله التصانيف وكانت له حلقة بجامع المنصور يُفتي ويشهد.

الحَسَن بن شِهاب بن الحَسَن أبو عليّ العُكبَري لازَمَ ابن بَطّة وله حظّ وافر من الفقه والحديث والفُتيا والأدب.

أحمد بن عمر بن أحمد أبو العبّاس البَرمَكي سمع أبا حفص بن شاهين وأبا القاسم بن حَبابة وكان صدوقًا.

أخوه إبراهيم بن عمر أبو إسحاق البرمكي قيل: إن سَلَفه كانوا يسكنون قرية تسمّى البرمكية فنُسبوا إليها، صحب ابن بطّة وسمع منه وكانت له حلقة بجامع المنصور.

---

[1] تركي: الروشناني.

ʿAbd al-Wāḥid ibn ʿAbd al-ʿAzīz ibn al-Ḥārith, Abū l-Faḍl al-Tamīmī. Transmitted reports citing Abū Bakr al-Najjād and Abū Bakr al-Shāfiʿī, among others. He worked in a variety of fields. He died in 410 [1019–20] and was buried next to Aḥmad's grave.

Aḥmad ibn Mūsā ibn ʿAbd Allāh al-Rūshnāʾī. Heard reports from Abū Bakr al-Qaṭīʿī and others. He was learned and worshipful.

Selected Members of the Fourth Generation

ʿAbd al-Salām ibn al-Faraj, Abū l-Qāsim al-Mazrafī. The associate of Ibn 100.42
Ḥāmid and an author of compilations.

Al-Ḥusayn ibn Muḥammad ibn Mūsā, Abū ʿAbd Allāh al-Fuqqāʿī (the brewer). A jurisprudent who engaged in debate. His study circle was at the mosque of Medina.

ʿAbd al-Wahhāb ibn ʿAbd al-ʿAzīz ibn al-Ḥārith, Abū l-Faraj al-Tamīmī. Heard and transmitted Hadith. He had a study circle in the mosque of al-Manṣūr where he delivered legal opinions and exhortations. He died in 425 [1033–34] and was buried near Aḥmad's grave.

Muḥammad ibn Aḥmad ibn Abī Mūsā, Abū ʿAlī l-Hāshimī, the judge. Heard Hadith from Muḥammad ibn al-Muẓaffar and others and authored some compilations. He held a study circle in the mosque of al-Manṣūr where he gave legal opinions and served as a notary.

Al-Ḥasan ibn Shihāb ibn al-Ḥasan, Abū ʿAlī l-ʿUkbarī. A longtime associate of Ibn Baṭṭah. He was well versed in legal reasoning, Hadith, legal opinions, and the language arts.

Aḥmad ibn ʿUmar ibn Aḥmad, Abū l-ʿAbbās al-Barmakī. Heard reports from Abū l-Ḥafs ibn Shāhīn and Abū l-Qāsim ibn Ḥabābah. He was trustworthy.

His brother Ibrāhīm ibn ʿUmar, Abū Isḥāq al-Barmakī. It is said that his ancestors lived in a village called al-Barmakiyyah, which gave them their name. He associated with Ibn Baṭṭah and heard reports from him. He had a study circle in the mosque of al-Manṣūr.

١٠٠،٤٣ محمّد بن عليّ بن الفتح أبو طالب العُشَارِي له الرواية الواسعة والدين الغزير.
سمعتُ شيخنا عبد الوهّاب الحافظ يقول: خرج أبو طالب العُشاري في أيّام فتنة وظلم فلقيه تُركي فقال: أي شيء معك؟

فقال: لا شيء.

فذهب التركي فصاح به أبو طالب فعاد فقال: اعلم أنّ رأس مالنا الصدق، ومعي درهمان فخُذهما.

قال: فتركه التركي وعرف منزله فحمى بذلك الفعل محلّته كلّها.

ومن الطبقة الخامسة

١٠٠،٤٤ القاضي أبو يعلى محمّد بن الحسين بن محمّد بن خلَف بن الفرّاء سمع الحديث الكثير ودرس الفقه على أبي عبد الله بن حامد وانتهى إليه علم المذهب وكانت له التصانيف الكثيرة في الأصول والفروع وله الأصحاب المتوافرون وكان فقيهاً نزهاً متعفّفاً وولي القضاء وأملَى الحديث بجامع المنصور على كرسيّ عبد الله ابن أحمد فكان المُبَلّغون عنه ثلاثة، أبو محمّد بن جابر وأبو منصور ابن الأنباري وأبو عليّ البَرداني، وحضر خلقٌ لا يُحصَى.

وتوفّي في ليلة الأثنين بين العِشاءين ودُفن يوم الاثنين التاسع عشر من رمضان سنة ثمان وخمسين وأربع مائة بمقبرة أحمد وكان الجمع يزيد على الحدّ وأفطر خلق كثير من شدّة ما لحقهم من الحرّ في الصوم.

ذكر المختارين من الطبقة السادسة

١٠٠،٤٥ أبو الغَنائِم عليّ بن طالب المعروف بابن زِبِيّا كان فقيهاً وله حلقة بجامع المهدي وتوفّي بعد القاضي أبي يعلى بنحو سنة ودُفن قريباً منه.

Muḥammad ibn ʿAlī ibn al-Fatḥ, Abū Ṭālib al-ʿUshārī. A prolific transmitter 100.43
and a man of abundant religious feeling.

I heard my teacher ʿAbd al-Wahhāb al-Ḥāfiẓ say, "Abū Ṭālib al-ʿUshārī once went out on a day of unrest when no one was safe. He was accosted by a Turk who asked him, 'What have you got to give me?'

"'Nothing,' he said.

"The Turk walked off but Abū Ṭālib called him back. 'I have to tell you,' he said, 'that our stock in trade is being honest. I have two dirhams—take them!'

"The Turk not only left him unmolested but found out where he lived and extended protection to the whole neighborhood in appreciation of his honesty."

From the Fifth Generation

The judge Abū Yaʿlā Muḥammad ibn al-Ḥusayn ibn Muḥammad ibn Khalaf 100.44
ibn al-Farrāʾ. Heard much Hadith, and studied legal reasoning with Abū ʿAbd Allāh ibn Ḥāmid. To him passed the knowledge of Aḥmad's way in his generation. He authored numerous compilations on the principles of jurisprudence and on particular applications of the law. He had many students. He was a man of propriety and integrity, and discerning in matters of law. He served as a judge and dictated Hadith in the mosque of al-Manṣūr from the chair formerly occupied by Ibn Ḥanbal's son ʿAbd Allāh. Vast crowds attended his sessions, and three men—Abū Muḥammad ibn Jābir, Abū Manṣūr ibn al-Anbāri, and Abū ʿAlī l-Baradānī—worked as his repeaters.[283] He died on Sunday night between the two night prayers and was buried on Monday, the nineteenth of Ramadan 458 [August 14, 1066]. So many people attended his funeral that a good number succumbed to the heat and had to break their fast.

Selected Members of the Sixth Generation

Abū l-Ghanāʾim ʿAlī ibn Ṭālib, known as Ibn Zibibyā.[284] A jurisprudent who 100.45
led a study circle in the mosque of al-Mahdī. He died about a year after Abī Yaʿlā and was buried near him.

أبو طاهر عبد الباقي بن محمّد البزّاز المعروف بصِهْر هبة المقرئ كان صالحًا معدّلاً.

أبو بكر محمّد بن عليّ بن محمّد بن موسى بن جعفر الخيّاط المقرئ ولد في سنة ستّ وسبعين وثلاث مائة وقرأ القرآن على أبي الحسين السُّوسَنْجِرْدي وأبي الحسن الحمّامي وسمع الحديث الكثير، وتوفّي في جمادى الأُولى من سنة سبع[1] وستّين وأربع مائة.

أبو الحسن عليّ بن الحسين بن جَدَا العُكْبَري سمع من أبي علي بن شِهاب وأبي عليّ بن شاذان وكان فقيهاً صالحًا فصيحًا. وتوفّي فجأة في الصلاة في رمضان سنة ثمان وستّين وأربع مائة ودُفن في مقبرة أحمد.

أبو جعفر عبد الخالق بن عيسى الهاشِمي سمع الحديث الكثير من أبي القاسم ١٠٠،٤٦
ابن بِشْران وأبي محمّد الخلال وأبي إسحاق البرمكي والعُشَاري وابن المُذْهب وغيرهم، وتفقّه على القاضي أبي يعلى وكان فقيهاً مصنّفاً دَيّناً عفيفاً وكان أحد شهود أبي عبد الله الدّامَغاني وتولّى تزكيته القاضي أبو يعلى ثم ترك الشهادة قبل وفاته. ولم يزل يُدرس في مسجد بسكّة الخِرَقي من باب البصرة وبجامع المنصور ثم انتقل إلى الجانب الشرقي يدرّس في مسجد مقابل لدار الخلافة ثمّ انتقل في سنة ستّ وستّين لأجل ما لحق نهر المُعَلّى من الغَرق إلى باب الطّاق وسكن في درب الديوان من الرُّصافة ودرّس بجامع المهدي وبالمسجد الذي بباب درب الديوان وكان له مجلس نظر.

ولمّا احتضر القاضي أبو يَعْلى أوصى أن يغسله الشريف أبو جعفر فلمّا احتضر ١٠٠،٤٧
القائم بأمر الله قال: يغسلني عبد الخالق.

ففعل ولم يأخذ مما هناك شيئاً فقيل له: قد وصّى لك أمير المؤمنين بأشياء كثيرة.

فأبى أن يأخذ. فقيل له: فقميص أمير المؤمنين تتبرّك به فأخذ فوطة نفسه فنشفه بها وقال: قد لحق هذه الفوطة بركة أمير المؤمنين.

ثم استدعاه في مكانه المقتدي فبايعه منفردًا.

---

١ هـ: تسع.

Abū Ṭāhir ʿAbd al-Bāqī ibn Muḥammad al-Bazzāz, known as the In-Law of Hibah al-Muqriʾ. He was righteous and considered a reliable witness.

Abū Bakr Muḥammad ibn ʿAlī ibn Muḥammad ibn Mūsā ibn Jaʿfar al-Khayyāṭ al-Muqriʾ. Born in 376 [986–87]. He studied the Qurʾan with al-Ḥusayn al-Sūsanjirdī and Abū l-Ḥasan al-Ḥammāmī, and heard many Hadith reports. He died in Jumādā I 467 [December 1074–January 1075].

Abū l-Ḥasan ʿAlī ibn al-Ḥusayn ibn Jadā l-ʿUkbarī. Heard reports from Abū ʿAlī ibn Shihāb and Abū ʿAlī ibn Shādhān. He was a jurisprudent, and a righteous and eloquent man. He died suddenly while at prayer during Ramadan 468 [April–May 1076] and was buried in Aḥmad's burial ground.

Abū Jaʿfar ʿAbd al-Khāliq ibn ʿĪsā l-Hāshimī. Heard much Hadith from Abū l-Qāsim ibn Bishrān, Abū Muḥammad al-Khallāl, Abū Isḥāq al-Barmakī, al-ʿUshārī, Ibn al-Mudhhib, and others, and studied jurisprudence with Judge Abū Yaʿlā. He was a jurisprudent and compiler, and a pious and self-restrained man. He was certified by Judge Abū Yaʿlā and served Abū ʿAbd Allāh al-Dāmaghānī as a notary-witness but stopped before he died. He taught at a mosque in the Ragdealer's Alley near the Basra Gate and at the mosque of al-Manṣūr, then moved to the East Side, where he taught at a mosque across from the caliphal palace. In '66, after the flooding of the Muʿallā Canal, he moved to the Archway Gate, settling in Dīwān Street in al-Ruṣāfah and teaching in the mosque there as well as the mosque of al-Mahdī. He also convened sessions where speculative discussions took place. 100.46

When Judge Abū Yaʿlā was on his deathbed he asked ʿAbd al-Khāliq to wash his corpse. Later, when the Caliph al-Qāʾim bi-Amr Allāh was on his deathbed, he made the same request. ʿAbd al-Khāliq did as he was asked but took nothing from the palace. He was told that the caliph had made him numerous bequests, but he refused to take anything. Finally they offered him the caliph's shirt, saying he could gain a blessing from it. In response, he took his own waist-cloth, dried the body with it, and said, "Now I've got the caliph's blessing." He was then summoned by al-Muqtadī to offer the oath of allegiance on the spot. ʿAbd al-Khāliq tendered his oath alone.[285] 100.47

٤٨،١٠٠ فلمّا وصل إلى بغداد ولدُ القُشَيْري وظهرت الفتن وكان هو شديداً على المبتدعة فقمعهم وكان النصر لطائفته إلّا أنّه أُخذ وحُبس فضجّ الناس من حبسه فأُخرج إلى الحريم الطاهري بالجانب الغربي فتوفّي هناك في يوم الخميس للنصف من صفر سنة سبعين وأربع مائة وكان يوماً مشهوداً وحُفر له إلى جانب قبر أحمد ولزم الناس قبره ليلاً ونهاراً فيقال: إنّه خُتم على قبره في مدّة شهور أكثر من عشرة آلاف ختمة.

ورآه بعضهم في المنام فقال: ما فعل الله بك؟

قال: لمّا وُضعت في قبري رأيت قبّة من دُرّة بيضاء لها ثلاثة أبواب وقائل يقول: هذه لك، ادخل من أيّ أبوابها شئت.

ورآه آخر في المنام فقال: ما فعل الله بك؟

قال: التقيتُ بأبي عبد الله أحمد بن حنبل فقال لي: يا أبا جعفر لقد جاهدتَ في الله حقّ جهاده وقد أعطاك الله الرضا.

٤٩،١٠٠ عبد الرحمن بن محمّد بن إسحاق بن مَنْدَة الأصبهاني أبو القاسم له التصانيف وكان من أهل السنّة الكبار توفّي سنة سبعين وأربع مائة.

أبو بكر أحمد بن محمّد الرازي المقرئ المعروف بابن حَمْدُوَيْه سمع من أبي الحسين بن سمعون وغيره وتفقّه على القاضي أبي يعلى وتوفّي في ذي الحجّة سنة سبعين.

أبو عليّ الحسن بن أحمد بن البنا سمع الحديث الكثير وقرأ بالقراءات وتفقّه على القاضي أبي يعلى ودرس وصنّف التصانيف الكثيرة في فنون العلوم. وقال: صنفت خمس مائة مصنّف وكانت له حلقة للفقه والحديث وتوفّي في رجب سنة إحدى وسبعين ودفن بمقبرة أحمد.

٥٠،١٠٠ أبو الوفاء طاهر بن الحسين بن القوّاس كانت له حلقة بجامع المنصور يُفتي ويَعظ وكان يدرّس الفقه ويُقرئ القُرآن وكان زاهداً أمّاراً بالمعروف أقام في مسجده نحواً من خمسين سنة وأجهد نفسه في العبادة وخُشونة العيش وتوفّي في ليلة الجمعة

When al-Qushayrī's boy came to Baghdad and unrest broke out, ʿAbd al-Khāliq, who was severe in his treatment of innovators, fought to keep them down, and succeeded, though he was arrested and jailed.[286] Hearing that he was in jail, the people raised an outcry. ʿAbd al-Khāliq was removed to the Harem of Ṭāhir on the West Side and died there on Thursday, the fifteenth of Ṣafar 470 [September 7, 1077], a day long remembered. He was buried in a grave next to Aḥmad's. People spent days and nights by the gravesite. It is said that within months the Qur'an had been read there in its entirety more than ten thousand times. 100.48

Someone saw ʿAbd al-Khāliq in a dream and asked how he had fared. "When they buried me," he replied, "I saw a dome of white pearl with three doors, and I head a voice say, 'This is yours; enter by whichever door you wish!'"

Another dreamer who saw him asked the same question and was told, "I met Aḥmad ibn Ḥanbal, and he told me, 'You've fought the good fight for God, and He's pleased with you.'"

ʿAbd al-Raḥmān ibn Muḥammad ibn Isḥāq ibn Mandah al-Iṣfahānī, Abū l-Qāsim. The author of compilations, and a great Sunni. He died in 470 [1077–78]. 100.49

Abū Bakr Aḥmad ibn Muḥammad al-Rāzī l-Muqri', known as Ibn Ḥamduwayh. Heard reports from Abū l-Ḥusayn ibn Samʿūn and others, and studied jurisprudence with Judge Abū Yaʿlā. He died in Dhu l-Hijjah '70 [June–July 1078].

Abū ʿAlī l-Ḥasan ibn Aḥmad ibn al-Bannā. Heard much Hadith, learned the different readings of the Qur'an, and studied jurisprudence with Judge Abū Yaʿlā. He studied and wrote numerous compilations covering the different branches of learning. He himself said that he had written five hundred compilations. He had a study circle where he taught jurisprudence and Hadith. He died in Rajab '71 [January–February 1079].

Abū l-Wafā' Ṭāhir ibn al-Ḥusayn ibn al-Qawwās. Had a study circle at the mosque of al-Manṣūr where he would answer legal questions and deliver exhortations. He also taught jurisprudence and the Qur'an. He was a renunciant and a caller to right action. He lived in his mosque for some fifty years, and exhausted himself with constant worship and a comfortless life. He died 100.50

سابع شعبان من سنة ثلاث وسبعين ودُفن إلى جانب الشريف أبي جعفر.

علي بن أحمد بن الفَرَج البزّاز المعروف بابن أخي نَصر العُكبَري سمع من أبي عليّ بن شاذان والحسن بن شِهاب العُكبري وكان له تَقدُّم في القرآن والحديث والفقه والفرائض وجمع إلى ذلك النُّسك والورع وتوفِي سنة ثلاث وسبعين.

أبو الفَتح عبد الوهّاب بن أحمد الحَرّاني سمع الحديث من أبي عليّ بن شاذان والبَرقاني وتَفقّه على القاضي أبي يَعلى وكان يدرّس ويُفتي ويعظ. واستُشهد في سنة ستّ وسبعين وأربع مائة.

أبو عليّ يعقوب بن إبراهيم البَرزَبيني وبَرزَبين قَرية بين بَغداد وأَوانا، سمع ٥١،١٠٠
الحديث من أبي إسحاق البرمكي وتفقّه على القاضي أبي يعلى وشهد في اليوم الذي شهد فيه الشريف أبو جعفر وزكّاهما القاضي أبو يعلى ودَرّس أبو عليّ في حياة شيخه وولاّه القاضي قضاءَ باب الأَزَج، وتوفّي في شوّال سنة ثمان – وقيل: سنة ستّ – وثمانين وأربع مائة ودُفن بباب الأزج إلى جانب عبد العزيز غُلام الخلاّل.

أبو محمّد شافع بن صالح بن حاتم الجيلي[1] سمع من أبي عليّ بن المُذهب وتفقه على القاضي أبي يعلى وكان مُتعففاً مُتقشفاً ذا صلاح، توفّي في سنة ثمانين.

أبو إسماعيل عبد الله بن محمّد بن عليّ الأنصاري الهَرَوي كان يُدعى ٥٢،١٠٠
شيخ الإسلام وكان شديداً على المبتدعة عالماً بالحديث وكان يقول: مذهبُ أحمدَ أحمدُ مذهبٍ. ومن شعره:

أنا حَنْبليٌّ ما حَيِيتُ فإنْ أَمتْ   فوَصِيّتي ذاكُمُ إلى إخواني
إذ دينُه ديني وديني دينُه   ما كنْتُ إمَّعةً له دينانِ

وتوفِّي في سنة إحدى وثمانين.

---

[1] ش: الجبلي.

Friday night, the seventh of Shaʿbān ’73 [January 21, 1081] and was buried next to the Prophet’s descendant Abū Jaʿfar.[287]

ʿAlī ibn Aḥmad ibn al-Faraj al-Bazzāz, known as the Nephew of Naṣr al-ʿUkbarī. Heard reports from Abū ʿAlī ibn Shādhān and al-Ḥasan ibn Shihāb al-ʿUkbarī. He enjoyed preeminence in the fields of Qur’an, Hadith, jurisprudence, and the calculation of inheritence, which he combined with asceticism and scrupulosity. He died in ’73 [1080–81].

Abū l-Fatḥ ʿAbd al-Wahhāb ibn Aḥmad al-Ḥarrānī. Heard Hadith from ʿAlī ibn Shādhān and al-Barqānī, and studied jurisprudence with Judge Abū Yaʿlā. He taught, issued legal opinions, and delivered exhortations. He was martyred in 476 [1083–84].

Abū ʿAlī Yaʿqūb ibn Ibrāhīm al-Barzabīnī. Barzabīn is a village between 100.51
Baghdad and Awānā. Heard Hadith from Abū Isḥāq al-Barmakī and studied jurisprudence with Judge Abū Yaʿlā. He presented himself as a notary-witness on the same day as al-Sharīf Abū Jaʿfar, and Judge Abū Yaʿlā declared both reliable.[288] Abū ʿAlī taught while his own teacher was still alive, and the judge granted him the jurisdiction of the Vaulted Gate. He died in Shawwāl 486 [October–November 1093] or 488 [October–November 1095] and was buried at the Vaulted Gate beside ʿAbd al-ʿAzīz, the Disciple of al-Khallāl.

Abū Muḥammad Shāfiʿ ibn Ṣāliḥ ibn Ḥātim al-Jīlī. Heard reports from Abū ʿAlī l-Mudhhib and studied jurisprudence with Judge Abū Yaʿlā. He was a self-restrained and righteous man who lived without comforts. He died in ’80 [1087–88].

Abū Ismāʿīl ʿAbd Allāh ibn Muḥammad ibn ʿAlī l-Anṣārī l-Harawī. Called 100.52
the Shaykh of Islam. He was unrelenting in his efforts against innovation and learned in Hadith. He used to say “Aḥmad’s way is the best.”[289] Among his verses are these:

My life I’ve spent with Aḥmad’s school of law
  And when at last I die, remember this:
I never left a doubt about my faith.
  His creed is mine, and my belief is his.[290]

He died in ’81 [1088–89].

أبو الفرج عبد الواحد بن محمّد الشيرازي تفقه على القاضي أبي يعلى واجتمع له العلم والزهد وله كرامات وتُوفّي بدمشق سنة ستّ وثمانين.

١٠٠،٥٣ أبو محمّد رزق الله بن عبد الوهّاب التَّميمي تفقه على القاضي أبي عليّ[١] بن أبي موسى، وكانت له المعرفة الحسنة بالقُرآن والحديث والفقه والأُصول والتفسير واللّغة والعربية والفرائض وكان حسن الأخلاق وكان يجلس في حلقة أبيه بجامع المنصور للوعظ والفَتوى ثم انقطع فصار يمضي في السنة أربع دفعات في رجب وشعبان فيعقد المجلس عند قبر أحمد. ومولده سنة أربع مائة[٢] وتوفي سَنة ثمان وثمانين وأربع مائة ودُفن في داره بباب المراتب ثم نُقل بعد ذلك إلى مقبرة أحمد لما توفي ابنه أبو الفضل سنة إحدى وتسعين.

١٠٠،٥٤ أبو عبد الله محمّد بن الحسن الراذاني سمع من القاضي أبي يعلى وكان كثير التهجُّد ملازماً للصيام وكانت له كرامات، وتوفّي سنة أربع وتسعين ودُفن بأوانا.

أبو عليّ أحمد بن محمّد البَرَداني تفقّه على القاضي أبي يعلى وسمع الحديث الكثير وله به المعرفة التامّة، وتوفّي في شوّال سنة ثمان وتسعين.

أبو منصور محمّد بن أحمد بن عليّ بن عبد الرزاق الخيّاط وكان من أهل القرآن الأخيار وسمع الحديث الكثير وتفقّه على القاضي أبي يعلى كان كثير الصيام والصلاة وله كرامات وتوفّي في محرم سنة تسع وتسعين وقد بلغ سبعاً وتسعين سنة ودفن في دكّة قبر أحمد.[٣]

١٠٠،٥٥ أبو بكر أحمد بن عليّ بن أحمد العُلَبي أحد المشهورين بالزهد والصلاح، سمع الحديث على القاضي أبي يعلى وقرأ عليه شيئاً من المذهب، وكان يعمل بيده تجصيص الحيطان ثمّ ترك ذلك ولازَمَ المسجد يُقرئ القرآن ويؤم الناس. وكان عَفيفاً لا يقبل من أحد شيئاً وكان يذهب بنفسه كل ليلة إلى دجلة فيأخذ في كوز له ماء يُفطر عليه، وكان يمشي بنفسه في حوائجه ولا يستعين بأحد.

---

١ هـ، د: يعلا. ٢ هـ: ومائة. ٣ د: احمد بن حنبل رضي الله عنه.

Abū l-Faraj ʿAbd al-Wāḥid ibn Muḥammad al-Shīrāzī. Studied jurisprudence with Judge Abū Yaʿlā. He combined learning and renunciation, and displayed manifestations of grace. He died in Damascus in '86 [1093–94].

Abū Muḥammad Rizq Allāh ibn ʿAbd Wahhāb al-Tamīmī. Studied jurisprudence with Judge Abū ʿAlī ibn Abī Mūsā. He had a good knowledge of Qur'an, Hadith, jurisprudence, foundations of jurisprudence, exegesis, lexicography, Arabic, and the calculation of inheritances. He was of a pleasing character. He used to sit in his father's study circle in the mosque of al-Manṣūr to give exhortations and legal opinions, but then he withdrew, coming out only four times a year in Rajab and Shaʿbān to hold sessions next to Aḥmad's grave. He was born in 400 [1009–10] and he died in 488 [1095–96]. He was buried at home, at the Marātib Gate,[291] but later, in '91 [1097–98], when his son Abū l-Faḍl died, he was moved to Aḥmad's burial ground. 100.53

Abū ʿAbd Allāh Muḥammad ibn al-Ḥasan al-Rādhānī. Studied jurisprudence with Judge Abū Yaʿlā. He frequently spent the night in prayer and was constantly fasting. He displayed signs of grace. He died in '94 [1100–1] and was buried in Awānā. 100.54

Abū ʿAlī Aḥmad ibn Muḥammad al-Baradānī. Studied jurisprudence with Judge Abū Yaʿlā and heard a great deal of Hadith, a field which he mastered completely. Died in Shawwāl '98 [1105].

Abū Manṣūr Muḥammad ibn Aḥmad ibn ʿAlī ibn ʿAbd al-Razzāq al-Khayyāṭ. Among the best on the Qur'an. He heard much Hadith and studied jurisprudence with Judge Abū Yaʿlā. He was much given to fasting and prayer, and he displayed signs of grace. He died in Muḥarram '99 [1105–6] at the age of ninety-seven and was buried by the *dikkah* at Aḥmad's tomb.[292]

Abū Bakr Aḥmad ibn ʿAlī ibn Aḥmad al-ʿUlabī. Among those renowned for righteousness and renunciation. He heard Hadith and studied some of our jurisprudence with Judge Abū Yaʿlā. He worked for a time plastering walls with his own two hands before giving that up and staying permanently at the mosque, teaching others to read the Qur'an and leading worshippers in prayer. He guarded his person and would accept nothing from anyone. Every night he would go by himself to the Tigris and fill a pitcher with water for his breakfast. He would run all his own errands rather than send someone else. 100.55

وكان إذا حجّ يزور القبور بمكّة ويجيء إلى قبر الفُضَيل بن عِياض ويخطّ بعصاه ويقول: يا ربّ ها هنا، يا ربّ ها هنا! فاتّفق أنّه خرج في سنة ثلاث وخمس مائة إلى الحجّ وكان قد وقع من الجمل في الطريق دفعتين فشهد عَرَفة مُحْرِماً، وتوفّي عشيّة ذلك اليوم في أرض عرفات فحُمل إلى مكّة وطيف به البيت ودُفن في يوم النّحْر إلى جنب قبر الفُضَيل بن عِياض.

٥٦،١٠٠ أبو الفتح محمّد بن عليّ الحُلْواني شاهد القاضي أبا يعلى لكنّه تفقّه على يعقوب البَرْزَبِيني[1] والشريف أبي جعفر، ثم درس في المسجد الذي كان يدرّس فيه الشريف بالحرم. وتوفّي في ذي الحجّة سنة خمس وخمس مائة.

أبو منصور عليّ بن محمّد بن الأنباري تفقّه على القاضي أبي يعلى وسمع الحديث الكثير وكان أحد الشُّهود والوُعّاظ، وتوفّي في سنة سبع وخمس مائة.

٥٧،١٠٠ أبو الوفاء عليّ بن عقيل بن محمّد بن عقيل البغدادي انتهت إليه الرئاسة في الأصول والفروع وله الخاطر العاطر والفهم الثاقب واللباقة والفطنة البغدادية والتبريز في المناظرة على الأقران والتصانيف الكبار، ومن طالع مُصنّفاته أو قرأ شيئاً من خواطره وواقعاته في كتابه المسمّى بالفُنون وهو مائتا مجلّد عرف مقدار الرجل، ووقع إليّ من هذا الكتاب نحو من مائة وخمسين مُجلّدة. سمع أبا بكر بن بِشْران وأبا الفتح بن شِيطا وأبا محمّد الجوهري والقاضي أبا يعلى وغيرهم. ومولده في سنة ثلاثين وأربع مائة وروى بعضهم سنة إحدى وثلاثين، وتوفّي في سنة ثلاث عشرة وخمس مائة.

٥٨،١٠٠ أبو الخطّاب محفوظ بن أحمد الكَلْوَاذي وُلد في شوّال سنة اثنتين وثلاثين وأربع مائة وسمع من الجوهري والعُشاري والقاضي أبي يُعلى، وبرع في الفقه وصنّف ونفع بتصنيفه لحسن قصده. وتوفّي سحرة يوم الخميس ودفن يوم الجمعة قبل الصلاة الثالث والعشرين من جمادى الآخرة سنة عشر وخمس مائة.

---

[1] ش،د: البرزبيني.

Whenever he went on the pilgrimage, he would visit the graves in Mecca. At the grave of al-Fuḍayl ibn ʿIyāḍ, he would draw his stick across the ground and say, "Here, Lord! Here!" In 503 [1109–10] he went out to perform the pilgrimage. On the way, he had twice fallen off his camel. He lived long enough to stand at ʿArafah in his pilgrim's garb, but died that evening[293] in ʿArafāt. His body was taken to Mecca and carried around the Kaʿbah, then buried on the Day of Sacrifice next to the tomb of al-Fuḍayl ibn ʿIyāḍ.

Abū l-Fatḥ Muḥammad ibn ʿAlī l-Ḥulwānī. Met Judge Abū l-Yaʿlā but stud- 100.56
ied jurisprudence with Yaʿqūb al-Barzabīnī and al-Sharīf Abū Jaʿfar. He later taught at the mosque where the latter had taught in Mecca. He died in Dhu l-Hijjah 505 [May–June 1112].

Abū Manṣūr ʿAlī ibn Muḥammad ibn al-Anbārī. Studied jurisprudence with Judge Abū Yaʿlā and heard much Hadith. He was a notary-witness and preacher. He died in 507 [1113–14].

Abū l-Wafāʾ ʿAlī ibn ʿAqīl ibn Muḥammad ibn ʿAqīl al-Baghdādī. Heir of 100.57
the school's expertise in both the principles and the applications of jurisprudence. He was possessed of a piquant turn of mind, a penetrating intelligence, and the sharp eyes and sharp wits that Baghdadis are famous for. Anyone who peruses his compilations or reads the reflections and experiences he describes in his book *Varieties*, in two hundred bound sections, will second my appreciation of the man. I have so far managed to get a hold of some 150 volumes. He heard Hadith from Abū Bakr ibn Bishrān, Abū l-Fatḥ ibn Shīṭā, Abū Muḥammad al-Jawharī, Judge Abū Yaʿlā, and others. He was born in 430 [1038–39], or according to some others, 431 [1039–40], and died in 513 [1119–20].

Abū l-Khaṭṭāb Maḥfūẓ ibn Aḥmad al-Kalwādhī. Born Shawwāl 432 [June– 100.58
July 1041]. He heard reports from al-Jawharī, al-ʿUshārī, and Judge Abū Yaʿlā. He excelled in jurisprudence and authored compilations which—by virtue of his good intentions—have proven useful to others. He died early in the morning on Thursday, the twenty-third of Jumādā II 520 [July 15–16, 1126].

ذكر المختارين من الطبقة السابعة

أبو سَعْد المُبارك بن علّي المُخَرِّمي سمع أبا الحسين بن المهتدي وابن المأمون ٥٩،١٠٠
وابن النَّقُور وتفقّه على يعقوب والشريف أبي جعفر وولي قضاء باب الأَزَج.
وتوفّي في محرّم سنة ثلاث عشرة وخمس مائة.

علي بن المُبارك بن الفاعوس أبو الحسن كان زاهدًا حسن الطريقة وسمع
من القاضي أبي يعلى وغيره، وتوفِي في شوّال سنة إحدى وعشرين وخمس مائة
وحَضر جنازته خلق لا يُحصون ودُفن بمقبرة أحمد.

وحدثني إبراهيم بن دينار الفقيه قال: كان ابن الفاعوس إذا صلّى الجُمعة جلس
يقرأ على أصحابه الحديث فيأتي ساقي الماء فيأخذ منه فيشرب لِيُريَهم أنّه مُفطر وربّما
صامها في بعض الأيّام.

محمّد بن أبي طاهر بن عبد[1] الباقي بن محمّد بن عبد الله بن محمّد بن عبد ٦٠،١٠٠
الرحمن بن الرَّبيع بن ثابت بن وهب بن مَشْجعة بن الحارث بن عبد الله بن
كعب بن مالك الأنصاري أحد الثلاثة الذين خُلِّفوا، وُلد في صفر سنة اثنتين
وأربعين بالكَرخ، وكان يقول: لمّا ولدتُ جاء مُنجّم من قِبل أبي ومنجم من جهة أمّي
وأخذا الطالع واتّفق حسابهما على أنّ عمري اثنتان وخمسون سنة فها أنا في عَشر
المائة.

وهو آخر من حدّث عن أبي إسحاق البَرْمَكي وأبي الطيّب الطَّبَري وأبي طالب
العُشاري وأبي الحسن الباقلاني وأبي محمّد الجوهري في آخرين. وكان يقول: حفظتُ
القرآن وأنا ابن سبع سنين وما من علم إلا وقد نظرتُ فيه وحصّلت منه الكُلّ
أو البعض وما أعرف أنّي ضيّعت ساعة من عمري في لهو أو لعب. وانفرد بعلم
الحساب والفرائض، ودخلنا إليه وقد تمّ له ثلاث وتسعون سنة وما تغيّر من
حواسّه شيء. وتوفّي في يوم الأربعاء قبل الظهر ثاني رجب من سنة خمس

---

١ د: بن عبد.

Selected Members of the Seventh Generation

Abū Saʿd al-Mubārak ibn ʿAlī l-Mukharrimī. Heard reports from al-Ḥusayn ibn al-Muhtadī, Ibn al-Maʾmūn, and Ibn al-Naqūr. He studied jurisprudence with Yaʿqūb and al-Sharīf Abū Jaʿfar, and served as a judge at the Vaulted Gate. He died in Muḥarram 513 [April–May 1119]. 100.59

ʿAlī ibn al-Mubārak ibn al-Fāʿūs, Abū l-Ḥasan. He was a renunciant and an admirable representative of our way of life. He heard reports from Judge Abū Yaʿlā and others. When he died in Shawwāl 521 [October–November 1127], countless people attended his funeral. He was interred in Aḥmad's burial ground.

I heard the jurisprudent Ibrāhīm ibn Dīnār report: "After the Friday prayer, Ibn al-Fāʿūs would sit and read Hadith to his associates. When the water-seller would pass by, he would take some water to show them that he wasn't fasting. On some days, though, he would be fasting."

Muḥammad ibn Abī Ṭāhir ibn ʿAbd al-Bāqī ibn Muḥammad ibn ʿAbd Allāh ibn Muḥammad ibn ʿAbd al-Raḥmān ibn al-Rabīʿ ibn Thābit ibn Wahb ibn Mashjaʿah ibn al-Ḥārith ibn ʿAbd Allāh ibn Kaʿb ibn Mālik al-Anṣārī (one of the three Helpers who stayed behind).[294] Born in Safar of '42 [June–July 1050] in al-Karkh. He used to say, "When I was born my father brought in one astrologer and my mother brought in another. They took my horoscope and agreed that I would live for fifty-two years. But here I am in my tenth decade!" 100.60

He is the last to have transmitted Hadith citing Abū Isḥāq al-Barmakī, Abū l-Ṭayyib al-Ṭabarī, Abū Ṭālib al-ʿUshārī, Abū l-Ḥasan al-Bāqillānī, Abū Muḥammad al-Jawharī, and others. He used to say, "I memorized the Qurʾan at the age of seven, and there's no branch of learning I haven't studied, either completely or in part. I don't think I've wasted a single hour of my life with distractions or diversions."

He was unique in his mastery of mathematics and inheritance calculation. I went to see him when he was ninety-three, and he hadn't lost any of his faculties. He died before noon on Wednesday, the second of Rajab 535

وثلاثين وخمس مائة ودُفن قريباً من بشر الحافي وبقي ثلاثة أيّام قبل موته لا يفتر عن قراءة القرآن.

أبو بكر محمّد بن الحُسين بن عليّ المَزْرَفي ولم يكن من المَزْرَفة وإنّما انتقل أبوه في زمان الفتنة إلى المَزْرَفة فأقام بها مدة فلمّا رجع قالوا: المَزْرَفي فعُرف بذلك. وُلد في سنة تسع وثلاثين وقيل في سنة أربعين. وكان إماماً في القرآن والفرائض وسمع الحديث الكثير من الكبار كابن المُسلمة وغيره، وتوفّي أول يوم من المحرّم سنة سبع وعشرين وخمس مائة. ١٠٠،٦١

أبو الحُسَيْن محمّد بن محمّد بن الفرّاء وُلد ليلة النِّصف من شعبان سنة إحدى وخمسين وسمع الحديث الكثير وتفقّه على الشريف أبي جعفر، وقتله اللصوص ليلة عاشوراء من سنة ستّ وعشرين وخمس مائة. ١٠٠،٦٢

أخوه أبو خازم محمّد بن محمّد بن الفراء كان فقيهاً زاهداً وتوفّي في صَفر سنة سبع وعشرين وخمس مائة.

أبو الحسن عليّ بن عُبيد الله بن نصر الزّاغُوني سمع الحديث الكثير من ابن النَّقور وابن المأمون وابن المُسلمة وغيرهم، وقرأ بالقراءات وتفقّه على يَعقوب البَرْزَبيني وصنّف في الأُصول والفروع وكان له في كلّ فنّ من العلم حظّ ووعظ مدّة طويلة. وُلد في سنة خمس وخمسين وتوفّي في محرّم سنة سبع وعشرين وخمس مائة.

ذكر المختارين من الطبقة الثامنة

أبو البركات عبد الوهّاب بن المبارك الأَنْماطي ما رأينا في مشايخ الحديث أكثر سماعاً منه ولا أكثر كتابة للحديث بيده مع المعرفة منه ولا أصبر على الإقراء ولا أسرع دمعة وأكثر بكاءً مع دوام البِشر وحُسن اللقاء. وُلد في رجب سنة اثنتين وستّين ومات في محرّم سنة ثمان وثلاثين وخمس مائة ودُفن بالشونيزيّة. ١٠٠،٦٣

[February 11–12, 1141], and was buried near Bishr al-Ḥāfī. He spent the last three days of his life tirelessly reciting the Qur'an.

100.61 ***Abū Bakr Muḥammad ibn al-Ḥusayn ibn ʿAlī l-Mazrafī.*** Not actually from al-Mazrafah: during the unrest, his father moved there and so Abū Bakr lived there for a time. When he returned, people started calling him al-Mazrafī. He was born in '39 or '40 [1047–49]. He was preeminent in the Qur'an and inheritance calculation, and heard much Hadith from senior figures such as Ibn al-Muslimah and others. He died on the first of Muḥarram 527 [November 12, 1132].

100.62 ***Abū l-Ḥusayn Muḥammad ibn Muḥammad ibn al-Farrāʾ.*** Born on the eve of the fifteenth of Shaʿbān '51 [September 26, 1059]. Heard much Hadith and studied jurisprudence at the hands of al-Sharīf Abū Jaʿfar. He was killed by thieves on the eve of ʿĀshurāʾ 526 [December 2, 1131].

His brother Abū Khāzim Muḥammad ibn Muḥammad ibn al-Farrāʾ. A jurisprudent and renunciant. He died in Ṣafar 527 [December 1132–January 1133].

Abū l-Ḥasan ʿAlī ibn ʿUbayd Allāh ibn Naṣr al-Zāghūnī. Heard much Hadith from Ibn al-Naqūr, Ibn al-Ma'mūn, Ibn al-Muslimah, and others. He could read the Qur'an according to its variant readings. He studied jurisprudence with Yaʿqūb al-Barzabīnī, and authored compilations on foundations as well as applications. He had some knowledge in every field, and served as a preacher for a long time. He was born in '55 [1063] and died in Muḥarram 527 [November–December 1132].

Selected Figures from the Eighth Generation

100.63 ***Abū l-Barakāt ʿAbd al-Wahhāb ibn al-Mubārak al-Anmāṭī.*** Of all the Hadith teachers I have seen, he had heard the most reports and copied the most despite knowing them by heart. I never had a teacher who corrected our reading more patiently, or one more likely to be moved to tears despite his customary cheerfulness and the warm welcome he extended. He was born in Rajab '62 [April–May 1070] and died in Muḥarram 538 [July–August 1143]. He is buried in al-Shūnīziyyah.

أبو بكر أحمد بن محمّد بن أحمد الدّينَوَري تفقّه على أبي الخطّاب الكَلْوَذاني ٦٤،١٠٠ وبرع في الفقه وتقدّم في المناظرة على أبناء جنسه حتّى كان أسعد المِيهَني يقول: ما اعترض أبو بكر الدينوري على دليل أحد إلاّ ثَلَمَ فيه ثُلْمة.

وكان يَرِقُّ عند ذكر الصالحين ويبكي ويقول: للعلماء عند الله قدر فلعلّ![1]

وحضرت درسه بعد موت شيخنا أبي الحسن الزاغوني نحوًا من أربع سنين، وأنشدني:

أَصِخْ لن تَنالَ العلمَ إلّا بستّةٍ ... سأُنبيكَ عن مَكْنونها ببَيانِ
ذَكاءٍ وحِرْصٍ وافتِقارٍ وبُلغَةٍ ... وإرْشادِ أُستاذٍ وطولِ زَمانِ

وأنشدني: ٦٥،١٠٠

تمنّيْتَ أن تُمسي فَقيهاً مُناظِراً ... بغَيرِ عَناءٍ فالجُنون فُنونُ
وليسَ اكتسابُ المالِ دونَ مشقّةٍ ... تلقّيتَها فالعِلمُ كَيفَ يَكونُ

وتوفّي في سنة اثنتين وثلاثين وخمس مائة ودفن قريباً من قبر أحمد.

أبو منصور موهوب بن أحمد الجَواليقي سمع الحديث الكثير وانتهى إليه علم اللغة[2] ٦٦،١٠٠ وكان مُتقناً في علمه متورّعًا في نطقه شديد التثبّت في قوله. وتوفّي في محرّم سنة أربعين وخمس مائة.

أبو محمّد عبد الله بن عليّ بن أحمد المقرئ سمع الحديث الكثير وقرأ ٦٧،١٠٠ بالقراءات الكثيرة وصنّف فيها التصانيف الحسان وكانت له معرفة بالعربية وما سمعنا أحسن قراءةً منه ولا أكمل أداة ولا أصحّ أداء. وكان قويّاً في السنّة وكان طولَ عمره منفرداً في مسجده. ومولده في شعبان سنة أربع وستّين، وتوفّي في يوم

---

١ تركي: فلعل [الله أن يجعلني منهم]. ٢ د: اللغة والفقه.

Abū Bakr Aḥmad ibn Muḥammad ibn Aḥmad al-Dīnawarī. Studied jurisprudence with Abū l-Khaṭṭāb al-Kalwadhānī and excelled in it. He also outdid his fellows in disputation to the point that As'ad al-Mīhanī said of him, "Abū Bakr al-Dīnawarī never saw an argument he couldn't poke a hole in." Whenever the righteous were mentioned, he would break down and weep, saying "Learned men have some standing with God, and perhaps..."[295] I began attending his lectures after the death of my teacher Abū l-Ḥasan al-Zāghūnī and continued with him for some four years. He once recited to me: 100.64

The things a scholar needs are six.
Here's a list of them in rhyme:
Brains, drive, ripe age, poverty,
His teacher's help, and time.[296]

He also recited to me: 100.65

You want to be well versed in law
And a whiz at disputation,
But without much work, or pain, or toil:
Now there's a mental aberration!
To make a dirham, as you know,
Means work and toil and pain;
Why should the learning that you seek
Be an easier thing to gain?[297]

He died in 532 [1137–38] and was buried near Aḥmad's grave.

Abū Manṣūr Mawhūb ibn Aḥmad al-Jawālīqī. He heard much Hadith and inherited all that was known of the science of language. He was a master of his field, careful in expression, and firm in his statements. He died in Muḥarram 540 [June–July 1145]. 100.66

Abū Muḥammad ʿAbd Allāh ibn ʿAlī ibn Aḥmad al-Muqriʾ. Heard much Hadith and could read the Qur'an in many variant readings, on which he authored well-executed compilations. He had some knowledge in the sciences of the Arabic language. I never heard anyone recite more beautifully, perfectly, or correctly. He was a strong Sunni who spent his whole life alone in his mosque. He was born in Shaʿbān '64 [April–May 1072] and 100.67

الاثنين ثامن عشرين ربيع الآخر سنة إحدى وأربعين وخمس مائة وكان له جمع يزيد على الحصر ما رأينا لأحد مثله.

١٠٠،٦٨ أبو الفضل محمّد بن ناصر بن محمّد بن عليّ وُلد في شعبان سنة سبع وستّين وسمع الحديث الكثير وكان له حظّ وافر من معرفته، وقرأ علم اللغة على أبي زكريّا وهو الذي جعله الله تعالى سَبباً لإرشادي إلى العلم فإنّه كان يجتهد معي في الصِّغر ويحملني إلى المشايخ وأسمعني مسند الإمام أحمد بقراءته على ابن الحُصين والأجزاء العوالي وأنا إذ ذاك لا أدري ما العلم من الصِّغر وكان يثبت لي كل ما أسمعه، وقرأت عليه ثلاثين سنة ولم أستفد من أحد كاستفادتي منه. وتوفّي في شعبان سنة خمسين وخمس مائة رضي الله عنه.

١٠٠،٦٩ عبد القادر بن أبي صالح الجِيلي تفقه على أبي سَعْد المُخَرِّمي وسمع الحديث ثم لازَمَ الانقطاع عن الناس في مدرسته مُتشاغلاً بالتدريس والتذكير وبلغ من العمر تسعين سنة. وتوفّي في ليلة السبت ثامن ربيع الآخر من سنة إحدى وستين وخمس مائة ودُفن بمدرسته.

١٠٠،٧٠ أبو العباس أحمد بن أبي غالب بن الطّلاّية كان كثير التعبّد حتى انطوى وكان رأسه إذا قام عند ركبتيه.

وحدثني أبو الحسن بن غرية قال: جاء إليه رجل فقال له: سَل لي فُلاناً في كذا. فقال: يا أخي قُم معي نُصلّي ركعتين ونسأل الله تعالى فأنا لا أترك باباً مفتوحاً وأقصد باباً مغلقاً.

وتوفّي في رمضان سنة ثمان وأربعين وخمس مائة ودُفن بمقبرة أحمد.

ذكر المختارين من الطبقة التاسعة

١٠٠،٧١ أبو العباس أحمد بن بَرَكة الحَرْبي تفقّه على أبي الخَطّاب وكان له فَهم حسن وفطنة في المناظرة، وتوفّي في جُمادى الأولى من سنة أربع وخمسين وخمس مائة.

died Monday, the twenty-eighth of Rabīʿ II 541 [October 7, 1146]. Countless people attended his funeral—more than I have ever seen attend for anyone.

Abū l-Faḍl Muḥammad ibn Nāṣir ibn Muḥammad ibn ʿAlī. He was born in Shaʿbān of '67 [March–April 1075]. He heard much Hadith and was gifted with a good deal of knowledge in that field. He also studied linguistics with Abū Zakariyyā. It is through him that God guided me toward a life of learning. When I was young he worked hard to bring me with him to the study circles. I first heard Aḥmad's *Authenticated Reports*, as well as collections of prized Hadith with short transmission chains,[298] when he read them aloud for Ibn al-Ḥuṣayn. At the time I had no idea what it meant to be involved in learning from a young age. He would check to make sure I understood everything I heard. I studied with him for thirty years and never learned as much from anyone else. He died in Shaʿbān of 550 [September–October 1155]. God be pleased with him! 100.68

ʿAbd al-Qādir ibn Abī Ṣāliḥ al-Jīlī. Studied jurisprudence with Abū Saʿd al-Mukharrimī and heard Hadith, then cut himself off from the scholars and stayed in his academy, busying himself with teaching and leading others in the remembrance of God. He died on Saturday night, the eighth of Rabīʿ II 561 [February 11–12, 1166], at ninety years of age, and was buried at his academy. 100.69

Abū l-ʿAbbās Aḥmad ibn Abī Ghālib ibn al-Ṭallāyah. Prayed so much that he became permanently stooped. When he rose his head was bent nearly to his knees. 100.70

Abū l-Ḥasan ibn Gharībah reported to me that a man once came to Abū l-ʿAbbās and said, "Ask So-and-So for me about this question."

"Brother," he replied, "come pray two cycles with me and we'll ask God. I won't leave an open door for one that's closed." He died in Ramadan of 548 [November–December 1153] and was buried in Aḥmad's burial ground.

Selected Figures from the Ninth Generation

Abū l-ʿAbbās Aḥmad ibn Barakah al-Ḥarbī. Studied jurisprudence with Abū l-Khaṭṭāb. He had a sharp mind and was a skillful debater. He died in Jumādā I of 554 [May–June 1159]. 100.71

أبو حكيم إبراهيم بن دينار النَّهْرُوَاني لقي أبا الخطّاب[١] الكَلْوَاذيّ وغيره من المشايخ وتفقّه وناظر وسمع الحديث الكثير وكانت له في علم الفرائض يدٌ حسنة وكان من العلماءِ العاملين بالعلم وكان كثير الصيام والتعبّد شديد التواضع موثِرًا للخُمول وكان المثل يضرب بحِلمه وتواضعه وما رأَينا له نظيرًا في ذلك. توفّي في يوم الثلاثاء ثالث عشرين جمادى الآخرة في سنة ستّ وخمسين وخمس مائة ودفن بُكْرَة الأَربعاء قريبًا من بشر الحافي.

أبو العلاء الحسن بن أحمد بن الحسن العطّار الهَمَذَاني له المعرفة الحَسنة بالقراءات والأَدب والحديث وسافر في طلب العلم وحَصَّل الكتب الكثيرة وهو مشهود له بالسيرة الجميلة. وتوفّي في سنة تسع وستّين وخمس مائة.[٢]

أبو محمّد عبد الله بن أحمد بن الخَشّاب النّحوي قرأ الحديث الكثير وجمع الكتب الكثيرة وانتهى إليه علم اللغة والنحو. وتوفِّي في رمضان سنة سبع[٣] وستين وخمس مائة.[٤]

أبو يعلى محمّد بن محمّد بن محمّد بن الفَرّاء تفقّه على أبيه أبي خازم وسمع الحديث ودرّس وكانت له فطنة وفهم، وبرع في المناظرة وولي القضاء ببغداد وبواسط. وتوفِّي في ليلة السبت الخامس من جمادى الأولى من سنة ستّين وخمس مائة ودُفن بمقبرة أحمد.

٧٢،١٠٠ ولو ذهبنا نذكر في كلِّ طبقة جميعَ أعيانها أو استقصينا[٥] أخبار المذكورين لَطال كتابنا لكنّا اقتصرنا على أعيان الأعيان من كلّ طبقة وأشرنا إلى أحوالهم والله المشكور وبالله المستعان.

آخر الكتاب والحمدُ لله حَمْدًا دائمًا وصَلواته على خير خلقه محمّد النبيّ الأُمّي وعلى آله وصحبه وسلّم.[٦]

١ د: أبا الخطاب محفوظ. ٢ ليس في د. ٣ ش: تسع. ٤ الجملة ناقصة في د. ٥ ش: واستقصينا.
٦ (والحمدُ لله . . .) الخ: ليس في هـ.

Abū Ḥakīm Ibrāhīm ibn Dīnār al-Nahrawānī. Met Abū l-Khaṭṭāb al-Kalwādhī and other teachers. Studied jurisprudence, engaged in disputation, and heard much Hadith. He was deft at calculating inheritances. He was a learned man who put what he knew into effect. He was given to fasting and worship, and he was extremely humble, preferring to be ignored. His forbearance and self-deprecation became proverbial; indeed I never saw anyone like him in that respect. He died Tuesday, the twenty-third of Jumādā II 556 [June 19–20, 1161], and was buried on Wednesday morning near Bishr al-Ḥāfī.

Abū l-ʿAlāʾ al-Ḥasan ibn Aḥmad ibn al-Ḥasan al-ʿAṭṭār al-Hamadhānī. Had a good knowledge of variant Qur'an readings, the language arts, and Hadith. He traveled in search of learning and amassed many books. He was well known for his goodly life. He died in 569 [1173–74].

Abū Muḥammad ʿAbd Allāh ibn Aḥmad ibn al-Khashshāb the Grammarian. Read much Hadith and collected many books. The knowledge of language and grammar in his day all came down to him. He died in Ramadan of 567 [April–May 1172].

Abū Yaʿlā Muḥammad ibn Muḥammad ibn Muḥammad ibn al-Farrāʾ. Studied jurisprudence with Abū Ḥāzim, heard Hadith, and taught. He was an intelligent man who excelled in disputation. He held the post of judge in Baghdad and Wāsiṭ. He died Saturday night, the fifth of Jumādā I 560 [March 20, 1165], and was interred in Aḥmad's burial ground.

If we had mentioned all the figures in each generation, or written complete biographies of the men we have listed, the book would have grown much longer. We have therefore confined ourself to mentioning only the most prominent figures in each generation and saying a few words about the sort of people they were. We give God our thanks and to Him direct our pleas for help. **100.72**

Here ends the book. We give praise to God always, and ask Him to bless and save Muḥammad, the unlettered[299] Prophet and the best of His creation, and his family and Companions.

[أختام المخطوطات]

١٠١،١ هـ : فرغ من كتابته محفوظ بن عيسى بن محفوظ الزملكاني وكان يملي على الشيخ الإمام الفقيه أبي محمد عبد الرحمن بن عبد الله من الأصل المنقول من خطّ مصنّفه الشيخ الإمام العالم الأوحد ناصر السنّة جمال الدين أبي الفرج عبد الرحمن بن عليّ بن محمّد بن عليّ بن الجوزي وذلك يوم الثلاثاء تاسع عشر من شعبان سنة ستّ وستّين وخمسمائة وصلّى الله على محمد خاتم النبيّين وعلى آله وأصحابه الأكرمين.

١٠١،٢ د: وافق الفراغ منه ضحى يوم الاثنين ثالث ذي القعدة سنة تسع وتسعين وخمسمائة وصلّى الله على سيّدنا محمّد وآله وصحبه الطاهرين.

١٠١،٣ ش: ووافق الفراغ منه في يوم السبت العشرين من شهر رمضان المعظّم قدره وحرمته سنة خمسين وثمان مائة على يد العبد الفقير الحقير المستجير المحتاج إلى رحمة ربّه العلي الكبير محمود بن محمّد بن عمر الششيني الشافعي مَذهباً، غفر الله له ولوالديه ولمن قرأ فيه ودعا له بالمغفرة والرحمة حيّاً ومَيتاً وذلك بمكة المشرفة بباب السلام تحت الأروقة تجاه البيت الحرام والحمدُ لله وحده. وصلّى الله على سيدنا محمّد وآله وصحبه وسلّمَ تسليماً كثيراً.

[Colophons]

[Colophon of H:] Copying completed by Maḥfūẓ ibn ʿIsā ibn Maḥfūẓ al-Zamlakānī, who read aloud for correction by the elder exemplar and jurisprudent Abū Muḥammad ʿAbd al-Raḥmān ibn ʿAbd Allāh from a copy of the original written by the author, the elder, exemplar, unique scholar, and pillar of the *sunnah*, Jamāl al-Dīn Abū l-Faraj ʿAbd al-Raḥmān ibn ʿAlī ibn Muḥammad ibn ʿAlī ibn al-Jawzī, on Tuesday, the nineteenth of Shaʿbān 566 [April 27, 1171]. May God bless Muḥammad, the Seal of the Prophets, and his noble family and Companions. 101.1

[Colophon of D:] Completed before noon on Monday, the third of Dhu l-Qaʿdah 599 [July 14, 1203]. May God bless our master, the Prophet Muḥammad, and his pristine family and Companions. 101.2

[Colophon of SH:] Completed on Saturday, the twentieth of the holy month of Ramadan 850 [December 9, 1446], by Maḥmūd ibn Muḥammad ibn ʿUmar al-Shishīnī, a Shāfiʿī in law, and an inadequate, unworthy, and suppliant servant of God needful of the mercy of his great and mighty Lord. May God forgive him, his parents, and anyone who reads any of this work and prays that God forgive him and be merciful unto him, whether he be living or dead. This work was completed in Mecca, at the Salām Gate under the porticos facing the Holy Mosque. Praise is God's alone. May God bless and keep our master, the Prophet Muḥammad, and his family and Companions. 101.3

Notes

1 The speaker is surprised that an Arab—that is, a descendant of the original Muslim conquerors—is poor. Indeed, Ibn Ḥanbal belonged to a prestigious tribe and his relatives occupied positions in the Abbasid administration (see chapters 1–3).

2 The problem was not the chair itself but the fact that it was decorated with silver, as becomes clear in the next report. I thank Hossein Modarressi for clarifying this point.

3 Al-Sawwāq seems to mean a banquet (apparently known to his audience) held in a house near the Bāb al-Muqayyir, which may mean "Pitch-Worker's Gate" but not "Pitched Gate," pace Le Strange, *Baghdad*, 224–26. The gate was located in al-Mukharrim, a quarter of northeast Baghdad.

4 Ibn Ḥanbal's ascetic contemporary Bishr ibn al-Ḥārith the Barefoot (see Glossary).

5 Identified by al-Turkī as Ibn ʿAbd al-Ḥakam ibn Nāfiʿ al-Warrāq (d. 251/865–66).

6 *Akhāfu an takraha l-rijl*, so voweled in H, which al-Turkī evidently understands to mean "I'm afraid you don't like crowds." For this unusual meaning of *rijl*, see Ibn Manẓūr, *Lisān*, *R-J-L*.

7 The rest of the thought apparently being "even when he's alone."

8 The various political interpretations of this term (discussed in Nagel, "Qurrāʾ," and Shah, "Quest") are based on references to earlier periods and none makes obvious sense here. From the passage itself it is clear that the *qurrāʾ*, whatever else they may have been, were associated, in Ibn Ḥanbal's milieu, with pious shabbiness.

9 The manuscripts read *asmārjūn*, the Arabic pronunciation of *āsemāngūn*, meaning "sky-colored" in Persian. Al-Turkī emends to *asmān jūn*, which is closer to the Persian but not attested in the manuscripts.

10 "They" would appear to be the Abbasid authorities, who tried to court his favor after the Inquisition.

11 Reportedly what ʿUmar ibn al-Khaṭṭāb said about having served as caliph. Here Ibn Ḥanbal seems to be talking about the Inquisition.

12 Sahl ibn Salāmah was a leader of the vigilante movement that sought to restore law and order in Baghdad after the siege of 813. See al-Ṭabarī, *Taʾrīkh*, 8:552/3:1009–10, 572–73/3:1035–36; van Ess, *Theologie*, 3:173–75.

13 The term *ṭunbūr*, "long-necked lute," is sometimes translated using the cognate term "pandore," which, however, is also used to describe many different forms of medium- and long-necked lutes, as well as certain unrelated European instruments. I thank

Dwight Reynolds for explaining these terms. On the pious smashing of musical instruments, see Cook, *Commanding Right*, 79, 90–91, 98, 100 (where this incident is discussed), 121, 149, 238, 300, 309, 383, 384, and 481.

14 Q Mulk 67:30.

15 Al-Shāfiʿī was a foundational Sunni legal theorist (see Glossary). Supplications at dawn were thought to be especially effective. This report, though not impossible in itself, is the sort of story that was circulated to paper over the differences between jurists who followed al-Shāfiʿī's approach and those who favored Ibn Ḥanbal's.

16 This story was clearly invented to make Ibn Ḥanbal look good, to argue that prayer is more important than scholarship, or both. But only the first half of the story makes the point effectively; the second part may have been added to avoid giving offense.

17 The word *ṣabr* (fortitude, patience) and its various derivatives appear ninety-six times (searched on tanzil.net).

18 Q 18, Sūrat al-Kahf. This chapter deals with the themes of ingratitude, quarrelsomeness, and impatience. It tells several well-known stories. One is that of the People of the Cave, fugitive believers whom God cast into a deep sleep and revived 309 years later as a sign and a test to humankind. Another is that of the ungrateful grower who comes to understand his absolute dependence on God when his crops fail. Yet another is that of Moses's travels with an unnamed servant of God who commits a series of apparently wicked actions, which are later explained as benevolent. It also contains the story of "the horned one," often identified as Alexander the Great, and his encounters with various peoples. It ends with a description of the Day of Judgment and a exhortation to the Prophet to proclaim that God is one and to urge humankind to good deeds.

19 The salutation, which ends the prayer, is "Peace be upon you, and the blessing of God."

20 One should not interrupt someone who is praying, or pass directly in front of him or her.

21 It is not clear who was keeping whom busy, though the preference should perhaps be given to Ibn Ḥanbal as the subject.

22 "The rest": the *nawāfil*, or "supererogatory prayers," that is, optional observances performed in addition to the ritual devotions.

23 Worshippers may choose which chapters to read during their prayers. Several reports say that Ibn Ḥanbal preferred this one. On the chapter itself, see 58.7.

24 That is, transported supernaturally to Mecca. In Sufi biography, the Allies of God can cross great distances instantly and can carry others with them.

25 This awkwardly constructed story was apparently intended to establish cordiality between exemplars of the religious sciences and exemplars of the mystical tradition. See Cooperson, *Classical*, 138–51, 178–84.

26 Q Sharḥ 94:5–6.

27 Q Fuṣṣilat 41:11.

28 H and SH have *mā yaṣnaʿu*, "what He does," though the *fatḥah* in H may also be a *ḍammah*, giving *mā yuṣnaʿu*, "what is done" (thus al-Turkī). Though odd, "what He does" makes sense if Ibn Ḥanbal believed that God has predestined all our actions (see 20.49). Since H and SH represent independent manuscript traditions, I have adopted *mā yaṣnaʿu* and translated accordingly. But theodicy aside, D's *mā naṣnaʿu*, "what we do," is the most natural reading.

29 H and D have *ṭibb*, commonly "medicine," and not attested as a plural of *ṭabīb*, "physician," but apparently being used in that sense here.

30 Evidently they were putting something up his nose to absorb the blood.

31 "Thirty years" appears to be wrong; see 62.8.

32 Rayḥāna is also identified (see 63.5) as Ibn Ḥanbal's concubine, though this claim seems less well documented.

33 Literally something cut off or cut out. Here it obviously refers to some kind of footwear but I have not found it attested in other sources.

34 Probably the head of a sheep.

35 This seems to mean that he has just spent the last dirham they have, and that she should not count on him to throw any more celebrations for her. Another possible reading is: "This is all you'll get from me today."

36 A dry measure whose value varied greatly by region, from approximately 926.7 grams to 1.6 kilograms (Ashtor, "*Mawāzīn*, 1").

37 It is unclear to me whether Ḥusn paid for the fabric or was paid for the work she did when she made the garment. *Kirā* usually means the rent, but here it seems to mean the fee paid for a service. I thank Isam Eido, Saud AlSarhan, and Julia Bray for discussing this problem with me. It is also unclear exactly why Ibn Ḥanbal did not want the garment. He may have disliked its being finely woven, or he may have disapproved of the transaction Ḥusn mentions (the *ghallah* being the money he collected from his tenants).

38 Ibn Ḥanbal decided immediately to use the cloth as a shroud and therefore asked Ḥusn not to cut it, as a shroud is simply a wrapper. At the end, though, she seems to be saying that he cut the cloth in order to use only the coarser part for the shroud.

39 Evidently a now-lost biography of Ibn Ḥanbal.

40 Since Rayḥānah is also given as the name of Ibn Ḥanbal's second wife (62.4) the most economical explanation of the discrepancy is that al-Munādī mistakenly applied the name to Ḥusn. The details about asking his wife's permission and following the *sunnah* may be pious embellishments.

41 Ibn Ḥanbal is referring to Q Aʿrāf 7:172, where God summons the souls of all those yet unborn and has them acknowledge Him as their Lord. Here, then, he is apologizing to his older son for fathering the younger ones. He leaves out the younger al-Ḥasan and al-Ḥusayn, who died young (see 63.2), though why he should leave out Muḥammad, the fourth of his young sons, is not clear. Following this understanding of the passage, I have translated based on the text of H, which reads "al-Ḥasan." For their part, D and SH both read Ḥusn (Ibn Ḥanbal's concubine) instead of Ḥasan. If this reading is adopted, the report means that Ibn Ḥanbal is apologizing for buying Ḥusn and fathering Saʿīd.

42 A *qanṭarah* is a masonry bridge as opposed to one supported by boats or inflated skins. Fūrān is using local shorthand to refer to a market near one such bridge. For a list of the possibilities, see Le Strange, *Baghdad*, 368, left column.

43 "The gate leading out from the [northwest] suburbs to the shrine of the Kâẓimayn," and for legal purposes "the northern limit of Western Baghdad." Le Strange, *Baghdad*, 115 and map 5.

44 One who measures cloth or plots of land (al-Samʿāni, *al-Ansāb*, 3:5).

45 Al-Turkī, drawing on a parallel text, emends *Aḥmad* to *aḥmadu l-Lāh*, but the original, which appears in all the manuscripts, strikes me as much more plausible.

46 To judge by third/ninth-century works intended to correct writing errors, "bad Arabic" (*laḥn*) in this period probably did not mean making errors in inflection (*iʿrāb*), as in the (probably contrived) stories told of early Islamic figures. Rather, it meant making errors such as mixing up Form I and Form IV verbs, or using *yāʾ* instead of the glottal stop. For examples, see Ibn Qutaybah, *Adab al-kātib*, passim. For "bad Arabic" as a matter of word choice, see 98.23.

47 *Qarāmil*: "twisted strips of hair, wool, or silk, used by women to pull back their hair" (*Lisān*, s.v. *Q-R-M-L*).

48 This report is not identical to the one attributed to Fāṭimah in ch. 61.

49 Ibn al-Jawzī's claim that the early Muslims held the Revelation to be uncreated is tendentious. Elsewhere in this volume (72.9–10, 72.13–14) his sources will argue that the subject is off limits precisely because the early Muslims announced no position on the matter.

50 Ibn al-Jawzī sees the Secessionists (Muʿtazilah) as the villains behind the Inquisition, and this is a commonly repeated view, but Ibn Ḥanbal himself casts the Jahmists in that role. See Jadʿān, *Miḥnah*, 47–109, and Melchert, "Adversaries."

51 It is unlikely that Ibn Nūḥ, an obscure student of Hadith (see chapter 67), would have been in a position to overhear the caliph say anything. This series of reports was probably invented in the course of the post-Inquisition rapprochement between the Hadith

community and the Abbasid regime. The point was to show that, except for two bad eggs—al-Ma'mūn and al-Wāthiq—the caliphs had always held the correct (that is, the Sunni) view of the Qur'an: that it was not created.

52 Modern scholarship has explained the Inquisition as al-Ma'mūn's attempt to make the caliphate the source of all guidance in matters of belief and law. This attempt can broadly be characterized as a Shi'i one. Al-Ma'mūn adopted several other pro-Shi'a positions, including the nomination of a descendant of 'Alī as his heir apparent. He did not, however, limit exemplary leadership to 'Alī's family. He included his own family, the Abbasids, among the potential imams or guides, and of course believed himself to be the imam in his own time. He seems to have developed these ideas in the course of the civil war between himself and his predecessor, the caliph al-Amīn. Intentionally or not, al-Ma'mūn's Shi'i self-positioning brought him into conflict with people like Ibn Ḥanbal, who believed that the Law was to be found in the *sunnah* rather than in the declarations of individuals. To force the Hadith-men and like-minded jurists to acknowledge his authority, al-Ma'mūn craftily decided to ask them about the createdness of the Qur'an. Unlike other points of contention between the two parties, this issue is not mentioned in the Book itself or in the Hadith. The caliph's plan was thus to force his opponents to engage in the kind of theological argument he was sure he could win. For discussions of the *miḥnah* and further references, see Patton, *Aḥmed ibn Ḥanbal*; Sourdel, "Politique religieuse"; Nagel, *Rechtleitung*, esp. 116–54, 430–46; Lapidus, "Separation"; Crone and Hinds, *God's Caliph*, esp. 80–96; Jad'ān, *Miḥnah*, 47–109; Steppat, "From *'Ahd Ardeshir*"; Nawas, "The Mihna"; van Ess, *Theologie*, 3:446–508; Nawas, *Al-Ma'mûn*, 25–78; Zaman, *Religion*, 106–18; Cooperson, *Classical*, 117–38; Hurwitz, *Formation*, 113–44; Cooperson, *Al-Ma'mun*, 107–28; Winkelmann-Liebert, "Die *miḥna*"; Yücesoy, *Messianic Beliefs*, 128–35; Turner, *Inquisition*; de Gifis, *Shaping*, 91–115.

53 Although Yaḥyā served as chief judge under al-Ma'mūn, he argued consistently for proto-Sunni positions. Ḥanbalī biographers therefore tend to treat him as a reliable source.

54 A parallel account by Aḥmad ibn Ḥanbal's cousin Ḥanbal ibn Isḥāq sheds additional light on Aḥmad's first encounter with the Inquisition. It begins with a list of the scholars summoned to meet with the caliph in al-Raqqah. (Here Ḥanbal seems to have confused the initial dispatch of scholars to al-Raqqah with the later transport of Ibn Ḥanbal and Ibn Nūḥ to the Byzantine front. As it stands, his account includes Ibn Ḥanbal among those who made the initial trip and proclaimed the Qur'an created: see Ḥanbal, *Dhikr*, 34-36. Van Ess, *Theologie*, 3:455n23, thinks the editor is wrong to supply Ibn Ḥanbal's name to complete the text here, though the mistake seems to be Ḥanbal's, not the editor's, as the

claim is repeated, the second time without emendation. As Ḥanbal's account continues, in any event, it comes into agreement with our other sources, which say that Ibn Ḥanbal was first questioned in Baghdad.) Ḥanbal's report quotes his father Isḥāq, who was also Aḥmad ibn Ḥanbal's uncle, as saying:

> At sunset a messenger arrived from the captain of the ward (*ṣāḥib al-rabʿ*) and took Aḥmad away. I went out with them. The ward captain said: "The chief wants to see you at his place tomorrow." After we left [the ward captain's house] I said to Aḥmad: "Why not go into hiding?"
>
> "How could I do that?" he replied. "If I did, I'd worry that something might happen to you, or to my children, your children, or the neighbors. I wouldn't want anyone to suffer on my account. Let's just see what happens" (Ḥanbal, *Dhikr*, 36).

55 Al-Ma'mūn was in al-Raqqah, having stopped there on his way to the Byzantine front. During his visit to Syria, the caliph may have realized the extent of anti-regime sentiment there, and the extent to which such sentiment correlated with what were to him heretical religious ideas. The trigger may have been his meeting with the Hadith scholar Abū Mushir al-Ghassānī, who at first refused to describe the Qur'an as created (see 78.19, and van Ess, *Theologie*, 3:452–53)

56 Ibn Ḥanbal and his circle avoided referring to the Abbasid caliphs by their regnal titles, evidently because they rejected their Shiʿi-millenarian implications. *Al-ma'mūn* means "the trustworthy" and was a common form of reference to the Prophet.

57 Q Shūrā 42:11.

58 Q Anʿām 6:102; Raʿd 13:16; Zumar 39:62; Ghāfir 40:62. Here al-Ma'mūn puts together parts of different Qur'anic verses to emphasize that God is fundamentally different from His creations, including the Qur'an. In this first letter, the full text of which we have from other sources, the caliph also emphasizes his duty to guide the community and protect Islam from the false teachings of the self-proclaimed people of the *sunnah* (al-Ṭabarī, *Ta'rīkh*, 3:1112–32/8:631–44, and van Ess, *Theologie*, 3:452–56).

59 That is, Ibn Ḥanbal completed the citation of Q Shūrā 42:11, of which the interrogators recited only the part given above. He thus reminded those present that one cannot simply ignore the passages that seem to describe God as if He has a physical body. He may have believed that God did have a physical body, all of whose attributes, including the voice that had spoken the Qur'an, were uncreated. Alternatively, he may have been trying to make the point that the problem of attributes could not be resolved by human reason. In any case, Ibn al-Jawzī might not be giving us an entirely reliable

account, as he himself was opposed to anthropomorphist interpretations of the Qur'an (Swartz, "Ḥanbalī Critique").

60 Called Raḥbat Ṭawq in another telling (see below). Perhaps the same as the place today called al-Raḥbah, which lies on the Euphrates between Baghdad and al-Raqqah.

61 That is, al-Ma'mūn. Some chroniclers state that he contracted a fever after being splashed with cold water, while others say he fell ill after dangling his feet in cold water while eating freshly delivered dates (that is, he presumably caused an imbalance in his humours, according to the Greco-Islamic medical theories of the day). See al-Ṭabarī, *Ta'rīkh*, 3:1134–41/8:646–651.

62 Or al-Mutawakkil, as the storyteller has forgotten to add. The third request—the one not granted—was presumably not to meet al-Muʿtaṣim. The story switches from first to third-person narration in mid-sentence and thus seems to have been garbled in transmission.

63 A town, also known as ʿĀnāh (67.14), on the Tigris in what is now northeastern Iraq, near the Syrian border (Longrigg, "ʿĀna").

64 An earlier report says that Ibn Ḥanbal got as far as Adana, which is plausible enough given that the news of al-Ma'mūn's death would not have reached al-Raqqah immediately.

65 A western suburb of Baghdad, located approximately two miles west of the Round City just northeast of the ʿĪsā Canal (Le Strange, *Baghdad*, index and map 6).

66 ʿUmārah ibn Ḥamzah was a freedman of the Caliph al-Manṣūr. His palace was located on the Trench of Tahir just west of the Upper Harbor on the Tigris (Le Strange, *Baghdad*, 117 and map 5).

67 There were at least two prisons in use in Baghdad at this time: the Muṭbaq (Le Strange, *Baghdad*, 27 and map 5) and the Prison of the Syrian Gate (ibid., 130–31 and maps 2, 5, and 6). It is not clear whether the "Commoners' Prison" was one of these, or another place altogether.

68 I have not been able to identify this street. In any case it seems that the authorities first intended to keep Ibn Ḥanbal confined inside a house, as seems to have been customary with high-profile figures, but then decided to put him in a prison for common criminals.

69 According to Ḥanbal, Ibn Ḥanbal's fetters were loose enough that he could slip them off, which he did in order to perform his prayers properly (Ḥanbal, *Dhikr*, 38–39).

70 According to the account (ignored by Ibn al-Jawzī) by Aḥmad ibn Ḥanbal's cousin Ḥanbal, it was Ḥanbal's father Isḥāq—Aḥmad's uncle—who persuaded the authorities to put Aḥmad on trial. The report runs as follows:

> With Aḥmad still in prison, my father, Isḥāq ibn Ḥanbal, made the rounds of the commanders and regime figures on his behalf, hoping to get him

released. Eventually, seeing that his efforts were leading nowhere, he went directly to Isḥāq ibn Ibrāhīm. "Commander," he said, "our families are bound together in a way I'm sure you appreciate. We were neighbors in Marw and my father Ḥanbal was with your grandfather al-Ḥusayn ibn Muṣʿab."

"So I've heard."

[My father continued:] I said: "So would the Commander not do something to honor that bond? Your position is one my nephew approves of. He has not denied Revelation; the only disagreement concerns its interpretation. Even so, you have deemed it lawful to keep him confined for a long time. Commander: put him together with some jurists and scholars." I didn't say anything to him about Hadith-men and transmitters of reports.

"Would you accept the outcome, whatever it was?"

"Yes!" I said. "Let the best argument win."

[My father continued:] "[Later, when I told] Ibn Abī Rabʿī, he said, 'What have you done? You want to gather your nephew's opponents--whatever Debaters and squabblers Ibn Abī Du'ād can find--and let them beat him in a debate? Why didn't you consult with me first?'"

[...]

Escorted by [Isḥāq ibn Ibrāhīm's] chamberlain, I went in to see Aḥmad.

"Your companions have surrendered," I told him. "You've discharged your responsibility before God. Everyone else has given in, and here you are, still locked up!"

"Uncle," he replied, "if those who know remain silent out of fear, and the ignorant remain silent out of ignorance, then when does the truth come out?"

Hearing this I stopped trying to change his mind (Ḥanbal, *Dhikr*, 41).

The failure of Isḥāq's plan, along with his later attempt to talk Ibn Ḥanbal down (Ḥanbal, *Dhikr*, 49), not to mention his alleged complicity in persuading the crowd that Ibn Ḥanbal was unharmed after the flogging (see 69.57), may have made him a *persona non grata* and his reports distasteful (van Ess, *Theologie*, 3:461–62).

71 The relevant part of the report reads: "You must know that, when I'm gone, princes will arise. Anyone who seeks them out, believes their lies, and abets their tyranny is not part of my community nor am I of his." See al-Turkī, 431n2.

72 Ḥanbal's account includes a tantalizing detail regarding this episode. The interrogators, he says, came to see Ibn Ḥanbal, carrying with them "a picture of the heavens and the

earth, and other things" (*ṣūratu al-samawāti wa-l-arḍi wa-ghayru dhālika*). Then, Ibn Ḥanbal is quoted as saying, "They asked me something I knew nothing about" (Ḥanbal, *Dhikr*, 42). Al-Ma'mūn is known to have sponsored the drawing of world maps and star charts (Sezgin, *GAS*, 10:73–149) so the claim is believable, but one can only speculate about why the interrogators would show those items to Ibn Ḥanbal. Perhaps they hoped to persuade him that the caliph had access to knowledge that could not be derived from the Hadith (Cooperson, *Al-Ma'mun*, 105).

73 The line of argument implied here runs as follows: If God is not created, none of His attributes, including knowledge, can be created either. Since it is encompassed by God's knowledge and spoken in His voice, the Qur'an must also be uncreated.

74 Q Zukhruf 43:3.

75 Q Fīl 105:5. In this verse and the one cited just before, the verb *jaʿala*, as Ibn Ḥanbal points out, means "to make" in the sense of "cause to have a certain attribute." It does not mean "to create."

76 Perhaps the Orchard Gate (or Garden Gate) located on the east side of the Tigris, near the palace of al-Muʿtaṣim (Le Strange, *Baghdad*, 221, 276, maps 5 and 8). Ibn Ḥanbal seems to have been taken there by boat.

77 That is, on the permissibility of performing one's ablutions by wiping one's shoes instead of removing them and washing the feet. This was a distinctively Sunni position. The story itself is obviously contrived. For one thing, protocol did not permit speaking without first being addressed by the caliph.

78 A longer version of this report appears in 69.30. Both reports overlook the twenty-eight months Ibn Ḥanbal spent in prison (69.28) and thus give an incorrect date for his trial, which took place in Ramadan 220/September 835 (van Ess, *Theologie*, 3:460).

79 The following accounts of the trial are based largely on testimony by Ibn Ḥanbal's son Ṣāliḥ (preserved independently in Ṣāliḥ, *Sīrat al-imām*, 49–65). In Ibn al-Jawzī's retelling, Ṣāliḥ occasionally returns as the frame narrator, but for easier reading I have maintained the first-person voice throughout. Ibn al-Jawzī was also aware of the testimony by Aḥmad ibn Ḥanbal's cousin Ḥanbal (preserved independently in Ḥanbal, *Dhikr*, 41–60), though he has ignored or suppressed certain problematic elements of it. In any event, neither of the family accounts is fully trustworthy. Their authors believed that Ibn Ḥanbal had, or should have had, a ready answer for every argument, and write accordingly. This bias will be evident in the present account as well. See Cooperson, *Classical*, 117–25; van Ess, *Theologie*, 3:456–57; Winkelmann-Liebert, "Die *miḥna*," 252–60.

80 According to Ḥanbal's account, the caliph was surprised that Ibn Ḥanbal was middle-aged: "You told me he was a young man!" (*a-laysa zaʿamtum li-annahu ḥadathun*). See Ḥanbal, *Dhikr*, 43.

81 Ibn Ḥanbal (or more likely one of his biographers) is using a report transmitted by Ibn ʿAbbās, the ancestor of the Abbasid caliphs, to argue by implication that the authorities have no business questioning Muslims who profess faith by the definition given here.

82 Q Anʿām 6:120; Raʿd 13:16; Zumar 39:62; Ghāfir 40:62.

83 Q Aḥqāf 46:24–25.

84 The point is that the expression "everything" is not always categorical.

85 Q Anbiyā' 21:2.

86 Q Ṣād 38:1. This verse, like several others, begins with the name of an Arabic letter or letters, in this case *ṣād*.

87 That is, you should seek nearness to God by reciting the Qur'an. The disputant understands this to imply that God and His word are two distinct entities.

88 I thank Tahera Qutbuddin for suggesting this interpretation of a puzzling passage. After the first hundred thousand I expected *mi'atay alf*, "two hundred thousand," which is written almost indistinguishably from *mi'at alf*, but the manuscripts agree on the latter.

89 Ḥanbal's account sets this remark in a different light. In his telling, Ibn Abī Du'ād says to Ibn Ḥanbal: "I hear you like to be a leader" (*balaghanī annaka tuḥibbu r-ri'āsah*; *Dhikr*, 51), and then the caliph makes his offer to parade Ibn Ḥanbal around as a hero. This question of Ibn Ḥanbal's popular following is a tantalizing one. Steppat ("From *Ahd Ardašīr*") notes that a Persian work on statecraft known to al-Ma'mūn urges rulers to crush any manifestations of religious leadership among the people, and may have inspired the Inquisition. Ḥanbal claims that during the Ibn Ḥanbal's flogging "people had gathered in the square, the lanes, and elsewhere; the markets had closed and crowds had gathered" (*Dhikr*, 60). Later Ḥanbalī accounts make much of the crowd, though these accounts are not very persuasive (Winkelmann-Liebert, "Die *miḥna*," 246). On the other hand, sources hostile to Ibn Ḥanbal and his followers speak fearfully of their supposed power to command the rabble (Qāḍī, "Earliest *Nābita*" and Cooperson, "Al-Jāḥiẓ").

90 This passage is puzzling, as the fast should already have ended after the sunset prayer mentioned just above.

91 That is, the scholars summoned to al-Raqqah at the beginning of the Inquisition (in 212/827–28) to be questioned regarding the Qur'an (see chapter 76). All of them reportedly agreed to say that it was created.

92 This list is an interpolation by a transmitter or by the author. Only three of these names agree with those listed by al-Ṭabarī, *Ta'rīkh*, 1116–67/8:634; cf. Ḥanbal, *Dhikr*, 34–36.

The descendants of the men involved doubtless tried to get their names off such an infamous list (van Ess, *Theologie* 3:455n23).

93 Q Nisā' 4:11.

94 The point is that one needs Hadith in order to understand the Qur'an properly. This was Ibn Ḥanbal's reply to those who sought to dismiss Hadith as a source of knowledge.

95 The day began at sunset, so for Ibn Ḥanbal the third night would be followed by the third day.

96 Literally, "my voice became louder than theirs." The text may indeed mean this, though it seems implausible for him to be depicted as shouting at his opponents.

97 At roughly this point in the parallel account by Ḥanbal, there is mention of an argument that the editor has omitted on the grounds that it contradicts what is known of Ibn Ḥanbal's opinions (Ḥanbal, *Dhikr*, 55, note 1). As the passage is of some interest, I reproduce it here from the Dār al-kutub manuscript (Ta'rīkh Taymūr no. 2000, microfilm no. 11159, folio no. 16). After *wa-kān min amrihi mā kan*, which appears in the printed edition (p. 55), the account continues:

> ... *wa-samiʿtu Abā ʿAbda l-Lāhi yaqūlu wa-ḥtajjū ʿalayya yawmaʾidin qāla tajīʾu l-baqaratu yawma l-qiyāmati wa-tajīʾu tabāraka fa-qultu lahum innamā hādhā th-thawābu qāla l-Lāhu wa-jāʾa rabbuka wa l-malāku ṣaffan ṣaffan innamā taʾtī qudratuhu innamā l-Qurʾānu amthālun wa-mawāʿiẓu wa-amrun wa-kadhā* [sc. *wa-hādhā*?] *fa-kadhā* [print edition resumes] *wa-qultu l-ʿAbdi r-Raḥmāni...*
>
> I heard Abu ʿAbd Allāh [Ibn Ḥanbal] say: "They argued against me that day by saying: '[Don't you say that the chapter called] the Cow and the [chapter called] Tabārak will come on the Day of Resurrection?'
>
> "I told them: 'This [sc. the thing that will come] is only the reward [for reading the Qur'an]. God [also] says: "Your Lord will come, with the angels arrayed in rows" [Q Fajr 89:22]. [By this is meant] only [that] His power comes. The Qur'an is only similitudes, exhortations, and commandment; and this [expression] is like that.'"

Here ʿAbd al-Raḥmān is accusing Ibn Ḥanbal of holding the anthropomorphist view that the chapters of the Qur'an would come to life on the Day of Resurrection. The chapters in question (Baqarah and Tabārak or Mulk) seem to have figured as part of the accusation because they mention creatures (cows and birds respectively) that were supposed to take on physical reality. The argument was that if God had literal, physical eyes and ears, as the Qur'an seems to say, then the cows and birds (for example) must have a real existence too. In this passage Ibn Ḥanbal rejects the *reductio ad absurdem* but as a consequence is forced to say that the Qur'an need not always be taken literally. This is the view that Naghsh, the editor, finds contradictory with Ibn Ḥanbal's known opinions. (I thank Josef van Ess for helping me understand this passage; any errors are of course mine.)

98 The copyists of D and SH appear not to have understood this passage, but H has a fairly clear *nābayi l-khashabatayn*, meaning literally "the two tusks" or "eye-teeth" of the posts. Al-Turkī reads *nāti'*, "the part sticking out," which is plausible in itself but requires emending H. Although I have not found either term attested as the name for part of a whipping apparatus, the instructions seem clear enough. The person being flogged was suspended from ropes or straps (the latter suggested by Winkelmann-Liebert, "Die *miḥnah*," 255) tied around the wrists and attached to the posts by a horizontal peg or bar. Ibn Ḥanbal is being told to hold on to this horizontal element, or the ropes, and pull himself up to ease the tension on his wrists.

99 Cooperson ("Two Abbasid Trials") argues that al-Mu'taṣim may here be calling for the unbarbed whips mentioned in the hostile account by al-Jāḥiẓ (*Rasā'il*, 3:295–96), in order to minimize Ibn Ḥanbal's injuries. Winkelmann-Liebert, by contrast, thinks the references to al-Mu'taṣim's soft-heartedness are much exaggerated ("Die *miḥnah*," 253ff.).

100 Lictors were ancient Roman officials who did many jobs besides flogging, but English does not have another common word for flogger, and "lictor" has the sanction of having been used by Patton in his 1897 rendering of this episode (*Aḥmed*, 108).

101 On the face of it, this curse suggests that the caliph was angry that the lictors were not striking more forcefully. Winkelmann-Liebert, however, suggests that the caliph was upset about having to flog Ibn Ḥanbal—or at least that the Ḥanbalī biographers wanted to depict him that way ("Die *miḥnah*," 255).

102 This account places the trial in a courtyard. Extant examples of Abbasid-era buildings indicate that they consisted of rooms, or complexes of rooms, arranged around a central courtyard (see, for example, Northedge, *Historical Topography*). Literary sources indicate that the yard was used for formal events and the rooms for intimate gatherings. Al-Mu'taṣim would have been sitting under a shade; when he got up to address Ibn Ḥanbal, he would have been exposing himself to the sun.

103 Or "I didn't know what I was doing." Ḥanbal's account says: "I passed out and came to more than once [*rubbamā lam a'qil wa-rubbamā 'aqaltu*]. When they hit me again I would pass out and not know [anything], and they would stop hitting me" (Ḥanbal, *Dhikr*, 57). Van Ess has argued that this way of putting things is intended to cover up some act of capitulation on Ibn Ḥanbal's part, without which he would never have

been released (*Theologie*, 3:465). Three sources (al-Jāḥiẓ, *Rasā'il*, 3:295–96; al-Ya'qūbī, *Ta'rīkh*, 2:576–77; Ibn al-Murtaḍā, *Ṭabaqāt*, 122–25) agree that he capitulated. One (al-Jāḥiẓ) even refers to the event as if to a matter of common knowledge (see further Hinds, "Miḥna" and Winkelmann-Liebert, "Die *miḥnah*," 267). References to *taqiyyah*, or dissimulation justified by circumstance (e.g., 69.28, and Ḥanbal, *Dhikr*, 37–38), indeed suggest that the principle was invoked by Ibn Ḥanbal's partisans to justify a lapse on his part during the trial. And the proliferation of fantastic reports exonerating him (Abū l-'Arab, *Miḥan*, 438–44; Abū Nu'aym, *Ḥilyah*, 9:204–5; Ibn Abī Ya'lā, *Ṭabaqāt*, 1:437–43 [the entry on Sulaymān ibn 'Abd Allāh al-Sijzī of the first *ṭabaqah*]; al-Maqdisī, *Miḥnah*, 109) implies there was indeed a scandal that needed to be narrated away (Cooperson, *Classical*, 129–38). However one chooses to evaluate the evidence, three points are worth bearing in mind. First, the circumstances of the trial—its being held inside the palace, the use of torture, and the lack of sympathetic witnesses—made the facts of the matter almost immediately irretrievable (a point some of the participants seem to have realized; see 69.56). Second, Ibn Ḥanbal made his opposition to rationalist theology and imamic pretentions clear enough on numerous occasions, such that there need be little doubt of his actual views, regardless of what happened at the trial. Finally, Sunni tradition is unanimous in its conviction that he did not capitulate, so that, even if he did, his having done so has effectively been abolished from history.

104 Ḥanbal gives a more detailed report of Ibn Ḥanbal's departure:

> At sunset, Aḥmad was led out of the house on a mount belonging to Isḥāq ibn Ibrāhīm and rode to his own house surrounded by the caliph's officials and his own people. When he reached the gate, I heard 'Ayyāsh, the Master of the Bridge, say, when he saw Aḥmad approaching—I heard 'Ayyāsh say to Isḥāq's man, with everyone standing there—"*Tāzīh tāzīh*," which means "Arab! Arab!" (Ḥanbal, *Dhikr*, 60).

Although the Persian word *tāzīh* means "Arab," and Ibn Ḥanbal was indeed of Arab origin, 'Ayyāsh seems to have meant something else: namely, that he was a rigid, legalistic scholar. This interpretation was suggested to me by Patricia Crone, who notes that Bābak referred to Muslims as *yahūd* for the same reason: both (he thought) believed in a distant God who issued "an endless stream of restrictive rules" (Crone, *Nativist Prophets*, 273).

105 Since Ibn Ḥanbal had been fasting all day, he could have eaten, though he is depicted as refusing to consume anything provided for him by the caliph. The second point regards *taqiyyah*, or "prudential dissimulation," according to which a Muslim may conceal his beliefs to protect himself from harm. Ibn Ḥanbal is depicted as rejecting this option.

106 *Al-hanbāzān*: perhaps from Persian *hambāz*, "companion" or "partner," here Arabized to mean the two parallel supports of the scaffold.

107 Q Nisā' 4:30.

108 This is the first of many reports invented to make Ibn Ḥanbal's ordeal into a test of the rightness of the Sunni creed.

109 Bilāl ibn Abī Rabāḥ, a slave who was one of the first to accept Islam, is described as suffering tortures at the hands of his masters but nevertheless refusing to recant.

110 Q Tawbah 9:51.

111 The sharply critical biographer Shams al-Din al-Dhahabī (d. 748/1348) denounces this report as "wrong" and condemns Abū Nuʿaym al-Iṣfahānī (but not Ibn al-Jawzī) for repeating "abominable fantastications" (*khurāfāt samijah*) about Ibn Ḥanbal's ordeal (al-Dhahabī, *Siyar*, 11:255). See al-Turkī, 488n3, and Cooperson, "Probability."

112 The most natural reading makes Ibn Ḥanbal the one who would have died. The day was still momentous for the caliph because killing Ibn Ḥanbal would entail being punished in the afterlife. The Arabic sentence can also mean that the caliph is the one who would have died—a possibility worth considering only because of the fantastic nature of these accounts. See also 69.58.

113 As used here, the verb *baṭṭala* (so voweled in H and D) seems to mean that Ibn Ḥanbal has given the lie to the bandits' claims to toughness. On this trope, see Cooperson, *Classical*, 138–41.

114 This sentence displays unusual pronoun agreement: the *-hu* suffix on *ḍarabtu* refers to the masculine singular *sawṭ*, but the verb *haddat* is feminine singular as if referring to the set of eighty blows.

115 This is the philologist Nifṭawayh (d. 323/935); his *History* is lost (Bencheikh, "Nifṭawayh").

116 This (probably invented) story is set in the period after the Inquisition.

117 Apparently meaning: join him in protesting to the caliph over what was being done to Ibn Ḥanbal.

118 Bishr's extreme asceticism and refusal to teach Hadith distinguished him from Ibn Ḥanbal. Stories like this were invented to help negotiate the conflict between the two visions of piety (Cooperson, *Classical*, 178–84).

119 Ibn al-Jawzī may have in mind reports claiming that Ibn Ḥanbal did capitulate (see 69.26). Conversely, he may be thinking of certain pro-Ḥanbalī fictions even less likely than the ones cited here (Cooperson, *Classical*, 129–38).

120 It is not clear which of the above-named transmitters is speaking here.

121 Catacombers: warriors based in, or near, the *maṭāmīr*, that is, the underground complexes of Cappadocia, on the the Byzantine frontier (Honignmann, *Ostgrenze*, 46).

122 A parallel text (al-Dhahabī, *Siyar*, 11:259; added in brackets by al-Turkī, 459) has here "Some will say he did give in," which is a plausible addition but not present in our manuscripts.

123 This speech provides a convenient explanation for Ibn Ḥanbal's release—so convenient, in fact, that it is likely to have been fabricated by one of his partisans.

124 "He" most likely refers to the Caliph al-Muʿtaṣim, though it might also refer to Isḥāq, Ibn Ḥanbal's uncle, who apparently went along with the trick.

125 The rough cloak would shrink painfully after being drenched.

126 "Rejoice!" may mean "Rejoice in the prospect of entering Paradise," to which the pious caliph replies that the innocent man would testify against him on the Day of Judgment.

127 A marginal note in D, partially cut off on the left, reads: "These [men] were not beaten under the same circumstances as Aḥmad. Had Aḥmad not stood firm, people would have strayed from right belief. The trials [of these men] are therefore not to be compared to his." A second marginal comment adds that Ibn Ḥanbal's trial can be compared only to that of ʿUmar, the second caliph. Ibn Ḥanbal's achievement is still greater, though, because he, unlike ʿUmar, had no one fighting with him.

128 This seems to be a (rather harsh) reference to al-Muʿtaṣim.

129 Q Shūrā 42:40.

130 Q Shūrā 42:40.

131 Ḥanbal tells us that his name was Abū Ṣubḥ (*Dhikr*, 61).

132 A reference to the Prophet's concealing himself in a cave during his flight from Mecca to Medina.

133 Abū Zurʿah seems to be asking "Why did al-Muʿtaṣim flog you instead of beheading you, and why didn't al-Wāthiq hurt you at all?" Ibn Ḥanbal appears to give him the answer to a different question, namely: "How did you survive the flogging?"

134 This apocryphal story, in its two variants, has a character very much like Ibn Ḥanbal make all of the arguments that Ibn Ḥanbal himself was unable or unwilling to make at his trial. See further van Ess, *Theologie*, 3:502–4. For much more elaborate fiction, in which al-Maʾmūn himself is bested, see van Ess, *Theologie*, 3:504–8, and Omari, "Kitāb al-Ḥayda."

135 Q Nisāʾ 4:86.

136 This putative recording of an insignificant variant seems to be an attempt on the part of the storyteller to give the impression that he is upholding the strictest standards of accurate transmission.

137 All the manuscripts have *yaṣba'*, "to go from one religion to another." Al-Turkī, drawing on a parallel text, emends to *yaṣbū*, "to suffer from youthful ignorance." This is a plausible reading but has no support in the manuscripts.

138 Addressing a stranger by his name instead of his *kunyah* (Ibn Abī Du'ād) was rude and dismissive.

139 Q Mā'idah 5:3.

140 What Ibn al-Jawzī does not tell us is that Ibn Ḥanbal was reportedly asked to join a rebellion against al-Wāthiq. During al-Wāthiq's reign, teachers were ordered to tell their pupils that the Qur'an was created, and scholars who did not accept the caliph's teaching were separated from their wives. A number of Baghdad jurisprudents came to Ibn Ḥanbal saying that they no longer acknowledged al-Wāthiq as caliph. Ibn Ḥanbal reportedly urged them not to make a bad situation worse by rejecting their obligation to obey the authorities. It was at this juncture that al-Wāthiq ordered him to make himself scarce (Ḥanbal, *Dhikr*, 69–73).

141 On the end of the Inquisition, see Melchert, "Religious Policies." The "reports on seeing God" were among those interpreted literally by the Sunnis and figuratively by their rivals; see further Omari, "Beatific Vision."

142 Meter: *kāmil.*

143 Q A'rāf 7:54.

144 The partisans of 'Alī—that is, the Shi'a—believed that the only legitimate religious exemplar, and by extension the ideal leader of the community, was a descendant of 'Alī ibn Abī Ṭālib. During the civil war between al-Amīn and al-Ma'mūn, Shi'i claimants had rebelled in Kufa, Yemen, and the Hijaz.

145 Here Ibn Ḥanbal seems to be saying that he has not disappeared from public life in order to signal disapproval of the regime, but rather because al-Mu'taṣim and al-Wāthiq had forbidden him to appear in public.

146 Jad'ān, who thinks of Ibn Ḥanbal as willing to countenance rebellion against the Abbasid regime, suggests that the accusation may have been true (Jad'ān, *Miḥnah*, 285–90).

147 This is presumably an error for Abū 'Alī Yaḥyā (al-Turkī, 488n5).

148 The word *ijjānah* usually means a large shallow drinking bowl, but since it is used here to cover a sizable bag of coins I have chosen the secondary meaning of washtub. It may have been green because it was made of oxidized copper. I thank Paul Cobb, Nancy Khalek, and Noura Elkoussy for their thoughts on this point.

149 Apparently Ibn Ḥanbal did not want to use the light without paying for it, a problem he addresses elsewhere; see Cooperson, *Classical*, 176.

150 The Arabic says only "after he passed Yaḥyā ibn Harthamah," leaving it unclear who passed Yaḥyā (a military commander), and what it meant to pass him. The translation is my best guess.

151 Ibn Abī Du'ād, who by this time had fallen out of favor, had pushed for broad adoption of the dogma of the created Qur'an. Al-Mutawakkil seems to be asking Ibn Ḥanbal to preach in favor of the opposite view and thus make up for the Abbasid adoption of a now-heretical creed.

152 The dictionaries define this word as "the horse that places second in a race," here perhaps meaning a horse of good but not superior quality. It may be that Yaḥyā is making a joke: *muṣallī* also happens to mean "engaged in prayer," which may have struck him as an appropriate name for an animal ridden by Ibn Ḥanbal.

153 Q Ṭā Hā 20:55.

154 Ḥanbal gives a more detailed account of this meeting. Upon seeing Ibn Ḥanbal, the caliph's mother says to her son: "I beg you: fear God in your dealings with that man. There's nothing you can offer him to tempt him, and it's no good trying to keep him here away from his home. So let him go: don't try and hold him!" Ibn Ḥanbal then enters the presence of the heir apparent, al-Muʿtazz, but fails to address him as "emir." Isḥāq ibn Ibrāhīm was reportedly minded to strike Ibn Ḥanbal with his sword, but the prince's tutor, Ibn Ḥanbal's former interrogator ʿAbd al-Raḥmān al-Ḍabbī, merely tells the boy, "This is the tutor your father has sent you." Ibn Ḥanbal then reports: "The boy replied that he would learn whatever I taught him. I was impressed with his clever answer given how little he was" (Ḥanbal, *Dhikr*, 90).

155 *Khayshah*: a strip of wet cloth suspended from the ceiling and moved back and forth by a servant to cool a room. The only English word for this seems to be punkah, which comes from Hindi.

156 Yaʿqūb's request seems to have been a trick intended to find out whether Ibn Ḥanbal indeed refused to teach anyone or just the caliph's sons.

157 Q Mā'idah 5:1.

158 Q Baqarah 2:156–7: «Those who say, when afflicted with a calamity, "We belong to God and to Him we shall return," are the ones who will have blessings and mercy from their Lord.»

159 Apparently the stipend granted by al-Mutawakkil.

160 Literally "some knots have slipped off me." Ibn Ḥanbal may be alluding to a report in which ʿUmar used the word "knots" to mean "appointments to positions of power." See Ibn Manẓūr, *Lisān*, s.v. *ʿ-Q-D*.

161 I am not entirely satisfied that I understand what *huwa muṣaddaq* means here, but al-Turkī's voweling imposes this reading. Other possibilities, e.g., *muṣaddiq* and *muṣṣaddiq*, mean payer or collector of the alms-tax, but neither fits the sense or the syntax of the passage.

162 Following the parallel text in Ṣāliḥ, *Sīrat al-imām*, al-Turkī has "the children of Sāliḥ and 'Abd Allāh, the two sons of Aḥmad ibn Muḥammad ibn Ḥanbal."

163 This description is not entirely clear to me, but it seems to refer to the sunken-eyed look that accompanies starvation.

164 That is, to exhort and admonish him. On this tradition, see Cook, *Commanding Right.*

165 Ibn Ḥanbal apparently means that he would remind the caliph of his duty to care for the descendants of the first Muslims.

166 The elaborate courtly style of the first paragraph, the omission of important details, and the direct reference to Ibn Ḥanbal's view of Disputation all suggest that this letter is a forgery intended to make his doctrine palatable to outsiders.

167 Q Tawbah 9:6.

168 Q Aʿrāf 7:54.

169 A reference to Q Furqān 25:63: «The true servants of the Gracious One are those who walk upon the earth with humility and when they are addressed by the ignorant ones, their response is, "Peace"» (or "Goodbye," *salāman*).

170 A less elaborate telling of this story is dismissed as a fabrication by al-Dhahabī, *Siyar*, 11:321; see Cooperson, "Probability," 71. The point of the fiction may be to rehabilitate Ibn Rāhawayh, of whom Ibn Ḥanbal disapproved.

171 That is, the property he coveted would appear to testify against him.

172 All the manuscripts read *ilā mā d.w.r.nā*, which makes no evident sense. Al-Turkī instead gives *balaghahu*, "and it reached him" (that is, the news reached Ibn Ḥanbal), from a parallel account.

173 Ibn Ḥanbal's two youngest children.

174 Leading the Muslims into battle, defending the frontier, and dividing up the spoils were among the duties of the imam or head of the community. Since al-Mutawakkil, in Ibn Ḥanbal's view, was not carrying out these tasks, the money he collected through taxation was misappropriated. Consequently, any gift of money from the treasury was unacceptable to the scrupulous.

175 Ibn 'Ulayyah reportedly died before the Inquisition; see al-Turkī, 519n1.

176 Q Baqarah 2:156, recited when affliction strikes.

177 The passage in context runs as follows: "God will not guide those who will not believe in the signs of God, and theirs will be a painful punishment. Only those fabricate lies

concerning God who do not believe in the signs of God, and these are the liars. As for one who denies God after he has believed—not one who is forced to do it while his heart rests securely in faith, but one who opens his heart to a denial of truth—such as these will have a terrible punishment" (Q Naḥl 16:104–06).

178 In the report, the pagans force ʿAmmār ibn Yāsir to curse the Prophet and praise their deities. He later confesses his misdeed to the Prophet, who tells him that as long as he remained a believer in his heart then no harm was done. The Hadith does not appear in the collections in the form cited here; see al-Turkī, 524n2.

179 Part of a report in which believers are told to act on the parts of the Qur'an they do understand and to leave the rest for God to clarify. See al-Turkī, 326n1.

180 ʿAlī seems to be trying to protect his shoes and clothing from getting dirty, a matter of concern if one were attending the state-sponsored prayer but presumably not an issue for Ibn Ḥanbal and his ascetic circle.

181 Q Ikhlāṣ 112:1–2. *Ṣamad* may once have meant "with no hollow" (Gardet, "Allāh") or "impenetrable," "dense to the absolute degree" (Böwering, "God"). English translations of the verse vary significantly, rendering *ṣamad* as, e.g., "the Self-sufficient One" (Wahiduddin Khan), "the Everlasting Refuge" (Arberry), "the eternally besought of all" (Pickthall), "immanently indispensable" (Ahmed Ali), "the Eternal, Absolute" (Yusuf Ali) (all translations at tanzil.net). Chapter 112 as a whole denies trinitarianism, so *ṣamad* may (also) carry the sense that God does not consist of distinct persons. In view of the divergent possibilities I have not ventured a translation.

182 Q Dhāriyāt 51:22.

183 Q Dhāriyāt 51:22.

184 It is unclear precisely who is meant.

185 Forty *raṭls* times four hundred grams, the approximate value of a Baghdad *raṭl* (Ashtor, "*Mawāzīn*").

186 Q Shuʿarāʾ 26:2.

187 An allusion to Q Ikhlāṣ 112:31; Dukhān 44:53.

188 *Laylat al-arbiʿāʾ*: in the Islamic calendar, the day begins at sunset, so "Wednesday night" in Arabic is Tuesday night in English. But the date seems wrong anyway, as the first of Rabīʿ I 241 [July 20, 855] was a Saturday.

189 It seems to have been ʿAlī ibn al-Jaʿd's son who came: ʿAlī himself was already dead by this time, and a parallel text has *ibn*. See al-Turkī, 541n2.

190 The manuscripts insist on *uʿṭiyat*, which provides the basis for my translation, though I am not certain it is right.

191 According to the common understanding of Q Anfāl 8:59, one who swears an oath and does not fulfill it may make expiation by (among other things) feeding ten destitute persons. See further Lange, "Expiation." Presumably Ṣāliḥ gave the dates away to the poor. Neither Ibn Ḥanbal nor his biographers tell us what vow it was he broke.

192 Al-Faḍl ibn al-Rabīʿ had been vizier to al-Rashīd and al-Amīn. He survived the civil war during which al-Maʾmūn overthrew al-Amīn, but was thereafter disgraced. His son's visit to Ibn Ḥanbal in prison shows that the old Abbasid order disapproved of the Inquisition. Like many of al-Maʾmūn's other initiatives, it undermined the legitimacy of the dynasty by suggesting that only some of its members—specifically, those that behaved like Shiʿi imams—could serve as rulers.

193 *Al-rukhaṣ* are cases of replacing a commandment "with a less onerous alternative in cases of need or duress" (Katz, "*ʿAzīmah* and *Rukhṣah*"). Presumably Ibn Ḥanbal was worried about having failed to complete all his religious duties during his illness and wanted reassurance that he had a good excuse.

194 For an analysis of this story, see Cooperson, "Probability," 78–81.

195 Unfortunately, this date, which corresponds to July 31, 855, was a Wednesday.

196 Muslim funeral practice requires that a man's body be wrapped in three pieces of cloth, each of which covers it entirely.

197 The Amānūs or Nur Dağları mountain range in what is today Turkey, just across the northwest border with Syria. God has given the visitors the power to travel instantly from there in time for the funeral.

198 For a caustic denunciation of this unlikely story, see al-Dhahabī, *Siyar*, 11:343, and Cooperson, "Probability," 74–75.

199 The passage in H and SH is garbled. Al-Turkī supplies *al-ḥuzn*, "sorrow," giving the more likely meaning that all virtuous households were in mourning. Here I have rendered what is in the manuscripts, garbled though it may be.

200 Or: "We keep them here so people can copy them." The point, in any case, seems to be that he knows these reports to have been properly transmitted. If they leave his hands, he cannot guarantee their authenticity should others someday wish to copy them.

201 Meter: *ṭawīl*.

202 Here meaning the Prophet Muḥammad.

203 The reference is to Muḥammad ibn Nūḥ ("son of Noah"), the otherwise undistinguished figure who joined Ibn Ḥanbal in defying the Inquisition and died during the return from Tarsus.

204 Q Naml 27:48: «There were in the city nine men who spread corruption in the land, and would not reform.»

205 Meter: *ṭawīl.*

206 "Aḥmad" means "most praiseworthy."

207 Meter: *sarīʿ.*

208 Meter: *ṭawīl.*

209 Meter: *kāmil.*

210 Meter: *ṭawīl.*

211 Meter: *wāfir.*

212 Meter: *ṭawīl.*

213 Meter: *ṭawīl.*

214 Meter: *ṭawīl.*

215 Meter: *kāmil.*

216 The original sentence seems patched together here, probably because a transmitter omitted the curse that appears in the version immediately following.

217 Q Zumar 39:74. This is what the blessed say after being admitted to the Garden.

218 The first person singular here and in the corresponding place in the parallel reports could be Ibn Ḥanbal and the one answering could be Sufyān. In 92.12, though, the questioner asks about Miskīnah, who says "If only you knew!" This means that the questioner must still be alive and dreaming rather than dead and in the Garden.

219 The storyteller has God refer to Himself in the third person, as in the Qur'an. The transmitters of this report evidently thought that hating ʿAlī was a grave fault in a Sunni. The transmitters of the variant immediately preceding either thought otherwise or simply did not wish to repeat God's supposed cursing of Jarīr.

220 Q Zumar 39:74.

221 Q Zumar 39:74.

222 Q Zumar 39:74.

223 Miskīna, whose name means "Wretched," was a pious Worshipper of the Followers' generation (Rāghib, *Muḥāḍarat,* 1: 609). She was of the Ṭufāwah, an Arab clan (Ibn Manẓūr, *Lisān,* s.v. *Ṭ-F-W*).

224 Q Anʿām 6:89.

225 Q Anʿām 6:89–90.

226 Q Anʿām 6:89.

227 Al-Fīrūzābādī (*al-Qāmūs al-muḥīṭ,* s.v. *Ṣ-Y-N*) mentions a place called al-Ṣīniyyah, but not specifically in al-Karkh (the district south of the Round City in Baghdad). The name suggests a connection with China or with Chinese wares, and Le Strange mentions such a market in Baghdad, though under another name, and again not in al-Karkh (*Baghdad,* 197).

228 Q An'ām 6:89.

229 From Q Baqarah 2:137: «If they believe as you have believed, then are they rightly guided; but if they turn back, then know that they are entrenched in hostility. God will surely suffice to defend you against them, for He is All Hearing, All Knowing.»

230 The text seems garbled here and the variant does not help. The likeliest way for the story to go is: "I noticed that many of them were carrying spears. The Prophet looked out, as if intending to dispatch an expedition, and saw a spear taller than any of the others."

231 Or: those whom Ibn Ḥanbal loves.

232 Evidently Yaḥyā ibn Ma'īn.

233 "Pelting" is explained as being struck by stones flung from the skies, and "disfigurement" as being changed into an uglier form, such as that of an animal. The report is described as referring to the punishments that will befall Muslims who commit certain transgressions.

234 Apparently Isḥāq ibn Rāhawayh.

235 That is, he was a Ḥanafī or a Shi'i.

236 The niche is the feature in a mosque that indicates the direction to Mecca. Ibn Ḥanbal seems to be saying, "Keep praying until you die."

237 A *sāq* is normally a leg or stalk. Here it is being used as a measure of length but I have not been able to pin down the meaning any more precisely.

238 For the story, see the second report following.

239 Q Baqarah 2:156.

240 The original story may have specified the caliph or governor involved, but later Sunni transmitters seem to have suppressed the name to protect his reputation.

241 The verb used means literally "to grasp someone's forearm." The gesture was used (among other things) to show allegiance to a newly appointed caliph.

242 That is, al-Khaḍir appeared to him in a dream.

243 A name for Baghdad, reportedly given because its first mosque was imperfectly aligned toward Mecca.

244 An expression of great esteem, based in the pre-Islamic practice of capturing members of rival tribes and releasing them in exchange for something valuable.

245 A reference to Q Nisā' 4:164, where God speaks directly to Moses.

246 A reference to Q Muṭaffifīn 83:18–21: «But, the record of the righteous is [preserved] in the 'Illiyyīn. And what will make you understand what the 'Illiyyīn is? A written record, which those angels closest to God will bear witness to.» Some exegetes also explain the word as referring to a high place in the Garden.

247 This seems to be an error for Aḥmad, as Ibn al-Jawzī points out.

248 That is, adopt his positions on law and the like.

249 A respected transmitter of reports from his father, ʿUmar, the second caliph.

250 This report offers a puzzling chronology. Aḥmad ibn Naṣr al-Khuzāʿī, who is sitting with the Prophet, was executed during the reign of al-Wāthiq—that is, long after al-Qawārīrī's forced capitulation to the Inquisition.

251 A quarter called Dār al-Quṭn (with the article) existed between the ʿĪsā Canal in al-Karkh (Le Strange, *Baghdad*, 84, and map 4, no. 32).

252 The word *ṭūbā* appears in Q Raʿd 13:29. Some exegetes explain it as the name of a tree in Paradise while others say that it means simply "bliss." See Waines, "Tree(s)" and Kinberg, "Paradise."

253 Q Kahf 18:63ff, where an unnamed servant of God teaches Moses about patience.

254 A reference to two nearly identical verses of the Qur'an: «Before you also the messengers We sent were but [mortal] men to whom We vouchsafed revelation. Ask the People of the *dhikr*, if you do not know» (Q Naḥl 16:43 and Anbiyā' 21:7). The term *ahl al-dhikr* in this verse has been explained as "the recipients of previous scriptures." More generally it can also mean people mindful of God.

255 So says the one manuscript that contains the story, though "he was wearing fine clothes" seems a likelier thing to say here.

256 Ar. *mukhannath*, originally a man, usually a musician, who dressed and acted like a woman for entertainment. In Ibn Ḥanbal's time, *mukhannathūn* associated with the court were famous for "savage mockery, extravagant burlesque, and low sexual humor" (Rowson, "Effeminates," quotation at 693). The word can also mean "hermaphrodite," but being a hermaphrodite was not a sin or a crime, so the speaker in this story would not need to be forgiven (at least, not for that).

257 Q Hūd 11:105.

258 In Arab folklore, every human being has a jinni counterpart of the opposite sex.

259 Based on the account in Lane, s.v. *T-N-R*, it seems we must imagine an oven open at the top which had to be turned over to create a closed space. It must also have had a door on the side for inserting the clover, which apparently served as a fireproof sort of bedding.

260 The historical Harthamah took part in the siege of Baghdad, which ended in the death of the Caliph al-Amīn. But he was himself executed shortly thereafter, during the reign of al-Ma'mūn: that is, several decades before al-Mutawakkil became caliph. Ḥanbalī storytellers seem to have had a confused idea of Abbasid prosopography.

261 Meter: *kāmil*.

262 This seems to mean that he did not send his son to school or hire a tutor for him but instead preferred to instruct him himself.

263 Unassimilated, this word would be *i'takhadhtum*, which as far as I know is not actually used.

264 For more on Ibn Ḥanbal's views on recitation, see Melchert, "Aḥmad ibn Ḥanbal and the Qur'ān," 25–26.

265 The speaker, al-Shāfiʿī, will defend Mālik ibn Anas, and the challenger will defend Abū Ḥanīfah.

266 The book written in Baghdad is apparently (the first draft of) the *Risālah* (*Epistle*, trans. Lowry) and the one written in Egypt is the *Umm*.

267 That is, one to clean the face and another to clean the arms as far as the elbows.

268 The Prophet is described as "striking his palms on the ground, blowing on them, and wiping his face and hands" (see references in al-Turkī, 666n1).

269 That is, if having met the Companions necessarily confers precedence, Saʿīd and others should outrank Abū Ḥanīfah.

270 That is, if certain Successors thought more highly of Mālik than they did of the Prophet's Companions then the premise that one gains precedence simply by having met the Companions cannot be valid.

271 That is, people preferred the word of transmitters more distantly related to the Prophet than Ibn ʿAbbās.

272 Q Nisāʾ 4:3.

273 That is, the person to whom I owe everything in my books is Ibn Ḥanbal. Al-Turkī, 668n5, inserts this phrase for clarity, but it is not there in the manuscripts. The original audience doubtless knew what was meant.

274 To take something from someone *min taḥt yadihi* ("from under his hand") elsewhere means to take what one is owed from another party without his knowledge or permission. As that is hardly likely here, I am guessing that a more literal meaning is intended. Possibly, too, the phrase is *man taḥt yadihi*, "those dependent on him," but then an additional word would be needed to complete the sentence.

275 I thank Christopher Melchert for suggesting an explanation for this passage.

276 I thank Peter Pormann for explaining the term *qiyām al-dam*.

277 The "City of Salvation" is Baghdad, so named (in my view) because its Abbasid founders and rulers considered themselves imams, meaning that allegiance to them implied salvation. Commonly, however, the title is translated as "City of Peace."

278 Q Hūd 11:79.

279 Apparently a reference to the promulgation of Shiʿi creeds during the ascendancy of the Buyids.

280 It is unclear which Sulaymān this is.

281 The neighbor is in the Garden but ʿUthmān is in Paradise, which evidently means a special place or higher level of blessedness.

282 A question motivated by *waraʿ* (scrupulosity): if, for example, the man had taken the water from someone else without permission, it would be wrong to drink it.

283 *Muballighūn*: people who repeat the words of the prayer leader or lecturer when the crowd is too large for everyone to hear him.

284 On the name, see al-Turkī, 694n1.

285 This is the oath of assent that formalized the accession of a new caliph. Normally a crowd of dignitaries would be involved.

286 In 469/1077, the Shāfiʿī jurist Abū l-Naṣr ʿAbd al-Raḥīm (d. 514/1120), son of the mystic and theologian ʿAbd al-Karīm al-Qushayrī, came to Baghdad to teach the speculative theology of al-Ashʿarī. Although the Ashʿarite system was intended to defend the texts and conclusions favored by the Ḥanbalīs, the latter were having none of it, and rioted. Eventually Abū l-Naṣr was sent back to Isfahan. See Halm, "al-Qushayrī."

287 See above, 100.46.

288 This may mean that Abū ʿAlī and Abū Jaʿfar (see above, 100.46) served as notary-witnesses in court on the same day of the week, or that the two gave testimony together in a particular case. I thank Ahmed El Shamsy, Mohammed Salama, and Adam Talib for their thoughts on this point.

289 *Madhhabu Aḥmada Aḥmadu madhhabin*: a pun in Arabic, as Aḥmad means "most praiseworthy."

290 Meter: *kāmil*.

291 See Le Strange, *Baghdad*, 296.

292 A *dikkah* can be a bench. It can also be "a platform usually standing on columns two to three metres high, situated in the covered part of the mosque between the *miḥrāb* [the niche indicating the direction to Mecca] and the court" (Jomier, "Dikka") where the repeater (*muballigh*) stands during prayer. But Ibn Ḥanbal's place of burial, though a popular place for visits, is not described as having a mosque attached (Le Strange, *Baghdad*, 158–59).

293 The ninth of Dhu l-Hijjah 503 [June 29, 1110].

294 Kaʿb ibn Mālik was one of three Helpers reportedly condemned and later forgiven for staying behind during the Prophet's raid on Tabūk.

295 ". . . God will make me one of them." The rest of the sentence does not appear in the manuscripts, perhaps because al-Dīnawarī was too modest to say it, but it does appear in a parallel text from *Shadharāt al-dhahab*, whence it is supplied by al-Turkī (see 705n1).

296 Meter: *ṭawīl*.

297 Meter: *ṭawīl.*

298 Such collections contained reports that not only had short chains of transmitters but also one transmitter, or some other distinctive feature, in common. I thank Devin Stewart for explaining this point.

299 There is some debate about what *ummī* may have meant in the Qur'an (for which see Sebastian Günther, "Ummī"). By Ibn al-Jawzī's time, though, it was understood to mean "illiterate," meaning that Muḥammad could not have been inspired by reading older scriptures.

Glossary of Names and Terms

ʿAbbāsah bint al-Faḍl Ibn Ḥanbal's first wife, and mother of his son Ṣāliḥ.

ʿAbd Allāh ibn Aḥmad ibn Ḥanbal one of Ibn Ḥanbal's sons, and a major transmitter of his Hadith reports (d. 290/903).

ʿAbd al-Raḥmān al-Shāfiʿī see Abū ʿAbd al-Raḥmān al-Shāfiʿī.

ʿAbd al-Razzāq a Yemeni Hadith scholar (d. 211/827).

ʿAbd al-Wahhāb al-Warrāq Ibn Ḥanbal's close friend, described as right-minded and pious (251/865 or 866).

Abū ʿAbd al-Raḥmān al-Shāfiʿī jurist and theologian who debated with Ibn Ḥanbal during his trial (d. ca. 230/845).

Abū Bakr (al-Ṣiddīq) a Companion of the Prophet and first caliph (r. 11–13/632–34).

Abū Bakr al-Khallāl a disciple of al-Marrūdhī (q.v.) and author of the formative compilations of the Ḥanbalī school (d. 311/923).

Abū Bakr (Aḥmad ibn Muḥammad) al-Marrūdhī a close associate of Ibn Ḥanbal and a transmitter of his reports (d. 275/888).

Abū Ḥanīfah early legal authority who favored judgment (*ra'y*) over *sunnah* (q.v.) (d. 150/767).

Abū Khaythamah Zuhayr ibn Ḥarb a Hadith scholar and compiler of reports (d. 243/857–58).

Abū Mushir al-Ghassānī Syrian Hadith scholar persecuted by al-Ma'mūn (q.v.) for his unwillingness to declare the Qur'an created; his resistance may have provoked al-Ma'mūn to pursue the Inquisition (q.v.) (d. 218/833).

Abū Zurʿah al-Rāzī major Hadith scholar known for his critical examination of chains of transmitters and his disapproval of Disputation (d. 264/878).

Aḥmad ibn Naṣr al-Khuzāʿī leader of a failed rebellion against the Caliph al-Wāthiq (q.v.) and much admired by the Sunnis (q.v.) (d. 231/845).

ʿAlī ibn Abī Ṭālib the Prophet's son-in-law and fourth caliph (q.v.) according to the Sunni (q.v.) count, or the first imam (q.v.) according to several Shiʿi (q.v.) groups (r. 35–40/656–61).

ʿAlī ibn al-Jaʿd Hadith scholar condemned by Ibn Ḥanbal for capitulating to the Inquisition (d. 230/845).

ʿAlī ibn al-Jahm an official at the court of al-Mutawakkil (q.v.).

ʿAlī ibn al-Madīnī major Hadith scholar, reportedly criticized by Ibn Ḥanbal for accepting the createdness (q.v.) of the Qur'an (d. 239/853).

Ascalon (modern Ashkelon) a town on the southeast Mediterranean coast in what is now Israel.

Basra a port city in southern Iraq, near the head of the Persian Gulf; a major intellectual center in early Islamic times.

Bishr ibn al-Ḥārith (the Barefoot) famous ascetic who was suspicious of Hadith study but admired Ibn Ḥanbal (d. 227/841–42).

Bishr al-Marīsī a Ḥanafī and Postponer influential during the reign of al-Ma'mūn (q.v.); he was hated by Ibn Ḥanbal and his followers for his belief that the Qur'an is created (d. 218/833).

Bughā the Elder a Turkish general who served several Abbasid caliphs (d. 248/862).

Commander of the Faithful the title of the caliph (q.v.).

Companions Muslims whose lives overlapped with that of the Prophet Muḥammad.

createdness (of the Qur'an) the belief that God's revelation to the Prophet Muḥammad is a created thing, as opposed to being eternal by virtue of its divine origin.

cycle (rakʿah) any of the rounds of standing, kneeling, and prostration that make up the Muslim ritual prayer.

dāniq a coin equal in value to one-sixth of a dirham (q.v.).

al-Dāraquṭnī a Hadith scholar and Shāfiʿī (q.v.) jurist fiercely opposed to Disputation (q.v.) (d. 385/995).

dinar a gold coin originally weighing 4.25 grams, and the most valuable coin in use during the early Abbasid period.

dirham a silver coin, until the mid-third/ninth century weighing between 2.91 and 2.96 grams.

Disputation (kalām, literally "talking") a discourse on physical or spiritual matters that employs syllogistic reasoning; theological or dogmatic speculation.

Emissary of God a title of the Prophet Muḥammad.

al-Fatḥ ibn Khāqān an administrator and scholar who served al-Mutawakkil (q.v.) (d. 247/861–62).

Fāṭimah Ibn Ḥanbal's daughter; possibly the same as Zaynab (q.v.)..

Fire (al-nār) according to the Qur'an, the place where the wicked spend eternity after death.

Fūrān ('Abd Allāh ibn Muḥammad) a Hadith scholar and close associate of Ibn Ḥanbal (d. 265/879).

Garden (al-jannah) according to the Qur'an, the place where the blessed spend eternity after death.

Hadith the entire corpus of hadiths (q.v.), used to determine the *sunnah* (q.v.).

hadith a report of something the Prophet Muḥammad said or did, including tacit expressions of approval or disapproval, consisting of the report itself as well as a list of those who transmitted it.

Ḥanafī a follower of the legal school named after Abū Ḥanīfah (q.v.).

Ḥanbal ibn Isḥāq Ibn Ḥanbal's cousin, and author of an account of the Inquisition; less often cited than other sources, perhaps because of his father Isḥāq ibn Ḥanbal's (q.v.) role in the episode (d. 273/886).

Harthamah (ibn A'yan) Abbasid general anachronistically used as a character in a story (96.9) about al-Mutawakkil and his court (d. 200/816).

Hāshimī a member of the clan to which the Prophet Muḥammad belonged.

Helpers (anṣār) those citizens of Medina who accepted Islam after the Prophet moved there from Mecca in 1/622.

Ḥusn Ibn Ḥanbal's concubine and mother of six of his children.

Ibn 'Abbās a cousin of the Prophet and the nominal ancestor of the Abbasid line; later generations of Sunnis (q.v.) credited him with vast knowledge of the Qur'an and the *sunnah* (q.v.) (d. ca. 68/687–88).

Ibn Abī Du'ād a Secessionist (q.v.) and adviser to the Caliphs al-Ma'mūn, al-Mu'taṣim, al-Wāthiq, and al-Mutawakkil (q.q.v.); hated by Ibn Ḥanbal and his followers for his role in the Inquisition (d. 240/854).

Ibn Māsawayh physician to several Abbasid caliphs (d. 243/857).

Ibn Rāhawayh see Isḥāq ibn Rāhawayh.

Ibn Ṭāhir see Muḥammad ibn 'Abd Allāh ibn Ṭāhir.

Ibn al-Zayyāt vizier under al-Mu'taṣim, al-Wāthiq, and al-Mutawakkil (q.q.v.) (d. 233/847).

imam one who in his capacity as a Muslim leads other Muslims, whether in group prayer, in pursuing a particular path in interpretation, or as head of state; among Sunnis (q.v.), an exemplary scholar; among Shi'a (q.v.), a member of the Prophet's family entitled to lead the community, usually by virtue of special knowledge of the law.

innovator a term used by Ibn Ḥanbal and his followers to condemn persons they believed responsible for introducing beliefs and practices not present in the *sunnah* (q.v.) and therefore bad.

Inquisition the interrogation of judges, notary-witnesses (q.v.), Hadith scholars, and miscellaneous other persons to determine their assent to the doctrine that the Qur'an is created, and by extension their acknowledgment that the Abbasid caliph had the final word in matters of belief and practice; introduced by the Caliph al-Ma'mūn (q.v.) in 218/833 and intermittently enforced until ended by al-Mutawakkil (q.v.) in 237/851.

Isḥāq ibn Ḥanbal Ibn Ḥanbal's uncle; reportedly responsible for having him put in trial, and described as urging him to compromise with the Inquisition.

Isḥāq ibn Ibrāhīm governor of Baghdad under al-Ma'mūn, al-Mu'taṣim, al-Wāthiq, and al-Mutawakkil (q.q.v.) (d. 235/849).

Isḥāq ibn Rāhawayh respected Hadith scholar who transmitted to Ibn Ḥanbal (d. 238/853).

Ītākh Khazar military commander under the Caliphs al-Mu'taṣim, al-Wāthiq, and al-Mutawakkil (q.q.v.) (d. 235/849).

Jahm ibn Ṣafwān early Muslim thinker to whom are attributed a number of teachings hateful to Ibn Ḥanbal and his associates, particularly the claim that the prototype of the Qur'an began to exist only at a particular point in time (d. 128/745).

jinni a sentient creature made of fire, often described as interfering in human affairs.

jurisprudence (fiqh) most broadly, the ability to discern the right course of action in ritual, legal, and ethical matters; more narrowly, formal text-based legal reasoning.

al-Karābīsī a jurist and theologian who argued that God's speech (including the Qur'an) is uncreated but human utterance of it is not (d. 245/859 or 248/862).

al-Karkh the general name for the region of Baghdad south of the caliphal compound in the Round City.

al-Khallāl see Abū Bakr al-Khallāl.

al-Khaḍir (also called al-Khiḍr) a figure who appears in the Qur'an (Q Kahf 18:60–82) and guides Moses; in popular belief, a perennially recurrent figure who provides guidance to Muslims in times of need.

Khurasan a region that includes what is today northeastern Iran, Afghanistan, and parts of Central Asia.

al-Khuzāʿī see Aḥmad ibn Naṣr al-Khuzāʿī.

Kufa city in central Iraq, on the Tigris River; an important center of learning in early Islamic times.

Magians (majūs) a term used by outsiders to refer to Zoroastrians.

Mālik (ibn Anas) early legal thinker (d. 179/795) associated with the doctrine that the practice of the people of Medina constituted the best precedent.

al-Ma'mūn seventh Abbasid caliph (r. 198–218/813–33).

manifestations of grace see signs of grace.

al-Manṣūr, mosque of the mosque built by the second Abbasid caliph (r. 136–58/754–75). The mosque continued to serve as a center for Friday worship even after the caliphs moved out of the purpose-built Round City.

al-Marīsī see Bishr al-Marīsī.

al-Marrūdhī see Abū Bakr al-Marrūdhī.

Maʿrūf al-Karkhī a Baghdadi ascetic prominent in Sufi (mystical) traditions (d. 200/815–16).

Marv city in what is now Turkmenistan; in early Islamic times, the capital of Khurasan (q.v.).

al-Miṣṣīṣah town near the northeast Mediterranean coast in what is today Turkey, and in early Abbasid times on the frontier with the Byzantines.

Muḥammad ibn ʿAbd Allāh ibn Ṭāhir military commander in Baghdad and representative of al-Muʿtaṣim (q.v.) at Ibn Ḥanbal's funeral.

Muḥammad ibn Idrīs see al-Shāfiʿī.

Muḥammad ibn Nūḥ a young man of little Hadith-learning who joined Ibn Ḥanbal in refusing to declare the Qur'an created (218/833).

al-Muhtadī fourteenth Abbasid caliph (r. 255–56/868–70).

al-Muʿtaṣim eighth Abbasid caliph (r. 218–27/833–42).

al-Mutawakkil tenth Abbasid caliph (r. 232–47/847–61).

Nishapur a town in northeastern Iran near present-day Mashhad.

notary-witness a person engaged by a judge to serve as a regular witness to the undertaking of contractual obligations or to the character of persons who appear in court.

Nuʿaym ibn Ḥammād a Hadith scholar imprisoned for refusing to declare the Qur'an created; also famous as a compiler of apocalyptic traditions (d. 228/843?).

Postponers (murji'ah) those who hold that latter-day Muslims cannot judge the Companions (q.v.) or resolve the disputes that divided them, and that any such resolution must be postponed until Judgment Day.

al-Qā'im bi-Amr Allāh twenty-sixth Abbasid caliph (r. 422–67/1031–75).

al-Qawārīrī Baghdadi Hadith scholar who at first refused, then agreed under duress, that the Qur'an is created (d. 235/850).

Qazwīn a town in north-central Iran west of present-day Tehran.

Quraysh the tribe to which the Prophet Muḥammad belonged.

al-Raqqah a town located on the Euphrates River in north-central Syria; a common stopping point on the journey between Baghdad and the Byzantine frontier.

al-Rashīd fifth Abbasid caliph (r. 170–93/786–809).

Rayḥanah Ibn Ḥanbal's second wife and mother of his son ʿAbd Allāh.

Rejectionist (rāfiḍi) a term of disparaging reference to a Shiʿi (q.v.).

Rey city in the north-central part of what is now Iran, just south of modern Tehran.

Riḍwān in Muslim tradition, the angel who receives the blessed into the Garden (q.v.).

al-Ruṣāfah the part of greater Baghdad that lay on the east bank of the Tigris River.

Saʿīd ibn al-Musayyab Successor (q.v.) renowned for his intense piety and great knowledge of *sunnah* (d. ca. 94/712–13).

Sajjādah (al-Ḥasan ibn Ḥammād) Baghdadi Hadith scholar who at first refused, then agreed under duress, that the Qur'an is created (d. 241/855).

Ṣāliḥ ibn Aḥmad ibn Ḥanbal Ibn Ḥanbal's eldest son and a major transmitter of his Hadith reports; served as judge in Isfahan (d. 265/879).

Samarra purpose-built city in central Iraq that served as the Abbasid capital from 221/836 to 279/892; the Caliph al-Mutawakkil (q.v) had Ibn Ḥanbal brought here from Baghdad.

scrupulosity (waraʿ) the pious practice of shunning not only forbidden objects and activities but also those which are merely suspicious or of unknown legality.

Secessionists (al-muʿtazilah, "those who set themselves apart") a name applied to scholars who were, broadly speaking, rationalist in their approach. For example, they favored metaphorical explanations for the apparently physical attributes of God.

al-Shāfiʿī (Muḥammad ibn Idrīs) legal theorist credited with laying the foundation for Sunni jurisprudence by developing methods for deriving law from the Qurʾan and *sunnah* (d. 204/820).

Shāfiʿī a follower of the legal school named after al-Shāfiʿī (q.v.).

Shiʿi (pl. Shiʿa) one characterized by the belief that certain members of the Prophet's family are the only legitimate leaders of the Muslim community, usually because of their special understanding of God's law.

signs of grace (karāmāt) violations of accustomed causality that serve as evidence that a person enjoys God's special favor. These are generally concealed, and differ from the evidentiary miracles performed by prophets.

Stopper one who, when asked about the Qurʾan, says "It is the speech of God" and stops. According to Ibn Ḥanbal, he should add "uncreated."

Successors the generation of Muslims after the Companions (q.v.).

Sufyān (al-Thawrī) transmitter and jurisprudent admired by the Sunnis for his pioneering emphasis on Hadith (q.v.) as well as his pro-Umayyad and anti-Abbasid sentiments (d. 161/778).

sunnah the exemplary practice of the Prophet, preserved in the Hadith (q.v.) and used as a source of law; sometimes also included the practice of the early Muslims (preserved in narratives called *āthār* or *akhbār*).

Sunnah (adj. Sunni) the mature form of the movement that began by proclaiming itself "the people of *sunnah* (q.v.) and Community"; it is characterized by solidarity with the historical caliphate, rejection of imamism, and reliance on Hadith (q.v.) rather than Disputation (q.v.).

Tarsus town on the Mediterranean coast of what is today Turkey; in the early Abbasid period, a popular destination for pious Muslims seeking to join the frontier wars against the Byzantines.

Tūzūn a Turkish general who siezed control of Baghdad in 331/943.

ʿUbayd Allāh ibn Khāqān vizier of al-Mutawakkil (q.v.) (d. 263/877).

ʿUkbarā town on the east bank of the Tigris north of Baghdad.

ʿUmar ibn ʿAbd al-ʿAzīz Umayyad caliph renowned for his piety and justice (r. 99–101/717–20).

ʿUmar ibn al-Khaṭṭāb Companion of the Prophet and second caliph; among Sunnis, an exemplar of just rule (r. 13–23/634–44).

ʿUthmān ibn ʿAffān Companion of the Prophet and third caliph (r. 23–35/644–56); often praised beyond his merits by Sunnis eager to counter the partisans of ʿAlī ibn Abī Ṭālib (q.v.).

variant readings (of the Qurʾan) In Aḥmad's time, any of several different traditions of reading aloud (and sometimes writing) the text of God's revelation to Muḥammad. The different traditions were partially standardized by Ibn Mujāhid (d. 324/936), though up to fourteen different ones remained acceptable.

Wakīʿ ibn al-Jarrāḥ pious Hadith scholar and transmitter to Ibn Ḥanbal (d. 197/812).

Waṣīf Turkish general who served and subsequently betrayed al-Mutawakkil (q.v.) (d. 253/867).

Wāsiṭ an agricultural town and administrative center located on the Tigris River in central Iraq. It was founded around 80/700 and seems to have last been inhabited in the tenth/sixteenth century.

al-Wāthiq ninth Abbasid caliph (r. 227–32/842–47).

witr a voluntary but very meritorious prayer consisting of an odd number of cycles (q.v.) performed at night.

Worshipper any especially pious Muslim who was not a scholar.

Yaḥyā ibn Khāqān an official at the court of al-Muʿtaṣim (q.v.).

Yaḥyā ibn Maʿīn famously learned Hadith scholar censured by Ibn Ḥanbal for capitulating to the Inquisition (d. 233/848).

Zaynab Ibn Ḥanbal's daughter.

Bibliography

Abbreviations

EI2 Encyclopaedia of Islam, Second Edition. Edited by P. Bearman, Th. Bianquis, C. E. Bosworth, E. van Donzel, and W. P. Heinrichs. Leiden: Brill Online, 2012. http://www.brill.com/publications/online-resources/encyclopaedia-islam-online.

EI3 Encyclopaedia of Islam, Third Edition. Edited by Gudrun Krämer, Denis Matringe, John Nawas, and Everett Rowson. Leiden: Brill Online, 2014. http://www.brill.com/publications/online-resources/encyclopaedia-islam-online.

Abū l-ʿArab Muḥammad ibn Aḥmad al-Tamīmī. *Kitāb al-Miḥan.* Edited by Yaḥyā Wahīb al-Jubūrī. Beirut: Dār al-Gharb al-Islāmī, 1403/1983.

Abū Nuʿaym al-Iṣfahānī. *Ḥilyat al-awliyāʾ.* Cairo: al-Khānjī, 1932–38. Reprint, Beirut: al-Maktabah al-ʿIlmiyyah, n.d.

Abu Zahra, Nadia. "Adultery and Fornication." In McAuliffe, *Encyclopaedia of the Qurʾān.*

Adang, Camilla. "Belief and Unbelief." In McAuliffe, *Encyclopaedia of the Qurʾān.*

Ahsan, M. M. *Social Life under the Abbasids.* New York: Longman, 1979.

Anvarī, Ḥasan. *Farhang-e bozorg-e sokhan.* 8 vols. Tehran: Intishārāt-e Sokhan, 1381/2002–3.

Ashtor, E. "Mawāzīn." In *EI2.*

ʿAsqalānī, al-. *See* Ibn Ḥajar.

Baer, E. "Dawāt." In *EI2.*

[Baghdādī], Muḥammad ibn al-Ḥasan ibn Muḥammad ibn al-Karīm al-. *A Baghdad Cookery Book.* Translated by Charles Perry. Totnes. UK: Prospect Books, 2005.

Ballian, Anna. "Country Estates, Material Culture, and the Celebration of Princely Life: Islamic Art and the Secular Domain." In Evans with Ratliff, *Byzantium and Islam,* 200–8.

Bencheikh, Omar. "Nifṭawayh." In *EI2.*

Bernards, Monique, and John Nawas, eds. *Patronate and Patronage in Early and Classical Islam.* Leiden: Brill, 2005.

Björkman, W. "Kāfir." In *EI2.*

Böwering, G. "God and His Attributes." In McAuliffe, *Encyclopaedia of the Qurʾān.*

Bukhārī, Muḥammad al-. *Al-Jāmiʿ al-ṣaḥiḥ.* 9 vols. Būlāq: al-Amīriyyah, 1311/1893–94.

Bulliet, Richard. "Conversion-Based Patronage." In Bernards and Nawas, *Patronate and Patronage,* 246–62.

Burton, J. "Muḥṣan." In *EI2*.

Chabbi, Jacqueline. "Zamzam." In *EI2*.

Clarity, Beverly E., Karl Stowasser, Ronald G. Wolfe, D. R. Woodhead, and Wayne Beene. *A Dictionary of Iraqi Arabic*. Washington, DC: Georgetown University Press, 2003.

Colburn, Kathrin. "Materials and Techniques of Late Antique and Early Islamic Textiles Found in Egypt." In Evans with Ratliff, *Byzantium and Islam* , 161–71.

Cook, Michael. *Commanding Right and Forbidding Wrong in Islamic Thought*. Cambridge: Cambridge University Press, 2000.

———. "The Opponents of the Writing of Tradition in Early Islam." *Arabica* 44:4 (October 1997): 437–530.

———. "The Origins of *Kalām*." *Bulletin of the School of Oriental and African Studies* 43, no. 1 (1980): 32–43.

Cooperson, Michael. *Classical Arabic Biography: The Heirs of the Prophet in the Age of al-Ma'mūn*. Cambridge: Cambridge University Press, 2000.

———. "Ibn Ḥanbal and Bishr al-Ḥāfī: A Case Study in Biographical Traditions." *Studia Islamica* 86 (1997): 71–101.

———. "Al-Jāḥiẓ, the Misers, and the Proto-Sunnī Ascetics." In *Al-Jāḥiẓ: A Muslim Humanist for Our Time*, edited by Arnim Heinemann, John L. Meloy, Tarif Khalidi, and Manfred Kropp, 197–219. Beiruter Texte und Studien 119. Beirut: Orient-Institut, 2009.

———. *Al-Ma'mun*. Oxford: Oneworld, 2005.

———. "Probability, Plausibility, and 'Spiritual Communication' in Classical Arabic Biography." In *On Fiction and* Adab *in Medieval Arabic Literature*, edited by Philip F. Kennedy, 69–83. Wiesbaden: Harrasowitz, 2005.

———. "Two Abbasid Trials: Aḥmad Ibn Ḥanbal and Ḥunayn b. Isḥāq." *Al-Qantara. Revista de estudios árabes* 22, no. 2 (2001): 375–93.

Crone, Patricia. *God's Rule: Government and Islam*. New York: Columbia University Press, 2004.

———. *The Nativist Prophets of Early Islamic Iran: Rural Revolt and Local Zoroastrianism*. Cambridge: Cambridge University Press, 2012.

Crone, Patricia, and Martin Hinds. *God's Caliph: Religious Authority in the First Centuries of Islam*. Cambridge: Cambridge University Press, 1986.

Crone, Patricia, and Shmuel Moreh. *The Book of Strangers: Medieval Arabic Graffiti on the Theme of Nostalgia*. Princeton: Markus Wiener, 2000.

De Gifis, Vanessa. *Shaping a Qur'anic Worldview: Scriptural Hermenutics and the Rhetoric of Moral Reform in the Caliphate of al-Ma'mūm*. New York: Routledge, 2014.

Dekhodā, ʿAlī Akbar. *Lughatnāmeh-ye Fārsī*. Tehran: University of Tehran, 1982. Online at http://www.loghatnaameh.org/.

Dhahabi, Shams al-Dīn. *Mīzān al-iʿtidāl*. Edited by ʿAlī Muḥammad al-Bījāwī. 4 vols. Cairo: al-Bābī l-Ḥalabī, 1963.

———. *Al-Mushtabih fī asmāʾ al-rijāl*. Edited by P. de Jong. Leiden: Brill, 1863.

———. *Siyar aʿlām al-nubalāʾ*. 25 vols. Beirut: Muʾassasat al-Risālah, 1403/1983.

Donner, Frederick M. "Maymūn b. Mihrān, Abū Ayyūb." In *EI2*.

Dozy, Reinhart. *Dictionnaire détaillé des noms de vêtements chez les Arabes*. Amsterdam: Jean Müller, 1845. https://archive.org/details/dictionnairedtaooiiigoog.

El Omari: *see* Omari.

[Encyclopaedia Judaica.] "Lamed Vav Ẓaddikim." In *Encyclopaedia Judaica*, 2nd ed., edited by Michael Berenbaum and Fred Skolnik, 12:445–46. Detroit: Macmillan Reference USA, 2007.

Evans, Helen C., ed., with Brandie Ratliff. *Byzantium and Islam: Age of Transition, 7th–9th Century*. New York: Metropolitan Museum of Art, 2012.

Fīrūzābādī, al-. *Al-Qāmūs al-muḥīṭ*. Cairo: Dar al-Maʾmūn, 1938. http://www.baheth.info/.

Fluck, Cäcilia. "Inscribed Textiles." In Evans with Ratliff, *Byzantium and Islam*, 183–85.

Gacek, Adam. *Arabic Manuscripts: A Vademecum for Readers*. Leiden: Brill, 2009.

Goitein, Shelomo Dov. *A Mediterranean Society: The Jewish Communities of the Arab World as Portrayed in the Documents of the Cairo Geniza*. 6 vols. Berkeley: University of California Press, 1967–93.

Goldziher, I. "Awtād." In *EI2*.

Goldziher, I., and H. J. Kissling. "Abdāl." In *EI2*.

Grabar, Oleg. *The Illustrations of the Maqamat*. Chicago: University of Chicago Press, 1984.

Günther, Sebastian. "Ummī." In McAuliffe, *Encyclopaedia of the Qurʾān*.

Guthrie, Shirley. *Arab Social Life in the Middle Ages: An Illustrated Study*. London: Saqi, 1995.

Halm, H. "Al-Qushayrī." In *EI2*.

Ḥanbal ibn Isḥāq ibn Ḥanbal. *Dhikr miḥnat al-Imām Aḥmad ibn Ḥanbal*. Edited by Muḥammad Naghsh. Cairo: Nashr al-Thaqāfah, 1398/1977.

Heller, B. "Lazarus." In *EI2*.

Hill, D. R. "Māʾ, 3. Hydraulic Machines." In *EI2*.

———. "Naʿūra." In *EI2*.

Hinds, Martin. "Miḥna." In *EI2*.

Hinz, W. "Dhirāʿ." In *EI2*.

Honigmann, Ernst. *Die Ostgrenze des Byzaninischen Reiches von 363 bis 1071.* Brussels: Institut de philologie et d'histoire orientales, 1935.

Hurvitz, Nimrod. *The Formation of Hanbalism: Piety into Power.* New York: RoutledgeCurzon, 2002.

Ibn Abī Ya'lā l-Farrā'. *Ṭabaqāt al-Ḥanābilah.* Edited by 'Abd al-Raḥmān ibn Sulaymān al-'Uthaymīn. 3 vols. Riyad: al-Amānah al-'Āmmah li-l-Iḥtifāl bi-Murūr Mi'at 'Ām, 1419/1999. https://archive.org/details/Tabaqat_Hanabila.

Ibn al-Athīr, 'Izz al-Dīn. *Usd al-ghābah fī ma'rifat al-ṣaḥābah.* 2nd ed. Edited by 'Alī Muḥammad Mu'awwaḍ and 'Ādil Aḥmad 'Abd al-Mawjūd. Beirut: Dār al-Kutub al-'Ilmiyyah, 1424/2003.

Ibn Ḥajar al-'Asqalānī. *Fatḥ al-bārī bi-sharḥ Ṣaḥīḥ al-Bukhārī.* Edited by Muḥammad Fu'ād 'Abd al-Bāqī, Muḥibb al-Dīn al-Khaṭīb, and Quṣayy Muḥibb al-Dīn al-Khaṭīb. 13 vols. N.p: Dār al-Rayyān, 1407/1986. http://islamweb.net.

———. *Tabṣīr al-muntabih bi-taḥrīr al-Mushtabih.* Edited by 'Alī Aḥmad al-Bajāwī and Muḥammad 'Alī l-Najjār. Beirut: al-Maktabah al-'Ilmiyyah, 1964. http://www.archive.org/details/TabsirAlmuntabih.

———. *Tahdhīb al-tahdhīb.* Edited by Ibrāhīm al-Zaybaq and 'Ādil Murshid. 4 vols. Beirut: Mu'assasat al-Risālah, 1416/1995.

Ibn Ḥanbal, Aḥmad. *Al-Jāmi' fī l-'ilāl wa-ma'rifat al-rijāl.* Edited by Muḥammad Ḥuṣām Bayḍūn. Beirut: Mu'assasat al-Kutub al-Thaqāfiyyah, 1410/1990.

———. *Kitāb al-Wara'.* Edited by Zaynab Ibrāhīm al-Qārūṭ. Beirut: al-'Ālamiyyah, 1403/1983.

———. *Kitāb al-Zuhd.* Edited by Muḥammad Jalāl Sharaf. Beirut: Dār al-Nahḍah, 1981.

——— [attr.]. *Al-Radd 'alā l-zanādiqah wa-l-jahmiyyah.* Cairo: al-Salafiyyah, 1393/1973–74.

Ibn al-Jawzī, Abū l-Faraj 'Abd al-Raḥmān ibn 'Alī. *Kitāb al-Quṣṣāṣ wa-l-mudhakkirīn.* Edited by Merlin L. Swartz. Beirut: Dār al-Mashriq, 1971.

———. *Manāqib al-Imām Aḥmad ibn Ḥanbal.* Edited by Muḥammad Amīn al-Khānjī l-Kutubī. Cairo: Maktabat al-Khānjī, 1349/1931–32.

———. *Manāqib al-Imām Aḥmad ibn Ḥanbal.* Edited by 'Abd Allāh ibn 'Abd al-Muḥsin al-Turkī. 2nd rev. ed. Giza: Hajr, 1988. First published in 1399/1979 by Maktabat al-Khānjī in Cairo.

———. *A Medieval Critique of Anthropomorphism: Ibn al-Jawzi's Kitab Akhbar as-Sifat: A Critical Edition of the Arabic Text with Translation, Introduction and Notes.* Edited and translated by Merlin Swartz. Leiden: Brill, 2002.

Ibn Manẓūr. *Lisān al-ʿarab*. Edited by ʿAbd Allāh ʿAlī al-Kabīr, Muḥammad Aḥmad Ḥasab Allāh, and Ḥāshim Muḥammad al-Shādhilī. Cairo: Dār al-Maʿārif, 1981. http://www.baheth.info/.

Ibn al-Murtaḍā, Aḥmad ibn Yaḥyā. *Kitāb Ṭabaqāt al-muʿtazilah. Die Klassen der muʿtaziliten.* Edited by Susanna Diwald-Wilzer. Wiesbaden and Berlin: Franz Steiner, 1961.

Ibn Qutaybah. *Adab al-kātib*. Edited by Muḥammad al-Dālī. Beirut: Mu'assasat al-Risālah, 1402/1982.

Inalcık, H. "Quṭn" (2). In *EI2*.

Iṣfahānī, Abū l-Faraj al-. *Kitāb al-Aghanī*. Edited by Ibrāhīm al-Ibyārī. 33 vols. Cairo: Dār al-Shaʿb, 1969–82.

Iṣfahānī, Abū Nuʿaym al-: *see* Abū Nuʿaym al-Iṣfahānī.

Jadʿān, Fahmī. *Al-Miḥnah: Baḥth fī jadaliyyat al-dīnī wa-l-siyāsī fī l-Islām*. Amman: Dār al-Shurūq, 1989.

Jāḥiẓ, al-. *The Book of Misers*. Translated by R. B. Serjeant. Reading: Garnet, 1997.

———. *Al-Bukhalā'*. Edited by Ṭāhā l-Ḥājiri. Cairo: Dār al-Kitāb al-Miṣrī, 1948.

———. *Rasā'il*. Edited by ʿAbd al-Salām Hārūn. 4 vols. Beirut: Dār al-Jīl, 1411/1991.

Jeffrey, A. "Āzār." In *EI2*.

Jomier, J. "Dikka." In *EI2*.

Juynboll, J. H. A. "Shuʿba b. al-Ḥadjdjādj." In *EI2*.

Katz, Marion H. "ʿAzīmah and Rukhṣah." In *EI3*.

Keller, Nun Ha Mim. *See* Misri, al-.

Kennedy, Hugh N. *The Armies of the Caliphs: Military and Society in the Early Islamic State*. London: Routledge, 2001.

Khaṭīb al-Baghdādī, al-. *Ta'rīkh Baghdād*. Edited by Muṣṭafā ʿAbd al-Qādir ʿAṭā'. 14 vols. Beirut: Dār al-Kutub al-ʿIlmiyyah, 1417/1997.

Kinberg, Leah. "Paradise." In McAuliffe, *Encyclopaedia of the Qur'ān*.

———. "What Is Meant by *Zuhd*." *Studia Islamica* 61 (1985): 27–44.

Lane, Edward William, and Stanley Lane-Poole. *An Arabic-English Lexicon*. London: Williams and Norgate, 1863–93. http://ejtaal.net.

Lange, Christian. "Expiation." In *EI3*.

Lapidus, I. M. "The Separation of State and Religion in the Development of Early Islamic Society." *International Journal of Middle East Studies* 6 (1975): 363–85.

Lassner, J. "Nahr ʿĪsā." In *EI2*.

Le Strange, Guy *Baghdad during the Abbasid Caliphate*. Oxford, 1900. Reprint, Westport, CT: Greenwood Press, 1983.

Longrigg, S. H. "ʿĀna." In *EI2*.

Lucas, Scott C. *Constructive Critics, Hadith Literature, and the Articulation of Sunni Islam: The Legacy of the Generation of Ibn Saʿd, Ibn Maʿīn, and Ibn Ḥanbal.* Leiden: Brill, 2004.

Madelung, Wilferd. "Mahdī." In *EI2*.

———. "The Origins of the Controversy Concerning the Creation of the Qur'ān." In *Religious Schools and Sects in Medieval Islam*, edited by Wilferd Madelung, 504–25. London: Ashgate, 1985.

Makdisi, George. *The Rise of Humanism in Classical Islam and the Christian West.* Edinburgh: Edinburgh University Press, 1990.

Maqdisī, Taqī l-Dīn. *Miḥnat al-Imām Aḥmad ibn Ḥanbal.* Edited by ʿAbd Allāh al-Turkī. Giza: Hajr, 1987.

Martin, Richard. "Createdness of the Qur'ān." In McAuliffe, *Encyclopaedia of the Qur'ān.*

Maṭlūb, Aḥmad. *Muʿjam al-malābis fī lisān al-ʿarab*. Beirut: Maktabat Lubnān, 1995.

McAuliffe, Jane Dammen, ed. *Encyclopaedia of the Qur'ān.* Leiden: Brill Online, 2012. http://www.brill.com/publications/online-resources/encyclopaedia-quran-online.

Melchert, Christopher. "The Adversaries of Aḥmad ibn Ḥanbal." *Arabica* 44 (1997): 234–53.

———. *Ahmad ibn Hanbal.* Makers of the Muslim World. Oxford: Oneworld, 2006.

———. "Ahmad ibn Hanbal and the Qur'an." *Journal of Qur'anic Studies* 6, no. 2 (2004): 22–34.

———. "Aḥmad ibn Ḥanbal's Book of Renunciation." *Der Islam* 85 (2008): 345–59.

———. "Early Renunciants as Hadith Transmitters." *Muslim World* 92 (2002): 407–18.

———. "Exaggerated Fear in the Early Islamic Renunciant Tradition." *Journal of the Royal Asiatic Society* 3, no. 21 (2011): 283–300.

———. *The Formation of the Sunni Schools of Law, 9th–10th Centuries C.E.* Leiden: Brill, 1997.

———. "The Ḥanābila and the Early Sufis." *Arabica* 48 (2001): 352–67.

———. "Hasan al-Basri, al-." In *Dictionary of Literary Biography 311: Arabic Literary Culture, 500–925*, edited by Michael Cooperson and Shawkat M. Toorawa, 121–27. Detroit: Thomson Gale, 2005.

———. "The *Musnad* of Ahmad ibn Hanbal: How It Was Composed and What Distinguishes It from the Six Books." *Der Islam* 82 (2005): 32–51.

———. "The Piety of the Hadith Folk." *International Journal of Middle East Studies* 34 (2002): 425–39.

———. "Religious Policies of the Caliphs from al-Mutawakkil to al-Muqtadir, AH 232–295/AD 847–908." *Islamic Law and Society* 3, no. 3 (1996): 316–42.

———. Review of *Virtues of the Imām Aḥmad Ibn Ḥanbal*, Vol. I. *Journal of Islamic Studies* (2014). Advance access published online March 24, 2014.

Mietke, Gabriele. "Vine Rinceaux." In Evans with Ratliff, *Byzantium and Islam*, 175–82.

Minorsky, V. "Ṣaḥna." In *EI2*.

Misri, Ahmad ibn Naqib al-. *Reliance of the Traveler*. Edited and translated by Nun Ha Mim Keller. Beltsville, MD: Amana, 1999.

Monnot, G. "Ṣalāt." In *EI2*.

Mourad, Sulaiman Ali. *Early Islam between Myth and History: Al-Ḥasan al-Baṣrī (d. 110H/728CE) and the Formation of His Legacy in Classical Islamic Scholarship*. Leiden: Brill, 2005.

Mubārakfūrī, Muḥammad ibn ʿAbd al-Raḥmān al-. *Al-Aḥwadhī bi-sharḥ Jāmiʿ al-Tirmidhī*. Beirut: al-ʿIlmiyyah, 1418/1997. http://islamweb.net.

Nagel, T. "Ḳurrāʾ." In *EI2*.

———. *Rechtleitung und Kalifat. Versuch über eine Grundfrage der islamischen Geschichte*. Studien zum Minderheitenproblem im Islam 2. Bonn: Selbstverlag des Orientalischen Seminars der Universität Bonn, 1975.

Nawas, John A. *Al-Maʾmūn. Miḥna and Caliphate*. Nijmegen, 1992.

———. "The Mihna of 218 A.H./833 A.D. Revisited: An Empirical Study." *Journal of the American Oriental Society* 116 (1996): 698–708.

Northedge, Alistair. *Historical Topography of Samarra*. London: British School of Archaeology in Iraq, 2005.

Omari, Racha El. "Beatific Vision." In *The Oxford Encyclopedia of the Islamic World*, edited by John L. Esposito, 1:331–32. Oxford: Oxford University Press, 2009.

———. "*Kitāb al-Ḥayda*: The Historical Significance of an Apocryphal Text." In *Islamic Philosophy, Science, Culture, and Religion: Studies in Honor of Dimitri Gutas*, edited by Felicitas Opwis and David C. Reisman, 419–51. Leiden: Brill, 2012.

Patton, Walter M. *Aḥmed Ibn Ḥanbal and the Miḥna*. Leiden: Brill, 1897.

Pellat, C. "Al-Masḥ ʿAlā l-Khuffayn." In *EI2*.

Perry, Charles. *See* Baghdādī, al-.

Pérès, H. "Al-Ramādī." In *EI2*.

Peters, R. "Zinā or Zināʾ." In *EI2*.

Picken, Gavin. "Ibn Ḥanbal and al-Muḥāsibī: A Study of Early Conflicting Scholarly Methodologies." *Arabica* 55 (2008): 337–61.

Qāḍī, Wadād al-. "The Earliest *Nābita* and the Paradigmatic *Nawābit*." *Studia Islamica* 78 (1993): 27–61.

Qurṭubī, Abū ʿAbd Allāh Muḥammad ibn Aḥmad, al-. *Al-Jāmiʿ li-aḥkām al-Qurʾān*. Edited by ʿAbd Allāh ibn ʿAbd al-Muḥsin al-Turkī. 24 vols. Beirut: Muʾassasat al-Risālah, 2006. http://www.archive.org.

Raddatz, H. P. "Sufyān al-Thawrī." In *EI2*.

Rāghib al-Iṣfahānī, al-. *Muḥāḍarāt al-udabā'*. Beirut: Dār Maktabat al-Ḥayāh, 1961.

Reinhart, A. K. "Sha'r, 2: Legal Aspects Regarding Human Hair." In *EI2*.

Rippin, A. "Al-Ṣiddīḳ." In *EI2*.

Robinson, Neal. "Antichrist." In McAufliffe, *Encyclopaedia of the Qur'ān*.

Rowson, Everett. "The Effeminates of Early Medina." *Journal of the American Oriental Society* 111, no. 4 (1991): 671–93.

Sadan, J. "Mafrūshāt." In *EI2*.

Ṣāliḥ ibn Aḥmad ibn Ḥanbal. *Sīrat al-Imām Aḥmad ibn Ḥanbal*. Edited by Fu'ād 'Abd al-Mun'im Aḥmad. Alexandria: Mu'assasat al-Jāmi'ah, 1401/1981.

Sam'ānī, Abū Sa'd 'Abd al-Karīm ibn Muḥammad. *Al-Ansāb*. Edited by 'Abd Allāh 'Umar al-Bārūdī. 5 vols. Beirut: al-Jinān, 1408/1988. http://www.archive.org.

Sarhan, Saud Al-. "Early Muslim Traditionalism: A Critical Study of the Works and Political Theology of Aḥmad Ibn Ḥanbal." PhD diss., University of Exeter, 2011.

———. "'Patience Is Better Than Sedition': The Political Thought of Ahmad Ibn Hanbal." Paper delivered at the second LIVIT (Legitimate and Illegitimate Violence in Early Islamic Thought) conference, Institute of Arab and Islamic Studies, University of Exeter, UK, September 5–6, 2011.

Schacht, J. "Ibn Nudjaym." In *EI2*.

Serjeant: *see* Jāḥiẓ, al-.

Sezgin, Fuat. *Geschichte des arabischen Schrifttums*. 12 vols. Leiden: E.J. Brill, 1967–2010.

Shāfi'ī, Muḥammad ibn Idrīs al-. *The Epistle on Legal Theory*. Edited and translated by Joseph E. Lowry. New York University Press, 2013.

Shah, Mustafa. "The Quest for the Origins of the Qurrā' in the Classical Islamic Tradition." *Journal of Qur'anic Studies* 7, no. 2 (2005): 1-35

Sizgorich, Thomas. *Violence and Belief in Late Antiquity: Militant Devotion in Christianity and Islam*. Philadelphia: University of Pennsylvania Press, 2009.

Sourdel, Dominique. "La politique religieuse du caliph 'abbaside al-Ma'mūn." *Revue des études islamiques* 20 (1962): 27–48.

Sourdel-Thomine, J. "Ḥammām." In *EI2*.

Steppat, Fritz. "From *'Ahd Ardašīr* to al-Ma'mūn: A Persian Element in the Policy of the Miḥna." In *Studia Arabica et Islamica. Festschrift for Iḥsān 'Abbās on His Sixtieth Birthday*, edited by Wadād al-Qāḍī, 451–54. Beirut: American University of Beirut, 1981.

Stillman, Y. K. "Libās." In *EI2*.

Swartz, Merlin. *Ibn al-Jawzi, a Study of His Life and Work as Preacher: Including a Critical Edition and Translation of His Kitāb al-Quṣṣāṣ wa 'l-mudhakkirīn, with Introduction and Notes*. Beirut: Institut de Lettres Orientales, 1971.

———. "A Ḥanbalī Critique of Anthropomorphism." *Proceedings of the Arabic and Islamic Sections of the 35th International Congress of Asian and North African Studies (ICANAS)*, Part Two, edited by A. Fodor, 27–36. Budapest: Csoma de Kőrös Society, 1999.

Ṭabarī, al-. *Ta'rīkh al-rusul wa-l-mulūk*. Edited by M.J. de Goeje. Leiden: E.J. Brill, 1879–1901. Edited by Muḥammad Abū l-Faḍl Ibrāhīm. 10 vols. Cairo: Dār al-Maʿārif, 1979. References in the notes give the page numbers in the Cairo edition, then the Leiden, separated by a slash.

Tillier, Mathieu. *Les cadis d'Iraq et l'État abbasside (132/750-334/945)*. Damascus: Institut français du Proche-Orient, 2009.

Tirmidhī, Abū ʿĪsā Muḥammad al-. *Sunan*. 2nd ed. Edited by Aḥmad Muḥammad Shākir. Cairo: Muṣṭafā l-Bābī l-Ḥalabī, 1398/1978. https://archive.org/details/thermidiosun.

Toorawa, Shawkat M. "Prayer." In *Key Themes for the Study of Islam*, edited by Jamal J. Elias, 263–80. Oxford: Oneworld, 2010.

Turkī, al-. *See* Ibn al-Jawzī, Abū l-Faraj ʿAbd al-Raḥmān.

Turner, John P. "Aḥmad b. Abī Du'ād." In *EI3*.

———. *Inquisition in Early Islam: The Competition for Political and Religious Authority in the Abbasid Empire*. London: I.B. Tauris, 2013.

Tyan, E. "ʿAdl." In *EI2*.

van Ess, Josef. *Theologie und Gesellschaft im 2. und 3. Jahrhundert Hidschra: Eine Geschichte des religiösen Denkens im frühen Islam*. Berlin and New York: Walter de Gruyter, 1991–97.

Waines, David. "Tree(s)." In McAuliffe, *Encyclopaedia of the Qur'ān*.

Wensinck, A. J. "Ḥawḍ." In *EI2*.

———. "Al-Khaḍir (Al-Khiḍr)." In *EI2*.

Williams, Wesley. "Aspects of the Creed of Imam Ahmad ibn Hanbal: A Study of Anthropomorphism in Early Islamic Discourse." *International Journal of Middle Eastern Studies* 34 (2002): 441–63.

Winkelmann-Liebert, Holger. "Die *miḥna* im Kalifat des al-Muʿtaṣim." *Der Islam* 80, no. 1 (2003): 224–83.

Yaʿqūbī, al-. *Ta'rīkh*. . Edited by M. Th. Houtsma. 2 vols. Leiden: Brill, 1883.

Yāqūt al-Ḥamawī. *Muʿjam al-buldān. Jacut's geographisches Wörterbuch*. Edited by Ferdinand Wüstenfeld. 6 vols. Leipzig: Brockhaus, 1866–73.

Yücesoy, Hayrettin. *Messianic Beliefs and Imperial Politics in Medieval Islam. The ʿAbbāsid Caliphate in the Early Ninth Century*. Columbia: University of South Carolina Press, 2009.

Zaman, Muhammad Qasim. *Religion and Politics under the Early ʿAbbāsids: The Emergence of the Proto-Sunnī Elite*. Leiden: Brill, 1997.

Further Reading

Brown, Jonathan A. C. *Hadith: Muhammad's Legacy in the Medieval and Modern World*. Oxford: Oneworld, 2009.

Cook, Michael. *Commanding Right and Forbidding Wrong in Islamic Thought*. Cambridge: Cambridge University Press, 2000.

Cooperson, Michael. *Al-Ma'mun*. Oxford: Oneworld, 2005.

Crone, Patricia. *God's Rule: Government and Islam*. New York: Columbia University Press, 2004.

Goitein, S. D., and Jacob Lassner. *A Mediterranean Society: An Abridgement in One Volume*. Berkeley: University of California Press, 1999.

Katz, Marion Holmes. *Body of Text: The Emergence of the Sunni Law of Ritual Purity*. Albany: SUNY Press, 2002.

Melchert, Christopher. *Ahmad ibn Hanbal*. Makers of the Muslim World. Oxford: Oneworld, 2006.

Shāfiʿī, Muḥammad ibn Idrīs al-. *The Epistle on Legal Theory*. Edited and translated by Joseph E. Lowry. New York: New York University Press, 2013.

Sizgorich, Thomas. *Violence and Belief in Late Antiquity: Militant Devotion in Christianity and Islam*. Philadelphia: University of Pennsylvania Press, 2009.

van Ess, Josef. *The Flowering of Muslim Theology*. Translated by Jane Marie Todd. Cambridge, MA: Harvard University Press, 2006.

Index

About the NYU Abu Dhabi Institute

The Library of Arabic Literature is supported by a grant from the NYU Abu Dhabi Institute, a major hub of intellectual and creative activity and advanced research. The Institute hosts academic conferences, workshops, lectures, film series, performances, and other public programs directed both to audiences within the UAE and to the worldwide academic and research community. It is a center of the scholarly community for Abu Dhabi, bringing together faculty and researchers from institutions of higher learning throughout the region.

NYU Abu Dhabi, through the NYU Abu Dhabi Institute, is a world-class center of cutting-edge research, scholarship, and cultural activity. The Institute creates singular opportunities for leading researchers from across the arts, humanities, social sciences, sciences, engineering, and the professions to carry out creative scholarship and conduct research on issues of major disciplinary, multidisciplinary, and global significance.

About the Typefaces

The Arabic body text is set in DecoType Naskh, designed by Thomas Milo and Mirjam Somers, based on an analysis of five centuries of Ottoman manuscript practice. The exceptionally legible result is the first and only typeface in a style that fully implements the principles of script grammar (*qawāʿid al-khaṭṭ*).

The Arabic footnote text is set in DecoType Emiri, drawn by Mirjam Somers, based on the metal typeface in the naskh style that was cut for the 1924 Cairo edition of the Qur'an.

Both Arabic typefaces in this series are controlled by a dedicated font layout engine. ACE, the Arabic Calligraphic Engine, invented by Peter Somers, Thomas Milo, and Mirjam Somers of DecoType, first operational in 1985, pioneered the principle followed by later smart font layout technologies such as OpenType, which is used for all other typefaces in this series.

The Arabic text was set with WinSoft Tasmeem, a sophisticated user interface for DecoType ACE inside Adobe InDesign. Tasmeem was conceived and created by Thomas Milo (DecoType) and Pascal Rubini (WinSoft) in 2005.

The English text is set in Adobe Text, a new and versatile text typeface family designed by Robert Slimbach for Western (Latin, Greek, Cyrillic) typesetting. Its workhorse qualities make it perfect for a wide variety of applications, especially for longer passages of text where legibility and economy are important. Adobe Text bridges the gap between calligraphic Renaissance types of the 15th and 16th centuries and high-contrast Modern styles of the 18th century, taking many of its design cues from early post-Renaissance Baroque transitional types cut by designers such as Christoffel van Dijck, Nicolaus Kis, and William Caslon. While grounded in classical form, Adobe Text is also a statement of contemporary utilitarian design, well suited to a wide variety of print and onscreen applications.

About the Editor–Translator

Michael Cooperson (PhD Harvard 1994) has taught Arabic language and literature at UCLA since 1995. He has also taught at Dartmouth College, Stanford University, and the Middlebury School of Arabic. His research interests include the cultural history of the early Abbasid caliphate, Maltese language and literature, and time travel as a literary device. His publications include *Classical Arabic Biography*, a study of four ninth-century celebrities and how they have been remembered; and *Al Ma'mūn*, a biography of the caliph. He has translated Abdelfattah Kilito's *The Author and His Doubles*, Khairy Shalabi's *Time Travels of the Man Who Sold Pickles and Sweets*, and Jurji Zaidan's *The Caliph's Heirs: Brothers at War*. He is a co-author, with the RRAALL group, of *Interpreting the Self: Autobiography in the Arabic Literary Tradition*; and co-editor, with Shawkat Toorawa, of *The Dictionary of Literary Biography: Arabic Literary Culture, 500–925*.